OFFICIAL STRATEGY GUIDE

INTRODUCTION

Welcome to the official strategy guide for Infinite Undiscovery. Thanks to the resources and access graciously provided by Square-Enix and tri-Ace, this guide offers remarkable depth of information and data for all levels of gameplay. Indeed, the author team spent several weeks in Square's Los Angeles offices, working side by side with Square-Enix's peerless QA team in crafting flawless strategies and unlocking all of the game's secrets for you.

THE LIBERATION FORCE

PRIMARY CHARACTERS

CAPELL

A simple flute player, an orphan, a drifter, and a lifelong loner, Capell the Soother is a boy with few ties and fewer worries…until one day, soldiers of the brutal Order of Chains suddenly seize him and toss him into the deepest dungeon of Graad Prison. Stunned by his jailers' contempt, Capell can't understand why his guards keep calling him "the Liberator." Perhaps even more stunning is his untrained skill with a shortsword that soon falls into his hands. When a spirited young girl named Aya leads a breakout, Capell finds himself swept up in chain of events destined to rock the very foundations of the world order…and challenge even the gods themselves.

AYA

Adept with a bow and low-level healing magic, Aya is a keen admirer of Lord Sigmund the Liberator and a fervent soldier of his Liberation Force. When her "rescue" of Sigmund turns out to be mistaken, she nonetheless drags a reluctant Capell into the cause. Her attitude toward Capell grows decidedly more complicated as she discerns not only his goodhearted nature but also the hidden strength that arises in the most unlikely circumstances. And her own hidden qualities will surprise the entire Force soon enough…

SIGMUND

A young man of remarkable leadership skills, Lord Sigmund leads a ragtag, but surprisingly effective, rebel group known as the Liberation Force, created from an effort to thwart the Dreadnight's plans. Sigmund sees something in Capell, his dead ringer—something far deeper than their striking resemblance. But he's a man who keeps his own counsel in personal matters, and he's got a grim and physically draining job to do—breaking the Dreadknight's evil chains that bind and harness the moon, before they lay waste to the land.

EDWARD

Edward is a powerful warrior whose skill with his massive sword is unrivaled. The only thing stronger than his battle prowess is his unquestioned dedication and loyalty to Sigmund and the Force. His contempt for Capell's "weakness" is almost palpable, and it becomes even more pronounced as it becomes clear that Sigmund sees special qualities in the ragged young musician.

EUGENE

A mage of great skill, Eugene is a boyhood friend of Sigmund and a great source of knowledge and level-headed guidance for the Liberation Force. His calm demeanor provides a perfect counterbalance to Edward's fiery intensity in their roles as Lord Sigmund's primary lieutenants. His healing and resurrection skills can be indispensable to a well-balanced party, but don't discount his offensive capabilities.

BALBAGAN

Edward calls him "Sir Muscles." A massive melee warrior with an axe the size of a city stop sign, Balbagan is a mighty man with simple needs. Give him a good meal, a good night's sleep, and a good cause, and he'll fight by your side with a nearly inhuman ferocity. The only man who's ever bested Balbagan in a physical challenge is Lord Sigmund himself. So now Balbagan is the heavyweight of Sigmund's Liberation Force, fighting with the twin goals of smashing the Order of Chains…and getting a rematch.

RICO & RUCHA

Capell meets these inseparable twins in the village of Nolaan soon after his escape from Graad Prison. Good-natured, playful, and full of spunk, both Rico and Rucha possess indispensable skills of a remarkable nature. In time, they become some of Capell's most reliable and upbeat partners as the mission veers into ever-darker territory.

GUSTAV

A stout, powerful crimson bear, Gustav is Aya's "pet"...a somewhat quaint term for such a massive and devoted creature. His presence in your party adds great physical power and launching skills, knocking foes into the air for easier KOs. Keep in mind that Aya's presence always brings out the best in him.

VIC

A street urchin met in Kolton, Vic is a master pickpocket who can pick locks and disarm even the most sophisticated trap. With Vic in your party, you may find yourself a distinctly wealthier person. But Vic also has a secret that complicates his friendship with his good "buddy" Capell.

TOUMA

This young aristo of Halgita is a friend of Lord Sigmund and a blade master of the highest level skill. His leadership qualities can make him a valuable party member.

KOMACHI

She wields a wicked katana and fights with unnatural grace. Yet perhaps her biggest assets are her elegant Trapmaster and Honeysuckle skills, which give you access to seemingly inaccessible treasure chests.

SECONDARY CHARACTERS

GENMA

This venerable member of the Nightwhisper Guild is always nearby with news from his secretive intelligence network. He also proves to be an invaluable provider of respite and re-supply. Expect his help in unlikely places, particularly when the road ahead looks grim and unforgiving.

SAVIO

Also known as Starseer, Savio is an aristo oracle with famous powers of foresight and magic. A master of ancient rites, he is a calming presence and, late in the game, will prove an indispensable one as well.

DOMINICA

A salty mercenary soldier with a penchant for straight talk, Dominica is Aya's friend and protector with connections to the inner circle at the Emirate of Fayel. She sees things as they are, unfiltered, and her realism is refreshing. Her weapon skills are also welcome in any party.

KIRIYA

A renowned and somewhat infamous healer and scholar, Kiriya dwells in the deepest reaches of the Cobasna Timberlands. His knowledge of lunar power can give the Liberation Force the edge it needs in countering the insidious machinations of the Dreadknight and his minions. But can Capell and crew find him?

KRISTOFER

A great lover of women in the classic Don Juan mold, Kristofer keeps things warm in icy Kolton. But despite all the sweet talk to any female within his radar range, Kristofer has only one true love: Seraphina. Ironically, she is as cool and seemingly emotionless as he is passionate.

SERAPHINA

Seraphina is an aristo of the highest rank with a probing intellect that questions even the most fundamental of constructs. Thus, she finds Kristofer's pronouncements of love somewhat illogical and slightly vexing.

THE ORDER OF CHAINS

LEONID THE DREADKNIGHT

Founder and iron-fisted leader of the Order of Chains, Leonid has engineered a horrifying plan to ensnare the moon and use its great power to establish a new world order. Lashing the world's satellite to the planet via a system of great chains linked to the ground, the Dreadknight has harnessed unspeakably dark lunar powers and unleashed them far and wide on the land.

SARANDA

A cruel, seemingly heartless sorceress of great power, Saranda is Leonid's most loyal and adoring servant. Her mastery of lunar influence augments (and warps) the strength of the Order knights who guard the Dreadknight's chain links throughout the land.

THE ORDER KNIGHTS

The Dreadknight's lunar chains are weakest at the points where they're anchored to the ground. Protecting these links are Leonid's most powerful followers, the Order knights. At each link, you must face and defeat one of these fearsome warriors.

Lester

Semberas

Dmitri

Niedzielan

Held

Iskan du Bal

CHARACTERS

GAME BASICS & SKILLS

CAPELL

In the world of *Infinite Undiscovery*, Capell is the only character directly under your control. Using the left analog stick moves him around the environment. Ⓐ is used to examine objects or speak to other people, like townsfolk. After drawing a weapon with 🔲, Ⓐ becomes quick attack, while Ⓑ is power attack. Holding down either Ⓐ or Ⓑ activates the battle skill assigned to that button. Abilities assigned to Ⓐ have standard power and MP cost, while abilities assigned to Ⓑ increase both power and cost by 20%. 🔲 attempts a Deflect Drive. This parries an enemy's strike just as it hits, stunning them and guaranteeing follow-up attacks are critical. This is a great tactic to use against single enemies who telegraph their attacks (or a cluster of enemies all to one side), but this is difficult to use in crowds, and won't work against magic, or certain attacks. Holding 🔲 brings up the Connect menu—press the button corresponding to the character you want to Connect with. While Connected, that ally ceases acting on his or her own and waits for Capell's directives. Ⓧ and Ⓨ issue direct orders to that party member. Battle skills, magic, and Connect askills can be assigned to these buttons. As with Ⓐ and Ⓑ, Ⓧ functions as the standard version of an action, while Ⓨ increases effect and cost by 20% (though this does not apply to spells). When not Connected to anyone, Ⓧ plays flute songs, whereas Ⓨ calls for healing aid from allies—they then use any magic or item you've left available to them (enable or disable spells and items by pressing Ⓨ over a given item in the menu; this is great for restricting the use of overly costly or relatively useless spells and items). Finally, 🔘 brings up the camp menu, which does not stop the action and can be used even in combat… occasionally essential when you need to perform emergency miraculous medicine triage on your unexpectedly disintegrating party!

Capell's Basic Attacks

Name	Command	Number of hits	Description and Special Effects	Purpose
Spinning Waltz	Ⓑ	1	Capell attacks with a 360 degree spin. Cannot cancel into battle skills.	Clearing out and disrupting foes when surrounded.
Crescendo Spike	ⒶⒷ	2	Capell attacks with two linear strikes; the 2nd hit launches foes if AP gauge is filled past target marker. Cancels to battle skills.	Popping foes into the air to score EXP bonuses with aerial combos.
Diminuendo Dive	ⒶⒶⒷ	3	Capell attacks with three linear strikes; the 3rd hit knocks foes down if AP gauge is filled past target marker. Cancels to battle skills.	Knocking foes down to replenish HP/MP with ground combos.
Dancing Rhapsody	ⒶⒶⒶⒷ	6	Capell follows three normal strikes with a swirling 3-hit attack. Cancels to battle skills.	Building AP, attacking foes impervious to AP effects, and chaining to battle skills.

CAPELL'S ATTACKS

For being the composer of such leisurely tunes as "The Slovenly Serenade," Capell is more nimble on his feet than you might expect. He's an effective fighter right from the game's first encounter, against two Order jailers. Even without abilities, Capell can use Ⓐ Ⓐ Ⓐ to deal damage in relative safety, going for special strings where appropriate—Dancing Rhapsody to build AP, and Crescendo Spike or Diminuendo Dive to use it. After launching

with Crescendo Spike, repeat Crescendo Spike over and over until Capell runs out of AP, or simply juggle with Dancing Rhapsody. After knocking down with Diminuendo Dive, Ⓐ Ⓐ can be used immediately to score a 2-hit downed combo (among other options). Finally, simply using Ⓐ Ⓐ Ⓐ without Crescendo Spike, Diminuendo Dive, or Dancing Rhapsody can be effective, especially on harder difficulty settings…if you use a full attack string without chaining into a Battle Skill or knocking down or launching a foe, Capell frequently gets hit immediately after his attack. In these cases, just Ⓐ Ⓐ Ⓐ and run away!

Status Effects

Through certain spells or attacks, enemies inflict Capell and his allies with various detrimental effects. Results can vary—allies may lose a little HP/MP over time, or they may become completely immobile, and so on. The following table details status effects and the items needed to restore healthy function. You can open the camp menu with ⊗ and apply the appropriate remedy manually, but it's faster and more efficient to simply call for healing with Ⓨ—as long as required items are stocked and unrestricted, Capell's friends helpfully take care of status ailments. If Capell is somehow incapacitated, unable to call for healing, you'll be relying on their autonomy for status curing anyway! The panacea, cornucopia, and mysterious curry bread items help by curing any status ailment, but the first is expensive and the latter two are rare. Alternative cures are listed in this table.

Icon/Graphic	Status Ailment	Effects	Cure
	Faint	Unable to act. If Capell is unconscious, he's unable to move, attack, or issue commands to allies.	Liquid Salt
	Sleep	Unable to act. If Capell is asleep, he's unable to move, attack, or issue commands to allies.	Getting hit, Coffee, Berry Bread
	Poison	1% of max HP is lost every 5 seconds.	Antidote, Cobasna Salad Sandwich
	Curse	1% of max MP is lost every 5 seconds.	Holy Water
	Paralysis	Unable to act. If Capell is paralyzed, he's unable to move, attack, or issue commands to allies.	Para-Gone, Soul Roll
	Silence	Unable to cast spells. If Capell is silenced, he's unable to Connect with allies or call for healing.	Cough Drop, Royal Herb Tea, Exquisite Bread Crusts
	Confusion	Capell's allies become confused, potentially attacking one another. In a creative twist, if Capell is confused, player controls are inverted.	Sedative, Toast of Dawn
	Freeze	Victim is encased in ice and cannot move. If Capell is frozen, he cannot move, Connect with allies, or call for healing.	Spring Warmth, Honey Tea, Jackpot Burger
	Stone	Victim is encased in stone and completely unable to act, and a timer begins. When the timer hits 0, the subject dies. If Capell is encased in stone and the timer reaches 0, it's Game Over!	Odious Eye, Rock Hard Stick of Bread

Icon/Graphic	Status Ailment	Effects	Cure
	Unseeing	Victim suffers lowered accuracy and cannot receive orders. If Capell is afflicted, the screen becomes blurry and he cannot lock-on to foes or Connect to allies.	Eye Drops, Hell's Egg Sandwich
	Unhearing	Victim cannot receive orders. If Capell is afflicted, hearing is muffled and he cannot Connect with allies, though he can still call for healing.	Angel Earpick
	Stink	Allies let off a pungent odor; can attract enemies.	Aroma Oil
	Untasting	Victim receives no benefits from food.	Toothbrush
	Stun	Victim is briefly stunned. Some abilities may cause a launch after the stun..	--
	Charm	Allies cease attacking foes and turn on one another. Extremely dangerous, as allies are stronger than most enemies that aren't bosses.	Maiden's Scorn, Oradian Chicken Sandwich
	Berserk	Victim experiences increased strength, but cannot receive orders or do anything but attack. If Capell is Berserk, he cannot issue orders to allies or sheathe his weapon.	Call of War
	Doom	Victim dies.	Miraculous Medicine, Holy Grail, Salva, Salvus

We Make Our Own Luck: A Word on Stats, Loot, & Treasure

Stats are important in gauging the usefulness of a character. HP, MP, ATK, DEF, HIT, AGL, and INT are determined by overall level, and also equipped gear. There is a hidden stat, too—luck (or LUC). Luck helps determine whether characters score criticals, whether they survive potentially fatal attacks, and the quality of drops awarded when that character scores a kill shot. LUC does not effect whether an item actually drops, however. Each enemy has a set percentage rate for whether items will drop upon defeat. Each foe can drop a wide variety of items, in one of four drop ranks (S, A, B, & C). The drop rank is determined by how effectively an enemy is defeated—score Player Advantage repeatedly and defeat a foe efficiently and you'll nab an S rank drop; simply score Player Advantage and you'll get A rank; defeat the enemy normally for B rank; and defeat the enemy after they score Enemy Advantage for C rank (usually a low-quality item, or junk). Then, within each rank, different items can be awarded. The quality of the item awarded within a rank is what LUC affects. As stated, LUC is a hidden stat, not displayed in-game. The table here shows you who the luckiest characters are relative to one another. There are also a few accessories that boost LUC a bit...while the game doesn't feature this information, this guide's chapter on Items does!

Stat	Effect
ATK	Determines physical attack power. Checked against target DEF.
DEF	Determines physical defense. Checked against attacker ATK.
HIT	Determines accuracy—a higher HIT rating causes enemies to guard less often. Checked against target AGL.
AGL	Determines whether blows will be guarded. Checked against attacker HIT.
INT	Determines magic attack power and magic defense. Checked against target/attacker INT.
LUC	Has an influence on above stats, and criticals, survival, and loot quality within a given drop rank—but not the drop rate itself (a set percentage), or the drop rank (determined by combat).

Character	Luck Rating
Kiriya	66
Gustav	65
Aya, Vic	60
Komachi, Touma	55
Sigmund	50
Rico, Rucha	45
Seraphina	43

Character	Luck Rating
Eugene	40
Michelle, Dominica	35
Savio	33
Edward	30
Balbagan	25
Kristofer	20
Capell	15

In addition to the loot gathered from felled enemies, Capell and friends frequently find treasure chests throughout the adventure. Most can be simply sprung open, but occasionally chests are locked, hidden, or out-of-reach. To snag the contents of these chests, you'll need certain allies to help you, or the aid of a certain flute song, or both...and while flimsier locked chests can be bashed apart, this brute force approach runs the risk of destroying the contents. Consider just waiting, since locked chests are usually worth the trouble to come back for later!

Capell's battle skills

Skill	Description	Learning Method	Execution Time	Ⓐ Battle skill MP Cost	Ⓑ Battle skill MP Cost	Lv.1 Hits/ Effect	Lv.2 Hits/ Effect	Lv.3 Hits/ Effect
Slashing Canon	A slash followed by a mighty kick. 2nd hit knocks foe down if AP gauge is filled past target marker.	Lv.2	Instant	5 MP	6 MP	2	2	2
Cutting Gavotte	Two quick slashes followed by a powerful shockwave. 1st hit launches foe if AP gauge is filled past target marker.	Lv.5	Instant	15 MP	18 MP	5	5	5
Symphonic Blade	A technique that draws power from a Connected ally. Depending on who Capell Connects to, different elements are added to his blade. Effect ends after a set duration, or if Capell's sword is sheathed. Does not work with Gustav, or with Sigmund before lunar rite. Allows Capell to directly damage vermiforms.	Lv.12	3.5 seconds	13 MP	15 MP	Ⓐ - 30 seconds; Ⓑ - 35 seconds	Ⓐ - 60 seconds; Ⓑ - 72 seconds	Ⓐ - 90 seconds; Ⓑ - 108 seconds
Marching Boots	A barrage of powerful kicks. 2nd-to-last hit launches foe if AP gauge is filled past target marker.	Lv.16	Instant	40 MP	48 MP	6	9	11
Eternal Refrain	A devastating series of lightning-quick slashes.	Lv.22	0.75 seconds	75 MP	90 MP	5	7	11
Reginleif	A powerful swing of the sword in a piercing arc. Knocks foe down if AP gauge is filled past target marker.	Lv.33	1.25 seconds	50 MP	60 MP	1	1	1
Grinn Valesti	An aerial assault that hits the enemy from above.	Lv.50	0.75 seconds	60 MP	72 MP	2	2	2
Alfheim	A shield-based attack followed by two sword attacks. Last hit launches foe if AP gauge is filled past target marker.	"Dance of the Sword"	0.75 seconds	80 MP	96 MP	3	3	3
Levantine Slash	A jumping sword attack that uses all of the wielder's might. 2nd hit knocks foe down if AP gauge is filled past target marker.	"Path of a Hero"	Instant	100 MP	120 MP	5	5	5

Symphonic Blade Elements	
Connected Friend	**Element Granted**
Aya	Fire
Rico	Air
Rucha	Air
Edward	Air
Sigmund	Air (only after lunar rite)
Eugene	Earth
Balbagan	Fire
Michelle	Aether
Gustav	None
Vic	Aether
Touma	Earth
Komachi	Earth

CAPELL'S BATTLE SKILLS

As Capell learns battle skills and allied Connect skills become available, combat options only open up further. Any of the basic attack strings can be canceled into battle skills, allowing you to easily land powerful hits or begin long combos. For example, with Cutting Gavotte assigned to Ⓑ, inputting ⒶⒶⒶⒷ, then pressing Ⓑ again and holding it, performs Dancing Rhapsody to Cutting Gavotte. Cutting Gavotte is a battle skill that launches if Capell has enough AP, so from here he'll often get a chance to juggle the enemy, especially with his friends attacking too.

Your allies attack with normal swings, assigned battle skills, and unrestricted magic. Their incidental attacks very frequently bridge the gaps in Capell's assault, leading to truly huge combos and juggles. This behavior can be encouraged by using Connect askills. While Connected to an ally, he or she can be made to perform assigned CAs at any time—even while Capell has his own attacks in progress. So, for another example: with Cutting Gavotte assigned to Ⓑ, Aya as an ally and her skill Sparrowrain assigned to Ⓨ, Capell at the ready, and Aya Connected, perform: ⒶⒶⒶⒷ+Ⓨ, press and hold Ⓑ. Capell then performs Dancing Rhapsody, striking six times, before leading into Cutting Gavotte for five more hits. The call for Sparrowrain, done at the same time as the button press to complete Dancing Rhapsody, causes Sparrowrain to land just in the middle of Cutting Gavotte, adding 3~5 more hits (depending on skill level). Whether Cutting Gavotte launched the enemy or not, Sparrowrain's presence allows the combo to continue—Cutting Gavotte either tosses the enemy right up into Sparrowrain, giving Capell time to recover and juggle further, or it simply holds them in place, where Sparrowrain hits long enough to allow Capell to land another Dancing Rhapsody…and so on!

MP often becomes an issue if you use high-cost abilities, assign high-cost battle skills to friends, or allow them to cast any magic they please. When outfitting Capell, assigning his skills, and constructing your parties, keep this in mind. To begin, choose a character with effective, low-cost abilities you can use as tools along with Capell's offense. Aya's Sparrowrain, Rico's Hydrill, Edward's Twinstream, Michelle's Astro, and Sigmund's Grinn Valesti serve as strong examples that are learned at relatively low levels but remain useful the entire game. Then, consider placing characters in your party who grant useful abilities—Rico for talking to animals, Balbagan for breaking rocks, and so on (see chart). Finally, make sure you have a strong healing contingent. Even if the Connect buddy you picked happens to have healing capabilities, they don't count—allies do not use curing magic while Connected. While any character employs items like berries to restore HP (as long as the items aren't restricted), you should always have a magic healer, and in difficult scraps you'll likely want to travel with two. Aya is capable of some light magical curing, as is Rico, but the heavy magical healers are Rucha, Michelle, and Eugene. Don't worry about giving up offense picking mages—all three are capable of dispensing severe pain.

Unique Ability	Party Member
Striking distant objects	Aya (Ravaging Raptor), Komachi (Honeysuckle)
Talking to animals	Rico
Charming foes	Rico (Penguin Parade, Rabbit Tail)
Reviving fallen friends with magic	Rucha, Eugene
Summoning	Rucha (Tir na Nog)
Finding raw materials occasionally	Rucha, Gustav, Komachi
Viewing elemental resistance of foes	Sigmund (while Connected)
Inflicting silence, unhearing, unseeing, unsmelling	Eugene (Soil Splitter)
Breaking cracked rocks	Balbagan (Gigatackle), Gustav (Explosive Ride)
Being a bear	Gustav
Disarming traps & lockpicking	Vic, Komachi
Stealing from enemies	Vic (Sneaky Scorpion)
Pulling in distant objects	Komachi (Honeysuckle)

Most enemies in the game, especially many lesser ones, can be defeated with parties built like this. Go for combos aggressively, using a Connected friend to bolster your offense. When assigning battle skills, consider whether it's even worth assigning two…for your allies who can pull their weight repeating one skill (and here we are staring at Edward); there's no reason to give them a chance to do anything else. This also levels that skill up faster, through more frequent use. Let your mage friends heal and fire away with offensive magic autonomously, encouraging them more toward the healing side as needed by breaking your Connection briefly (🆁🅱) then pressing 🆈. Turn off the more expensive offensive spells until late in the game, though. It's also worth disabling redundant spells—skills are far more useful when they're leveled up, but it takes quite a lot of use on any one spell or skill to get it to Lv.3. Letting a mage use their full spellbook may never get them anywhere! At first, pick one or two cheap offensive spells you like to lean on. Later on in the game, as Fol piles up and your level increases, MP becomes less of an issue. Higher levels mean bigger pools of MP, and deeper pockets allow more liberal purchase of items for MP replenishment. Very late in the game, there are even some items that grant MP regeneration over time (between 1~3% of max MP every 5 seconds). In practice, this essentially grants the user infinite MP, and changes the game dramatically—here, you can loosen your collar a bit and start swapping out mainstays like Cutting Gavotte for Grinn Valesti, Sparrowrain for Raven Venom, and so on.

USING THE FLUTE

Capell's Flute skills—up to four songs can be assigned at a time in the Menu under Flute Skills. Tap the D-pad left or right to switch between them. Hold ❎ to play the selected song. It takes one second to begin playing any song.

Song	Description	Learning Method	MP Cost	Target/Area of Effect
Valere	An exciting song which increases the party's attack but decreases its defense while song is played.	Concerto Score	30 MP initially, then extremely rapid MP drain for duration of song	Allies in surrounding area
Obduratus	A calming song which increases the party's defense but decreases its attack while song is played.	Suite Score	30 MP initially, then extremely rapid MP drain for duration of song	Allies in surrounding area
Precari	A song of prayer which increases all the abilities of the party while song is played.	Symphony Score	100 MP initially, then extremely rapid MP drain for duration of song	Allies in surrounding area
Fortuna	An uplifting song which gives a feeling that one's luck will improve.	Prelude Score	10 MP initially, then very rapid MP drain for duration of song	Allies in surrounding area
Obstreperus	An original song which is just a very noisy racket.	1	0	Surrounding area
Prudentiae	A song which creates an area canceling lunaglyph effects and magic.	Granted during story by Saruleus	3 MP initially, then MP drain for duration of song	Surrounding area
Percipere	A song which shares the sight of Saruleus, enabling hidden objects to be seen. Reveals false walls and hidden treasure chests. Allows the party to target vermiforms.	Granted during story by Saruleus	0	Surrounding area
Mare Lunaris	A song which defuses the power of the moon and hurts those with too much of its power.	Overture Score	2 MP initially, then MP drain for duration of song	Surrounding area
Alucinari	A song which distracts enemies' attention by creating an image of Capell. This decoy explodes after a short countdown, or if contacted by an enemy.	Fantasia Score	5 MP	Foes near decoy
Placare	A song which, when played in town, has the potential of earning some money.	Training Score	3 MP initially, then MP drain for duration of song	Randomly rewards 5 Fol when played in towns
Perturbare	A song which turns the targeted enemy against other enemies for a limited time.	Sonata Score	3 MP initially, then MP drain for duration of song	Targeted foe
Angere	A song which irritates the targeted enemy.	Fugue Score	5 MP initially, then rapid MP drain for duration of song	Targeted foe
Hypnoticus	A comforting song which puts enemies to sleep.	Nocturne Score	10 MP initially, then very rapid MP drain for duration of song	Foes in surrounding area
Irritatus	A song which agitates both friend and foe and causes them to act irrationally.	Capriccio Score	20 MP initially, then extremely rapid MP drain for duration of song	Everyone in surrounding area

Some encounters, however (especially in the Seraphic Gate, unlocked after a playthrough on Normal difficulty or greater) require an altered approach. Against difficult groups of enemies and bosses, simply cutting your way forward can quickly get Capell into trouble. Apart from the physical risk from Capell rushing in, difficult enemies often use harsh magic that can annihilate your party in seconds. Sometimes you'll get a warning in red at the top of the screen, but sometimes you won't, and are only given audio or visual queues that a heavy nuke is coming. In these circumstances, Prudentiae becomes your party's saving grace. Anyone standing within the bubble of influence of the song is protected from nearly every spell in the game. Incoming Hydrill shards, Geocrush boulders, and even Astro meteors simply get deflected harmlessly. Aside from this, certain enemies cannot even be targeted or attacked unless they are made visible by the song Percipere. However, readying Saruleus's flute at a moment's notice requires a more measured approach. You won't want to remain Connected often, because it prevents immediate emergency healing calls or flute use. You won't want to attack much with standard strikes, since they require you to be too close for too long, and you won't be launching many hard enemies or bosses. And you just might not be as inclined to bring characters along that you didn't want to actually fight with, just because they can, say, break rocks (no offense meant to Balbagan or Gustav, even if it's doubtful either can read). Instead, you'll want to use powerful skills when the opportunity arises, while surrounded with a solid, balanced group that can deal damage and take care of itself. In this capacity, Capell also has more opportunity to use other songs to boost his ally's abilities, or to debilitate foes. The need to be careful becomes much more pressing on harder difficulties, where almost every encounter becomes a challenge—beating the game on Normal difficulty unlocks the grueling Seraphic Gate dungeon, as well as Hard difficulty. Hard difficulty isn't too bad; enemies have their stats and HP multiplied by 1.2, but by the time you've cleared the Seraphic Dungeon on Normal, this shouldn't be too daunting. Infinity difficulty, unlocked by beating the

game on Hard, is another story…enemy stats and HP are multiplied by 1.8, and Capell and his friends do drastically less damage to them. The very first encounter on Infinity difficulty is more challenging that almost any encounter in Hard mode!

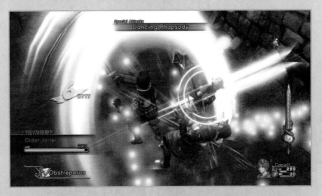

Yes, those are 1s; yes, this is the first fight in the game.

ALLY SKILLS

AYA

Aya's AP Portrait Position ① 1

Aya's Skills

Skill ②	Description ③	Learning Method ④	Execution Time ⑤	BS 1/⊗ CS MP Cost	BS 2/Ⓨ CS MP Cost	Lv.1 Hits/ Effect	Lv.2 Hits/ Effect	Lv.3 Hits/ Effect
Peacock Plume	An attack aimed at the enemy's feet. Launches foe if Aya's portrait is above target marker on AP gauge.	Lv.3	1.5 seconds	5 MP	6 MP	1	1	1

⑥ ⑦

① *Portrait Position: Just as Capell has a target marker on the Attack Point (or AP) gauge representing when his attacks gain special effects, so too do his allies. Rather than the target marker, this position is marked by a portrait of a character's face that appears only while Connected to him or her. While Capell's target marker varies from one monster to another, his allies' portraits do not. If this portrait is equal to or above Capell's target marker, a given character's skills and Magic may gain special advantages against the targeted foe. The effect can involve launching the enemy, stunning them, or knocking them down. If this portrait is below Capell's target marker, no special effect occurs. Finally, note that Capell's target marker only appears on the AP gauge after he has registered a special effect on the foe himself, such as launching them with Crescendo Spike or knocking them down with Diminuendo Dive. Many lesser enemies (like Order soldiers and Lumper denizens) have low target marker values, while sturdier adversaries (basilisks, for example) place the target marker higher on the AP gauge. Thus, characters with a higher AP portrait position are more likely to register special effects on a larger variety of enemies. Finally, while Capell must build AP past the target marker before registering his special hit effects, his allies have no such restriction—if their portrait is above the target marker, their actions always have special properties. Rucha and Michelle have the lowest portrait values, at position 2 out of 10, while Gustav's is the highest at 9 out of 10—if something can be launched, Gustav will launch it! Some foes, particularly most bosses, are immune to special hit effects altogether.*

② *Skill/Spell Name*

③ *Description: Describes a skill or spell, and points out whether any special hit effects exist with sufficient portrait position.*

④ *Learning Method: Most abilities are earned simply by leveling up. Later on, some advanced abilities are learned through books that must either be found, or written using the IC (Item Creation) system. Where this is the case, the title of the required tome is listed.*

⑤ *Execution/Casting Time: The time it takes an ally to unleash a skill or spell after being ordered. Abilities that take longer to execute run a larger risk of being interrupted by enemy blows. These execution times assume weapons are already drawn and allies are in position to execute commands—actions take longer to initiate if weapons aren't drawn, if allies are busy performing other actions, or if they must move to a different position first (such as closing the distance to a foe before using a melee skill). Execution time is not affected by the skill level of an ability, though some late-game items cut down on casting times.*

⑥ *MP Cost: The mana expended when a skill or spell is used. Every ally has two slots for battle skills (BS), which they use autonomously depending on Tactic orders. There are also ⊗ and Ⓨ slots for Connect skills (CS). Actions assigned to battle skill 1 or ⊗ Connect skill expend standard MP and deal normal damage. Actions assigned to battle skill 2 or Ⓨ Connect skill deal 20% more damage (or have an enhanced duration/effect, for certain skills), at the cost of 20% more MP. MP cost is not affected by the skill level of an ability.*

⑦ *Hits/effects at different skill levels: battle skills, Connect actionskills, and spells start at lv. 1 out of 3. Through repetitious use, these actions level up. Level up progress can be tracked by pressing ⊗ on a given skill within the battle skill, Connect actionskill, and Magic menus. Abilities deal more damage (or have enhanced effects or duration) at higher levels and often gain a larger number of hits, extending how long a foe reels while being struck and enhancing combo potential. Restorative spells do not level up.*

AYA

Aya's Skills

Skill	Description	Learning Method	Execution Time	BS 1/ⓧ CS MP Cost	BS 2/ⓨ CS MP Cost	Lv.1 Hits/ Effect	Lv.2 Hits/ Effect	Lv.3 Hits/ Effect
Peacock Plume	An attack aimed at the enemy's feet. Launches foe if Aya's portrait is above target marker on AP gauge.	Lv.3	1.5 seconds	5 MP	6 MP	1	1	1
Ravaging Raptor (CS)	A powerful attack that pierces the enemy. (Connect skill)	Lv.3	Aya draws her bow as soon as she reaches Capell	0 MP	0 MP	1	1	1
Sparrowrain	A harrowing attack from the heavens.	Lv.8	1.25 seconds	15 MP	18 MP	3	4	5
Falcon Spread	A dash followed by a close-range shot.	Lv.13	Instant	30 MP	36 MP	1	2	3
Moa Impaler	A jump kick followed by a flashing blast. Launches and freezes foe in midair if Aya's portrait is above target marker on AP gauge.	Lv.21	Instant	45 MP	54 MP	2	2	2
Cardinal Cloak	A blazing blast that takes the form of a fiery bird.	Lv.25	2.25 seconds	50 MP	60 MP	1	1	1
Phoenix Feather	A fiery barrage of arrows.	Lv.32	3 seconds	100 MP	120 MP	6	6	6
Snipe Arrow	An aerial attack that unleashes a flurry of arrows.	Lv.40	1.75 seconds	120 MP	144 MP	5	7	10
Raven Venom	A powerful attack that hits the enemy from all sides.	Lv.52	3.25 seconds	200 MP	240 MP	7	15	22
Devouring Vulture	An attack that hits a concentrated area with arrows. Nearby enemies are rendered immobile during this attack.	Lv.64	4.25 seconds	150 MP	180 MP	4	4	4
Simorgh Zal	A fiery bird that decimates the enemy. Knocks foe down if Aya's portrait is above target marker on AP gauge.	"Memos of a Master Marksman"	4.25 seconds	220 MP	264 MP	2	2	2

Aya's Magic

Spell	Learning Method	Casting Time	MP Cost
Levi	Lv.3	2.75 seconds	5 MP
Megalevi	Lv.17	2.75 seconds	10 MP

Capell's liberator and fast friend is a versatile ally. In battle, Aya normally fires arrows at foes while hanging back. She also performs a shin kick up close to prolong combos. She comes equipped with Levus and eventually learns Megalevi. This makes her a great supplemental character—she offers decent, low-risk offense while providing spot healing. She's lacking as a main healer, especially later in the game, so consider grouping her with at least one of Eugene, Michelle, or Rucha in difficult areas. Her Ravaging Raptor Connect skill is great for gaining Player Advantage against distant foes, and for striking objects, such as fruit hanging in trees. Sparrowrain is an excellent offensive staple for her for the majority of the game. Later on, when her MP pool and equipment are sufficient to justify its use, Raven Venom is even more potent. Aya provides a small stat boost to Gustav while he is in the party. She can also become an excellent cook.

RICO

Rico's skills

Skill	Description	Learning Method	Execution Time	BS 1/ⓧ CS MP Cost	BS 2/ⓨ CS MP Cost	Lv.1 Hits/ Effect	Lv.2 Hits/ Effect	Lv.3 Hits/ Effect
Penguin Parade (CS)	A taming technique that takes control of an enemy. (Connect skill)	Lv.2	3 seconds	3 MP	3 MP	Puppet	Puppet	Puppet
Rabbit Tail	An ability that turns a foe into an ally for a short time.	Lv.5	2.75 seconds	5 MP	6 MP	Charm	Charm	Charm
Serpent Head	Launches a blast of energy at the enemy.	Lv.27	2.75 seconds	25 MP	30 MP	1	1	1

Rico's Magic

Spell	Learning Method	Casting Time	MP Cost
Volt	Lv.2	3 seconds	5 MP
Levi	Lv.2	3.25 seconds	5 MP
Hydrill	Lv.9	3 seconds	8 MP
Levus	Lv.13	3.25 seconds	15 MP
Voltsweep	Lv.18	3 seconds	15 MP

Rico's Magic

Spell	Learning Method	Casting Time	MP Cost
Hydrain	Lv.21	4 seconds	20 MP
Aerwhirl	Lv.31	4 seconds	20 MP
Levusti	Lv.34	4.25 seconds	45 MP
Voltscourge	Lv.37	5 seconds	50 MP
Geocrush	"Molding of Earth"	4 seconds	80 MP

The male sibling in the precocious, musically-inclined pair, Rico wields a baton. When fighting he'll perform single swings or a 3-hit chain with his batons, but he's usually disinclined to use them, and instead favors running from foes to cast from afar. Hydrill is great to use from range, as it hits many times, doesn't cost much MP, and can freeze foes in place, leaving them totally vulnerable. Aerwhirl can launch large numbers of lesser foes (such as Order soldiers), while Geocrush can knock them down. Penguin Parade can be useful

to control foes, but requires that you command the foe to attack each time. This is the puppet effect, rather than charm. It's vital to an early mission. Rabbit Tail is more useful, as it charms enemies and doesn't require micro-management to make them attack. Foes charmed from Rabbit Tail's influence attack other enemies, and cannot be targeted by your party. This, coupled with its low MP cost, makes Rabbit Tail an easy choice as Rico's active battle skill, unless you'd prefer he spend more time using offensive magic. Rico can provide healing, but his lack of area-of-effect curing makes him most effective as a supplemental healer rather than a primary one, just like Aya. Despite his youth, Rico can become a prodigious writer, authoring several exclusive skill books and musical scores. Rico's stats are slightly enhanced when he's grouped with Rucha.

RUCHA

Rucha's skills

Skill	Description	Learning Method	Execution Time	BS 1/❌ CS MP Cost	BS 2/Ⓨ CS MP Cost	Lv.1 Hits/ Effect	Lv.2 Hits/ Effect	Lv.3 Hits/ Effect
Tir na Nog (CS)	Summons an elemental beast from nearby. (Connect skill)	Lv.2	4 seconds	10 MP	12 MP	Increases power	Increases Power	Increases Power

Rucha's Magic

Spell	Learning Method	Casting Time	MP Cost
Aerowave	Lv.2	3.25 seconds	5 MP
Megalevi	Lv.2	3 seconds	10 MP
Pyros	Lv.3	3.25 seconds	3 MP
Pyre	Lv.5	3.25 second	5 MP
Pyrwall	Lv.10	3.25 seconds	20 MP
Megalevus	Lv.13	3 seconds	30 MP
Pyrdance	Lv.18	4.25 seconds	30 MP

Rucha's Magic

Spell	Learning Method	Casting Time	MP Cost
Pyrsweep	Lv.21	3.25 seconds	40 MP
Salva	Lv.28	2.75 seconds	50 MP
Hydryser	Lv.32	5.25 seconds	50 MP
Pyrburst	Lv.36	4.25 seconds	50 MP
Miasma	"Power of Fog"	3.25 seconds	30 MP
Pyrgeddon	"Will of the Universe"	4.25 seconds	100 MP

Rico's sister is less rambunctious and more disciplined. Like her brother, she uses a musical implement (in this case, drums) as her weapon. She too shares a connection with nature, though instead of communing with animals, she summons and controls a diminutive elemental beast, Tir na Nog. To keep Tir na Nog active, Rucha must be Connected. This presents an ideal opportunity to use Capell's Symphonic Blade against foes weak to air, the element Rucha grants. Tir na Nog itself can spawn as any of the elements, though it's inherently unpredictable—you've no control over which element it chooses to represent on a given summon. As a summoner, Rucha is also skilled at magic, and can serve, like Eugene or Michelle, as either a primary healer or a fierce source of magic offense. Foes susceptible to fire won't stand before spells like Pyrwall, or later Pyrburst, for long. Like Aya, Rucha can cook. She also occasionally finds raw materials while simply running around. Rucha's stats are slightly enhanced when she's grouped with her brother.

Tir na Nog Incarnations & Elements

Name	Element
Aerry	Air
Pyrool	Fire
Geogar	Earth
Astrogul	Aether
Hydrake	Water

EDWARD

Edward's skills

Skill	Description	Learning Method	Execution Time	BS 1/❌ CS MP Cost	BS 2/Ⓨ CS MP Cost	Lv.1 Hits/ Effect	Lv.2 Hits/ Effect	Lv.3 Hits/ Effect
Expert Slash	A well-timed sequence of three slashes.	Lv.8	0.75 seconds	8 MP	9 MP	3	3	3
Swordsquall (CS)	A volcanic downward thrust. Knocks foe down if Edward's portrait is above target marker on AP gauge. (Connect skill)	Lv.8	1.5 seconds	5 MP	6 MP	2	4	6
Twinstream	Two fearsome thrusts.	Lv.11	0.5 seconds	10 MP	12 MP	2	2	2
Turbulent Swing	A spinning attack that knocks the enemy into the air. 2nd hit launches foe if Edward's portrait is above target marker on AP gauge.	Lv.13	1.25 seconds	15 MP	18 MP	2	2	2
Galvanic Strike	A lightning-packed thrust.	Lv.15	0.5 seconds	23 MP	27 MP	5	5	5
Rising Current	A running upward slash. Launches foe if Edward's portrait is above target marker on AP gauge.	Lv.21	1 second	40 MP	48 MP	1	1	1
Thornrain	An attack from below that impales the enemy. Immobilizes foe briefly if Edward's portrait is above target marker on AP gauge.	Lv.25	2 seconds	50 MP	60 MP	1	5	8
Billowing Blade	A powerful thrust of the sword.	Lv.30	1.25 seconds	65 MP	78 MP	1	1	1
Dragonic Hail	A mighty thrust followed by a dragonic blast. Immobilizes foe during duration if Edward's portrait is above target marker on AP gauge.	Lv.45	1 second	75 MP	90 MP	2	4	6
Burning Sun	An explosive downward swing fueled by glyph energy. Knocks foe down if Edward's portrait is above target marker on AP gauge.	Lv.55	2.25 seconds	100 MP	120 MP	2	2	2
Tempest Clash	A furious barrage of attacks.	"Live by the Sword"	3 seconds	125 MP	150 MP	9	9	9

Edward is one of Sigmund's strongest allies. His giant greatsword and extremely useful skill set make him the most well-rounded pure melee character. When simply attacking, he favors a reverse hammer slash, or 2-hit chain. His skills are where he shines, however...in particular, Twinstream wins the title of best pound-for-pound physical skill in the game, from both this guide's staff and Square-Enix's testers! It executes very quickly, doesn't require much MP, and features two very heavily damaging hits. Since Edward doesn't provide a secondary role such as healing, there is no reason not to Connect with him when he's in the party, encouraging him to use this skill over and over. He won't need the MP for spells or curing, after all. This stoic knight also shines as an artisan—if you want the best close-range melee weapons (admit it, you do), you'll need to keep up Edward's smithing skill.

SIGMUND

Sigmund's skills

Skill	Description	Learning Method	Execution Time	BS 1/Ⓧ CS MP Cost	BS 2/Ⓨ CS MP Cost	Lv.1 Hits/ Effect	Lv.2 Hits/ Effect	Lv.3 Hits/ Effect
Grinn Valesti	An aerial assault that hits the enemy from above.	Lv.10	1 second	10 MP	12 MP	2	2	2
Alfheim	A shield-based attack followed by two sword attacks. Last hit launches foe if Sigmund's portrait is above target marker on AP gauge.	Lv.10	0.75 seconds	15 MP	18 MP	3	3	3
Levantine Slash (CS)	A jumping sword attack that uses all of the wielder's might. 2nd hit knocks foe down if Sigmund's portrait is above target marker on AP gauge. (Connect skill)	Lv.10	0.5 seconds	10 MP	12 MP	3	3	3
Reginleif	A powerful swing of the sword in a piercing arc.	Lv.16	1.5 seconds	25 MP	30 MP	1	1	1

The mysterious and noble liberator is as useful an ally as you'd expect, for someone capable of such astounding feats as severing the Order's chains. Like Capell, Sigmund wields a one-handed blade. Sigmund comes standard with battle skills that Capell doesn't learn until very late in the game, and what's more, Sigmund doesn't require nearly as much MP to use them. Grinn Valesti is generally the best; like Edward's Twinstream, for the cost and effectiveness there's not much point in even assigning a skill to Ⓐ. Putting Grinn Valesti in the Ⓑ slot and calling it a day definitely can serve you well. When attacking normally, Sigmund employs a jumping slash or a 3-hit chain. Concerning crafts, he's a jack-of-all-trades, capable of minor feats of creation in any trade. He's a master of none, however, so avoid "grinding" too much skill on Sigmund, as it is better served on other, more specialized allies. When in the party, Sigmund raises everyone's stats slightly. When Connected to Sigmund, the enemy's elemental affinities are revealed under their HP bar.

EUGENE

Eugene's skills

Skill	Description	Learning Method	Execution Time	BS 1/Ⓧ CS MP Cost	BS 2/Ⓨ CS MP Cost	Lv.1 Hits/ Effect	Lv.2 Hits/ Effect	Lv.3 Hits/ Effect
Soil Splitter (CS)	A random attack utilizing different ores. Pick between attempting to inflict silence, unhearing, unseeing, or unsmelling on a targeted foe. (Connect skill)	Lv.8	2 seconds	30 MP	36 MP	1	1	1

Eugene's Magic

Spell	Learning Method	Casting Time	MP Cost
Geos	Lv.8	3.5 seconds	10 MP
Levi	Lv.8	3 seconds	5 MP
Megalevi	Lv.8	3.25 seconds	10 MP
Geowall	Lv.8	3.5 seconds	20 MP
Volt	Lv.13	3.75 seconds	5 MP
Levus	Lv.15	3.25 seconds	15 MP
Geoclaw	Lv.17	3.5 seconds	30 MP
Megalevus	Lv.20	3.5 seconds	30 MP

Eugene's Magic

Spell	Learning Method	Casting Time	MP Cost
Salva	Lv.27	3 seconds	50 MP
Levusti	Lv.29	4.5 seconds	45 MP
Geopale	Lv.31	3.5 seconds	40 MP
Salvus	Lv.33	4 seconds	100 MP
Astro	Lv.35	3.5 seconds	15 MP
Geocrush	Lv.36	4.5 seconds	80 MP
Pyrdance	"Rage of Fire"	4.25 seconds	30 MP
Geoquake	"Flow of the Land"	5.5 seconds	100 MP

Childhood friend and constant companion of Sigmund, Eugene is a part-time archaeologist, ore collector, priest, healer, pain dispenser, and woodsmith. He crafts some of the game's best light weapons, has the most complete suite of healing magic, and commands the forces of earth in his offensive spells. He'll use his staff to hurl ore at foes, but is more effective sending forth spells like Geoclaw. Like Michelle, if you're ever in doubt over a final party slot, Eugene will never let you down. He even learns Astro eventually!

BALBAGAN

Balbagan's skills

Skill	Description	Learning Method	Execution Time	BS 1/Ⓧ CS MP Cost	BS 2/Ⓨ CS MP Cost	Lv.1 Hits/ Effect	Lv.2 Hits/ Effect	Lv.3 Hits/ Effect
Blitz Brigade	A rolling attack that finishes with a jumping body slam. Last hit knocks foe down if Balbagan's portrait is above target marker on AP gauge.	Lv.8	2.25 seconds	20 MP	24 MP	5	5	5
Gigatackle (CS)	An attack that can be charged for higher damage. Knocks foe down if Balbagan's portrait is above target marker on AP gauge. (Connect skill)	Lv.8	0.5 seconds	5 MP	6 MP	1	1	1
Barrier of Brawn	Concentrates lunaglyph energy into a defensive shield. Balbagan's DEF increases for a set duration. The effect is an increase of roughly 12% at Lv.15, and grows more potent as Balbagan gains levels.	Lv.15	3 seconds	15 MP	18 MP	Ⓧ - 30 seconds; Ⓨ - 35 seconds	Ⓧ - 45 seconds; Ⓨ - 50 seconds	Ⓧ - 60 seconds; Ⓨ - 70 seconds
Grandslammer	A mighty swing that raises the earth up into the air. Knocks foe down if Balbagan's portrait is above target marker on AP gauge.	Lv.20	2 seconds	35 MP	42 MP	1	1	1
Axle Drive	A clumsy—but effective—spinning attack. Last hit knocks foe down if Balbagan's portrait is above target marker on AP gauge.	Lv.43	1.75 seconds	50 MP	60 MP	4	4	4
Triple Threat	A three-tiered attack useful against multiple enemies.	Lv.53	1 second	75 MP	90 MP	5	5	5

If Edward is Sigmund's more cerebral (if overly passionate) melee companion, Balbagan is…not. He holds to the theory that if you can't break it with a hammer, get a bigger hammer. Balbagan wields a huge axe, which he'll apply liberally to enemy skulls with either a reverse hammer swing or 3-hit string. Concerning skills, Balbagan is interesting tactically; while some of his later skills are especially powerful, he lacks the MP pool to use them at will like many other characters. For much of the game until this becomes a non-issue, he's often better served simply using Barrier of Brawn to bolster his defense, and swinging away normally, rather than using some of his earlier, mostly awkward battle skills. Balbagan lacks a craft, but can instead bash apart fragile rocks strewn throughout the adventure, often opening the way to secret areas.

MICHELLE

Michelle's skills

Skill	Description	Learning Method	Execution Time	BS 1/Ⓧ CS MP Cost	BS 2/Ⓨ CS MP Cost	Lv.1 Hits/ Effect	Lv.2 Hits/ Effect	Lv.3 Hits/ Effect
Lover's Cuirass (CS)	A protective shell of paper that envelops an ally. Use Ⓧ for a 10-second shield, or Ⓨ for a 12-second shield. (Connect skill)	Lv.9	3.5 seconds	10% of max MP	12% of max MP	Grants shield that absorbs damage equaling up to 30% of max HP	Grants shield that absorbs damage equaling up to 50% of max HP	Grants shield that absorbs damage equaling up to 70% of max HP

Michelle's Magic

Spell	Learning Method	Casting Time	MP Cost
Astro	Lv.9	3.25 seconds	15 MP
Levi	Lv.9	3.25 seconds	5 MP
Megalevi	Lv.9	3.25 seconds	10 MP
Levus	Lv.9	3.25 seconds	15 MP
Hydrop	Lv.9	3.25 seconds	10 MP
Megalevus	Lv.15	3.25 seconds	30 MP
Astrovoid	Lv.18	3.25 seconds	30 MP

Michelle's Magic

Spell	Learning Method	Casting Time	MP Cost
Megalevusti	Lv.20	4.25 seconds	90 MP
Astrobeam	Lv.23	4.25 seconds	50 MP
Miasma	Lv.26	3.25 seconds	30 MP
Astroluminous	Lv.30	5.25 seconds	60 MP
Astrocalypse	Lv.34	5.25 seconds	80 MP
Nekros	"Tide of Water"	4.25 seconds	80 MP
Voltsweep	"Whispers of a Tree"	5.25 seconds	15 MP

There is much to be said in praise of Michelle, some of it printable, some of it not. She's very forward with certain male companions, and receives a small stat boost when in a party with either Capell or Sigmund. Along with Eugene or Rucha, she's one of the best main healers available. Her unique weapon of choice is the grimoire—a magical spellbook. She attacks by tossing an endless supply of enchanted pages from her tomes, or using them to summon a ground wave to prolong juggles up close. Her aether spell, Astro, is the magic equivalent to Edward's Twinstream—it's cheap and powerful, and becomes something approaching ridiculous when used enough to attain Lv.3 skill. What's more, enemies are stunned for the duration of its hits, and no enemy absorbs aether damage (the same cannot be said of any other element). Michelle is a practitioner of alchemy, which she uses to transmogrify seemingly worthless materials into useful ingredients for *other* crafts. Her unique Connect skill, Lover's Cuirass, can also be useful in quick skirmishes where Capell (or other allies) are virtually guaranteed to take damage—it grants a "stoneskin" effect, applying a percentage of max HP as an extra lifebar that lasts for a certain duration, and must be exhausted before any actual damage is taken. If Michelle is being used an Astro slingshot, it's worth setting up Lover's Cuirass as her other Connect ability, and using it on Capell before rushing toward a difficult foe or boss (before returning to her regularly scheduled Astro programming).

GUSTAV

Gustav's skills

Skill	Description	Learning Method	Execution Time	BS 1/ⓍCS MP Cost	BS 2/ⓨCS MP Cost	Lv.1 Hits/ Effect	Lv.2 Hits/ Effect	Lv.3 Hits/ Effect
Inferno Breath	A fiery breath attack.	Lv.13	2.25 seconds	10 MP	12 MP	1	1	1
Explosive Ride (CS)	An ability that combines Gustav's and Capell's strength. (Connect skill)	Lv.13	Capell mounts Gustav as soon as he is near	15 MP	18 MP	1	1	1
Grizzly Swing	A ferocious swing of the bear claw. Launches foe if Gustav's portrait is above target marker on AP gauge.	Lv.14	1 second	25 MP	30 MP	1	1	1
Crimson Burst	A blazing aura that increases ATK for a short time. The effect is an increase of roughly 10% at Lv.25, and grows more potent as Gustav gains levels.	Lv.25	2.75 seconds	40 MP	48 MP	Ⓧ - 30 seconds; ⓨ - 35 seconds	Ⓧ - 60 seconds; ⓨ - 70 seconds	Ⓧ - 90 seconds; ⓨ - 105 seconds
Volcanoblast	A raging concentration of heat that incinerates all in its path.	Lv.48	2.5 seconds	50 MP	60 MP	1	1	1

Gustav has the strength of a…OK, so, Gustav is a bear. Aya's pet bear, in fact. He's the rawest, most dominating physical force in the game by a fair margin; while he can't equip any gear except bear claws and accessories, his base HP and ATK stats surpass everyone else anyway. He provides Capell the only alternative transport in the game beyond simply running—during Explosive Ride our hero hops on Gustav's back for a speedy ride. However, run into any object or foe and Capell falls off. Explosive Ride can be used to break fragile rocks just like Balbagan's Gigatackle. When attacking, Gustav has a 3-slash string with

his claws. He can also rip chunks out of the very earth beneath his feet to hurl at far-away adversaries. In another similarity to Balbagan, Gustav frequently seems more useful *refraining* from using skills in battle. His MP pool isn't sizeable and his attacks do plenty of damage anyway…in particular his ranged rock toss matches his ranged skills in damage, with faster execution and no cost to MP. Consider simply assigning Crimson Burst as his Ⓑ battle skill. Gustav will then buff himself on his own when MP is available, before attacking normally. When the buff wears off, he'll re-apply it (just like assigning Balbagan's Barrier of Brawn to Ⓑ). Grizzly Swing can also be worthwhile when hunting for juggles, as no one has a higher AP gauge position than Gustav. If something can be launched, he is launching it. For all his advantages, using Gustav presents some unique problems. The expense of having a bear in the party is that he takes up two slots, forcing you to use only three characters. Although Gustav's stats are boosted slightly when grouped with his master, Aya, her healing capability may prove lacking in difficult encounters. Gustav may be a powerhouse, but three people (err, mammals) in the party rather than four means there's one less ally healing or dealing damage, and one less target for enemies to focus on. Depending on the encounter, these cons can outweigh the pros of bringing a bear to a swordfight. Finally, though you probably already knew this, Gustav has no crafting ability, though he does occasionally find raw materials while wandering around.

VIC

Vic's skills

Skill	Description	Learning Method	Execution Time	BS 1/ⓍCS MP Cost	BS 2/ⓨCS MP Cost	Lv.1 Hits/ Effect	Lv.2 Hits/ Effect	Lv.3 Hits/ Effect
Sneaky Scorpion (CS)	An attack from behind with varying effects. Vic dashes to the foe's back, striking them, before performing the follow-up of choice—choose between weakness up, steal, doom, and trip. The first hit stuns foes briefly if Vic's portrait is above target marker on AP gauge. Doom may kill susceptible foes outright. Trip knocks foes down if they are not still stunned from the first hit of Sneaky Scorpion and Vic's portrait is above target marker on AP gauge. (Connect skill)	Lv.25	Variable depending on action	15 MP	18 MP	2~3	2~3	2~3
Sliding Stinger	A sliding attack that knocks enemies off their feet. Knocks foe down if Vic's portrait is above target marker on AP gauge.	Lv.25	Instant	10 MP	12 MP	1	1	1
Dragon Flyer	A somersault kick that launches the enemy into the air. Launches foe if Vic's portrait is above target marker on AP gauge.	Lv.25	0.5 seconds	25 MP	30 MP	1	2	3
Mantiscissors	A distracting slap followed by a devastating slash.	Lv.28	0.75 seconds	40 MP	48 MP	2	2	2
Roly-poly	A stealthy attack that fakes out the enemy.	Lv.31	0.75 seconds	50 MP	60 MP	1	1	1
Grasshopper Stomp	A speedy stomp attack from above.	Lv.35	0.75 seconds	60 MP	72 MP	1	1	1
Butterfly Rush	A blinding flurry of strikes with the knife.	Lv.52	1 second	75 MP	90 MP	12	12	12

Vic's a young thief, wise beyond his years and eager (strangely eager…) to impress Capell, for reasons not entirely plain. He's the first ally you'll pair with who can open locked chests, which often makes him worth a party slot regardless of other factors. He's competent in combat too, however, attacking with upward dagger slashes or a double backhand slice. Sneaky Scorpion is a Connect skill that allows for some variation—Vic can increase the target's elemental weaknesses, inflict instant doom (not guaranteed, of course), trip them up, or even steal loot. Komachi is a more versatile, powerful fighter who duplicates and improves on the lock-picking function, however, so Vic is essentially outdated eventually. Vic has no craft skills, but can knock the price off store costs if you shop while Connected.

TOUMA

Touma's skills

Skill	Description	Learning Method	Execution Time	BS 1/ ⊗ CS MP Cost	BS 2/ Ⓨ CS MP Cost	Lv.1 Hits/ Effect	Lv.2 Hits/ Effect	Lv.3 Hits/ Effect
Nimble Zephyr	A quick swing of the sword that produces a sonic burst.	Lv.28	1.25 seconds	15 MP	18 MP	1	1	1
Steady Will	An astonishingly fast flurry of deadly strikes.	Lv.28	1.5 seconds	20 MP	24 MP	4	4	4
Seamless Fury (CS)	A swift attack utilizing rapid button pressing. (Connect skill)	Lv.28	1.5 seconds	15 MP	18 MP	1~11	1~16	1~21
Infallible Self	A magical sheathing of the sword that creates a vacuum.	Lv.28	2 seconds	25 MP	30 MP	1	1	1
Momentary Spite	A quick spin followed by a powerful shockwave.	Lv.33	2 seconds	40 MP	48 MP	3	3	3
Encompassing Rend	A swift and deadly attack that affects a group of enemies.	Lv.46	1.5 seconds	50 MP	60 MP	1	1	1
Cosmic Gambol	An adept combination of skilled sword strikes.	Lv.54	0.75 seconds	60 MP	72 MP	7	7	7
Peerless Valor	A courageous step forward followed by a heroic swing.	"Palm of the Hand"	1.5 seconds	100 MP	120 MP	2	2	2

Don't let Touma's stature fool you; this samurai doesn't need size to match up with hardened foes. Touma has a 2-hit string or draws and strikes in one motion with his katana. His Connect skill, Seamless Fury, is more effective the faster you mash the button, and can help pile on the damaging hits in a combo very quickly. His later skills are even more powerful. His stats are enhanced slightly when grouped with Komachi, his servant. Touma has no craft skills.

KOMACHI

Komachi's skills

Skill	Description	Learning Method	Execution Time	BS 1/ ⊗ CS MP Cost	BS 2/ Ⓨ CS MP Cost	Lv.1 Hits/ Effect	Lv.2 Hits/ Effect	Lv.3 Hits/ Effect
Ash	A burning breath attack.	Lv.28	3 seconds	10 MP	12 MP	3	3	3
Honeysuckle (CS)	Pulls in far away items or enemies. (Connect skill)	Lv.28	Komachi draws her chain as soon as she reaches Capell	0 MP	0 MP	1	1	1
Crowfoot	An aerial attack that stuns the enemy. Foes are briefly stunned if Komachi's portrait is above target marker on AP gauge.	Lv.28	1 second	18 MP	21 MP	1	1	1
Hornbeam	A giant shuriken that smashes everything in its path.	Lv.28	1.5 seconds	23 MP	27 MP	2	2	2
Water Lily	A powerful splash that smites nearby foes with water. Launches foe if Komachi's portrait is above target marker on AP gauge.	Lv.35	3 seconds	35 MP	42 MP	1	1	1
Windflower	An aerial attack that strikes the enemies with petals. Launches foe if Komachi's portrait is above target marker on AP gauge.	Lv.42	1.75 seconds	45 MP	54 MP	1	2	3
Thistle	A rapid succession of deadly kicks. Last hit of Lv.3 version knocks foe down if Komachi's portrait is above target marker on AP gauge.	Lv.56	0.5 seconds	55 MP	66 MP	5	7	9
Nightshade	A teleportation strike.	"Legend of a Shadow"	1.5 seconds	75 MP	90 MP	3	5	9

Komachi is Touma's loyal servant and a great ally in her own right. She's the only character besides Vic who can pick locked chests, but what's more, she can snag out-of-reach chests with Honeysuckle. This grappling ability is aimed just like Aya's Ravaging Raptor. Although she has no craft skills, the ability to spring chests or snag distant treasure makes Komachi extremely appealing as a constant companion. It helps that she's no slouch in battle either; while she's not as heavily armored as other melee characters like Balbagan or Edward, and thus a little more vulnerable, she makes up for this somewhat with Hornbeam, an excellent and long-ranged stylish shuriken attack. In function, this skill is like a slightly more expensive Twinstream, except that Komachi doesn't have to be anywhere close to her foe to use it. When attacking up close, she'll either slash upward with both daggers, or perform a double dagger slice into a kick. She receives a slight stat boost when grouped with her master, Touma. While she has no crafts, she'll sometimes find raw materials while simply running around.

MAGIC

Determining which spells a character uses is a little different than assigning battle skills. Tap ⓨ on a given spell within a character's magic menu to enable or disable it. Disable MP-inefficient or less useful spells, and place situational or high-cost spells as Connect abilities. Leave healing spells on, along with low-cost, high-hit spells (Hydrill, Astro, etc.). When frequently fighting foes that completely resist or absorb given elements, disable spells of that element. When MP is short, consider using abilities like Diminuendo Dive, Slashing Canon, and so on to knock foes down, then combo them on the ground to replenish some MP. Otherwise, rest at inns, accept Genma's invitations to rest, or use items that restore MP. Late in the game, pieces of gear and enchantments become available that restore a percentage of max MP every five seconds. This MP regeneration essentially removes MP as a concern, enabling more frequent, careless spellcasting, and allows you to swap from using low-cost spells to more costly ones with a stronger ultimate potential. Finally, when assigning both a skill and a spell as Connect skills for an ally, avoid placing the spell in the ⓨ slot, needlessly robbing a skill of a 20% effectiveness boost…spells do not get this bonus (or an increase in cost) by being in the ⓨ slot.

Restorative magic

Spell	Description	MP Cost	Aya	Rico	Rucha	Eugene	Michelle
Levi	Heals around 30% of an ally's HP.	5 MP	Lv.3	Lv.2	--	Lv.8	Lv.9
Levus	Heals around 60% of an ally's HP.	15 MP	--	Lv.13	--	Lv.15	Lv.9
Megalevi	Heals around 30% of HP for allies within range.	10 MP	Lv.17	--	Lv.2	Lv.8	Lv.9
Levusti	Heals 100% of an ally's HP.	45 MP	--	Lv.34	--	Lv.29	--
Megalevus	Heals around 60% of HP for allies within range.	30 MP	--	--	Lv.13	Lv.20	Lv.15
Megalevusti	Heals 100% of HP for allies within range.	90 MP	--	--	--	--	Lv.20
Salva	Revives a fallen ally and heals 30% of HP.	50 MP	--	--	Lv.28	Lv.27	--
Salvus	Revives a fallen ally and heals 100% of HP.	100 MP	--	--	--	Lv.33	--

Air magic

Spell	Description	MP Cost	Level 1 Hits	Level 2 Hits	Level 3 Hits	Aya	Rico	Rucha	Eugene	Michelle
Aerowave	Sends a condensed whirlwind towards the enemy.	5 MP	1	1	1	--	--	Lv.2	--	--
Aerwhirl	Sends a tornado towards the enemy, tearing up everything nearby. Launches foes if caster's portrait is above target marker on AP gauge.	20 MP	1	1	1	--	Lv.31	--	--	--
Volt	Creates a spark above the enemy that hits them with a bolt of lightning.	5 MP	1	3	6	--	Lv.2	--	Lv.13	--
Voltsweep	Sends out a bolt of electricity from the caster.	15 MP	2	3	4	--	Lv.18	--	--	"Whispers of a Tree"
Voltscourge	Creates an electrical sphere around the enemy which hurts any foe it touches.	50 MP	3	6	9	--	Lv.37	--	--	--

Fire magic

Spell	Description	MP Cost	Level 1 Hits	Level 2 Hits	Level 3 Hits	Aya	Rico	Rucha	Eugene	Michelle
Pyros	Sends a ball of fire hurtling towards the enemy.	3 MP	1	1	1	--	--	Lv.3	--	--
Pyre	Throws a fiery ember at the feet of the enemy, creating a pillar of fire.	5 MP	2	2	2	--	--	Lv.5	--	--
Pyrwall	Creates a wall of fire at the feet of the enemy, engulfing them in flames.	20 MP	5	5	5	--	--	Lv.10	--	--
Pyrdance	Sends a huge ball of fire which splits up, attacking nearby enemies.	30 MP	2	--	--	--	--	Lv.18	"Rage of Fire"	--
Pyrsweep	Sends a flame hurtling along the ground towards the enemy.	40 MP	1	1	1	--	--	Lv.21	--	--
Pyrburst	A ball of energy which grows above the enemy and engulfs them in an explosion.	50 MP	1	1	1	--	--	Lv.36	--	--
Pyrgeddon	A magic seal appears in the sky and showers the enemy with flaming boulders.	100 MP	5	7	9	--	--	"Will of the Universe"	--	--

Earth magic

Spell	Description	MP Cost	Level 1 Hits	Level 2 Hits	Level 3 Hits	Aya	Rico	Rucha	Eugene	Michelle
Geos	Sends rocks hurtling towards the enemy.	10 MP	1	1	1	--	--	--	Lv.8	--
Geowall	Creates a barrier of earth to protect the caster. Launches foe if caster's portrait is above target marker on AP gauge.	20 MP	1	1	1	--	--	--	Lv.8	--
Geoclaw	Creates an earthen claw which rushes along the ground to smash the enemy.	30 MP	3	3	3	--	--	--	Lv.17	--
Geopale	Sharp rocks spring up from the ground in front of the enemy.	40 MP	1	3	5	--	--	--	Lv.31	--
Geocrush	Sends a boulder hurtling along the ground towards the enemy. Knocks foe down if caster's portrait is above target marker on AP gauge.	80 MP	1	1	1	--	"Molding of Earth"	--	Lv.36	--
Geoquake	Causes an earthquake which hurts all nearby enemies.	100 MP	3	3	3	--	--	--	"Flow of the Land"	--

Aether magic

Spell	Description	MP Cost	Level 1 Hits	Level 2 Hits	Level 3 Hits	Aya	Rico	Rucha	Eugene	Michelle
Astro	Smashes an enemy with a small meteor and shocks them momentarily. Stuns foe briefly is caster's portrait is above target marker on AP gauge.	15 MP	3	9	15	--	--	--	Lv.35	Lv.9
Astrovoid	Creates an energy force that sucks in everything in the surrounding area. Has a small chance to kill foes outright.	30 MP	1	1	1	--	--	--	--	Lv.18
Astrobeam	Fires a beam of energy at a group of enemies.	50 MP	1	1	1	--	--	--	--	Lv.23
Astroluminous	Rays of light shine from the sky, causing enemies that touch them to explode.	60 MP	3	3	3	--	--	--	--	Lv.30
Astrocalypse	Two balls of opposing energy collide to create an immense explosion.	80 MP	3	3	3	--	--	--	--	Lv.34

Water magic

Spell	Description	MP Cost	Level 1 Hits	Level 2 Hits	Level 3 Hits	Aya	Rico	Rucha	Eugene	Michelle
Hydrill	Sends a barrage of ice arrows at the enemy. May freeze foe if caster's portrait is above target marker on AP gauge.	8 MP	4	6	8	--	Lv.9	--	--	--
Hydrop	Creates a ball of ice above the enemy, which drops down to crush them. Knocks foe down if caster's portrait is above target marker on AP gauge.	10 MP	1	1	1	--	--	--	--	Lv.9
Hydrain	Showers the enemy with acid rain.	20 MP	4	4	4	--	Lv.21	--	--	--
Hydryser	Freezes the enemy where they stand and shoots up a geyser from under them. Lv.1 version launches foe if caster's portrait is above target marker on AP gauge.	50 MP	2	2	2	--	--	Lv.32	--	--
Miasma	Emits a cloud of poison gas from the caster, damaging nearby enemies.	30 MP	1	1	1	--	--	"Power of Fog"	--	Lv.26
Nekros	Soaks the enemy with poisonous liquid, potentially causing instant death.	80 MP	--	--	--	--	--	--	--	"Tide of Water"

HOW TO USE THIS WALKTHROUGH

Welcome to the official story walkthrough for *Infinite Undiscovery*. This section contains detailed maps and step-by-step guidance for all of the game's main story missions. Note that in this book, side quests are considered separate from the main story. **See Part 4: Side Quests** for walkthroughs of all *Infinite Undiscovery* side quests.

IMPORTANT: Our story walkthrough focuses on showing you "where to go" in detail, but it tells you "what to do" in only a general sense.

For in-depth info and strategies on combat, equipment choice, battle skills, Connect skills, magic, party formation, item creation, status ailments, tactics against specific enemies, and other important aspects of gameplay, refer to this book's four separate sections on Game Basics, Skills, Data, and the Bestiary.

SIDE QUESTS

Your arrival in each new village or city usually unlocks optional side quests. To trigger these quests, explore the town area and talk to townsfolk. Some ask favors of Capell. Each favor initiates a side quest that usually requires the completion of several tasks.

In the story walkthrough, all new side quests are listed as they become available. However, instructions are not given for where you need to go or what you need to do. To get those details (including maps), refer to **Part 4: Side Quests**. Check the introduction to that section for other useful tips about triggering and completing side quests.

PRIVATE EVENTS

Your arrival at each new village or city also unlocks a number of special conversations when Capell talks to certain people. These "private events" explore deeper aspects of the story, its characters, and their relationships to one another. The conversations almost always involve dialogue between Capell and other party members, but some exceptions exist—Capell may learn something from a local fisherman or shopkeeper, for example.

Private events are short but revealing, so the walkthrough indicates each one and how to trigger it. As with side quests, sometimes Capell must be Connected to a specific party member in order to trigger the private event dialogue with another character.

SITUATION BONUSES

The game rewards you with special bonuses when you complete certain story-related tasks with distinction. For example, if you escort a group of unblessed citizens across the dangerous Oradian Dunes to their hometown without losing a single citizen, you earn a bonus of 7500 EXP. These "situation bonuses" are all noted in the walkthrough; in each case both the challenge and the reward are listed.

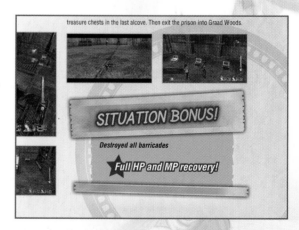

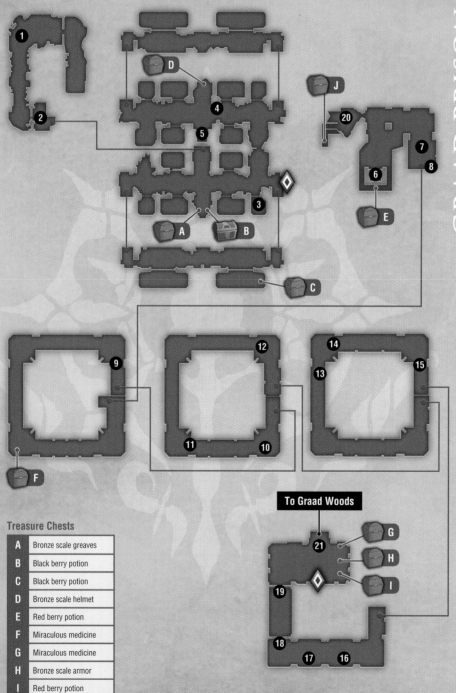

GRAAD PRISON

MISSION MAPS

1. Start
2. Capell's cell
3. Young villager (side quest contact)
4. Explosive barrel
5. Elevator (lower level)
6. Elevator (upper level)
7. Alarm triggered!
8. Barricade
9. Barricade (barrel)
10. Order archers (barrel)
11 - 15 Barricades
16 - 17 Barrels
18. Locked door
19. Last barricade
20. Vembert's room
21. Exit door to woods

LEGEND

Wooden Chest

Gold Chest

Save Point

To Graad Woods

Treasure Chests

A	Bronze scale greaves
B	Black berry potion
C	Black berry potion
D	Bronze scale helmet
E	Red berry potion
F	Miraculous medicine
G	Miraculous medicine
H	Bronze scale armor
I	Red berry potion
J	Black berry

RESCUE

A young musician named Capell the Soother sits in Graad Prison, the grim destination for enemies of the Dreadknight and his legions. But it's a case of mistaken identity—Capell, a mild-mannered flute player, is a dead ringer for Lord Sigmund, the man known as "The Liberator" and head of the underground force working to defeat the Order.

MISSION
ESCAPE GRAAD PRISON

The Order of Chains is not alone in its identity error. A young woman warrior named Aya suddenly drops in, overcomes the jailer, and unlocks Capell's cell. Aya believes she's rescuing Lord Sigmund! But as she learns the truth, she gets caught off-guard and knocked unconscious. Capell is left facing two angry prison guards. Time to fight!

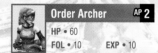

ACTION CHECKLIST

1 • Escape your prison cell.

2 • Explore the main cell block area.

3 • When the alarm sounds, flee upstairs to the front gate.

4 • Defeat Vembert.

5 • Exit the prison.

ENEMIES

	Order Jailer	AP 2
	HP • 120	
	FOL • 10	EXP • 15

	Order Archer	AP 2
	HP • 60	
	FOL • 10	EXP • 10

	Vembert the Ogre	AP ?
	HP • Vembert cannot be killed.	
	FOL • ?	EXP • ?

NEW SIDE QUESTS AVAILABLE

Deliver the Gold Coin

PRIVATE EVENTS AVAILABLE

None.

MISSION WALKTHROUGH

As the mission opens, Capell stands facing two Order jailers. He picks up a sword…and has little choice but to fight. Your overall objective in this mission is to work together with Aya to reach the prison exit door alive. Most of the prison structure is underground, so to escape you must work your way upward.

VIEW THE BATTLE TUTORIALS

Before you can fight, however, you get your first set of in-game tutorials. These ones, entitled Battle 1, Battle 2, and Battle 3, are several pages long and cover the very basics of combat. Read tutorial pages carefully whenever they appear onscreen! They give instructions and offer good advice.

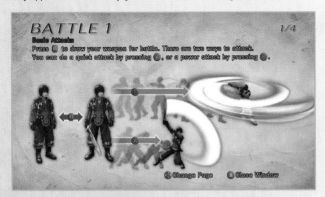

DEFEAT THE GUARDS

This first fight is straightforward. Attack the Order jailers, testing out your new moves. Mix up quick and power attacks, and try some combos. Add a Deflect Drive or two to parry enemy strikes and immobilize the attacker for a moment.

After your foes fall, Aya revives, and convinces Capell to escape with her. Here, she officially joins your party. (You get an onscreen notification whenever someone joins or leaves your party.) Time to make your first move across the map.

Step through the doorway at the corridor's end to trigger a short scene— Aya gives you several useful medicinal items, and then another tutorial appears, this one is about the Camp screen. Then follow the corridor and head upstairs.

Don't Camp If Danger Lurks...

Don't use the Camp menu as a pause function! Remember that the game progresses in real time when you camp. Enemies don't care if you're camping peacefully; they attack regardless. Camp only if you're sure the area is clear. Press the Start button to actually pause the game.

EXPLORE THE MAIN CELL BLOCK

This is the main cell block area, which includes two raised levels, located up the side stairs to the north and south. Approach the two treasure chests in the alcove opposite the stairs. Open the wooden chest on the right to nab a nice pair of bronze scale greaves. Immediately equip the greaves to improve your DEF (defense) stat by 4 and your AGL (agility) stat by 2.

Protect Yourself

Whenever you find equipment that improves your stats, equip it as soon as possible.

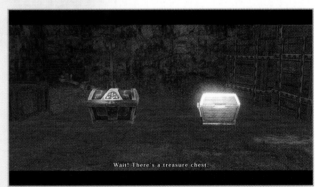

The gold chest on the left is locked. Smash it open with quick attacks; if the contents survive, you get a black berry potion. If not, you get a nice piece of junk. (You cannot return to Graad Prison once completed; however, if you don't want to risk losing the items in other locked chests you find early in the game, you can return later with someone who knows how to unlock chests.)

Now start exploring the cell block. Talk to various prisoners in cells to pick up information. Always speak to everyone at least twice; most NPCs have two messages. Don't miss chatting with the "Young villager" in the southeast cell, the one nearest the glowing blue save point. He asks you to deliver a special gold coin to his wife and son. Select "Very well" if you want to take on the first side quest available in the game. This puts an "eagle emblem gold coin" in your Items inventory, listed under Special Items.

Quest Contact

Talk to the young villager a second time to learn that his wife's name is Anne and his son's is Ralph. You can meet them later in Burgusstadt.

Now save your game at the save point. From there you can go upstairs to the south and find an unlocked cell with a treasure chest inside. Nab the bottle of black berry potion from the chest, then come back downstairs. Go due north past the save point into the northern half of the cell block.

This triggers a tutorial sequence: Aya points out an elevator, a guard, and an explosive barrel just down the corridor. View the tutorial pages on Connect and Connect actions (CA), then Connect to Aya and use her bow-based CA, "Ravaging Raptor," to fire an arrow into the barrel. The resulting explosion knocks out the Order jailer posted nearby. This technique—Connecting to Aya and then shooting her arrows into explosive barrels—will prove very useful during the rest of the mission.

TAKE THE ELEVATOR TO THE PRISON'S UPPER LEVEL

Finish exploring the cell block area—in particular, don't miss the bronze scale helmet in the treasure chest across from the elevator. Put it on immediately! Then, approach the elevator to trigger another cutscene. Aya stumbles briefly in pain, then delivers a quick history lesson on Lord Sigmund's struggle against the Order of Chains. After the cutscene, examine the control lever; Capell uses it to bring down the elevator. Enter and use the lever inside to ride up to the next level.

Exit on the upper level. Don't miss the treasure chest tucked behind the elevator. A tall wooden door across from the elevator is locked; it will be open later, but for now, move on. Find the nearby stairs and start climbing to trigger a cutscene. An Order jailer spots you and sounds the alarm! (You can't avoid this detection; you must trigger the event in order to proceed.) A powerful ogre appears. His name is Vembert, he's head of the jail guard, and he hates you quite a lot.

As you climb stairs with Vembert breathing down your neck, remember that you can target explosive barrels with Aya's "Ravaging Raptor" to clear an easier path through enemies ahead. In fact, barrels are placed near barricades in several spots. By targeting these for detonation, you can take out guards *and* barricades with a single arrow. Note also that when you see Vembert climbing up the banister, you can strike his hand with your sword to make him fall, buying you more ogre-free time.

FLEE UPSTAIRS TO THE PRISON EXIT

Run! Eventually, you want to take the advice of the "Fleeing" tutorial that appears—i.e., sheathe your weapon to run faster. But right now you need your sword in hand to bash through the wooden barrier blocking your escape at the top of the first staircase.

Vembert is essentially invincible, and his Brandishbane stomp attack is brutal, so don't try to tangle with him. The big ogre stays on your tail all the way to the top. Note that his bullish charge smashes through friend, foe, and barricade alike, so the big guy can actually *help* you in some cases. If you get cornered by Order jailers or archers, fight back just enough to get free, but then sheathe your sword and run away. Keep running until you reach the top and trigger the cutscene where Capell finds the door locked. Guess who has the keys?

A Smashing Bonus

You gain a Situation Bonus if you destroy every barricade as you escape the prison. This includes one last barricade reachable only after you defeat Vembert and unlock the exit door. Also: after Vembert falls, you have plenty of time to go back and smash any barricades you missed while fleeing.

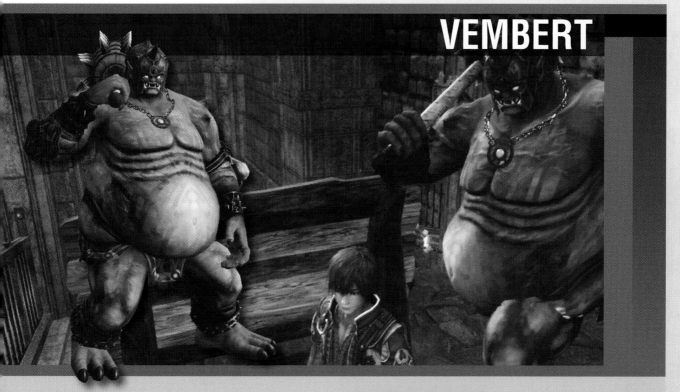

VEMBERT

Vembert is very tough if you let the fight turn into a close-range slugfest. But you can take him out easily if you simply follow the onscreen suggestion: use Aya's "Ravaging Raptor" to target the clusters of explosive barrels in the corridor as Vembert passes them. If the ogre is close enough to the explosions, you can knock him out before he reaches your end of the corridor.

BACKTRACK TO VEMBERT'S ROOM!

Here's a fun tip: after you knock Vembert off the stairwell, all of his troops disappear from the prison! Before you exit, you can go back downstairs and open any treasure chests or smash any barricades you missed as you were fleeing upstairs. In fact, you can backtrack all the way down to where Vembert lies unconscious in front of the elevator!

Nearby, the door to Vembert's bunkroom is now open. (It was locked earlier—see **20** on the mission map.) Raid the treasure chest next to the bed for a black berry. Then go all the way back upstairs to the locked exit door.

EXIT THE PRISON INTO GRAAD WOODS

After the fight, you automatically gain Vembert's key ring. Open the locked door, smash through the final barrier to score your Situation Bonus (a full recovery of HP and MP), then help yourself to the goodies in the three treasure chests in the last alcove. Then exit the prison into Graad Woods.

SITUATION BONUS!

Destroyed all barricades

⭐ *Full HP and MP recovery!*

MISSION

TRAVERSE GRAAD WOODS

Capell and Aya plunge into the dangerous, wasp-infested darkness of Graad Woods. Unfortunately, the Order of Chains patrols the paths…and you haven't seen the last of Vembert yet, either. The big ogre recovers and deploys his troops and his hounds into the dense forest in pursuit. Your goal is to follow the long, winding route until you reach a footbridge more than halfway across the forest.

MISSION MAPS

1. Start
2. First beacon
3. Beacon (2 Burguss apples)
4. Hounds triggered!
5. Beacon (2 Burguss apples)
6. Wasp attack!
7. Beacon (2 Burguss apples)
8. Medical herb
9. Beacon (1 Burguss apple)
10. Vembert appears!
11. Footbridge

LEGEND

Wooden Chest
Jeweled Cabinet
Save Point

Treasure Chests

A	Red berry potion
B	Blue berry potion
C	Miraculous medicine
D	Black berry potion
E	Miraculous medicine
F	Charming perfume

GRAAD WOODS (EAST)

To Graad Prison

ACTION CHECKLIST

1 · Move stealthily from beacon to beacon across the woods.

2 · Fight off the Order hounds.

3 · Optional: Shoot down and gather all the Burguss apples.

4 · Reach the footbridge deep in the forest.

NEW SIDE QUESTS AVAILABLE

None.

PRIVATE EVENTS AVAILABLE

None.

ENEMIES

	Order Jailer	AP 2
	HP • 120	
	FOL • 10	EXP • 15

	Order Archer	AP 2
	HP • 60	
	FOL • 10	EXP • 10

	Order Hound	AP 5
	HP • 600	
	FOL • 30	EXP • 50

	Giant Wasp	AP 1
	HP • 70	
	FOL • 3	EXP • 10

	Vembert the Ogre	AP ?
	HP • Vembert cannot be killed	
	FOL • ?	EXP • ?

MISSION WALKTHROUGH

Here's another mission where escape is the primary goal. This time, however, use stealth in the early going to score quick KO's against Order foes, boost EXP, and get better drop items. You can spend some time swatting down killer wasps as well; it's a good way to build EXP. But once Vembert gets back in the picture, your best bet is to simply sprint hard for safety.

WIN THE ADVANTAGE BATTLE

The onscreen tutorials continue in this mission. You learn about detection and the attack advantages of surprise hits. When you score a surprise hit on an enemy, your entire party gains attack bonuses against that foe for a short time, including landing every blow as an unblockable critical hit. Surprised foes are more likely to drop rare items. You also gain infinite AP and bonus EXP.

Use what you learn in the darkness of these woods. Capell can sneak up on the Order of Chains soldiers for stealthy hits. Aya's long distance strikes are particularly good for getting in surprise first hits, but be sure to rush Capell forward for quick follow-up to take advantage of the attack bonuses.

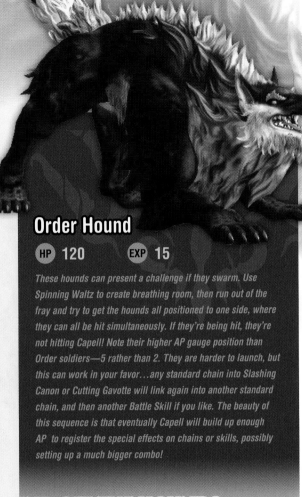

Surprise!

Surprise attacks give you a big advantage in a fight. But remember: the reverse is true as well. If a foe lands a surprise blow on your party from behind while Capell's sword is sheathed, all enemy blows become critical hits, and your AP Gauge drops to zero for a while.

OPTIONAL: APPLE HUNT

Shortly after you enter the woods, Aya points out the luscious red Burguss apples hanging from the tree above a beacon fire. Use Aya's "Ravaging Raptor" CA to target and shoot down the pungent fruit. A total of seven apples hang from trees on your route through the woods—three pairs and a single. If Aya shoots them all down, you earn a Situation Bonus.

FOLLOW THE BEACON FIRES

Graad Woods is dark, and even your minimap goes fuzzy when you're deep in the trees. But the path is narrow and marked by a line of beacon fires. Keep moving from beacon to beacon, watching for Order guards and the occasional wasp attack. Don't miss the treasure chests and healing herbs scattered through the trees.

And listen carefully: you'll hear guards give away their position by saying, "Where are they hiding?" Some of the Order soldiers carry light globes.

These illuminate a small area, which makes it harder to sneak past. But it also lets you spot the foe from afar.

Order Hound

HP 120   **EXP** 15

These hounds can present a challenge if they swarm. Use Spinning Waltz to create breathing room, then run out of the fray and try to get the hounds all positioned to one side, where they can all be hit simultaneously. If they're being hit, they're not hitting Capell! Note their higher AP gauge position than Order soldiers—5 rather than 2. They are harder to launch, but this can work in your favor...any standard chain into Slashing Canon or Cutting Gavotte will link again into another standard chain, and then another Battle Skill if you like. The beauty of this sequence is that eventually Capell will build up enough AP to register the special effects on chains or skills, possibly setting up a much bigger combo!

FEND OFF THE HOUNDS

When you exit one of the first clearings (see ④ on the mission map), you trigger a quick cutscene of a vicious pack of Order hounds on the hunt nearby. Be ready, because they'll close in on your position soon enough.

FEND OFF THE WASPS

A little farther down the path, you pass a beacon light that triggers an attack by nasty giant wasps. These insects are not particularly tough, one on one. But they can swarm, and if a wasp manages to stick you with its odor-inducing Stinksting attack, the resulting smell (which appears as a yellowish smoke coming off Capell or Aya) attracts a steady stream of wasps until it wears off.

This isn't an entirely bad thing, however. Once you figure out how to kill wasps effectively without taking much damage in return, let a wasp mark you with stink and then swat wasp after wasp to boost your EXP.

Let Rotten Fruit Lie?

The odor of rotten fruit immediately marks you as a target for wasps. If you want to whack wasps for awhile to build EXP, go ahead and pick up the fruit. Otherwise, don't touch it.

SITUATION BONUS!

Shot down all Burguss apples.

⭐ **Obtained a bottle of blue berry potion!**

OUTRUN VEMBERT!

In another clearing deep in the woods (see ❿ on the map), Vembert reappears. You don't have far to go from here to reach safety, but the going sure gets tough. Take Aya's advice: "Ignore him, Capell! Let's run!"

Sprint past him and follow the narrow path as it curves south then sharply north again. Wasps, Order jailers, and Order archers abound in the next couple of clearings, and Vembert stays right behind you, making the occasional bull rush and following up with his Brandishbane jump-slam.

Just keep running and weaving through the final clearing, then veer west toward the footbridge. Once you reach the bridge, you complete the mission and trigger a cinema in which your pursuers meet their fate…and Capell finally meets his look-alike. Welcome to Lord Sigmund's Liberation Force.

Here you're introduced to the Liberator himself, his lieutenant Edward, the powerful Balbagan, the wise Genma, and Eugene the priest. Eventually, all but Genma end up joining you as active party members. In the next mission, however, these characters function as independent guest NPCs.

Once the scenes of the initial meeting end, Capell can move about the Liberation Force camp. Explore a bit and talk to other characters, saving Aya for last. (If you talk to her once, she suggests that you get to know the others first.) Don't miss the fresh herb growing near the fire where Aya sits. When you talk to Aya a second time, you trigger a long sequence in which she's eventually stricken by the effects of her battle wound.

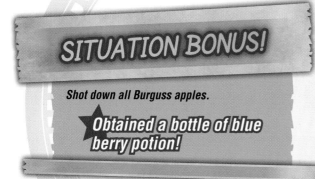

GRAAD WOODS (WEST)

Treasure Chests

A	Red Berry Potion

MISSION MAPS

1. Liberation Force camp
2. Start
3. Cracked rock
4. Novo herb
5. Mission ends

LEGEND

Jeweled Cabinet

A

To Luce Plains

SECRET OF THE CLARIDION

The next series of missions focuses on healing Aya's mysterious battle wound. Capell must carry her out of Graad Woods to a nearby town. There, you pick up unlikely new allies and unlock new side quests and private events. Then you explore the forbidding temple of the Claridian in search of a cure for Aya's ailment.

MISSION

GET AYA OUT OF GRAAD WOODS

Eugene calls Aya's wound a "lunaglyph curse." She needs healing that the Force cannot provide now; their all-important mission is to break the Azure Chain at Castle Prevant. Thus Sigmund decides that Capell should take Aya to Nolaan, a nearby village with ties to a great healer. He gives Capell a sword with a royal emblem that grants safe passage through the land.

ACTION CHECKLIST

1 · Follow your Force escort through the woods.

2 · Carry Aya into the Luce Plains.

NEW SIDE QUESTS AVAILABLE

None.

PRIVATE EVENTS AVAILABLE

None.

ENEMIES

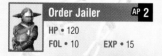

Order Jailer	AP 2
HP • 120	
FOL • 10	EXP • 15

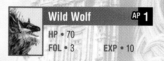

Wild Wolf	AP 1
HP • 70	
FOL • 3	EXP • 10

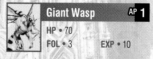

Giant Wasp	AP 1
HP • 70	
FOL • 3	EXP • 10

MISSION WALKTHROUGH

In this simple mission, you carry Aya out of the forest, working your way south to the Luce Plains where you'll eventually head west to Nolaan. In order to reach Castle Prevant where the Azure Chain is anchored, the rest of the Liberation Force must also exit Graad Woods to the south. So Sigmund, Edward, Eugene, and Balbagan will escort you to the edge of the plains—as Sigmund says, "Until the road splits."

FOLLOW THE ESCORT PARTY

Again, Capell is carrying the stricken Aya. As a result, you cannot fight or talk to anyone, although you can pick up items dropped by defeated foes. (Just walk over them.) You can also examine items, such as herbs, to gather them. Just follow your escort team. They happen to be world-class fighters, so stay behind them and let them protect you. But don't let them get too far away. Enemies can come from any direction in Graad Woods.

Healing Request

This mission introduces the healing request function. Don't hesitate to press Ⓨ if your health is low.

NOTES FOR A RETURN VISIT

See the large reddish boulder (at ❸ on the map) in the alcove just before your route bends east? If you approach it, you see it targeted and called a "Cracked Rock." Swing the camera to the side; you'll see a gleaming treasure chest behind it! But you can't smash the rock just yet. Note it for later when you have party members who can use Connect actions to bash through a boulder.

When you finally clear the woods, Eugene sends you west toward Nolaan. Then you're given the opportunity to save your game.

MISSION
GET AYA TO NOLAAN

The Luce Plains are home to unfriendly beasts and a curious race of hostile hominids known as Lumpers. Still carrying Aya, Capell cannot fight back if attacked, but he's fast enough to outrun foes if necessary. However, there is a new menace in the plains.

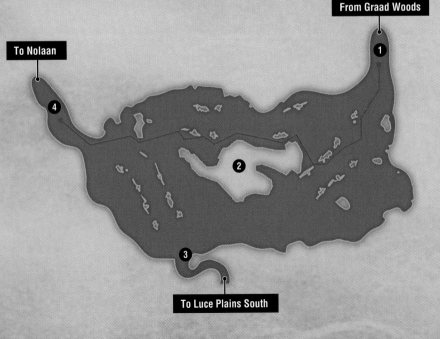

From Graad Woods

To Nolaan

To Luce Plains South

LUCE PLAINS (NORTH)

MISSION MAPS

❶ Start
❷ Saruleus
❸ Blocked tunnel
❹ Finish
●━● Recommended route

ACTION CHECKLIST

1 • Carry Aya west across the Luce Plains.

2 • Avoid the angry dragon's fireballs.

3 • Enter the village of Nolaan.

NEW SIDE QUESTS AVAILABLE

None.

PRIVATE EVENTS AVAILABLE

None.

ENEMIES

Lumper Marksman	AP **2**
HP • 675	
FOL • 20	EXP • 25

Thorn Cobra	AP **3**
HP • 800	
FOL • 30	EXP • 35

Saruleus	AP **?**
HP • Saruleus cannot be killed.	
FOL • ?	EXP • ?

MISSION WALKTHROUGH

This mission is about as painfully simple as it gets. The great dragon Saruleus settles atop the central plateau and fires streams of explosive fireballs down at you. Your goal is to run west past the raging reptile and carry Aya safely into the village.

USE RUINS AS SHIELDS

Ancient stone ruins line the roads running across the northern Luce Plains. Saruleus is so powerful that his blasts actually obliterate some of the old rubble—and if the flying debris hits you, you take damage. However, the bases of the bigger columns are sturdy enough to hold up under fire. Use these for protection from the dragon's fireball attacks. You can also cut off the dragon's firing angle in some (but not all) spots right up under the cliff face.

Dragons Inhale Eventually

Saruleus takes a brief pause to catch his breath after every 10 to 12 rapid-fire blasts. Time your dashes from pillar to pillar to these pauses.

OR TRY THE END AROUND

Another route that works well is to turn left immediately when the mission starts, then run along the outer wall of the area. Don't stop running! Stick to the wall, and keep moving through the fire barrage. It doesn't always work, but from time to time, you might earn the Situation Bonus by taking this route.

When you finally reach the western exit that leads to Nolaan, Saruleus turns his attention from you to the poor Lumpers and other creatures on the plains around him. Run up the hill to enter the village.

SITUATION BONUS!

Reached Nolaan without being hit.

★ *Bonus 500 EXP!*

INTERLUDE: NOLAAN

As Capell approaches Nolaan carrying Aya, a pair of energetic (and quite talented) children confront him: Rico the beastmaster, and Rucha the summoner. Rico and Rucha are twins. Seeing the emblazoned sword on Capell's belt, the siblings mistake him for Lord Sigmund and lead him into their village. But they have bad news about the Claridian you seek.

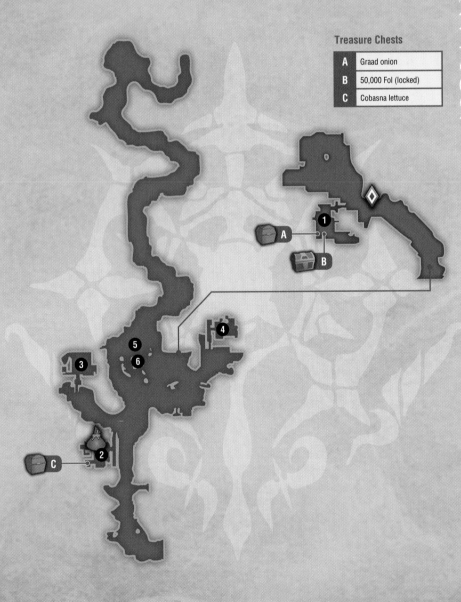

Treasure Chests

A	Graad onion
B	50,000 Fol (locked)
C	Cobasna lettuce

NOLAAN

MISSION MAPS

1. Twins' house (Rico, Rucha, Mother, Aya)
2. General Store (Shopkeeper)
3. Old couple's house
4. Young couple's house (Distracted man)
5. Spirited kid
6. Town well

LEGEND

- Wooden Treasure Chest
- Jeweled Cabinet
- Gold Treasure Chest (Locked)
- Shop
- Save Point

ACTION CHECKLIST

1. Carry Aya to the twins' house.
2. Optional: Pick up two side quests.
3. Optional: Trigger two private events.
4. Optional: Explore the town, talk to villagers, and shop at the general store.
5. Exit the village in search of the Dragonbone Shrine.

ENEMIES

None.

NEW SIDE QUESTS AVAILABLE

Where's Snouty?

The Old Ring

PRIVATE EVENTS AVAILABLE

Aya's Delirium

Rocco's Legacy

INTERLUDE WALKTHROUGH

Before you move on to the story's next mission, spend some time in Nolaan. You can pick up two more side quests and trigger a couple of "private events," those special extended conversations between Capell and other party members. As you enter town, you can talk to the "Helpful young woman" who explains that Nolaan was protected by a Claridian named Saruleus until the Order of Chains invaded the land.

TAKE AYA TO THE TWINS' HOUSE

First off, carry Aya up the ramp-like hill just past the well. It curves up to a house at the top. The twins stand near the porch; this is their home. Approach them to trigger another cutscene in which the twins' mother explains the nature of Claridians. You learn that Order of Chains forces attacked the nearby shrine of Saruleus.

You also learn that her husband is Saruleus' priest, but he's been missing since the invasion. The twins tell Capell, "Go to the shrine and help our dad!" Hard to say no to such a request. When the scene ends, Capell ends up outside, Rico and Rucha officially join your party, and Aya is removed from the party.

Connecting Conversations

You get an in-game tutorial on this, but this aspect of the game is very important. Some citizens (and even creatures) tend to speak more openly if Capell is Connected to other members of his party. Connect to Rico and talk to the dog, for example. Being a beastmaster, Rico can speak with animals!

EXPLORE THE HOUSE

Before you explore the village, go back inside the twins' house to accomplish some optional (but useful) tasks. Talk to Aya. Connect to each twin and talk to the other twin. Open the wooden treasure chest and nab the Graad onion. (The locked gold chest can't be opened until much later in the game when you have a lock-picking character in the party.)

Twins' Treasure

The treasure locked inside the gold chest in the twins' house is 50,000 Fol—easily worth the long trip back to Nolaan after you gain a party member who can open locked chests!

Finally, talk to the twins' mother until she asks if you'd like to rest. If you answer "Sounds good," you rest and restore all of your HP and MP. Thus the twins' house functions as a restorative spot, much the same as the inns you'll find in other locations later in the game.

Aya's Delirium

The first time you talk to Aya when she's lying on the bed in the twins' house, she speaks to Capell but calls him Lord Sigmund. It's just a few sentences, but you can see her loyalty to the man and his cause. Among other effects (all good), this event raises the emotional bond between Capell and Aya. Obviously, you must complete it before Aya is cured.

Rocco's Legacy

Before you go to Dragonbone Shrine, connect to Rico and talk to Rucha; she explains how both twins learned their special skills from their father, Rocco. Note that Rucha wants to be a doctor and mentions an old woman in the village who's always in pain. Then connect to Rucha and talk to Rico. He talks about his father too, and about his desire to be a priest like Rocco.

After you complete the mission in Dragonbone Shrine and revive Aya back in Nolaan, repeat the process—i.e., connect to each twin and talk to the other twin. Completing these four conversations raises the emotional bond between Capell and both of the twins.

EXPLORE THE VILLAGE

Exit the house to trigger a short cutscene; Rucha tells Capell to gather ingredients for her to cook up, then you get an onscreen tutorial on Creation. Now you can create items. Time to go explore Nolaan.

If you want to fully master and enjoy *Infinite Undiscovery*, you should explore every nook and cranny of every location you visit in the game. We'll walk you through Nolaan here, but in future locations we'll leave more of the exploration up to you.

Try the following in the village:

 *Talk to villagers to gather items they donate. Examples: the anxious old woman by the save point gives you a black berry potion; the energetic old man offers a panacea; the two women by the well ("Worried old woman" and "Fretful woman") each donates a red berry potion.*

 Talk to the spirited kid twice; the second time he says, "Only Rico is smart enough to think like me." This is a hint. Go Connect to Rico and come back to talk to the kid again. This triggers the side quest entitled "Where's Snouty?" The kid wants you to find his pet mouse, Snouty.

 Connect to Rico and talk to the forgetful dog and other creatures you find in the village. Rico uses his "Beastspeaker" skill to have actual conversations with animals. The mouse over near the house tells Rico his "friend" went to Dragonbone Shrine. Hmmm. Could that friend be Snouty?

 Note the odd sound and the rippling, wavy look of the area behind the old couple's house. That indicates a hidden chest, but you can't see/open it until Capell acquires a special flute song upon completing the Dragonbone Shrine mission.

 Enter the general store and nab the Cobasna lettuce from the wooden treasure chest in the back corner. The three chests behind the counter may look tempting, but they are strictly property of Nolaan!

 While in the General Store, buy a Nolaan potato, some fresh milk, and a couple of antidote herbs.

 After you gather and buy items, Connect to Rucha and access the Creation menu. Then have her use her cooking skill to whip up some fruit milk and a veggie salad.

 While still Connected to Rucha, talk to the spirited kid. He gives you an antidote. (Capell can't get this by talking to the kid by himself, or even with Rico.)

 Enter the easternmost house and talk to the distracted man. The first time you talk, he mentions something he buried in the rubble at the shrine's entrance. Wonder what it is? After that, he just tells you to go away.

EXIT NOLAAN TO THE NORTH

When you're done exploring the village, exit north by going under the arch that runs up to the twins' house. (The nearby sign reads "Dragonbone Shrine" and points the way.) Follow the path to the entrance of the Dragonbone Shrine and go inside.

FIND THE ALTAR IN DRAGONBONE SHRINE

Rico and Rucha automatically appear with Capell as you enter the outer caverns of the shrine area. Get ready for combat with nasty cave creatures. And here's a starter tip: be sure to equip Capell with the emblazoned sword! It's much deadlier than his old shortsword.

MISSION MAP

1. Start
2. Rubble
3. Dragontail lever (Bloodsuckers!)
4. Snakes!
5. Cracked rock
6. Scamper
7. Dragontail lever (triggers aerial ambush)
8. Miss Sewaria
9. Dragontail lever
10. Door to secret room
11. Snouty
12. Shrine doors
13. "Offerings" respawn here
14. Rambert
15. Secret exit door (reveal with flute)
16. Exit to Nolaan

LEGEND

Wooden Treasure Chest

Gold Treasure Chest (Locked)

DRAGONBONE SHRINE

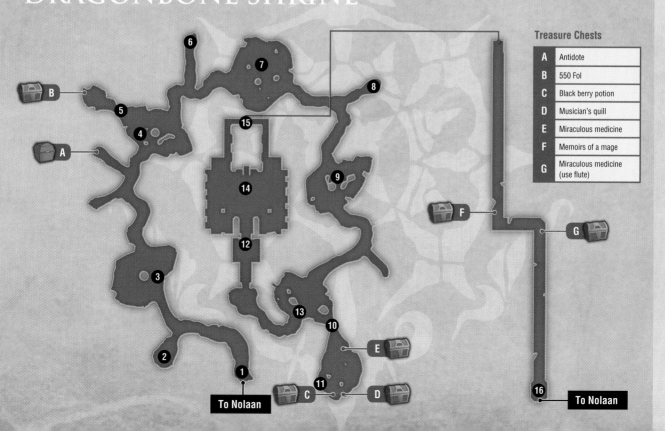

Treasure Chests

A	Antidote
B	550 Fol
C	Black berry potion
D	Musician's quill
E	Miraculous medicine
F	Memoirs of a mage
G	Miraculous medicine (use flute)

To Nolaan

To Nolaan

ACTION CHECKLIST

1. Reach the big entry doors leading into the shrine's altar room.

2. Use Rico to lure the two appropriate "offerings" to the doors.

3. Enter the altar room and defeat Rambert.

4. Return to Nolaan.

NEW SIDE QUESTS AVAILABLE

None.

PRIVATE EVENTS AVAILABLE

None.

ENEMIES

Bloodsucker AP **1**
HP • 80
FOL • 15   EXP • 20

Fleshbiter AP **1**
HP • 600
FOL • 55   EXP • 60

Thorn Cobra AP **3**
HP • 800
FOL • 30   EXP • 35

Rambert the Ogre AP **7**
HP • 10000
FOL • 300   EXP • 500

MISSION WALKTHROUGH

The route to Dragonbone Shrine's altar room runs through a series of connected caverns, some of which have fallen into pitch black darkness. These rooms are overrun with your usual cave-dwelling beasts—bloodsuckers, fleshbiters, and thorn cobras, to be precise.

Twin Effects

Rico and Rucha boost each other's stats when they're in a party together. Note the green stat modifier arrows indicating this boost above the Rico/Rucha icons in the Party Status area (lower right hand corner of the screen).

LIGHT THE CAVES!

Draw your sword, then follow the tunnel and defeat the first bloodsucker. Veer left at the fork into the alcove to find two mice, Toothy and Cheddar; Connect with Rico and talk to each mouse for some info. Optional: examine the nearby rubble (see ❷ on the map) to officially trigger a side quest, "The Old Ring." Then exit the alcove and continue northwest.

Stop just outside the first large cavern, at the edge of the darkness, and make sure your sword is sheathed. See that bluish glowing object ahead? It's a light switch called a "Dragontail lever." Run directly to use it; when you pull the lever, a central torch lights up the cave. Bloodsuckers awaken and swarm you immediately, but focus on pulling the lever first, then draw your weapon and fight. Remember that Spinning Waltz is a good move to use when you find yourself in a swarm of foes.

Use Connect Actions

Be sure to take advantage of Rico's and Rucha's Connect actions, too. Rucha's Tir na Nog summons a cute but tough elemental beast, and Rico's Volt zaps bats hard and fast.

FIGHT THROUGH THE SNAKE PIT

Proceed north up the passage. Knock out the thorn cobra waiting for you, then take the second left into a dead-end tunnel. There you find a wooden treasure chest holding an antidote. Antidotes are very nice to have when poisonous snakes lurk ahead. Continue up the passage to the next big cavern, where a family of seven thorn cobras warms itself around the fire.

Fleshbiter

HP 600

EXP 60

Lightweight flying foes are among the easiest foes to juggle repeatedly. Simply repeating Dancing Rhapsody can be enough, if your allies join in the action too! Encourage this behavior by issuing the Focus or Combo tactics by pressing up or down on the D-pad.

SECRET OF THE CLARIDION

Connect with Rico and use his Volt attack for a surprise hit, then wade into serpentine flesh with your sword swinging. This is a tough fight; be ready to call for healing and use antidotes when party members are poisoned by

cobra bites. If you see a snake wind up for a Tailwhip special attack, target it with a quick attack before it can strike.

When you finally clear the snake-infested cavern, note that another "cracked rock" (**5** on the map) blocks passage to the northwest. Behind the boulder sits yet another gorgeous jeweled cabinet treasure chest; unfortunately, you still can't smash through rock yet. As with the cracked rock back in Graad Woods, you'll have to just note its location for later.

MEET SCAMPER

Proceed north to the next fork, then veer left into the dark, dead-end tunnel. Find a rodent named Scamper hiding in the tall grass at the end of the passage. Connect to Rico and talk to Scamper; he says the temple has a secret room, but he refuses to tell you where it is. However, Scamper admits he'd give the secret to "Miss Sewaria" because he likes her. Okay, you little rat. Exit the dead end, turn left and proceed to the next room, lit by an open roof.

Scamper scampers off pretty quickly, but don't worry—even if you lose him, you'll find him again shortly. He is waiting at the secret entrance. Proceed south into the next cavern. You can try to stay on Scamper's tail, but enemies lurk in the darkness, so you may want to head straight for the glowing Dragontail lever to light up the room. Fight off the snakes and flyers, then continue south to the next fork, where a fleshbiter and two more cobras attack from the left. Eliminate them, and proceed southwest into the next large cavern.

OPTIONAL: TRIGGER THE LEVER TRAP

You can just pass right through this well-lit cavern unmolested, if you want. But see that Dragontail lever installed in the room's center? The room's roof provides plenty of light, so what's the purpose of this switch? If your curiosity gets the better of you and you pull the Dragontail lever… you trigger an aerial ambush by a mixed squad of bloodsuckers and fleshbiters. Ouch! Swat them down and exit the cavern, heading east.

MEET SEWARIA

Veer left at the next fork, heading up the next dead-end passage to find another mouse. This is Sewaria—the "Miss Sewaria" mentioned earlier by Scamper. Connect to Rico and talk to her, then go back to Scamper (at **6** on the map) and report the meeting. The mouse tells you to follow him to the secret room.

FIND THE SECRET ROOM

Eradicate the monsters in this open, lighted cavern, then find Scamper in the southeast end of the room, waiting at a blocked passageway. Connect to Rico and talk to the rodent to learn that the blocked way is actually a rock door to the secret room. Examine the door to open it, then enter to pick up a Situation Bonus of 1000 EXP. You also find three ornate jeweled cabinets. Each one holds a very nice prize.

After you pick the chests clean, don't miss one more optional "prize" in this room. Find the mouse cowering just to the right of the two chests in the back (southern end) of the room. Connect to Rico and talk to the small creature to learn that this is Snouty, the friend of the "Spirited kid" back in Nolaan. To exit the secret room, approach the rock door and examine it again to open it.

LURE A "BLACK WINGS" SACRIFICE TO THE SHRINE DOORS

Continue along the passage until you reach the big doors leading into the shrine's altar room. This triggers a cinematic cutscene—apparently the doors demand a sacrifice of "black wings and poisonous fangs" before you can enter. Indeed, the two icons etched on the door depict a bat and a snake.

Here's where Rico's Penguin Parade Connect action comes in handy. Backtrack into the last cavern; you find one fleshbiter bat (black wings) and one thorn cobra (poisonous fangs). Sheathe your sword and make sure you're Connected to Rico! Approach the fleshbiter first to draw its attention, then turn and let it chase you back toward the shrine doors.

As you near the stairs leading up to the doors, turn and press ⊗ to trigger Rico's Penguin Parade. He fires it at the fleshbiter; when the action hits, the bat glows a smoky, sparkling blue and docilely follows Capell. (You may need to try several times before Rico scores a hit.) Lead the flying beast to the altar doors, then press Ⓐ to examine the doors. The doors automatically accept the "black wings" sacrifice. Note that the wings icon on the doors turns blue to indicate the completion of the task.

Endless Wing/Fang Supply

If you accidentally kill one of the beasts that you're trying to lure as an offering to the altar doors, just approach the doors. This spawns a new fleshbiter (black wings) or thorn cobra (poisonous fangs) back in the cavern around the corner to replace the beast you killed. Thus, you have an endless supply of the two beast-types you need to lure back to the doors.

LURE A "POISONOUS FANGS" SACRIFICE TO THE SHRINE DOORS

Now go back to the cavern and repeat the process with a thorn cobra. This time, quickly KO the aggressive fleshbiter that attacks first, then lure the thorn cobra toward the shrine without attacking it. At the staircase, turn and direct Rico to zap your slithery pursuer with Penguin Parade. When the spell takes effect, lead the snake to the shrine doors and examine them to complete the offering. The fangs icon turns blue, and the doors unlock.

ENTER THE SHRINE TO FACE RAMBERT

Open the shrine doors and enter to trigger a cutscene. The twins find what they seek. The great ogre Rambert and a pair of thorn cobras face you in front of the altar, where Saruleus the Claridian sits in captivity. It's boss-fight time!

RAMBERT p.293

HP 10000   **EXP** 500

Rambert is tough, but somewhat slow. The real problem here is Saruleus, who spits fireballs down at Capell and the twins if you take too long to defeat your ground foes. The two snake minions can cause major problems too, if you ignore them. Your best bet is to KO the thorn cobras first, then turn full attention to Rambert. Another variation: immediately zing one of the cobras with Rico's Penguin Parade to pull it over to your side and distract the boss.

Ogre attacks tend to be slow in coming, so a good tactic is to parry them with Deflect Drive, then follow up with quick slashes and combos. Timing is everything, of course, but it shouldn't take long to recognize when Rambert's attack animation is gearing up. You can also try a more conservative method—move aside as the ogre attacks, dive in with a quick strike combo, then move away and repeat. If you catch the Ogre during his attack recovery, or parry his attacks with Deflect Drive, cut him down quickly with Dancing Rhapsody into Slashing Canon. If one of the twins is Connected, toss Pyros or Volt into the mix for good measure.

After Rambert finally falls, watch as Saruleus is released and offers help for Aya in the form of a healing stone called the Saruleus Amarlista. The great Claridian also gives Capell the divine Saruleus Flute; you receive the flute tunes Prudentiae and Percipere as well. An onscreen flute tutorial appears after the scene. Percipere becomes your default flute tune, appearing in the lower left corner of the screen. Prudentiae might be easy to overlook right now, as enemies have not yet wielded strong magic. Keep it in mind for later in the game, though…this song shields those within its reach from magical effects!

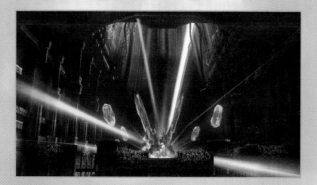

RETURN TO NOLAAN

The main doors are locked; you must exit the shrine via a secret passage. You can access the passage by finding the door behind the altar. Note the rippling effect on the door and the strange sound that indicates a hidden object. Make sure your sword is sheathed, then hold down ⊗ to play Percipere, a flute tune described as "a song which shares the sight of Saruleus, enabling hidden objects to be seen." The tune reveals the hidden passage.

Hidden Indicators

Listen for the distinctive metallic warbling sound that indicates a hidden object is nearby. When you hear it, start looking for a rippling area in the visual field that pinpoints the location of the object.

Go down the passage, looking for treasure chests along the way—the first chest is in plain sight, but a second chest is magically hidden and must be revealed using the flute tune, Percipere. Continue to the corridor's end and then follow the path back south into Nolaan.

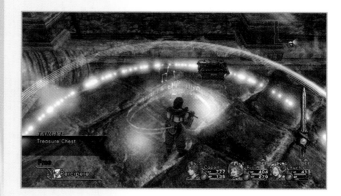

HERO OF LIGHT

The next series of missions leads you across Luce Plains to Castle Prevant, where you must aid Lord Sigmund in his effort to break the Azure Chain.

MISSION

INTERLUDE: NOLAAN

Back in Nolaan, your first concern should be caring for the stricken Aya. Then you can finish up existing side quests and take on a few new ones. Finally, if you want, go upgrade your equipment at the general store.

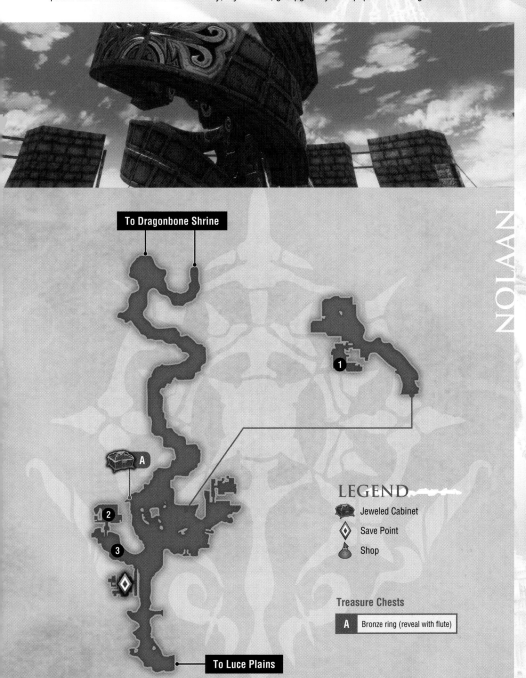

To Dragonbone Shrine

A

2

3

To Luce Plains

LEGEND

🪨 Jeweled Cabinet

◇ Save Point

🛍 Shop

Treasure Chests

| A | Bronze ring (reveal with flute) |

NOLAAN

MISSION MAP

1 Aya in bed

2 Cranky old man

3 Doleful man

ACTION CHECKLIST

1 · Visit Aya to use the Saruleus Amarlista.

2 · Optional: Complete side quests, upgrade equipment, and find a hidden chest using Percipere.

3 · Exit Nolaan to the south into Luce Plains.

NEW SIDE QUESTS AVAILABLE

Clay for Pots

Nolaan Delivery Boy

A Letter for Denton

PRIVATE EVENTS AVAILABLE

None.

ENEMIES

None.

INTERLUDE WALKTHROUGH

As mentioned, you want to reach Aya with your healing item, but for the sake of efficiency, you can find a hidden object (circled here) just past the rock arch as you reenter town on your return trip from Dragonbone Shrine. This is the first step in this section of the walkthrough.

FIND THE HIDDEN CHEST

Go to the rippling spot at the back corner of the old couple's house (see **A** on the map) and play Percipere on the flute. Open the chest to grab a bronze ring. Equip it right away; it boosts the wearer's DEF stat by 5 points.

CURE AYA

Now approach the front door of the twins' house to trigger a cinematic cutscene: Capell and the kids report Rocco's fate to his wife. Then Capell uses the amarlista stone from Saruleus to heal Aya. The twins are ready to join you in the fight against the Order of Chains. When the scene ends, Aya rejoins the party. Now you can go about town and pick up new side quests, if you want. (See the Nolaan side quests listed in **Part 4: Side Quests**.)

UPGRADE YOUR GEAR

Before you leave Nolaan, consider making the equipment upgrades now available at the General Store. You probably aren't fabulously wealthy yet, but you should have enough cash for a nice broadsword for Capell, a tracker's bow for Aya, a training baton for Rico, and a clay drum for Rucha. Equip the new gear immediately, but hesitate to sell outdated pieces. In order to get the best gear, you'll need to get some friends familiar with Item Creation (IC), and to do that, you'll need raw materials! Save gear over selling it unless it's absolutely vital that some Fol be generated. With sufficient craft level and materials, your upgrades can come from Item Creation rather than the general store, with the more exclusive creations surpassing goods available anywhere! Stock up on items such as antidotes and berry potions if you have extra Fol.

EXIT NOLAAN TO THE SOUTH

Walk south out of Nolaan to trigger a cutscene in which a carrier pigeon arrives with a note from Eugene. He asks Capell to come to Castle Prevant without delay once Aya has recovered; Sigmund's team has slipped

in through the back, but the Liberation Force needs help at the front gates. After the scene, Aya points out that Castle Prevant is to the east of Luce Plains. Thus you have your new destination.

TRAVEL TO CASTLE PREVANT

Capell, Aya, and the twins must now traverse the dangerous Luce Plains, heading east for Castle Prevant. You might want to explore the plains for a while, gathering berries and herbs, and bashing foes to gain EXP. It helps to level up for the big battle ahead.

ACTION CHECKLIST

1 • Find the tunnel passage leading from northern to southern Luce Plains.

2 • Cross the southern plains to Castle Prevant.

NEW SIDE QUESTS AVAILABLE

None.

PRIVATE EVENTS AVAILABLE

None.

ENEMIES

	Harpy	AP 2
	HP • 1500	
	FOL • 40	EXP • 120

	Order Servant	AP 2
	HP • 1200	
	FOL • 70	EXP • 90

	Gior	AP 5
	HP • 3750	
	FOL • 100	EXP • 200

	Order Jailer	AP 2
	HP • 120	
	FOL • 10	EXP • 15

	Thorn Cobra	AP 3
	HP • 800	
	FOL • 30	EXP • 35

	Lumper Marksman	AP 2
	HP • 675	
	FOL • 20	EXP • 25

MISSION MAP

1 Start

2 Cracked rock

3 Passage to southern plains

4 Arrive at castle gates

LUCE PLAINS (EAST)

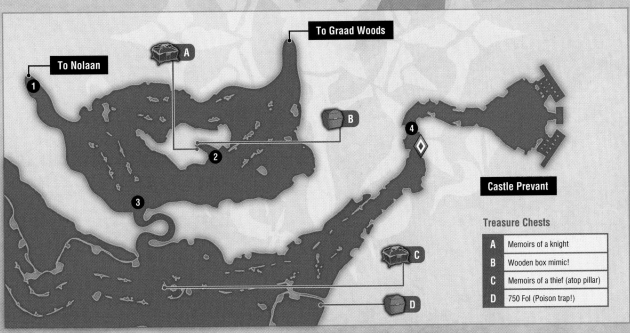

To Nolaan

To Graad Woods

Castle Prevant

Treasure Chests

A	Memoirs of a knight
B	Wooden box mimic!
C	Memoirs of a thief (atop pillar)
D	750 Fol (Poison trap!)

MISSION WALKTHROUGH

This is a straightforward sprint across the plains. To reach Castle Prevant most directly, exit Nolaan and stick to the right-side boundary of the northern Luce Plains until you reach the tunnel. Take the tunnel into the southern Luce Plains. Watch out for the thorn cobra camped halfway through!

You run into new enemies in the southern region of Luce Plains. In particular, beware the harpy. It likes to perch atop pillars and other high spots, then dive down into a brutal swoop called Wing Attack. When you see a harpy tuck for the dive, hit it immediately with a quick attack or dodge to the side. Watch out for the tough giors and the Order servant as well.

By now, Capell has probably reached level 5 and learned a new battle skill: Cutting Gavotte. When this happens, you may want to go to the Battle menu, set Cutting Gavotte in Capell's Ⓐ or Ⓑ slot, and then use it frequently.

Cutting Gavotte

Capell's "Cutting Gavotte" battle skill deserves special mention—its MP cost is cheap, it strikes fast, it launches with sufficient AP, it always works for air juggles, and it combos into itself on heavy foes (any chain -> Cutting Gavotte -> any chain -> Cutting Gavotte etc). It also pays for the MP it expends and then some if you use the ground combo of Diminuendo Dive -> Cutting Gavotte on foes that Capell can knock down.

In the southern plains, stick to the left boundary as you head northeast toward Castle Prevant. Important: be sure to take advantage of the save point just off the road to the right as you approach Castle Prevant.

FORCE OPEN THE CASTLE GATE!

This mission tosses you into a wild melee outside the gates of Castle Prevant. The army of Burguss lays siege to the castle, and the Order of Chains fights back furiously. Your task is to hammer open the gates for the good guys.

ACTION CHECKLIST

1 • Fight off the Order troops until the Burguss catapults start arriving.

2 • As each catapult arrives, take control and target the castle gate.

3 • Keep firing boulders at the gate until it opens.

NEW SIDE QUESTS AVAILABLE

None.

PRIVATE EVENTS AVAILABLE

None.

ENEMIES

Order Servant	AP 2
HP • 1200	
FOL • 70	EXP • 90

Order Jailer	AP 2
HP • 120	
FOL • 10	EXP • 15

Ogre	AP -
HP • N/A	
FOL • N/A	EXP • N/A

MISSION MAP

1 Castle gate

2 Catapult stops here

3 Catapult stops here

CASTLE PREVANT (GATE)

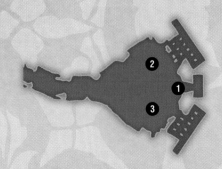

MISSION WALKTHROUGH

This mission has a blue bar across the top of the screen labeled "Castle Prevant Gate." This is the castle gate's health gauge. Any damage you inflict on the gate lowers the bar. When the gauge hits zero (i.e., when the blue bar disappears), the gate opens and the mission is completed. You win a Situation Bonus if you can do this in under three minutes.

FIGHT UNTIL THE ARTILLERY ARRIVES

As the mission opens, Burguss soldiers (in azure blue) tangle with Order forces all over the field in wild melee action. Jump in with your party and start slashing away. Ignore the castle gate for now; your strikes do very little damage to it, and you've got bigger, better gate-busters on the way.

This is an "infinite infantry" situation—you cannot stop the flow of enemy troops just by fighting them. Every time a batch of Order soldiers goes

down, new ones always jump down from the ramparts to take their place. For now, just keep fighting! This is a good place to rack up KO's for EXP and Fol as you kill time, waiting for your friendly siege engines to show up.

Free Party

It's a good idea to set your tactics to Free in a free-for-all like this. With so many targets in the field, you want to let your comrades use their own initiative. You also want them drawing attention away from you when the catapults start arriving.

TARGET THE GATE WITH THE CATAPULTS

After about two minutes, a pair of big ogres appears on the castle ramparts, one on each side of the gate; each ogre starts whacking big rocks at you, swinging his hammer like a golf club.

Not long after that, a cutscene depicts the arrival of the first Burguss catapult, a big stone-tossing machine that can inflict huge amounts of damage on the castle door with each hit. However, you must aim and fire it yourself. Unfortunately, the enemy ogres fire stones with great accuracy at your war engines; generally, you have enough time to get off only one or two shots before your catapult gets smashed. But when one is destroyed, another rolls up seconds later in a different spot.

Run up quickly behind each catapult, sheathing your sword as you run. The moment you reach the machine, hit Ⓐ to take control, then use the left stick to quickly swivel the catapult until it faces directly at the castle gate. Press and hold Ⓐ to build up the distance gauge (the circle that appears onscreen at upper right), then release the button to hurl the stone. You need to fill most of the distance gauge to reach the castle door. After the shot, the circular gauge turns into a reload timer; when it fills up with red, the catapult is ready to fire again.

Smashing the Ogres!

If you like, take some time to fire the catapult at the ogres up on the wall—you'll unlock an Achievement ("Rock, Stock, and Barrel") for smashing ten of them! The catapult registers startling damage totals (approaching 40000) on the enemies up on the wall, figures you won't see again for some time. Going for the Achievement assures you won't score the Situation Bonus for bashing down the gate within three minutes, however.

Order Servant

HP 1200

EXP 90

Enemies like Order servants have more HP than you're accustomed to thus far. This places a premium on effective attacks and juggles. No matter how strong a foe's offense is, or how resilient it is, it won't fight back while it's bouncing in the air. Also, be wary of simply using Dancing Rhapsody on enemies with higher HP totals—they'll survive the barrage, and simply hit Capell back immediately. Instead, use Crescendo Spike, or be sure to tack a skill on after Dancing Rhapsody.

Keep this up (ignoring Order troops around you as best you can) until the Castle Prevant Gate gauge drops to zero and the gate opens. Your team automatically rushes inside, where Balbagan waits. He says he's the Force party's rear guard; Lord Sigmund and the rest of the group are up ahead in the castle.

SITUATION BONUS!

Opened the castle gate within 3 minutes.

⭐ **Bonus 3000 EXP!**

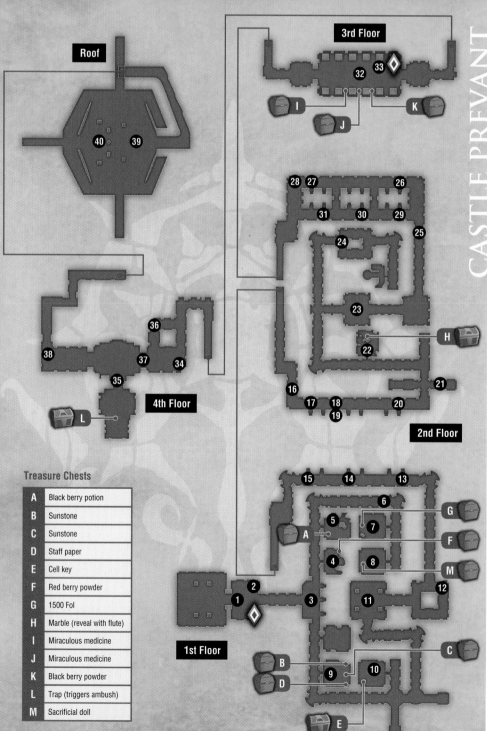

Roof

3rd Floor

4th Floor

2nd Floor

1st Floor

CASTLE PREVANT

Treasure Chests

A	Black berry potion
B	Sunstone
C	Sunstone
D	Staff paper
E	Cell key
F	Red berry powder
G	1500 Fol
H	Marble (reveal with flute)
I	Miraculous medicine
J	Miraculous medicine
K	Black berry powder
L	Trap (triggers ambush)
M	Sacrificial doll

MISSION MAP

1. Start
2. Genma (rest & supplies)
3. Gargoyle trap
4. - 5. Locked cells
6. Order servant (cell key)
7. - 8. Locked cells
9. - 10. Open cells
11. Burguss soldiers under attack
12. Explosive barrel
13. - 15. Gargoyle traps
16. Darkness begins
17. - 18. Gargoyle traps
19. Mouse (cell key)
20. Gargoyle trap
21. Explosive barrel & pots
22. Room with hidden object
23. Burguss soldiers under attack
24. Explosive barrels
25. Darkness begins
26. - 27. Gargoyle traps
28. Mouse (iron metal)
29. - 31. Gargoyle traps
32. Reunion
33. Genma relocated
34. Wooden box mimic
35. Sigmund
36. Pots & barrel
37. Order squad
38. Illusory wall (use flute)
39. Lester
40. Saranda

LEGEND

 Wooden Treasure Chest

 Gold Treasure Chest (Locked)

 Save Point

GET TO THE AZURE CHAIN!

The Azure Chain is on the castle roof, but Castle Prevant is crawling with Order troops. You'll have to fight your way up to the top, but your Liberation Force friends are waiting for you somewhere inside.

ENEMIES

Stone Gargoyle	AP 4
HP • 2500	
FOL • 100	EXP • 200

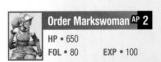

Order Jailer	AP 2
HP • 120	
FOL • 10	EXP • 15

Wooden Box Mimic	AP 4
HP • 10000	
FOL • 4000	EXP • 10

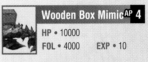

Saranda	AP ?
HP • ?	
FOL • ?	EXP • ?

Order Servant	AP 2
HP • 1200	
FOL • 70	EXP • 90

Order Markswoman	AP 2
HP • 650	
FOL • 80	EXP • 100

Lester	AP 5
HP • 25000	
FOL • 700	EXP • 1450

ACTION CHECKLIST

1. Optional: Find cell keys to unlock three cells on the first floor.

2. Fight your way up to the castle's fourth floor and meet up with Edward and Eugene.

3. Optional: Craft a cell key to unlock the fourth cell on the first floor.

4. Find the hidden staircase to the castle roof and climb to the Azure Chain.

NEW SIDE QUESTS AVAILABLE

None.

PRIVATE EVENTS AVAILABLE

None.

MISSION WALKTHROUGH

Start by going immediately to Genma. Talk to him and select "I want to rest" to restore all party stats, then stock up on items from him too. Make sure you have a store of antidotes—Order markswomen with poisoned arrows are posted throughout the castle. Save your game at the glowing save point across the entry hall.

Buy a Sunstone

Dark passages lie ahead in Castle Prevant. A sunstone is an inexpensive purchase that brightens up dark areas. Buy two or three from Genma. You'll find some in treasure chests as you progress, too.

WATCH OUT FOR GARGOYLE TRAPS

A Burguss soldier in blue waits for Capell's party in the first hallway. As you approach, he runs ahead down the corridor. But when he reaches the intersection, the unfortunate fellow springs a trap—red glyphs on the floor start glowing and inflict damage, then the stone gargoyle in the alcove comes to life and attacks. Defeat the beast and learn your lesson: don't trust gargoyles. Castle Prevant features numerous traps just like this. To test whether a gargoyle is a trap or merely ornamentation, Connect to Aya and have her shoot it with Ravaging Raptor. If her target was indeed a gargoyle lying in wait, the trap becomes disabled, granting Player Advantage to the party.

After you defeat the stony menace, note the red floor glyphs that triggered the trap. Keep an eye out for these as you proceed. Also note that stone gargoyles have a special attack called Crash Ball in which they fling a stone sphere at you. When you see a gargoyle raise both arms over his head, Crash Ball is coming. Dodge to the side, then dash in with a good combo.

EXPLORE THE NORTHERN CELLBLOCK

From the first stone gargoyle attack, the way to Sigmund and the others is to the right, down the south corridor. But a number of Burguss soldiers are imprisoned in cells reached via the north corridor to the left. Not only is freeing prisoners a nice thing to do, it's a tactically advantageous thing to do as well. Every Burguss soldier that you spring from a cell joins the fight on your side.

Go north past the first two locked cells and around the first corner heading east. At the end of this hall, you confront an Order servant who leaves a

small wooden box behind when you defeat him. Pick up this box to obtain a cell key. (The key now appears in your Special Items inventory.) This key unlocks any cell in the northern cellblock. But use it to unlock one of the three cells that hold Burguss prisoners first (**5**, **7**, and **8** on the map).

MOVE THROUGH THE SOUTHERN CELLBLOCK

Backtrack to the first intersection and head south now. The second cell on the left (**9** on the map) holds three treasure chests. Seems too good to be true, doesn't it? The two sunstones you find can definitely come in handy very soon. Around the corner (**10** on the map) you find another cell key in a treasure chest. This opens another one of the cells back in the north cell block. Go back and use it to free another Burguss prisoner.

Pottery Lure

Enemies come running to investigate nearly every time you break a pot in Castle Prevant. So if you see any pots near an explosive barrel, use this neat trick: Connect to Aya and have her shoot a Ravaging Raptor arrow into a pot, wait for foes to check it out, then fire another arrow into the explosive barrel to inflict good damage.

Order Markswoman HP 650 EXP 100

Ranged foes, like Order markswomen or Lumper marksmen, will do their best to stay away from Capell and his allies. Be wary of them in larger groups, as they'll stay on the fringes and pepper Capell with projectiles while he's otherwise occupied with close-range adversaries. Connect with allies and have them use strong ranged spells or attacks on Order markswomen, while using Capell to chase them down and launch them. Once upon them, don't let them get away and establish long range again!

Continue along the corridor to the large room (at **11**) where Order soldiers are hammering your Burguss allies. Jump into the fight and save the Burgess soldiers, who subsequently run off to fight for your side.

Proceed down the hallways—the route is linear for the rest of the floor—with a sharp eye out for any telltale red floor glyph that indicates a stone gargoyle trap.

When you find such a glyph, don't step on it! Instead, have Aya zap the gargoyle nearest the glyph with a Ravaging Raptor arrow to trip the trap safely and also give you a Player Advantage. Then go smash the creature into pebbles. You'll find three such traps (**13**, **14**, **15**) in the northernmost corridor. Climb the stairs to the second floor of the castle.

2ND FLOOR: FIND THE MOUSE WITH THE CELL KEY

Follow the corridor until you reach the dark area. Then open your Usable Items inventory, select "Sunstone," and assign it to Capell. Now you can see ahead well enough to spot glyph traps on the floor before you step on them. Work your way slowly and carefully along the southernmost corridor to the stone gargoyle's trap at **18**; defeat the gargoyle and look into his alcove to see a mouse.

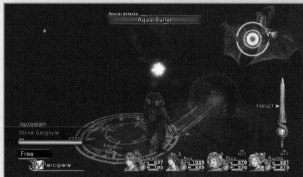

Sunstone Speed

Sunstones move slowly. If you start running with a sunstone, the stone lags behind. Don't outrun your light source!

Connect to Rico and talk to the mouse. (To do this you need an active sunstone shining.) The mouse gives you a cell key. Go back downstairs to unlock another cell in the northern cellblock.

Heal at Genma

Visit Genma for a full healing each time you come back to the first floor cellblock with a new cell key.

FIND THE HIDDEN CHEST

Come back upstairs and find the distinctive warbling sound and rippling visual effect of a hidden object (room ㉒ on the map). Play Percipere on your flute to reveal a treasure chest that holds some valuable marble.

SURVIVE THE GARGOYLE GAUNTLET

Keep working your way up to the northernmost hallway, a dark stretch lined with gargoyles, five of which are traps. You may have to burn through more than one sunstone in this area if you want to fully explore. The only thing of value, however, is a mouse in the hall's northwest corner who gives you a piece of iron metal if you Connect to Rico and talk to the rodent. When you finally reach the dark hall's west end, climb the long staircase up to the next floor.

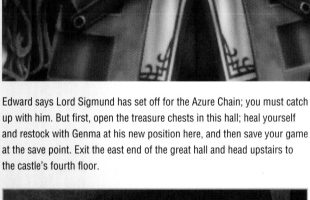

Edward says Lord Sigmund has set off for the Azure Chain; you must catch up with him. But first, open the treasure chests in this hall; heal yourself and restock with Genma at his new position here, and then save your game at the save point. Exit the east end of the great hall and head upstairs to the castle's fourth floor.

3ᴿᴰ FLOOR: WATCH THE PARTY REUNION

When you push through the big doors on the castle's third floor, you trigger a cutscene. Capell, Aya, and the twins reunite with Eugene and Edward in the great hall. This reconfigures the party. Capell goes on with Aya and Edward; the twins leave your party and stay with Eugene.

BEWARE THE BOX MIMIC

Don't try the pots/barrels trick here; no enemies are in the area yet. Approach the treasure chest in the southeast corner with your sword drawn. It's a "wooden box mimic" taking the shape of a chest, and it springs up to attack as you approach. It's a tough foe, with 10000 HP, but Edward and Aya are stout allies. Mimics are fun to juggle, so try to get it airborne with a Crescendo Spike or Cutting Gavotte.

 Killer Mimics

Very tough monsters called mimics can take the shape of treasure chests and spring up to attack as you draw near. Always approach chests with your weapon drawn.

MEET SAVIO THE STARSEER

After you dispatch the wooden box mimic, approach Lord Sigmund, who stands at the tall wooden doors leading south. This triggers a cutscene in which you meet the honorable Savio, also known as Starseer. Sigmund asks Capell to escort Savio back downstairs to Eugene.

En route, Savio demonstrates the power of lunaglyphs and discusses their origin. He also speaks of "the unblessed" who have none and are ostracized. You soon learn that Lord Sigmund doesn't use lunaglyphs at all. Downstairs, Eugene is happy to see Savio, who now joins the group waiting in the great hall on the third floor.

CRAFT A KEY TO UNLOCK THE LAST CELL

Okay, right here is where you get the full value of a strategy guide. Now that Edward is in your party, open up your Creation menu and scroll to Edward. He's a "Bronzesmith," a Level 2 IC forger. Note that he can create a cell key using marble (which you got from the hidden treasure chest on the second floor) and iron metal (you should have several pieces by now). Make the key and backtrack all the way down to the last locked cell on the first floor cellblock and open it. You'll run into a lot of enemies on the way, but your party is strong.

The western end of the main hall seems like a dead end, but you can hear the telltale sound of a hidden object and see the stone wall rippling in the northeast corner. Use Percipere to reveal the wide staircase behind the illusory wall. Then climb up to the castle's top floor to trigger a cutscene.

SITUATION BONUS!

Freed all Burguss soldiers.

⭐ **Bonus 3500 EXP!**

REVEAL THE HIDDEN PASSAGE

Head back upstairs to the fourth floor. Connect to Aya, then use Ravaging Raptor to shoot one of the pots (at), wait for the squad of five Order troops (posted at 37) to come investigate, then shoot the explosive barrel right next to the pot to damage them. Eliminate the survivors.

 Chest Trap

Don't open the treasure chest in the fourth floor's south hall. It triggers a nasty ambush.

If you go through the big doors leading south to enter the room where you met Savio, you see a gleaming treasure chest (at **L** on the map) in the middle of the room. It's a trap, so unless you're looking for a fight, leave it be. If you open it, you get a measly 1 Fol and trigger an ambush

that includes Enemy Advantage, which drops your AP to zero and makes your party susceptible to critical hits.

DEFEAT LESTER AND BREAK THE AZURE CHAIN

Lord Sigmund faces a powerful Order knight named Lester, who guards the chain. Lester calls for an infusion of power from Saranda, a woman who seems to be some sort of sorceress; in response, Sigmund calls upon his allies to support him.

LESTER p.293

HP 25000   EXP 1450

The easier way to beat Lester is to run around and let Sigmund do the heavy lifting. The secret is that Sigmund cannot be KO'd in this fight. You can hang back, Connect with Aya, and use Ravaging Raptor to sling arrows up at Saranda to prevent her from augmenting Lester's attack with her power spells. In fact, you can drive her away, eventually.

If you rely entirely on that tactic, you may also gain the Situation Bonus available for beating Lester within two minutes.

Sigmund fights as an independent party; he doesn't follow your lead, and you can't Connect to him. Again, you can use Aya from time to time to shoot Saranda, but focus most of your energy on nailing Lester with your Cutting Gavotte battle skill chained with combos, again and again. Sigmund and Edward are strong allies; you can chain your hits with theirs to keep Lester on the defensive.

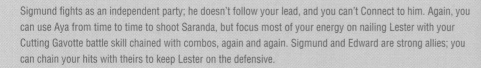

SITUATION BONUS!

Defeated Lester within 2 minutes.

★ **Obtained a yellow berry potion and a white berry potion!**

Once Lester falls, Sigmund turns his attention to the Azure Chain and shows why he's considered a hero…but it's at a price. Aya insists that Capell join the Force on their mission to free the land. To Capell's alarm, Sigmund concurs, and calls for a victorious return to Burgusstadt.

Sigmund, Eugene, Balbagan, and Savio all join your party now, and the Party menu becomes available for the first time. In general, there is no strictly "correct" grouping at any given time; all of your potential party members are strong in their own ways. But keep in mind that some characters boost other character's stats when both are in a party together. And some characters have complementary skills. You always want a good healer in the group, for example, and it's often nice to have someone with ranged capabilities.

For this next journey you may want to choose Balbagan, Aya, and Sigmund to join Capell in Party A as you leave Castle Prevant and make some detours to previous locations before you move on to Burgusstadt.

To Dragonbone Shrine

To Luce Plains

NOLAAN

MISSION MAP

1. Twins' house (Aya, Rico, Rucha)
2. Balbagan
3. Sigmund
3. Edward
3. Savio
3. Eugene

LEGEND

◇ Save Point

Refer to previous mission maps as well. See also the maps for the two side quests listed below in **Part 4: Side Quests**.

TRIUMPHANT RETURN

This chapter takes you on some optional backtracking to pick up previously inaccessible items and side quests, then sends you triumphantly into the capital of the Kingdom of Burguss. After arriving in Burgusstadt, Capell can get to know his new friends better in a few private events.

OPTIONAL ACTIVITIES

UNFINISHED BUSINESS, PART 1

Before you make your glorious entry into Burgusstadt, you may want to spend some time checking out areas that were previously inaccessible. You can also take a detour back to Nolaan to complete side quests you've already begun, and pick up some new ones.

ACTION CHECKLIST

1 • Optional: Use Balbagan to access areas blocked by cracked rocks.

2 • Optional: Complete Nolaan side quests you've already begun, and pick up new ones.

NEW SIDE QUESTS AVAILABLE

Monsters in the Shrine

Back Pain Medicine

PRIVATE EVENTS AVAILABLE

Sigmund and the Saruleus Flute

ENEMIES

None.

MISSION WALKTHROUGH

Again, this is a backtracking mission, and it's entirely optional. But you'll score some good items if you take the time. It's also good to wander through the plains and woods defeating monsters and enemy troops—you can level up your party and fatten your wallet with Fol.

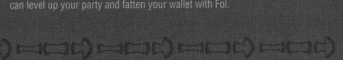

REVISIT THE CRACKED ROCKS

The addition of Balbagan to your party gives you the ability to smash through those three "cracked rocks" that blocked access to treasure chests in Graad Woods, the northern Luce Plains, and Dragonbone Shrine. Go back to each boulder, Connect to Balbagan, then use his Gigatackle action to shatter the rock.

 Luce Mimic

Keep your sword drawn as you approach the two treasure chests behind the cracked rock in the northern Luce Plains. The wooden chest is actually a hostile box mimic!

IC Opportunities

Some of your new party members have very useful IC skills. Sigmund can create a wide range of items; he can whip up those red berries you've been gathering into red berry potions for healing. Eugene and Edward are excellent blacksmiths as well, so look to create upgraded equipment whenever you can. Keep grinding!

REVISIT NOLAAN

When you reach Nolaan, start by taking a rest in the twins' house (by talking to their mother). As mentioned, a return to Nolaan lets you get involved in more side quests, completing old ones and starting new ones. But there's one important private event available here too. Don't miss out on the chance to talk to Sigmund by the well.

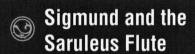

Sigmund and the Saruleus Flute

Talk to Sigmund, who stands next to the town well. He asks to see the flute Capell received from Saruleus. Select "Okay, just a quick peek." This triggers a quick cutscene in which Sigmund plays a flute song. When he returns the flute, Capell has learned some concerto notations.

Have this chat with Sigmund before you head off to Fayel, or else you lose the opportunity for good. The exchange increases the bond between Capell and Sigmund.

When you've finished off your unfinished business, save your game and exit Nolaan to the south into the Luce Plains.

OFF TO BURGUSSTADT

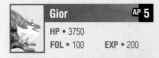

This mission takes you to the capital city. It's a simple trek across the Luce Plains. But this might be a good time to explore the full expanse of the plains.

ACTION CHECKLIST

1. • Optional: Explore the Luce Plains.
2. • Cross the Luce Plains heading west to Burgusstadt.
3. • Enter the capital city.

NEW SIDE QUESTS AVAILABLE

None.

PRIVATE EVENTS AVAILABLE

None.

ENEMIES

Gior	AP 5
HP • 3750	
FOL • 100	EXP • 200

Harpy	AP 2
HP • 1500	
FOL • 40	EXP • 120

Lumper Marksman	AP 2
HP • 675	
FOL • 20	EXP • 25

Thorn Cobra	AP 3
HP • 800	
FOL • 30	EXP • 35

Fleshbiter	AP 1
HP • 600	
FOL • 55	EXP • 60

Order Servant	AP 2
HP • 1200	
FOL • 70	EXP • 90

Order Jailer	AP 2
HP • 120	
FOL • 10	EXP • 15

MISSION MAP — LEGEND

1 Cracked rock
2 Path to Burgusstadt

🟫 Wooden Treasure Chest
🟫 Jeweled Cabinet

◆ Save Point

LUCE PLAINS

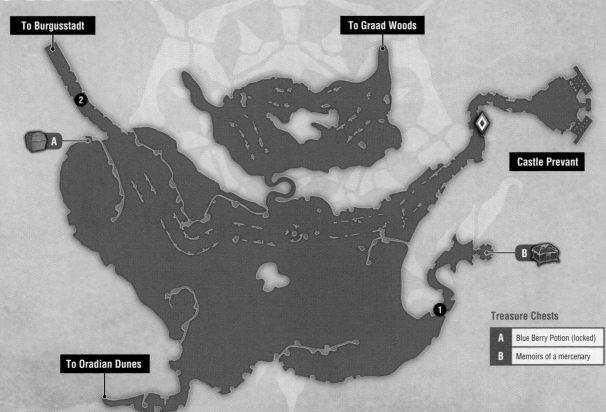

To Burgusstadt

To Graad Woods

Castle Prevant

To Oradian Dunes

Treasure Chests

A	Blue Berry Potion (locked)
B	Memoirs of a mercenary

MISSION WALKTHROUGH

You must traverse the open plains west to reach Burgusstadt, but consider heading east first and exploring. Be ready! Unless you've fully explored the Luce Plains already, you may run into new enemy types along the way.

HEAD ACROSS THE PLAINS

Work your way down into the large southern region of the Luce Plains, then—and again, it's optional—head off into regions you haven't explored yet. You'll find another cracked rock blocking a passage in the southeast (at **1** on the map) that leads to a pack of beasts and a gorgeous, waterfall-ringed canyon where an open temple-like structure sits. Inside sits a treasure chest that holds "memoirs of a mercenary"—a valuable prize that significantly raises

the max HP of the party member on whom you bestow it. Different memoir books can raise various stats, but they can also be saved and used in high-level writing creations.

Keep an eye out for berries and herbs as you jog through the vast southern Luce Plains. When your traveling itch is finally satisfied, head northwest along the old stone road lined with crumbling pillars as it veers up to Burgusstadt. Up ahead, you can see the Order's evil chains rising through the sky to the moon above.

MISSION

INTERLUDE: BURGUSSTADT

Lord Sigmund and crew indeed make a triumphant return. Then Capell gets a warm, warm introduction to Michelle, a major-league healer who mistakes Capell for Lord Sigmund. But Sigmund appears, setting the poor woman straight…

ACTION CHECKLIST

1 · Optional: In Burgusstadt, talk to various party members to complete a set of six private events.

2 · Find the Chamber of Rites in the Castle Burguss.

NEW SIDE QUESTS AVAILABLE

None.

ENEMIES

None.

PRIVATE EVENTS AVAILABLE

Note: these become available only after you arrive in Burgusstadt.

Rustic Capell

Boyhood Friends

Rico's Impressions of the Hero

Rucha's Impressions of the Hero

The Hero's Right Hand

The Fortune Teller

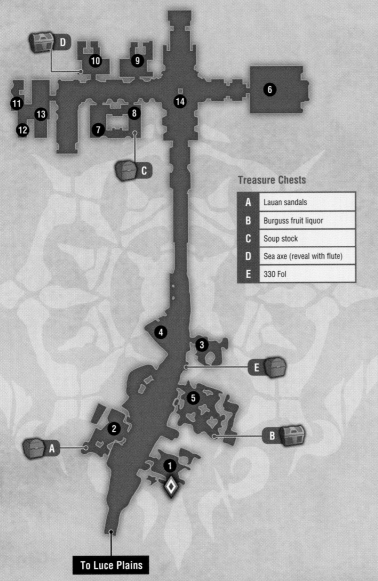

To Luce Plains

MISSION MAP

1. Inn (Aya, Genma)
2. General Shop
3. Anne's house (Anne, Ralph)
4. Rico & Rucha
5. Bar (Balbagan)
6. Chamber of Rites
7. Michelle
8. Edward (before private event)
9. Savio
10. Sigmund
11. Nestor, Azure King
12. Eugene
13. Smiling minister
14. Edward (after private event)

Treasure Chests

A	Lauan sandals
B	Burguss fruit liquor
C	Soup stock
D	Sea axe (reveal with flute)
E	330 Fol

LEGEND

- Wooden Treasure Chest
- Gold Treasure Chest (Locked)
- Save Point

MISSION WALKTHROUGH

Now you can trigger a number of private events that become available when you first reach the city. Don't forget that you can continue or finish three Nolaan side quests in Burgusstadt now too. After the lunar rite that triggers the next "mission," a new set of side quests open up as well.

TRIGGER THE RITE ANNOUNCEMENT

When you first enter Castle Burguss and take the first right turn inside, you trigger another cutscene with Michelle and Capell, and then Aya. The others join, and Edward announces that Lord Sigmund must undergo a lunar rite that night, a great honor to be performed by the Azure King of Burguss himself. Everyone is invited. Tea, anyone? Here, Michelle officially joins your party.

MEET SIGMUND AND FIND THE HIDDEN CHEST

When you approach the room where Sigmund waits (at ❿ on the map), you trigger another cutscene. This time it's a brief meeting between Capell and Sigmund. Afterwards, play Percipere with your flute to reveal the hidden chest in the corner.

TRIGGER THE PRIVATE EVENTS

After the long cutscene ends, start exploring the castle and town and talking to folks in your own party. Try connecting to different characters before you make the rounds. You can complete private events in any order you want.

Note that the first time you enter the castle's Chamber of Rites, you trigger the lunar rite cutscene and this initial interlude period ends. But don't worry, you can still engage in all the private conversations after the ceremony as well.

🐾 Rustic Capell

Find Rico on the main street and Connect to him, then go into the General Shop and talk to the shopkeeper. This triggers a conversation between Capell and Rico. Twice you get the choice of two responses. To increase your bond with Rico and end up with some berry ice cream, pick the second choice each time.

🐾 Rico's Impression of the Hero

Talk to Rico on the street. He raves about Sigmund's strength and skills, and wonders why Capell looks so much like him.

Rucha's Impression of the Hero

Talk to Rucha on the street. Like her brother, she gives Capell an honest appraisal of Sigmund. She finds his "fire and ice" personality kind of scary, especially when he's fighting.

TRIUMPHANT RETURN

The Hero's Right Hand

Go into the inn and Connect to Aya, then head for Castle Burguss. Find Edward in one of the side rooms (see on the map) and talk to him. When Edward "thanks" Capell in a somewhat insulting manner, Aya sticks up for Capell. After that, Aya and Capell are alone; Aya asks if Edward annoys Capell, and you get two response choices.

To strengthen your bond with Aya, choose "He definitely gets on my nerves." She likes your response. If you answer "Not really…" instead, you lose points with Aya but gain some with Sigmund (and lose less with Edward, although you lose with him either way). Meanwhile, Edward picks up a new personal skill after the event: "Sigmundite." As the description puts it, "He worships Sigmund like a god!"

Boyhood Friends

In Castle Burguss, find Eugene in the library (see 12 on the map) and talk to him. He explains that he's Lord Sigmund's strategist, but also a childhood friend; they grew up together. Eugene also fills in Capell on some of Sigmund's behavior.

The Fortune Teller

In Castle Burguss, find Michelle in the side room (see 7 on the map) and Connect to her. Then find Savio in his room across the hall and talk to him. Michelle asks him to look into her future. You can choose one of three topics for her, but all choices increase your bond with her equally.

GO TO THE CHAMBER OF RITES

When you're ready to view Sigmund's lunar rite and kick the story forward again, go to the Chamber of Rites (on the map). Your approach triggers a new cutscene.

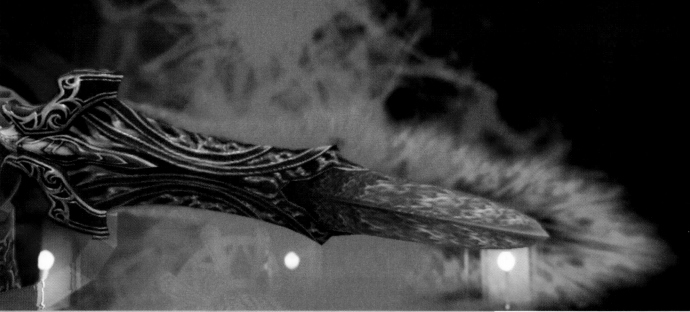

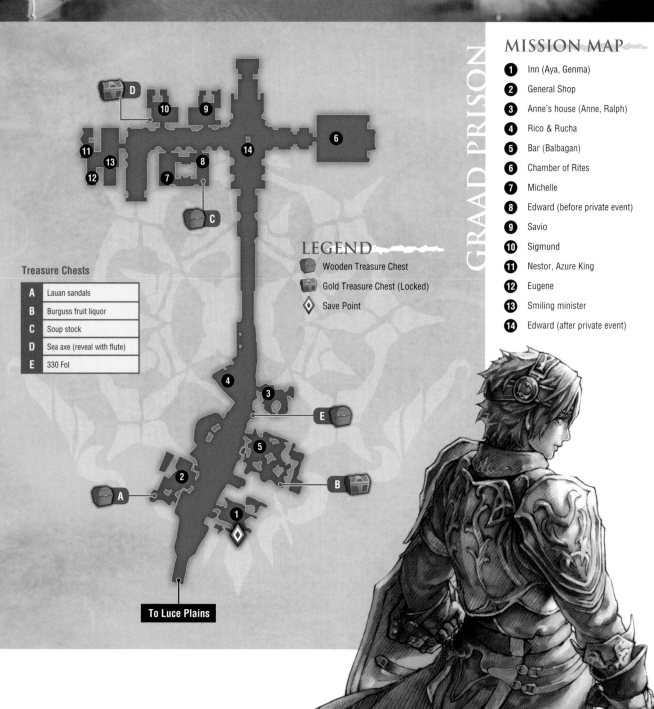

GRAAD PRISON

Treasure Chests

A	Lauan sandals
B	Burguss fruit liquor
C	Soup stock
D	Sea axe (reveal with flute)
E	330 Fol

LEGEND

- Wooden Treasure Chest
- Gold Treasure Chest (Locked)
- Save Point

To Luce Plains

MISSION MAP

1. Inn (Aya, Genma)
2. General Shop
3. Anne's house (Anne, Ralph)
4. Rico & Rucha
5. Bar (Balbagan)
6. Chamber of Rites
7. Michelle
8. Edward (before private event)
9. Savio
10. Sigmund
11. Nestor, Azure King
12. Eugene
13. Smiling minister
14. Edward (after private event)

LUNAR RITE

This short chapter opens with a powerful ritual performed in the holiest sanctum within Castle Burguss, and ends by sending your party across Luce Plains to the scorched sands of the Oradian Dunes.

RITE TO DUNES

Lord Sigmund undergoes the dramatic lunar rite as a reward for smashing the Azure Chain. Newly bestowed with a lunaglyph, Sigmund is tasked by King Nestor to protect the people of the realm. Then the Force (now including Michelle) heads off across the plains to the desert dunes that lead to the next chain.

ACTION CHECKLIST

1. Watch Sigmund's lunar rite.
2. Optional: Start on six new side quests.
3. Exit Burgusstadt to the Luce Plains.
4. Cross the plains south to the Oradian Dunes.

PRIVATE EVENTS

None.

ENEMIES

None.

NEW SIDE QUESTS AVAILABLE

Monster Exterminator

The Unblessed Son

Decipher the Letter

Budding Diva

Fur for the Minister's Daughter

Risky Meat Delivery

MISSION WALKTHROUGH

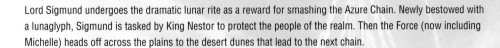

The next chain is anchored in Fayel, and you'll head there soon enough. But after Sigmund's lunar rite ends, you can embark on a new batch of Burgusstadt-based side quests. Some can be completed without leaving Burgusstadt; others call for you to travel on to Fayel or even back to Nolaan.

Again, all side quests are optional, but each includes a nice reward and is fairly easy to accomplish, so why not give it a shot? Go to the Burgusstadt section in **Part 4: Side Quests** for walkthroughs of each quest.

HEAD FOR THE ORADIAN DUNES

When you're ready to embark for Fayel, exit Burgusstadt and cross the Luce Plains heading southeast to the passage that leads into the Oradian Dunes. (If necessary, refer to the full Luce Plains map back in the "Off to Burgusstadt" mission.)

Upgrade! Upgrade!

Keep Eugene and/or Edward grinding out equipment upgrades for your entire party. And whatever you can't make, buy from the General Shop. Progress is much easier when you have top-notch weapons, armor, and accessories.

Treasure Chests

A	10,000 Fol!
B	Staff paper
C	Eagle eye (locked)
D	Memoirs of an alchemist (out of reach)
E	1000 Fol

To Luce Plains

To Oradian Dunes (West)

MISSION MAP

1 Cracked rock
2 Whirlwind area
3 Old stone road
4 Ruins (1st visit triggers cutscene)
5 Rock arch
6 Whirlwind (blocks passage)
7 Sapran gate

ORADIAN DUNES (EAST)

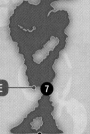

LEGEND

Gold Treasure Chest (Locked)

Wooden Treasure Chest

Jeweled Cabinet

Save Point

To Sapran

BLAZING DESERT

Welcome to the Oradian Dunes, an arid wasteland where only the nasty thrive. This chapter takes you to its central oasis, then south to an imprisoned desert settlement overrun by the Order of Chains. You get your first opportunity to create a second group in the Party B slot of the Party menu.

MISSION

CROSS THE DUNES TO SAPRAN

Yes, your overall goal here is to reach Fayel, but halfway across the Oradian Dunes you pick up a new interim destination. The Order of Chains hasn't deployed any troops in the open dunes, but the desert is crawling with an entirely new assortment of monsters and other menaces.

ACTION CHECKLIST

1 • Create two well-balanced parties.

2 • Cross the Oradian Dunes to its central oasis to change your destination.

3 • Head south to the village of Sapran.

NEW SIDE QUESTS AVAILABLE

None.

PRIVATE EVENTS AVAILABLE

None.

FIND THE BIG FOL

Be ready for huge flying garudas, and the annoying impfish that slither under the sand and suddenly pop up to attack; you sometimes have to face both at the same time, so it's nice to have two parties of four on this trek.

ENEMIES

	Impfish	AP 1
	HP • 1659	
	FOL • 100	EXP • 150

	Swamp Serpent	AP 3
	HP • 3000	
	FOL • 200	EXP • 250

	Amigo	AP 3
	HP • 2750	
	FOL • 250	EXP • 300

	Garuda	AP -
	HP • 3650	
	FOL • 300	EXP • 350

	Narbear	AP 7
	HP • 10000	
	FOL • 450	EXP • 500

From where you enter the dunes, stick to the right-hand cliff wall; it leads you into an enclosed canyon with a cracked rock at its west end. Use Balbagan's Gigatackle to smash the rock, then climb to the treasure chest on the rise. It holds a whopping 10,000 Fol, so don't miss this prize.

MISSION WALKTHROUGH

Keep Balbagan in your main party with Sigmund; another cracked rock is up ahead, blocking passage to a treasure chest. But consider adding Michelle for Astro, her cheap but powerful spell that can also be used as Connect action, and for her excellent healing skills. Like Balbagan and Edward, her stats are enhanced by being in a party with Sigmund, although it could be assumed for entirely different reasons. Remember to keep the twins together if you want them in Party B, and you might want to add Edward to your support party as leader.

Don't let whirlwinds hit you! A lot of sand blows across the dunes, so be careful—sometimes a whirlwind can sneak

up on you. Each is marked by swirling chunks of debris visible in its vortex.

FIND THE RUINS

Now work your way south, but avoid the towering whirlwind that sweeps back and forth across the open sands. Lead your team around the edge of the area; the whirlwind inflicts painful damage if you run into its swirling debris. When you finally get past it, you find an old stone road in the pass (at ❸ on the map) that leads to some ruins and, just beyond them, a spectacular stone arch.

Your approach to the ruins triggers a cutscene: Eugene reads "South: Sapran" on a road direction marker, and Aya spots the small village to the south. Genma reports that a nearby canyon was recently enchained and overrun with monsters. The village was abandoned before the Order attacked; some villagers are still

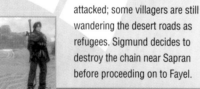

wandering the desert roads as refugees. Sigmund decides to destroy the chain near Sapran before proceeding on to Fayel.

After the cutscene, you must reset Party A and lose the sub-party. Before you head through the arch toward Sapran, turn around and use the save point near the oasis. Two treasure chests are in the oasis area, but one is locked and the other is out of reach in the middle of the oasis lagoon.

Northwest Passage Denied

The Oradian Dunes extend far north and west of the central oasis, but a large whirlwind blocks the only passage to these areas until after you complete the Sapran mission.

HEAD SOUTH TO SAPRAN

Go through the rock arch and work your way south over the dunes. Keep alert—the closer you get to the chain, the more monsters you face. Soon you see the rough wooden gates of Sapran up ahead. Proceed into the village.

Narbear   **HP** 10000   **EXP** 500

These towering beasts represent the most significant challenge Capell and friends have yet seen from a standard, roaming foe. Despite their heft, narbears can be launched—make sure AP is built beyond the seventh tick mark on the gauge, then freeze them with Deflect Drive before cutting loose with Crescendo Spike or Cutting Gavotte. Otherwise, Capell is just likely to get smacked down immediately after delivering his attack, since narbears are stout foes that won't recoil from blows unless they are sent aloft. Rely on strong allied Connect abilities to start an offense, distracting the narbear before moving Capell in to either build AP or parry before launching to an extended juggle.

CHAINED VILLAGE

This chapter takes you into a heated battle around the village of Sapran where you must destroy the infrastructure that protects the Orange Chain. Then you face another powerful Order knight who guards the chain in the canyon above Sapran. Quick work in these endeavors can earn you two separate Situation Bonuses!

THE BATTLE OF SAPRAN

The cutscene triggered as you enter Sapran gives you a glimpse of the challenge you face. The Orange Chain is protected by a barrier powered by a set of orange crystals placed throughout the village. The crystals themselves are guarded by Order forces and some very tough new monster types, including the powerful hill gigas and the pebbleshell crab.

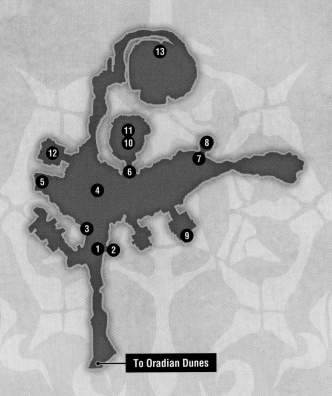

MISSION MAP

SAPRAN

1. Crystal
2. Hidden crystal (reveal with flute)
3. High crystal (use Aya)
4. Crystal
5. Crystal
6. High crystal (use Aya)
7. Crystal
8. Hidden crystal (reveal with flute)
9. Hidden crystal (reveal with flute)
10. Crystal
11. High crystal (use Aya)
12. Crystal
13. Orange Chain & Semberas

To Oradian Dunes

ACTION CHECKLIST

1· Destroy the orange crystals to liberate Sapran.

2· Defeat Semberas.

NEW SIDE QUESTS AVAILABLE

None.

PRIVATE EVENTS AVAILABLE

None.

ENEMIES

Order Jailer `AP 2`
HP • 120
FOL • 10   EXP • 15

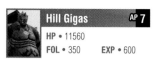

Hill Gigas `AP 7`
HP • 11560
FOL • 350   EXP • 600

Pebbleshell Crab `AP 4`
HP • 2000
FOL • 250   EXP • 400

Semberas `AP -`
HP • 40000
FOL • 1200   EXP • 5000

MISSION WALKTHROUGH

An impenetrable energy field blocks the path leading up the hill behind Sapran to the Orange Chain. To dissolve the field you must smash a total of 12 orange crystals placed around the village. As Sigmund says, "We will destroy our enemies and *all* of those crystals."

CREATE YOUR PARTIES

You start by creating three parties. Capell leads Party A which automatically includes Aya; you need her Ravaging Raptor in this mission, as you'll see shortly. Add two more to this main group. Then set up the other parties with characters who enhance each other: Rico and Rucha always belong together, for example, and Michelle performs better when in either Capell's or Sigmund's party. (Of course, Sigmund boosts *everyone* in his party.)

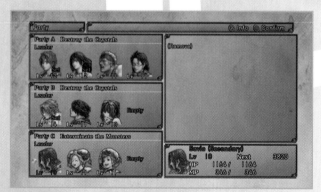

DESTROY THE ENERGY FIELD

Again, you must shatter all 12 orange crystals in order to destroy the energy field so you can reach the chain. A blue bar gauge labeled "Energy Field" appears across the top of the screen. Each time you smash a crystal, the bar drops by one-twelfth. When it drops to zero, the energy field dissipates.

In general, focus on the crystals as much as you can. Yes, bad guys and monsters are everywhere, and you may need to fend off swarms from time to time; they can make your crystal-bashing efforts very painful if you don't thin their ranks occasionally. But the minute you smash the final remaining orange crystal, you successfully complete the first part of the mission regardless of how many enemy troops and/or monsters are left in Sapran.

Hill Gigas

`HP` **11560**   `EXP` **600**

Even more sizeable than narbears, gigas enemies pack a mean punch. Their languid gait and attack speed makes them prime targets for Deflect Drive, however—this parrying skill is even more important against them, because only after being frozen by a parry can they be launched with Crescendo Spike or knocked down with Diminuendo Dive. Play hit-and-run with Connect abilities and quick battle skills like Cutting Gavotte, then go for Deflect Drive into a launch once AP is built past 7.

Note that Party B automatically attacks crystals on its own, so you may not need to smash all 12 with Party A. Also keep in mind that if you smash all 12 crystals within 3 minutes, you earn a nice Situation Bonus for saving Sapran.

Here's where to look for crystals:

DEFEAT THE ORDER KNIGHT SEMBERAS

When the last crystal shatters, you trigger a cutscene in which the party approaches the chain and confronts its protector, an Order knight named Semberas. As with Lester at the Azure Chain, this knight is infused with extra power by the sorceress Saranda. Get ready for your toughest fight so far.

- ▶ Six crystals are in plain sight on the ground, easy to smash with melee attacks. Two of these six crystals are inside structures.

- ▶ Three crystals are installed in high places and must be destroyed with ranged shots using Aya's Ravaging Raptor.

- ▶ Three crystals are hidden behind illusory walls and must be revealed by flute music (Percipere) before you can destroy them.

SITUATION BONUS!

Liberated Sapran within 3 minutes.

⭐ **Bonus 5000 EXP!**

p.293

SEMBERAS

HP 40000 **EXP** 5000

Start by quickly eliminating the Order jailer minions. As in the last boss fight against Lester, Sigmund cannot be KO'd, so you can let him take point versus Semberas while you mop up the minions; in fact, as before, you can let Sigmund do *all* the hard work against Semberas, keeping Capell back and safe. But then you'll likely forego the Situation Bonus earned by beating Semberas within two minutes. Better to wade in with Cutting Gavotte, combo, Cutting Gavotte, combo, and help Sigmund knock big HP off the enemy knight quickly.

Semberas summons an energy orb every so often, which he then unleashes on the party. Direct Capell to smash this sphere immediately,

then return to your Semberas-bashing. Avoid the boss's combo moves, strike quickly, and then hang back. Keep calling for healing and keep guzzling MP-replacing potions if necessary so you can unleash your battle skills.

SITUATION BONUS!

Defeated Semberas within 2 minutes.

Obtained some granite and some steel!

Once Semberas finally falls, Lord Sigmund summons Capell forward to complete a surprising task. When the Orange Chain is destroyed, Sapran is released from its evil power.

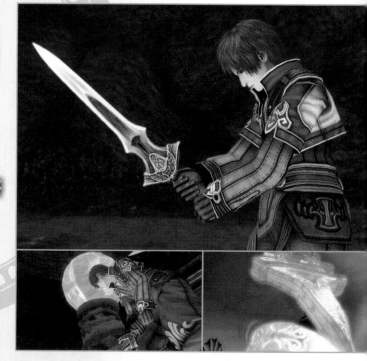

REFUGEES

Sapran is entirely deserted after your epic battle, and as Genma has heard, the inhabitants are likely wandering the desert. In this chapter's pair of missions, you head north and then west for Fayel. En route, you find a distressed group of Sapran townsfolk who need escort back to their village. But halfway home another complication arises…

MISSION
ESCORT THE SAPRAN REFUGEES HOME

The Order's assault and installation of the Orange Chain has driven off the citizens of Sapran. Now they're lost in the desert. In this mission, you come upon them while working your way west toward Fayel. Will you help them?

ORADIAN DUNES (WEST)

MISSION MAP

1. Rock arch
2. Fallen rocks (blocks passage north)
3. Find refugees here
4. Lumper mages!
5. Refugee destination

LEGEND

⬢ Wooden Treasure Chest
— Refugees route

A

2

4 5

1

To Fayel

3

Treasure Chests

A	Silver berry potion

To Sapran

ACTION CHECKLIST

1. Exit Sapran and backtrack north to the oasis area.
2. From the oasis, head west toward Fayel.
3. Meet the Sapran refugees.
4. Escort the refugees safely back to Sapran.

NEW SIDE QUESTS AVAILABLE

None.

PRIVATE EVENTS AVAILABLE

None.

ENEMIES

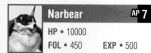

Narbear	AP 7
HP • 10000	
FOL • 450	EXP • 500

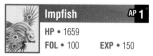

Impfish	AP 1
HP • 1659	
FOL • 100	EXP • 150

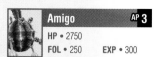

Amigo	AP 3
HP • 2750	
FOL • 250	EXP • 300

Lumper Mage	AP 2
HP • 1825	
FOL • 150	EXP • 200

Garuda	AP -
HP • 3650	
FOL • 300	EXP • 350

MISSION WALKTHROUGH

This starts as a simple cross-desert trek and turns into an escort mission. Your team's HP and MP is automatically replenished after the battle with Semberas. Put together a good monster-fighting party and head out into the Oradian Dunes.

GET TO THE OASIS

The oasis to the north is a nice interim destination to shoot for. Work your way across the hot sands toward the rock arch, fighting through the usual desert beasts. When you reach the oasis, save your game and start heading west.

FIND THE SAPRAN REFUGEES

This step is easy; you can't miss them, really. They're camped next to a save point in a narrow pass that you must go through on your way to Fayel. As you approach, you trigger a cutscene; Eugene sends Capell over to talk to the refugees. When control returns, walk over and talk to various folk, including the woman Faina, her brother Leif, and the refugee leader, Levan. You learn that these are "unblesseds" from Sapran, which is in fact an entire village of unblesseds. Important: *be sure to use the save point before you return to report to Sigmund!* It won't be there after the next cutscene.

Good Save

Be sure to use the save point sometime during your initial conversations with the refugees. It won't be there later.

Now go back and talk to Sigmund to trigger the next cutscene. Sigmund wants to press on to Fayel, but Aya doesn't want to just leave the refugees to their plight. So Capell volunteers to take them back to Sapran. Sigmund at first forbids it…then he relents and gives Capell seven days to complete the task and rejoin the party in Fayel. Aya and the twins join Capell too. The others move on west.

Here the game gives you a nice bounty of four red berry potions, two black berry potions, and three miraculous medicines. Then you get a quick cutscene of the grateful villagers, ready to roll.

ESCORT THE REFUGEES TO SAPRAN

Your task is to escort the slow-moving crowd of Sapran villagers back to the safety of their home town. A red bar gauge labeled "Refugees" appears across the top of the screen. This is the group health bar. If it drops to zero, you fail the mission. Each refugee has an individual health bar too.

Desert monsters along the route target the refugees first rather than your party members, so try to get out in front of the group's frontrunners. But don't get lured too far away; some monsters (particularly the sneaky impfish) may slip past you or approach the crowd from different directions.

Things really get tough as you cross the last open stretch, because a tribe of Lumper mages joins in the assault on the refugees. These fellows add particular challenge because they're ranged attackers; they sling fireballs from their staffs from a distance, and they're spread across the field. Hustle quickly from mage to mage, but don't ignore the prickly amigos who try to roll over your escort. Try hard to keep all refugees alive. The Situation Bonus you earn by delivering the entire group safely to the mission endpoint is 7500 EXP—a very nice bonus indeed.

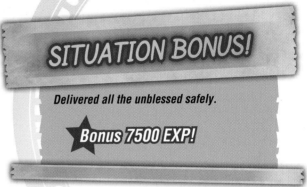

SITUATION BONUS!

Delivered all the unblessed safely.

⭐ Bonus **7500 EXP!**

MISSION

FIND LEIF!

When the refugees finally reach the safe area near the oasis, your job seems done. But then a young woman named Faina reports that her little brother, Leif, is missing. Capell decides to find out who might have seen him last.

MISSION MAP

1 Start
2 Find Leif here

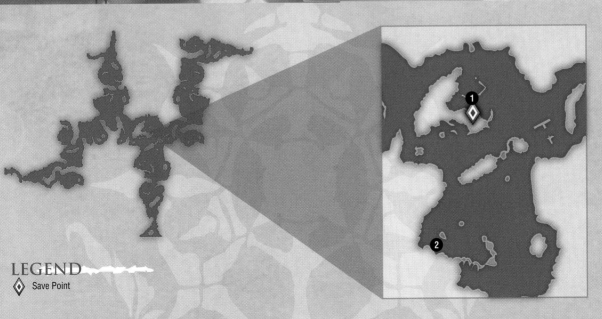

LEGEND
◇ Save Point

ORADIAN DUNES

ACTION CHECKLIST

1. Talk to the refugees for clues to Leif's whereabouts.
2. Head south through the rock arch.
3. Use Aya to shoot down the garuda that holds Leif.

NEW SIDE QUESTS AVAILABLE

None.

PRIVATE EVENTS

None.

ENEMIES

Narbear		AP 7
HP • 10000		
FOL • 450	EXP • 500	

Garuda		AP -
HP • 3650		
FOL • 300	EXP • 350	

Swamp Serpent		AP 3
HP • 3000		
FOL • 200	EXP • 250	

MISSION WALKTHROUGH

Certainly somebody must have seen Leif wander off. Better ask around for clues.

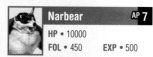

FIND OUT WHERE LEIF WENT

Start talking to refugees to get reports on Leif. The "Disheartened woman" saw a kid wander off towards some rocks. Hey, that's helpful. Rocks lie in every direction. But the "Servile man" saw a kid heading south. Now we're getting somewhere. In fact, that's all you need to know.

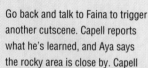

Go back and talk to Faina to trigger another cutscene. Capell reports what he's learned, and Aya says the rocky area is close by. Capell takes only Aya with him to look for Leif, leaving Rico and Rucha behind to protect the refugees. (Aya seems a little funny about the way Faina is looking at Capell, doesn't she?)

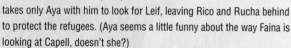

Raptor Ready

Connect to Aya before you set off looking for Faina's brother Leif. Get ready to quickly use her Ravaging Raptor Connect action.

FIND LEIF

Connect to Aya and follow the old stone road through the rock arch to trigger a cutscene: Leif is menaced by a narbear. When you regain control, start fighting! The narbear is bad enough, but an entire den of swamp serpents slithers up to eat the poor kid too. Kill them all, then get ready to use Aya's Connect action.

SHOOT THE GARUDA!

After the last foe falls, a hungry garuda suddenly drops from the sky and snatches up little Leif. A red time limit bar appears onscreen and starts dropping quickly. Hurry! Press ✕ to activate Aya's Ravaging Raptor interface, then aim and fire at the big bird before the time limit runs out. One good hit forces the garuda to drop Leif and fly off.

Watch the cutscene afterwards as Leif is returned to his sister in Sapran. Faina is immensely grateful…yes, especially toward Capell. As Aya says, "What's *with* her, anyway?" Then Rico and Rucha reappear with reports that the refugees are home and happy.

FAINA

Well, it looks like Capell has a new admirer. You've been working hard, so take an interlude in Sapran. Here you can rest up, restock, take care of some side quests and private events, and get ready to rejoin the main party in Fayel.

MISSION
INTERLUDE: SAPRAN

The citizens of the wind-powered village of Sapran are all unblessed and simply seek for a place to live peacefully. The place is a little ragged after the occupation, but folks are slowly getting their lives back together.

To Oradian Dunes

MISSION MAP

1 Faina's house (Faina and Leif)
2 Aya
3 Rico & Rucha
4 Despairing man's house
5 Mayor's house (Levan and Relieved old woman)
6 Grieving young man's house
7 Exhausted old man
8 Bone comb

LEGEND

 Inn
◆ Save Point

ACTION CHECKLIST

1. Have dinner with Faina and Leif.

2. Optional: Finish one old quest and start a new one.

3. Optional: Trigger two private events.

4. Exit Sapran and head west for Fayel.

ENEMIES

None.

NEW SIDE QUESTS AVAILABLE

The Memento

PRIVATE EVENTS AVAILABLE

The Fayel Claridian   **Boy Talk**

MISSION WALKTHROUGH

Make the rounds and meet the good and grateful people of Sapran. You can rest up at the inn, have a good meal with Faina, then get on with your larger mission.

DINE WITH FAINA AND LEIF

Approach the entrance to Faina's house (**①** on the map) to trigger a cutscene. Capell, Aya, and the twins join Faina and Leif for a nice feast and some very interesting interaction.

🐦 The Fayel Claridian

After your meal with Faina and Leif in Sapran, talk to Aya just outside Faina's house. She explains that the village was formerly protected by a Claridian named Avifir whose fire was the symbol of life. The Order has been killing off the great Claridians, or enslaving them as they did Saruleus.

🐦 Boy Talk

After your meal at Faina's house, Connect to Rico and talk to Leif. (He's in Faina's house afterwards.) Listen to the boys talk about brotherhood, rivalry, and...the girls.

After you've wrapped up all your business in Sapran, save your game at the inn and head out into the Oradian Dunes again. As you exit town, Levan the mayor, Faina, and Leif see you off and thank you again. Then Levan lets you in on the secret practice of enchantment, and that creation ability becomes available to you. Now you can boost certain stats and bestow other qualities (such as elemental attributes to your attacks, or immunity to a status effect) for a period of time.

RESPITE

This is another short chapter. Here, you cross the dunes until you reach a remarkable campsite—a place of true respite overlooking the forbidding beauty of the high desert. The next day, it's off to Fayel at last!

MISSION

TREK TO FAYEL

As our title indicates, this "mission" is just a trek, most of it over ground you've already covered before the refugee escort mission. But it includes a pleasant night interlude.

MISSION MAP

1 Start
2 Whirlwind area!
3 Trigger camp scene here
4 Campsite
5 Fayel's outer gate
6 Cracked Rock

ORADIAN DUNES

LEGEND

 Firewood

Note that the campsite save point disappears after the night camp cutscene, so use it before you gather firewood.

To Oradian Dunes (East)

To Fayel

To Sapran

ACTION CHECKLIST

1 • Work your way north then west across the Oradian Dunes.

2 • Find a place to camp for the night..

3 • Gather enough wood for a campfire.

4 • The next day, continue west to Fayel.

NEW SIDE QUESTS AVAILABLE

None.

PRIVATE EVENTS AVAILABLE

None.

ENEMIES

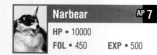

Narbear	AP 7
HP • 10000	
FOL • 450	EXP • 500

Garuda	AP -
HP • 3650	
FOL • 300	EXP • 350

Amigo	AP 3
HP • 2750	
FOL • 250	EXP • 300

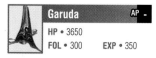

Impfish	AP 1
HP • 1659	
FOL • 100	EXP • 150

MISSION WALKTHROUGH

Off you go over the desert sands again. This time, use your new enchant ability to create immunity to the poison inflicted by desert snakes. You should have plenty of the metal fragments you need to create the anti-poison enchantment bonus. Remember, each anti-poison bonus lasts five minutes.

FIND THE CAMPSITE

Head north from Sapran up to the oasis area, then veer northwest into the open desert (**2** on the map) where the whirlwind rages. Skirt the twister and follow the passes as they curve southwest. When you reach the rock arch (at **3** on the map), you trigger a cutscene. Aya leads your party to a high promontory and asks Capell to gather enough firewood for the night.

GATHER TEN PIECES OF FIREWOOD

If you talk to Aya before you start your search, you learn that ten pieces of firewood ought to be plenty. Look for crossed sticks that indicate firewood; you'll find them scattered all around the area. The first piece of firewood is near the ledge not far from where Aya stands, and two more are on the path leading up to the site.

ENJOY THE DESERT NIGHT

This is one of our favorite scenes in the game. After the twins fall asleep near the campfire, Aya and Capell sit marveling at the pristine, starry sky and the desert's dark beauty. Then Capell takes out his flute…

Save First, Gather Later

Note that the save point at the top of the hill by the campsite disappears after the night camping cutscene, so save your game *before* you talk to Aya when gathering your firewood.

Your movement is restricted to the campsite area and the canyon below, so don't worry, your search won't take long. Note the glowing spots on the sandy dunes. Each is a useful item (including some firewood) buried in the sand, so gather them up too. Don't miss the piece of firewood hidden in grass up against the south canyon wall, next to a red berry.

When you've gathered all the items, including ten pieces of firewood, go save your game at the save point. Then talk to Aya to trigger a long cutscene.

Despite Capell's joke about the song title, the new music he composes gives you training notations that can be written by Rico into Placare, a flute tune that you can play in towns to earn money from citizens.

HEAD WEST TO FAYEL

If you look west from the westernmost ledge of your campsite you can see Fayel's great domes gleaming on the horizon. Head downhill and proceed west down the final canyon. Fight past two last garudas and enter the city.

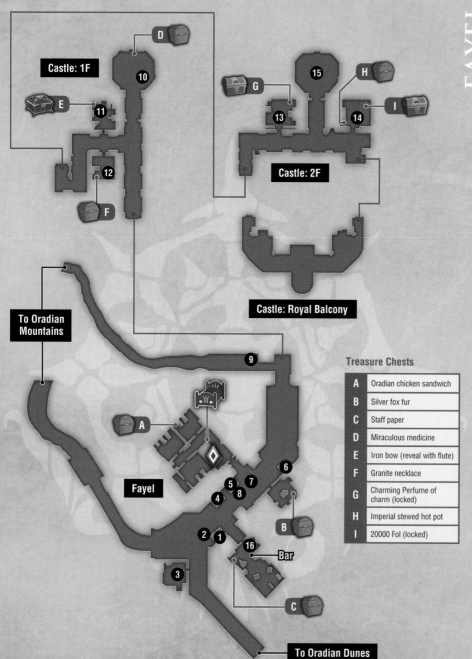

Castle: 1F

Castle: 2F

Castle: Royal Balcony

To Oradian Mountains

Fayel

To Oradian Dunes

Bar

FAYEL

MISSION MAP

1. Item shop
2. Rico & Rucha
3. Matilda's house
4. Weapons shop!
5. Armor shop
6. Accessory shop

* Note: the following can be found in these locations only after the "Gustav is missing" cutscene with Gina.

7. Gina
8. Eugene
9. Edward
10. Chamber of Rites (Michelle)
11. Sigmund
12. Savio
13. Aya's chambers
14. King & queen's chambers
15. Throne room
16. Balbagan

LEGEND

🗃 Wooden Treasure Chest
🗃 Gold Treasure Chest (Locked)
🗄 Jeweled Cabinet
🏠 Inn
◆ Save Point

Treasure Chests

A	Oradian chicken sandwich
B	Silver fox fur
C	Staff paper
D	Miraculous medicine
E	Iron bow (reveal with flute)
F	Granite necklace
G	Charming Perfume of charm (locked)
H	Imperial stewed hot pot
I	20000 Fol (locked)

PRINCESS OF FAYEL

At last, you've reached the teeming capital of Fayel. This chapter gives you the opportunity for some long-awaited supply restocking and equipment upgrades. Get ready for a surprise or two as you explore the city and palace.

INTERLUDE: FAYEL

Fayel's town center is a bustling marketplace with a number of shops filled with useful goods. You should have a healthy purse by now, so you can go on a shopping spree if you want. But keep in mind that you want your party to use its IC skills to create items and equipment as well. Remember that it's always cheaper to make your own stuff from the materials you've collected.

ACTION CHECKLIST

1. Optional: Shop for items and equipment upgrades.
2. Approach the castle to trigger Edward's rite along with subsequent scenes.
3. Exit the inn to trigger the next mission.

ENEMIES

None.

NEW SIDE QUESTS AVAILABLE

Blood of Fayel

PRIVATE EVENTS AVAILABLE

Proper Oasis Attire?

Edward in Training

Savio's Self-Abnegation

MISSION WALKTHROUGH

This interlude features a lot of cinematic exposition. Start by taking a little time to explore the main street and its establishments, and talk to the citizens wandering through the marketplace and in the local bar. Approach the royal palace's outer gate to trigger a long series of cutscenes.

WATCH EDWARD'S LUNAR RITE... AND MEET THE PRINCESS

The emir performs the lunar rite upon Edward. Capell arrives too late to see it...and then the princess of Fayel makes her royal appearance. Does this look familiar?

After the commotion dies down, the princess and the emir have what appears to be a somewhat barbed father-daughter exchange. Aya exits, and Sigmund announces to his stunned party that they'll set out for the next chain as soon as Edward recovers from the rite. Now the full party is reunited.

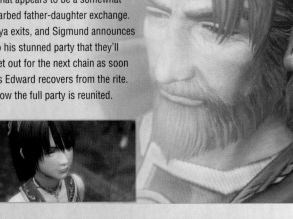

WATCH THE ROYAL FAMILY SCENE

Time for one last cutscene. That night, Capell accidentally eavesdrops on a family discussion. It seems the princess plans to stick with the mission, in spite of her father's wishes. When she catches Capell listening in, she takes him out on the royal balcony for a chat. Then Capell the Soother plays his flute...and gains some prelude notations.

LEARN ABOUT THE MISSING PET

When the scene ends, Capell ends up in his room at the Rosy Bear Inn on Fayel's main street. When you step outside the inn, you trigger another cutscene—a young woman named Gina, thinking Capell is Sigmund, asks for help finding Gustav, the princess's pet crimson bear. Gina can't seem to help speaking exactly what's on her mind!

Now you can chat with locals to pick up some clues. For example, the young boy called "Aspiring warrior" near the city gates says he saw a massive bear running really fast out of the city; the Merchant from Halgita at the produce stand saw him exit the city too. Then, return and talk to Gina once more, giving your report.

Now, before exiting the city to seek Gustav, you can pick up a new side quest and engage in some private event conversations. (See the first Fayel side quest, "Blood of Fayel," in **Part 4: Side Quests**.)

OPTIONAL: TRIGGER 3 PRIVATE EVENTS

There are three distinct private events now available to you in Fayel. All of them take you through the palace's outer gates, but only two occur within the palace itself.

Edward in Training

Go through the outer gates of the royal palace, but then turn left before you reach the inner gates. Follow the path to Edward and talk to him. This triggers a quick scene of Edward working hard on his swordsmanship. Then click through the conversation between the two. Capell is impressed by Edward's work ethic.

Proper Oasis Attire?

Enter the Chamber of Rites in the royal palace and talk to Michelle. (You can do this while Connected to any of the male adult characters as well, but *not* with Aya.) Michelle asks you about appropriate attire at an oasis. If you choose "Sarong," you get a small boost in your bond with Michelle. You get a bigger boost if you answer "Swimsuit"...and bigger still if you answer "Nothing at all."

Hidden Chest

Don't miss the hidden chest in Sigmund's room in the royal palace. Hit it with a refrain of Percipere!

Savio's Self-Abnegation

Find Savio in the first floor palace room, left side, and talk to him. He explains to Capell that he remains fully hooded even in the hottest weather as a way to master his "inner forces." Savio's opinion of Capell goes up after this exchange.

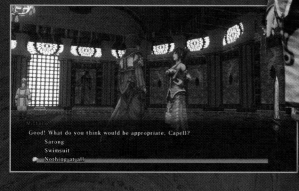

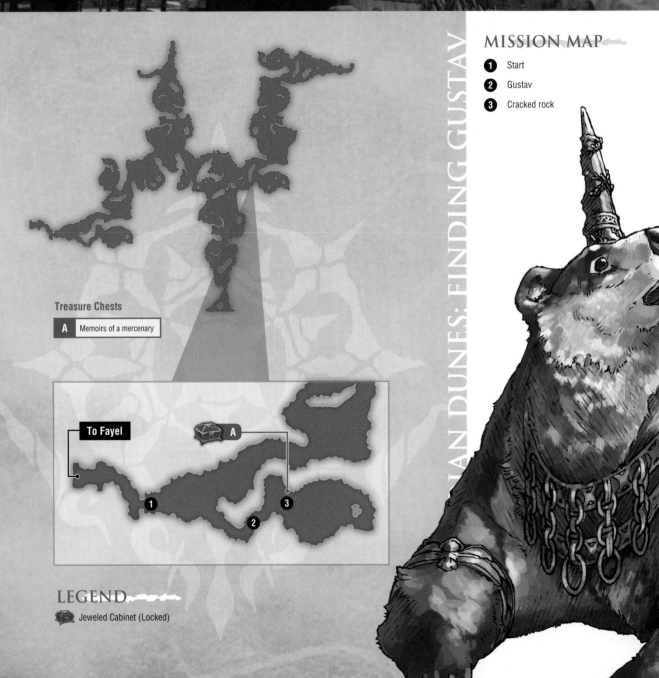

Treasure Chests

A	Memoirs of a mercenary

To Fayel

IAN DUNES: FINDING GUSTAV

MISSION MAP

1 Start

2 Gustav

3 Cracked rock

LEGEND

Jeweled Cabinet (Locked)

A DAY IN THE CITY

This short chapter includes the rescue of Aya's pet bear, the addition of a new party member along with one new side quest, and the opportunity to finish up any quests or private events you didn't complete earlier.

MISSION

RESCUE GUSTAV THE CRIMSON BEAR

Aya's pet bear Gustav has run off into the Oradian Dunes. Yes, he's big and tough, but the beast has run into something equally big and tough out in the desert. Put together a strong party that includes Balbagan (to smash a nearby cracked rock), and go rescue Gustav!

ACTION CHECKLIST

1 • Exit Fayel and find Gustav in the Oradian Dunes.

2 • Defeat the creatures attacking Gustav.

3 • Use Balbagan to smash the nearby cracked rock.

PRIVATE EVENTS AVAILABLE

None.

NEW SIDE QUESTS AVAILABLE

Deliver Nina's Letter

ENEMIES

Garuda		AP **2**
HP • 3650		
FOL • 300	EXP • 350	

Hill Gigas		AP **7**
HP • 11560		
FOL • 350	EXP • 600	

SITUATION BONUS!

Rescued Gustav without him getting hit.

★ **Obtained a bottle of yellow berry potion!**

MISSION WALKTHROUGH

There's a bear out there somewhere in the dunes. Go find him! Exit Fayel and immediately veer to the right through the nearby rock arch.

Not far beyond the arch, you trigger a quick cutscene in which the party finds Gustav…and picks up the help of a tough mercenary named Dominica. The help is welcome, because Gustav is standing toe to toe with a powerful hill gigas. Slam into the fellow quickly with Cutting Gavotte so you can get his full attention and earn the Situation Bonus if Gustav isn't hit.

After this battle, you discover that Dominica and Gustav know each other. And she knows Aya too. "I know *lots* of people," she says. The scene changes to Fayel, where Gina is overjoyed to see Gustav again.

SMASH THE CRACKED ROCK

You *do* have Balbagan in your party, right? If not, go back to Fayel and switch him in. Then find the cracked rock just past where you rescued Gustav (at ❸ on the map) and use Balbagan's Gigatackle to shatter it. Then, nab the memoirs of a mercenary from the chest that was behind the rock.

Return to Fayel. Now you're free to take up side quests and explore areas of the city you may have missed before.

TALK TO EUGENE AT THE ROSY BEAR INN

When you're ready to move on, enter the inn to trigger a meeting with Eugene. He says the party is moving out to Vesplume Tower tomorrow to destroy the Crimson Chain. From this point on, every time you talk to Eugene, he asks if you're ready. If you've restocked supplies, upgraded equipment, explored everywhere, and completed all the side quests and private events possible, answer "Yes."

You automatically rest at the inn for the night (replenishing all your stats) and awaken refreshed and ready to go. Exit the inn to trigger a cutscene of the party's exit from Fayel. Guess who rejoins you? She has a couple of new protectors now…both of whom join the party as well.

NEW ALLIES

This chapter features a single mission that takes you up the treacherous Oradian Mountains. You ascend with two parties; Party B takes its own route up. Climb to a resting point where your parties reunite. Your "new allies," Gustav and Dominica, are now available, though Dominica can only join sub-parties.

MISSION

CLIMB THE ORADIAN MOUNTAINS

Start by setting up two parties for the ascent. Gustav is so big and powerful that he takes up two slots; if you use him, remember that he's Aya's pet, so her presence in the party boosts the bear's stats. (Capell, Aya, and Gustav make a nice trio on Party A.) Remember also that Dominica's Title 1 is "Big Sis"—she's looking out for Aya too. So, like Gustav, she's a good option in a party that contains Aya.

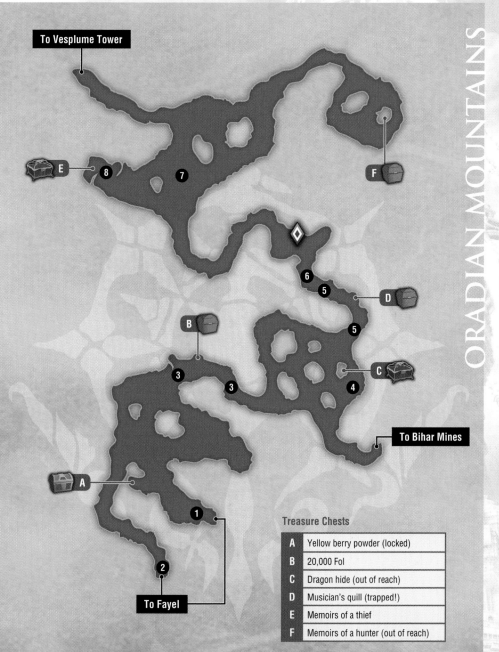

To Vesplume Tower

To Bihar Mines

To Fayel

ORADIAN MOUNTAINS

MISSION MAP

1 Party A start
2 Party B start
3 Boundaries of rockslide area
4 Fire gigas!
5 Boundaries of rockslide area
6 Rendezvous with Party B
7 Fire gigas!
8 Cracked rock

LEGEND

🧰 Wooden Treasure Chest

🧰 Gold Treasure Chest (Locked)

🗄 Jeweled Cabinet

◈ Save Point

Treasure Chests

A	Yellow berry powder (locked)
B	20,000 Fol
C	Dragon hide (out of reach)
D	Musician's quill (trapped!)
E	Memoirs of a thief
F	Memoirs of a hunter (out of reach)

ACTION CHECKLIST

1. Fight your way up the mountain passes.
2. Avoid rolling boulders in the rockslide areas.
3. Reach the rendezvous point halfway up to reorganize.
4. Continue climbing to the Vesplume Tower gates.

NEW SIDE QUESTS AVAILABLE

None.

PRIVATE EVENTS AVAILABLE

None.

ENEMIES

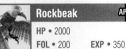

	Rockbeak	AP 2
	HP • 2000	
	FOL • 200	EXP • 350

	Lumper Soldier	AP 2
	HP • 4500	
	FOL • 150	EXP • 300

	Lumper Mage	AP 2
	HP • 1825	
	FOL • 150	EXP • 200

	Fire Gigas	AP 7
	HP • 20000	
	FOL • 400	EXP • 800

MISSION WALKTHROUGH

The first part of the mission takes you up to a spot about halfway up where your two parties reunite. The climbing is complicated by a bevy of tough new foes (including the monstrous fire gigas) along with three nasty rockslide passes.

CLIMB AND FIGHT TO THE RENDEZVOUS SPOT

Your goal here is simple: fight your way up to the Vesplume Tower gate at the top of these Oradian Mountains. Your second party makes its own way up, and does a nice job against monsters in the passes. Get underneath the flying rockbeaks when they attack; they're not particularly tough, and they're easy to air juggle. But they can swarm around you, so keep the camera rotating so you can spot multiple flying foes hovering in an area.

BEWARE THE ROCKSLIDE AREAS!

When you step into rockslide areas—which are clearly marked by brown, rocky soil—huge boulders start rolling down the pass, bouncing side to side. These rocks knock down and damage Capell and crew if they make contact. The only good news is that the boulders do the same damage to enemies. In fact, if you lure foes into the path of falling rocks and you manage to get five of them killed, you pick up a nice Situation Bonus of 10,000 EXP. It's very difficult, though—chances are good you'll take a lot of boulder damage trying to pull off this feat.

"Wait" at Rockslides

Assign the "Wait" tactic to your party and let Capell open treasure chests in rockslide areas.

Your party members aren't too good at dodging the rolling rocks, so keep them out of rockslide areas as much as possible. Try to lure enemies out from rockslide passes onto safe green ground. A good trick is to issue the "Wait" tactic command to your party on safe ground, run Capell up to foes in rockslide areas, then run him back down to lure the enemies down to your party.

SITUATION BONUS!

Defeated more than 5 enemies using rocks.

★ Bonus 10,000 EXP!

BEWARE THE FIRE GIGAS!

A lumbering fire gigas with 20,000 HP roams in the southeastern canyons. As with all gigas foes, he's very powerful but a tad slow, telegraphing his strikes so much that you can use Deflect Drive against them most of the time. But if you time your parry wrong, you can suffer a lot of damage. Keep out of his range until he strikes, then dash in with Cutting Gavotte and a follow-up combo before backing off again. Watch out for annoying Lumper mages tossing fireballs at you from the periphery. Go strike them down quickly, then return to the big guy. If you do score a parry with Deflect Drive

while the AP gauge is above the 7th mark, use the opportunity to launch the gigas and put him out of commission with a juggle combo.

AT THE RENDEZVOUS

Once you clear the second rockslide area, you reach the rendezvous point and trigger a short scene. Here, Sigmund admits privately to Capell that his powers are fading; Capell is now the key to the mission. After their talk, Edward has a few choice words for Capell as well. When the scene is over, save your game at the save point and proceed onward.

CONTINUE ON TO THE VESPLUME TOWER GATE

Keep working your way upward. One more rockslide pass lies directly ahead; in the clearing at the top of this deadly pass you run into another fire gigas. After you eliminate him, look for the cracked rock to the west (at **8** on the map). Behind it you'll find a chest holding "memoirs of a thief." Then, proceed up the last pass to the northwest leading to Vesplume Tower, where you're given the option to save your current data.

MISSION MAP

1 Start

2 Grate-like fence

3 Orb dais (place orb of chaos)

4 Door unlocked by orb of chaos

5 - 6 Teleport platforms

7 Door puzzle (1 globe)

8 Balcony

9 Mirror puzzle

10 Jeweled cabinet mimic

11 Ambush! (fire gigas, Order rangers)

12 Door puzzle (2 globes)

13 - 14 Teleport platforms

15 Meet Aya

16 Rampart (side view)

17 Fire gigas!

18 Ambush! (shadow warriors, Order rangers)

19 Mirror puzzle (to 2 doors)

20 Orb dais (place orb of patience)

21 Rampart (side view)

22 Ambush (Order soldiers)

23 Door puzzle (4 globes)

24 Teleport platform

25 Genma (rest and resupply)

26 Teleport platform

27 Mirror puzzle (to 2 doors)

28 Door to orb chest

29 Rampart (side view)

30 Begin "black orb gauntlet"

31 Forge orb of rebirth & give to Aya

32 Door puzzle (2 globes)

33 - 34 Teleport platforms

35 Door puzzle (4 globes)

36 Kron!

37 Dmitri, Saranda, and Leonid

LEGEND

⬠ Wooden Treasure Chest

⬠ Jeweled Cabinet

◆ Save Point

VESPLUME TOWER

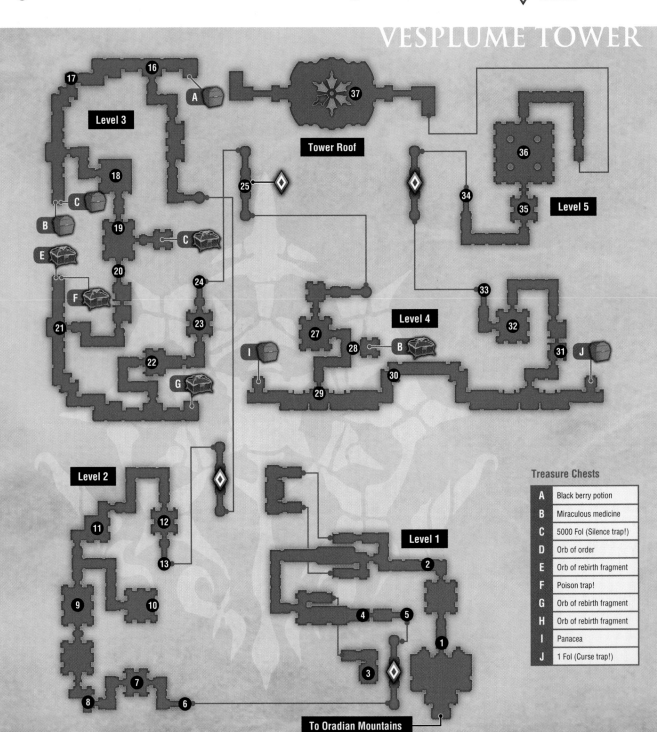

	Treasure Chests
A	Black berry potion
B	Miraculous medicine
C	5000 Fol (Silence trap!)
D	Orb of order
E	Orb of rebirth fragment
F	Poison trap!
G	Orb of rebirth fragment
H	Orb of rebirth fragment
I	Panacea
J	1 Fol (Curse trap!)

A PLACE OF DEFEAT

This chapter takes you all the way to the Crimson Chain anchored atop Vesplume Tower. There you find not one, but two boss enemies waiting for you, including the Dreadknight himself, Leonid. On the way up, you encounter not only hordes of minions but a creepy sub-boss capable of wiping out your party on its own.

MISSION

REACH THE TOWER'S TOP

The party arrives, and the place is far too quiet. As Dominica says, "So they're waiting for us." Vesplume Tower is a vexing maze with various puzzles you must solve in order to advance. Some involve gathering and placing orbs, others call for redirection of light via mirrors, and still others require tricky simultaneous strikes on podiums to disable locks.

ACTION CHECKLIST

1. Fight your way upward from level to level to the Vesplume Tower roof.
2. Solve three types of door puzzles to advance.
3. Defeat Kron the Vicious Eye, a sub-boss.
4. Defeat Dmitri, the Order knight guarding the Crimson Chain.
5. Defeat Leonid the Dreadknight.

NEW SIDE QUESTS AVAILABLE

None.

PRIVATE EVENTS AVAILABLE

None.

ENEMIES

Order Fighter AP 2	**Gigas** AP 7
HP • 3630	HP • 20000
FOL • 180 EXP • 400	FOL • 400 EXP • 800

Order Ranger AP 2	**Dire Wolf** AP 5
HP • 2315	HP • 5650
FOL • 250 EXP • 350	FOL • 300 EXP • 750

Order Conjurer AP 2	**Crystal Gargoyle** AP 4
HP • 1500	HP • 8000
FOL • 160 EXP • 400	FOL • 50 EXP • 800

Order Warrior AP 2	**Kron the Vicious Eye** AP -
HP • 3630	HP • 43150
FOL • 180 EXP • 400	FOL • 1800 EXP • 7000

Order Soldier AP 2	**Dmitri** AP -
HP • 7000	HP • 45650
FOL • 400 EXP • 550	FOL • 2200 EXP • 5000

Order Witch AP 2	**Leonid** AP -
HP • 2315	HP • 30000
FOL • 200 EXP • 450	FOL • 2500 EXP • 6500

Soulcrusher AP 1
HP • 1315
FOL • 150 EXP • 250

MISSION WALKTHROUGH

Eugene explains that the tower has three entrances, but they must be opened simultaneously or else they remain locked. Inside, each group must find and operate a lever to reach the top floor. You'll face a higher level of troops here: Order fighters, rangers, and conjurers.

CREATE YOUR PARTIES

Start by splitting your team into three parties; the leaders are already set, and Sigmund is in Capell's group. Remember to combine characters that enhance each other's stats— for example, put Gustav and Dominica in Aya's group, Party B.

LEVEL 1: FIND THE ORB DAIS

Capell's group, Party A, moves in through the central entrance (see ❶ on the map); the others move through the side doors. Eliminate the Order fighters in the entry vestibule and move through the first jeweled door. You see Edward's team fighting its way down a corridor on the other side of a grate-like fence (❷ on the map). This is where you'll make an important exchange with Edward soon. But for now, move on down the hall.

The route is linear; just follow it, but be ready for combat around every corner. Keep following the corridor up one staircase, and then down another one. Eventually, you reach a fork—the door at the end of the great hall down the right fork is locked, so fight your way up the left fork staircase. There you discover a dais with a small recession on top. Examine it to trigger a short scene: if you place the correct orb on the dais, the door in the great hall below opens.

Door Jewels

If a door's jewel is pink, the door is impassable. If its jewel is blue, the door dissipates when you approach.

FIND THE ORB OF CHAOS

Time to backtrack. En route, you trigger a quick cutscene of Edward nabbing an orb from a chest. Shortly after, a carrier pigeon arrives with the message from Edward: "Lord Sigmund, I found an orb." Continue all the way back to the grate-like fence (again, ❷ on the map) near the tower entry to find Edward. When you examine him, he hands over the "orb of chaos."

With the orb of chaos now in your inventory, return to the dais and examine it to place the orb. The jewel in the door below turns from pink to blue, and the doorway "unlocks." Go downstairs and head through the doorway to the teleport platform (❺ on the map). Step onto the platform to warp to another platform in a small corridor with a save point in the middle. Save your game and use the teleport platform on the far side to warp to the next level of the tower.

LEVEL 2: DOOR PUZZLE X 1

This route is linear too, so just keep following the hallways. Around the first corner you run into a flight of red, bat-like soulcrushers. Watch out! Their bite can inflict the confusion status effect, which moves Capell in the opposite direction of your control commands and causes other afflicted party members to attack each other for a short time. Whack the winged menace out of the air and move on.

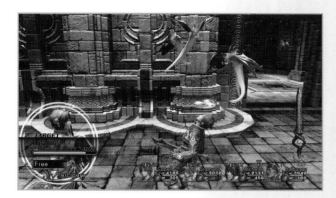

In the next chamber, the door jewel is pink, indicating no passage. Just attack the big globe-like stand in the middle of the room—one good hit turns the door jewel blue and activates the doorway. Then go on through into the next corridor. (Note: this door puzzle is quite simple, but it's just an introduction to the puzzle type. You'll run into trickier ones as you move through the tower.)

SOLVE THE MIRROR PUZZLE, PT. 1

Follow the halls until you emerge onto a balcony overlooking a heated battle below between Edward's party and a squad of Order foes. You can't get down there, so Capell can't help. But if you have a ranged attacker in your party, they can join in—Michelle's Astro attack, for example. Once Edward's group mops up the last foes and moves on, you do the same, moving through the next door into another great hall where Order troops await your arrival.

Continue into mirror puzzle room. Here, you find five mirrors and a light projector. Each mirror is two-sided and can be rotated. The idea is to use the projector to shoot a beam of light into the pink jewel in the far door; a hit turns the jewel blue, activating the door. To do this, you must align the mirrors to create a path for the light beam from the projector, then reflecting the beam from mirror to mirror until it hits the door jewel. The correct alignment is shown in the screenshot below. Head through the doorway.

BEWARE THE "JEWELED CABINET"

Next, you reach an intersection. If you turn right, you eventually end up in a roomful of Order troops. Stay near the doorway to fight them. The reason: the gleaming treasure chest across the room (at ❿ on the map) is actually a jeweled cabinet mimic, a brutal beast with 30,000 HP. The mimic pops up the moment you approach it. So try to keep your distance and clean up the Order fighters and conjurers before you take on the mimic. (Or, just skip the mimic entirely.) Remember that mimics can be juggled relatively easily. Once you get this one up in the air, you can inflict lots of heavy damage without taking hits in return.

SURVIVE THE AMBUSH!

Now prepare yourself for an intense ambush. Go back to the intersection and proceed north through the doors. This triggers a cutscene in which a massive fire gigas suddenly drops into your midst from above. And that's not all—a squad of Order rangers starts raining down arrows on you from the balcony above. Fortunately, Edward's party arrives on the balcony as well, and starts plowing into the Order troops.

The key to survival here is to immediately sheathe your sword. No, this is not a joke. If you get locked into a static toe-to-toe slugfest with the gigas, the Order rangers can perforate Capell pretty quickly. A better tactic is to start running around full speed to avoid the arrows (and the fire gigas) until your comrades up on the balcony can wipe out the archers. Once the arrows stop flying, pull out your sword and introduce Cutting Gavotte to some gigas guts.

DOOR PUZZLE X 2

Continue along the passageways to the next chamber, where another colony of soulcrusher bats drops onto your party. Wipe them out and approach the two globe stands in the middle of the room. To activate the exit door, you must hit the globes almost simultaneously. To do so, stand between the stands and then unleash your Spinning Waltz attack.

Proceed through the door and step onto the teleport platform to warp to another connecting hall with a save point. Save your game and step onto the opposite platform to teleport up to the tower's next level.

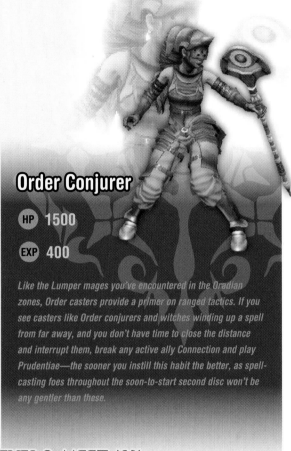

Order Conjurer

HP 1500

EXP 400

Like the Lumper mages you've encountered in the Oradian zones, Order casters provide a primer on ranged tactics. If you see casters like Order conjurers and witches winding up a spell from far away, and you don't have time to close the distance and interrupt them, break any active ally Connection and play Prudentiae—the sooner you instill this habit the better, as spell-casting foes throughout the soon-to-start second disc won't be any gentler than these.

LEVEL 3: MEET AYA

Move down the long corridor until you trigger the cutscene where Aya and her party meets you at another grated fence. Sheathe your sword, approach Aya, and press Ⓐ to receive three red berry potions and two black berry potions from her.

FIGHT ALONG THE RAMPARTS

Continue along the corridor and emerge through the door onto a wide rampart. Now the camera perspective changes, scrolling sideways along the ramparts as you move. You can't see enemies coming either, so be ready. Dire wolves join the Order troops out here. Be sure to fully explore from end to end so you don't miss any treasure chests. Watch out for another fire gigas who also climbs up the wall onto the rampart (at ⑰ on the map).

*One of the chests (at **C** on the map) at the end of the rampart is a trap. Opening it afflicts anyone nearby with damage and the silence status effect. However, it also contains 5000 Fol, so it may be worth it.*

DEFEAT THE SHADOWS

After you reenter the tower from the ramparts, the first big chamber (**18** on the map) features an enemy squad composed of shadow versions of your party and another ring of Order rangers shooting arrows down at you from the balcony. Use the same tactic as before—run around avoiding combat until Edward's party upstairs defeats the enemy archers. Then draw your weapon and focus on wiping out the shadow warriors.

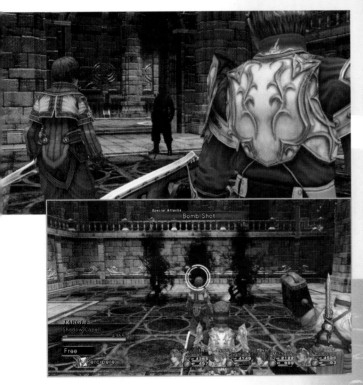

SOLVE THE MIRROR PUZZLE, PT. 2

The next room features another light projector and a set of seven mirrors. This time there are two doors you can open by directing the light beam from projector to mirrors to door jewel. Again, rotate the mirrors to direct the beams to each door. The solutions are shown here in this guide's two screenshots.

The east door leads to a treasure chest (**D** on the map) that holds the orb of order.

The south door lets you continue on through the tower.

ACQUIRE THE ORB OF PATIENCE

The next room holds an orb dais. But it's the "dais of patience"—the orb of order doesn't open the door when placed on the dais! Not only that, but your party gets locked into the room as well. But in a cutscene, Sigmund sends a carrier pigeon, and soon Aya arrives to give you the orb you need—the orb of patience. She needs the orb of order over on her side, so Capell automatically gives it to her. Place the orb of patience in the dais on your side to activate the door, then move on to the next area.

BACK ONTO THE RAMPARTS

More side-scrolling action as you move out onto the southwest ramparts (at **21** on the map). Again, don't miss the treasure chests at each end of the ramparts—in particular, the two that hold the orb of rebirth fragments (**E** and **G** on the map). Go through the door at the south end of the rampart.

SURVIVE THE ORDER AMBUSH

Entering the next room (**22** on the map) triggers a quick cutscene in which Order soldiers spot you and leap down at you from a balcony. The door ahead is locked and the passage behind is blocked by an energy barrier, so you have no choice but to fight. (As if you would do anything else?) This is a three-wave ambush—four Order fighters drop in per wave.

After the last of the twelve ambushers is KO'd, you see a quick scene of Edward placing an orb and moving ahead. Move on into the next room.

DOOR PUZZLE X 4

Soulcrushers are amassed in this chamber, so slash the bats down. This time, you find four globe stands in the room. But they're bunched close enough together to let you stand in the center and unleash Spinning Waltz, hitting all four in a split-second. This activates the door, so you can reach another teleport platform.

Don't Miss Genma!

Genma waits near the save point in the passage connecting the teleport platforms to Levels 3 and 4. Use him to restore all party stats to 100 percent and stock up on items.

Teleport to another connecting hall with a save point. This time, however, Genma waits patiently nearby (at **25** on the map). Don't miss this opportunity! Talk to Genma and select "I want to rest" to restore all of your party's stats, then talk to him again and restock your item supplies. When you're finished, proceed south to the platform that teleports you up to Level 4 of the tower.

LEVEL 4: SOLVE THE MIRROR PUZZLE, PT. 3

This time your arrival draws immediate attention, so be armed and ready to rock. KO the Order warriors and one dangerous Order witch in the first hall, then proceed into the mirror room. Once again, you must open two different doors using the projector/mirror setup, and this time, both doors are actually outside the projector room. But the mirror rotation process is

the same. Before you start adjusting mirrors, however, go into the hall, find the mirror-less podium, and then use your flute song Percipere to reveal the mirror.

Since the whole setup cannot be shown in a single screenshot, this pair of mini-maps demonstrates how to rotate the mirrors to open each door:

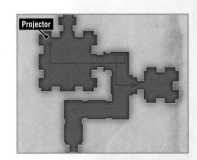

When you get the first door activated, enter that room (**28** on the map) and open the treasure chest to obtain another orb of rebirth fragment. (You should have three fragments now.) Set the mirrors to activate the second door at the end of the corridor and go through onto another side-scrolling tower rampart section.

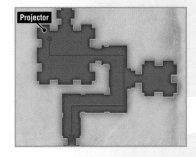

GET PAST THE FALLING BOULDER MAGIC

Head west first to face a new foe, a crystal gargoyle, then score a panacea from the nearby treasure chest. Then fight your way east until you reach a section (starts at **30** on the map) lined with four Order witches who seal off

the passage on both ends and then summon four black magic orbs. These orbs generate huge boulders that drop onto the rampart and inflict heavy damage on your party if you move underneath them.

Meanwhile, Order warriors rush along the rampart to attack you. Two solutions here: one is to whack the warriors then just wait until your comrades in Aya's party eliminate the witches above. Or you can quickly dispatch the warriors, then sheathe Capell's sword and play the flute song Prudentiae before moving across the rampart beneath the orbs. This song casts a protective magic dome over your party! Continue east along the rampart to the door.

O Cursed Chest!

Don't open the wooden treasure chest at the end of the rampart (at **J** *on the map). It contains only 1 Fol and afflicts all nearby characters with the curse status effect, which slowly drains MP.*

FORGE THE ORB OF REBIRTH FOR AYA

As you move north, you trigger a scene in which Aya finds an orb dais that requires the orb of rebirth. All you have are fragments of this orb. But if you have all three fragments (from treasure chests **E**, **G**, and **H**), you

can use Sigmund's IC skill to forge the pieces together into a complete orb. When it's done, give it to Aya and move on north, fighting your way into the next puzzle room.

LEVEL 5: DOOR PUZZLE X 4

This last door puzzle isn't as difficult as it might seem at first. The four globes are spaced well apart in the room, but if you strike one, you

learn that it stays active (turns pink) for several seconds before turning back to blue. So here's your strategy: stand next to a globe, Connect to a party member, and target a second globe with a Connect action. Launch the Connect action, then spin and launch a quick attack at the globe next to Capell. Sprint to each of the other two globes and nail them each with a quick attack too. You should have just enough time to turn all four globes pink, which activates the door. Head north into the next chamber.

DEFEAT KRON!

Entering the chamber triggers the appearance of a creepy beast called Kron the Vicious Eye. Kron is accompanied by two dire wolves. Eliminate both wolves first—they can be a real annoyance if you don't! Then start circling Kron, dashing in to hit with Cutting Gavotte, then running back out of range again.

Kron can stun characters with his ray attack at close range, then teleport to a new spot and strike, so don't spend too much time right in front of the big eye. Keep moving to avoid Kron's various attacks, including Paralyzing Gaze. If you stray too far from Kron, beware of Pyrburst or Volt, and keep moving laterally to avoid these spells as well. Keep your party's healer busy healing everyone: stunned characters may take fearsome damage while they're immobile, especially if either of the dire wolves is still roaming the area. If Michelle is present and not preoccupied with main healing, Connect with her and cast Astro repeatedly. Aether is the only element that does normal damage to Kron—this ocular fiend is half-resistant to all other elements save air, which Kron resists completely. When the room is finally cleared, exit north and take the stairs up to the tower roof.

DOOR PUZZLE X 2

This room has only two globe stands, but they're too far away from each other to reach both with a Spinning Waltz attack as in the previous door puzzles. But don't worry, you actually have two solutions here.

First, try this: your first time here, rush quickly into the room and engage the three Order witches near the globe stands where they're posted. In the wild swinging fight that follows, chances are good that the globes end up getting simultaneously struck by weapons, thus activating the far door.

But if that doesn't happen, you'll have to set up a simultaneous hit after the witches fall. With your sword drawn, Connect to a party member, target one of the globes, and use a Connect action to attack it. Immediately after triggering the Connect action attack, spin Capell and swing his sword in a quick attack on the other globe. The two attacks should strike the two globes at about the same time, activating the door. Follow the passage beyond to the usual teleport setup, including one last save point before the final stretch.

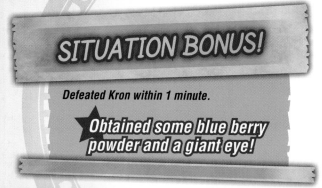

SITUATION BONUS!

Defeated Kron within 1 minute.

⭐ *Obtained some blue berry powder and a giant eye!*

DEFEAT DMITRI AND LEONID!

Your arrival at the Crimson Chain triggers a cinematic introduction to Leonid the Dreadknight, leader of the Order of Chains. He's accompanied by the red witch Saranda, whom you've met before, and an Order knight, a teleporting bowmaster named Dmitri. When the action starts, you should target Dmitri first. Both Aya and Edward arrive in the course of the fight, but the bosses have plenty of Order minions arrive on the rooftop too—rangers and warriors.

SITUATION BONUS!

Defeated Dmitri within 2 minutes.

⭐ **Obtained some lentesco wood and some down feather cloth!**

DMITRI

p.294

HP 45650   **EXP** 5000

Dmitri is a ranged fighter with a powerful bow and the ability to teleport away to keep his distance from your close-in melee attacks. Several Order rangers join him in firing arrows at you; keep zigzagging to avoid taking too many hits. Hunt down the minions quickly when they're nearby; otherwise, keep closing the distance on Dmitri as he warps from spot to spot. Note that Eternal Refrain teleports with Dmitri if he warps while it's active.

Combo quickly whenever you reach Dmitri. Open with a good battle skill because he'll disappear soon, teleporting away. (Tip: if you lose track of Dmitri, check the minimap for his red blip.) Beware the Exopto spell that blurs your vision; eye drops in your inventory can counter this. But note that even when the screen is blurred, you can spot Dmitri's position clearly on the minimap, so rely on that if you run out of eye drops. Also watch out for the arrival of Order warriors as the battle intensifies. Finally, if Eugene's around and not busy healing everyone (sound familiar?), Dmitri can be pushed down much more easily. He's *extremely* vulnerable to earth—Connect with Eugene, activate Symphonic Blade, then go after Dmitri while having Eugene cast Geoclaw over and over. Capell's attacks deal out 2.5 times normal damage, same as Geoclaw—which, like Eternal Refrain, can track Dmitri even if he teleports! This Order knight won't withstand the barrage of granite for long.

Important: until Dmitri's demise, keep away from the area where Sigmund is battling Leonid! If you get caught in the midst of their duel, you can get trapped in Leonid's chains and take significant damage.

LEONID

p.294

HP 30000 **EXP** 5500

After Dmitri falls, it's time to take the fight to Leonid. But Leonid is quite powerful, and since there's no Situation Bonus associated with beating him, you can just hang back and let Sigmund handle the bulk of the fighting here.

Leonid falls within seconds because Sigmund has already inflicted so much damage. (Once, Leonid was defeated without Capell landing a single blow!)

Connect with party members who have ranged attacks (like Michelle's Astro; avoid earth or water spells, however, which Leonid half-resists) and use those, then slip in some quick slashes and combos when Leonid is vulnerable, which is right after he finishes a special attack. The Dreadknight usually falls fairly quickly; in fact, sometimes in the battle,

After the battle, watch the dramatic conclusion of the confrontation between the Liberator and the Dreadknight…and then the somber aftermath. Capell receives Sigmund's pendant and makes a difficult, fateful decision. There are more chains to be cut; the mission must go on.

BURDEN OF THE LIBERATOR

This is primarily a "movie" chapter. It opens with the party's return to Fayel with Capell in his new role. Then, you trigger a set of cutscenes with various party members as everyone adjusts to the new realities of the mission.

INTERLUDE: FAYEL

The "Liberator" leads his somber party into Fayel and the joyous welcome of its grateful citizens. He gets a lot of "helpful" suggestions from the others on his demeanor and behavior as the new Liberator.

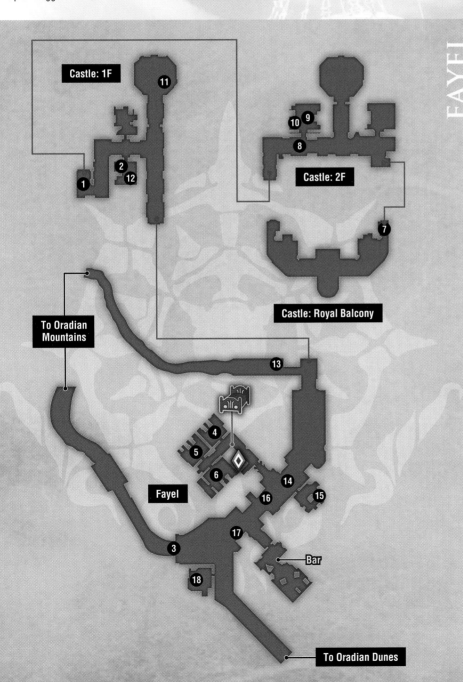

FAYEL

MISSION MAP

(First 7 locations are during Fayel night sequence only)

1. Start
2. Meet Edward
3. Meet Balbagan
4. Meet Rico & Rucha
5. Meet Eugene
6. Meet Michelle
7. Meet Aya

(Locations below are next morning)

8. Gina
9. Aya
10. Gustav
11. Michelle
12. Savio
13. Edward
14. Unlucky woman
15. Dominica
16. Eugene
17. Rico & Rucha
18. Matilda, former adventurer

LEGEND

 Inn

◇ Save Point

ACTION CHECKLIST

1 • Meet Edward in the palace.

2 • Meet Balbagan in the street.

3 • Meet the twins, Eugene, and Michelle in their rooms at the Rosy Bear Inn.

4 • Go onto the royal balcony to meet Aya.

5 • Optional: The next morning, take on side quests in Fayel and Burgusstadt.

NEW SIDE QUESTS AVAILABLE

Unlucky's Relative

Gustav's Memories

PRIVATE EVENTS AVAILABLE

Zalacrest Wine

The Lost Sword

ENEMIES

None.

MEET BALBAGAN

Everything but the Rosy Bear Inn is closed down for the night. Before you visit the inn, approach Balbagan (**3** on the map) under the great arch that leads west to the Oradian Mountains. The mighty man makes an impulsive decision to leave the party. Say, these first two meetings went really well for Capell, didn't they?

MISSION WALKTHROUGH

After the arrival movie, the interlude continues in the middle of the night, with Capell waking up restless in his palace room. Your task is to explore Fayel and see if Capell's comrades are experiencing the same sleeplessness. You start out on the staircase in the palace, halfway between floors.

MEET EDWARD

Go downstairs to the main floor of the palace and approach the first room on the right (**2** on the map). Edward has some pent-up anger issues, doesn't he? After the scene, exit the palace into the streets of Fayel.

SUGGESTIONS ON HOW TO PLAY: TIPS ON SETTING SKILLS

Welcome back to Fayel. Now that you're in town, take some time to adjust your full party's battle, Connect, and magic skills. You can find extensive advice on this in **Part 1: Game Basics & Skills**, but here's a quick distillation of some of that advice.

First and foremost: assign low-cost skills that can be used repeatedly to each character's battle, Connect, and (if applicable) magic skill slots. If these skills stun, or launch, or knock down, or otherwise confound the enemy too, that's great. If they have a large number of hits, even better. This creates a short-list of extremely effective skills that are head-and-shoulders above other options. Edward's Twinstream, in particular, is fantastic—two heavily-damaging hits that execute very quickly, with negligible MP cost. Why would Edward use anything else? (Well, his Galvanic Strike is excellent too.)

Other notable skills include Michelle's Astro (area-of-effect damage and stun, extremely damaging with a large number of hits at Lv.3, low MP cost, no enemy absorbs ether damage, arguably pound-for-pound the best spell in the game), Aya's Sparrowrain (basically a melee Astro, minus the stun), Rico's Hydrill (low MP cost, possible freeze effect, decent number of hits), and Capell's Cutting Gavotte, which deserves special mention yet again. As stated earlier in the walkthrough, Cutting Gavotte is cheap, fast, launches with sufficient AP, always works for juggles, combos into itself on heavy foes, and pays for itself (and then some) when used in a combo of Diminuendo Dive -> Cutting Gavotte on foes that Capell can knock down.

Here are some other notes on individual characters:

Michelle can serve your party as both the main healer and a serious dealer of heavy damage. A good suggestion is to disable every offensive spell on her magic list except Astro. Astro is fantastic and cheap, and should be used repeatedly. If you use Astro as a staple throughout the game, it should be nearing Lv.3 skill just around the time the feeble cape is found, an item that regenerates 1% of max MP every 5 seconds for the wearer—enough MP regeneration to allow Michelle to cast Astro almost infinitely without worrying about her MP ever again. If you turn off all her other offensive magic (and some of the earlier healing spells like Levi and Megalevi) she'll cast Astro on her own, but you can certainly encourage this by frequently Connecting to Michelle and forcing her to recast Astro over and over—unless you need her autonomous healing, of course.

Eugene is an excellent healer alternative to Michelle: he can use Salva and Salvus (Michelle cannot, forcing your party to rely on miraculous medicine for revivals), has a few great offensive spells (mainly Geoclaw), and learns Astro later on (though he'll have to grind in order to increase his skill with it to catch up to Michelle, if she's been in play).

MEET RICO AND RUCHA

Enter the inn and go upstairs. Approach the first door on the right to trigger a scene with the sleeping twins, Rico and Rucha. Finally, a word of support from your teammates…

MEET EUGENE

In the upstairs hall of the inn, approach the second door on the right to trigger a scene with Eugene. He speaks of his days with Sigmund, going back to boyhood…and points out that Sigmund saw something in Capell "that goes far deeper then mere resemblance."

MEET MICHELLE

In the upstairs hall of the inn, approach the lone door on the left to trigger a scene with Michelle. She and Capell take turns passing words of wisdom to each other.

MEET AYA

Now you can enter the palace and go upstairs onto the royal balcony, where you trigger one last cutscene. Capell wanders out alone to play his flute, and then Aya joins him. They discuss Sigmund's ideals and resolve to carry on as best they can. You also gain fantasia notations after the encounter.

The scene automatically changes to the next morning as Capell and the others (minus Balbagan) gather together and head out into the Oradian Dunes. Then it's off to Port Zala…well, after a U-turn back into Fayel for some cleanup work, if you want.

OPTIONAL: GET SOME SIDE WORK DONE

Two new side quests are now available in Fayel, along with two more new ones back in Burgusstadt. So you might want to tackle those now. See **Part 4: Side Quests** for the details.

Good Connect skill buddies include Edward (Twinstream! Twinstream! Twinstream!) and Aya (Sparrowrain, Ravaging Raptor for Player Advantage). However, in certain fights (and in particular, during a significant portion of the late game and the Seraphic Gate) you won't want to be Connected to anyone, because you'll need to quickly play Prudentiae for protection against powerful enemy attack spells.

Here are a few suggestions for setting your battle and/or magic skills:

* For Capell, consider setting both his Ⓐ and Ⓑ battle skills to Cutting Gavotte. Otherwise, keep Cutting Gavotte on Ⓑ and set a situational skill, or one you'd like to level up, on Ⓐ. No reason not to have the 20% damage boost for such a consistent attack as Cutting Gavotte.

* For Edward, set his Ⓑ battle skill to Twinstream, and set Ⓐ to "None."

* For Balbagan, until Axle Drive or Triple Threat become available (both of which are late-game skills), it's a smart idea to place Barrier of Brawn as his Ⓑ battle skill once it's available, and set "None" as the Ⓐ skill. It seems Balbagan is better off just attacking nonstop with the defensive buff active. Also, his MP pool is low, so even if you do assign him attack skills, he won't be using them consistently in the early going.

* On magic lists, you might want to turn off any offensive spell that isn't Astro for Michelle, or Geoclaw (and later Astro) for Eugene. You could also turn off their earliest healing spells, Levi and Megalevi, the ones that only heal 30 percent per individual. In a heated battle, it's often counterproductive for characters to spend 4-7 seconds positioning and casting a minor cure, when by the time their cure goes off, the target likely took more severe damage.

One final tip: you can never have too many red berry potions or miraculous medicines. Another recommendation is having a sacrificial doll as one of the accessories for every character. Instant resurrection is a far better benefit than a +3% critical hit rate or +5 ATK or whatever other boost you might get out of an accessory slot. If you're in the middle of a rough battle, pull out for a bit and quickly re-equip new sacrificial dolls if you have them, because each works only once and then changes into a hopeless charm.

MISSION MAP

1. Start
2. Rock arch (formerly blocked)
3. Port entry

LEGEND

Jeweled Cabinet

ORADIAN DUNES (WEST)

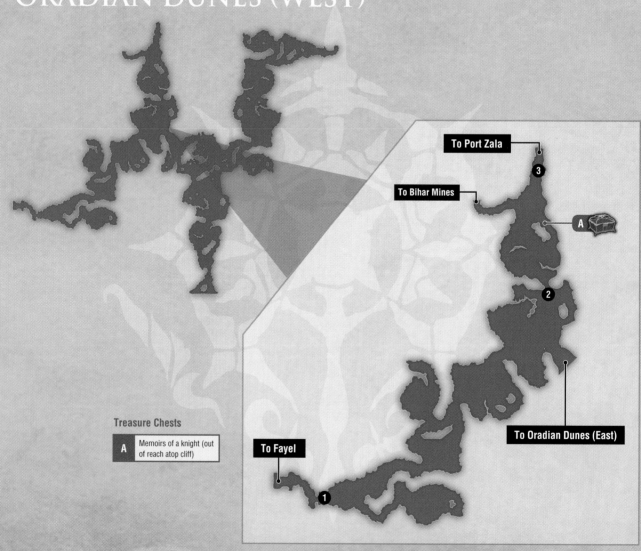

To Port Zala

3

To Bihar Mines

A

To Oradian Dunes (East)

To Fayel

1

2

Treasure Chests

A | Memoirs of a knight (out of reach atop cliff)

This chapter features another cross-desert sojourn, this time heading north to Port Zala…a town suffering the wrath of the sea itself, or so it seems.

MISSION

CROSS THE DUNES TO PORT ZALA

This travel mission takes you to a previously blocked archway, then across the northernmost stretch of the Oradian Dunes and into the waterfront city of Port Zala.

ACTION CHECKLIST

1. Exit Fayel into the Oradian Dunes.
2. Cross the dunes east.
3. Head north to Port Zala.

NEW SIDE QUESTS AVAILABLE

None.

PRIVATE EVENTS AVAILABLE

None.

ENEMIES

Narbear	AP 7
HP • 10000	
FOL • 450	EXP • 500

Amigo	AP 3
HP • 2750	
FOL • 250	EXP • 300

Garuda	AP -
HP • 3650	
FOL • 300	EXP • 350

Impfish	AP 1
HP • 1659	
FOL • 100	EXP • 150

MISSION WALKTHROUGH

As you leave Fayel, put together a single party and head northeast across the Oradian Dunes. Then, veer north through the previously blocked pass. Continue north until you enter Port Zala. As you approach, you can see the Cerulean Chain rising into the sky.

There, you trigger an entrance cutscene—the town has been heavily damaged by great waves and its citizens are hurt and panicked. An injured citizen blames the tsunamis on the great chain anchored north of town, just up the coast. Michelle does what healing she can…and the locals are uplifted by the news that "the Liberator" has come to save them!

STORMY SEAS

Tsunamis triggered by the dark power of the nearby Cerulean Chain threaten to wipe Port Zala off the map. This walkthrough takes you directly to the chain and the brutal Order knight who guards it. You can explore Port Zala at your leisure afterward.

MISSION

DESTROY THE CERULEAN CHAIN!

With tsunamis coming, logic suggests you shouldn't take time right now to explore this coastal town—although, let's be clear, you *can* if you want. In particular, before you head for the chain you might want to visit the shopkeeper at Port Zala's general store to stock up on health items, and then go save your game at the inn. Otherwise, head straight for the source of the town's affliction.

Zalan Coast

To Oradian Dunes

Port Zala

MISSION MAP

1. General store
2. Inn
3. Faina & Leif
4. Beach path
5. Niedzielan & Cerulean Chain
6. Rock barrier (protection from tsunamis)

LEGEND

◇ Save Point

* Note: this first map of Port Zala is minimal, pointing out only the few places you might visit before heading to the chain. A more complete map of the town is given in the interlude section after this mission.

ACTION CHECKLIST

1 • Optional: Stock up on items at Port Zala shops.

2 • Meet Faina and Leif.

3 • Follow the beach path to the Zalan Coast.

4 • Continue along the coast to the Cerulean Chain.

5 • Defeat Niedzielan and destroy the chain.

NEW SIDE QUESTS AVAILABLE

None.

PRIVATE EVENTS AVAILABLE

None.

ENEMIES

Gremlinfish `AP 1`

HP • 1500
FOL • 150   EXP • 166

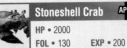

Stoneshell Crab `AP 4`

HP • 2000
FOL • 130   EXP • 200

Niedzielan `AP -`

HP • 62500
FOL • 2500   EXP • 5660

MISSION WALKTHROUGH

Get ready for what is likely your toughest boss fight yet. En route to the Cerulean Chain, you can make a couple of optional stops in town—remember, you have the choice to stock up and save your game. But you must make one mandatory stop as well.

MEET FAINA AND LEIF AGAIN

As you walk toward the waterfront and the beach path that runs north up the coast, you trigger a meeting with none other than Faina, Capell's ardent admirer from Sapran, and her young brother Leif. Faina is an itinerant peddler of goods now, and her selection is actually quite good, so check out her wares.

The crew sees the chain roiling the waters into swirling tornadoes. Edward wants to seek high ground, but Capell wants to save the villagers and leads the party onward.

DEFEAT NIEDZIELAN AND DESTROY THE CERULEAN CHAIN

Continue west along the path until you finally encounter Niedzielan and the Cerulean Chain. This is slightly different than previous boss battles in that you must not only defeat the Order knight, but also smash the chain in the course of the fight.

TAKE THE BEACH PATH TO THE COAST

Now head north along the beach (littered with wreckage from the tsunami) past the twins and Gustav and toward the big cliffs; you see the chain rising to the moon behind them. Keep going until you reach the Zalan Coast to trigger a cutscene.

NIEDZIELAN AND THE CERULEAN CHAIN

p.294

HP 62500   **EXP** 5660

The key to this battle is knowing the sequence of events. First, note that Niedzielan and the Cerulean Chain have a powerful symbiotic relationship, feeding off each other's energy. You cannot win this fight simply by attacking Niedzielan; the Order knight is unbeatable as long as the chain is still intact. The chain has two layers of protection: (1) an impenetrable force field fed by Niedzielan's own power, and (2) a coating of armor crystals that can be smashed once the force field is down.

So here's the trick: your attacks eventually stun Niedzielan, temporarily. When stunned, he slumps, his power ebbs, and the force field around the chain dissipates. At this point, you can start smashing through the chain's armor crystals. But when Niedzielan recovers from being stunned, his power surge rebuilds the force field, knocking you away from the chain.

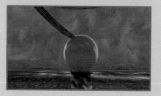 

You must then go and stun the Order knight again and repeat the process until the chain's crystal armor is smashed, at which point Niedzielan finally falls. This triggers a cutscene of Capell delivering the final blow to the chain itself. Niedzielan takes excessive damage from earth attacks, so Connect with Eugene, activate Symphonic Blade, then attack with Capell while casting Geoclaw to expedite the battle. Avoid using water spells, which the Order knight simply resists.

But here's another trick, one that can earn you a hefty Situation Bonus. The Cerulean Chain unleashes occasional tsunamis that crash onto the beach, knocking down every exposed member of your party. The key word here is "exposed"—rock formations on the beach can provide protection, letting you can ride out the wave without being knocked down. You get warnings about each tsunami's arrival—the wave rises in

the distance, the water on the beach starts to recede faster (sucking you out if you're not careful), your controller starts vibrating, and then one of your party members calls out that a tsunami is coming. When these signs occur, hustle behind one of the rock barriers on the high part of the beach. If you make it in time, Capell stays on his feet as the great wave sweeps through.

As usual, the boss has minions. Beware the annoying stoneshell crabs and gremlinfish that attack as you move through the area. They're fairly weak, so take a few seconds to whack them into oblivion. The whole process is much easier if fewer minions are harassing you.

SITUATION BONUS!

Destroyed all barricades

⭐ *Full HP and MP recovery!*

After the fight, one last monstrous wave knocks Capell for a loop. But he wakes up a hero…and Edward isn't too happy about it.

CONFLICT

This chapter lets you explore Port Zala, a town full of grateful residents with a few favors to ask. You also see some fractures forming in the party—hence the chapter title. The first time you enter the town's inn after smashing the chain, you trigger a party meeting that airs out a few grievances.

INTERLUDE: PORT ZALA

Now that the tsunamis have stopped, you can wander around town looking for treasure, side quests, and private conversations with your party.

Item Bags

The following item bags are washed up by the tsunami and appear after the Cerulean Chain is destroyed:

a	Strange-colored bag
b	Dentures
c	Wooden box
d	Piece of wood
e	Rag
f	Doll
g	Battered notebook
h	Bouquet
i	Vase
j	Tail

Zalan Coast

To Oradian Dunes

Port Zala

PORT ZALA & ZALAN COAST

MISSION MAP

1. Inn (Savio)
2. Mayor's house (Mayor's wife)
3. General store (Eugene)
4. Bar (waitress, Martin, fisherman)
5. House (Aya, Dominica)
6. Toothless old man
7. Michelle
8. Faina & Leif (item sellers)
9. Rico, Rucha, Gustav
10. Lost dog
11. Edward
12. Fish warehouse (Ivan)

LEGEND

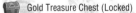

Wooden Treasure Chest

Gold Treasure Chest (Locked)

Jeweled Cabinet

Save Point

Treasure Chests

A	Memoirs of a warrior (out of reach in water)
B	15000 Fol (locked)
C	Premium Karathos (locked and hidden; reveal with flute)
D	Zala rock salt
E	Musician's quill
F	Zala rock salt
G	Sliced fish
H	Sliced deviant fish
I	Sliced salmon
J	Sliced deviant fish
K	Fish fin
L	Fish fin
M	Sliced fish

ACTION CHECKLIST

1 • Optional: Take on side quests and private events.

2 • Enter the inn to trigger a scene.

3 • Go find Edward on the dock.

4 • Take the ship to Kolton.

ENEMIES

None.

NEW SIDE QUESTS AVAILABLE

In Port Zala:

Lost Gift

Lost Dentures

Lost Secret

In Burgusstadt:

Multi-Item Exchange

Lost Amulet

Tsunami Junk Pickup

PRIVATE EVENTS AVAILABLE

The Stray Dog

Reeling in the Catch

Tsunami's Aftermath

First Ocean Visit

Gustav the Cub

MISSION WALKTHROUGH

Again, this is a time for exploration and side quests. The tsunamis have washed around a lot of debris; many townsfolk are looking for lost items. Help people find stuff and pick up some nice rewards in the process. See the Port Zala section in **Part 4: Side Quests** for details.

GO TO THE INN

The first time you enter the inn after destroying the Cerulean Chain, you trigger a cutscene in which Edward and the other party members disagree on fundamental issues of leadership. Edward leaves and Capell goes after him.

GO FIND EDWARD

After the inn meeting, head east toward the dock at the east end of town to trigger an encounter between Capell and Edward. You hear the story of how Edward first met Sigmund…and you see his anger issues. Afterwards, Aya joins Capell and notices some odd changes in the moon. Following this exchange, you end up back in the inn.

Exit the inn to trigger one more cutscene. As Capell steps outside, he notices that a large sailing vessel has just arrived at the dock. This is the ship slated to take you to your next destination, Kolton, whenever you're ready to leave Port Zala.

TALK TO OTHER FOLKS

You can trigger five private events and five side quests around Port Zala. You can also get the item you need from the Port Zala bar to complete the Burgusstadt side quest, "Zalacrest Wine," which (when completed) unlocks another Burgusstadt side quest, "Multi-Item Exchange."

The Stray Dog

Go to the beach area and Connect to Rico, then go talk to the dog standing near the seawall to find out that he's lost. By doing this, Capell improves his relationship with Rico, Rucha, and Gustav.

First Ocean Visit

Go to the beach area and talk to Rucha. You learn that this is her first-ever visit to the ocean, and she's full of questions and theories about it.

Reeling in the Catch

Find Michelle in the alley between the inn and the general store. Connect to Michelle, then enter the general store and talk to Eugene. He's thinking about going fishing. Michelle finds the idea interesting...but she has a different kind of fishing in mind.

Gustav the Cub

Enter the house nearest the town's exit to the Oradian Dunes and Connect with Dominica. Then head to the beach area and "talk" to Gustav, who is actually asleep. Dominica tells Capell about the bear's younger days, and his devotion to Aya.

Tsunami's Aftermath

Enter the inn and Connect with Savio. Head to the local bar and talk to the "Fisherman" standing by himself over on the east side of the room. The poor fellow's livelihood was almost wiped out by the tsunami. But Savio predicts better days ahead.

SHIP OUT FOR KOLTON

When you're ready to move on to the next mission, go to the dock and talk to the "Town-loving fisherman" who stands by the ship. He asks if you're leaving for Kolton. If you're ready to go, simply answer "Yes" to trigger your journey to the snowy city.

DEFEAT THE INVISIBLE ENEMY!

Kolton is frigid and beautiful, but something's wrong here. The party finds shattered statues and other signs of recent violence. Soon they come upon a monster that's menacing civilians—a monster who can't be seen by anyone but Capell!

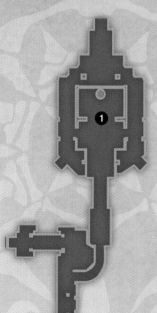

KOLTON DOCKS

MISSION MAP

1 Mysterious foe

ACTION CHECKLIST

1 · Play Percipere to reveal the invisible enemy.

2 · Let your party defeat the foe.

NEW SIDE QUESTS AVAILABLE

None.

PRIVATE EVENTS AVAILABLE

None.

ENEMIES

 Mysterious Foe **AP ?**

HP • ?

FOL • ? EXP • ?

MISSION WALKTHROUGH

Note in the cutscene that Capell's flute tune Percipere reveals the monster to the others in the party. As the tutorial page on "Invisible Enemies" explains, this is the key to your strategy in this fight.

After the battle, the citizens of Kolton greet "Sigmund the Liberator" and provide rooms for the party. Meanwhile, Edward discovers that his lunaglyph seems attracted to the mysterious monster he just defeated. Later, Capell and Aya have their first encounter with "lunar rain."

Not long after that, Edward comes down with a strange affliction…one that doesn't respond to the healing efforts of either Michelle or Eugene. A kid named Vic (the one you saved from the mysterious foe) knows of a healer in Halgita who might help. He says he can get you there, no problem, and joins your party. Edward and Michelle (decide to stay behind with Edward) leave the party for now.

SITUATION BONUS!

Defeated the mysterious foe within 1 minute.

★ *Obtained some blue berry powder!*

DEFEAT THE MYSTERIOUS FOE

This is a simple fight. Just play Percipere and keep the invisible foe within the radius of the song's influence, so that your comrades can see him. If your party is at good levels (mid to late 20's at least) they should defeat the foe quickly, earning the Situation Bonus for beating the mysterious foe within one minute.

BEDRIDDEN

With Edward afflicted by a mysterious, seemingly incurable ailment, the team decides to take Vic's word that healers can be found in Halgita. Before you venture out into the Cobasna Timberlands headed for Halgita, you should fully explore Kolton.

INTERLUDE: KOLTON

Take some time to shop and explore the chilly city of Kolton. Your first visit here unlocks three new side quests and several private events as well. And your new buddy Vic adds a very useful new skill to the party; you definitely want to take advantage of it.

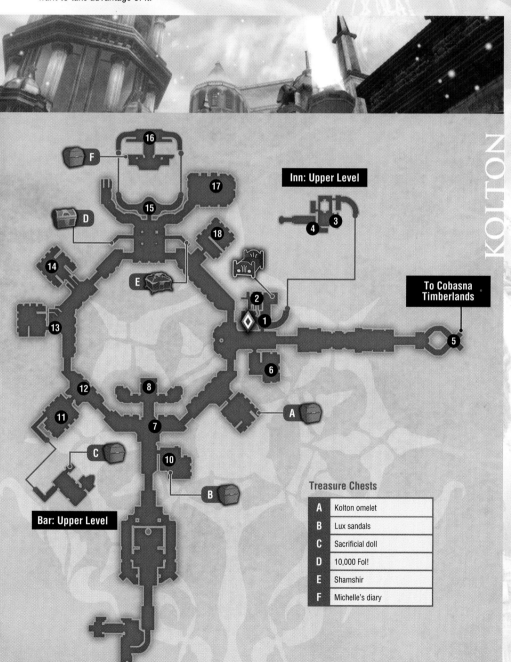

Inn: Upper Level

To Cobasna Timberlands

Bar: Upper Level

MISSION MAP

1. Inn: Ground Level (Vic)
2. Edward & Michelle
3. Aya
4. Dominica
5. Teleport to Cobasna Timberlands
6. General shop
7. Eugene
8. Locked gate
9. Sea transport (out of service)
10. The Emporium (Savio)
11. Bar: Ground Level (barkeeper)
12. Oreg
13. Rico & Rucha
14. House (Simon's grandparents)
15. Church: Upper Level
16. Church: Main Level
17. Gustav
18. House (senior apprentice, master confectioner)

LEGEND

- Wooden Treasure Chest
- Gold Treasure Chest (Locked)
- Jeweled Cabinet
- Inn
- Save Point

Treasure Chests

A	Kolton omelet
B	Lux sandals
C	Sacrificial doll
D	10,000 Fol!
E	Shamshir
F	Michelle's diary

ACTION CHECKLIST

1. Optional: Take up side quests and trigger private events.

2. Use Vic to open the locked treasure chest near the church.

3. Exit Kolton into the Cobasna Timberlands.

ENEMIES

None.

NEW SIDE QUESTS AVAILABLE

Simon Is Missing, Pt. 1

Confection Contest

The Surrogate Parent

PRIVATE EVENTS AVAILABLE

Michelle and Edward

Gustav's Secret

Snow Fairy

Aya's Slip

MISSION WALKTHROUGH

Get some things done here in Kolton before you head off to Halgita via the Cobasna Timberlands.

TRY OUT VIC'S "TRAPMASTER" SKILL

Vic has a personal skill called Trapmaster that lets him pick the locks on locked treasure chests. He can also open trapped chests without triggering the trap. So from now on, whenever you have Vic in your Party A group, make sure you Connect to him before opening any treasure chest.

An example of the great value his skill brings to your party is up in the north part of Kolton. Connect to Vic and find the locked chest at the end of a small walkway near the church entrance (see **D** on the map).

Vic opens it and nabs a sweet 10,000 Fol for your party.

Unfortunately, you can't leave Kolton for Port Zala and backtrack to other locked chests yet; ship transport is unavailable right now. But later, after you return from Halgita, you can go back to previous locations and use Vic to pick all the locked chests you couldn't open before—especially all those chests inside towns where you couldn't even draw your sword to smash them open.

OPTIONAL: DO THE QUESTS AND PRIVATE EVENTS

Three new side quests and four private events are available now in Kolton, with more to come later. Take care of this optional business before you leave town.

Michelle and Edward

Enter the inn and find Michelle watching over the stricken Edward in the back room on the main level (on the map). Talk to Michelle. She plans to stay and watch over Edward while the rest of your party heads off to Halgita looking for help.

Snow Fairy

Climb the stairs to the upper level of the Kolton inn and find Dominica outside on the balcony. Connect to her, then exit the inn. Work your way around Kolton's ring to find Rucha (with Rico, of course) in the westernmost part of town. Still Connected, talk to Rucha to trigger a cutscene in which Rucha exults in the falling snow.

Gustav's Secret

Find Rico on the westernmost street of Kolton and Connect to him. Head to Kolton's northeast courtyard, the area directly east of the church, and talk to Gustav. The bear shares secrets about Aya with Rico, but Rico won't pass them along to Capell.

Aya's Slip

Climb to the upstairs room at the Kolton inn and Connect with Aya, then exit the inn. This triggers a cutscene—Aya, mesmerized by the falling snow's beauty, slips and falls. Then she demands to know if Capell "saw that." You have a choice of three answers. The answer that gives you the best overall results in terms of Capell's relationship with Aya is: "Sorry, I just missed it."

TELEPORT TO THE COBASNA TIMBERLANDS

When business is completed in Kolton, exit the city via the east gates and continue all the way to the circular platform. Step aboard to get teleported into the lush wilderness of the Cobasna Timberlands.

MISSION

TRAVERSE COBASNA TO HALGITA

The Cobasna Timberlands features heavily-wooded terrain and a number of trails blocked by a teleporting mist. Stepping into this mist warps your entire party to new locations in the forest, so it helps to know exactly where each patch of mist sends you. For this first crossing, however, just follow Vic. He knows exactly where he's going, and he leads you directly to Halgita. You'll find the rest of the forest mapped out in detail for you later.

To Kolton

1

Treasure Chest

| A | Malus wood (trapped!) |

A

LEGEND

→ Vic's route to Halgita

~~~ Teleporting Mist

To Halgita **2**

COBASNA TIMBERLANDS (WEST)

MISSION MAP

1 Teleport to/from Kolton

2 Entrance to Halgita

ACTION CHECKLIST

1 · Follow Vic to Halgita.

2 · Enter the city when you arrive.

NEW SIDE QUESTS AVAILABLE
None.

PRIVATE EVENTS AVAILABLE
None.

ENEMIES

	Green Drogo Warrior	**AP 5**
HP • 6000		
FOL • 270	EXP • 550	

	Green Drogo Chief	**AP 5**
HP • 13170		
FOL • 350	EXP • 1000	

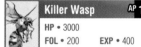

	Killer Wasp	**AP 1**
HP • 3000		
FOL • 200	EXP • 400	

MISSION WALKTHROUGH

Start by appointing two parties, with Vic leading Party B. You arrive via a teleport platform on the west edge of the forest. Your goal is to work your way east for awhile, then south to Halgita.

FOLLOW VIC TO HALGITA

Again, Vic knows the way, so just follow him and his group. Be ready for killer wasps and hostile jungle folk known as the Drogo. Note the gently falling lunar rain and the effect it seems to have on various party members—in particular, the ones who have lunaglyphs. Everybody feels great! But what's up with those glowing wings that seem to be growing on people's backs?

Note that lunar rain doesn't fall in certain parts of the forest, and if you spend some time in these areas, the glowing wings dissipate and eventually disappear. So there's an obvious, direct correlation between the rain and the wings.

Beware the Galloping Orthros

A huge beast called the orthros gallops in circles through the area where you must travel. You can't fight it yet, but if you get in its way, it can unfortunately trample you and inflict damage. Get out of its way!

AVOID THE MIST!

Watch out for the mist that blocks some of the forest trails. Vic warns you about "space being distorted" if you approach. Stepping into the mist teleports your party to a different part of the forest. Later, you will actually use this property to move through Cobasna, but for now you want to avoid getting sidetracked.

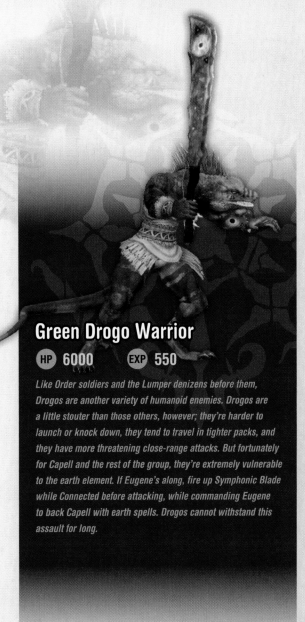

Green Drogo Warrior

HP 6000   **EXP** 550

Like Order soldiers and the Lumper denizens before them, Drogos are another variety of humanoid enemies. Drogos are a little stouter than those others, however; they're harder to launch or knock down, they tend to travel in tighter packs, and they have more threatening close-range attacks. But fortunately for Capell and the rest of the group, they're extremely vulnerable to the earth element. If Eugene's along, fire up Symphonic Blade while Connected before attacking, while commanding Eugene to back Capell with earth spells. Drogos cannot withstand this assault for long.

DON'T OPEN THE CHEST

You come upon only one treasure chest as you follow Vic to Halgita. It happens to be a trap, but you can't Connect to Vic here, since he's the head of Party B. You can open this chest and just take the damage, or leave it for later when you can put Vic in your party and use his Trapmaster skill.

INTERLUDE: HALGITA

Start by paying a courtesy visit to Svala, Empress of Halgita. (This is well worth the time.) Afterwards, poor Capell meets some of Sigmund's friends, then Vic brings the information you need regarding Edward's mysterious disease. Now you can spend some time exploring and shopping in the great city.

MISSION MAP

1. Gustav
2. Savio
3. Eugene
4. Materials shop
5. Elevator: 1F
6. Elevator: 2F
7. Elevator: 3F
8. Throne room
9. Aya
10. Vic
11. Item shop
12. Accessory shop
13. Weapon shop
14. Armor shop
15. Rucha
16. Rico
17. Dominica
18. Royal chambers

LEGEND

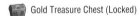

- Wooden Treasure Chest
- Gold Treasure Chest (Locked)
- Jeweled Cabinet

Treasure Chests

A	Panacea
B	Silk shawl (reveal with Percipere)
C	Ebony wood
D	Miraculous medicine
E	Karathos wristband (upstairs on balcony; locked)
F	Sacrificial doll (locked)
G	Staff paper
H	Malus wood
I	Black berry potion
J	Malus wood (locked)
K	Black berry potion
L	Miraculous medicine (locked)
M	5000 Fol (locked)
N	Bishop staff (upstairs on balcony; locked)

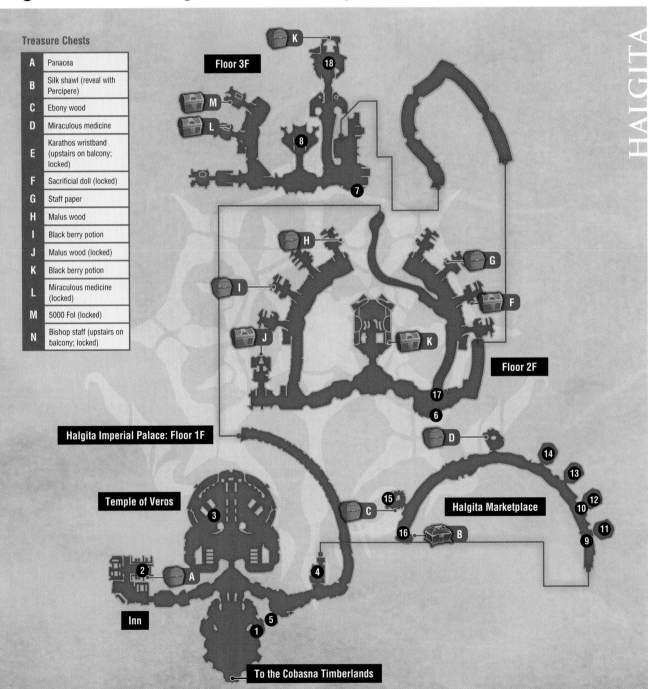

Floor 3F

Floor 2F

Halgita Imperial Palace: Floor 1F

Temple of Veros

Halgita Marketplace

Inn

To the Cobasna Timberlands

HALGITA

ACTION CHECKLIST

1 · Go to the throne room to meet Empress Svala.

2 · Meet Touma and Komachi.

3 · Learn about the healer in the Timberlands from Vic.

4 · Optional: Explore with Vic, shop to upgrade equipment, and trigger private events.

5 · Exit Halgita into the Cobasna Timberlands to seek the healer.

NEW SIDE QUESTS AVAILABLE

None.

ENEMIES

None.

PRIVATE EVENTS AVAILABLE

Note: all five events are available only after the meeting with Empress Svala and the subsequent cutscenes.

A Second Home   *A Different Culture*   *Rico and His Veggies*   *Gustav's Dream*   *A Sage's Solitude*

MISSION WALKTHROUGH

Eugene tells you to follow him to the throne room. It's a good idea to do so right away, because you get a reward from the empress that gives you a lot of buying power afterwards down in the Halgita marketplace. Meanwhile, Vic promises to dig up information, which is his specialty.

GO TO THE THRONE ROOM

The elevator is just down the corridor to the right from the entrance hall. Use the elevator controls to ride up to floor 3F. When you arrive, exit the car and head left past the staircase to the big doors guarded by two soldiers. Approach them to trigger the movie of Capell's meeting with Empress Svala of Halgita.

The empress confirms that eight chains have been destroyed and thanks Capell, Aya, and Eugene for their service. "Lord Sigmund" (Capell) tells her about his friend fallen ill who needs help fast. She bestows a gift… "a small token," she says. Small, indeed—it's a chest with 100,000 Fol inside! Afterwards, Capell runs into two of Sigmund's friends, Touma and Komachi, who think he is Sigmund.

Before you head off to explore, you get one last cutscene. In the Halgita inn, Vic reports that he's learned of a healer who cured someone with an illness like Edward's. The fellow lives deep in the Cobasna Timberlands.

EXPLORE HALGITA WITH VIC

Now take some time to explore the three levels of the Halgita royal palace, and then spend some of your windfall in the Halgita marketplace. Be sure to Connect with Vic before you set off. Six locked treasure chests are stored in the area, and Vic can pick them open with ease. One locked chest in a private chamber up on floor 3F holds another 5,000 Fol!

After you plunder the chests of Halgita, talk to your compatriots to trigger some private events too. All five available are outlined below. Remember that private events can increase Capell's bond with various party members.

A Different Culture

Find Aya by the item shop in the marketplace area and talk to her. She marvels at Halgita's size and diversity.

A Second Home

Enter the Temple of Veros on floor 1F of the palace and talk to Eugene. He reveals his actual profession, and tells Capell about his first meeting with Sigmund.

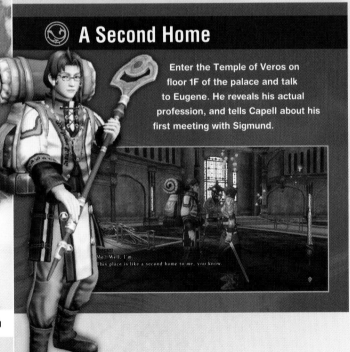

Rico and His Veggies

Connect to Rico at the bottom of the Halgita marketplace area and go talk to Rucha, who is in the first house on your left as you head up the stairs. You learn Rico hates vegetables, and his sister wants him to try some new recipes. This unlocks Rico's "Fish Lover" palate.

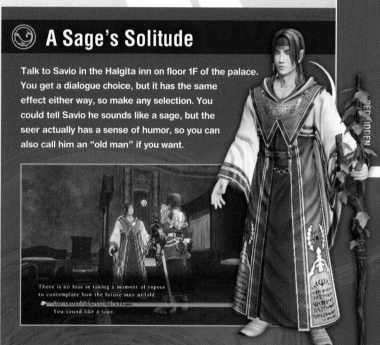

A Sage's Solitude

Talk to Savio in the Halgita inn on floor 1F of the palace. You get a dialogue choice, but it has the same effect either way, so make any selection. You could tell Savio he sounds like a sage, but the seer actually has a sense of humor, so you can also call him an "old man" if you want.

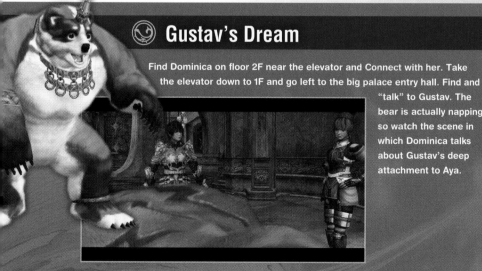

Gustav's Dream

Find Dominica on floor 2F near the elevator and Connect with her. Take the elevator down to 1F and go left to the big palace entry hall. Find and "talk" to Gustav. The bear is actually napping, so watch the scene in which Dominica talks about Gustav's deep attachment to Aya.

HEAD INTO THE TIMBERLANDS

Time to help Edward by finding the rumored healer out in the wild forest. Exit Halgita into the Cobasna Timberlands.

MISSION MAPS

1. Start
2. Den of the orthros
3. Walk into mist
4. Walk into mist

LEGEND

→ Teleport Route

Teleporting Mist

Route to Kiriya's Hut

Gold Treasure Chest (Locked)

Wooden Treasure Chest

Jeweled Cabinet

COBASNA TIMBERLANDS

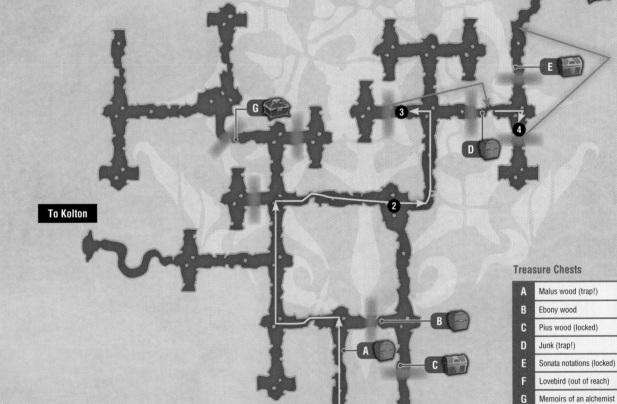

Kiriya's Hut

To Kolton

To Halgita

Treasure Chests

A	Malus wood (trap!)
B	Ebony wood
C	Pius wood (locked)
D	Junk (trap!)
E	Sonata notations (locked)
F	Lovebird (out of reach)
G	Memoirs of an alchemist

THROUGH THE JUNGLE

Somewhere in the deepest glades of the Cobasna Timberlands, a great healer is rumored to live in seclusion. The trek to his hut is long, winding, dangerous, and blocked at one point by a great monster of the woods. But there's a trick to staying on the correct path without getting sidetracked by the space-warping Cobasna mists.

MISSION
FIND THE HEALER'S HUT

It's a long haul through the maddening maze of the forest, and it's easy to get lost or frustrated by the mists. But there's a map in this guide for you, along with a killer tip that lets you reach the hut even without a map. One other tip: Eugene's Geoclaw is a great CS and battle skill to have active in your party, especially since Edward's vaunted Twinstream is bedridden right now. It's also good to have Vic on your crew for lock picking.

ACTION CHECKLIST

1. Follow the white sparks that mark the correct path at each intersection.
2. Defeat the orthros.
3. Find and enter the healer's hut.

NEW SIDE QUESTS AVAILABLE

None.

PRIVATE EVENTS AVAILABLE

None.

ENEMIES

	Killer Wasp	AP 1
	HP • 3000	
	FOL • 200	EXP • 400

	Green Drogo Chief	AP 5
	HP • 13170	
	FOL • 350	EXP • 1000

	Mandragora	AP 4
	HP • 13170	
	FOL • 290	EXP • 700

	Tequilo	AP 3
	HP • 13170	
	FOL • 300	EXP • 620

	Green Drogo Warrior	AP 5
	HP • 6000	
	FOL • 270	EXP • 550

	Orthros	AP -
	HP • 70000	
	FOL • 2800	EXP • 6180

MISSION WALKTHROUGH

Here's your Triple-A travel secret: every time you come to a trail crossing, look for a shower of white sparks rising from the ground at the head of one of the trails leading away from the intersection. These sparks mark the direction you should take. (It's such a neat trick that it's been called out in a tip box just to make sure you don't miss it.) Look carefully, though—the falling lunar rain sometimes obscures the sparks. But the lunar rain is yellow and falls down, whereas the trail-marking sparks are white and rise upward.

Follow the White Sparks

Whenever you come to a trail crossing while seeking the healer's hut in the Cobasna Timberlands, follow the trail marked by rising white sparks.

Killer Wasp

HP 3000

EXP 400

Killer wasps travel in trios and can inflict stench, which attracts even more wasps. You can allow this to happen intentionally if you'd like to gain easy battle skill levels, items, EXP, and Fol. Wasps are extremely weak to fire, so let Rucha cut loose if she's around, and keep Symphonic Blade active with Aya. The mandragoras in this area also burn easily.

USE THE MIST TO YOUR ADVANTAGE

When the orthros has been dispatched, its den reopens and you can move on. Follow the white sparks east, then veer left heading north. At the next intersection, the white sparks appear to lead you astray, sending you west and then directly into a shroud of mist! But guess what? You actually *want* to teleport this time. Step into the mist (at ❸ on the map) to warp east into a clearing.

DEFEAT THE ORTHROS

When you reach the clearing marked on the map as ❷, you trigger the appearance of the orthros, a galloping monster you may have encountered briefly on your first sojourn across Cobasna to Halgita. He's a horrible beast, with fire-spewing serpents sprouting from his back, and he seals off his "den" so you cannot escape. Here's where Eugene's Geoclaw combined with Capell's Cutting Gavotte can work wonders against a heavy opponent. Hydrill and Hydrain, which the orthros is weak to, work even better. Exploit these spells if you have Rico along, and keep your distance to avoid the serpents' spinning fire attacks.

This clearing has three exits, and all three are blocked by mist shrouds. But just follow the white sparks; this time they lead you into the mist barrier to the south. You teleport again and end up north of the last mist barrier. The white sparks ahead of you lead you north to a stream, which triggers a cutscene (although you can find a treasure chest if you head south first).

South of the Orthros

After you defeat the orthros, you can head south to nab a couple of treasure chests. Each one sits near a barrier of teleporting mist, so approach them carefully.

134

The cutscene is interesting—Capell and Vic hop rocks across the stream while Vic reveals a bit of his past. Suddenly, he slips and Capell lunges to catch him. After the grab, Capell lets Vic go and mutters, "Something's not right." Then Vic screams, pushes Capell into the stream, and starts hollering. Hmmm...what's *that* all about?

This leads right into another cutscene in which we see Komachi, the friend of Sigmund we met briefly back at Halgita. At the behest of Touma, she's tailing the party to protect "the Liberator."

FIND THE HEALER'S HUT

From here you just follow the trail almost due north. Another cutscene shows how the lunar rain is raising spirits; Aya even calls it a "blessing." But Capell watches as the local vegetation does some pretty strange things.

Continue north, plucking the various herbs and berries that you find along the trail. Eventually, you reach a hut with a save point. Approach the door to trigger a scene.

Mandragora

HP 13170 **EXP** 15700

These plant nymphs present themselves as harmless foliage, but if you wander too close, they'll get the jump on you with Shrillshriek, a multi-hit attack that can defeat characters outright if you're not careful. Use ranged skills to gain a Player Advantage on them, rousing them from their slumber and avoiding a surprise Shrillshriek. Defeat them as usual after leading off, peppering them with fire magic if available.

MISSION MAPS

1 Cracked rock

2 Iron chest mimic!

3 - 4 Cracked rocks

LEGEND

→ Teleport Route

Teleporting Mist

Route from Hut to Kolton

Jeweled Cabinet

FROM KIRLYA'S HUT TO KOLTON

Kiriya's Hut

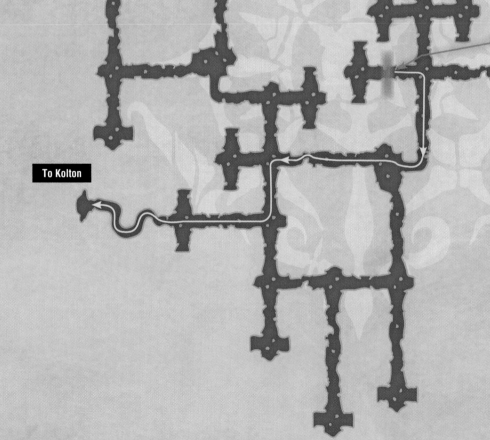

To Kolton

Treasure Chests

A	Malus wood
B	Staff paper
C	Ebony wood (reveal with Percipere)
D	Gold chainmail

TRUTH BEHIND LUNAGLYPHS

This chapter introduces a great healer and scholar, Kiriya, young but wise beyond his years. As the chapter title indicates, Kiriya is an expert on the true nature of lunaglyphs and lunar power. This new knowledge puts the beauty and exhilaration of the lunar rainfall into a new perspective.

GET THE ELIXIR CURE TO EDWARD

A young man named Kiriya emerges from the jungle hut. He seems to know and respect Savio. Kiriya calls Edward's illness a "glyph disease" and gives Capell a special elixir called Lunytol that can suppress lunar power. Then he speaks of lunaglyphs and "vermification," a state in which a human is overwhelmed by too much lunar power. Kiriya describes it as "a transformation into a living monster."

ACTION CHECKLIST

1 · Watch the cutscenes to learn more about the nature of lunar power.
2 · Return to Kolton.

NEW SIDE QUESTS AVAILABLE

None.

PRIVATE EVENTS AVAILABLE

None.

ENEMIES

 **Killer Wasp** AP 1
HP • 3000
FOL • 200   EXP • 400

 **Green Drogo Chief** AP 5
HP • 13170
FOL • 350   EXP • 1000

Mandragora AP 4
HP • 13170
FOL • 290   EXP • 700

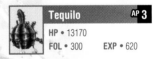 **Tequilo** AP 3
HP • 13170
FOL • 300   EXP • 620

 **Green Drogo Warrior** AP 5
HP • 6000
FOL • 270   EXP • 550

MISSION WALKTHROUGH

You must get the Lunytol elixir back to Edward in Kolton. As the team prepares to head back to Halgita, Savio and Kiriya speak of someone named Held who has joined the Order of Chains. Then Savio convinces Kiriya to join the party on their journey back.

OPTIONAL: EXPLORE BEYOND KIRIYA'S HUT

Now control returns to you. If you have Gustav in your party, you can continue north past Kiriya's hut and use the bear's Explosive Ride to smash through a trio of cracked rocks. (If you don't have Gustav in Party A now, just come back later when you do.) This provides access to areas with more herbs and four treasure chests, including one that contains gold chainmail.

Careful, though—the first "treasure chest" you find (right after the first cracked rock) turns out to be a powerful and very hostile iron chest mimic.

HEAD BACK TO KOLTON

Refer to the map for the route from Kiriya's hut back to Kolton. Use mist to make one teleport jump as you head south from the hut, then zigzag your way west to the teleport platform that takes you back to Kolton.

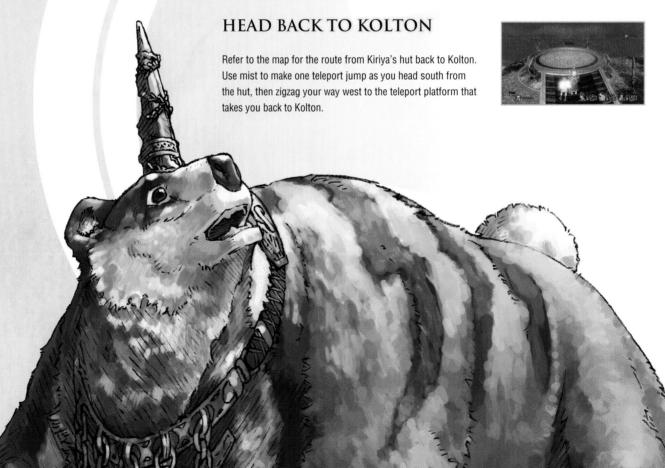

VERMIFICATION

The party returns to find Kolton in a state of general panic. Citizens are fleeing through the city gates! Michelle appears and reports that Edward has vermified and gone on a rampage. Is it too late for the Lunytol elixir?

MISSION

HALT EDWARD'S VERMIFORM

This is a fast-moving mission. Edward is in the advanced stages of vermification. His vermiform self is very powerful, highly mobile, and like the first vermified monster you faced, invisible too. Capell must keep him in everyone's sight with his Percipere flute tune.

ACTION CHECKLIST

1 • Play Percipere to keep Edward visible to your party.

2 • Follow Edward from location to location in Kolton until you stop him.

NEW SIDE QUESTS AVAILABLE

None.

PRIVATE EVENTS AVAILABLE

None.

ENEMIES

Vermified Edward	**AP 5**
HP • 20000	
FOL • 3000	EXP • 6530

KOLTON

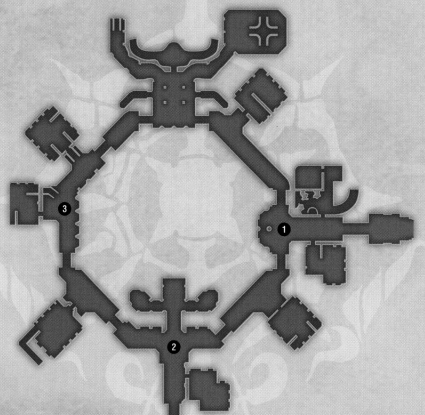

MISSION MAP

1 Edward's first appearance

2 Edward's second appearance

3 Edward's final appearance

MISSION WALKTHROUGH

As the vermification maddens Edward, he leaps from building to building, forcing you to chase him through the city. The lunar power has a strong grip, but Kiriya claims he can still be saved. Capell starts playing Percipere to reveal Edward's first location atop the Kolton clock tower.

FIGHT EDWARD IN EAST KOLTON

You start out in east Kolton near the inn. As the fight begins, a red "Time Limit" bar appears at the top of the screen. The first thing you should do against Edward is activate Symphonic Blade while Connected to either Eugene or Vic (Michelle would be a poor choice, since Capell cannot directly hit vermiforms without Symphonic Blade on). Once Symphonic Blade is going, break the Connection and play Percipere near Edward. Once Edward's visible, join your allies in damaging him, re-applying Symphonic Blade and Percipere as necessary. If you have Symphonic Blade active and build the AP gauge to at least half, you can pop him up with Crescendo Spike or Cutting Gavotte before juggling along with allies, so long as you're watchful for when the sight of Saruleus granted by Percipere wears off.

Get close enough so that the flute song's circle of effect covers Edward, but also keep enough distance from him to avoid getting attacked (which forces Capell to stop playing). After Edward takes a bit of damage, he leaps away to a new location.

FIGHT EDWARD IN SOUTH KOLTON

Next, Edward lands in south Kolton near the emporium. Repeat your strategy of firing up Symphonic Blade with Eugene or Vic, playing the flute to keep Edward visible, then getting in a few Cutting Gavottes and such. Soon he's off again.

FIGHT EDWARD IN WEST KOLTON

In west Kolton, you don't see Edward right away. Run forward a few steps and he bursts out to attack. Play Percipere as your comrades attack him. If you've kept your team upgraded and leveled up, you should be able to take Edward down quickly in this area and earn a generous Situation Bonus of 20,000 EXP.

SITUATION BONUS!

Stopped Edward within 3 minutes.

⭐ **Bonus 20,000 EXP!**

WATCH THE AFTERMATH

Stopping Edward triggers a long series of cutscenes. First, you see Capell use the Lunytol elixir on Edward, trying to halt the vermification process. Then Capell becomes privy to a series of scenes from Edward's troubled past, including his first meeting with Sigmund. Finally, in a trail of purple-black smoke, the vermification exits his body.

MISSION MAP

1. Vic
2. Aya
3. Gustav
4. Savio
5. Eugene
6. Kiriya
7. Dominica
8. Edward
9. Faina & Leif (shop)
10. Michelle
11. Rico & Rucha
12. Barkeeper
13. Aspiring animal breeder
14. Dog

KOLTON 2ND VISIT

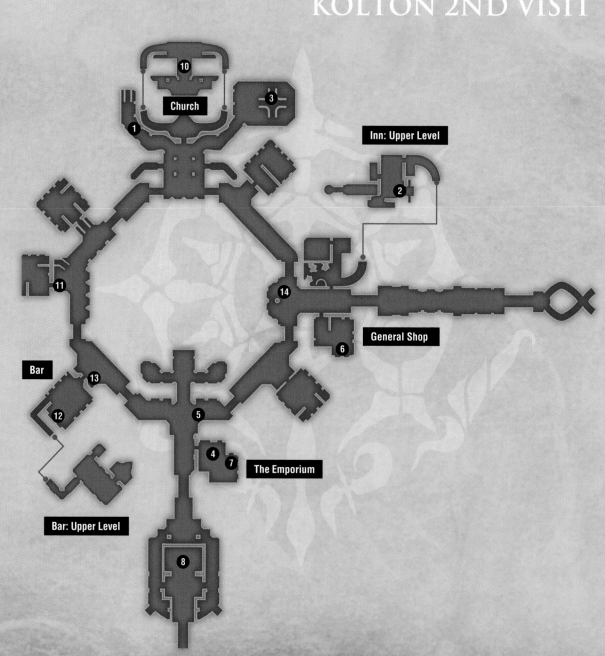

RECONCILIATION

This chapter features the forging of new bonds in your party, with new concerns about lunar power arising as well. It also lets you wrap up some side business in Kolton Union's cold capital.

MISSION

INTERLUDE: KOLTON

Capell and the party have issues to thrash out in the wake of Edward's vermiform episode, and this interlude opens with a series of cutscenes full of conflict, compromise, and new bonds formed. After that, Capell learns more from Kiriya about lunaglyphs and the deadly lunar rain.

ACTION CHECKLIST

1. Watch the scenes of party reconciliation.
2. Optional: Do side quests and private events.
3. Return to Halgita.

NEW SIDE QUESTS AVAILABLE

The Aspiring Animal Breeder

PRIVATE EVENTS AVAILABLE

The Secret of Off-Street

Lunaglyph and Magic

Rivals

The Secret of Battle

ENEMIES

None.

MISSION WALKTHROUGH

This interlude opens with a long series of post-battle cutscenes. Afterwards, it becomes clear that your next destination is back to Halgita. But before you go, finish up old side quests, pick up some new ones, and engage in some private events around town.

AFTER THE BATTLE...

Once Edward's vermification is reversed, the scene switches to a short while later at the Kolton inn. The full party, including Kiriya now, gathers around their recovering comrade. Amends are made and the team regains its fiercest fighter.

 Kiriya makes it clear that the madness could happen to anyone with a lunaglyph. And then Capell makes an angry admission that stuns the crowd.

Later that day, Capell, sitting on the Kolton dock, gets a visit from his number one fan, Faina. Just as things get interesting, Aya shows up. And then things get *really* interesting...Aya drags Capell off to a party meeting in which their "leader" sets the next destination: Halgita.

HEED KIRIYA'S WARNING

Before you move on to side questing and so forth, pay attention to one last scene. Kiriya warns Capell about lunar power and lunaglyphs. What happened to Edward could happen to anyone. After a quick tutorial on "Glyph Rates," you receive eight lunar suppressants.

OPTIONAL: TRIGGER FOUR PRIVATE EVENTS

Move around town and talk to folks. Note that some of your party members hang out in different places than before. You can finish some of the side missions you started earlier and take on a new one too.

The Secret of Off-Street

Go find Vic in the alley on the west side of the church (at on the map). Talk to him to trigger a heartwarming scene: Vic distributes his newly-earned cash to a pack of street orphans. In the subsequent conversation, you come to a dialogue option with three choices. For the best results overall, select: "Why don't you become a nightwhisper?" Capell suggests that Vic go to Halgita and train under Genma.

Lunaglyphs and Magic

Find Savio inside the emporium in the southern section of Kolton and Connect with him. Exit the emporium, then talk to Eugene who stands just up the street to the north. Eugene is troubled about his use of lunaglyphs and magic, but Savio reassures him that it's okay as long as one uses glyphs only when necessary. After the conversation, you gain the book entitled "Rage of Fire."

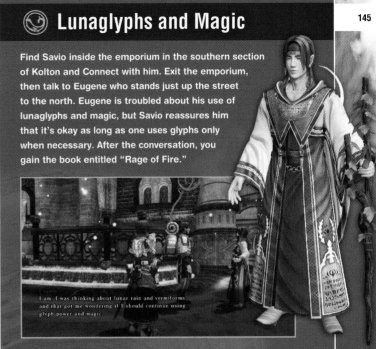

Rivals

Go to the upstairs room in the Kolton inn and Connect to Aya. Then go to the courtyard east of the church and talk to Gustav. The big bear gets worked up about Capell's attempt to pluck a string out of Aya's hair.

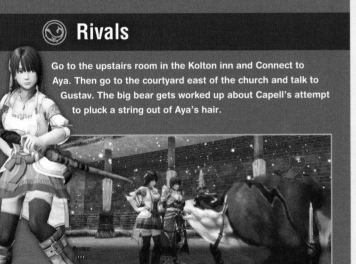

RETURN TO HALGITA

Exit Kolton into the Cobasna Timberlands and follow the same route you took to Halgita the first time when you were following Vic. (You can refer back to the map in the guide if you get lost.) When you get down the last stretch of trail heading south to Halgita, you hear Eugene ask, "Hmmm, do you smell something burning?" A little further south, you trigger a cutscene—the party sees smoke rising from Halgita up ahead!

The Secret of Battle

Find Dominica inside the emporium and talk to her. She wants Capell's help buying some weapons. When she asks the most important thing to keep in mind during battle, you get three choices of response. Pick any answer.

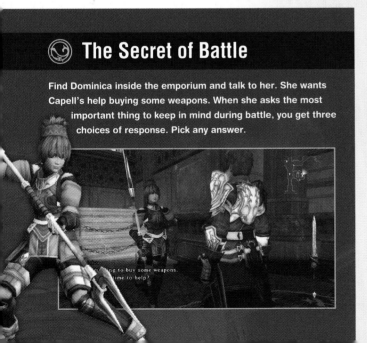

MISSION MAP

 Passage blocked   - **5** Storm gigas   **6** - **7** Vermiforms

HALGITA UNDER ATTACK

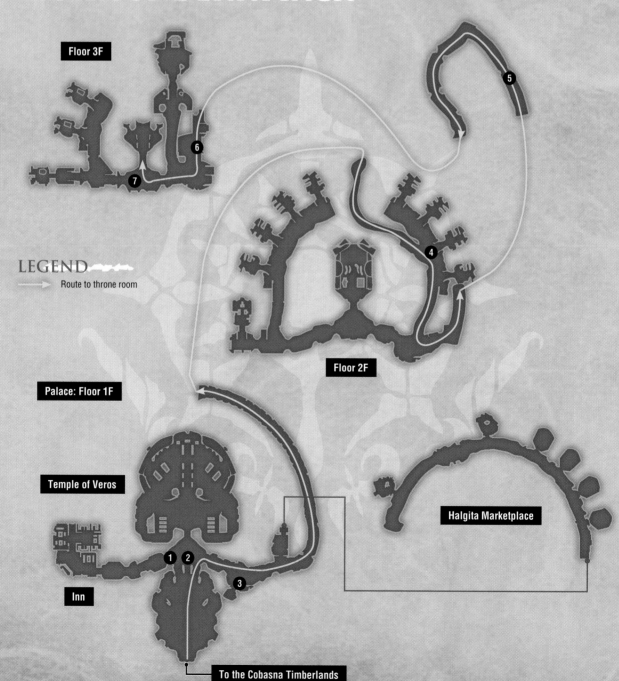

Floor 3F

5

6

7

4

Floor 2F

LEGEND
→ Route to throne room

Palace: Floor 1F

Temple of Veros

Halgita Marketplace

1 **2**

3

Inn

To the Cobasna Timberlands

DREADKNIGHT RETURNS

Invisible vermiform warriors are wreaking havoc in the Halgita royal palace. All citizens and current visitors, including Faina and Leif, are in grave peril.

MISSION

RESCUE EMPRESS SVALA!

All hell is breaking loose in the imperial city. As the mission opens, Halgita is a madhouse as Order troops and vermiform monsters run amok in the palace. Faina and Leif are nearly cornered, but Genma rescues them. Can Capell and the others arrive in time to save Svala and her people?

ACTION CHECKLIST

1 • Fight your way upstairs to floor 3F.

2 • Defeat the squad of vermified foes on 3F.

3 • Enter the throne room.

NEW SIDE QUESTS AVAILABLE

None.

PRIVATE EVENTS AVAILABLE

None.

ENEMIES

Order Soldier	AP 2
HP • 7000	
FOL • 400	EXP • 550

Storm Gigas	AP 7
HP • 30000	
FOL • 800	EXP • 1000

Order Sharpshooter	AP 2
HP • 3500	
FOL • 300	EXP • 450

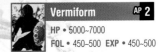

Vermiform	AP 2
HP • 5000~7000	
FOL • 450~500	EXP • 450~500

MISSION WALKTHROUGH

The party arrives at Halgita's devastated entry hall as a wounded Genma staggers out to meet them. As Michelle uses her healing glyph on him, he reports that the enemy is inside the palace. The empress must be saved!

The Mad Dash Strategy

You don't have to defeat a single enemy to complete this mission. Your mission objective is simply to reach the throne room. If you want, you can just run past every foe, including the vermiforms on the top floor. This way, you earn the Situation Bonus with ease.

However, the Situation Bonus reward is only a piece of malus wood, whereas defeating the four storm gigas and the entire squad of vermiforms en route earns you a huge boatload of EXP and Fol. So if your party is strong and healthy, fight. If your HP/MP are dropping and health items are scarce, just run.

GET TO THE THRONE ROOM IN TIME

Get ready for some insane stair climbing. A red time limit bar appears onscreen designating how much time you have to reach the throne room. The palace elevator is disabled, so you must run up the long, long staircases that lead up to the throne room on floor 3F. This entire route is teeming with Order soldiers and sharpshooters, and also four storm gigas monsters.

Or…just run past the fools. Simply approaching the throne room completes the mission and triggers a long, mission-ending cutscene. You enter to see none other than Leonid the Dreadknight threatening the Empress Svala.

Twinstream! Twinstream!

If you have Edward in Party A, be sure Twinstream is in his Battle Skill 2 slot and also set as his Connect actions for Ⓑ. In any fight, but especially against storm gigas, Connect to Edward and use Twinstream again and again for quicker victories.

At the top of your climb, on floor 3F, you run into a squad of deadly vermiform warriors outside the throne room doors. Play Percipere to reveal them to your party, then quickly Connect to your favorite party member and "spam" (hit repeatedly) your favorite Connect action attack (one great choice is Edward's Twinstream) on the vermiform targets.

Vermiform

HP 5000~7000 **EXP** 450~500

The vermiforms found while roaming through Halgita (or in Oradian Dunes) are much less threatening than Edward was in his vermified state. If you simply play Percipere, and Capell's allies aren't otherwise occupied, the allies can handle undoing vermiforms readily enough. If you want to speed up the process, Connect with a friend and activate Symphonic Blade prior to revealing the vermiform with Percipere. Launch the vermiform or nail it with a flurry of skills, and it won't survive long enough to require re-applying Percipere.

WATCH THE DRAMATIC PAYOFF

Completing the race to the throne room triggers a long series of cutscenes that kick the story up to a new level. Leonid has indeed returned, as Genma had hinted.

You also meet Held, a man well known to Kiriya and Savio.

Leonid seems as powerful as ever— *more* powerful, perhaps. And in the ensuing confrontation, Capell and the party seemingly can do little to stop him.

SITUATION BONUS!

Reached Svala within 3 minutes.

⭐ *Obtained some malus wood!*

MISSION MAP

1. Savio
2. Faina & Leif
3. Gustav
4. Eugene
5. Michelle
6. Owen, old nightwhisper
7. Aya
8. Vic
9. Rico
10. Rucha, Komachi, and Genma
11. Swordmaster Shido
12. Lavie, fashion designer
13. Kiriya
14. Dominica
15. Edward
16. Touma
17. Karin, aristo
18. David, lover of shiny things

HALGITA: AFTER THE ASSAULT

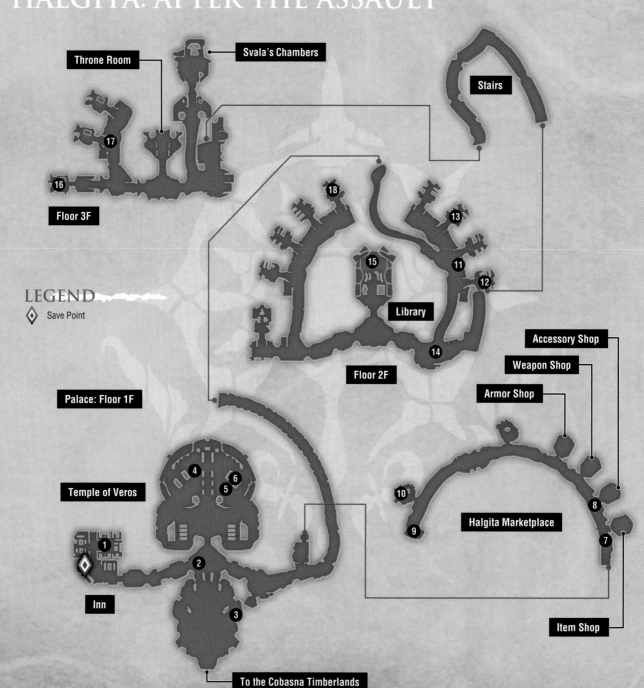

Throne Room

Svala's Chambers

Stairs

17

16

Floor 3F

18

13

15

11

12

Library

Accessory Shop

Weapon Shop

Armor Shop

14

Floor 2F

LEGEND

◇ Save Point

Palace: Floor 1F

Temple of Veros

4

6

5

10

8

1

9

Halgita Marketplace

7

Inn

2

Item Shop

3

To the Cobasna Timberlands

DREAM OF THE PAST & PROMISES

After the confrontation with Leonid, Capell drifts into a dream world in which he sees past events, beginning with the young Svala holding an infant. A familiar-looking, brown-eyed young boy is watching. Who is it?

MISSION
INTERLUDE: HALGITA

Resilient Halgita gets back to normal remarkably soon after repelling the Order of Chains assault. This interlude features quite a few side quests and private events. It also adds two formidable new members to your Liberation Force.

NEW SIDE QUESTS AVAILABLE

Lost Memories

Rebirth of Halgita

Dressed Up Vic

The Lost Katana

ACTION CHECKLIST

1. Watch Capell's "dream of the past."
2. Watch the scenes introducing Touma and Komachi.
3. Watch Capell's private meeting with Empress Svala.
4. Optional: Engage in side quests and private events.
5. Exit Halgita into the Cobasna Timberlands.

ENEMIES

None.

PRIVATE EVENTS AVAILABLE

Book Junkie

Dwell On Tea

Old Friend

I Am the Cat

Shopping

Master and Apprentice

Reconciled

MISSION WALKTHROUGH

This mission starts with a series of cutscenes, then gives you time to explore before you return to chain-busting. Here you can take on four new side quests and engage in seven interesting private events. You can also leave Halgita to finish up any quests in Kolton you may have missed earlier.

WATCH THE STORY UNFOLD

After Capell awakens from his "dream of the past," he joins his comrades before the empress, and promises hope for her people. Then, Touma

and Komachi join the Force in its mission to destroy the rest of the chains. Both already see Capell for who he truly is…and both offer their full support and strength to the cause.

Finally, Capell meets with Svala alone, and learns more of the truth about Sigmund's past. Then he learns from Touma that nightwhisper agents have located the next chain in the mountains north of the Cobasna Timberlands—an area called Dais.

OPTIONAL: EVENTS AND QUESTS

Again, you have seven private events available now in post-siege Halgita. Four new side quests are unlocked too. As before, see **Part 4: Side Quests** for quest details. Note that Kolton ship traffic is still out of commission, so you can't get back to previous areas of the game yet.

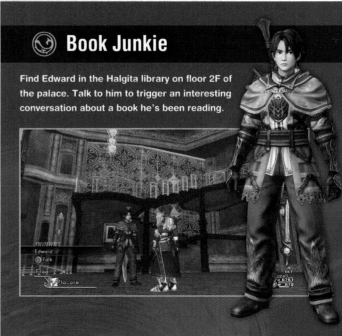

Book Junkie

Find Edward in the Halgita library on floor 2F of the palace. Talk to him to trigger an interesting conversation about a book he's been reading.

Old Friends

Connect to Eugene in the Temple of Veros on the palace's floor 1F, then go find Touma in his room in the southwest corner of floor 3F. Talk to Touma to trigger a long exchange between him and his longtime friend and ally, Eugene.

We had promised to protect this country together. It will not be possible now...

Reconciled

Connect to Aya near the item shop in the Halgita marketplace area, then go talk to Gustav in the palace entry hall on floor 1F. This triggers a scene in which Aya tries to broker a friendship between Capell and the crimson bear.

Dwell on Tea

Connect to Michelle in the Temple of Veros on floor 1F, then go find Komachi in the westernmost house, toward the bottom of the Halgita marketplace area. Talk to Komachi to trigger a tea party and discussion.

Shopping

Connect to Dominica, who stands near the elevator on floor 2F, then find Vic in the Halgita marketplace at the accessory shop. Talk to Vic; Capell and Dominica find him shopping for jewelry...for a friend, he says. Dominica ends up helping him pick out something.

Ah, it's Capell...and Dominica.

I Am the Cat

Find Rucha inside the westernmost house of the Halgita marketplace and Connect to her. Exit the house, turn right, and go talk to Rico at the end of the area. He's in the middle of a strained conversation with a Halgitian cat.

Master and Apprentice

Connect to Savio in the back room of the Halgita inn and go find Kiriya in the residence area of floor 2F; his room is the second from the end of the hall (see **13** on the map). Talk to Kiriya to learn something of his checkered Halgitian past, and his subsequent tutelage under Savio.

Kiriya
Honorable Savio...and Capell.

FIND DAIS

Touma's nightwhisper network has spotted the next chain north of the Cobasna Timberlands in an area called Dais. Prep for departure, then traverse the jungle once more, this time heading for a northwest exit.

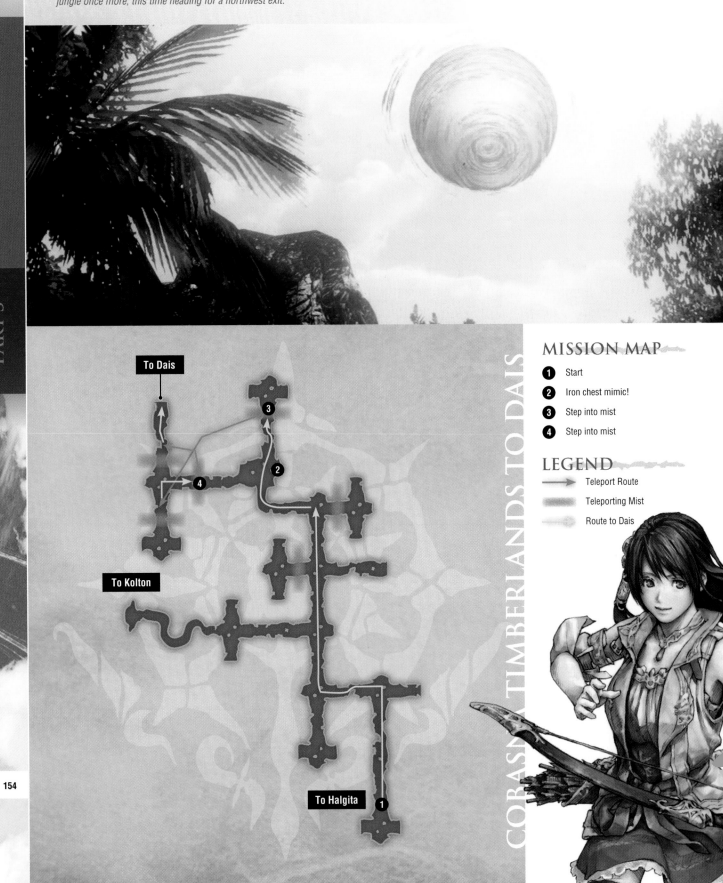

MISSION MAP

1 Start

2 Iron chest mimic!

3 Step into mist

4 Step into mist

LEGEND

→ Teleport Route

Teleporting Mist

Route to Dais

To Dais

To Kolton

To Halgita

COBASNA TIMBERLANDS TO DAIS

ACTION CHECKLIST

1. Put together a bug-fighting party and stock up on key items.

2. Exit Halgita into the Cobasna Timberlands.

3. Work your way north to Dais.

NEW SIDE QUESTS AVAILABLE

None.

PRIVATE EVENTS AVAILABLE

None.

ENEMIES

Green Drogo Warrior AP 5
HP • 6000
FOL • 270   EXP • 550

Mandragora AP 4
HP • 13170
FOL • 290   EXP • 700

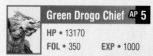

Green Drogo Chief AP 5
HP • 13170
FOL • 350   EXP • 1000

Tequilo AP 3
HP • 13170
FOL • 300   EXP • 620

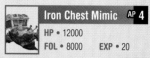

Killer Wasp AP 1
HP • 3000
FOL • 200   EXP • 400

Iron Chest Mimic AP 4
HP • 12000
FOL • 8000   EXP • 20

MISSION WALKTHROUGH

Your next destination, the Dais, presents some unique challenges that you want to prepare for in Halgita. Then it's out into the lunar rain again, this time heading northwest across the Cobasna Timberlands.

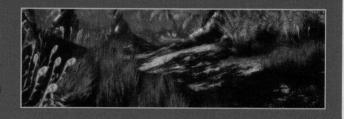

STOCK UP ON NECESSARY GOODS

Stock up on para-gone and sedative—have *plenty* of both on hand. Dais is filled with nasty mushrooms that, if struck in the heat of battle, spread confusion and turn party members on each other; you need sedatives to counter this. You also encounter some webs that paralyze you when you touch them, even if you're using a weapon to do the touching; you need para-gone to dispel the paralysis.

PUT TOGETHER A TOUGH PARTY

Dais literally crawls with insects, and under Aya's personal skills you may have noticed that her Trait 5 is "Bug Hater"! However, her Sparrowrain skill can be very effective in Dais, so consider her in one party slot. It's a very good idea to include Eugene and his excellent healing and resurrection (Salvus) abilities. Turn off all of Eugene's offensive spells other than Geoclaw or Astro, if he's leveled up high enough to acquire it. Note that Michelle is a great alternative to Eugene for reasons mentioned earlier—a fine healer, she already has Astro available, a highly effective area-of-effect spell that's very useful against hordes of weak minions like the ones you encounter in Dais.

Also, consider putting Komachi in your party. You'll find several locked treasure chests in Dais, and you want to use/improve her Trapmaster personal skill. A good alternative to Aya is Edward, who is tough as nails, and his Twinstream attack is relentlessly good against boss foes like the ones you'll meet in Dais. But keep in mind that Edward's very susceptible to vermification via the lunar rain, so if you put him in Party A, be ready to use lunar suppressants at any time in "rainy" areas. (Edward's fine once you get him inside Dais, of course.)

FOLLOW THE GREEN SPARKS TO DAIS

Remember the rising white sparks that led you across Cobasna to Kiriya's hut? You get the same travel directional aid here. This time the rising sparks are green. Follow them from Halgita right into the warping mist at two different points (**3** and **4** on the map), then all the way to Dais. Watch out for the iron chest mimic (**2** on the map) en route, though! He's tough, and a swarm of killer wasps lurk in the same area. Lunar rain falls on parts of the forest, so move through those areas quickly.

Don't Play in the Rain

Minimize the amount of time your lunaglyph-bearing characters spend out in the lunar rain. Edward in particular is very susceptible to vermification. You don't want to use up any more lunar suppressant than is absolutely necessary.

MISSION MAP

1 Start

2 Scissorclaw centipede

3 - **5** Iron chest mimic

6 - **10** Silk bridge made

11 Three scissorclaw centipedes

12 - **13** For bridge, use Rico's CS on cave rachnuvus

14 Silk bridge made

15 Iron chest mimic

16 Queen rachnuvus

17 Held and Amber Chain

18 Iron chest mimic

DAIS

LEGEND

- 🗃️ Wooden Chest
- 🗃️ Gold Chest
- 🗃️ Jeweled Cabinet
- ◈ Save Point

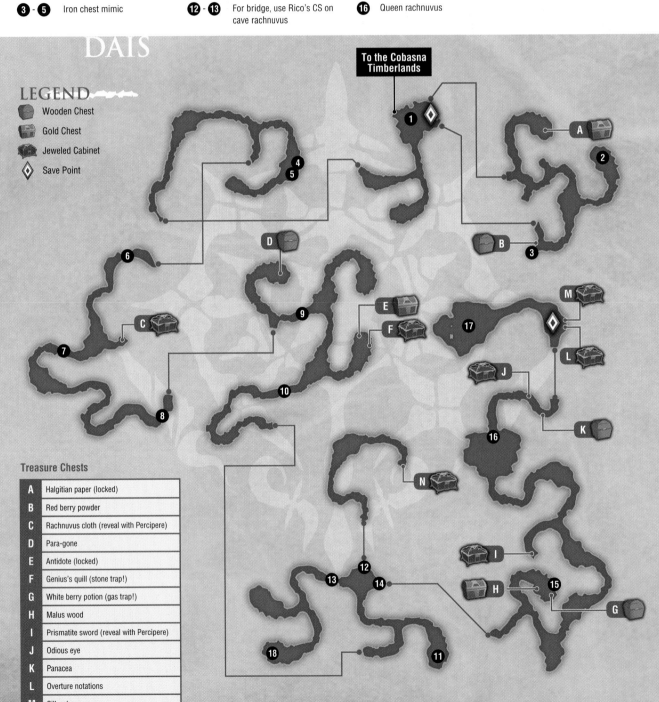

To the Cobasna Timberlands

Treasure Chests

A	Halgitian paper (locked)
B	Red berry powder
C	Rachnuvus cloth (reveal with Percipere)
D	Para-gone
E	Antidote (locked)
F	Genius's quill (stone trap!)
G	White berry potion (gas trap!)
H	Malus wood
I	Prismatite sword (reveal with Percipere)
J	Odious eye
K	Panacea
L	Overture notations
M	Silk robe
N	Rachnuvus pumps (out of reach)

NATURE'S MAZE

This chapter is all about combat. First, you weave your way through the creepy underground colony inhabited by a weird species of arachnid with ant-like communal instincts called the rachnuvus. Once you defeat the nest queen, you move on to the Amber Chain and its familiar protector.

MISSION
THE RACHNUVUS NEST

Touma explains that this hive is the best way up to the chain. But you'll have to fight your way past some nasty rachnuvus swarms, killer centipedes, and highly-dangerous mushrooms that can turn team members against each other. Then Komachi gives you a quick overview of the rachnuvus species. Note her mention of their monstrous size…and of "the queen."

ACTION CHECKLIST

1 • Fight your way through the rachnuvus nest to the queen's chamber.
2 • Defeat the queen rachnuvus.
3 • Exit the nest to find the Amber Chain.
4 • Defeat Held and destroy the chain.

NEW SIDE QUESTS AVAILABLE

None.

PRIVATE EVENTS AVAILABLE

None.

ENEMIES

Cave Rachnuvus AP 4
HP • 5000
FOL • 600   EXP • 800

Larva AP 1
HP • 150
FOL • 30   EXP • 200

Scissorclaw Centipede AP 3
HP • 5300
FOL • 400   EXP • 705

MISSION WALKTHROUGH

The rachnuvus nest is, believe it or not, filled with rachnuvae, both big (cave rachnuvus) and small (larva). An occasional scissorclaw centipede blocks a passage too, but the big menace is of the spidery variety.

SURVIVE THE FIRST ASSAULT

Things get hairy, literally, right off. All exit passages are sealed by force fields, and an onslaught of big cave rachnuvae and their annoying little larvae suddenly rolls at your party. (Note that a dying cave rachnuvus spawns larvae from its body.) Keep moving and try to avoid the web-shooting and paralyzing bites. Afterwards, to Aya's disgust, Capell and the twins muse on the taste properties of boiled rachnuvus. Meanwhile, Touma suggests that if you can defeat the queen, you'll be able to get out safely.

WATCH FOR MIMICS AND TRAPS

You can find good things stashed in treasure chests throughout the rachnuvus colony, but five of them turn out to be iron chest mimics. Always approach treasure chests with your weapon drawn. If you walk into the chest and no mimic pops up, then it's safe. Avoid letting mimic chests score Enemy Advantage against the party, which voids the possibility of getting items from them upon defeat. Remember that some chests are trapped too, like the one at **F** on the map which inflicts the stone status on anyone nearby if Capell opens it. (You can cure petrified characters with odious eyes.) Always Connect to either Vic or Komachi so they can open chests (even unlocked ones) with their Trapmaster skill.

BEWARE OF WEBS

Watch out for other hazards in the nest as well. Some passages are blocked by large webs that open only when you touch them; ranged attacks won't work. But the moment a character touches the web, he/she is temporarily paralyzed. (This is why you need a healthy supply of para-gones.) At the same time, larvae pop out of nearby nests and attack. The safest choice is to Connect to a party member with a physical attack and then use the Connect action to bust the web. Afterwards, you or your healer can toss a para-gone over the afflicted character to dispel the paralysis quickly.

BEWARE OF MUSHROOMS

A far worse hazard are the patches of translucent mushrooms found growing in many caves and passages. When struck by a weapon, these fungi emit a gas that inflicts the confusion status ailment on any party member caught in the emission. Confused comrades then turn against each other—a situation that can turn critical quickly.

Lure Foes Away from Mushrooms

When you see monsters near mushrooms, sheathe your sword and run up to the beasts, then turn and sprint away so they chase you to a mushroom-free area. You always want to avoid accidentally hitting a mushroom and unleashing its confusion-inducing spew.

FIND THE QUEEN

This becomes your first primary objective. Naturally, she's at the very end of the map. Although the rachnuvus nest seems to be a maze, it really isn't. The way forward is usually clear…with the exception of a few side chambers. These detours, however, are almost always worth taking for treasure chests or good EXP-boosting fights.

Except for the previously mentioned iron chest mimics (at **3**, **4**, **5**, and **15** on the map), none of the creatures are particularly tough until you reach the queen rachnuvus, although in many places you face large swarms of larvae mixed in with larger monsters.

Cave Rachnuvus **HP** 5000 **EXP** 800

As you might expect, these creatures are extremely weak to fire. Take advantage of this if Rucha is present. Spiders are half-resistant to aether, so Astro cannot execute its full damage. But it's still a useful spell against swarms of insects, since Astro strikes and stuns multiple targets.

WAIT FOR THE SILK BRIDGES

In several places the route seems blocked by a chasm (at **6** through **10** on the map, for example). But if you see a cave rachnuvus or larva on the other side, get close enough to trigger its aggressive instinct (when the exclamation point "!" appears over its head) then wait for the beast to weave silk strands that span the gap. Cross the new silk bridge and show your thanks…with extreme prejudice.

Two chasms (at **12** and **13** on the map) have no rachnuvus on the other side, however. So how do you get across? If you have Rico in your party, Connect to him and use his Penguin Parade skill to take control of a nearby cave rachnuvus (at **14** on the map). (If you defeat the cave rachnuvus here, a new one spawns and moves to this spot if you exit the cave then come back.) Lead the beast over to the gaps at **12** and then **13** and press the "Command" button when he's aiming across the chasm so he shoots web across to the other side.

One of the new areas across these enemy-built bridges leads to a treasure chest up out of reach (at **N** on the map), so you'll need Komachi's Honeysuckle skill to open it. The other area leads to an iron chest mimic, unfortunately.

DEFEAT THE QUEEN RACHNUVUS

Eventually, you reach the large cavern where the queen rachnuvus emerges. You must defeat her and the minions she spawns in order to get through the passage she blocks on the far side of the cave and proceed to the Amber Chain.

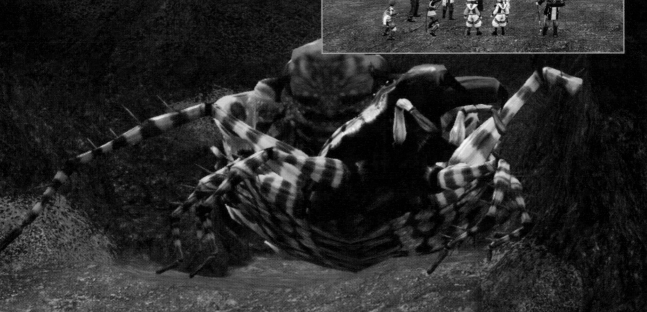

QUEEN RACHNUVUS

p.295

HP 76850   **EXP** 6000

The queen isn't an overwhelming fighter and isn't that tough to kill… if you can get at her. The problem is her spidery minions. She moves forward from the far tunnel and fills the cavern with cave rachnuvae and their ugly little larva spawn, then retreats. This moment, when she's out into the cavern, is when she's most vulnerable. Unfortunately it's also when the most rachnuvus minions are running around, zapping you with web shots.

One way to deal with the problem is to focus on area-of-effect attacks. In particular, Aya's Sparrowrain and Eugene or Michelle's Astro are very good effects to rain down on the teeming minions and clear them out fast. Astro in particular is cheap in MP cost, inflicts stun, and deals a ton of damage. Once the little rachnuvae are dead, wait for the queen to waddle out of the far cave again and then start whacking her with Capell's Cutting Gavotte and Edward's Twinstream (or whatever your favorite high-damage CS attack happens to be).

SITUATION BONUS!

Used stalactite to finish the rachnuvus queen.

★ **Obtained some rachnuvus cloth!**

DEFEAT HELD AND DESTROY THE AMBER CHAIN

After the queen falls, head up the tunnel behind her and snag the goods out of the two treasure chests along the way. Outside, open two more treasure chests, use the save point, then proceed up into the clearing to the Amber Chain. Savio's former apprentice Held waits for you there.

HELD AND THE AMBER CHAIN

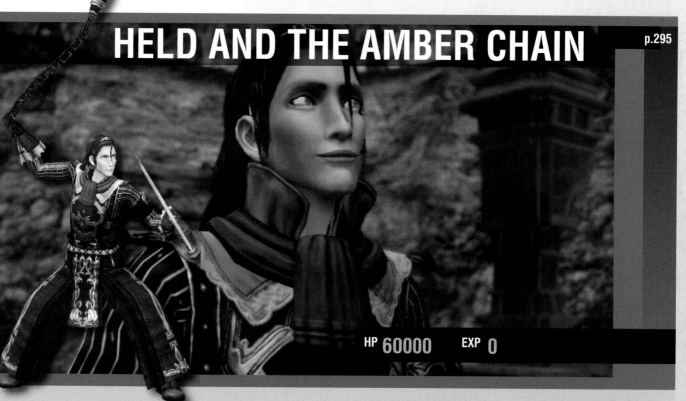

p.295

HP 60000   **EXP 0**

A force field surrounds the Amber Chain's link; the field drops only when Held is stunned. Held can also teleport from spot to spot on the field. Thus this fight proceeds much like your battle with Niedzielan earlier at the Cerulean Chain, except this one has two phases. In phase one, you simply attack Held until he staggers in defeat, which doesn't take very long. (If you defeat him within two minutes, you earn a Situation Bonus.) Then, Saranda appears to give him a boost.

In phase two, Held is infused with Saranda's lunar power and transforms into an invisible vermiform. Now you must play Percipere on Capell's flute to keep Held visible for the others. Let everybody attack Held until he's stunned, then hurry over to hammer away at the Amber Link until Held revives and the barrier reactivates. Repeat this until Held falls, then get in one last hit on the chain to end the battle. If Eugene and Michelle are present, have them use Astro—Held is extremely weak to the aether element.

Watch out for Held's deadly Spin Axis attack: it inflicts repeated heavy damage, so try to hustle out of its range until it subsides. Be wary of Held's black orbs as well. When he conjures them, spend a few seconds smashing any nearby to reduce the overall damage your team is taking. But keep your primary focus on Held himself. If he's stunned, he can't produce orbs!

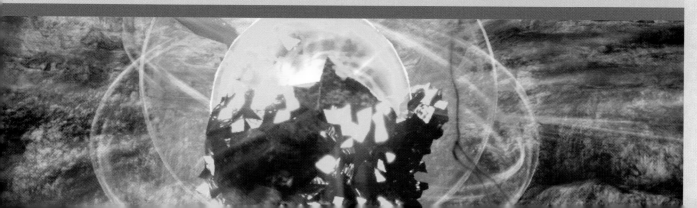

SITUATION BONUS!

Defeated Held within 2 minutes.

★ Obtained the memoirs of a mage!

After the battle, Held tries to pass on one last bit of information about the Dreadknight's source of power. But he cannot provide details to his master Savio. Then the scene changes to the royal court at Halgita, where the Liberation Force is celebrated for living up to their name.

MESSENGER OF PERIL

Over the objection of her imperial advisors, Empress Svala is convinced to spread the word about the dangers of the lunar rain. Then, as the Force readies to leave Halgita for Kolton, Genma brings word to Aya from her father of trouble brewing back home in Fayel. Reports are murky, but Genma believes vermiforms are involved! Time for the princess to head back home.

MISSION

BACK TO KOLTON

This mission wraps up business in Halgita, then takes you back across the Cobasna Timberlands to Kolton, the first leg of your return to Fayel. But before you leave Halgita, you can start a new side quest by talking to Faina.

FROM HALGITA TO KOLTON

To Kolton

LEGEND
→ Route from Halgita to Kolton

To Halgita

ACTION CHECKLIST

1. Step into the Halgita entry hall to trigger Genma's message from Fayel.

2. Optional: Talk to Faina to start a side quest, and complete quests previously started.

3. Cross the timberlands to Kolton.

NEW SIDE QUESTS AVAILABLE

Promised Dolls

PRIVATE EVENTS AVAILABLE

None.

ENEMIES

Green Drogo Warrior AP 5
HP • 6000
FOL • 270   EXP • 550

Green Drogo Chief AP 5
HP • 13170
FOL • 350   EXP • 1000

Killer Wasp AP 1
HP • 3000
FOL • 200   EXP • 400

MISSION WALKTHROUGH

Start in Halgita by stepping into the main entry hall to trigger Genma's arrival with the message for Aya. Capell leaves no doubt as to their next course of action. The princess seems to have a new respect for Capell, doesn't she?

OPTIONAL: FAINA'S SIDE QUEST

You most likely have some old side quests to wrap up—the "Lost Katana" or "Rebirth of Halgita" tasks, for example. You can also approach Faina near the Temple of Veros entrance and get a new quest in the works.

RETURN TO KOLTON

Exit Halgita and cross the Cobasna Timberlands back to Kolton. (See the provided map for the best route.)

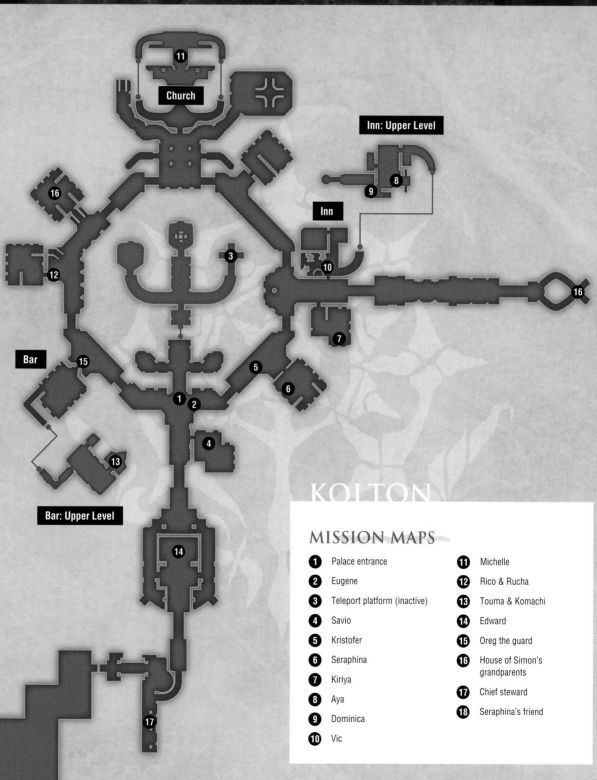

Church

Inn: Upper Level

Inn

Bar

Bar: Upper Level

KOLTON

MISSION MAPS

1. Palace entrance
2. Eugene
3. Teleport platform (inactive)
4. Savio
5. Kristofer
6. Seraphina
7. Kiriya
8. Aya
9. Dominica
10. Vic
11. Michelle
12. Rico & Rucha
13. Touma & Komachi
14. Edward
15. Oreg the guard
16. House of Simon's grandparents
17. Chief steward
18. Seraphina's friend

AUDIENCE WITH THE KING

Your arrival in Kolton triggers a cutscene in which Edward suggests you meet the king. The royal audience garners more support for the Force, adds an interesting pair of new party members, and unlocks new private events as well as a new side quest in Kolton.

ACTION CHECKLIST

1. Enter the Kolton palace to meet the king.

2. Watch as the Force meets Kristofer and Seraphina.

3. Optional: Restock supplies, take on one more Kolton side quest, and trigger a new set of private events.

4. Go to the dock and board the ship for Port Zala.

NEW SIDE QUESTS AVAILABLE

Simon is Missing, Pt. 2

PRIVATE EVENTS AVAILABLE

Broken Toy

Bashful Type

Pickup Artist

Under a Mask

Becalmed World

What is Aristo?

ENEMIES

None.

MISSION WALKTHROUGH

Approach the palace gate (at ❶ on the map) and enter to trigger a cutscene set in the huge Kolton throne room.

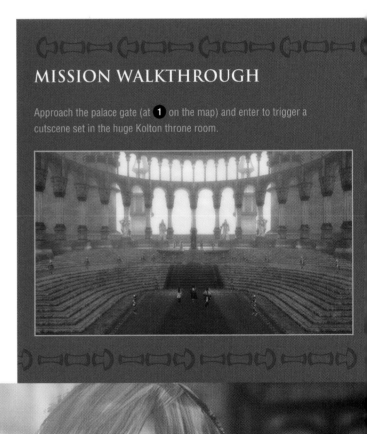

MEETING THE KING

The Liberation Force finally gets to meet Miro, King of Kolton Union. Capell and the others explain the dire situation to the king, and he pledges his support. Then two Kolton warriors, Kristofer and Seraphina, join the party.

Afterward, you get to know Kristofer and Seraphina a little better…and you really couldn't find an odder pairing.

OPTIONAL: SIDE QUESTS AND PRIVATE EVENTS

Now you can get your "side work" done. Check the map for character locations.

Broken Toy

Find Kristofer on the street in southeast Kolton and talk to him. This triggers a scene in which he returns a toy he fixed for a kid. He fills in Capell on some of his past research "accomplishments" and his meeting with Seraphina.

Pickup Artist

Here's a fun one. Connect with Kristofer and then go talk to Aya, Michelle, Komachi, Seraphina, Rucha, and Dominica. He gets some interesting reactions to his pickup lines. Note that the event isn't completed until you talk to all six females in the party.

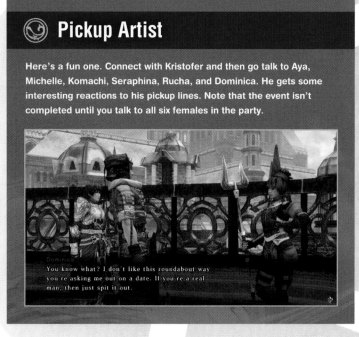

Becalmed World

Enter the house in southeast Kolton to find Seraphina and talk to her. Here you get a glimpse of the depth of her questioning and thought. Answer her questions however you want; all answers have the same effect on your emotional bond. But you might want to make a questioner like Seraphina feel that her existence has value.

Under a Mask

Go to the balcony off the upstairs room over the Kolton bar and talk to Touma. He speaks of his mask and the purposes it serves for him.

Bashful Type

Go into the house in southeast Kolton and Connect with Seraphina. Then, go to the church in northernmost Kolton and talk to Michelle, who is inside near the altar downstairs. Enjoy the amusing exchange between the two women.

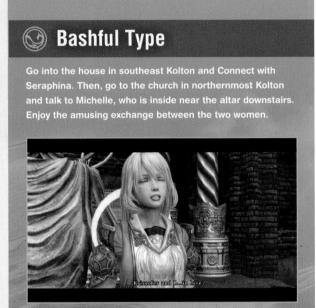

What is Aristo?

Connect with Savio in The Emporium and then enter the Kolton palace. Go straight up the stairs into the central room and find the aristo called "Seraphina's friend."

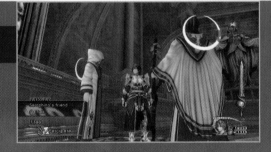

BOARD THE SHIP FOR PORT ZALA

When you're ready to ship out for Fayel, exit town via the south gate and find the chief steward on the dock. Talk to him and answer "I'll get on board." Then, you're off to Port Zala.

INTERLUDE: PORT ZALA

MISSION

When the Force arrives, they're stunned to see lunar rain falling on Fayel in the distance. Before you head out across the dunes to Aya's home, take on the new side quest and the eight new story-rich private events unlocked by your arrival here from Kolton. You can also open the previously inaccessible treasure chests, now that you have a couple of lock-pick experts in your party.

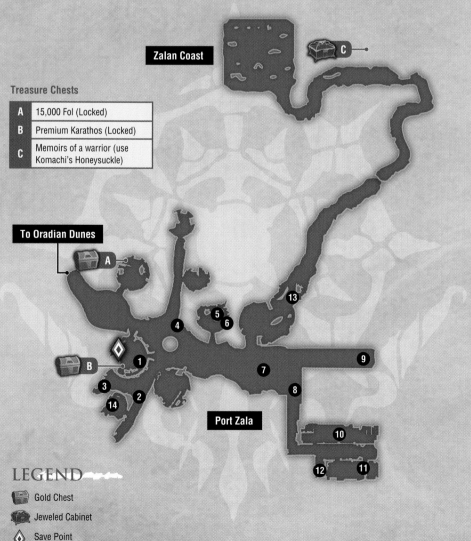

Zalan Coast

Treasure Chests

A	15,000 Fol (Locked)
B	Premium Karathos (Locked)
C	Memoirs of a warrior (use Komachi's Honeysuckle)

To Oradian Dunes

Port Zala

LEGEND

🧰 Gold Chest

🧰 Jeweled Cabinet

◈ Save Point

Vertical text: PORT ZALA

Vertical text: AUDIENCE WITH THE KING

MISSION MAPS

1. Savio
2. Kiriya
3. Michelle
4. Vic
5. Dominica
6. Fisherman
7. Touma
8. Aya
9. Edward
10. Ivan
11. Kristofer
12. Komachi
13. Rico, Rucha, and Gustav
14. Seraphina

* Note that the treasure chests marked on this map were shown on the previous Port Zala map too. But they are shown again here because now you have characters who can unlock chests (Vic and Komachi), and also because Komachi can use Honeysuckle to reach the submerged chest on the Zalan Coast.

ACTION CHECKLIST

1• Optional: Complete the private events and a side quest.

2• Connect with Komachi and open previously inaccessible chests.

3• Exit the town into the Oradian Dunes.

NEW SIDE QUESTS AVAILABLE

Rat Extermination

ENEMIES

None.

PRIVATE EVENTS AVAILABLE

Hard Bargaining

Sword Demo

Drinking Buddies

Best Couple

Someone to Watch Over Me

Sign of Recovery

The Twin Quiz

Encouraging Tone

MISSION WALKTHROUGH

Lunar rain is falling on Fayel, so the Force is needed there. But take the time to get to know your team better in some private events around Port Zala. Some encounters actually earn you rewards.

GO TREASURE CHEST HUNTING WITH KOMACHI

Open your Party screen and make sure Komachi is in Party A, then head up the beach path to the Zalan Coast. Find the underwater treasure chest a few feet out from the shore (at **C** on the map). Connect with Komachi, make sure Honeysuckle is one of her Connect actions, and then use it to snag the submerged chest. Back in town, find Komachi in the small alley near the fish warehouses (see **12** on the map), Connect to her, then take her to the two locked chests in town. (You can use Vic to open locked chests too, of course.)

OPTIONAL: COMPLETE ALL EIGHT PRIVATE EVENTS

A lot of good conversation with your crew is available this time in Port Zala. Don't miss these events!

Hard Bargaining

Talk to Seraphina in the general store. Capell gets into the middle of an economic discussion between Seraphina and the weapon shopkeeper.

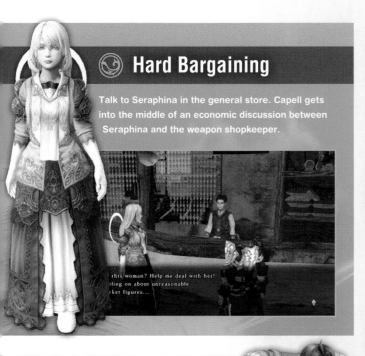

The Twin Quiz

Connect to Rucha out on the beach and talk to Rico, who is right next to her as usual. Take the "Twins Quiz" from the kids. (The answers are Rico, Rico, Rucha, Rico and...well, your choice on question number five.) If you get the questions right, you win a green berry potion.

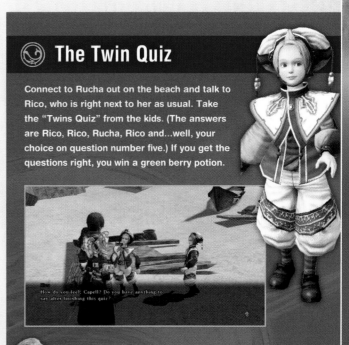

Drinking Buddies

Connect to Eugene in the general store, then go find Dominica in the bar and talk to her. Watch the amusing scene as she challenges Eugene's "toughness"...and he takes up the challenge with a few drinks.

Sword Demo

Connect to Edward at the end of the dock, then head toward town until you run into Touma, who stands in the middle of the cobblestone road. Talk to Touma to trigger an esoteric discussion of swordsmanship that quickly leads to some "demonstrations" of technique. Afterwards, Touma hands over a copy of memoirs of a warrior.

Someone to Watch Over Me

Connect to Vic out in the street near the circular planter in the center of town. Go talk to Komachi in the alley next to the fish warehouses (at **12** on the map) to learn about her affinity for dark places. She also keeps a close eye on those she is protecting—maybe a bit too close?

AUDIENCE WITH THE KING

Best Couple

Connect to Kristofer in the southernmost fish warehouse and then go talk to Michelle, who chats with the repetitive woman in the alley between the inn and general store. We learn more about Kristofer's first meeting with Seraphina on the battlefield. (Note: after this event, Michelle temporarily moves to a nearby location next to the "charming woman.")

Encouraging Tone

Find Aya near the ship at the dock and talk to her. She's clearly concerned about her homeland, and Capell makes an attempt to ease her mind with a goofy story and a little flute music. The song Capell composes adds suite notations to your inventory.

Signs of Recovery

If you've already completed the "Tsunami's Aftermath" private event earlier in Port Zala, Connect to Savio in the inn and then go talk to the fisherman in the bar again. The fisherman reports good news to Savio and thanks him for the earlier encouragement. Then he gives you two pieces of crab meat and three slices of deviant fish.

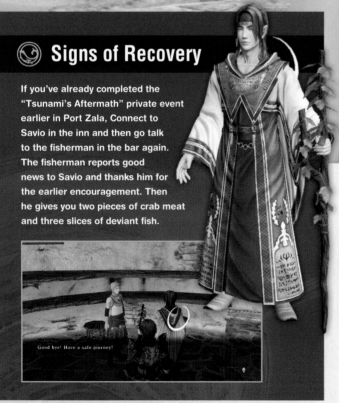

SET OUT FOR FAYEL

Exit Port Zala into the Oradian Dunes and start working your way south. Be ready—new monsters are roaming the sands now. Your goal is to reach Fayel.

172

OFF TO FAYEL

The desert is now filled with new species of flyers, a powerful new wolf called a vallin, and a few unfortunate humans mutated into vermiform monsters.

ACTION CHECKLIST

1. Cross the Oradian Dunes to Fayel.
2. Be ready for vermiform attackers en route.

NEW SIDE QUESTS AVAILABLE

None.

PRIVATE EVENTS AVAILABLE

None.

ENEMIES

 Miragebeak AP **2**
HP • 4722
FOL • 350   EXP • 550

 Vermiform AP **2**
HP • 15000
FOL • 500   EXP • 950

Quetzalcoatl AP **1**
HP • 6000
FOL • 710   EXP • 900

Vallin AP **5**
HP • 17740
FOL • 800   EXP • 1000

ORDANIAN DUNES FROM PORT ZALA TO FAYEL

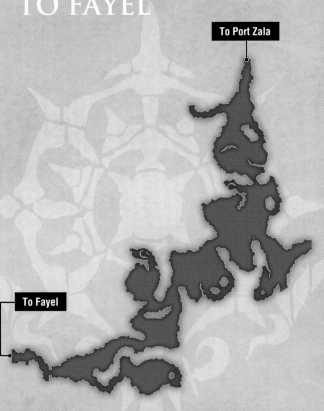

To Port Zala

To Fayel

MISSION WALKTHROUGH

The lunar rain is falling on and off in the desert now, so you can't linger, or your lunaglyph-bearing party members may suffer vermification. Make a beeline south through the gap into the open central basin, defeating monsters as you go. Then, veer west toward Fayel.

BEWARE VERMIFORMS

The lunar rain has done its job on a few desert denizens, so vermiforms are running around the dunes now. Have Capell's Percipere ready to play, and make sure Symphonic Blade is in one of your battle skill slots. (One good option is placing Symphonic Blade in Ⓐ for vermiforms and Cutting Gavotte in Ⓑ for your regular foes.) Once Percipere turns the vermiform "black" (visible), you can Connect to a comrade and activate Symphonic Blade for a few good hits. But be ready to jettison the Connect quickly and get your flute going again when the vermiform goes back to transparent (invisible to the others). If you aren't caught unaware by a vermiform, Connect and activate Symphonic Blade first before revealing the vermiform with Percipere and starting off combat—Symphonic Blade requires a Connection to initiate, but once it's active, the Connection can be broken without losing the effect.

ENTER FAYEL

As you approach Fayel, the lunar rain picks up a bit. Get inside the city gate to escape it.

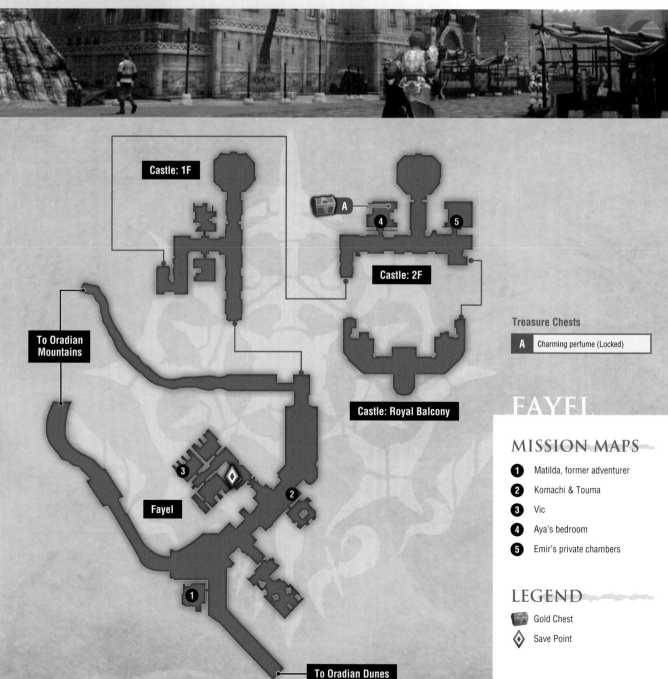

Castle: 1F

Ⓐ

Castle: 2F

4

5

Castle: Royal Balcony

To Oradian Mountains

Fayel

3

2

1

To Oradian Dunes

Treasure Chests

A	Charming perfume (Locked)

FAYEL

MISSION MAPS

1 Matilda, former adventurer

2 Komachi & Touma

3 Vic

4 Aya's bedroom

5 Emir's private chambers

LEGEND

🎁 Gold Chest

◇ Save Point

MEET EMIR SHARUKH

Aya's father, the emir, has called you to Fayel with news of vicious vermiform monsters across the countryside. Your goal is to reach him with the truth about lunaglyphs and the lunar rain.

ACTION CHECKLIST

1. Optional: Pick up the "Halgitian Memories" side quest from Matilda.
2. Go to the emir's private chambers on the top floor of the palace.
3. Optional: Connect to Vic or Komachi, so you can open a locked treasure chest.

NEW SIDE QUESTS AVAILABLE

Halgitian Memories

PRIVATE EVENTS AVAILABLE

None.

ENEMIES

None.

MISSION WALKTHROUGH

There's not much to do in Fayel other than shop for items and upgrades and take on one side quest before your meeting with Aya's father, the emir, in his private chambers. However, there is one thing you can do now that you couldn't the previous times you were in Fayel.

OPTIONAL: OPEN THE LOCKED CHEST

Connect to either Komachi (on the street near the accessory shop) or Vic (upstairs in a room at the inn) and proceed into the palace. Climb to the top floor and pick open the locked chest in Aya's bedroom (at ④ on the map). There's another locked chest in the emir's private chambers, but you can't open it now. (The cutscene ends with your party outside Fayel, and you can't get back in until later.)

GO TO THE EMIR'S PRIVATE CHAMBERS

Approach the door to Emir Sharukh's private chambers on the top floor of the palace at the end of the hall. This triggers a cutscene in which the emir reports invisible monsters ravaging the land. Aya and Capell explain the nature of vermiforms and the great danger posed by lunar rain and lunaglyphs.

LUNAR RAIN & VERMIFORM

Unfortunately, the emir's plans have included increasing his people's lunaglyph powers to fight the monsters, but he trusts his daughter's word on the matter and dispatches aristos to halt the process. However, he refuses to send help to Sapran, "home to the unblessed." This angers Capell, who rushes off to help Sapran himself. His loyal Liberation Force mates follow.

MISSION
HURRY TO SAPRAN

Your objective here is to cross the increasingly dangerous Oradian Dunes to besieged Sapran.

ORADIAN DUNES: FAYEL TO SAPRAN

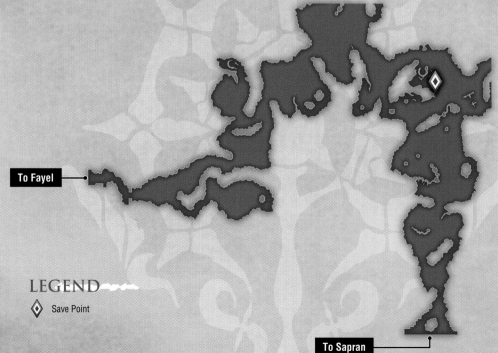

To Fayel

To Sapran

LEGEND

◆ Save Point

ACTION CHECKLIST

1 • Cross the Oradian Dunes south to Sapran.

2 • Enter the besieged village.

NEW SIDE QUESTS AVAILABLE

None.

PRIVATE EVENTS AVAILABLE

None.

ENEMIES

Miragebeak `AP 2`

HP • 4722

FOL • 350   EXP • 550

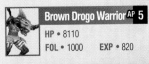

Vallin `AP 5`

HP • 17740

FOL • 800   EXP • 1000

Quetzalcoatl `AP 1`

HP • 6000

FOL • 710   EXP • 900

Brown Drogo Warrior `AP 5`

HP • 8110

FOL • 1000   EXP • 820

Vermiform `AP 2`

HP • 15000

FOL • 500   EXP • 950

Dune Harpy `AP 2`

HP • 7000

FOL • 600   EXP • 740

MISSION WALKTHROUGH

Hustle across the dunes to Sapran. Don't waste too much time monster-hunting when lunar rains start falling. Be quick with the lunar suppressant if vermification overtakes one of your party members. Remember, Capell is unblessed—he has no lunaglyph—so the rains don't affect him. So you're always able to dispense suppressants if necessary.

Head northeast up the canyons, then veer south at the oasis area and head through the rock arch with the Sapran sign at its base (the same one you passed on your earlier trips to Sapran). From there, continue south to Sapran's gate. Your arrival triggers a grim cutscene: Sapran is under assault!

SITUATION BONUS!

Reached Sapran within 3 minutes.

⭐ *Bonus 30,000 EXP!*

MISSION

DEFEND SAPRAN!

The Force arrives in Sapran to the horrifying sight of vermiforms slaughtering defenseless civilians. Capell's shock and anger is uncontrollable as he seeks to defend the helpless Saprans.

SAPRAN UNDER ATTACK

ACTION CHECKLIST

1. Defeat the vermiforms attacking Sapran.
2. Return to Fayel.

NEW SIDE QUESTS AVAILABLE

None.

PRIVATE EVENTS AVAILABLE

None.

ENEMIES

Vermiform AP **2**

HP • 15000
FOL • 500   EXP • 950

MISSION WALKTHROUGH

Follow the anti-vermiform strategy you've been using—play Percipere to reveal the first vermiforms to your party, then Connect to someone and use Symphonic Blade to get in a few blows. After the first enemies fall, the team splits up to look for survivors. Capell sprints off looking for Faina and Leif.

Capell and Aya find Leif being menaced by vermiform warriors. Then Faina emerges to help. They struggle fiercely to save their friends…

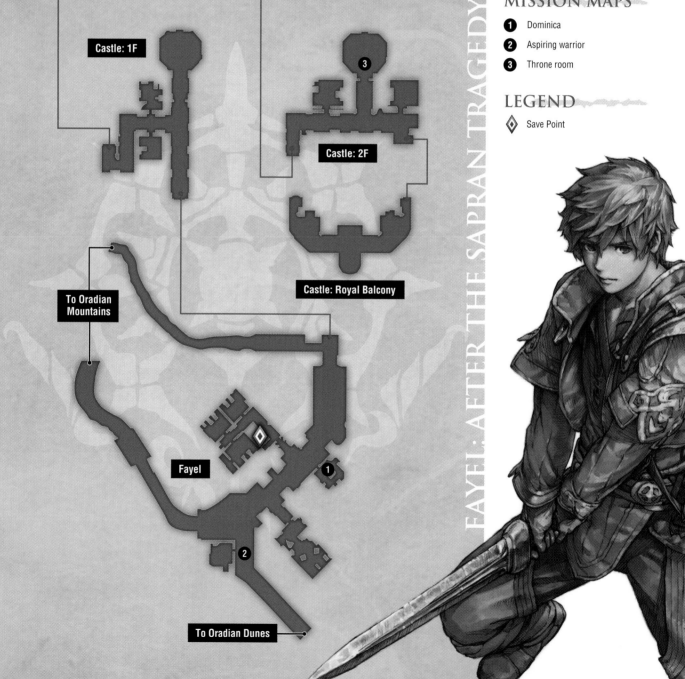

MISSION MAPS

1 Dominica

2 Aspiring warrior

3 Throne room

LEGEND

◇ Save Point

FAYEL: AFTER THE SAPRAN TRAGEDY

Castle: 1F

3

Castle: 2F

Castle: Royal Balcony

To Oradian
Mountains

Fayel

1

2

To Oradian Dunes

IMPOSTER

Capell, stunned by the tragedy at Sapran, leads the party back to Fayel to confront Emir Sharukh. But their arrival at the palace in Aya's hometown soon brings another shock.

FAYEL ESCAPE

Before leaving for Sapran, Aya made a verbal slip when talking to "Lord Sigmund" in front of her father. Now, if you talk to your comrades or other folks in town, you'll notice that the Fayel citizenry has noticeably cooled in its regard for Capell and crew. In fact, some are calling him an imposter.

ACTION CHECKLIST

1 • Go to the top floor of the palace and approach the throne room.

2 • Watch the scene with the emir.

3 • Cross the Oradian Dunes to Port Zala.

4 • Approach the dock to board the ship for Kolton.

5 • Watch the Force's arrival in Kolton.

ENEMIES

None.

NEW SIDE QUESTS AVAILABLE

In Fayel: Fayel Warrior

PRIVATE EVENTS AVAILABLE

In Sapran: Sapran Memorial

MISSION WALKTHROUGH

After completing the Sapran mission and viewing the subsequent cutscenes, you automatically end up in Fayel with the Oradian Dunes now off limits. Your simple task in this mission is to go see the emir once again, this time in the throne room.

OPTIONAL: NEW SIDE QUEST

You can pick up another side quest before you enter the palace in Fayel this time. See "Fayel Warrior" in **Part 4: Side Quests**.

Dominica, you're a warrior of Fayel, right? I bet you can beat a wendigo with your hands tied behind your back!

GO TO THE THRONE ROOM

Enter the palace and approach the throne room upstairs to trigger a cutscene. The emir's soldiers, led by Dominica's own sister, General Emmie, attempt to put the Force under arrest. The accusation: Capell is an imposter.

Hard to argue with that…and so Capell doesn't. But he won't be "captured" either. As the team escapes Fayel, they run into an old and very apologetic friend. And Capell makes an executive decision about their next destination: Casandra, the Order of Chains stronghold.

RETURN TO PORT ZALA

Balbagan rejoins the party, adding some much-needed inside muscle to your lineup. You should be quite familiar with the Oradian Dunes by now, so it's sufficient to just tell you to head back to Port Zala. (If you need a map, just refer to one of the earlier Oradian Dunes maps.) But if you want, you can first take a detour south to Sapran to trigger a somber private event.

Sapran Memorial

Return to Sapran and enter the large building that looks like a lighthouse; it's actually the village church. Examine the "flower pedestal" in front of the altar to trigger a scene in which Capell plays a flute nocturne for Faina and Leif. Afterwards, you obtain some nocturne notations.

Goodbye.

SHIP OUT TO KOLTON

No new events or quests are unlocked this time in Port Zala, so just save your game at the inn, rest up, stock up, and then ship out. This time, all you have to do is run onto the dock to trigger the travel sequence. When you arrive in Kolton…well, as Edward puts it, "*This* looks familiar," as soldiers meet the Liberation Force at the dock.

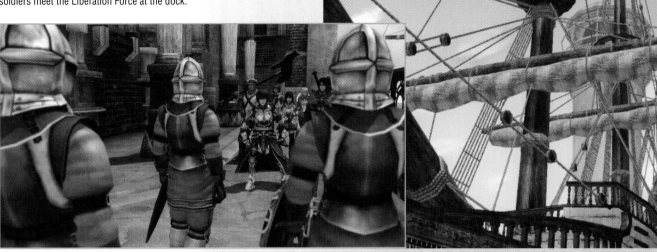

Edward and Balbagan are ready to fight. Fortunately, Seraphina's cooler head prevails.

MISSION MAP

1. Balbagan
2. Eugene
3. Teleporter (inactive)
4. Savio
5. Kristofer
6. Seraphina
7. Kiriya
8. Aya
9. Dominica
10. Vic
11. Michelle
12. Rico & Rucha
13. Touma & Komachi
14. Edward
15. Meeting chamber (Svala)
16. Teleporter to Castle Valette

KOLTON: AFTER SARANDA'S ATTACK

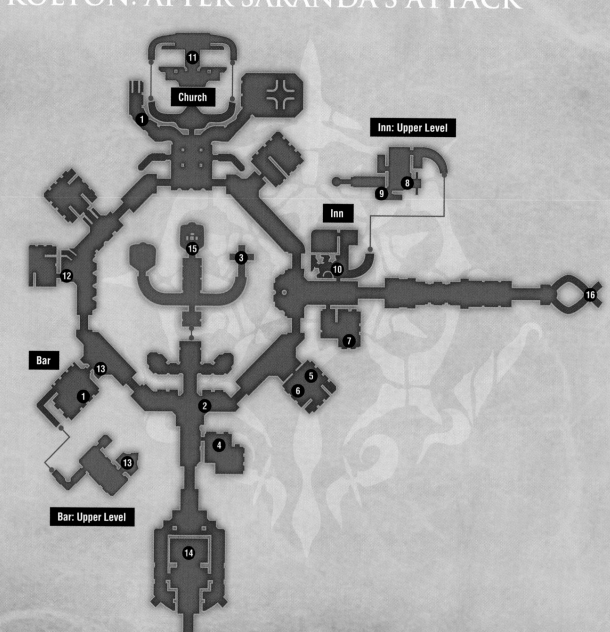

SARANDA'S ATTACK

A royal meeting between Fayel and Kolton is interrupted by the lady in red whose presence at every chain has complicated the Force's mission. Then it's off to a new and sinister destination. Time to take the fight to the Order! This chapter is primarily a series of cinematic scenes that deepen the plot considerably.

MISSION
INTERLUDE: KOLTON REVELATIONS

King Miro is not pleased with what he considers your betrayal of his people. But Seraphina's word carries great weight with the monarch; she vouches for Capell, his purity of heart, and his mission. Then a surprise visitor makes an appearance in the Kolton throne room.

ACTION CHECKLIST

1 · Watch the Kolton throne room scenes and Empress Svala's tales of the past.

2 · Enter the palace's meeting chamber to get more back-story from Svala.

3 · Exit the palace to trigger scenes with Eugene, Aya, and a Kolton guard.

4 · Step onto the Kolton inn's upstairs balcony to visit Dominica.

5 · Use the east teleporter to Castle Valette.

NEW SIDE QUESTS AVAILABLE

None.

PRIVATE EVENTS AVAILABLE

Family Man

Idiots

ENEMIES

None.

MISSION WALKTHROUGH

Yes, Aya's father, Emir Sharukh, intercedes on behalf of the Force and its mission. But just as the matter seems settled, Saranda makes a guest appearance. She ensnares Capell in her red chains and then tries to nail Aya with a death spell. But Sharukh will have none of that…

After the confrontation, the Empress Svala arrives to speak with Capell, Touma, and Komachi. She tells them of Sigmund's hidden past, a tale she's kept secret for many years.

MEET SVALA AGAIN

When Svala's story is finished, you end up outside the palace's meeting chamber. You can go out into the city and complete tasks or shopping. Or, you can turn around and go back into the chamber to trigger a private meeting with the empress. When you do this, Svala asks a favor of Capell—one difficult to accomplish or even contemplate. Then she reveals sad secrets of Leonid the Dreadknight's past as well.

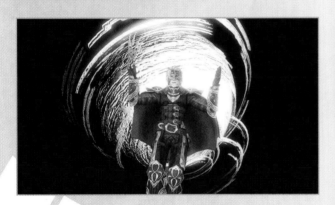

EXIT THE PALACE

Go through the palace's outer gates into the city to trigger another set of cutscenes, this time starting with Eugene. He's becoming a good friend who looks out for Capell. Then in another scene, Capell tries to comfort Aya in light of her loss.

Then one more scene: a Kolton soldier appears with news from King Miro. Scouts have determined the location of the Ashen Chain. It's in enemy territory: Casandra, protected by Castle Valette, the Order's stronghold. This is your next destination. The Cobasna teleporter has been adjusted to take you to the outskirts of the castle.

TRIGGER SOME PRIVATE EVENTS

Now, full control finally returns to you. Two private events are available at this point.

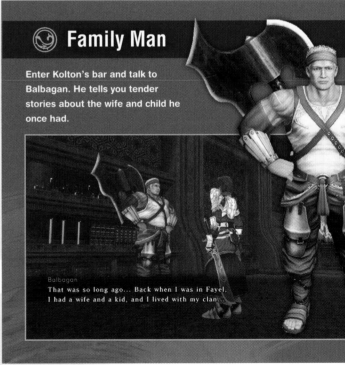

🐾 Family Man

Enter Kolton's bar and talk to Balbagan. He tells you tender stories about the wife and child he once had.

Balbagan
That was so long ago... Back when I was in Fayel, I had a wife and a kid, and I lived with my clan...

Idiots

Go talk to Kiriya in the general shop. He rails against the idiocy of politics. When you get a dialogue choice, pick the one that suits you best. Either choice increases your emotional bond with Kiriya.

DOMINICA'S PROMISE

Enter the inn and go upstairs, then step out onto the balcony to trigger a scene with Dominica. She makes a vow to protect Aya.

Stock Up on Antidotes

Before you leave Kolton for Castle Valette, buy up a good supply of antidotes. The castle features a number of poison traps. (Of course, you can avoid all of them if you follow this walkthrough!)

TELEPORT TO CASTLE VALETTE

Go through the city's east gate to the teleporter (16 on the map) and use it to reach Castle Valette.

MISSION MAP

1. Start
2. Iron box mimic
3. Skeleton ambush!
4. Trial of Colors orb
5. Trial of Colors orb
6. Skeleton ambush!
7. Trial of Colors orb
8. Skeleton ambush!
9. Envy
10. Begin Chamber of Elements
11. Iron box mimic
12 - 13. Crystal ball puzzle
14. Crystal ball puzzle (play Percipere to reveal)
15. Saranda and the Ashen Chain

LEGEND

Route
Gold Chest
Wooden Chest
Jeweled Cabinet
Save Point

CASTLE VALETTE

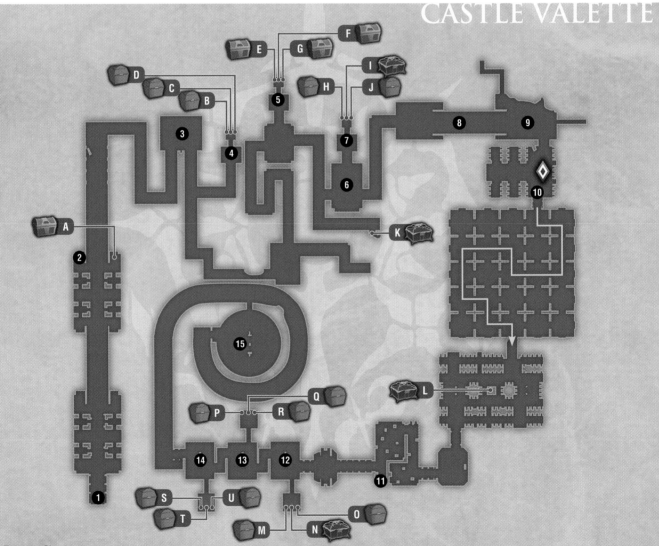

Treasure Chests

A	Miraculous medicine	F	Viper fang	K	Memoirs of a mage	O	40,000 Fol	T	Blaze metal
B	1000 Fol	G	Glacial Delight	L	Instrumental sword (out of reach; use Komachi's Honeysuckle)	P	Rachnuvus cloth	U	Blaze metal
C	5000 Fol	H	Junk			Q	Capriccio notations		
D	3000 Fol	I	Memoirs of a thief	M	6550 Fol	R	Rachnuvus shell		
E	Feather wristband	J	Crystallite metal	N	Memoirs of a hunter	S	Salamander skin		

SIEGE

This chapter takes you to the Ashen Chain through the puzzles, traps, and skeleton troop ambushes of Casandra's key defensive structure, Castle Valette—a grim, dark, bat-infested fortress.

MISSION

DESTROY THE ASHEN CHAIN IN CASTLE VALETTE

Led by Capell, the party enters the dank underground fortification. Be ready to face tough Order of Chains troops and plenty of flyers called lifestealers, plus a few waves of supernatural foes. You'll also encounter three types of color-themed puzzles.

ACTION CHECKLIST

1 • Survive the skull soldier ambushes.

2 • Optional: Solve the Trial of Colors to open three secret doors leading to treasure chests.

3 • Defeat the great lich, Envy.

4 • Negotiate the Chamber of Elements maze.

5 • Solve the crystal ball door puzzles to advance.

6 • Defeat Saranda and destroy the Ashen Chain.

NEW SIDE QUESTS AVAILABLE

None.

PRIVATE EVENTS AVAILABLE

None.

ENEMIES

Order Mage	AP 2
HP • 4000	
FOL • 800	EXP • 1000

Skull Soldier	AP 2
HP • 3000	
FOL • 800	EXP • 400

Order Fencer	AP 2
HP • 9000	
FOL • 1150	EXP • 1500

Dancing Sword	AP 1
HP • 2500	
FOL • 410	EXP • 850

Lifestealer	AP 1
HP • 1500	
FOL • 400	EXP • 500

Dancing Crossbow	AP 1
HP • 8240	
FOL • 400	EXP • 800

Burning Lantern	AP 1
HP • 4240	
FOL • 500	EXP • 844

Envy	AP -
HP • 230000	
FOL • 4100	EXP • 8440

Skull Knight	AP 2
HP • 6240	
FOL • 1300	EXP • 1300

Saranda	AP -
HP • 250000	
FOL • 4100	EXP • 8440

MISSION WALKTHROUGH

Except for the Chamber of Elements maze about halfway through, the route through Castle Valette is essentially linear, with six secret side chambers stuffed full of valuable items in treasure chests. Start by assigning your team to three full parties. Put Komachi in your party so you can open locked and/or trapped chests and also snag an out-of-reach chest deep in the castle. Then watch as two Order mages destroy the exit teleporter behind you!

BE AMBUSH-READY

The Order mages who cut off your escape route are joined by a squad of Order fencers as well, and the passage is sealed off by force fields; wipe them all out to unseal the way forward. This ambush is a sample of what lies ahead.

Fight through bats, soldiers, and one sneaky iron box mimic (at ❷ on the map) until you reach the first large chamber (at ❸ on the map). Again, the exit passages seal shut and a deadly liche named Envy appears to summon wave after wave of skull soldiers and knights. Don't waste your time going after Envy; you can't attack him now, and he disappears in seconds. (You'll get your shot at him later, though.) Just whack away at the bony guys until they stop appearing and the force field barriers dissipate.

Dodge the Hydrop!

Keep moving throughout the first skeleton ambush. An Order mage drops Hydrop spells on you from the other side of the force field during the battle. You can't reach her until after you clear out all skull attackers and the barrier deactivates.

Bones and Air

Skull soldiers and knights are particularly susceptible to the air element, as is their summoner, Envy. Use enchantment skills to imbue your party members' attacks with the air attribute before entering large rooms that look like possible ambush areas.

You'll run into similar Envy-directed skeleton ambushes in two more places (at ❻ and ❽ on the map) as you move through the castle. In both cases, the area is sealed off until you defeat all of the skull knights and soldiers that spawn into the room.

OPTIONAL:
SOLVE THE TRIAL OF COLORS

In the first side chamber (at ❹ on the map), you find some "strange writing" projected in blue light on the wall. Examine it to read a riddle

suggesting that red is bad, blue is good. Now spot the lighted orb over the closed door across the room. It alternately glows red and blue.

Now Connect to a party member with a ranged Connect action that you can aim (both Aya's Ravaging Raptor and Komachi's Honeysuckle works well). Activate the Connect action, move the targeting reticule over the orb, and shoot. Depending on the orb's color when your shot hits, the following happens:

▶ *If your shot hits the orb while its light is red, you trigger the release of a swarm of dancing swords and crossbows that start attacking you.*

▶ *If your shot hits the orb while its light is blue, the door below the orb opens, giving you access to three treasure chests.*

(Note: the best timing seems to be firing just as the light turned red; this makes the shot hit just after the light switched to blue. However, your experience may vary.)

You'll run into similar Trial of Color chambers in two other locations (at ❺ and ❼ on the map) as you move through the castle. Solve both in the same manner.

DEFEAT ENVY

When you reach the northeast corner of the map, Envy appears and summons another ambush of his skull troops. But this time, he joins the fight himself. Focus your attacks on Envy so he can't summon any more skeletons. Remember that Envy and his skull troops are weak against the air element. Be ready with holy water to dispel the Curse status ailment as well.

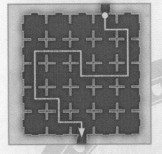

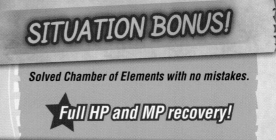

The riddle sequence begins with red to white ("crimson flame engulfs the alabaster bird"), so turn left and approach the white door to open it. Continue moving from door to door following the gems that correspond to the colors in the riddle sequence, then repeat the sequence a second time to get through the maze without error. (Or you can just follow the elegant map here.) If you do make a mistake, you trigger a trap that poisons the party, stuns everyone, and teleports you back to start over.

SITUATION BONUS!

Solved Chamber of Elements with no mistakes.

★ **Full HP and MP recovery!**

SOLVE THE CHAMBER OF ELEMENTS

Just south of the save point you find more "strange writing" projected on the wall. Basically, this riddle lists a sequence of colors that goes in the following order:

Red ("crimson flame") to white ("alabaster bird") to blue ("azure skies") to yellow ("amber lands") to purple ("onyx seas") to red ("wild fire"), then repeat the cycle.

Now approach the door with the white gem; it opens automatically. Walk onto the red glyph in the next room's center. When all party members are

standing on the red glyph, it dims and the element puzzle begins. Glowing, colored gems activate in the other three doors that surround you.

SNAG THE INSTRUMENTAL SWORD

You exit the Chamber of Elements into a room with a raised walkway across its center and skull troops posted everywhere. Order mages are up on the balcony, slinging Hydrop spells down at you. Fortunately, one of your other parties is up there too. Keep moving to avoid getting "Hydropped" until your comrades up on the balcony eliminate the mages, then focus on clearing out skull knights and soldiers down on the ground floor where you are.

Now, spot the treasure chest up on the balcony. It's out of your reach, so Connect to Komachi and use her Honeysuckle skill to snag the item from the chest: a sleek weapon known as an "instrumental sword." It's

probably more powerful than your current sword, so equip it on Capell immediately.

SOLVE THE CRYSTAL BALL DOOR PUZZLES

Soon you come to a room (**12** on the map) with more strange writing on the wall. Read the riddle—it suggests that red is bad, blue is good, and green is the way forward. You also see two sealed doors and two crystal balls, each alternating between red, blue, and green. When you hit either crystal ball with your sword, for a few seconds the ball stays the color it was when you hit it.

The trick is to whack one crystal ball to briefly lock in its color, then rush to the other ball and hit it when it turns the same color as the first. If you hit both crystal balls so that they're locked into the same color, it triggers an event associated with that color:

- ▶ *If both crystal balls are locked into red, a swarm of dancing swords and crossbows appear and attack you.*

- ▶ *If both crystal balls are locked into blue, the smaller door opens, giving you access to a trio of treasure chests.*

- ▶ *If both crystal balls are locked into green, the larger door opens, letting you proceed to the next area of the castle.*

After you get through the first crystal ball room, you come to two more (at **13** and **14** on the map) that work exactly the same. (In the third room, you must use the flute tune Percipere to reveal the two crystal balls.) Use the same method to first open the side doors and gain valuable items from chests, and then move on.

DEFEAT SARANDA AND DESTROY THE AMBER CHAIN

Once you get past the third crystal ball room, follow the winding corridor to the chamber where Saranda protects the Amber Chain's link. Aya and Dominica in particular are ready to tangle with the woman who so brutally attacked Sharukh.

HP **250000**   EXP **8440**

By now you should be adept at recognizing the lulls in boss foe attacks and taking advantage of them by launching your own counterattacks. But Saranda's magic presents a new challenge that calls for increased use of Capell's protective flute tune Prudentiae. This song's dome of protection wards off her spells such as Pyrgeddon that can inflict great area-of-effect damage, crippling your entire party in one fell swoop.

So, if you're not that interested in the lunatite and mercurius metal earned as a Situation Bonus for beating Saranda quickly, then consider using Capell largely in a support role. You can sneak in some combos in Saranda's lulls, but focus on watching like a hawk for her spellcasting

animation, then quickly play Prudentiae to shield your team. There's nothing wrong with hanging back and letting your powerful friends skewer the red sorceress while you protect them from the worst of her magic.

But remember, only you (Capell) can attack the Ashen Chain itself. As with previous links, your task is to attack the boss until she's stunned, then hustle to slash away at the chain's link until Saranda revives and puts her force field back up around it. Keep in mind that you have some help from your secondary party comrades in this fight. So there are plenty of folks hitting Saranda. Your job is to protect them, then hammer the chain.

SITUATION BONUS!

Defeated Saranda within 2 minutes.

⭐ **Obtained some lunatite and some mercurius metal!**

After the fight, Saranda expresses her primary motivation for all she's done—a motivation that strikes a surprising and sympathetic chord with Aya. Then Capell makes his final approach to the Ashen Chain, which triggers a mighty shock wave that shatters the castle's very foundation, forcing the team to escape into the Plodhif Caverns below.

MISSION MAP

1. Start
2. Juggernaut centipede!
3. See rest of party
4. - 5. Juggernaut centipede!
6. False wall (play Percipere)
7. False wall (play Percipere)
8. Iron box mimic
9. Juggernaut centipede!
10. Centipede & Balbagan
11. Cracked rock

LEGEND

Gold Chest

Wooden Chest

Jeweled Cabinet

Save Point

PLODHIF CAVERNS

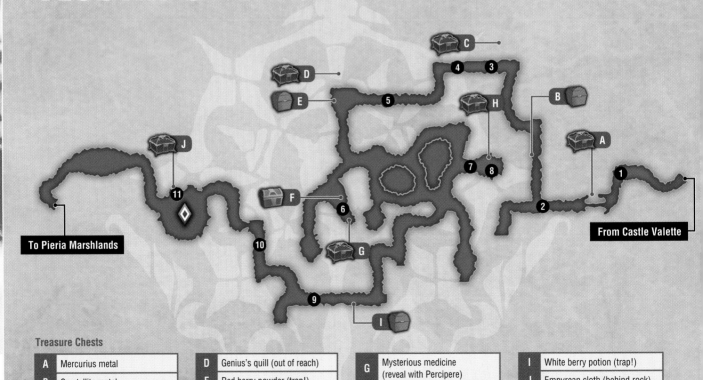

To Pieria Marshlands

From Castle Valette

Treasure Chests

A	Mercurius metal	D	Genius's quill (out of reach)	G	Mysterious medicine (reveal with Percipere)
B	Crystallite metal	E	Red berry powder (trap!)	H	160,000 Fol!
C	Mercenary helmet (out of reach)	F	Rachnuvus cloth (locked)		

I	White berry potion (trap!)
J	Empyrean cloth (behind rock)

TO CASANDRA

You're in the home stretch now. The heartland of Casandra is just through the old cave system beneath the fortress. But for a short time you're on your own, thanks to a rare rumbling monstrosity known as a juggernaut centipede. Beyond that lie the Pieria Marshlands, home to many slimy beasts rising from the coastal waters.

MISSION

PASS THROUGH PLODHIF CAVERNS

Thankfully, a save point is in the first cavern, as is Genma with the welcome offer of rest and re-supply; be sure to buy some antidotes and angel earpick doses to counteract Poison and Unhearing status ailments. This straightforward and refreshingly simple mission sends you through the bug and bat filled ancient caverns alone…

ACTION CHECKLIST

1 · Fight your way through Plodhif Caverns alone.

2 · Reunite with your party.

3 · Exit into the marshlands beyond.

NEW SIDE QUESTS AVAILABLE

None.

PRIVATE EVENTS AVAILABLE

None.

ENEMIES

Larva	AP 1
HP • 3248	
FOL • 100	EXP • 200

Swordtail Viper	AP 3
HP • 8200	
FOL • 390	EXP • 700

Lifestealer	AP 1
HP • 1500	
FOL • 400	EXP • 500

Forest Rachnuvus	AP 4
HP • 16000	
FOL • 600	EXP • 900

MISSION WALKTHROUGH

Not long after this mission begins, an unstoppable centipede roars through the cavern walls (at **2** on the map), shattering rock and cutting Capell off from the rest of the party. You can't fight the beast, so just let it go.

WORK YOUR WAY THROUGH THE CAVERNS

Nothing too tricky about the Plodhif Caverns. Just get through them, fighting off insects, bats, and snakes, and suffering the occasional bull rush of the juggernaut centipede. (The

big bug's runs through the walls may hurt a bit, but they also keep clearing the path ahead.) While it's not pitch-black, it is dark in the caverns, so you might consider activating a sunstone.

Soon after you start, you see your party (❸ on the map) across an open chasm and make plans to meet up again. Note the treasure chest next to them; you can come back with Komachi later and use Honeysuckle to open it. A little further beyond that, the big centipede rumbles up from behind you and smashes through another wall.

Continue through the new hole into another passage, fighting off the poison-spitting forest rachnuvae and their larva swarms plus a few snakes en route. The larvae spew out a status effect called Deafening Spray that inflicts Unhearing on you, rendering your flute useless, so use your Creation skills to cast an anti-unhearing enchantment on yourself when you get a moment. (You should have plenty of the bat wings you need for this enchantment in your inventory.)

At two separate places in the caverns (❻ and ❼ on the map), you'll hear the telltale sound and see the rippling effect that indicates a hidden object. Play Percipere to reveal some false walls. Behind one wall (at ❼) sits a chest with 160,000 Fol...but also one nasty iron box mimic, so stay sharp.

REUNITE WITH THE TEAM

When you reach the final passage, you trigger a cutscene in which Balbagan takes care of your ongoing centipede problem at last. Now you can reconfigure your party and save your game in the big cavern. One good idea is putting Komachi and Balbagan in your new party so you can try the next step. (You can substitute Gustav for Balbagan too.)

OPTIONAL: SNAG THE INACCESSIBLE CHESTS

Several treasure chests along the cavern route were either locked or out of reach. Once you reconfigure your team as suggested, first Connect to Balbagan and use his Gigatackle to smash through the cracked rock (at ❿ on the map) near the save point and plunder the chest stashed there. (Gustav's Explosive Ride works to smash through cracked rocks too.) Then, Connect to Komachi and go back into the caverns to open the one locked chest and then snag the contents of the two out-of-reach chests using her Honeysuckle skill.

EXIT INTO THE PIERIA MARSHLANDS

Now simply head northwest to exit the caverns into the rainy, ruined marshlands of Pieria.

MARSHLAND MENACE

The bleak marshlands of Pieria are close enough to the final chain that the wetlands now host an endless infestation of monsters—and we mean, literally, endless. As you'll see, this actually can be beneficial for your party's long-term health as you head into the final confrontations beyond Pieria. But first you must defeat the dragon of the marsh.

MISSION MAPS

1 Start
2 Dragon!
3 Cracked rock
4 Teleporter to Kolton
5 Teleporter to Underwater Palace

LEGEND

Wooden Chest
Gold Chest
Jeweled Cabinet
Save Point

ACTION CHECKLIST

1 • Defeat the dragon.

2 • Optional: Spend time leveling up near the water.

3 • Watch the Force party cutscenes.

4 • Optional: Teleport back to Kolton for final preparations.

NEW SIDE QUESTS AVAILABLE

None.

PRIVATE EVENTS AVAILABLE

None.

ENEMIES

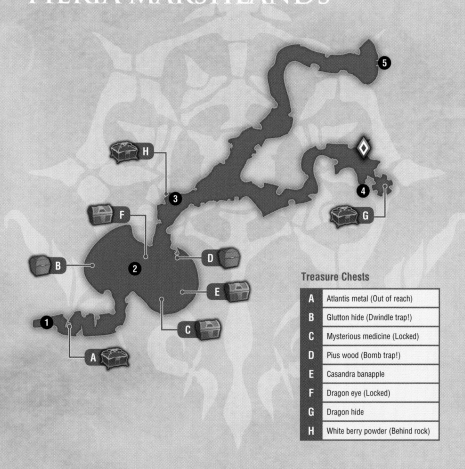

PIERIA MARSHLANDS

Treasure Chests

A	Atlantis metal (Out of reach)
B	Glutton hide (Dwindle trap!)
C	Mysterious medicine (Locked)
D	Pius wood (Bomb trap!)
E	Casandra banapple
F	Dragon eye (Locked)
G	Dragon hide
H	White berry powder (Behind rock)

Enemy	AP	Stats
Moss Glutton	6	HP • 10000 FOL • 800 EXP • 1000
Blue Drogo Warrior	5	HP • 10700 FOL • 1500 EXP • 1878
Mantifish	1	HP • 5300 FOL • 650 EXP • 700
Dragon	-	HP • 160000 FOL • 4300 EXP • 8780

MISSION WALKTHROUGH

This mission wastes no time in getting to the point. Moments after you start climbing uphill from the Plodhif Caverns exit to the open marsh, you trigger the appearance of the great dragon. Then you can reconfigure your party. With a number of locked/trapped chests out in the marshes, it's best to put Komachi or Vic in your party, although you can come back for these chests later if you want.

DEFEAT THE DRAGON

Yes, the dragon is very powerful, as you would expect. But he's a slow turner, and he can't hit you if you're behind him. So keep running in circles around him, then hit him from the side or back. This tactic is complicated by the hostile marsh minions that clog the area, so you might need to clear them out to create more room for your dragon-circling. The dragon is very weak against the water element, but absorbs fire. If Rico is in the party, have him use Hydrill and Hydrain to speed up the kill. Unfortunately, no character grants water as a Symphonic Blade element.

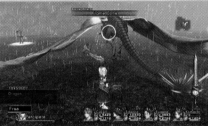

You can also Connect with a Trapmaster (Vic or Komachi) if you have one in your party and open all chests in the area. Some are locked, and some are trapped.

SITUATION BONUS!

Defeated the dragon within 2 minutes.

★ Obtained a dragon eye and a dragon fang!

Moss Glutton

HP 10000   **EXP** 1000

Gluttons are big, lumbering targets. If Capell begins striking one, with the right sequence of attacks he can sustain a combo until any of them are dead. With Cutting Gavotte assigned as a battle skill, simply start striking a glutton with ⒶⒶⒶⒷ for Dancing Rhapsody, then immediately press and hold whatever button Cutting Gavotte is assigned to. If Capell doesn't have enough AP to launch the glutton, begin pressing Ⓐ over and over again as Cutting Gavotte ends—a new string of attacks soon creates a combo on these big foes even without ally assistance. Chain into another Dancing Rhapsody to Cutting Gavotte, and wash, rinse, repeat until the glutton is either launched or defeated.

OPTIONAL: DO SOME "FARMING"

"Farming" is gamer slang for camping someplace where enemies spawn and wiping them out for their drop items and EXP. This marsh is one such farming location. The moss gluttons, blue Drogo warriors, and mantifish just keep coming out of the water, so you can hack away and keep leveling up for as long as you want.

HEAD UP THE NORTHEAST CANYON

When you've finished with the marsh, head northeast up the canyon to trigger a cutscene. The team fights through the driving rain toward the Underwater Palace, but Eugene convinces Capell to take shelter for the night.

This leads to a long series of scenes in which we see individual party members prepare for the coming battle and muse on the state of things.

THE NEXT MORNING: GO MEET THE TEAM

After the last cutscene with Capell and Aya, you end up just outside the temple-like structure on the promontory above the marshlands, not far from a save point. Save your game and head down the narrow pass until you find Edward, Eugene, and Dominica waiting for you. Approach them to trigger a cutscene—the entire team gathers, ready to move out.

OPTIONAL: TELEPORT BACK TO KOLTON

By now you've probably accumulated a lot of cash, perhaps even hundreds of thousands of Fol. Before you head off to your final set of battles in the Underwater Palace and beyond, you can hop aboard the teleporter (at ④ on the map) next to the temple-like structure and warp back to Kolton.

You can stock up on supplies and upgrade equipment in Kolton, or you can cross the timberlands and shop in the better-stocked Halgita marketplace. Don't hoard your money now! If you haven't been steadily grinding out IC items using your party's crafting skills, then you'd better buy the best equipment you can afford. Be sure to have a good supply of health potions too.

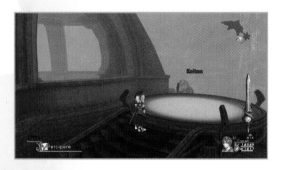

TELEPORT TO THE UNDERWATER PALACE

Once you're ready to fight, climb up the narrow canyon that leads to the teleporter overlooking the ocean (at ⑤ on the map). Your approach triggers a final cutscene as the party marvels at the sight of the stunning Underwater Palace. When control returns, step onto the teleporter to zap over to the palace.

SHOWDOWN

The Underwater Palace is packed full of formidable foes on level after level, including great brutal beasts of enormous power. And at the top waits your nemesis, looking for a final chapter to this story...

MISSION

REACH THE ONYX CHAIN

This marathon mission opens with a boss fight against an Order knight, then sends you up the many levels of the Underwater Palace in a series of fights against enemy swarms and powerful sub-boss foes until you reach the Dreadknight himself at the base of the Onyx Chain.

ACTION CHECKLIST

1 · Defeat Iskan du Bal.

2 · Fight your way up the palace's eight levels.

3 · Defeat Karathos.

4 · Defeat the Dreadknight.

NEW SIDE QUESTS AVAILABLE

None.

PRIVATE EVENTS AVAILABLE

None.

ENEMIES

Iskan du Bal AP - HP • 350000 FOL • 5000 EXP • 9000	**Order Sorceress** AP 2 HP • 4490 FOL • 780 EXP • 800	**Skull Warrior** AP 2 HP • 8000 FOL • 450 EXP • 600
Fountainbeak AP 2 HP • 7000 FOL • 650 EXP • 700	**Frost Gigas** AP 7 HP • 45000 FOL • 1670 EXP • 2000	**Flying Sword** AP 1 HP • 3000 FOL • 200 EXP • 300
Garm AP 5 HP • 17200 FOL • 1500 EXP • 1800	**Queen Wasp** AP 1 HP • 5000 FOL • 800 EXP • 1000	**Kraken** AP - HP • 287250 FOL • 4000 EXP • 5000
Veld the Evil Eye AP 1 HP • 120000 FOL • 4000 EXP • 5000	**Lava Glutton** AP 6 HP • 13930 FOL • 1150 EXP • 1300	**Karathos** AP - HP • 250000 FOL • 4700 EXP • 7000
Order Sniper AP 2 HP • 4600 FOL • 900 EXP • 950	**Greed** AP - HP • 277777 FOL • 4000 EXP • 5000	**Leonid the Dreadknight** AP - HP • 300000 FOL • 4700 EXP • 8000
Order Officer AP 2 HP • 10000 FOL • 900 EXP • 900	**Rib Forager** AP - HP • 18000 FOL • 0 EXP • 0	

MISSION WALKTHROUGH

Your ultimate goal is to reach the Onyx Chain at the top of the palace. But you've got a *lot* of fighting to do before you reach it. And it all starts with an Order knight in the very first chamber.

MISSION MAPS

1. Teleporter to Pieria Marshlands
2. Iskan du Bal
3 - 4. Side routes taken by secondary parties
5. Teleporter to 6
6. Teleporter to 5
7. Fountainbeak & garm
8. Teleporter to 9
9. Teleporter to 8

10. Veld the Evil Eye
11. Teleporter to 12
12. Teleporter to 11
13. Order troops & frost gigas
14. Teleporter to 15
15. Teleporter to 14
16. Orthros
17. Teleporter to 18
18. Teleporter to 17

19. Queen wasp & lava glutton
20. Teleporter to 21
21. Teleporter to 20
22. Greed & minions
23. Teleporter to 24
24. Teleporter to 23
25. Save point & Genma
26. Teleporter to 27
27. Teleporter to 26

28. Kraken!
29. Teleporter to 30
30. Teleporter to 29
31. Karathos & Leonid the Dreadknight
32. Onyx Chain

* Note: The save point near the Onyx Chain appears only after you win the final boss battle.

UNDERWATER PALACE

LEGEND

🪙 Jeweled Cabinet

◇ Save Point

Treasure Chests

A	Solar necklace
B	Feeble cape
C	Phoenix feather jacket
D	Feeble wristband
E	Phoenix feather hood
F	Phoenix feather boots
G	Amarlista
H	Sovereignty ring

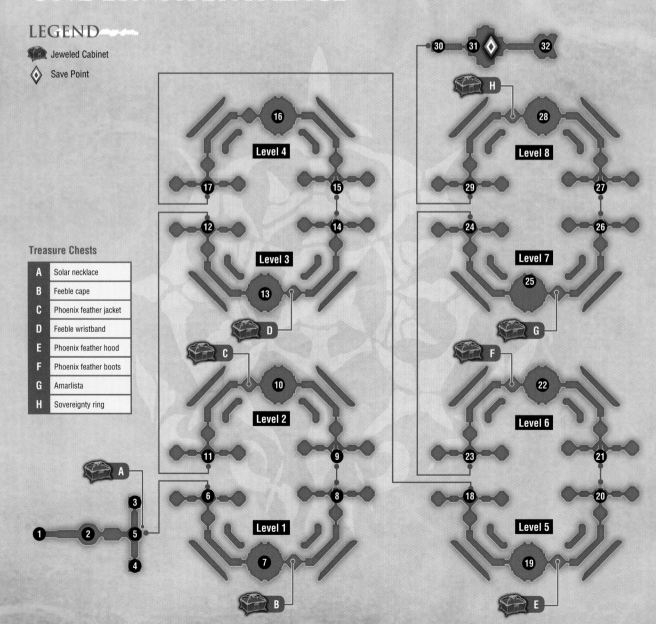

DEFEAT ISKAN DU BAL

No slow buildup here. Once you arrive at the Underwater Palace, proceed up the entry hall and approach the doors to trigger a meeting with Iskan du Bal, Leonid's last Order knight, in the palace's entry hall.

ISKAN DU BAL p.XXX

HP 350000   EXP 9000

Iskan fights much like Sigmund did, including a wide, sweeping sword stroke called Heraldic Edge that can strike your entire party with a single vicious swing. Keep your distance until Iskan completes this attack, then counter quickly with a good combo to get him reeling. Dodge away quickly before he unleashes his swing again! Note that Iskan is weak against the earth element, so consider an enchantment that adds the earth attribute to your physical attacks or use Symphonic Blade while Connected to Eugene, Touma, or Komachi,

and unleash Eugene's Geoclaw on the Order knight.

Note also that you can earn a big EXP bonus if you let someone other than Capell strike the finishing blow against Iskan. It isn't easy to judge when Iskan is on his last legs, so consider hanging back after the first minute of blows and focus on providing support via flute. Prudentiae won't help much because Iskan's primary attacks are physical rather than magic, but remember that other tunes like Valere boost your party's stats. Of course, you need a good healer in your party to pull this off.

SITUATION BONUS!

Didn't finish off Iskan via Capell.

★ **Bonus 35,000 EXP!**

After the fight, Iskan reveals some shocking information about Capell and Lord Sigmund that puts the adventure in an entirely new light. Then he pays homage to the memory of pre-Dreadknight Casandra one last time… by helping Capell and the party into the heart of the palace. When the cutscene ends, proceed through the newly opened doors to the next teleporter, which zaps you up to Level 1. (Don't miss the treasure chest behind the teleporter, though.)

DEFEAT THE LEVEL 1 FOES

Now your daunting task is to work your way up the eight levels of the palace. Your two secondary parties do so as well, fighting beside you up separate but parallel routes. Each level's basic layout is the same, so your tasks on each level are the following:

▶ *Move up a long staircase to a central hall filled with enemies (except level 7, which features just a save point and Genma).*

▶ *Clear the central hall of foes.*

▶ *After the fight, proceed into an antechamber to nab a valuable item in a treasure chest (except at level 4).*

▶ *Continue up another long staircase to a teleporter, which warps you to the next level of the palace.*

You encounter a different set of foes in each level's central hall. Some are collections of regular enemies, but a few are powerful "sub-boss" types. The first level's central hall features flyers called fountainbeaks along with a new type of wolf called a garm. Afterwards, step through the hall's exit doors and open the treasure chest to acquire a feeble cape. Equip it right away on your party's primary healer/ magician.

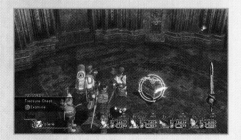

DEFEAT THE LEVEL 2 FOES

This level features two sub-boss "eye" creatures who are collectively called "Veld the Evil Eye." Fight these eye-beasts just as you did their cousin Kron way back in Vesplume Tower; keep circling to hit them from the side or back. For magic damage, stick to aether spells—other elements are ineffective. The treasure chest in the next room contains a phoenix feather jacket.

DEFEAT THE LEVEL 3 FOES

This level features Order troops (officer, sniper, and sorceress) and two frost gigas in the central hall. The treasure chest in the next room contains a feeble wristband.

DEFEAT THE LEVEL 4 FOES

This level features an orthros in the central hall; you see it transported in from the Cobasna Timberlands. Fight him the same way you did back in the jungle. Stay away from in front of the orthros, whose Charge is lightning-quick and deadly. As always, keep circling around to the side and back, but hustle away when the beast unleashes its all-directional fire attack. As with the dragon not too long ago in Pieria Marshlands, abuse Hydrill and Hydrain if available. This level has no treasure chest in the antechamber.

DEFEAT THE LEVEL 5 FOES

This level features queen wasps and lava gluttons in the central hall. The treasure chest in the next room contains a phoenix feather hood.

DEFEAT THE LEVEL 6 FOES

This level's central hall features Greed, a powerful conjuring lich (like Envy back in Castle Valette), and the skull warrior and flying sword minions that he summons. Greed is also surrounded by a screen of rib foragers that you must smash through to reach him. Hammer away at them, but pull back when they turn red and start spinning, as this inflicts great damage. Like his lich brethren, Greed is susceptible to wind magic—if Rico is along and at least level 37, Voltscourge can punish Greed heavily, while Rucha's Pyrburst (learned at level 36) is able to make extremely short work of the waves of rib foragers. The treasure chest in the next room contains phoenix feather boots.

DEFEAT THE LEVEL 7 FOES

Whew! This level features no enemies, but rather a save point and Genma (for rest and re-supply) in the central hall. The treasure chest in the next room contains an amarlista.

DEFEAT THE LEVEL 8 FOES

This level's central hall features a huge tentacled monster called a kraken. As with other large foes, the kraken is a slow turner. If you can keep circling and hitting without letting him face up on you (where he can strike you with Ink Blast), you can patiently wear him down while taking little damage. Be ready to dash away when the kraken starts rapidly flapping its tentacles, an attack that lets the big squid-beast nail you with multiple painful hits. Earth damage is very strong against the kraken, while water is not. The treasure chest in the next room contains a sovereignty ring.

DEFEAT THE DREADKNIGHT AND HIS PET

Climb the last set of stairs and teleport up to the top room of the palace to meet none other than Leonid. Go get him! He has a big buddy, a turtle-snake hybrid named Karathos, who you must meet and defeat first...but then you get a piece of the Dreadknight at last.

KARATHOS AND THE DREADKNIGHT p.297

| KARATHOS: | HP 250000 | EXP 7000 |
| LEONID: | HP 300000 | EXP 8000 |

This fight starts as a duel with the mighty but lumbering Karathos. This is yet another occasion in which your primary tactic should be running in circles around the beast to strike from the side or behind. Like the kraken, this large fellow has a very slow turn rate. Don't get caught in front, or he'll ram you with his head or spit out a bubbly Poison Rain special attack. When you're hitting him at close range, be prepared to dodge away when Karathos goes into his Jet Spin, which can knock you down hard. Note that Karathos is weak against the earth attribute and strong (as you might expect from a turtle) against water.

After the monster drops (you gain a sturdy Karathos helmet when he does), it's time for the Dreadknight. This is a relatively straightforward encounter. Stay clear of Leonid's various chain attacks and counterattack immediately after he finishes any major special attack. For VIIth Violation, you'll want to get far away, while the best way to avoid XIIIth worth is to circle to Leonid's back. As with Iskan du Bal, you get a huge EXP bonus if you let one of your party members deal Leonid the finishing blow. So as before, spend some time slashing at the Dreadknight to lower his health, then switch to a support role with your flute, playing Valere or Obduratus to boost your teammate's stats as they finish him off. Leonid is half-resistant to earth and water, so use other elemental spells and attacks if available.

SITUATION BONUS!

Didn't finish off Leonid via Capell.

⭐ *Bonus 40,000 EXP!*

After the battle, Leonid seems pathetic and beaten, but he revives with an infusion of red power bestowed from somewhere above! The bell tolls, and a light appears in the sky…

After the cutscene, use the save point and proceed through the doors directly ahead to the base of the Onyx Chain. (This is your last chance to save until the end of the story, so use it!) Watch as Capell takes his best shot at the chain…and then the team figures out what the next step should be.

HUBRIS OF VEROS

The party's aristos—Savio, Touma, and Seraphina—perform an ancient lunar rite that creates a passage to the moon up the Onyx Chain. The party then takes off walking, yes, walking to the moon. (To be clear, the moon is very close because of the chains.) Eventually, they reach the Lunar Sanctuary of the moon god, Veros.

MISSION

DEFEAT LEONID AND VEROS

Here it is, your final mission. All you have to do is defeat two of the most powerful forces in the known universe. Good luck!

LUNAR SANCTUARY

HUBRIS OF VEROS

MISSION MAP

1 Start

2 Staircase

3 Leonid and Veros

ACTION CHECKLIST

1 • Defeat Leonid.

2 • Defeat Veros the moon god.

3 • Watch the finale.

ENEMIES

 **Leonid** `AP -`
HP • 300000
FOL • 6000   EXP • 9650

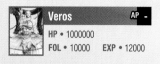 **Veros** `AP -`
HP • 1000000
FOL • 10000   EXP • 12000

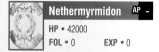 **Nethermyrmidon** `AP -`
HP • 42000
FOL • 0   EXP • 0

NEW SIDE QUESTS AVAILABLE

None.

PRIVATE EVENTS AVAILABLE

None.

MISSION WALKTHROUGH

This is it, the big finale. Just follow the long passageway through several doors and up the long staircase to the sanctuary where the Onyx Chain is anchored. Then say hello to Veros, the moon god, the Crimson One. He presents Capell with a momentous decision. A vision of the past influences Capell, and he makes his choice.

DEFEAT LEONID AND VEROS

Veros is not happy with Capell's choice, and soon you face a resurrected and extremely blue Leonid in one last fight. His attacks are basically the same as before, although he adds vicious area-of-effect attacks called XIIIth Word and VIIth Violation. He also becomes immune to melee attacks for periods of time. When these things happen, protect your team with Prudentiae and hold on until you can inflict melee damage again. As before, water and earth are less useful than other elements.

SITUATION BONUS!

Defeated Leonid within 2 minutes.

⭐ **Obtained some amarlista!**

After Leonid falls again, it's time for the final battle of the *Infinite Undiscovery* main story. Time to stand up to the ruthless plans of the Crimson One.

VEROS

p.298

HP 1000000 **EXP** 12000

Veros is the final boss, so naturally he's tough. But if you've prepared well, equipped well, and leveled up your characters steadily (so Capell and his party are in the high 50s to mid 60s) you should be in very good shape for this last fight.

The first thing to note is that Veros is protected by a ring of colored discs called nethermyrmidons. You cannot hurt the moon god until you bash through these discs. You can attack the discs easily enough, but when they start rotating or spinning, back away! Spinning discs can inflict painful damage. Bide your time and play Prudentiae to ward off magic attacks like Fanatic Lunaseer until the discs are stationary again. Veros also summons faespheres to assist him in battle; destroy these as they appear to prevent them from assisting him too much.

Once the discs are down, wade into Veros with your favorite battle skill and get in combos with your party members. Soon he starts deploying fiery red and magnetic black orbs. Run away out to the periphery of the area until they dissipate, then sprint back in to deal damage to the moon god. Halfway through the battle, the background begins to rotate and the moon god's attacks become more powerful. If you've survived up until now, however, persevering should just be a matter of time.

After Veros finally falls, you've successfully completed *Infinite Undiscovery*. Congratulations! Watch the dramatic game-ending movie and the epilogue set two years later. And here's a big-time tip: *Don't miss the scene after the credits!* After the conclusion, you'll be prompted to save your game. If you've beaten the game on at least Normal difficulty, the Seraphic Gate opens—load the save later to access this huge additional challenge in Kolton. Beating the game on Normal unlocks Hard difficulty, while beating Hard unlocks the ludicrously difficult Infinity mode.

THE SERAPHIC GATE

The adventure is done, wrongs made right, and the curtain closes. But not so fast—the battle is far from over, provided you've completed the game on at least Normal difficulty. After the final battle and the full ending, you'll be prompted to save. Loading this save places the party in the Pieria Marshlands. Head back to Kolton and check inside the main building—a formerly-dormant teleporter now leads to a location known as the Seraphic Gate.

Fighting in the Seraphic Gate spans locations from the whole game, under a blazing kaleidoscope sky—altogether, the Seraphic Gate is far, far larger than any other dungeon in *Infinite Undiscovery*. The foes are leaner and meaner than in the main game, too…while normal game enemies top out at level 50, with around 100,000 HP, enemies in the Seraphic Gate can be as high as level *200*, with HP totals up to 2.5 *million*! This challenge is only greater on Hard or Infinity difficulty, where enemy stats are multiplied by 1.2 or 1.8, respectively; on Infinity, that means an HP total of 2.5 million becomes 4.5 million!

The rewards are commensurate to the risk, however—many of the best pieces of equipment in the game are found in the Seraphic Gate (and many upper-tier crafting recipes only become available, for that matter, once the Seraphic Gate is unlocked). The stat jumps you'll see once you start equipping some of these items are startling, but necessary—the further you delve into the Seraphic Gate, the harder it gets.

The dynamics of combat change in the Seraphic Gate, too. By the time the way to the Seraphic Gate is open, allies should be at least level 50. Finally, MP pools are deep enough to drop old staples like Cutting Gavotte and Sparrowrain, replacing them with more powerful, MP-costly skills like Grinn Valesti and Raven Venom. In addition to the feeble cape found in the Underwater Palace, you'll find (and craft, if you've kept IC skill levels up) even more gear in the Seraphic Gate that replenishes MP over time, making conservation even less of a concern. Fol drops in abundance and money isn't a great worry after the main game is done, so there's no harm in stocking up on MP-replenishment items like white berry powder. The moral of the story is that you'll have to really cut loose to succeed in this odd place, but at least you'll have the tools to do so. Finally, there is no mini-map or menu map in the Seraphic Gate. You'll have to get by on familiarity with old environments, but most areas are downsized from their original incarnations, or made more linear. The lack of a map really only presents a problem in the more convoluted sections—in the Seraphic Gate's versions of Bihar Mines and Cobasna Timberlands.

MISSION
1F: GRAAD PRISON

ENEMIES

Blue Drogo Warrior AP 5
HP • 17000
FOL • 1840   EXP • 2300

Tiger Rachnuvus AP 4
HP • 20000
FOL • 1600   EXP • 2000

Larva AP 1
HP • 7000
FOL • 400   EXP • 500

Vembert AP 7
HP • 340000
FOL • 10400   EXP • 13000

TREASURE

1 ∘ Memoirs of a warrior—treasure chest

2 ∘ Sacrificial doll—treasure chest

3 ∘ Maestro's baton—defeat Vembert (finally!)

The first section resembles Graad Prison, from which Aya sprang Capell so long ago. Capell's come a long way, but so have his enemies. Waves of drogo and insects attack as you descend the prison staircase. This is a good barometer for further progress into the gate;

if you have trouble with these first waves, spend some time "grinding" EXP on them and experimenting with/leveling up different skills and spells to build up the party. To leave, simply step on the teleporter that brought you here. Our old friend Vembert is near the bottom. Unlike encounters against him early in the game, Vembert is no longer invulnerable. Watch out for his Brandishbane stomp, running away from allies when Vembert directs it at Capell, minimizing damage to the party. He's extremely weak to water, and somewhat weak to Astro. Vembert absorbs fire completely, however, so muzzle Rucha if she's along. A teleporter beyond Vembert at the bottom leads to the next section.

MISSION
2F: ORADIAN DUNES

ENEMIES

Dune Harpy AP 2
HP • 20000
FOL • 1920   EXP • 2400

Fountainbeak AP 2
HP • 10000
FOL • 1200   EXP • 1500

Fire Gigas AP 7
HP • 35000
FOL • 2400   EXP • 3000

Quetzalcoatl AP -
HP • 30000
FOL • 2240   EXP • 2800

TREASURE

1 ∘ Atlantis metal—treasure chest behind cracked rock near teleporter to Luce Plains; requires Balbagan or Gustav

2 ∘ Avifir headdress—treasure chest inside whirlwind near teleporter to Vesplume Tower roof; requires Komachi

Every foe in the Oradian Dunes except the gigas is extremely weak to aether. Against fire gigas, use water instead, if available. There are two paths to take from the teleporter from Graad Prison. To reach a special battle against an old friend, hug the left wall until you reach a teleporter. To advance to the next area, a demented copy of Luce Plains, hug the right wall. No boss creature is present in this area. If this is your first time in the gate, you'll want to head to Vesplume Tower first, so hug the left wall initially.

MISSION
VESPLUME TOWER ROOF

ENEMIES

Shadow Sigmund AP 5
HP • 130000
FOL • 49610   EXP • 15000

TREASURE

1 ∘ Pius wood—treasure chest

2 ∘ Gold berry potion—treasure chest

Long ago, Sigmund gave his life spiriting Leonid away from Vesplume Tower, allowing Capell and friends to cut the Crimson Chain and continue on their quest. Or did he? Sigmund and Leonid were both feared dead, but obviously that wasn't telling the full story, as Leonid reappears several times after that sequence. Here, we find what's befallen Sigmund, who stands brainwashed at the summit of a facsimile of the tower he disappeared from. If Capell can knock some sense into him, solo, Sigmund rejoins the group! The fight is no easy task, however. Capell has no friends to rely on to heal him, or to distract Sigmund. Sigmund attacks with either normal swings, or a few extremely damaging skills—Grinn Valesti and Alfheim. The key to defeating Sigmund is Deflect Drive. Anything Sigmund does can be parried, and only while Sigmund is stunned after a parry can he be launched or floored. Parrying Sigmund's powerful skills is easier said than done, however, and mistiming Deflect Drive often leads to Capell losing at least half his life. Therefore, make it count when you *do* parry Sigmund—get him airborne and try for the most damaging juggle possible, maximizing the opportunity. If Capell gets hit, wait near Sigmund until he's ready to attack again. Then move out of the way just before he swings, causing him to whiff his attack. This buys time to open up the menu and quickly use a couple potions from the top of the item list. You might also consider keeping a sacrificial doll equipped, and swapping in new ones as necessary. After successful completion of this fight, Capell is returned to the Oradian Dunes segment, with the option to rebuild the party—complete with Sigmund, if desired! His level may be lacking, but the huge EXP earned in the Seraphic Gate helps bring him up to speed quickly.

MISSION
3F: LUCE PLAINS

ENEMIES

Avalanche Harpy AP **2**
HP • 30000
FOL • 2000   EXP • 2500

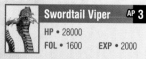
Swordtail Viper AP **3**
HP • 28000
FOL • 1600   EXP • 2000

Storm Gigas AP **7**
HP • 40000
FOL • 2400   EXP • 3000

Wyvern AP **-**
HP • 500000
FOL • 20000   EXP • 25000

TREASURE

1. Lubricus cloth—out-of-reach treasure chest; requires Komachi
2. Saruleus helmet—treasure chest
3. Hrotti—defeat wyvern

Luce Plains is teeming with hostile wildlife. Harpies perch above stone columns, ready to swoop down, while gigas and vipers patrol the area. A great wyvern—bigger brother to the dragon fought in Pieria Marshlands—also traverses the plain. It absorbs fire (of course), but is extremely weak to water. It follows the same pattern as the dragon, peppering the party with attacks from above, settling occasionally to attack from the ground. The hrotti, one of the two best greatswords, is obtained upon defeat (and almost certainly becomes your most powerful weapon at this point). A teleporter at the opposite end of the plains from where you start leads to the Bihar Mines segment.

MISSION
4F: BIHAR MINES

ENEMIES

Lumper Baron AP **2**
HP • 20000
FOL • 1000   EXP • 2885

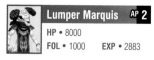
Lumper Marquis AP **2**
HP • 8000
FOL • 1000   EXP • 2883

Lumper Duke AP **2**
HP • 10000
FOL • 1000   EXP • 2882

Gold Chest Mimic AP **4**
HP • 50000
FOL • 60000   EXP • 30

TREASURE

1. Dragon hide—locked treasure chest; requires Vic or Komachi

The Bihar Mines, an optional zone in the main game, is excerpted and upgraded for the Seraphic Gate. It's split into a few different areas connected by elevators. From the first area, an elevator leads up to the second. This second area has two more elevators—one to the right, another ahead and to the left. The left elevator leads to a dead end. The right elevator goes to another floor where traveling ahead leads to a teleporter to the Cobasna Timberlands, while a door on the right hides an elevator that leads to a teleporter to Port Zala. The Lumper foes in these sections aren't too different from any before them, though being residents of the Seraphic Gate, they naturally have drastically upgraded stats. The Bihar Mines has no boss. If this is your first time in the Seraphic Gate, you should explore Port Zala before coming back through the Bihar Mines and heading to Cobasna.

MISSION
PORT ZALA

ENEMIES

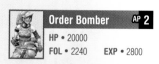
Order Bomber AP **2**
HP • 20000
FOL • 2240   EXP • 2800

Mantifish AP **1**
HP • 9000
FOL • 1440   EXP • 1800

Order Officer AP **2**
HP • 22000
FOL • 2320   EXP • 2900

TREASURE

1. Avifir garb—hidden chest on pier; requires Percipere
2. Dragon scale—out-of-reach chest; requires Komachi

Port Zala is relatively tame in comparison to other areas of the Seraphic Gate. There are a couple pieces of hidden treasure, but mostly Port Zala serves to lead to the Zalan Coast, which can be accessed from a teleporter tucked away in the buildings by the pier.

MISSION
ZALAN COAST

ENEMIES

Mantifish AP 1
HP • 9000
FOL • 1440   EXP • 1800

Leviathan AP -
HP • 425000
FOL • 23000   EXP • 28000

TREASURE

1 • Memoirs of a knight—treasure chest

2 • Moon blade—defeat the leviathan

Along the coastline, Capell and friends run into the monstrous leviathan. This upgrade to the kraken fought in the Underwater Palace has the same deficiency—its turn speed leaves something to be desired (for the leviathan, anyway). You can use this to your advantage by circling the foe continually. It never quite catches up, allowing you to circle and strike it repeatedly without taking damage in return. Earth spells also can help demolish the leviathan much more quickly, while water spells are simply absorbed. Upon defeat, the leviathan gives up the moon blade, an excellent upgrade for Vic. After the leviathan is defeated, you must backtrack through the coast and Port Zala to take the other teleporter from Bihar Mines.

MISSION
5F: COBASNA TIMBERLANDS

ENEMIES

Alraune AP 4
HP • 55000
FOL • 6000   EXP • 6000

Tequilo AP 3
HP • 28000
FOL • 2400   EXP • 3000

Lava Glutton AP 6
HP • 35000
FOL • 2100   EXP • 3500

Peluda AP -
HP • 350000
FOL • 24000   EXP • 30000

Queen Wasp AP 1
HP • 20000
FOL • 600   EXP • 1500

TREASURE

1 • Empyrean cloth—behind cracked rock; requires Balbagan or Gustav

2 • Gold berry potion—behind cracked rock

3 • Sabris claws—defeat the peluda

With no map, no compass, no mist directing the way, and no defining landmarks (the thick canopy even obscures a consistent view of the ever-present moon), the Cobasna Timberlands can be extremely frustrating if you lose your bearings. Take great care to avoid stepping on the plant-like alraunes; Shrillshriek was annoying during the main game, but eating it in the Seraphic Gate usually means multiple characters die outright at the very beginning of the fight. During your first run through of the Seraphic Gate, it's recommended that you simply hug the right wall at all times, which eventually takes you to a battle with peluda and then a teleporter leading to Nolaan. Peluda, like tarasque before it, absorbs fire and belches potent circular fire attacks, but is very weak to water. Keep your distance when it spews forth flame from its many maws, using ranged spells and skills when it's not safe to attack directly. Gustav will be pleased with the reward from defeating peluda: the Sabris claws. If you choose to explore Cobasna Timberlands more fully, bring along Balbagan, as several cracked rocks block the way to treasure chests and mimics.

MISSION

6F: NOLAAN

ENEMIES

 Pebbleshell Crab AP **4**
HP • 35000
FOL • 2400   EXP • 3000

Wendigo AP **7**
HP • 55000
FOL • 3000   EXP • 3800

Scissorclaw Centipede AP **3**
HP • 40000
FOL • 3200   EXP • 4100

This short segment brings back memories, doesn't it? After having your fill of battling bears and crushing crabs, take the teleporter to Vesplume Tower. Nolaan has no boss or treasure.

MISSION

7F: VESPLUME TOWER INTERIOR

ENEMIES

 **Frost Gigas** AP **7**
HP • 60000
FOL • 3000   EXP • 6000

Order Ranger AP **2**
HP • 30000
FOL • 2650   EXP • 3000

Order Adept AP **2**
HP • 38000
FOL • 3690   EXP • 3700

Gabriel Celeste AP **-**
HP • 1000000
FOL • 32000   EXP • 40000

Order Expert AP **2**
HP • 33000
FOL • 3200   EXP • 4000

TREASURE

1 ○ Charming perfume—treasure chest

2 ○ Nighthawk—treasure chest

3 ○ "Genesis"—defeat Gabriel Celeste

After much fighting with Order minions on this floor, you'll run into one of the Seraphic Gate's two strongest baddies, Gabriel Celeste. Take a good look at this character, as he should be very familiar…like many

bosses, he'll summon faespheres, which you should destroy as quickly as possible. He'll also use strong magic, such as Nekros, Hydrain, Pyrburst, Geocrush, and Aerwhirl. Depending on your party, Pyrburst and Geocrush might be strong enough to finish some allies in one shot, so keep Prudentiae at the ready to deflect spells. Up close, Gabriel Celeste employs a powerful skill called Noble Play, spinning his weapon rapidly. This is your obvious cue to get away! This boss has one million HP, so the fight will not be brief. As his HP gets low, Gabriel Celeste begins using an electrical attack called Critical Flare, striking all around him in a wide swath. If you are not far away or casting Prudentiae during this attack, defeat is basically assured, so be careful. "Genesis," Michelle's strongest grimoire, is obtained after defeating Gabriel Celeste. A teleporter leads to Kolton just past the battle.

MISSION
8F: KOLTON

TREASURE

1. Amarlista—treasure chest
2. Atlantis metal—treasure chest
3. Pius wood—treasure chest
4. Feet of Saruleus—treasure chest

The Seraphic Gate's incarnation of Kolton is the one safe haven for your party. There is a save point, as well as Genma. As usual, he can sell the party items, or help them rest and recover from battle. Four treasure chests provide valuable materials and items as well. There are two teleporters leading to new areas—the one to Genma's left leads to Castle Valette, while the one past him, up the stairs and through the door, leads to Graad Woods. There is also a teleporter, up the stairs and to the right, which exits the Seraphic Gate altogether and heads back to *actual* Kolton. Don't step through this teleporter accidently, as you'll have to trudge all the way back through the Seraphic Gate to get here again! It's best to save and take on Castle Valette first, since you'll just be coming back to Kolton before heading to Graad Woods.

MISSION
CASTLE VALETTE

ENEMIES

Burning Lantern AP 1
HP • 10000
FOL • 10   EXP • 1000

Skull Soldier AP 2
HP • 35000
FOL • 2800   EXP • 3500

Dancing Sword AP 1
HP • 25000
FOL • 1700   EXP • 2900

Atro the Cursed Eye AP -
HP • 240000
FOL • 2500   EXP • 7000

Gold Chest Mimic AP 4
HP • 50000
FOL • 60000   EXP • 30

Wrath AP -
HP • 450000
FOL • 1970   EXP • 34000

Skull Knight AP 2
HP • 40000
FOL • 3120   EXP • 3900

TREASURE

1. Claridian medicine—treasure chest
2. Okedo taiko drum—treasure chest
3. Discipline staff—defeat Wrath

Castle Valette is crawling with undead. More dangerous, though, are the dancing swords…do not underestimate these ethereal floating weapons, as they attack very quickly, meaning they'll continually interrupt the actions of whoever they're attacking. If that character doesn't get help from someone, death is inevitable. Make floating swords (and crossbows, where present) your total priority when they're present. Atro the Cursed Eye serves as a mid-boss on this stage, and can be dispensed with just the same as

Veld and Kron before it. Wrath serves as the boss, and is similar to Envy and Greed—he calls forth a set of Rib Forager swords to guard him, and teleports around the room to strike. Area-of-effect fire spells like Pyrburst can successfully *demolish* Rib Foragers and Wrath all at the same time, while Eternal Refrain (and spells like Geoclaw) can track Wrath even when he teleports. Upon defeat, Wrath gives up Eugene's second-best weapon, the discipline staff. There is no teleporter away from the Castle Valette section—you must walk back to the entrance and teleport back to Kolton before heading to the Graad Woods portion.

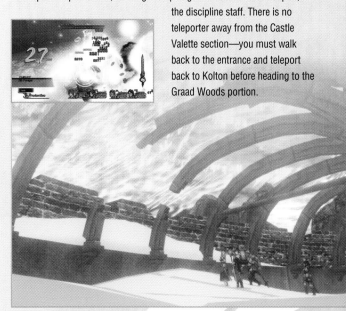

MISSION
9F: GRAAD WOODS

ENEMIES

Garm AP 5
HP • 40000
FOL • 3200   EXP • 4000

Hill Gigas AP 7
HP • 70000
FOL • 4000   EXP • 7000

Gold Chest Mimic AP 4
HP • 50000
FOL • 60000   EXP • 30

Larva AP 1
HP • 20000
FOL • 2   EXP • 100

TREASURE

1. Sabris garb—locked treasure chest; requires Vic or Komachi
2. Magic amplio—hidden treasure chest; requires Percipere

Beware of the wolves here in the woods, as they've been upgraded considerably in offense from the main game, and can do severe damage or kill instantly with their lunging attacks. A teleporter across the woods leads to Dragonbone Shrine. There is no boss in the woods.

MISSION

10F: DRAGONBONE SHRINE

ENEMIES

Inferno Glutton `AP 6`
HP • 60000
FOL • 4800   EXP • 5000

Scissorclaw Centipede `AP 3`
HP • 40000
FOL • 3200   EXP • 4100

Lifestealer `AP 1`
HP • 30000
FOL • 2400   EXP • 2500

Seaspawn `AP -`
HP • 550000
FOL • 3440   EXP • 43000

TREASURE

1 ◦ Karathos suit—defeat the seaspawn

Dragonbone Shrine is one of the shortest, simplest areas. It's guarded at the end by a seaspawn, a similar creature to Karathos. It's accompanied by many inferno gluttons, so take these out first before focusing on the big turtle. Like kraken or leviathan, seaspawn turns slowly. Take advantage of this by circling around it constantly while attacking. This causes its dangerous Killer Bite and Poison Rain to miss. However, as its hit points get lower, it begins turning more quickly, making this strategy ineffective. It also starts using Jet Spin, propelling itself around the arena and damaging whatever it strikes. Stand behind the pillars to avoid this attack, and keep plugging away with strong skills and earth spells to defeat it. The Karathos suit is obtained upon victory, and the way is opened to a teleporter leading to Castle Prevant.

MISSION

11F: CASTLE PREVANT

ENEMIES

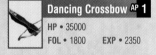

Crystal Gargoyle `AP 4`
HP • 70000
FOL • 3500   EXP • 4500

Order Expert `AP 2`
HP • 10000
FOL • 1000   EXP • 1050

Dancing Crossbow `AP 1`
HP • 35000
FOL • 1800   EXP • 2350

Order Master `AP 2`
HP • 100000
FOL • 4000   EXP • 5000

Gold Chest Mimic `AP 4`
HP • 50000
FOL • 60000   EXP • 30

Rockshell Crab `AP 4`
HP • 95000
FOL • 2840   EXP • 4800

TREASURE

1 ◦ Atlantis metal—locked treasure chest; requires Vic or Komachi

2 ◦ Symphony notations—locked treasure chest

Castle Prevant has no boss, just a lot of standard combat with supercharged Order enemies. As mentioned previously, go after the floating weapons above all else—perhaps no normal enemy in the game can ruin a party more unexpectedly than these. A teleporter at the end of this section leads to Halgita.

MISSION

12F: HALGITA

ENEMIES

Forest Rachnuvus `AP 4`
HP • 42000
FOL • 3400   EXP • 4300

Narbear `AP 7`
HP • 60000
FOL • 4800   EXP • 6000

Gold Chest Mimic `AP 4`
HP • 50000
FOL • 60000   EXP • 30

Order Sorceress `AP 2`
HP • 35000
FOL • 3700   EXP • 4700

Green Drogo Chief `AP 5`
HP • 50000
FOL • 4400   EXP • 5500

Doogadoola `AP 7`
HP • 120000
FOL • 4444   EXP • 10000

Halgita Soldier (F) `AP 2`
HP • 38000
FOL • 2300   EXP • 2890

Grymon `AP -`
HP • 500000
FOL • 7000   EXP • 47000

Halgita Soldier (M) `AP 2`
HP • 40000
FOL • 2400   EXP • 3000

TREASURE

1 ◦ Seven-star blade—treasure chest

2 ◦ Divinity—hidden treasure chest behind altar; requires Percipere

3 ◦ Executioner—defeat Grymon

Here there are shades of an earlier flight up the stairs in Halgita, in reverse. You'll have to progress past many waves of a large variety of foes before facing the toughest gigas, and a knight deadlier than any the Order had to offer. The most threatening minor enemy here is the Order sorceress—these mages utilize Geocrush liberally, a spell that can cause major trouble to multiple party members if you don't destroy the rolling boulders with Prudentiae. At the end of the zone, Grymon awaits behind closed doors, while Doogadoola idles with two narbears in an open area. If you decide to fight the king of gigas, take out the narbears first before going after Doogadoola with fire spells. Note that aether is completely ineffective against him. Against Grymon, move laterally continuously. His deadliest attacks (Heraldic Edge and Crestfallen) have a "cone" area-of-effect extending forward from him. When he misses with these skills, you have a chance to move in and strike. Beware that he also has close-range countermeasures in Flickering Sphere and Crushing Cube, so don't get overzealous while pressing the attack. When Grymon falls, he drops the most powerful axe, and opens the way to the final area.

13F: LUNAR SANCTUARY

ENEMIES

 Leonid - Celestial Sword AP -
HP • 1800000
FOL • 15000   EXP • 50000

 Ethereal Queen - Tri-emblem AP -
HP • 2500000
FOL • 20000   EXP • 70000

TREASURE

1 • Sabris boots—treasure chest

2 • Tri-emplem—treasure chest

3 • Halgitian paper—treasure chest

4 • Dragon meat—treasure chest

5 • Celestial sword—defeat Leonid

6 • Tri-emblem—defeat Ethereal Queen

As it is in the normal game, Lunar Sanctuary is the last area in the Seraphic Gate. After a trek past many worthwhile treasure chests, you'll have to take on Leonid and then the Seraphic Gate's ruler, the Ethereal Queen. Leonid can be defeated with the same tactics that work on his other forms—keep your distance to avoid VIIth Violation, and move laterally behind him to avoid XIIIth Word. Leonid has a staggering amount of HP, but if you've made it this far, his defeat should be a matter of time. Of more pressing concern is the Ethereal Queen, who you fight *immediately* after defeating Leonid.

Thee must desire respite from thy empty existence…thou shall have it!

First things first, if you haven't forged an azureal blade, equip Capell with the celestial sword. Sure, it damages Capell's HP and MP to the tune of 1% of maximum every 5 seconds, but at this level that amounts to a few hundred HP and a few dozen MP—essentially nothing compared to the damage even normal enemies output by now. The extra damage is worth it. Second things second, doesn't Ethereal Queen—like Gabriel Celeste—look exceedingly familiar? Nevermind. More importantly, she aims to kill Capell and his allies, and she's very good at doing it. To begin, like many bosses, she summons faespheres to assist her. She uses the highest-tier spell of each element: Geoquake, Astrocalypse, Voltscourge, and Pyrgeddon. Any character caught in the swath of these spells while unprotected by Prudentiae (which does work against them) is almost guaranteed to die. For this reason, Connecting at all in this battle is not really advisable.

If the spells weren't enough, she also has very threatening skills both up-close and far away. Her Southern Cross is similar to Gabriel Celeste's Noble Play, striking many times at a short distance, while Seraphic Law is an arcing series of projectiles that can severely damage or kill multiple friends. As the fight drags on (and it does, as the queen has 2.5 million HP on Normal difficulty!), she'll eventually begin to use an attack called Accused. The queen taunts the party with the statement from the caption before stamping the ground, stunning everyone nearby. She then unleashes a flurry of energy that is unlikely to leave anyone it touches alive. When she initiates this attack, get as far away as possible, and be prepared to use miraculous medicines to get defeated allies back into the fight quickly.

Stay alive long enough to wear the queen down and you'll be rewarded with the tri-emblem, one of the best items in the game. You'll also be spirited out of the Seraphic Gate. Upon re-entry from Kolton, however, you'll find all the bosses have respawned, and can be defeated for their spoils again, including the queen herself! Alas, previously opened treasure chests remain opened, though you can certainly search for any you missed. Playing through the Seraphic Gate multiple times is a great way to find raw materials for high-level crafts, to earn the amazing items granted for defeating certain bosses, and to level up—a first completion of the main game once found Capell at level 53. After one completion of the Seraphic Gate, he was level 88. After two completions? 117. And then, there's always the challenge of defeating the game on Hard or Infinity difficulty, and tackling a vastly revved-up Seraphic Gate. Keep your blade sharp, and good luck!

SIDE QUESTS

Whenever you reach a new village or city, you frequently unlock a series of optional side quests. To trigger these quests, explore the town area and talk to townsfolk you meet. Some of these people end up asking favors of Capell. Each favor is a side quest and usually requires the completion of several tasks. Complete these tasks to earn rewards from grateful citizens.

However, there are two important things to remember about side quests:

First, be aware that sometimes townsfolk won't ask their favors unless Capell is connected to a specific party member. For example, children often won't ask favors of Capell unless he's connected to Rico or Rucha at the time. Kids feel more comfortable talking to other kids, right?

Second, note that some side quests aren't available the first time you enter a village or city. You may be required to complete other main story tasks first, some of which inevitably take you away to new locations. For example, three side quests in Burgusstadt are unlocked only after you complete missions in Sapran, Fayel, and Vesplume Tower first, and then return.

So after you finish major story events and return to previous locations, be sure to chat again with townsfolk you've already met. They always have new observations, and some may trigger new side quests for Capell.

GRAAD PRISON

01 DELIVER THE GOLD COIN

QUEST CONTACT
Young villager

AVAILABLE
Immediately at game start

 REWARD
White berry potion
OR
1000 Fol

WALKTHROUGH

Shortly after the game begins, find the "Young villager" in the cell next to the save point in Graad Prison's main cell block. Talk to him once and select "Very well" to accept the quest: he wants you to deliver a special eagle emblem gold coin to his wife so that she knows he's alive. Talk to the young villager again to learn that his wife's name is Anne, and his son's name is Ralph.

Later, when you reach the town of Burgusstadt, enter the last house on the right as you're headed toward the palace. Talk to the woman; this is Anne, the prisoner's wife. Capell automatically hands over the eagle emblem gold coin. She asks about her husband, and you have a choice:

If you select "Tell her about him," the grateful Anne gives you a white berry potion as reward.

If you select "Don't tell her anything," Anne feels a sense of grief but gives you 1000 Fol.

NOLAAN

02 WHERE'S SNOUTY?

QUEST CONTACT
Spirited kid

AVAILABLE
After you leave Aya in the twins' house during first visit to Nolaan

 REWARD
Red berry powder

WALKTHROUGH

After you first arrive in Nolaan and leave Aya in the twins' house, Connect to Rico and talk to the "Spirited kid" running around the well in the village square. He tells Rico that his "bestest friend" Snouty is missing.

As you move across the Dragonbone Shrine map, look for a mouse in the secret room next to the two treasure chests (see "Find the Secret Room" in the Dragonbone Shrine section of our Story Walkthrough) down in the southeast corner of the area. Connect to Rico and talk to the mouse. It's Snouty, and he's lost. Select "Show him the way." Snouty automatically hops into Capell's pocket.

After you complete the mission in the shrine (or before completion, if you wish), go back to the spirited kid and talk to him to return Snouty.

03 THE OLD RING

QUEST CONTACT
Distracted man & Forgetful dog

AVAILABLE
After you leave Aya in the twins' house during first visit to Nolaan

 REWARD 500 Fol

WALKTHROUGH

After you first arrive in Nolaan and leave Aya in the twins' house, you can enter the easternmost house and talk to the "Distracted man." He first mentions something he buried in the rubble at the shrine entrance...but when you talk to him after that, he just tells you to keep away.

When you enter the Dragonbone Shrine, look for the disturbed pile of rubble in the first side alcove not far from where you enter the shrine area. Looks like somebody dug up the object buried there. This discovery actually triggers the side quest.

After you complete the shrine mission, return to Nolaan. Connect to Rico and talk to the "Forgetful dog" that keeps following you around town. He admits to Rico that he picked up something at the shrine...but doesn't remember where he put it. (If you talk to the Distracted man again, he can't believe that a dog dug up his item.)

After the Azure Chain is destroyed at Castle Prevant, return to Nolaan and talk to the Forgetful dog again. He remembers that he was thirsty after he returned from the shrine, and dropped what he dug up. Find the shining spot near the town well (next to where Sigmund is standing) and examine it to pick up the old ring. Return it to the Distracted man for your reward.

04 CLAY FOR POTS

QUEST CONTACT
Cranky old man

AVAILABLE
After you defeat Rambert and complete the Dragonbone Shrine mission

REWARD
If you give poor clay, you receive sandstone.
If you give soft clay, you receive ceramic.
If you give golden clay, you receive hearthstone.

WALKTHROUGH

After you complete the mission in Dragonbone Shrine and return to Nolaan, go into the old couple's house (the one nearest the well) and talk twice to the "Cranky old man." He asks if you'd pick up some clay for his pottery hobby.

From then on, look for the glowing lumps of clay that appear on the ground in various locations. You can find three different grades of clay: poor, soft, and golden. Poor clay is found around Nolaan, including a sample just outside the entrance to the Dragonbone Shrine outer caves; a soft clay sample sits not far away, just inside the shrine entrance. Golden clay is found in more distant locations.

You can return one sample of each type of clay to the cranky old man for rewards. When you give him a sample of golden clay (rarest of the three types), the quest ends.

05 A LETTER FOR DENTON

QUEST CONTACT
Doleful man

AVAILABLE
After you defeat Rambert and complete the Dragonbone Shrine mission

REWARD Karathos wristband

WALKTHROUGH

After you complete the mission in Dragonbone Shrine and return to Nolaan, talk to the "Doleful man" pacing near the general store. He asks if you'd deliver a letter to a friend of his named Denton in Burgusstadt. Select "Okay" and he gives you the letter, which now appears in your Special Items inventory.

When you arrive in Burgusstadt, enter the bar and talk to Denton, the man with the red headband sitting at one of the tables. Capell automatically hands over the letter and Denton thanks him with the gift of a Karathos wristband.

06 NOLAAN DELIVERY BOY

QUEST CONTACT	AVAILABLE
Shopkeeper in Nolaan General Store	After you defeat Rambert and complete the Dragonbone Shrine mission

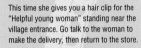 **REWARD** Miraculous medicine

WALKTHROUGH

After you complete the mission in Dragonbone Shrine and return to Nolaan, enter the general store and talk to the shopkeeper. She asks if you'd mind helping with her deliveries. Say "Yes, I will" and she gives you a potter's wheel. Go talk to the "Cranky old man" to deliver the wheel, then return to the store and talk to the shopkeeper again.

This time she gives you a hair clip for the "Helpful young woman" standing near the village entrance. Go talk to the woman to make the delivery, then return to the store.

The final delivery is a set of iron arm weights, but the shopkeeper can't remember who they're for! You can get clues from other villages…or you can just take them to the correct customer, the "Energetic old man." Return to the shopkeeper one last time to get a nice reward.

07 MONSTERS IN THE SHRINE

QUEST CONTACT	AVAILABLE
Forgetful dog	After the Azure Chain is destroyed

 REWARD Ogre's hammer

WALKTHROUGH

After the Azure Chain is destroyed in Castle Prevant, return to Nolaan, Connect to Rico, and then talk to the "Forgetful dog." He tells you he saw some strange creatures at the shrine. (If you haven't completed "The Old Ring" side quest, talk to the forgetful dog a second time here.)

Go to Dragonbone Shrine and move through the caves until you reach the northernmost cavern, the one with the open roof. There you find a big hill gigas with a pair of giors at his side. Defeat this very tough trio to earn your reward—an ogre's hammer. Afterwards, equip Balbagan with the new hammer; it most likely provides a huge increase in his ATK stat.

BURGUSSTADT

08 BACK PAIN MEDICINE

QUEST CONTACT	AVAILABLE
Worried old woman	After the Azure Chain is destroyed

 REWARD Sacrificial doll

WALKTHROUGH

Here's a quest with multiple steps. After the Azure Chain is destroyed at Castle Prevant, return to Nolaan and talk to the "Worried old woman" standing by the town well. She tells you she's out of pain medicine and asks if you'd pick up some for her. Answer "Sure" to trigger the quest. She gives you a prescription for the shopkeeper in Burgusstadt; it appears in your Special Items inventory.

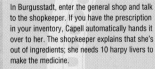

In Burgusstadt, enter the general shop and talk to the shopkeeper. If you have the prescription in your inventory, Capell automatically hands it over to her. The shopkeeper explains that she's out of ingredients; she needs 10 harpy livers to make the medicine.

Exit Burgusstadt into the Luce Plains and start hunting harpies. Every harpy's drop item is a harpy liver now that this quest is active, so you need to hunt only 10 harpies. A good place to start is at the south end of the tunnel that connects the northern and southern Luce Plains. Several harpies hang out on the south side; after you slay them, go through the tunnel to the north side, where a pair of harpies lurks on the central rock formation. Then come back through the tunnel again to find the southern-side harpies that have reappeared in the same locations!

Once you gather 10 harpy livers, return to Burgusstadt and talk to the shopkeeper to hand them over. She whips up the back pain medicine and gives it to you. Now you must trek all the way back to Nolaan to deliver the goods to the Worried old woman for a generous reward. Here's a timesaver tip: some of the Burgusstadt side quests (see the next section) require that you return to Nolaan too. So wait until you pick up those quests before you deliver the back pain medicine.

09 MONSTER EXTERMINATOR

QUEST CONTACT	AVAILABLE
Mid-career officer in Castle Burguss	After Sigmund's lunar rite

 **REWARD** 1500 Fol

WALKTHROUGH

After Sigmund's lunar rite, talk to the "Mid-career officer" patrolling the entry hall to the Chamber of Rites in Castle Burguss. He asks if you'd mind listening to a request. Select "Not at all." The soldier explains that fleshbiters are running rampant near the city, but the Burguss military is too busy with other problems. Would you mind hunting them? Select "Not at all" again. He thanks you and asks you to kill 30 fleshbiters.

Double Duty

Complete this quest in conjunction with "Risky Meat Delivery." For that quest you must go to Nolaan, and the way is well-populated with fleshbiters.

Head outside the city into Luce Plains with a good party and start whacking fleshbiters out of the sky. (They're suddenly everywhere along the road, and they flock heavily in the tunnel connecting the northern and southern Luce Plains.) When you get 30 kills, head back to the mid-career officer for your reward.

10 FUR FOR THE MINISTER'S DAUGHTER

QUEST CONTACT	AVAILABLE
Smiling minister in Castle Burguss	After Sigmund's lunar rite

★ REWARD Wisdom coin

WALKTHROUGH

After Sigmund's lunar rite, talk to the "Smiling minister" in the library of Castle Burguss. He tells you his daughter wants some gior fur and asks for help. Select "Well, okay then." He suggests you check out the giors in the Luce Plains.

Head out to the Luce Plains and veer to the southeast. Only one gior in the plains drops its fur when defeated; it's in the sunken section at the south boundary of the plains (see the map shot). Once you've got the fur, head back to the smiling minister for your reward.

Gior drops fur

Luce Plains

12 DECIPHER THE LETTER

QUEST CONTACT	AVAILABLE
Denton in bar	After Sigmund's lunar rite and completion of "A Letter for Denton" side quest

★ REWARD 2000 Fol

WALKTHROUGH

After Sigmund's lunar rite, go into the bar on Burgusstadt's main street and talk to Denton again. He says the letter you delivered is in "some cryptic language" and he can't read it. When he asks you to find someone who can read it, answer: "I'll try."

Exit the bar, turn right, and find the "Talented man" near the castle's outer gates. Talk to him; his lunaglyph gives him the ability to speak and read words backwards. He quickly deciphers Denton's letter. Return to Denton for your reward.

11 BUDDING DIVA

QUEST CONTACT	AVAILABLE
Waitress in bar	After Sigmund's lunar rite

★ REWARD Blue berry potion

WALKTHROUGH

After Sigmund's lunar rite, enter the bar on the main street of Burgusstadt and talk to the waitress. She tells you she's trying to make it as a singer, and is writing songs too. Agree to listen to her sing.

When she asks for your opinion, resist the temptation to answer, "I've heard ogres sing better than that." (You get no reward for that.) Instead, be realistic but gentle by answering, "The lyrics might need a little tweaking." She appreciates your honesty and gives you a nice potion.

13 THE UNBLESSED SON

QUEST CONTACT	AVAILABLE
Lonely old man on Burgusstadt street	After Sigmund's lunar rite

★ REWARD Gold ring

WALKTHROUGH

After Sigmund's lunar rite, talk to the "Lonely old man" standing in front of the park bench on the main street of Burgusstadt. Since you're heading to Fayel soon, he wonders if you might do him a favor. Answer "Sure." He wants you to find his unblessed son, whose life the old man saved by sending him off with a trader. An entire village of unblessed folks exists in Fayel; the old man just wants to know if his son is living there. Answer "Sure, I'll try to find him." The old man says you can recognize his son by the white birth mark on his shoulder. Note that he asks you not to tell his son about his true father.

En route to Fayel's capital city during the game's main story, you are sidetracked to the unblessed desert town of Sapran. After you destroy the Orange Chain there and escort the refugee villagers back to their homes, you can find the "Grieving young man" in the house next door to the mayor's. (It's a very small village, so the house is easy to find.) Talk to him; he tells Capell that the fellow with the white birthmark on his shoulder died quite a while ago.

Now go talk to the "Relieved old woman" in the mayor's house. She remembers a boy with the white birthmark, and adds that he's alive and well. Hmmm, seems to be a discrepancy here. Go back to the grieving young man and talk to him again. He admits that he was the kid with the birthmark. Return to Burgusstadt and talk to the old man to get your reward.

Relieved old woman
A boy with a white birthmark on his shoulder... About twenty years ago, you say...

14 RISKY MEAT DELIVERY

QUEST CONTACT
Energetic old woman on Burgusstadt main street

AVAILABLE
After Sigmund's lunar rite

★ **REWARD** 2000 Fol

WALKTHROUGH

After Sigmund's lunar rite, talk to the "Energetic old woman" who walks up and down Burgusstadt's main street. She asks you to deliver a package of cured meat to "the priest's home" in Nolaan—i.e., the twins' house. She warns you that the smell might attract monsters. Select "Okay," and she gives you the cut of cured meat.

Two "Birds" with One Stone

Complete this quest in conjunction with "Monster Exterminator." You face a lot of fleshbiters en route to Nolaan, so you can get the 30 kills you need for the other quest.

Head off to Nolaan, but be aware that beasts en route do find you particularly interesting. Go up the hill to the twins' house and talk to their mother to deliver the cured meat. Return to the energetic old woman in Burgusstadt to receive your reward.

15 ZALACREST WINE

QUEST CONTACT
Barkeeper

AVAILABLE
After return from Vesplume Tower

★ **REWARD** Burgano Special

WALKTHROUGH

After you return to Fayel from destroying the Crimson Chain at Vesplume Tower, go back to Burgusstadt and enter the bar. Talk to the barkeeper; he asks if you'd pick up a famous Zalan wine called Zalacrest for him. Answer "Okay, I'll see what I can do."

After you destroy the Cerulean Chain on the Zala Coast, head into Port Zala and visit the bar there. The barkeeper is happy to give you a bottle of Zalacrest. Take the wine back to the barkeeper in Burgusstadt to get a reward. Note that this reward, some Burgano Special beer, gives you the ability to start the "Multi-Item Exchange" side quest.

16 THE LOST SWORD

QUEST CONTACT
Ralph (kid in Anne's house)

AVAILABLE
After return from Vesplume Tower

★ **REWARD** Rabbit's foot

WALKTHROUGH

After you destroy the Crimson Chain and return to Fayel from Vesplume Tower, go to Burgusstadt and enter Anne's house (the house on the right just before the castle entrance). Talk to the kid named Ralph; he tells you his best buddy lost a toy sword out on the Luce Plains.

You may have to smash through a cracked rock en route to the sword location. So before you leave town to look for the sword, make sure you have a "rock buster" Connect skill in your party: Balbagan's Gigatackle (if he's available) or Gustav's Explosive Ride. For Explosive Ride, remember that Capell must hop aboard Gustav first, then you guide the bear in the direction you want him to "explode."

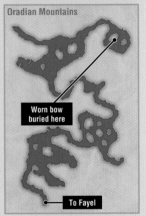

Oradian Mountains

Worn bow buried here

To Fayel

Exit Burgusstadt into the Luce Plains and head east to the opposite end of the vast area (refer to the provided map). Smash through the cracked rock and defeat all of the fleshbiters, wolves, and Lumper soldiers in the temple area surrounded by waterfalls. Run up to the temple and defeat the Lumper leader inside—careful, he's tough. When he falls, you obtain the toy sword. Take it back to Ralph in Burgusstadt to get your reward.

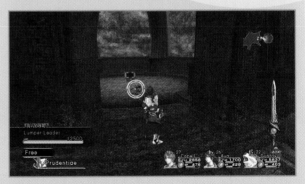

17 MULTI-ITEM EXCHANGE

QUEST CONTACT	AVAILABLE
Sober soldier	After you complete the Zalacrest wine quest

REWARD Cerebral staff

WALKTHROUGH

After you destroy the Cerulean Chain, pick up a bottle of Zalacrest wine from the Port Zala bartender, then deliver it to the Burgusstadt bartender to get a bottle of Burgano Special. Walk over to the "sober soldier" in the Burgusstadt bar and talk to him. When he asks for the Burgano Special, answer "Sure." He gives you a special cocktail recipe in return.

Now talk to the "lecherous old man" who has his eye on the cocktail waitress. He asks for a special cocktail recipe. Select "Tell him the recipe." In return, he gives you a secret pain reliever.

Exit the Burgusstadt bar and go talk to Mina, the little girl standing by the town well with her dog named Flash. When she asks for medicine for her dad, answer "Okay." She gives you her special stone called a "Veros's teardrop" in return.

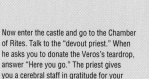

Now enter the castle and go to the Chamber of Rites. Talk to the "devout priest." When he asks you to donate the Veros's teardrop, answer "Here you go." The priest gives you a cerebral staff in gratitude for your generosity.

18 THE CUPID QUEST

QUEST CONTACT	AVAILABLE
Rookie soldier	After Saranda attacks emir in Kolton (late in game)

REWARD Blue berry powder
Blue berry

WALKTHROUGH

Talk to the "rookie soldier" patrolling the entry hallway inside the Burgusstadt castle. When he asks if you'll help him out, then if you'll deliver a ring to a girl for him, answer "Sure" both times. He gives you the "ring for delivery" and says the girl is guarding the restricted area just around the corner.

But two different female soldiers stand guard in that area: a "guarding soldier" and a "bored guarding soldier." Whichever one you talk to first accepts the ring and earns you a reward, but picking the correct girl earns you a better reward (blue berry powder rather than just a blue berry). So which is the right one?

You can ask the other soldiers in the castle for hints—for example, the mid-career officer tells you that the rookie soldier likes well-spoken women, and the worshipping soldier says the rookie's woman takes her job very seriously. Or, you can continue reading this sentence to easily learn that the correct woman is the guarding soldier, not the bored guarding soldier. After you deliver the ring, return to the rookie soldier for your reward.

SAPRAN

19 THE MEMENTO

QUEST CONTACT	AVAILABLE
Exhausted old man	After Capell and Aya rescue Leif

REWARD Marble necklace

WALKTHROUGH

After you return Leif to Sapran, find the "exhausted old man"—he stands in front of the secret alcove you opened earlier when you were smashing orange crystals to liberate Sapran. He asks you to find a bone comb he lost; it's a memento of his late granddaughter.

Find the flashing spot of light on the ground in the western part of town, not far from the water. Pick it up—it's the bone comb—and talk to the exhausted old man again to hand it over. He gives you your reward.

FAYEL

20 BLOOD OF FAYEL

QUEST CONTACT
Accessory-selling girl

AVAILABLE
After Gina reports that Gustav is missing

 REWARD Ring of life

WALKTHROUGH

After you learn that Aya's pet bear is missing, you can connect to Eugene, who stands at the armor shop tent on the main street of Fayel. Now go talk to the "accessory-selling girl" just down the street in the accessory shop tent. When she asks for a favor, answer "Sure, what's up?" She asks you to find a rare jewel called "Blood of Fayel."

Exit Fayel into the Oradian Dunes and keep your eyes peeled for a glowing spot on the ground somewhere over the expanse of sand; a Blood of Fayel gem is buried there. (The shot here shows one area where you can find it, but it could appear elsewhere.) Nab it and head back to Fayel. Be sure to Connect to Eugene before you take the Blood of Fayel to the accessory-selling girl for a nice reward; she won't take it from just Capell.

21 DELIVER NINA'S LETTER

QUEST CONTACT
Nina the cautious girl

AVAILABLE
After you rescue Gustav

 REWARD Metetite

WALKTHROUGH

Connect to Rucha and talk to Nina the cautious girl who stands in front of the abandoned shop tent on Fayel's main street. She asks Rucha to deliver a letter to her dad, identified by the blossom ring that he wears.

On your way up the Oradian Mountains, you reach a spectacular vista overlooking a deep canyon. Find the shining spot near the ledge and pick up the item buried there: a blossom ring! After you complete the Vesplume Tower mission (you can't return to Fayel until you do this), go back to Fayel and give the ring to Nina. She rewards you with a valuable material called metetite.

22 UNLUCKY'S RELATIVE

QUEST CONTACT
Unlucky woman on Fayel main street

AVAILABLE
After return from Vesplume Tower

 REWARD Para-gone

WALKTHROUGH

Once all the cutscenes are finished after your return from Vesplume Tower, go back into Fayel and talk twice to the "unlucky woman" who paces past the shops on the main street. The first time she mentions that she's looking for a relative. The second time she says, "If only someone could treat this disease of mine…I could start looking for him."

Let's see—who can heal a disease? Go into Fayel's palace and talk to Michelle in the Chamber of Rites, then Connect to her and return to the unlucky woman. While Connected to Michelle, talk to the woman to heal her and to learn that her relative's name is Burenelice. You can disconnect from Michelle now, then go into the Fayel bar.

In the bar, talk to the bearded "customer" sitting alone at a table. He says that Burenelice moved to Kolton a month ago. Return to the unlucky woman with your report and she gives you a reward.

23 GUSTAV'S MEMORIES

QUEST CONTACT
Gina

AVAILABLE
After return from Vesplume Tower

REWARD Panacea

WALKTHROUGH

Once all the cutscenes are finished after your return from Vesplume Tower, go back into Fayel and enter the palace. Find Gina upstairs in the second floor hallway and talk to her. When she asks if you'd like to get to know Gustav better, answer, "Yes, I want to be his friend." She asks you to find the princess's practice bow; Gustav took it someplace, but Gina doesn't know where.

For a clue, go into Aya's nearby bedroom and talk to Aya. She tells you about a mountain outside the city where she first met Gustav. The bear often goes there, considering it a special place. If you talk to Gina again, she says Gustav has a habit of burying his important things in the ground.

Exit Fayel into the Oradian Mountains and fight your way up to the far northeast canyon. You'll see several glowing spots indicating buried objects on the way up, but the "worn bow" is the glowing spot indicated on the map. Pick it up and return it to Gina in Fayel to get your reward.

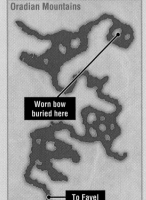

Oradian Mountains

Worn bow buried here

To Fayel

24 HALGITIAN MEMORIES

QUEST CONTACT
Matilda in Fayel house

AVAILABLE
When you first enter Fayel after destroying the Amber Chain

⭐ **REWARD** Lovebird

WALKTHROUGH

When you enter Fayel after destroying the Amber Chain in Kolton, and meeting King Miro in Kolton, Connect to Komachi next to the accessory stand on Fayel's main street. Find the house where Genma stands outside; it's not far from the city gate to the Oradian Mountains. Enter and talk to the old woman named Matilda. She reminisces about Halgita and longs for a bowl of Halgitian jelly.

Here's where Aya's Cooking IC skill comes in handy. Her specialty is sweets, and by Level 2 she can make Halgitian jelly. The recipe is 2 parts wood syrup, 1 part Zala rock salt, and 1 Nolaan potato. The potato, as its name implies, can be found/purchased in Nolaan, and the rock salt is in a couple of treasure chests in Port Zala. You have to cook up the wood syrup x 2 (2 parts honey, 1 part lauan wood), but that's one of Aya's recipes too. Once you have Halgitian jelly in your inventory, head back to Matilda and give it to her for your reward.

25 WARRIOR OF FAYEL

QUEST CONTACT
Aspiring warrior on the main street of Fayel

AVAILABLE
After the attack on Faina and Leif in Sapran

⭐ **REWARD** Poleaxe

WALKTHROUGH

After you return to Fayel from the tragedy in Sapran (the vermiform attack on Faina and Leif), Connect to Dominica inside the house behind the accessory stand (Touma and Komachi stand in front of it). Find the "aspiring warrior" pacing on the street by Genma, not far from the city gates, and talk to him. He issues a challenge: "Show me that the warriors of Fayel are the strongest!"

Now head off into the Oradian Dunes. Just outside of Fayel, veer to the right through the arch into the enclosed canyon where you'll find a powerful wendigo. Defeat this beast, then return to the aspiring warrior for your reward.

26 STRONGMAN COMPETITION

QUEST CONTACT
Samson the soldier patrolling the palace

AVAILABLE
After Saranda's attack on the emir in Kolton

⭐ **REWARD** Blaze axe

WALKTHROUGH

Connect with Balbagan in Fayel's bar and enter the palace. Talk to the guard named Samson patrolling the first floor. Samson says he lost a battle to a monster called a quetzalcoatl. If you can defeat one of these flying beasts, Samson says he'll give you a reward.

Now head out to the Oradian Dunes where the quetzalcoatl is a fairly common menace. But not just any quetzalcoatl will do. You must find and defeat one of the flyers, then return and talk to Samson again.

27 MR. RIGHT

QUEST CONTACT
General Emmie

AVAILABLE
After Saranda's attack on the emir in Kolton and subsequent scenes

⭐ **REWARD** Mysterious medicine

WALKTHROUGH

Enter the palace and go upstairs into the throne room. Talk to General Emmie, who happens to be Dominica's sister. Exit the palace and talk to Dominica inside the house behind the accessory stand on Fayel's main street (Touma and Komachi stand in front of it). Then talk to Aya in her private chambers on the second floor. Aya says Emmie never thinks about herself, then suggests introducing her to the Force men.

Connect to Aya and go talk to Emmie, who agrees the matchmaking idea. Now go Connect with each one of the adult guys in the Force (Eugene, Edward, Touma, Kristofer, Balbagan, Savio, and Kiriya), bringing them to Emmie one at a time. She tells you what she thinks of each one—but no match. Then talk to Emmie while unconnected; she apologizes for being too critical, then admits she's already seeing someone, but went along with meeting the Force guys because Aya seemed so excited about it. She apologizes for wasting your time and gives you a mysterious medicine.

PORT ZALA

28 LOST GIFT

QUEST CONTACT
Waitress in bar

AVAILABLE
After Cerulean Chain is destroyed

 **REWARD** Yellow berry powder

WALKTHROUGH

After you've destroyed the Cerulean Chain and returned to town, find Aya in the house nearest the town's exit to Oradian Dunes. Connect to Aya, then talk to the waitress in Port Zala's bar. When she asks Aya if she'll listen, answer "Yes." The waitress wants to tell the barkeeper her true feelings about him, and had a special gift for him. But the tsunami washed it away. She wants you to find it for her.

After the tsunami, a number of item bags were washed up all around Port Zala. Your quest here is to find the "strange-colored bag." Stay Connected to Aya! You'll find it almost directly across the street from the bar, behind the stack of barrels next to the mayor's house. Pick it up and, while still Connected to Aya, take it back to the waitress and talk to her to receive your reward. (She won't take the item from just Capell.)

29 LOST DENTURES

QUEST CONTACT
Toothless old man on Port Zala side street

AVAILABLE
After Cerulean Chain is destroyed

 **REWARD** 800 Fol

WALKTHROUGH

After you've destroyed the Cerulean Chain and returned to town, find the "toothless old man" about halfway up the side street that runs north from the town center. Talk to him—all he can say is, "Harumph." Not fun being old and toothless.

After the tsunami, a number of item bags were washed up all around Port Zala. Your quest here is to find the "dentures." Now head up the alley between the inn and the general store, where Michelle stands talking to the "repetitive woman." The dentures item bag is tucked behind the shelf holding the blankets and other wares. Pick it up and talk to the toothless old man. He gives you a nice cash reward…and his in-game title now becomes "old man with dentures."

30 LOST SECRET

QUEST CONTACT
Martin in the Port Zala bar

AVAILABLE
After Cerulean Chain is destroyed

⭐ **REWARD**   500 Fol

WALKTHROUGH

After you've destroyed the Cerulean Chain and returned to town, enter the Port Zala bar and talk to Martin, the fellow sitting alone at the big table. He tells you the tsunami washed away a "treasure" he'd been hiding. Could you find it for him? Martin doesn't give you much detail about the item.

After the tsunami, a number of item bags were washed up all around Port Zala. Your quest here is to find the "wooden box." Head toward the two warehouses on the waterfront (the area south of where the ship is docked). On the walkway between the warehouses, enter the door on the right as you head toward the water. You'll find the wooden box item bag in the back corner on a raised platform that holds some rolled rugs. Take it back to Martin for your cash reward.

31 LOST AMULET

QUEST CONTACT
Superstitious fisherman between Port Zala warehouses

AVAILABLE
After Cerulean Chain is destroyed

⭐ **REWARD**   1000 Fol

WALKTHROUGH

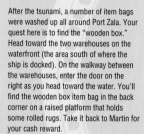

After you've destroyed the Cerulean Chain and returned to town, find the "superstitious fisherman" pacing at the end of the walkway between buildings in the warehouse area (south of where the ship is docked). Talk to him to learn that he's lost his amulet.

After the tsunami, a number of item bags were washed up all around Port Zala. Your quest here is to find the "piece of wood." This item bag is at the very end of the dock where the ship is moored, not far from Edward. Pick it up and take it to the superstitious fisherman to get a nice cash reward.

32 TSUNAMI JUNK PICKUP

QUEST CONTACT
Mayor's wife in the mayor's house

AVAILABLE
After Cerulean Chain is destroyed

⭐ **REWARD**
Red berry potion   Green berry potion
Blue berry potion   Gold berry potion
Yellow berry potion

WALKTHROUGH

Here's a great quest with lucrative rewards. After you've destroyed the Cerulean Chain and returned to town, go into the mayor's house (directly across from the inn) and talk to the "mayor's wife," the old woman by the fireplace. She wants to know if you'll help rebuild the town by collecting trash.

After the tsunami, a number of item bags were washed up all around Port Zala. (You can see their locations on the Port Zala map in the "Conflict" chapter of the story walkthrough.) Five of these bags contain items considered trash for the purposes of this quest. The items you seek are a doll, a battered notebook, a bouquet, a vase, and a rag.

Here's where you find them:

- *The battered notebook and bouquet can be found in the beach area, both not far from where the twins and Gustav hang out.*
- *The vase is against the building near the dock, not far from where Faina and Leif are standing. (See the provided shot.)*
- *The doll is in the darkened side alley between buildings in the warehouse area south of where the ship is docked.*
- *The rag is along the low wall leading to the dock, near where the "fatalistic old woman" paces back and forth.*

Take all five items back to the mayor's wife. She rewards you with a potion for each one you give her.

33 RAT EXTERMINATION

QUEST CONTACT
Ivan in the north fish warehouse

AVAILABLE
Return to Port Zala after meeting King Mino of Kolton

⭐ **REWARD**
Lux baton
Yellow berry potion

WALKTHROUGH

When you return to Port Zala after destroying the Amber Chain at the dais and meeting Kolton's king, go to the fish warehouse area south of the ship and enter the northern building—the one with rodents running around inside. Talk to Ivan, the guy pacing back and forth. He tells you the mice are causing problems with his cargo.

You have three choices of solution for this infestation. If you picked up all the tsunami-strewn item bags around town to help clean up for the "Tsunami Junk Pickup" side quest, you should have one with a "tail" inside. (If you don't have it yet, it's located on the beach not far from where the twins and Gustav hang out.) If you have it, talk to Ivan again to hand over the tail. As it turns out, the tail is a "famous mouse repellent." He gives you a lux baton in return.

34 BROKEN HEART

QUEST CONTACT	AVAILABLE
Waitress in Kolton bar	After Saranda's attack on the emir in Kolton

 REWARD Panacea
Silver fur pumps

WALKTHROUGH

Connect to Aya in the house near the Port Zala town gate and then talk to the waitress in the bar. She's upset because the man she loves, the bartender, is dating someone else: the girl at the inn's front desk. She wants you to find out why.

With Aya in tow, go talk to the girl in the Kolton inn. She explains how her relationship with the bartender got started. It turns out that Capell had something to do with it, indirectly, so she gives you a panacea in thanks. Report this to the waitress in the bar, and she thanks you with a pair of silver fur pumps.

KOLTON

35 SIMON IS MISSING, PT. 1

QUEST CONTACT	AVAILABLE
Oreg the patrolling guard	First arrival in Kolton, after defeating the invisible foe

 REWARD Quilt wristband

WALKTHROUGH

After the cutscenes following your defeat of the mysterious invisible enemy when you first arrive at Kolton, go to the southwest quadrant of Kolton and find Oreg, the guard patrolling the street. Talk to him to receive a broken pair of glasses that belonged to someone named Simon. Oreg thinks the monster killed Simon, and wants you to deliver the glasses to his family.

Now, head north through the gate and enter the house in the northwest quadrant of Kolton. Talk to Simon's grandmother to hand over the pair of broken glasses; she's upset, and won't speak to you after the first time. Talk to Simon's grandfather, who asks you to come back later. Now you must let some time pass before you return. Continue with other side quests, private events, or main story missions, then come back later.

When you return, Simon's grandmother tells you more about Simon and mentions the crimson orb pendant he always wore. If you find this pendant, she'll admit he's really gone. Now exit the town via the south gate leading down to the docks. Go back downstairs to the plaza where you defeated the invisible foe when you first arrived in Kolton. Look for the pulsing white glow on the ground, right in front of the round platform with the blue crystal lights. (See the screen shot to the right—the glow can be hard to see because of the falling snowflakes.)

Examine the glowing spot to pick up a "damaged pendant." Take this back to Simon's grandparents. (If you talk to Oreg on the way, he verifies that it is indeed Simon's pendant.) Talk to Simon's grandfather to receive your reward for helping them: a quilt wristband.

36 CONFECTION CONTEST

QUEST CONTACT	AVAILABLE
Senior apprentice in master confectioner's house	First arrival in Kolton, after defeating the invisible foe

 REWARD Wedding Special

WALKTHROUGH

After the cutscenes following your defeat of the mysterious invisible enemy when you first arrive at Kolton, go to the upstairs room of the Kolton inn and Connect to Aya. Exit the inn and head to the northeast quadrant of the city; enter the only house on that street. Talk to the woman designated "senior apprentice" and answer "Please continue" when she asks for Aya's help. Go back and forth between the apprentice and the master for details of their plan. They want Aya to be a judge of a baking contest. Answer "Yes, I will help you" when you get the second dialogue choice. The apprentice says they'll contact you at the inn when they're ready.

Now some time must pass, so go about your other business. Return after your first visit to Halgita and talk to the senior apprentice again. She shows Aya the contest poster and says she'll be in touch about the judging. Go on with the game; later, after your meeting with King Miro of Kolton, go back to the confectioner's house one more time and talk to the senior apprentice. She tells you the government ordered the event discontinued, and explains their new plans. Then talk to the master confectioner to get a reward—a slice of his famous Wedding Special. Eat it right away! It raises your entire party's MAX AGL stat by +2.

37 THE SURROGATE PARENT

QUEST CONTACT	AVAILABLE
Barkeeper in Kolton bar	First arrival in Kolton, after defeating the invisible foe

 REWARD Main gauche

WALKTHROUGH

After the cutscenes following your defeat of the mysterious invisible enemy when you first arrive at Kolton, go to the Kolton inn and Connect to Vic. Then head to the Kolton bar and talk to the barkeeper. He greets Vic in a friendly, familiar way. Disconnect from Vic and talk to the barkeeper again to learn that he's protective of Vic.

Later, after Edward has his vermiform episode and things get back to normal, you can return to the bar while Connected with Vic again, who now hangs out in an alley just west of the Kolton church. The bartender hands over a sweet weapon that used to belong to Vic's brother: a main gauche. Disconnect from Vic, then talk to the bartender again. Pay attention to the bartender's slip of the tongue about who Vic's older brother always looked out for. (Note: after you complete this side quest, Vic returns to his normal waiting location on the main floor of the Kolton inn.)

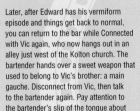

38 ASPIRING ANIMAL BREEDER

QUEST CONTACT
Aspiring animal breeder

AVAILABLE
After vermified Edward is stopped

REWARD Mercurius wristguard

WALKTHROUGH

Connect to Rico over in west Kolton, then go talk to the "aspiring animal breeder" in front of the bar in southwest Kolton. Since Rico can speak with animals, she wants him to ask her dog why he likes to run away.

Still Connected to Rico, go find the dog over on the east side of Kolton, near the light-stand not far from the inn. Talk to him to learn that he runs away because his owner cooks "weird-smelling food." Go back to the aspiring animal breeder in southwest Kolton and report the dog's reason. She's happy to make adjustments to his food, and the dog's happy now too.

The quest isn't done yet, however. After some time passes as you complete another story mission or two, Connect to Rico and return to the aspiring animal breeder. Her dog ran away again! As before, she wants you to ask the dog what's wrong. Go find the dog in east Kolton and talk to him. He says he runs away…for the exercise. Report this back to the aspiring animal breeder. She thanks you, but have you earned a reward yet? Not quite.

Let more time pass, then return to the aspiring animal breeder yet again. She tells you she's getting along great with her dog, finally, and she gives you a mercurius wristguard in return.

39 SIMON IS MISSING, PT. 2

QUEST CONTACT
Oreg the patrolling guard

AVAILABLE
Arrival in Kolton after you destroy the Amber Chain at the dais (also must complete "Simon Is Missing, Pt. 1")

REWARD Memoirs of a knight
AND
2 blue berry potions, 2 panacea, and 1 miraculous medicine

WALKTHROUGH

Talk to Oreg the guard patrolling in the southwest area of Kolton. You learn that the damage to Simon's pendant was from Edward's sword. The reason: Simon was the invisible monster you defeated back when you first arrived in Kolton! He isn't sure how to inform Simon's grandparents without hurting them.

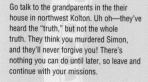

Go talk to the grandparents in the their house in northwest Kolton. Uh oh—they've heard the "truth," but not the whole truth. They think you murdered Simon, and they'll never forgive you! There's nothing you can do until later, so leave and continue with your missions.

Later, after you fight off the vermiforms in Sapran and return to Kolton, return and talk to Simon's grandfather, then Simon's grandmother. They acknowledge that they've made a terrible mistake and now know the truth about Simon. They give you a gift copy of memoirs of a knight. But that's not all! Make sure you talk to Oreg one more time to get a nice reward from him, too.

HALGITA

40 LOST MEMORIES

QUEST CONTACT
Karin the aristo on floor 3F

AVAILABLE
After you save Empress Svala from the Order assault on Halgita

REWARD Casandra ring

WALKTHROUGH

After the series of cutscenes triggered by your arrival at the throne room during the battle of Halgita, head up to west wing of floor 3F and find Karin the aristo in the hallway. Talk to her and she'll ask you to bring Eugene to her. Go down to the Temple of Veros on floor 1F and Connect to Eugene, then return to Karin and talk to her. She says that in the battle's chaos, Svala lost a ring. Karin suggests you look around the empress's room first, then ask soldiers about the item.

Head down the 3F hall and then up the stairs toward Svala's chambers. Before you enter, talk to the "imperial guard" on the right. She says animals were causing trouble during the post-battle cleanup—maybe one took the ring?

No need to search the royal chambers; it's time to start talking to animals. Release Eugene, head down to the Halgita marketplace, and find Rico at the bottom of the stairs. Connect with Rico and climb a few stairs to talk to Shibuff, the old dog (next to the polite old man" on the bench.) Shibuff tells Rico he saw a mouse "parading around with something" after the battle.

Other animals also provide tips, but let's cut to the chase. Head upstairs to the west residential wing of floor 2F. Enter the last of the four rooms on the left to find a mouse named "David, lover of shiny things." Talk to David, who reluctantly hands over the crested ring.

Let Rico go, head back downstairs to the Temple of Veros, and Connect to Eugene again. Take the crested ring back to Karin the aristo. (She won't acknowledge the ring from just Capell.) She tells you to present it to Svala. Go down the hall to the throne room and talk to Empress Svala to hand over the crested ring and receive your reward. The Casandra ring that Svala gives you is very valuable, giving you a +10 percent bonus whenever you acquire HP or MP.

41 DRESSED UP VIC

QUEST CONTACT

Lavie the fashion designer in room on floor 2F

AVAILABLE

After you save Empress Svala from the Order assault on Halgita

REWARD   Golden fur jacket

WALKTHROUGH

After the series of cutscenes triggered by your arrival at the throne room during the battle of Halgita, go to the Halgita marketplace and Connect with Vic by the accessory shop. Head up to the east residential wing on floor 2F and enter the first (southernmost) room to find Lavie, the fashion designer. Talk to her; she asks Vic to try on some clothes she designed. But you need to bring her the material she needs first.

First, she asks for 1 barkcloth and 3 golden wolf furs. You may have these materials in your inventory already. If not, you can buy barkcloth from Faina or the lively shopkeeper near the entrance to the Halgita marketplace. Golden wolf fur can be acquired as a rare drop by vallins out in the Oradian Dunes after the lunar rains starts falling there. Nail a vallin with a ranged attack to get the Player Advantage before you attack with your full party; if you do, the odds are good that you'll recover a golden wolf fur.

When you have everything you need, Connect to Vic again and take the items back to Lavie. She'll tell you to come back in a day's time. Go off and complete other tasks for awhile, then return while Connected to Vic and talk to Lavie again. She dresses up Vic, then gives you an armor clothing reward.

42 REBIRTH OF HALGITA

QUEST CONTACT

Owen, old nightwhisper in Temple of Veros

AVAILABLE

After you save Empress Svala from the Order assault on Halgita

REWARD   Blue berry powder   White berry powder   Symphonic baton   Flying swallow   Garuda hood

WALKTHROUGH

After the series of cutscenes triggered by your arrival at the throne room during the battle of Halgita, go to the Temple of Veros and talk to Owen, the old nightwhisper standing over on the walkbridge. He says reconstruction is ongoing after the Dreadknight's attack, but the shopkeepers need help. He suggests you ask them what they need.

Talk to the "lively shopkeeper" in the window just before you enter the Halgita marketplace. She says the shop owners need three pieces of lentesco wood. You may have enough already in your inventory, but if not, Faina sells lentesco wood for 400 Fol apiece. When you have three pieces of lentesco wood, go back to the lively shopkeeper and talk to her to hand over the wood. She gives you some blue berry powder as a token of her appreciation.

Next, go down and talk to the "hardworking weaponsmith" in the weapon shop down in the marketplace. He wants to repair his shop but he's short on cash. He requests a whopping 150,000 Fol in donations. That's a *lot* of money, of course, but if you can come up with the cash for him, he rewards you with a symphonic baton and a dagger called the flying swallow.

Finally, talk to the "quiet armor shopkeeper" at the armor shop. He wants you to get rid of the lizardmen on the route to Kolton who are blocking trade. Exit Halgita and follow the route through the Cobasna Timberlands to Kolton. At the western end of the forest, the final tunnel before you reach the teleport platform to Kolton is now filled with Drogo tribesmen, warriors and chiefs. If you eliminate all of these enemies and return to the quiet armor shopkeeper, he gives you a garuda hood.

43 THE LOST KATANA

QUEST CONTACT
Swordmaster Shido

AVAILABLE
After you save Empress Svala from the Order assault on Halgita

REWARD Herosong

WALKTHROUGH

After the series of cutscenes triggered by your run to the throne room during the battle of Halgita, go into the last open house at the western end of Halgita marketplace and Connect to Komachi. Go up to the east residential wing of floor 2F and talk to Swordmaster Shido, who stands in the hallway near the stairs. He says he lost the special katana he got from Master Shinkai. Can you help him find it?

Still Connected to Komachi, find Shinkai, an aristo, in the library on 2F. When you talk to him, he asks you to make a replica. The materials required are one lizard fang, one rachnuvus cloth, and one titanium metal.

You very likely have a lizard fang from traveling in the Cobasna Timberlands, and you can buy the titanium metal from Faina near the Temple of Veros entrance, or from the lively shopkeeper near the Halgita marketplace entrance. But getting rachnuvus cloth is trickier. When you travel to the dais looking for the Amber Chain, you can find rachnuvus cloth in a hidden treasure chest in the rachnuvus caves.

Once you get all three materials, find Edward in the library on 2F (he stands not far from Shinkai) and Connect to him. Use Edward's "Blacksmith" IC skill to craft the "Replica of a Kylin Sword." Once it's forged, you must Connect to Komachi again and return to Swordmaster Shido to hand over the replica to Shinkai. In return for your help, he gives you a herosong katana.

44 PROMISED DOLL

QUEST CONTACT
Faina near Temple of Veros doors

AVAILABLE
After you destroy the Amber Chain

REWARD
Capell doll
Faina doll
Leif doll

WALKTHROUGH

After you return from destroying the Amber Chain at the dais, talk to Faina, who stands in the 1F hall near the Temple of Veros entry doors. She asks you to bring her three pieces of damask cloth.

Where to get it? Michelle can create damask cloth when her IC skill reaches Level 4. But damask isn't cheap; each piece requires 2 gold metal, 2 silver metal, and 1 metetite, so multiply each times 3 for the amount of cloth you need for Faina. You can buy the gold and metetite materials from the lively shopkeeper, but silver is harder to come by in Halgita if you don't have it already.

45 VERMIFORM PROPAGATION

QUEST CONTACT
Shinkai the aristo in the library

AVAILABLE
After you see the "lunar rain falling on Fayel" scene from Port Zala

REWARD Laughter

WALKTHROUGH

Connect to Touma inside the room at the far west end of the floor 3F hallway, then go to the Halgita library on floor 2F and talk to Shinkai the aristo. He's getting reports of vermiform monsters around the city, and he wants you to kill all you encounter.

Now head out into the Cobasna Timberlands and start hunting vermiforms; they're all over the jungle. Keep defeating them until you can find no more. A good tip is to return to Halgita, then exit again. If the quest is still ongoing, a vermiform is always lurking nearby just as you arrive in the timberlands. But if you exit Halgita and no vermiform is there on the first trail, you've cleared the jungle. Go back into Halgita and Connect with Touma, then return to Shinkai in the library for your reward: a deadly katana blade for Touma called "laughter."

46 SHADOW OF VERMIFORM

QUEST CONTACT
Sara the flower girl in the Halgita entry hall

AVAILABLE
After you see the "lunar rain falling on Fayel" scene from Port Zala

REWARD 50,000 Fol!

WALKTHROUGH

This quest has a very lucrative payoff, so make sure you give it a try. Talk to Sara the flower girl in the Halgita entry hall on floor 1F. She's curious about what a vermiform carries with it, and wants you to check. It seems like a simple request, but it's a tough task to complete.

Now head out into the wilds of the Cobasna Timberlands and hunt for a special vermiform that drops an item called the "blood-stained seal." You'll find the jungle filled with vermiforms, and that's good—you need a bunch of vermiform kills in order to complete the "Vermiform Propagation" side quest anyway. If you follow the route you took to Kiriya's hut earlier in the main story missions, you'll nail the vermiform with the blood-stained seal eventually, most likely in the big intersection where you fought the orthros. Bring this seal back to Sara and get a cool 50,000 Fol as a reward!

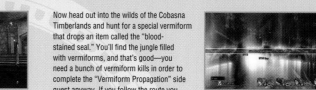

ITEMS & ITEM CREATION

Items come from many sources. You'll find Fol from treasure chests and fallen enemies throughout the game—this currency can be used to buy most items from shops. Defeated foes also frequently drop items. The Item Creation system can also make just about anything in the game. The best pieces of gear cannot be purchased or found as battle spoils—they come from treasure chests late in the game, or from the Item Creation system. With this system, characters can attempt to fuse items and materials into a superior result. There are five different crafts. The following table shows the characters that are skilled in each craft, as well as their initial IC level.

Craft	Artisan
Enchanting	Capell (Lv.1, acquired in Sapran)
Forging	Eugene (Lv.2), Sigmund (Lv.3), Edward (Lv.2), Kristofer (Lv.4)
Alchemy	Michelle (Lv.2), Kiriya (Lv.4), Seraphina (Lv.4), Sigmund (Lv.3)

Craft	Artisan
Cooking	Aya (Lv.2), Rucha (Lv.1), Dominica (Lv.3), Sigmund (Lv.2)
Writing	Rico (Lv.1), Savio (Lv.3), Sigmund (Lv.3)

All of these characters except Sigmund gain new craft recipes by increasing their IC level. This is accomplished simply by making many items. The higher the level of the recipe, the more it contributes. However, higher-level recipes are also more likely to fail, breaking some of the ingredients. For this reason, you might want to save the game before attempting Item Creation with rare ingredients, like when making the best weapons and armor in the game—most of which are obtained through crafting, rather than from a treasure chest or foe.

Weapon	Name	Description	Value	Rarity	ATK	HIT	DEF	AGL	INT	LUC	Effects	Special Acquisition
	Gladius	A light thin blade perfect for a beginner swordsman. ①	②	③	150	10	④	--	--	--	⑤	⑥

Forging

Rarity	Creation Result	1st Ingredient	Qty.	2nd Ingredient	Qty.	3rd Ingredient	Qty.	Sigmund IC Lv.	Edward IC Lv.	Kristofer IC Lv.
1	Cork Bow ⑦	Cork Wood	2	-- ⑧	--	--	--	1	1 ⑨	1

① **Name & Description:** *As you might guess, this is the name and description of the item in question.*

② **Value:** *For items available in stores, this is the cost. For all items, the amount of Fol received for selling the item is half this number.*

③ **Rarity:** *Indicates how exclusive and hard-to-come-by an item is. Items with higher rarity numbers come from very specific sources only (say, beating a particular boss) or from higher-level Item Creation recipes involving rare ingredients. Wearing pieces of gear with higher rarity values also helps increase grades during multiple party battles.*

④ **Stats:** *The attributes granted by an item. ATK and HIT determine melee effectiveness, while DEF and AGL dictate how much damage is taken from melee attacks, or whether it's avoided altogether through guarding. INT determines both magic effectiveness and magic defense. LUC is a hidden stat, granted only by certain accessories—increasing luck has a positive effect on quality of enemy drops, critical hits, guarding, and survival.*

⑤ **Effects:** *Special bonuses or penalties granted or accrued by an item are listed here.*

⑥ **Special Acquisition:** *The majority of items in the game are available in shops, or can be made through Item Creation. However, some items are only available as loot from certain monsters or spoils from certain chests, and others can only be crafted with IC after certain parameters are fulfilled. Special locations or conditions, if any, are listed here.*

⑦ **Item Creation Result:** *The result from a given IC recipe. This is the item you'll receive if the synthesis is successful!*

⑧ **Ingredients Needed:** *These are the items and quantities needed to attempt a particular IC recipe.*

⑨ **Crafter & Skill Level Required:** *Not everyone learns every trade, nor can everyone within a given trade make all items available from it. These columns note who can go to work on which recipe, and what IC Lv. he or she must attain as a prerequisite (6 is the highest level).*

WEAPONS

ONE-HANDED SWORDS

Capell

Sigmund

Weapon of choice for the Liberator and his imposter, one-handed swords have great stats, effects, and battle skills. Edward is the finest crafter of these blades—bump him up to IC Lv.6, and *do not* sell the emblazoned sword in order to make an azureal blade. The Seraphic Gate is also home to several elite swords. Don't miss the instrumental sword, with its unique sound effects, located in Castle Valette inside a chest that requires Honeysuckle to access.

Weapon	Name	Description	Value	Rarity	ATK	HIT	DEF	AGL	INT	Effects	Special Acquisition
	Dented Sword	An old sword covered with dents.	50	1	25	10	--	--	--	Unbreakable	--
	Shortsword	A bronze weapon often used by warriors in their first battle.	100	1	45	10	--	--	--	--	--
	Broadsword	A bronze weapon that can inflict great damage with its heavy frame.	250	1	100	10	--	--	--	--	--
	Gladius	A light iron blade perfect for a beginner swordsman.	500	2	150	10	--	--	--	--	--
	Longsword	A sturdy and dependable iron blade used by cavalry forces throughout the land.	800	2	195	20	--	--	--	--	--
	Scimitar	A curved sword made of copper that is often used in Fayel, where it is called a shamshir.	2000	3	260	20	--	--	--	--	--
	Hunting Sword	A shortsword that nobles of Burguss often carry with them on deer hunts.	1500	2	210	30	--	--	--	Critical hit rate +3%	--
	Falchion	A steel broadsword known as a falx in Fayel, where it is standard army-issue equipment.	3200	3	315	50	--	--	--	--	--
	Rapier	A titanium rapier with a pointed tip that makes it ideal for lunging.	5500	3	450	30	--	--	--	--	--
	Silver Sword	A silver longsword used in the lunar rite. It is also useful for fending off demons.	10000	4	500	--	--	--	--	MP Regeneration 1%	--
	Ceramic Sword	A ceramic longsword forged in Kolton. Its material is light yet durable.	7200	4	530	30	--	--	--	--	--
	Prismatite Sword	A prismatite longsword with a navy-colored blade that can withstand great stress.	15000	5	570	45	--	--	--	--	--
	Aqua Blade	A mercurius longsword imbued with the element of water and used by the Casandran cavalry.	25000	5	640	45	--	--	--	Water attack	--
	Crescent Sword	A longsword adorned with lunatite. Enhances the wielder's lunaglyph powers.	34000	6	670	30	--	--	--	--	--
	Holy Sword	A deadly lunatite-adorned sword with a glyph engraved into the blade.	40000	6	700	35	--	--	--	MP +10%	--
	Instrumental Sword	A blade designed with musical qualities. Creates a beautiful sound with each swing.	45000	6	800	30	--	--	--	Strange noise	Castle Valette Treasure Chest (Honeysuckle)
	Crystallite Blade	A highly refined crystallite longsword covered in intricate engravings.	50000	7	750	40	--	--	--	Critical hit rate +3%	--
	Eclipse Sword	A longsword with amarlista fragments embedded in its blade. Forged by unblesseds.	70000	8	820	50	--	--	--	Silence attack, MP +10%	--

Weapon	Name	Description	Value	Rarity	ATK	HIT	DEF	AGL	INT	Effects	Special Acquisition
	Emblazoned Sword	A silver-colored sword bearing the crest of Saruleus. Given to those King Nestor deems worthy.	10000	8	80	30	--			--	Story Event
	Seven-Star Blade	A straight sword marked with seven stars. Once worn by ancient Halgitian regents.	150000	9	950	50	--			--	Seraphic Gate
	Ancient Sword	An ancient sword left behind by the creator. Its sharp blade is a match for any spell or magic.	200000	9	1050	--				--	Must complete Private Event "Secret of Smithery" to make
	Gram	According to Casandran mythology, this blade is from the gods. Its name means "wrath."	320000	9	1800	50	--	--	--	Critical hit rate +3%	Must have access to Seraphic Gate to make
	Celestial Sword	A blade forged by Veros. Drains the energy of the wielder in exchange for divine power.	380000	10	2500	30	--			HP drain 1%, MP drain 1%	Seraphic Gate
	Balmung	A sword created to celebrate the birth of King Volsung's child that vanished along with the prince.	450000	10	2000	30	--	--		--	Seraphic Gate
	Azureal Blade	The true form of the emblazoned sword.	500000	10	2600	50	--			MP Regeneration 1%, MP +10%, HP +10%	Must have access to Seraphic Gate to make

Sword Forging

Rarity	Creation Result	1st Ingredient	Qty.	2nd Ingredient	Qty.	3rd Ingredient	Qty.	Sigmund IC Lv.	Edward IC Lv.
1	Shortsword	Bronze Metal	1	--	--	--	--	1	1
1	Broadsword	Bronze Metal	2	Shortsword	1	--	--	1	1
2	Gladius	Iron Metal	2	Broadsword	1	--	--	2	1
2	Longsword	Iron Metal	2	Granite	1	Shortsword	1	3	2
2	Hunting Sword	Iron Metal	2	Lauan Wood	2	Gladius	1	--	2
3	Scimitar	Copper Metal	2	Granite	1	Hunting Sword	1	--	2
3	Falchion	Steel Metal	2	Granite	1	Scimitar	1	--	3
3	Rapier	Titanium Metal	2	Marble	1	Falchion	1	--	3
4	Silver Sword	Silver Metal	2	Marble	1	Longsword	1	--	3
4	Ceramic Sword	Ceramic	2	Copper Metal	1	Longsword	1	--	4
5	Prismatite Sword	Prismatite Metal	2	Ceramic	1	Silver Sword	1	--	4
5	Aqua Blade	Mercurius Metal	2	Metetite	1	Ceramic Sword	1	--	4
6	Crescent Sword	Lunatite	2	Mercurius Metal	1	Silver Sword	1	--	5
6	Holy Sword	Lunatite	2	Holy Water	2	Crescent Sword	1	--	5
7	Crystallite Blade	Crystallite Metal	2	Hearthstone	1	Holy Sword	1	--	5
8	Eclipse Sword	Amarlista	2	Crystallite Metal	1	Instrumental Sword	1	--	6
9	Ancient Sword	Atlantis Metal	3	Amarlista	1	Seven-Star Blade	1	--	6
9	Gram	Atlantis Metal	3	Quartz	1	Aqua Blade	1	--	6
10	Azureal Blade	Amarlista	2	Gram	1	Emblazoned Sword	1	--	6

*Eugene and Kristofer cannot forge swords.

BOWS

Aya

Kristofer

Bows allow quick attacks from a distance. Crafting the best bow requires that Kristofer has IC Lv.6. Another ultimate bow is found in the Seraphic Gate.

Weapon	Name	Description	Value	Rarity	ATK	HIT	DEF	AGL	INT	Effects	Special Acquisition
	Worn Bow	A bow with a frayed string.	30	1	20	10	--	--	--	Unbreakable	--
	Cork Bow	A cork bow whose simple design makes it easy to draw.	80	1	40	15	--	--	--	--	--
	Tracker's Bow	A lauan bow whose light weight makes it a favorite among hunters.	480	2	70	20	--	--	--	--	--
	Laminated Bow	A layered lauan bow with improved power and range.	800	2	110	20	--	--	--	--	--
	Iron Bow	An iron bow designed for increased accuracy and range.	1800	3	130	30	--				--

Weapon	Name	Description	Value	Rarity	ATK	HIT	DEF	AGL	INT	Effects	Special Acquisition
	Backed Bow	A balsa bow reinforced for improved power and range.	2600	3	155	30	--	--	--	--	--
	Hunting Bow	An ebony bow that is light and easy to draw. A favorite among hunters.	4500	4	180	--	--	--	--	--	--
	Longbow	An ebony longbow that requires a great amount of strength to draw properly.	6500	4	230	30	--	--	--	--	--
	Great Bow	A large lux bow. More versatile than a longbow, but harder to handle.	12000	5	245	30	--	--	--	--	--
	Pointer	A titanium bow whose elaborate aiming mechanism gives it great accuracy.	20000	5	275	45	--	--	--	--	--
	Composite Bow	A large composite bow chiefly made from lentesco.	35000	6	300	30	--	--	--	--	--
	Broken Heart	A large malus bow that is effective against mages. The target loses magic power.	40000	7	300	30	--	--	--	MP absorb attack	
	Moon Bow	A placidus longbow that fires destructive, lunatite arrows.	50000	7	330	40	--	--	--	MP +10%	--
	Blaze Bow	A golden bow imbued with the element of fire that shoots deadly flaming arrows.	38000	6	290	30	--	--	--	Fire attack	--
	Commander Bow	A pius longbow reinforced with Cobasna cane vines. The best bow in Halgita.	65000	8	350	40	--	--	--	--	--
	Sagittarian Bow	Prototype of a large bow that is in development for use by Royal Burguss Archers.	85000	8	370	30	--	--	--		Must complete Private Event "Secret of Smithery" to make
	Royal Bow	A Halgitian royal family heirloom said to never miss its mark.	180000	9	390	60	--	--	--	Critical hit rate +3%	Must complete Private Event "Secret of Smithery" to make
	Kolt Bow	A metal bow created using the most advanced techniques of Kolton's weaponsmiths.	250000	9	470	40	--	--	--	--	Must have access to Seraphic Gate to make
	Sarnga	A bow of light once used by the creator. Its arrows are aided in flight by magical forces.	360000	10	830	40	--	--	--	MP +10%	Seraphic Gate
	Avifir Bow	A divine bow of Fayel said to contain the power of Avifir. Reduces its victims to ashes.	500000	10	1370	50	--	--	--	Fire attack, MP consumption -20%	Must have access to Seraphic Gate to make

Bow Forging

Rarity	Creation Result	1st Ingredient	Qty.	2nd Ingredient	Qty.	3rd Ingredient	Qty.	Eugene IC Lv.	Sigmund IC Lv.	Kristofer IC Lv.
1	Cork Bow	Cork Wood	2	--	--	--	--	1	1	1
2	Tracker's Bow	Lauan Wood	2	Cork Bow	1	--	--	1	1	1
2	Laminated Bow	Lauan Wood	3	Tracker's Bow	1	--	--	2	2	1
3	Iron Bow	Lauan Wood	2	Iron Metal	1	Cork Bow	1	2	3	2
3	Backed Bow	Balsa Wood	2	Iron Metal	2	Laminated Bow	1	3	--	2
4	Hunting Bow	Ebony Wood	2	Granite	1	Laminated Bow	1	--	--	2
4	Longbow	Ebony Wood	2	Marble	1	Hunting Bow	1	--	--	3
5	Great Bow	Lux Wood	2	Marble	1	Longbow	1	--	--	3
5	Pointer	Titanium Metal	2	Ceramic	1	Iron Bow	1	--	--	3
6	Composite Bow	Lentesco Wood	2	Silver Metal	2	Backed Bow	1	--	--	4
6	Blaze Bow	Blaze Metal	2	Gold Metal	1	Pointer	1	--	--	5
7	Moon Bow	Placidus Wood	2	Lunatite	1	Composite Bow	1	--	--	4
7	Broken Heart	Malus Wood	2	Silver Metal	1	Blaze Bow	1	--	--	4
8	Commander Bow	Pius Wood	2	Vine	4	Great Bow	1	--	--	5
8	Sagittarian Bow	Mercurius Metal	3	Quartz	1	Composite Bow	1	--	--	5
9	Royal Bow	Malus Wood	2	Pius Wood	2	Commander Bow	1	--	--	6
9	Kolt Bow	Crystallite Metal	3	Amarlista	1	Moon Bow	1	--	--	6
10	Avifir Bow	Pius Wood	3	Eye of Avifir	1	Vermillion Wing Piece	1	--	--	6

*Edward cannot forge bows.

STAFFS

Eugene

Savio

Staffs give manly mages another offensive option outside of their spells. The holy staff and the ancient staff both have effects that greatly enhance Eugene's casting ability. Eugene at IC Lv.6 can make the even more powerful caduceus.

Weapon	Name	Description	Value	Rarity	ATK	HIT	DEF	AGL	INT	Effects	Special Acquisition
	Bent Staff	A staff bent from constant use by its portly owner.	35	1	15	10	--	--	60	Unbreakable	--
	Beginner Staff	A cork staff often used by aspiring mages.	150	1	25	10	--	--	150	--	--
	Acolyte Staff	A lauan staff given to priests who have begun their training.	350	2	30	10	--	--	180	--	--
	Iron Staff	A strong iron staff used by priests who have excelled in their training.	600	2	50	10	--	--	200	--	--
	Preaching Staff	A balsa staff made light for waving around when preaching.	1500	3	80	10	--	--	210	--	--
	Ebony Staff	An ebony staff made strong for long journeys.	3000	3	120	10	--	--	230	--	--
	Cerebral Staff	A staff made with benevolence. It heals the soul and raises the spirit of the wielder.	8000	4	160	10	--	--	260	MP +10%	Complete Side Quest "Straw"
	Bishop Staff	A lux staff wielded by bishops as a symbol of their authority.	5000	4	150	10	--	--	300	--	--
	Light Staff	A silver staff. Purified by a high bishop, it has the power to repel evil spirits.	8500	5	200	10	--	--	315	--	--
	Pilgrim Staff	A lentesco staff made sturdy to withstand the long journeys taken by pilgrims.	12000	5	215	10	--	--	350	--	--
	Might Staff	A malus staff. Reduces reliance on magic by raising the wielder's strength.	40000	7	350	30	--	--	420	ATK +5%	--
	Glory Staff	A placidus staff with the power to ward off evil.	23000	6	250	10	--	--	400	--	--
	Holy Staff	A placidus staff imbued with holy power by a priest over a long period of time.	30000	6	280	30	--	--	450	MP Regeneration 1%	--
	Dominance Staff	A lunatite staff used as a symbol of power by those in authority.	42000	7	310	30	--	--	500	--	--
	Sage Staff	A pius staff carried by sages.	68000	8	380	10	--	--	550	--	--
	Seeker Staff	A staff wielded by those in search of themselves. Has the power to dispel worries.	80000	8	410	10	--	--	600	--	Must complete Private Event "Secret of Smithery" to make
	Ancient Staff	A staff which priests serving under Claridians use to control the flow of magic.	180000	9	500	30	--	--	780	Casting time down	Must complete Private Event "Secret of Smithery" to make
	Moon Staff	A staff with a fragment of the moon embedded in it. Amplifies the wielder's lunaglyph power.	260000	9	560	30	--	--	1000	Earth damage +10%	Must have access to Seraphic Gate to make
	Discipline Staff	A staff with powerful magic created to punish criminals guilty of terrible sins.	380000	10	600	30	--	--	1300	--	Seraphic Gate
	Caduceus	A staff of two entwined snakes. Heals the injured and revives the dead.	500000	10	700	30	--	--	1450	Earth damage +30%, HP Regeneration 3%, MP Regeneration 1%	Must have access to Seraphic Gate to make

Staff Forging

Rarity	Creation Result	1st Ingredient	Qty.	2nd Ingredient	Qty.	3rd Ingredient	Qty.	Eugene IC Lv.	Sigmund IC Lv.
1	Beginner Staff	Cork Wood	2	--		--		1	1
2	Acolyte Staff	Lauan Wood	2	Beginner Staff	1	--		1	1
2	Iron Staff	Iron Metal	2	Acolyte Staff	1	--		1	2
3	Preaching Staff	Balsa Wood	2	Holy Water	1	Acolyte Staff	1	2	3
3	Ebony Staff	Ebony Wood	2	Sandstone	1	Acolyte Staff	1	2	--
4	Cerebral Staff	Ebony Wood	2	Granite	1	Preaching Staff	1	2	--
4	Bishop Staff	Lux Wood	2	Holy Water	2	Iron Staff	1	3	--
5	Light Staff	Silver Metal	2	Granite	1	Bishop Staff	1	3	--
5	Pilgrim Staff	Lentesco Wood	2	Marble	1	Ebony Staff	1	3	--
6	Glory Staff	Placidus Wood	2	Holy Water	3	Light Staff	1	4	--
6	Holy Staff	Placidus Wood	3	Holy Water	4	Glory Staff	1	4	--
7	Might Staff	Malus Wood	1	Metetite	1	Pilgrim Staff	1	4	--
7	Dominance Staff	Lunatite	2	Hearthstone	1	Light Staff	1	5	--
8	Sage Staff	Pius Wood	2	Lunatite	1	Pilgrim Staff	1	5	--
8	Seeker Staff	Pius Wood	2	Quartz	1	Sage Staff	1	5	--
9	Ancient Staff	Atlantis Metal	1	Amarlita	1	Holy Staff	1	6	--
9	Moon Staff	Atlantis Metal	2	Lunatite	2	Ancient Staff	1	6	--
10	Caduceus	Atlantis Metal	2	Amarlista	2	Moon Staff	2	6	--

*Edward and Kristofer cannot forge staffs.

GRIMOIRES

Michelle

Seraphina *

Grimoires are powerful tomes that enhance the user's magic power. Savio can learn to write most of the better ones, but the strongest book, "Genesis," is in the Seraphic Gate.

	Name	Description	Value	Rarity	ATK	HIT	DEF	AGL	INT	Effects	Special Acquisition
	Moth-Eaten Grimoire	A tattered mage's book. Falling apart due to the ravages of insect infestation."	20	1	1	10	--	--	80	Unbreakable	--
	"The World of Magic"	A mage's book for beginners. Teaches the basics of lunaglyphs and magic.	100	1	5	10	--	--	185	--	--
	"The Art of Making Tea"	An in-depth guide to making the perfect cup of tea.	260	2	10	10	--	--	200	--	--
	"Dimensional Journey"	A mage's book about the magic and monsters in a realm beyond the world with two moons.	550	2	18	10	--	--	220	--	--
	"Romancing for Women"	A love manual for women. Reveals the science behind snagging the perfect guy.	1400	3	25	10	--	--	230	Charm attack	--
	"The Shadow Codex"	A mage's book compiled in Casandra. A valuable piece of work from a lost kingdom.	2400	3	30	10	--	--	250	--	--
	Michelle's Diary	An embarrassing diary containing Michelle's feelings for Sigmund.	3000	4	35	10	--	--	300	--	--
	"Fear of the Unseen"	A book full of unconfirmed stories about mysterious spirits.	4500	4	40	10	--	--	350	--	--
	"The Forbidden Grimoire"	A mage's book said to contain magic so powerful it could destroy the caster.	10000	5	46	10	--	--	380	MP +10%, DEF-10%	--
	"Endless Tale"	A book about a boy's endless adventures. Its voluminous text makes for an excellent weapon.	14500	5	52	10	--	--	420	--	--
	"Seven Secrets"	An ancient book containing the seven secrets of the gods preceding Veros.	19500	6	65	30	--	--	450	--	--
	"Science of Magic"	Kolton research paper on experiments combining magic with science.	35000	6	70	30	--	--	500	Aether damage +10%	--

	Name	Description	Value	Rarity	ATK	HIT	DEF	AGL	INT	Effects	Special Acquisition
	"End of Ages"	A banned book written in detail about the end of the creator's reign.	40000	7	83	10	--	--	580	MP Regeneration 1%	--
	"Apocalypse of Darkness"	A companion book to "Apocalypse of Light." Increases air and water magic.	50000	7	95	30	--	--	650	Water damage +30%	--
	"Apocalypse of Light"	A companion book to "Apocalypse of Darkness." Increases earth and fire magic.	66000	8	100	30	--	--	710	Aether damage +30%	--
	"The Book of Judgment"	The confessions of a lauded saint and his abandonment of his god for the black arts.	72000	8	120	10	--	--	760	--	--
	"Papyrus Magicus"	A book on the secret art of manipulating paper.	165000	9	150	30	--	--	830	MP +10%	--
	"The Tales of Volsung"	A collection of tales from the young King Volsung's epic adventures.	260000	9	200	30	--	--	1100	--	Must have access to Seraphic Gate to make
	"Tale of Two Moons"	A book about the truth behind Veros and the period before the crimson and blue moon.	450000	10	250	30	--	--	1620	MP Regeneration 1%	Must have access to Seraphic Gate to make
	"Genesis"	A book about the creation of the world. Gives its bearer limitless wisdom.	500000	10	300	30	--	--	1850	Magic damage +10%, Casting time down	Seraphic Gate

Grimoire Writing

Rarity	Creation Result	1st Ingredient	Qty.	2nd Ingredient	Qty.	3rd Ingredient	Qty.	Rico IC Lv.	Savio IC Lv.	Sigmund IC Lv.
1	"The World of Magic"	Papyrus Paper	1	Bat Wing	1	--	--	1	1	1
2	"The Art of Making Tea"	Papyrus Paper	2	Fresh Herb	1	--	--	1	1	2
2	"Dimensional Journey"	"The World of Magic"	1	Monster Claw	2	Lentesco Wood	1	2	1	2
3	"Romancing for Women"	"The Art of Making Tea"	1	Papyrus Paper	2	Lentesco Wood	1	2	2	3
3	"The Shadow Codex"	"Dimensional Journey"	1	Pulp Paper	1	Lentesco Wood	1	2	2	3
4	Michelle's Diary	--	--	--	--	--	--	--	--	--
4	"Fear of the Unseen"	"The Shadow Codex"	1	Papyrus Paper	2	Writer's Quill	1	3	3	--
5	"The Forbidden Grimoire"	"The Shadow Codex"	1	Pulp Paper	2	Writer's Quill	1	3	3	--
5	"Endless Tale"	"Fear of the Unseen"	1	Pulp Paper	3	Writer's Quill	1	4	3	--
6	"Seven Secrets"	"The Forbidden Grimoire"	1	Parchment	1	Writer's Quill	1	4	4	--
6	"Science of Magic"	Parchment	2	Prismatite Ring	1	Writer's Quill	1	4	4	--
7	"End of Ages"	"Seven Secrets"	1	Parchment	2	Writer's Quill	2	5	4	--
7	"Apocalypse of Darkness"	Lentesco Wood	1	Rachnuvus Cloth	1	Clerk's Quill	1	5	5	--
8	"Apocalypse of Light"	Salamander Skin	1	Ceramic Ring	1	Clerk's Quill	1	5	5	--
8	"The Book of Judgment"	"End of Ages"	1	Feeble Cloth	1	Clerk's Quill	2	6	5	--
9	"Papyrus Magicus"	Halgitian Paper	4	Genius's Quill	1	--	--	6	5	--
9	"The Tales of Volsung"	"Endless Tale"	2	Michelle's Diary	1	Genius's Quill	1	--	6	--
10	"Tale of Two Moons"	"The Tales of Volsung"	1	"Papyrus Magicus"	1	Genius's Quill	2	--	6	--

GREATSWORDS

Edward

Dominica

Heavier counterpart to one-handers, greatswords require both hands to manipulate. They are bested in power only by axes and claws. Edward crafts the better greatswords, including the incredible Karathos blade at IC Lv.6. The hrotti, almost as powerful, can be found in the Seraphic Gate.

	Name	Description	Value	Rarity	ATK	HIT	DEF	AGL	INT	Effects	Special Acquisition
	Rusted Greatsword	A rusted and damaged greatsword.	65	1	100	10	--	--	--	Unbreakable	--
	Hand-and-a-Half Sword	A bronze greatsword with a long hilt. Can be held with either one or two hands.	200	1	150	10	--	--	--	--	--
	Bastard Sword	A copper greatsword designed for both slashing and lunging.	1000	2	240	20	--	--	--	--	--
	Two-Handed Sword	A copper greatsword requiring the use of both hands. Unleashes devastating blows.	2500	3	260	20	--	--	--	--	--

	Name	Description	Value	Rarity	ATK	HIT	DEF	AGL	INT	Effects	Special Acquisition
	Greatsword	An iron greatsword used by many swordsmen due to its easy handling.	600	2	200	20	--	--	--	--	--
	Claymore	A titanium greatsword. Surprisingly light for its large size.	4000	3	350	20	--	--	--	--	--
	Shamshir	A titanium greatsword with a long curved blade.	7500	4	380	30	--	--	--	--	--
	Estoc	A two-handed steel greatsword made for lunging and piercing armor.	9300	4	410	30	--	--	--	--	--
	Katzbalger	A steel greatsword with fine craftsmanship favored by Kolton mercenaries.	16000	5	440	30	--	--	--	--	--
	Flamberge	A silver greatsword. Its flame-like blade is deceivingly deadly.	22000	5	560	30	--	--	--	--	--
	Defender	A greatsword whose size and shape allow it to be used as a shield in combat.	40000	6	530	30	--	--	--	Autoguard rate +3%	--
	Prismatite Blade	A prismatite greatsword. Shining a brilliant purple, the blade is extremely sharp.	32000	6	600	30	--	--	--	--	--
	Crescent Blade	A lunatite greatsword. Engraved with a lunaglyph, its blade can cut through anything.	58000	7	730	30	--	--	--	--	--
	Atlantis Blade	An atlantis greatsword whose flawless blade never rusts or nicks.	200000	9	1000	30	--	--	--		Must complete Private Event "Secret of Smithery" to make
	Dullahan	A cursed sword said to have used to behead many men. Boasts great strength and reach.	80000	8	800	--	--	--	--	--	--
	Braveheart	The greatsword of a legendary mercenary who faced and won many battles.	68000	7	760	30	--	--	--	--	--
	Ascalon	A greatsword of Georgio, a hero from Burguss. Venerated as a holy sword after his death.	280000	9	1850	30	--	--	--	HP Regeneration 3%	Must have access to Seraphic Gate to make
	Caladbolg	A greatsword from Kolton mythology. Said to call forth lightning with each hit.	380000	9	2000	30	--	--	--	Paralysis attack	Must have access to Seraphic Gate to make
	Hrotti	A sword once guarded by Fafnir, the ravager of Casandra. Taken by King Volsung after his victory.	450000	10	2500	30	--	--	--	--	Seraphic Gate
	Karathos Blade	Volsung's sword containing the power of Karathos. Its watery blade cuts all before it.	500000	10	3050	30	--	--	--	HP absorb attack, MP absorb attack	Must have access to Seraphic Gate to make

Greatsword Forging

Rarity	Creation Result	1st Ingredient	Qty.	2nd Ingredient	Qty.	3rd Ingredient	Qty.	Sigmund IC Lv.	Edward IC Lv.
1	Hand-and-a-Half Sword	Bronze Metal	3	--	--	--	--	1	1
2	Greatsword	Iron Metal	3	Hand-and-a-Half Sword	1	--	--	1	1
2	Bastard Sword	Copper Metal	3	Hand-and-a-Half Sword	1	--	--	2	1
3	Two-Handed Sword	Copper Metal	4	Greatsword	1	--	--	3	2
3	Claymore	Titanium Metal	3	Bastard Sword	1	--	--	--	2
4	Shamshir	Titanium Metal	4	Two-Handed Sword	1	--	--	--	2
4	Estoc	Steel Metal	3	Rapier	1	--	--	--	3
5	Katzbalger	Steel Metal	4	Claymore	1	--	--	--	3
5	Flamberge	Silver Metal	3	Katzbalger	1	--	--	--	3
6	Defender	Blaze Metal	2	Silver Ring	1	Katzbalger	1	--	4
6	Prismatite Blade	Prismatite Metal	3	Flamberge	1	--	--	--	4
7	Crescent Blade	Lunatite	3	Flamberge	1	--	--	--	4
7	Braveheart	Mercurius Metal	3	Prismatite Blade	1	--	--	--	5
8	Dullahan	Crystallite Metal	3	Braveheart	1	--	--	--	5
9	Atlantis Blade	Atlantis Metal	3	Dullahan	1	--	--	--	5
9	Ascalon	Atlantis Metal	3	Ring of Life	2	Atlantis Blade	1	--	6
9	Caladbolg	Atlantis Metal	3	Prismatite Ring	2	Ascalon	1	--	6
10	Karathos Blade	Ascalon	1	Karathos Sandals	1	Karathos Necklace	1	--	6

*Eugene and Kristofer cannot forge swords.

DUAL DAGGERS

Komachi's weapon of choice, dual daggers can be upgraded by Kristofer. The best, Nighthawk, is found in the Seraphic Gate.

Komachi

	Name	Description	Value	Rarity	ATK	HIT	DEF	AGL	INT	Effects	Special Acquisition
	Nicked Dagger	A dull nicked dagger. Rather useless now.	60	1	50	10	--	--	--	Unbreakable	--
	Sparrow	A bronze dagger used in the training of Nightwhisper Guild members.	220	1	300	15	--	--	--	--	--
	Lark	A copper dagger made for stealthy assassinations.	800	2	350	20	--	--	--	--	--
	Nightingale	A copper dagger used for self-defense. Given to Halgitian women when they come of age.	3000	3	370	30	--	--	--	--	--
	Seagull	An iron dagger. Commonly used in Halgita.	500	2	320	20	--	--	--	--	--
	Peacock	A silver dagger adorned with many jewels. Might as well be called a piece of art.	8000	4	390	30	--	--	--	--	--
	Swallow	A steel dagger. Official weaponry for the Nightwhisper Guild.	7000	3	350		--		--	AGL +10	--
	Kingfisher	A steel dagger designed for close-range combat.	6800	3	380	30	--	--	--	--	--
	Owl	A titanium dagger with a black blade made to blend in with the darkness of night.	18000	5	385	50	--	--	--	Unseeing attack	--
	Falcon	A ceramic dagger made light for swift attacks.	15000	5	400	50	--	--	--	--	--
	Flying Swallow	A mercurius dagger. A customized version of the swallow that is very rare.	50000	7	465	40	--	--	--	AGL +20	Complete Side Quest "Rebirth of Halgita"
	Cuckoo	A blaze dagger. The heated blade burns through enemies with ease.	35000	6	420	45	--	--	--	Fire attack	--
	Lovebird	A prismatite dagger for dual wielders. Enables simultaneous attacking and defending.	40000	6	450	30	--	--	--	Autoguard rate +3%	Complete Side Quest "History of Women"
	Raven	A crystallite dagger made for Nightwhispers who possess great skill.	48200	7	480	30	--	--	--	--	--
	Shrike	An amarlista dagger that neutralizes lunaglyph power.	75000	8	500	40	--	--	--	Anti-magic	Must complete Private Event "Secret of Smithery" to make
	Jacana	An easily-concealed dagger for stealth attacks against an enemy's weak point.	80000	8	555	30	--	--	--	Critical hit rate +3%	Must complete Private Event "Secret of Smithery" to make
	Vulture	A dagger with a disturbing history of leaving a trail of bodies behind it.	156000	9	700	60	--	--	--	--	Must complete Private Event "Secret of Smithery" to make
	Eagle	A dagger passed down to the leaders of the Guild. Gives the wielder agility and power.	245000	9	1150	40	--	--	--	AGL +30	Must have access to Seraphic Gate to make
	Plovers	A dagger designed for dual wielding. Enables quick stabs to the enemy's weak points.	380000	10	1700	40	--	--	--	Critical hit rate +3%	Must have access to Seraphic Gate to make
	Nighthawk	A cursed dagger that emits a ghastly sound with every strike.	500000	10	2000	50	--	--	--	Curse attack, Weird Noise	Seraphic Gate

PART 5

Dual Dagger Forging

Rarity	Creation Result	1st Ingredient	Qty.	2nd Ingredient	Qty.	3rd Ingredient	Qty.	Kristofer IC Lv.
1	Sparrow	Bronze Metal	1	--	--	--	--	1
2	Seagull	Iron Metal	1	Sparrow	2	--	--	1
2	Lark	Copper Metal	1	Seagull	2	--	--	2
3	Nightingale	Copper Metal	2	Lark	2	--	--	2
3	Kingfisher	Steel Metal	1	Nightingale	2	--	--	3
4	Swallow	Steel Metal	2	Kingfisher	2	--	--	3
4	Peacock	Silver Metal	2	Marble	1	Nightingale	2	3
5	Owl	Titanium Metal	1	Kingfisher	2	--	--	4
5	Falcon	Ceramic	1	Owl	2	--	--	4
6	Cuckoo	Blaze Metal	1	Falcon	2	--	--	5
6	Lovebird	Prismatite Metal	1	Falcon	2	--	--	5
7	Flying Swallow	Mercurius Metal	1	Swallow	2	--	--	5
7	Raven	Crystallite Metal	1	Lovebird	2	--	--	5
8	Shrike	Amarlista	1	Raven	2	--	--	5
8	Jacana	Amarlista	2	Eagle Eye	2	Raven	2	6
9	Vulture	Atlantis Metal	1	Shrike	2	--	--	6
9	Eagle	Atlantis Metal	2	Flying Swallow	2	--	--	6
10	Plovers	Atlantis Metal	2	Vulture	1	Jacana	1	6

Eugene, Sigmund, and Edward cannot forge Dual Daggers.

BATONS

Rico

Wielding it like a conductor's implement, Rico uses a baton to aid him in controlling animals and casting spells. The best baton is found in the Seraphic Gate, but Kristofer can make some exquisite ones as well.

	Name	Description	Value	Rarity	ATK	HIT	DEF	AGL	INT	Effects	Special Acquisition
	Cracked Baton	A baton that is so beaten up, it looks ready to break at any moment.	20	1	20	10	--	--	45	Unbreakable	--
	Toy Baton	A cork baton. Perfect as a toy for kids.	150	1	35	10	--	--	55	--	--
	Training Baton	A lauan baton often used by aspiring conductors for practice.	300	2	50	10	--	--	70	--	--
	Novice Baton	A lauan baton often used by those training to become conductors.	550	2	65	10	--	--	120	--	--
	Ebony Baton	An ebony baton. Only for true music aficionados.	2800	3	145	10	--	--	200	--	--
	Battle Baton	An ebony baton converted for use on the battlefield.	4300	4	180	10	--	--	250	Critical hit rate +3%	--
	Marching Baton	A balsa baton usually used when conducting a military band.	1650	3	100	10	--	--	170	--	--
	Lux Baton	A lux baton. Enchants those who catch the performance. Used by a famous conductor.	7000	4	200	10	--	--	280	Charm attack	Complete Side Quest "Rat Extermination"
	Marble Baton	A marble baton with intricate engravings. Might as well be called a piece of art.	8500	5	220	10	--	--	300	--	--
	Silver Baton	A silver baton. A light but durable piece that also exhibits a sense of style.	10000	5	250	10	--	--	340	--	--
	Symphonic Baton	A placidus baton for advanced users which can weave together the many sounds of battle.	32000	6	280	30	--	--	370	--	Complete Side Quest "Rebirth of Halgita"
	Healing Baton	A placidus baton with the power to heal both the body and soul.	40000	6	320	30	--	--	400	HP Regeneration 3%	--
	Prismatite Baton	A beautiful, yet deadly, rainbow-colored prismatite battle baton.	42000	7	360	10	--	--	430	Critical hit rate +3%	--
	Metronome Baton	A magical atlantis baton that puts those who watch it to sleep.	160000	9	550	30	--	--	750	Sleep Attack	Must complete Private Event "Secret of Smithery" to make

	Name	Description	Value	Rarity	ATK	HIT	DEF	AGL	INT	Effects	Special Acquisition
	Energico Baton	A pius baton. Strengthens both users and observers.	73000	8	400	10	--	--	520	Air damage +10%	--
	Scemando Baton	A magical baton that drains energy from those who watch its wicked performance.	45000	7	380	30	--	--	470	Curse attack	--
	Spiritoso Baton	A magical baton that raises the wielder's spirit and recharges the magic of those who watch.	85000	8	420	10	--	--	600	MP Regeneration 1%	--
	Animato Baton	A baton that increases the talent of the user, allowing for beautiful and lively gestures.	235000	9	600	30	--	--	820	--	Must have access to Seraphic Gate to make
	Grandioso Baton	A baton able to take control of various things. Its grandeur moves all who watch.	480000	10	620	30	--	--	1050	Air damage +30%	Must have access to Seraphic Gate to make
	Maestro's Baton	A legendary baton with a large area of influence. Increases the user's conducting speed.	500000	10	750	30	--	--	1350	Casting time down, Gold +10%	Seraphic Gate

Baton Forging

Rarity	Creation Result	1st Ingredient	Qty.	2nd Ingredient	Qty.	3rd Ingredient	Qty.	Eugene IC Lv.	Sigmund IC Lv.	Kristofer IC Lv.
1	Toy Baton	Cork Wood	2	--	--	--	--	1	1	1
2	Training Baton	Lauan Wood	2	Toy Baton	1	--	--	1	1	1
2	Novice Baton	Lauan Wood	2	Training Baton	1	--	--	2	2	1
3	Marching Baton	Balsa Wood	2	Novice Baton	1	--	--	2	3	2
3	Ebony Baton	Ebony Wood	2	Marching Baton	1	--	--	3	--	2
4	Battle Baton	Ebony Wood	2	Ebony Baton	1	--	--	3	--	2
4	Lux Baton	Lux Wood	2	Vine	2	Ebony Baton	1	4	--	3
5	Marble Baton	Marble	2	Lux Baton	1	--	--	4	--	3
5	Silver Baton	Silver Metal	2	Marble Baton	1	--	--	4	--	3
6	Symphonic Baton	Placidus Wood	2	Marble Baton	1	--	--	5	--	4
6	Healing Baton	Placidus Wood	2	Aroma Oil	3	Symphonic Baton	1	5	--	4
7	Prismatite Baton	Prismatite Metal	2	Battle Baton	1	--	--	--	--	4
7	Scemando Baton	Malus Wood	2	Healing Baton	1	--	--	--	--	5
8	Spiritoso Baton	Crystallite Metal	2	Scemando Baton	1	--	--	--	--	5
8	Energico Baton	Pius Wood	2	Prismatite Baton	1	--	--	--	--	5
9	Metronome Baton	Atlantis Metal	1	Spiritoso Baton	1	--	--	--	--	6
9	Animato Baton	Atlantis Metal	2	Pius Wood	2	--	--	--	--	6
10	Grandioso Baton	Atlantis Metal	2	Pius Wood	2	Malus Wood	2	--	--	6

*Edward cannot forge Batons.

DRUMS

Rucha

Rucha plays her drums while casting spells or summoning Tir na Nog, her ethereal pet. The second-best drumset, okedo taiko drums, are found in the Seraphic Gate. Eugene at IC Lv.6 can then upgrade them to the best set, mystic drums!

	Name	Description	Value	Rarity	ATK	HIT	DEF	AGL	INT	Effects	Special Acquisition
	Ripped Drum	A broken drum that cannot be played.	35	1	15	10	--	--	70	Unbreakable	--
	Toy Drum	A cork drum. Perfect as a toy marching drum for kids.	150	1	20	10	--	--	150	--	--
	Clay Drum	A sandstone drum of primitive design with hide stretched over a dried clay tube.	300	2	28	10	--	--	180	--	--
	Bodhran	A lauan instrument made from hide stretched over a shallow drum.	550	2	35	10	--	--	200	--	--
	Tarabuka	A vase-shaped granite drum that creates a clear, crisp sound.	1250	3	55	10	--	--	210	--	--
	Bayan	A bowl-shaped balsa drum with hide stretched over a simple shell.	2500	3	100	10	--	--	225	--	--
	Conical Drum	A cone-shaped lux drum with hide stretched over the rim.	5000	4	150	10	--	--	250	--	--

242

	Name	Description	Value	Rarity	ATK	HIT	DEF	AGL	INT	Effects	Special Acquisition
	Banana Drum	A ceramic drum with a long thin shell.	10000	4	185	10	--	--	300	MP +10%	--
	Ceramic Drum	A robust ceramic drum.	8300	5	200	10	--	--	320	--	--
	Silver Drum	A silver drum whose shell looks beautiful and makes a great sound.	9200	5	220	10	--	--	350	--	--
	Dholak	A heavy barrel-shaped lentesco drum. Hard to master, but effective as a weapon.	25000	6	250	30	--	--	400	--	--
	Taiko Drum	An hourglass-shaped drum from ancient Halgita. Makes an elegant sound.	30000	6	280	30	--	--	440	--	--
	Timpani	A perfected prismatite drum that deafens all those within earshot.	40000	7	300	10	--	--	470	Unhearing attack	--
	Fire Beat	A blazing drum that lets out a raging beat.	45000	7	320	30	--	--	500	Fire damage	--
	Taiko War Drum	A pius drum used on the battlefield to raise the morale of troops.	68000	8	350	10	--	--	520	--	--
	Dance Tambourine	A simple drum that contains a surprising amount of magic.	74500	8	380	10	--	--	620	MP +10%	--
	Talking Drum	A remarkable drum known for its speech-like sound that drives people mad.	180000	9	420	30	--	--	800	Confusion attack	Must complete Private Event "Secret of Smithery" to make
	Beatdown	A drum with magical beats that smash the enemy's souls.	250000	9	460	30	--	--	1000	Fire damage +30%	Must complete Private Event "Secret of Smithery" to make
	Okedo Taiko Drum	An ancient Halgitian drum that enchants all those who hear its hypnotic beats.	450000	10	550	30	--	--	1450	Charm attack	Seraphic Gate
	Mystic Drum	A drum shrouded in mystery for its unidentifiable material and unique sound.	500000	10	600	30	--	--	1650	Magic damage +10%, Casting time down, EXP +10%	Must have access to Seraphic Gate to make

Drum Forging

Rarity	Creation Result	1st Ingredient	Qty.	2nd Ingredient	Qty.	3rd Ingredient	Qty.	Eugene IC Lv.	Sigmund IC Lv.	Kristofer IC Lv.
1	Toy Drum	Cork Wood	1	--	--	--	--	1	1	1
2	Clay Drum	Sandstone	1	Kenaf Cloth	1	Toy Drum	1	1	1	1
2	Bodhran	Lauan Wood	1	Rabbit Hide	1	Clay Drum	1	1	2	1
3	Tarabuka	Granite	1	Silver Fox Fur	1	Bodhran	1	2	3	2
3	Bayan	Balsa Wood	1	Ramie Cloth	1	Tarabuka	1	2	--	2
4	Banana Drum	Ebony Wood	1	Buffalo Hide	1	Bayan	1	2	--	2
4	Conical Drum	Lux Wood	1	Golden Wolf Fur	1	Bayan	1	3	--	3
5	Ceramic Drum	Ceramic	1	Barkcloth	1	Banana Drum	1	3	--	3
5	Silver Drum	Silver Metal	1	Cotton Cloth	1	Ceramic Drum	1	3	--	3
6	Dholak	Lentesco Wood	1	Chameleon Skin	1	Ceramic Drum	1	4	--	4
6	Taiko Drum	Placidus Wood	1	Silk Cloth	1	Dholak	1	4	--	4
7	Fire Beat	Blaze Metal	1	Salamander Skin	1	Silver Drum	1	5	--	5
7	Timpani	Prismatite Metal	1	Damask Cloth	1	Dholak	1	4	--	5
8	Taiko War Drum	Pius Wood	1	Rachnuvus Cloth	1	Taiko Drum	1	5	--	--
8	Dance Tambourine	Mercurius Metal	1	Garuda Skin	1	Fire Beat	1	5	--	--
9	Talking Drum	Crystallite Metal	1	Lubricus Cloth	1	Dance Tambourine	1	6	--	--
9	Beatdown	Malus Wood	1	Dragon Hide	1	Talking Drum	1	6	--	--
10	Mystic Drum	Atlantis Metal	1	Empyrean Cloth	1	Okedo Taiko Drum	1	6	--	--

*Edward cannot forge Drum.

AXES

Balbagan

Balbagan is a straight-forward melee combatant with that giant axe of his. For brute force, the Seraphic Gate's executioner can't be beat. Edward at IC Lv.6 can make Mjolnir, which hits almost as hard as executioner, without the sapping side effects. However, the penalties inflicted by executioner can be largely offset with Barrier of Brawn.

Weapon	Name	Description	Value	Rarity	ATK	HIT	DEF	AGL	INT	Effects	Special Acquisition
	Worn Axe	A blunt axe with nicked edges.	100	1	200	10	--	--	--	Unbreakable	--
	Bronze Axe	A double-edged bronze axe. A favorite of powerful warriors.	200	1	270	10	--	--	--	--	--
	Woodcutter Axe	Converted from a simple chopping axe into a weapon.	950	2	400	10	--	--	--	--	--
	Sea Axe	An iron axe. A favorite among warriors for its ease of use.	500	2	360	10	--	--	--	--	--
	Ogre's Hammer	A hammer made from granite. An extremely heavy weapon favored by ogres.	3200	3	500	--	--	--			Complete Side Quest "Monster in Shrine"
	Broad Axe	A steel axe with an oversized head that smashes and slices the enemy's armor to pieces.	4100	3	480	10	--	--			--
	Battleaxe	A steel axe converted from a broad axe to be better suited for battle.	8000	4	550	10	--	--			--
	Poleaxe	A sturdy and powerful titanium axe. Takes great skill to master.	25000	5	750	10	--	--			Complete Side Quest "Fayel Warrior"
	Mithril Axe	A beautiful silver great axe. Its light weight and sharp blade make it a deadly weapon.	18000	5	700	10	--	--			--
	Halberd	A special steel great axe that is perfectly balanced for combat.	11000	4	620	10	--	--			--
	Metetite Axe	An axe made from a sharp chunk of metetite. Smashes targets with its weight.	35000	6	800	10	--	--			--
	Blaze Axe	A blaze great axe that has the ability to burn through even the toughest of armor.	38000	6	850	10	--	--	--	Fire attack	Complete Side Quest "Strongest Guard"
	Crescent Axe	A lunatite axe. Its crescent head cuts through things with magic-like power.	40000	7	900	10	--	--	--	MP +10%	--
	Crystallite Axe	A crystallite axe. Its crystal-forged blade is a sign of its extreme solidity.	58000	7	950	10	--	--	--	--	--
	Bardiche	An amarlista axe that can chop through any armor, even if it is enhanced by lunaglyphs.	78000	8	1040	10	--	--	--	--	--
	Bloody Bat	A great axe with a head shaped like a bat. Drains the life of its victims.	86000	8	1100	10	--	--	--	HP absorb attack	Must complete Private Event "Secret of Smithery" to make
	Berserker	A great axe imbued with the soul of a berserker. Allows for all-out attacks.	200000	9	2500	10	--	--	--	DEF-10%	Must complete Private Event "Secret of Smithery" to make
	Groundbreaker	A magical great axe able to strike with a force that can split the earth beneath it.	280000	9	2150	10	--	--	--	Earth attack	Must have access to Seraphic Gate to make
	Executioner	A cursed great axe once used by executioners.	450000	10	4000	--	--	--	--	HP drain 1%, DEF-10%	Seraphic Gate
	Mjolnir	A hammer that is said to never miss its target. Once used by a god of war.	500000	10	3450	40	--	--	--	HP +10%	Must have access to Seraphic Gate to make

Axe Forging

Rarity	Creation Result	1st Ingredient	Qty.	2nd Ingredient	Qty.	3rd Ingredient	Qty.	Sigmund IC Lv.	Edward IC Lv.
1	Bronze Axe	Bronze Metal	3	--	--	--	--	1	1
2	Sea Axe	Iron Metal	3	Bronze Axe	1	--	--	1	1
2	Woodcutter Axe	Copper Metal	3	Sea Axe	1	--	--	2	1
3	Broad Axe	Steel Metal	3	Woodcutter Axe	1	--	--	--	2
4	Battleaxe	Steel Metal	3	Broad Axe	1	--	--	--	2
4	Halberd	Steel Metal	3	Battleaxe	1	--	--	--	3
5	Mithril Axe	Silver Metal	3	Battleaxe	1	--	--	--	3
5	Poleaxe	Titanium Metal	3	Monster Claw	2	Halberd	1	--	3
6	Metetite Axe	Metetite	3	Mithril Axe	1	--	--	--	4
6	Blaze Axe	Blaze Metal	3	Poleaxe	1	--	--	--	4
7	Crescent Axe	Lunatite	3	Metetite Axe	1	--	--	--	4
7	Crystallite Axe	Crystallite Metal	3	Metetite Axe	1	--	--	--	5
8	Bardiche	Amarlista	2	Crystallite Axe	1	--	--	--	5
8	Bloody Bat	Amarlista	2	Bat Wing	10	Crystallite Axe	1	--	5
9	Berserker	Atlantis Metal	2	Dragon Fang	1	Ogre's Hammer	1	--	6
9	Groundbreaker	Atlantis Metal	2	Ceramic Ring	3	Bardiche	1	--	6
10	Mjolnir	Atlantis Metal	3	Eye of Avifir	1	Groundbreaker	1	--	6

Eugene and Kristofer cannot forge Axes.

KATANA

Touma

Despite Touma's diminutive build, he strikes swiftly and heavily with his katana. Kristofer can make a few of the most effective versions, but the cream of the crop is found in the Seraphic Gate.

	Name	Description	Value	Rarity	ATK	HIT	DEF	AGL	INT	Effects	Special Acquisition
	Blunt Katana	A sword with a blade nicked beyond use.	60	1	80	10	--	--	--	Unbreakable	--
	Weather Fox	The weather fox katana. Equip it with a mask to receive its divine protection.	200	1	400	15	--	--	--	DEF +5	--
	Wind	The wind demon katana. Equip it with a mask to receive its divine protection.	1000	2	450	20	--	--	--	DEF +5	--
	Blindeye	The silent nobleman katana. Equip it with a mask to receive its divine protection.	1800	2	500	20	--	--	--	DEF +5	--
	Ogre	The destructive ogre katana. Equip it with a mask to receive its divine protection.	3500	3	510	30	--	--	--	DEF +5	--
	Herosong	The brave lion katana. Equip it with a mask to receive its divine protection.	6200	3	520	30	--	--	--	DEF +5	Complete Side Quest "Lost Katana"
	Foresight	The katana of unyielding peace. Equip it with a mask to receive its divine protection.	10000	4	500	--	--	--	--	DEF +5, Paralysis attack	--
	Resentment	The vengeful spirit katana. Equip it with a mask to receive its divine protection.	12000	4	515	30	--	--	--	DEF +5, Curse attack	--
	Seagaze	The mariner katana. Equip it with a mask to receive its divine protection.	25000	5	530	70	--	--	--	DEF +5, Water attack	--
	Honor	The blade warrior katana. Equip it with a mask to receive its divine protection.	28000	5	580	45	--	--	--	DEF +5, Unseeing attack	--
	Thunder	The katana of the thunder god. Equip it with a mask to receive its divine protection.	40000	6	600	30	--	--	--	DEF +5, Air attack	--
	Laughter	The katana of the droll man. Equip it with a mask to receive its divine protection.	43000	6	620	30	--	--	--	DEF +5, Fire attack	Complete Side Quest "Vermiform propagation"
	Ease	The katana of the carefree woman. Equip it with a mask to receive its divine protection.	45000	7	640	40	--	--	--	DEF +10	--

	Name	Description	Value	Rarity	ATK	HIT	DEF	AGL	INT	Effects	Special Acquisition
	Pity	The katana of the sad old man. Equip it with a mask to receive its divine protection.	53000	7	700	30	--	--	--	DEF +10	--
	Scorn	The katana of the scornful woman. Equip it with a mask to receive its divine protection.	75000	8	750	40	--	--	--	DEF +10	Must complete Private Event "Secret of Smithery" to make
	Affection	The katana of the affectionate eye. Equip it with a mask to receive its divine protection.	80000	8	820	30	--	--	--	DEF +10	Must complete Private Event "Secret of Smithery" to make
	Dragonedge	The katana of the dragon god. Equip it with a mask to receive its divine protection.	170000	9	910	60	--	--	--	DEF +10	Must have access to Seraphic Gate to make
	Rage	The katana of the raging snake. Equip it with a mask to receive its divine protection.	265000	9	1600	40	--	--	--	DEF +10, Poison attack	Must have access to Seraphic Gate to make
	Holy King	The katana of sovereignty. Equip it with a mask to receive its divine protection.	450000	10	2200	40	--	--	--	DEF +10, Silence attack	Must have access to Seraphic Gate to make
	Divinity	The divine katana of Kylin. Equip it with a mask to receive its divine protection.	500000	10	2500	50	--	--	--	DEF +10, Stone attack	Seraphic Gate

Katana Forging

Rarity	Creation Result	1st Ingredient	Qty.	2nd Ingredient	Qty.	3rd Ingredient	Qty.	Kristofer IC Lv.
1	Weather Fox	Bronze Metal	2	Cork Wood	2	--	--	1
2	Wind	Iron Metal	2	Cork Wood	3	Weather Fox	1	1
2	Blindeye	Copper Metal	2	Lauan Wood	2	Wind	1	2
3	Ogre	Copper Metal	2	Lauan Wood	3	Blindeye	1	2
3	Herosong	Steel Metal	2	Balsa Wood	2	Ogre	1	3
4	Foresight	Steel Metal	2	Balsa Wood	3	Herosong	1	3
4	Resentment	Silver Metal	2	Ebony Wood	2	Foresight	1	3
5	Seagaze	Titanium Metal	2	Ebony Wood	3	Resentment	1	4
5	Honor	Ceramic	2	Lux Wood	2	Seagaze	1	4
6	Thunder	Hearthstone	2	Lux Wood	2	Honor	1	5
6	Laughter	Blaze Metal	2	Lentesco Wood	2	Thunder	1	5
7	Ease	Mercurius Metal	2	Lentesco Wood	3	Laughter	1	5
7	Pity	Crystallite Metal	2	Placidus Wood	2	Ease	1	5
8	Scorn	Amarlista	2	Placidus Wood	3	Pity	1	5
8	Affection	Amarlista	2	Malus Wood	2	Scorn	1	6
9	Dragonedge	Atlantis Metal	2	Malus Wood	3	Affection	1	6
9	Rage	Atlantis Metal	2	Pius Wood	2	Dragonedge	1	6
10	Holy King	Atlantis Metal	2	Pius Wood	2	Rage	1	6

Eugene, Sigmund, and Kristofer cannot forge Katanas.

DAGGERS

Vic

Kiriya

The sprightly Vic wields a dagger well. Kristofer makes good ones, but the best is in the Seraphic Gate.

	Name	Description	Value	Rarity	ATK	HIT	DEF	AGL	INT	Effects	Special Acquisition
	Old Dagger	A dagger with a broken and crumbling blade.	30	1	150	20	--	--	--	Unbreakable	--
	Flint Dagger	A bronze double-edged dagger. Not very powerful as a weapon.	180	1	200	30	--	--	--	--	--
	Kris	A copper dagger. Many assassinations have been carried out using this dagger.	700	2	300	30	--	--	--	--	--
	Pugio	A wide double-edged iron dagger. Often used as a backup weapon for soldiers.	400	2	250	30	--	--	--	--	--

	Name	Description	Value	Rarity	ATK	HIT	DEF	AGL	INT	Effects	Special Acquisition
	Chilanum Dagger	A copper dagger. A favorite among Fayel officers.	1800	3	320	30	--	--	--	--	--
	Scramasax	A basic steel dagger. Although primitive, it is a powerful weapon.	3500	3	350	30	--	--	--	--	--
	Main Gauche	A steel dagger made from hard ore. Ideal for parrying attacks.	12000	4	350	35	--	--	--	Autoguard rate +3%	Complete Side Quest "Parental Surrogate"
	Kukri	A steel dagger with a uniquely curved blade that can leave a vicious wound.	7000	4	380	35	--	--	--	--	--
	Baselard	A titanium dagger. Its ease of use makes it a favorite among thieves.	10500	5	410	35	--	--	--	--	--
	Stiletto	A silver dagger made for stabbing through cracks in armor.	17500	5	400	35	--	--	--	Critical hit rate +3%	--
	Ceramic Dagger	A ceramic dagger. Built for functionality using Kolton's finest techniques.	23000	6	420	40	--	--	--	--	--
	Deadly Needle	A mercurius dagger. With its poison-edged blade, it is ideal for assassinations.	50000	7	400	45	--	--	--	Doom attack	--
	Blaze Dagger	A blaze dagger. Hot enough to set fire to its victims.	32000	6	450	40	--	--	--	Fire attack	--
	Quartz Dagger	A quartz dagger whose resonating blade can cut through almost anything.	63000	8	480	40	--	--	--	--	--
	Katar	A crystallite dagger that tears apart its victim with each stab.	74000	8	550	45	--	--	--	Critical hit rate +3%	--
	Cinquedea	A prismatite dagger. The blade is adorned with engravings.	40000	7	430	45	--	--	--	Faint attack	--
	Viper Fang	A dagger made from the fangs of a monstrous viper. Poisons those it cuts.	175000	9	650	45	--	--	--	Poison attack	--
	Carnwennan	A legendary dagger of a king from a lost kingdom. This treasure holds great power.	245000	9	1100	50	--	--	--	Critical hit rate +3%	Must complete Private Event "Secret of Smithery" to make
	Jambiya	A valuable dagger said to have been used by Ruslan of Fayel during the emirate's founding.	450000	10	1500	50	--	--	--	--	Must have access to Seraphic Gate to make
	Moon Blade	A dagger carved from a piece of one of the chains. Drains energy with every cut.	500000	10	1700	50	--	--	--	HP absorb attack	Seraphic Gate

Dagger Forging

Rarity	Creation Result	1st Ingredient	Qty.	2nd Ingredient	Qty.	3rd Ingredient	Qty.	Edward IC Lv.	Kristofer IC Lv.
1	Flint Dagger	Bronze Metal	2	--	--	--	--	3	1
2	Pugio	Iron Metal	2	Flint Dagger	1	--	--	3	1
2	Kris	Copper Metal	2	Pugio	1	--	--	3	1
3	Chilanum Dagger	Copper Metal	2	Kris	1	--	--	4	2
3	Scramasax	Steel Metal	2	Chilanum Dagger	1	--	--	4	2
4	Kukri	Steel Metal	2	Scramasax	1	--	--	--	3
5	Stiletto	Silver Metal	2	Scramasax	1	--	--	--	3
5	Baselard	Titanium Metal	2	Stiletto	1	--	--	--	3
6	Ceramic Dagger	Ceramic	2	Baselard	1	--	--	--	4
6	Blaze Dagger	Blaze Metal	2	Ceramic Dagger	1	--	--	--	4
7	Cinquedea	Prismatite Metal	2	Ceramic Dagger	1	--	--	--	4
7	Deadly Needle	Mercurius Metal	2	Poison Stinger	10	Main Gauche	1	--	5
8	Quartz Dagger	Quartz	2	Cinquedea	1	--	--	--	5
8	Katar	Crystallite Metal	2	Quartz Dagger	1	--	--	--	5
9	Viper Fang	Crystallite Metal	2	Poison Stinger	10	Deadly Needle	1	--	6
9	Carnwennan	Amarlista	2	Viper Fang	1	--	--	--	6
10	Jambiya	Atlantis Metal	2	Carnwennan	1	--	--	--	6

*Eugene and Sigmund cannot forge Daggers.

CLAWS

Gustav

For raw ripping power, it's hard to beat a clawed bear. That's exactly what Gustav is, and no one approaches his ferocity. This performance comes at a price—Gustav takes up two slots in the party. Kristofer makes the best craftable claws, but the strongest set is in the Seraphic Gate.

Name	Description	Value	Rarity	ATK	HIT	DEF	AGL	INT	Effects	Special Acquisition
Broken Claws	Broken claws that don't seem to be of any use to anyone.	80	1	400	10	--	--	--	Unbreakable	--
Bronze Claws	Bronze battle claws used to tear apart enemies.	160	1	650	10	--	--	--	--	--
Honey Hunters	Bent-tip claws originally used for scooping honey. These deal out some serious damage.	450	2	750	10	--	--	--	--	--
Iron Claws	Iron battle claws for beasts.	2000	3	980	10	--	--	--	--	--
Wolf Claws	Bronze battle claws modeled after those of a wolf.	800	2	920	10	--	--	--	--	--
Panther Claws	Copper battle claws modeled after the flexible claws of a panther.	4500	3	1030	10	--	--	--	--	--
Eagle Claws	Silver battle claws modeled after the pointed talons of an eagle.	20000	5	1150	10	--	--	--	Autoguard rate +3%	--
Metetite Claws	Metetite battle claws. Too heavy for human use.	26000	6	1200	10	--	--	--	--	--
Bear Claws	Titanium claws modeled after the formidable claws of a bear.	25000	5	1100	10	--	--	--	HP Regeneration 3%	--
Tiger Claws	Steel battle claws modeled after the powerful claws of a tiger.	8000	4	1050	10	--	--	--	--	--
Lion Claws	Steel battle claws modeled after the mighty claws of a lion.	10000	4	1000	10	--	--	--	Critical hit rate +3%	--
Blaze Claws	Blaze battle claws that cut into the enemy and set them ablaze.	38000	6	1300	10	--	--	--	Fire attack	--
Wild Claws	Battle claws that awaken the mighty beast within the wielder.	85000	8	1650	10	--	--	--	--	--
Dragon Claws	Battle claws made from the extraordinarily sharp fangs of a dragon.	100000	8	1800	10	--	--	--	--	--
Salmon Killers	Battle claws modeled after the claws of a legendary bear.	220000	9	2050	10	--	--	--	--	Must complete Private Event "Secret of Smithery" to make
Crescent Claws	Crescent-shaped lunatite battle claws that enhance the wielder's lunaglyph power.	40000	7	1550	10	--	--	--	MP +10%	--
Prismatite Claws	Prismatite claws. The radiant blue shine asserts their sharpness.	45000	7	1420	10	--	--	--	--	--
Claws of Glory	Legendary battle claws that bring honor and victory to their wielder.	450000	10	3800	20	--	--	--	Critical hit rate +3%, Autoguard rate +3%	Must have access to Seraphic Gate to make
Eclipse Claws	Amarlista battle claws that repel lunaglyph effects and allow physical attacks.	285000	9	3500	10	--	--	--	--	Must complete Private Event "Secret of Smithery" to make
Sabris Claws	Legendary battle claws of Sabris that give the wielder the power of ice.	500000	10	4000	20	--	--	--	HP +20%, Freeze attack	Seraphic Gate

Claw Forging

Rarity	Creation Result	1st Ingredient	Qty.	2nd Ingredient	Qty.	3rd Ingredient	Qty.	Eugene IC Lv.	Sigmund IC Lv.	Kristofer IC Lv.
1	Bronze Claws	Bronze Metal	3	--	--	--	--	2	1	1
2	Honey Hunters	Sandstone	3	Honey	2	Bronze Claws	1	2	1	1
2	Wolf Claws	Bronze Metal	3	Bronze Claws	1	--	--	3	2	1
3	Iron Claws	Iron Metal	3	Bronze Claws	1	--	--	3	3	2
3	Panther Claws	Copper Metal	3	Wolf Claws	1	--	--	4	--	2
4	Tiger Claws	Steel Metal	3	Panther Claws	1	--	--	4	--	2
4	Lion Claws	Steel Metal	3	Tiger Claws	1	--	--	--	--	3
5	Eagle Claws	Silver Metal	3	Lion Claws	1	--	--	--	--	3
5	Bear Claws	Titanium Metal	3	Bear Paw	2	Lion Claws	1	--	--	4
6	Metetite Claws	Metetite	3	Iron Claws	1	--	--	--	--	4
6	Blaze Claws	Blaze Metal	3	Metetite Claws	1	--	--	--	--	4
7	Prismatite Claws	Prismatite Metal	3	Blaze Claws	1	--	--	--	--	5
7	Crescent Claws	Lunatite	3	Prismatite Claws	1	--	--	--	--	5
8	Wild Claws	Mercurius Metal	3	Bear Claws	1	--	--	--	--	5
8	Dragon Claws	Quartz	3	Dragon Fang	1	Wild Claws	1	--	--	6
9	Salmon Killers	Crystallite Metal	3	Sliced Rare Salmon	5	Bear Claws	1	--	--	6
9	Eclipse Claws	Amarlista	3	Crescent Claws	1	--	--	--	--	6
10	Claws of Glory	Atlantis Metal	3	Dragon Claws	1	--	--	--	--	6

*Edward cannot forge Claws.

ARMOR

HEAVY ARMOR

Capell

Sigmund

Edward

Balbagan

Dominica

Heavy armors are intended for front-line allies. The strongest craftable heavy armor is made by Edward...the last in the line can even negate magic, or resist status ailments! The best heavy armor is found in the Seraphic Gate.

Name	Description	Value	Rarity	ATK	HIT	DEF	AGL	INT	LUC	Effects	Special Acquisition
Dented Armor	Old plate armor dented all over.	150	1	--	--	5	--	--	--	Unbreakable	--
Bronze Scale Armor	Scale armor reinforced with bronze. Heavy, but doesn't offer much protection.	500	1	--	--	10	--	--	--	--	--
Iron Scale Armor	Scale armor reinforced with iron. Heavy, but offers ample protection.	1250	2	--	--	20	--	--	--	--	--
Steel Scale Armor	Scale armor reinforced with steel. Light and durable, making it easy to wear.	2650	3	--	--	45	--	--	--	--	--
Copper Chainmail	Copper chainmail that is official wear in many countries.	2000	2	--	--	35	--	--	--	--	--
Silver Chainmail	A suit of chainmail sewn of silver.	3400	3	--	--	50	--	--	--	--	--
Gold Chainmail	A suit of chainmail sewn of gold.	6500	4	--	--	80	--	--	--	--	--
Banded Armor	This armor is known for its ease of equipping.	4500	4	--	--	70	--	--	--	--	--
Bronze Plate Armor	Plate armor forged from bronze.	8500	5	--	--	85	--	--	--	--	--
Iron Plate Armor	Plate armor forged from iron.	14500	5	--	--	95	--	--	--	--	--
Steel Plate Armor	Steel plate armor created using Kolton's finest techniques.	20000	6	--	--	105	--	--	--	--	--
Assault Suit	Plate armor built focusing on offense rather than defense.	45000	6	--	--	110	--	--	--	ATK +10%	--
Prominence Armor	Blaze plate armor that protects against fire attacks.	50000	7	--	--	115	--	--	--	Fire damage -50%	--
Prismatite Suit	Prismatite armor that is both extremely beautiful and highly protective.	58000	7	--	--	120	--	--	--	--	--
Crescent Armor	Plate armor embedded with lunatite. Enhances the wearer's lunaglyph power.	65000	8	--	--	125	--	--	--	MP +10%	--
Crystallite Suit	A crystallite suit designed by an aristo armorsmith. Transparent and colorless.	86500	9	--	--	280	--	--	--	--	Must complete Private Event "Secret of Smithery" to make
Mercurius Suit	A mercurius suit created using Casandra's finest techniques.	78000	8	--	--	130	--	--	--	Water damage -50%	--
Eclipse Armor	Plate armor embedded with amarlista to repel lunaglyph power.	123500	9	--	--	350	--	--	--	Anti-ailment (50%)	Must complete Private Event "Secret of Smithery" to make
Hydra Armor	Armor layered in the scales of a beast. Has the ability to reflect magic.	165200	10	--	--	450	--	--	--	Anti-magic	Must have access to Seraphic Gate to make
Karathos Suit	A suit with the power of Karathos. Revitalizes the wearer's energy.	182000	10	--	--	500	--	--	--	ATK +5%, HP +10%	Seraphic Gate

Heavy Armor Forging

Rarity	Creation Result	1st Ingredient	Qty.	2nd Ingredient	Qty.	3rd Ingredient	Qty.	Sigmund IC Lv.	Edward IC Lv.
1	Bronze Scale Armor	Bronze Metal	3	--	--	--	--	1	1
2	Iron Scale Armor	Iron Metal	3	Bronze Scale Armor	1	--	--	1	1
2	Copper Chainmail	Copper Metal	3	Bronze Scale Armor	1	--	--	2	2
3	Steel Scale Armor	Steel Metal	3	Iron Scale Armor	1	--	--	3	2
3	Silver Chainmail	Silver Metal	3	Copper Chainmail	1	--	--	--	2
4	Banded Armor	Titanium Metal	3	Steel Scale Armor	1	--	--	--	3
4	Gold Chainmail	Gold Metal	3	Silver Chainmail	1	--	--	--	3
5	Bronze Plate Armor	Bronze Metal	5	Bronze Scale Armor	2	--	--	--	3
5	Iron Plate Armor	Iron Metal	5	Iron Scale Armor	2	--	--	--	4
6	Steel Plate Armor	Steel Metal	5	Steel Scale Armor	2	--	--	--	4
6	Assault Suit	Titanium Metal	2	Steel Plate Armor	1	--	--	--	4
7	Prominence Armor	Blaze Metal	3	Assault Suit	1	--	--	--	5
7	Prismatite Suit	Prismatite Metal	3	Steel Plate Armor	1	--	--	--	5
8	Crescent Armor	Lunatite	3	Prominence Armor	1	--	--	--	5
8	Mercurius Suit	Mercurius Metal	3	Prismatite Suit	1	--	--	--	6
9	Crystallite Suit	Crystallite Metal	3	Prismatite Suit	1	--	--	--	6
9	Eclipse Armor	Amarlista	3	Crescent Armor	1	--	--	--	6
10	Hydra Armor	Atlantis Metal	3	Feeble Cloth	2	Eclipse Armor	1	--	6

*Edward cannot forge Heavy Armor.

HEAVY HELMET

Capell

Sigmund

Edward

Balbagan

Dominica

Heavy helmets complement heavy armor, keeping our heroes' noggins safe. Edward can craft strong helmets. Of the two best, one comes from a storyline boss and the other from the Seraphic Gate.

Name	Description	Value	Rarity	ATK	HIT	DEF	AGL	INT	LUC	Effects	Special Acquisition
Dented Helmet	A dented helmet that is of no use to anyone.	100	1	--	--	2	--	--	--	Unbreakable	--
Bronze Scale Helmet	A scale helmet reinforced with bronze. Heavy, but doesn't offer much protection.	250	1	--	--	8	--	--	--	--	--
Iron Scale Helmet	A scale helmet reinforced with iron. Heavy, but offers ample protection.	1200	2	--	--	15	--	--	--	--	--
Steel Scale Helmet	A scale helmet reinforced with steel. Light and durable, making it easy to wear.	2000	3	--	--	25	--	--	--	--	--
Copper Chain Helmet	A copper chain helmet that is official wear in many countries.	1750	2	--	--	20	--	--	--	--	--
Silver Chain Helmet	A silver chain helmet. Favored by spearmen.	2800	3	--	--	35	--	--	--	--	--
Gold Chain Helmet	A gold chain helmet. High in defense, but low in mobility.	5800	4	--	--	55	--	--	--	AGL-20	--
Banded Headgear	A banded headgear worn by a savage tribe from the south.	4000	4	--	--	45	--	--	--	--	--
Bronze Plate Helmet	A bronze plate helmet that covers the entire head. Usually worn by knights.	8000	5	--	--	70	--	--	--	--	--
Iron Plate Helmet	An iron plate helmet. Quite heavy, but offers good protection.	12000	5	--	--	75	--	--	--	HIT-20	--
Steel Plate Helmet	A steel plate helmet created using Kolton's finest techniques.	18000	6	--	--	80	--	--	--	--	--
Mercenary Helmet	A helmet of a legendary mercenary that has been dyed red from the blood of battle.	35000	6	--	--	85	--	--	--	HP +10%	--
Prominence Helmet	A blaze plate helmet.	55000	7	--	--	90	--	--	--	--	--
Prismatite Headgear	A helmet reinforced with prismatite.	63500	7	--	--	95	--	--	--	--	--
Crescent Helmet	A plate helmet embedded with lunatite. Enhances the wearer's lunaglyph power.	72000	8	--	--	100	--	--	--	MP +10%	--
Crystallite Headgear	A crystallite helmet designed by an aristo armorsmith. Transparent and colorless.	95000	9	--	--	110	--	--	--	--	Must complete Private Event "Secret of Smithery" to make
Mercurius Headgear	A helmet reinforced with mercurius created using Casandra's finest techniques.	88000	8	--	--	105	--	--	--	--	--
Eclipse Helmet	A plate helmet embedded with amarlista to repel lunaglyph power.	112000	9	--	--	120	--	--	--	Magic damage -50%	Must complete Private Event "Secret of Smithery" to make
Saruleus Helmet	A plate helmet with the power of Saruleus. Greatly increases the wearer's attack power.	120000	10	--	--	150	--	--	--	ATK +10%	Seraphic Gate
Karathos Helmet	A plate helmet with the power of Karathos. Used by the young Volsung.	135000	10	--	--	180	--	--	--	Anti-freeze	Defeat Karathos (Underwater Palace)

Heavy Helmet Forging

Rarity	Creation Result	1st Ingredient	Qty.	2nd Ingredient	Qty.	3rd Ingredient	Qty.	Sigmund IC Lv.	Edward IC Lv.
1	Bronze Scale Helmet	Bronze Metal	2	--	--	--	--	1	1
2	Iron Scale Helmet	Iron Metal	2	Bronze Scale Helmet	1	--	--	1	1
2	Copper Chain Helmet	Copper Metal	2	Bronze Scale Helmet	1	--	--	2	2
3	Steel Scale Helmet	Steel Metal	2	Iron Scale Helmet	1	--	--	3	2
3	Silver Chain Helmet	Silver Metal	2	Copper Chain Helmet	1	--	--	--	2
4	Banded Headgear	Titanium Metal	2	Steel Scale Helmet	1	--	--	--	3
4	Gold Chain Helmet	Gold Metal	2	Silver Chain Helmet	1	--	--	--	3
5	Bronze Plate Helmet	Bronze Metal	4	Bronze Scale Helmet	1	--	--	--	3
5	Iron Plate Helmet	Iron Metal	4	Iron Scale Helmet	1	--	--	--	4
6	Steel Plate Helmet	Steel Metal	4	Steel Scale Helmet	1	--	--	--	4
6	Mercenary Helmet	Titanium Metal	2	Steel Plate Helmet	1	--	--	--	4
7	Prominence Helmet	Blaze Metal	2	Mercenary Helmet	1	--	--	--	5
7	Prismatite Headgear	Prismatite Metal	2	Steel Plate Helmet	1	--	--	--	5
8	Crescent Helmet	Lunatite	2	Prominence Helmet	1	--	--	--	5
8	Mercurius Headgear	Mercurius Metal	2	Prismatite Headgear	1	--	--	--	6
9	Crystallite Headgear	Crystallite Metal	2	Prismatite Headgear	1	--	--	--	6
9	Eclipse Helmet	Amarlista	2	Crescent Helmet	1	--	--	--	6

*Eugene and Kristofer cannot forge Heavy Helmets.

HEAVY BOOTS

Capell

Sigmund

Edward

Balbagan

Dominica

Edward crafts most of the better pieces of footwear for the melee-oriented. The Feet of Saruleus, found in the Seraphic Gate, are the zenith of offense for feet, but Edward at IC Lv.6 can turn them into Kylin greaves, which bestow a benefit irreplaceable to close-range combatants.

Name	Description	Value	Rarity	ATK	HIT	DEF	AGL	INT	LUC	Effects	Special Acquisition
Rusted Greaves	Greaves rusted all over.	60	1	--	--	1	--	--	--	Unbreakable	--
Bronze Scale Greaves	Greaves reinforced with bronze. Heavy, but don't offer much protection.	200	1	--	--	4	2	--	--	--	--
Iron Scale Greaves	Greaves reinforced with iron. Heavy, but offer ample protection.	950	2	--	--	10	4	--	--	--	--
Steel Scale Greaves	Greaves reinforced with steel. Light and durable, making them easy to wear.	1750	3	--	--	20	10	--	--	--	--
Copper Chain Greaves	Copper chain greaves that are official wear in many countries.	1400	2	--	--	15	8	--	--	--	--
Silver Chain Greaves	Silver chain greaves. Favored among spearmen.	2400	3	--	--	30	12	--	--	--	--
Gold Chain Greaves	Gold chain greaves. High in defense, but low in mobility.	5500	4	--	--	50	--	--	--	AGL-20	--
Banded Greaves	Banded greaves worn by a savage tribe from the south.	3500	4	--	--	40	15	--	--	--	--
Bronze Plate Greaves	Bronze plate greaves that don't get in the way when riding on horseback.	8000	5	--	--	55	25	--	--	--	--
Iron Greaves	Iron plate greaves. Quite heavy, but offer good protection.	11000	5	--	--	65	--	--	--	AGL-20	--
Steel Greaves	Silver plate greaves created using Kolton's finest techniques.	14500	6	--	--	70	30	--	--	--	--
Heavy Greaves	Heavy and durable greaves focusing on defense. Require great strength to wear.	25000	6	--	--	75	--	--	--	AGL-20	--
Prominence Leggings	Blaze plate leggings.	35000	7	--	--	80	30	--	--	--	--
Prismatite Greaves	Greaves reinforced with prismatite.	43000	7	--	--	85	35	--	--	--	--
Crescent Leggings	Plate leggings embedded with lunatite. Enhance the wearer's lunaglyph power.	60000	8	--	--	90	40	--	--	MP +10%	--
Crystallite Greaves	Crystallite greaves designed by an aristo armorsmith. Transparent and colorless.	92000	9	--	--	105	50	--	--	--	--
Mercurius Greaves	Mercurius greaves created using Casandra's finest techniques.	76000	8	--	--	100	45	--	--	--	--
Eclipse Leggings	Plate leggings embedded with amarlista to repel lunaglyph power.	140000	9	--	--	110	45	--	--	Anti-magic	Must complete Private Event "Secret of Smithery" to make
Kylin Greaves	Greaves with the power of Kylin. Revitalize the wearer's energy with every step.	145000	10	--	--	130	45	--	--	HP Regeneration 3%	Must have access to Seraphic Gate to make
Feet of Saruleus	Greaves with the power of Saruleus. Increase the wearer's attack power.	150000	10	--	--	150	50	--	--	ATK/DEF +5%	Seraphic Gate

Heavy Boot Forging

Rarity	Creation Result	1st Ingredient	Qty.	2nd Ingredient	Qty.	3rd Ingredient	Qty.	Sigmund IC Lv.	Edward IC Lv.
1	Rusted Greaves	Metal Fragment	1	--	--	--	--	1	--
1	Bronze Scale Greaves	Bronze Metal	1	--	--	--	--	1	1
2	Iron Scale Greaves	Iron Metal	1	Bronze Scale Greaves	1	--	--	1	1
2	Copper Chain Greaves	Copper Metal	1	Bronze Scale Greaves	1	--	--	2	2
3	Steel Scale Greaves	Steel Metal	1	Iron Scale Greaves	1	--	--	3	2
3	Silver Chain Greaves	Silver Metal	1	Copper Chain Greaves	1	--	--	--	2
4	Banded Greaves	Titanium Metal	1	Steel Scale Greaves	1	--	--	--	3
4	Gold Chain Greaves	Gold Metal	1	Silver Chain Greaves	1	--	--	--	3
5	Bronze Plate Greaves	Bronze Metal	3	Bronze Scale Greaves	1	--	--	--	3
5	Iron Greaves	Iron Metal	3	Iron Scale Greaves	1	--	--	--	4
6	Steel Greaves	Steel Metal	3	Steel Scale Greaves	1	--	--	--	4
6	Heavy Greaves	Titanium Metal	3	Steel Greaves	1	--	--	--	4
7	Prominence Leggings	Blaze Metal	1	Heavy Greaves	1	--	--	--	5
7	Prismatite Greaves	Prismatite Metal	1	Steel Greaves	1	--	--	--	5
8	Crescent Leggings	Lunatite	1	Prominence Leggings	1	--	--	--	5
8	Mercurius Greaves	Mercurius Metal	1	Prismatite Greaves	1	--	--	--	6
9	Crystallite Greaves	Crystallite Metal	1	Prismatite Greaves	1	--	--	--	6
9	Eclipse Leggings	Amarlista	1	Crescent Leggings	1	--	--	--	6
10	Kylin Greaves	Atlantis Metal	1	Feet of Saruleus	1	--	--	--	6

*Eugene and Kristofer cannot forge Heavy Boots.

LIGHT ARMOR

Aya   Kiriya   Vic   Komachi   Touma   Kristofer

Light armor is intended for more nimble fighters. Eugene crafts some solid light armor, but the best comes from the Underwater Palace and Seraphic Gate.

Name	Description	Value	Rarity	ATK	HIT	DEF	AGL	INT	LUC	Effects	Special Acquisition
Torn Clothes	Shabby clothes with holes all over.	90	1	--	--	3	--	--	--	Unbreakable	--
Patched Leather Jacket	Simple leather armor made from pieced-together patches of rabbit hide.	250	1	--	--	8	--	--	--	--	--
Soft Leather Jacket	Simple leather armor made from sheep hide. Has good mobility, but poor defense.	750	2	--	--	15	--	--	--	--	--
Hard Leather Jacket	Leather armor made from buffalo hide. Restricted in mobility, but high in defense.	1800	2	--	--	25	--	--	--	--	--
Crested Vest	Leather armor reinforced in certain areas with ceramic.	2400	3	--	--	30	--	--	--	--	--
Silver Fur Jacket	Simple leather armor adorned with silver fox fur.	3000	3	--	--	40	--	--	--	--	--
Lizard Skin Vest	Simple leather armor reinforced with lizard skin.	4000	4	--	--	55	--	--	--	--	--
Nightwhisper Garb	Official Nightwhisper Guild equipment. Perfect for covert missions.	6000	4	--	--	60	--	--	--	--	--
Woodchip Vest	Leather armor reinforced with lentesco. The lentesco helps absorb impact.	8000	5	--	--	75	--	--	--	--	--
Patchwork Vest	Artificial leather armor. Made from patching together various imitation leathers.	15000	6	--	--	80	--	--	--	--	--
Garuda Jacket	Leather armor made from garuda skin. Light, with good mobility.	20000	6	--	--	85	--	--	--	AGL +10	--
Salamander Jacket	Leather armor made from salamander skin covered in a thick liquid. Fireproof.	32000	7	--	--	95	--	--	--	Fire damage -50%	--
Nightwhisper Uniform	Official equipment for mid- ranked Nightwhisper Guild members. Offers good mobility.	40000	8	--	--	110	--	--	--	AGL +10	--
Golden Fur Jacket	Simple leather armor adorned with golden wolf fur. Absorbs all sorts of impacts.	5200	5	--	--	70	--	--	--	--	Complete Side Quest "Dressed up Vic"
Mirage Vest	Leather armor made from chameleon skin. Camouflages its wearer.	28000	7	--	--	90	--	--	--	--	--
Solid Leather Jacket	Leather armor made from glutton hide. Magically created to be hard yet light.	50000	8	--	--	115	--	--	--	Anti-stone	--
Fierce Leopard Garb	A garb made from the fur of a beast. Gives the wearer great agility.	62000	9	--	--	180	--	--	--	AGL +20	Must complete Private Event "Secret of Smithery" to make
Dragon Hide Vest	Leather armor made from dragon hide. Hardens according to its wearer's reflexes.	100000	9	--	--	200	--	--	--	--	Must complete Private Event "Secret of Smithery" to make
Phoenix Feather Jacket	Leather armor with the power of Avifir. The feathers protect against fire attacks.	128000	10	--	--	250	--	--	--	Fire damage -50%	Underwater Palace Treasure Chest
Sabris Garb	A garb with the power of Sabris. The fur sharpens the wearer's senses.	154000	10	--	--	300	--	--	--	Anti-ailment (30%)	Seraphic Gate

Light Armor Forging

Rarity	Creation Result	1st Ingredient	Qty.	2nd Ingredient	Qty.	3rd Ingredient	Qty.	Eugene IC Lv.	Sigmund IC Lv.
1	Patched Leather Jacket	Rabbit Hide	3	--	--	--	--	1	1
2	Soft Leather Jacket	Sheep Hide	3	Patched Leather Jacket	1	--	--	1	1
2	Hard Leather Jacket	Buffalo Hide	3	Patched Leather Jacket	1	--	--	2	2
3	Crested Vest	Ceramic	2	Hard Leather Jacket	1	--	--	2	3
3	Silver Fur Jacket	Silver Fox Fur	3	Soft Leather Jacket	1	--	--	2	--
4	Lizard Skin Vest	Lizard Skin	3	Crested Vest	1	--	--	3	--
4	Nightwhisper Garb	Cotton Cloth	3	Crested Vest	1	--	--	3	--
5	Golden Fur Jacket	Golden Wolf Fur	3	Silver Fur Jacket	1	--	--	3	--
5	Woodchip Vest	Lentesco Wood	3	Lizard Skin Vest	1	--	--	4	--
6	Patchwork Vest	Hard Leather Jacket	3	Lizard Skin Vest	2	--	--	4	--
6	Garuda Jacket	Garuda Skin	3	Nightwhisper Garb	1	--	--	4	--
7	Mirage Vest	Chameleon Skin	3	Crystallite Metal	1	Lizard Skin Vest	1	5	--
7	Salamander Jacket	Salamander Skin	3	Lizard Skin Vest	1	--	--	5	--
8	Nightwhisper Uniform	Damask Cloth	3	Nightwhisper Garb	1	--	--	5	--
8	Solid Leather Jacket	Glutton Hide	3	Salamander Jacket	1	--	--	6	--
9	Fierce Leopard Garb	Feeble Cloth	3	Nightwhisper Uniform	1	--	--	6	--
9	Dragon Hide Vest	Dragon Hide	3	Solid Leather Jacket	1	--	--	6	--

*Edward and Kristofer cannot forge Light Armor.

LIGHT HELMET

Aya

Kiriya

Vic

Komachi

Touma

Kristofer

The best light helmets are either made by Eugene or found in the Underwater Palace and Seraphic Gate.

Name	Description	Value	Rarity	ATK	HIT	DEF	AGL	INT	LUC	Effects	Special Acquisition
Shabby Hat	An old shabby hat.	45	1	--	--		--	--	--	Unbreakable	--
Patched Leather Cap *	A cap made from pieced-together patches of rabbit hide.	150	1	--	--	5	--	--	--	--	--
Soft Leather Cap	A leather cap made from sheep hide. Soft and devilishly comfortable.	650	2	--	--	10	--	--	--	--	--
Hard Leather Cap	A leather cap made from buffalo hide. Durable and gives great protection.	1450	2	--	--	15	--	--	--	--	--
Crested Mask	A mask reinforced with ceramic.	1600	3	--	--	20	--	--	--	--	--
Silver Fur Hood	A hood made from silver fox fur.	2400	3	--	--	25	--	--	--	--	--
Lizard Skin Cap	A cap made from lizard skin.	3500	4	--	--	30	--	--	--	--	--
Nightwhisper Hood	Official Nightwhisper Guild equipment. Made black to blend into the shadows.	5500	4	--	--	40	--	--	--	HIT +10	--
Woodchip Mask	A mask reinforced with lentesco. Resistant to heavy impact.	8500	5	--	--	55	--	--	--	--	--
Patchwork Cap	An artificial leather cap. Made from patching together various imitation leathers.	13500	6	--	--	65	--	--	--	--	--
Garuda Hood	A hood made from garuda skin. Surprisingly light and comfortable.	19500	6	--	--	70	--	--	--	AGL +10	Complete Side Quest "Rebirth of Halgita"
Salamander Cap	A cap made from salamander skin covered in a thick liquid. Fireproof.	32000	7	--	--	75	--	--	--	Fire damage -50%	--
Nightwhisper Mask	Official equipment for mid-ranked Nightwhisper Guild members. Covers entire face.	38000	8	--	--	85	--	--	--	HIT +20	--
Golden Fur Hood	A hood adorned with golden wolf fur. Absorbs all sorts of impacts.	6200	5	--	--	48	--	--	--	--	--
Mirage Cap	A cap made from chameleon skin. Camouflages its wearer.	28000	7	--	--	80	--	--	--	--	--
Solid Leather Cap	A cap made from glutton hide. Magically created to be hard yet light.	68000	8	--	--	90	--	--	--	--	--
Dragon Hide Cap	A cap made from dragon hide. Hardens according to its wearer's reflexes.	76500	9	--	--	95	--	--	--	--	Must complete Private Event "Secret of Smithery" to make
Phoenix Feather Hood	A hood with the power of Avifir. The feathers protect against fire attacks.	95000	10	--	--	120	--	--	--	Fire damage -50%	Underwater Palace Treasure Chest
Avifir Headdress	A headdress with the power of Avifir. Grants the wearer intelligence and agility.	110000	10	--	--	130	--	--	--	INT +10, AGL +20	Seraphic Gate
Eye of Avifir	An eyepatch with the power of Avifir. Allows for flawless accuracy.	82000	9	--	--	105	--	--	--	HIT +40	Must have access to Seraphic Gate to make

Light Helmet Forging

Rarity	Creation Result	1st Ingredient	Qty.	2nd Ingredient	Qty.	3rd Ingredient	Qty.	Eugene IC Lv.	Sigmund IC Lv.
1	Shabby Hat	Kenaf Cloth	1	--	--	--	--	--	1
1	Patched Leather Cap	Rabbit Hide	1	--	--	--	--	1	1
2	Soft Leather Cap	Sheep Hide	1	Patched Leather Cap	1	--	--	1	1
2	Hard Leather Cap	Buffalo Hide	1	Patched Leather Cap	1	--	--	2	2
3	Crested Mask	Ceramic	1	Hard Leather Cap	1	--	--	2	3
3	Silver Fur Hood	Silver Fox Fur	1	Soft Leather Cap	1	--	--	2	--
4	Lizard Skin Cap	Lizard Skin	1	Crested Mask	1	--	--	3	--
4	Nightwhisper Hood	Cotton Cloth	1	Crested Mask	1	--	--	3	--
5	Golden Fur Hood	Golden Wolf Fur	1	Silver Fur Hood	1	--	--	3	--
5	Woodchip Mask	Lentesco Wood	1	Lizard Skin Cap	1	--	--	4	--
6	Patchwork Cap	Hard Leather Cap	1	Lizard Skin Cap	1	--	--	4	--
6	Garuda Hood	Garuda Skin	1	Nightwhisper Hood	1	--	--	4	--
7	Mirage Cap	Chameleon Skin	1	Crystallite Metal	1	Lizard Skin Cap	1	5	--
7	Salamander Cap	Salamander Skin	1	Lizard Skin Cap	1	--	--	5	--
8	Nightwhisper Mask	Damask Cloth	1	Nightwhisper Hood	1	--	--	5	--
8	Solid Leather Cap	Glutton Hide	1	Salamander Cap	1	--	--	6	--
9	Dragon Hide Cap	Dragon Hide	1	Solid Leather Cap	1	--	--	6	--
9	Eye of Avifir	Salamander Skin	2	Garuda Skin	2	Amarlista	1	6	--

Edward and Kristofer cannot forge Light Helmets.

LIGHT BOOTS

 Aya

 Kiriya

 Vic

 Komachi

 Touma

 Kristofer

The best light boots are made by Eugene, or found in the Underwater Palace and Seraphic Gate.

Name	Description	Value	Rarity	ATK	HIT	DEF	AGL	INT	LUC	Effects	Special Acquisition
Soleless Shoes	Worn-out boots that are missing their soles.	30	1	--	--	--	--	--	--	Unbreakable	--
Patched Leather Boots	Boots made from pieced- together patches of rabbit hide.	120	1	--	--	3	4	--	--	--	--
Soft Leather Boots	Boots made from sheep hide. Soft and comfortable.	550	2	--	--	6	8	--	--	--	--
Hard Leather Boots	Boots made from buffalo hide. The hard leather makes them durable, though uncomfortable.	1100	2	--	--	10	10	--	--	--	--
Balsa Clogs	Clogs made of balsa. Light in weight and ideal for walking in.	1800	3	--	--	15	12	--	--	--	--
Solid Leather Boots	Boots made from glutton hide. Magically created to be hard yet light.	67000	8	--	--	80	80	--	--	--	--
Lux Clogs	Expensive clogs made of lux. These were clearly not designed with comfort in mind.	4800	3	--	--	20	5	--	--	--	--
Hearthstone Boots	Soft leather boots with soles made of hearthstone. Comfortable on long treks.	11000	5	--	--	45	30	--	--	--	--
Nightwhisper Shoes	Official Nightwhisper Guild equipment. Enable silent movement.	8500	4	--	--	35	35	--	--	Critical hit rate +3%	--
Lentesco Clogs	Clogs made of lentesco. Comfortable to wear due to their elasticity.	16000	5	--	--	50	40	--	--	--	--
Patchwork Boots	Artificial leather boots. Made from patching together various imitation leathers.	20000	6	--	--	55	55	--	--	--	--
Garuda Shoes	Shoes made from garuda skin. Make the wearer light-footed.	25000	6	--	--	60	60	--	--	--	--
Salamander Boots	Boots made from salamander skin covered in a thick liquid. Fireproof.	52400	7	--	--	70	70	--	--	Fire damage -50%	--
Mirage Boots	Boots made from chameleon skin. Camouflage their wearer.	42000	7	--	--	75	50	--	--	--	--
Lizard Skin Boots	Boots made from lizard skin.	5000	4	--	--	25	30	--	--	--	--
Dragon Hide Boots	Boots made from dragon hide. Harden according to their wearer's reflexes.	76500	9	--	--	85	85	--	--	--	Must complete Private Event "Secret of Smithery" to make
Phoenix Feather Boots	Boots with the power of Avifir. The feathers protect against fire attacks.	110000	10	--	--	100	95	--	--	Fire damage -50%	Underwater Palace Treasure Chest
Sabris Boots	Boots with the power of Sabris. Allow the wearer to run like the wind.	95000	10	--	--	95	90	--	--	--	Seraphic Gate
Kylin Boots	Boots with the power of Kylin. Enable silent movement.	82000	9	--	--	90	80	--	--	Earth damage -50%	Must complete Private Event "Secret of Smithery" to make
Kylin Sandals	Sandals with the power of Kylin. Allow lightning-fast movement.	120000	10	--	--	110	90	--	--	--	Must have access to Seraphic Gate to make

Light Boot Forging

Rarity	Creation Result	1st Ingredient	Qty.	2nd Ingredient	Qty.	3rd Ingredient	Qty.	Eugene IC Lv.	Sigmund IC Lv.
1	Soleless Shoes	Kenaf Cloth	1	--	--	--	--	--	1
1	Patched Leather Boots	Rabbit Hide	1	--	--	--	--	1	1
2	Soft Leather Boots	Sheep Hide	1	Patched Leather Boots	1	--	--	1	1
2	Hard Leather Boots	Buffalo Hide	1	Patched Leather Boots	1	--	--	1	2
3	Balsa Clogs	Balsa Wood	1	Hard Leather Boots	1	--	--	2	3
3	Lux Clogs	Lux Wood	1	Balsa Clogs	1	--	--	2	--
4	Lizard Skin Boots	Lizard Skin	1	Soft Leather Boots	1	--	--	2	--
4	Nightwhisper Shoes	Cotton Cloth	1	Hearthstone Boots	1	--	--	3	--
5	Hearthstone Boots	Hearthstone	1	Lizard Skin Boots	1	--	--	3	--
5	Lentesco Clogs	Lentesco Wood	1	Lux Clogs	1	--	--	3	--
6	Patchwork Boots	Hard Leather Boots	1	Lizard Skin Boots	1	--	--	4	--
6	Garuda Shoes	Garuda Skin	1	Nightwhisper Shoes	1	--	--	4	--
7	Mirage Boots	Chameleon Skin	1	Crystallite Metal	1	Lizard Skin Boots	1	4	--
7	Salamander Boots	Salamander Skin	1	Lizard Skin Boots	1	--	--	5	--
8	Solid Leather Boots	Glutton Hide	1	Salamander Boots	1	--	--	5	--
9	Dragon Hide Boots	Dragon Hide	1	Solid Leather Boots	1	--	--	5	--
9	Kylin Boots	Empyrean Cloth	1	Amarlista	1	--	--	6	--
10	Kylin Sandals	Atlantis Metal	2	Kylin Boots	1	--	--	6	--

*Edward and Kristofer cannot forge Light Boots.

MAGIC ARMOR

 Rico

 Rucha

 Eugene

 Michelle

 Savio

 Seraphina

* Males can't wear silk shawl.

Magic armor provides casters some defense and enhances their magic abilities. The feeble cape, found in the Underwater Palace, is probably the best pound-for-pound, simply because it grants MP regeneration on any caster not named Aya. However, there are better options for some casters once they have equipment that grants MP regeneration in other slots. Other great pieces are made by Eugene or found in the Seraphic Gate.

Name	Description	Value	Rarity	ATK	HIT	DEF	AGL	INT	LUC	Effects	Special Acquisition
Moth-Eaten Robe	Worn and torn traveling clothes.	50	1	--	--	1	--	--	--	Unbreakable	--
Kenaf Tunic	A tunic made from kenaf. Rigid and easily torn.	180	1	--	--	5	--	--	--	--	--
Bark Robe	A robe made from barkcloth. Often worn by novice priests and mages.	1000	2	--	--	10	--	--	--	--	--
Ramie Chiton	A robe made from ramie. Made thick for use in battle conditions.	600	2	--	--	15	--	--	--	--	--
Linen Toga	A robe made from linen. Favored by mages due to its magic powers.	6500	4	--	--	30	--	--	--	INT +10	--
Cotton Cloak	A cloak made from cotton. Made durable for long journeys.	1700	3	--	--	20	--	--	--	--	--
Linen Cape	A cape made from linen. Perfect for semi-formal occasions.	2000	3	--	--	25	--	--	--	--	--
Silk Cloak	A cloak made from silk. Resistant to hot and cold conditions.	15000	5	--	--	40	--	--	--	Water damage -50%, Fire damage -50%	--
Damask Coat	A coat made from damask.	28000	6	--	--	75	--	--	--	--	--
Rachnuvus Sari	A sari made of rachnuvus cloth. Has a beautiful sheen.	82000	8	--	--	100	--	--	--	--	--
Beast Fur Garb	A garb made from the fur of a beast.	36000	7	--	--	80	--	--	--	--	--
Down Feather Cloak	A cloak made of down feather cloth. Worn by priests who serve the Claridians.	18000	6	--	--	65	--	--	--	--	--
Silk Shawl	A shawl made from silk. Usually worn by women.	4500	4	--	--	40	--	--	--	--	--
Silk Robe	A robe made from silk. Feels nice on the skin and is comfortable to wear.	7000	5	--	--	50	--	--	--	--	--
Damask Gown	A gown made from damask. Adorned with gems; gives the wearer energy.	44000	7	--	--	85	--	--	--	HP +10%	--
Shadow Cloak	A cloak made from lubricus. Wear it in the dark for maximum effectiveness.	115500	9	--	--	150	--	--	--	--	Must complete Private Event "Secret of Smithery" to make
Mage Robe	A robe made of rachnuvus cloth. Gives the wearer great magic powers.	99800	9	--	--	100	--	--	--	MP +10%	Must complete Private Event "Secret of Smithery" to make
Blessed Garb	A garb made from empyrean. Only permitted for aristos to wear.	120500	10	--	--	200	--	--	--	INT +50	Must have access to Seraphic Gate to make
Feeble Cape	A shoulder cape made of feeble cloth. Increases magic powers in place of energy.	75000	8	--	--	90	--	--	--	HP drain 1%, MP +20%, MP Regeneration 1%	Underwater Palace Treasure Chest
Avifir Garb	A garb with the power of Avifir. Grants the wearer fire magic power.	148000	10	--	--	220	--	--	--	Fire damage +30%	Seraphic Gate

Magic Armor Forging

Rarity	Creation Result	1st Ingredient	Qty.	2nd Ingredient	Qty.	3rd Ingredient	Qty.	Eugene IC Lv.	Sigmund IC Lv.
1	Kenaf Tunic	Kenaf Cloth	2	--	--	--	--	1	1
2	Ramie Chiton	Ramie Cloth	2	Kenaf Tunic	1	--	--	1	1
2	Bark Robe	Barkcloth	2	Ramie Chiton	1	--	--	2	2
3	Cotton Cloak	Cotton Cloth	2	Bark Robe	1	--	--	2	3
3	Linen Cape	Linen Cloth	2	Cotton Cloak	1	--	--	2	--
4	Linen Toga	Linen Cloth	2	Linen Cape	1	--	--	3	--
4	Silk Shawl	Silk Cloth	2	Linen Cape	1	--	--	3	--
5	Silk Robe	Silk Cloth	2	Silk Shawl	1	--	--	3	--
5	Silk Cloak	Silk Cloth	2	Silk Robe	1	--	--	4	--
6	Down Feather Cloak	Down Feather Cloth	2	Silk Robe	1	--	--	4	--
6	Damask Coat	Damask Cloth	2	Down Feather Cloak	1	--	--	4	--
7	Damask Gown	Damask Cloth	2	Damask Coat	1	--	--	5	--
7	Beast Fur Garb	Feeble Cloth	2	Damask Gown	1	--	--	5	--
8	Rachnuvus Sari	Rachnuvus Cloth	2	Beast Fur Garb	1	--	--	6	--
9	Mage Robe	Rachnuvus Cloth	2	Rachnuvus Sari	1	--	--	6	--
9	Shadow Cloak	Lubricus Cloth	2	Rachnuvus Sari	1	--	--	6	--
10	Blessed Garb	Empyrean Cloth	2	Mage Robe	1	--	--	6	--

Edward and Kristofer cannot forge Magic Armor.

MAGIC HELMET

Rico   Rucha   Eugene   Michelle   Savio   Seraphina

* Females can't wear rachnuvus turban or silk hat.

Eugene makes the best helmets for mages. These hats typically boost MP or INT.

Name	Description	Value	Rarity	ATK	HIT	DEF	AGL	INT	LUC	Effects	Special Acquisition
Tarnished Circlet	A dirty circlet that has lost its shine.	25	1	--	--	--	--	--	--	Unbreakable	--
Sandstone Circlet	A circlet made of sandstone. Fragile and offers almost no protection.	100	1	--	--	3	--	--	--	--	--
Granite Circlet	A circlet made of granite. Hard to carve, but durable and offers good protection.	520	2	--	--	6	--	--	--	--	--
Marble Circlet	A circlet made of marble. The stone in the center helps the wearer to focus.	950	2	--	--	10	--	--	--	INT +10	--
Cotton Hat	A hat with a large brim made from cotton. Favored by mages.	1200	3	--	--	15	--	--	--	--	--
Linen Hat	A hat with a large brim made from linen.	1800	3	--	--	20	--	--	--	--	--
Metetite Circlet	A circlet made of metetite with a polished black stone at the front.	3800	4	--	--	30	--	--	--	MP +10%	--
Rachnuvus Turban	A turban made of rachnuvus cloth. Formal headgear for men in certain regions.	6500	5	--	--	40	--	--	--	--	--
Mage Hat	A hat with a large brim made of rachnuvus cloth. Grants the wearer great magic powers.	25000	7	--	--	60	--	--	--	INT +10	--
Beast Fur Bandana	A bandana made from the fur of a beast.	20000	6	--	--	45	--	--	--	--	--
Blaze Tiara	A tiara made of blaze. Increases fire magic power.	22000	6	--	--	50	--	--	--	Fire damage	--
Quartz Tiara	A tiara made of quartz. Increases water magic power.	42000	8	--	--	65	--	--	--	Water damage +10%	--
Prismatite Tiara	A tiara made of prismatite. Increases earth magic power.	50000	8	--	--	70	--	--	--	Earth damage +10%	--
Down Feather Hat	A hat with a large brim made of down feather cloth. Increases aether magic power.	4400	4	--	--	25	--	--	--	Aether damage +10%	--
Silk Hat	A cylindrical hat made from silk cloth. Lustrous formalwear for men.	4500	5	--	--	35	--	--	--	--	--
Mercurius Crown	A crown made of mercurius. Changes its size according to the wearer.	80000	9	--	--	80	--	--	--	--	--
Pius Tiara	A tiara made of pius. Increases air magic power.	96000	9	--	--	90	--	--	--	Air damage +10%	Must complete Private Event "Secret of Smithery" to make
Blessed Hat	A hat made from empyrean. Only permitted for aristos to wear.	120000	10	--	--	100	--	--	--	MP +20%	Must complete Private Event "Secret of Smithery" to make
Bloody Hat	A hat with a large brim made of feeble cloth.	30000	7	--	--	55	--	--	--	HP Regeneration 3%	--
Vermillion Wing Piece	A headpiece with the power of Avifir. Suppresses magic powers.	150000	10	--	--	110	--	--	--	INT +30, MP Consumption -20%	Must have access to Seraphic Gate to make

Magic Helmet Forging

Rarity	Creation Result	1st Ingredient	Qty.	2nd Ingredient	Qty.	3rd Ingredient	Qty.	Eugene IC Lv.	Sigmund IC Lv.	Kristofer IC Lv.
1	Tarnished Circlet	Stone Statue Fragment	1	--	--	--	--	--	1	--
1	Sandstone Circlet	Sandstone	1	--	--	--	--	1	1	1
2	Granite Circlet	Granite	1	Sandstone Circlet	1	--	--	2	1	1
2	Marble Circlet	Marble	1	Sandstone Circlet	1	--	--	2	2	1
3	Cotton Hat	Cotton Cloth	2	Barkcloth	2	--	--	3	3	2
3	Linen Hat	Linen Cloth	2	Cotton Hat	1	--	--	3	--	2
4	Metetite Circlet	Metetite	2	Marble Circlet	2	--	--	3	--	2
4	Down Feather Hat	Down Feather Cloth	1	Linen Hat	1	--	--	--	--	3
5	Silk Hat	Silk Cloth	1	Down Feather Hat	1	--	--	--	--	3
5	Rachnuvus Turban	Rachnuvus Shell	2	Silk Hat	1	--	--	--	--	4
6	Beast Fur Bandana	Feeble Cloth	1	Rachnuvus Turban	1	--	--	--	--	4
6	Blaze Tiara	Blaze Metal	2	Metetite Circlet	2	--	--	--	--	4
7	Bloody Hat	Feeble Cloth	2	Beast Fur Bandana	1	--	--	--	--	4
7	Mage Hat	Rachnuvus Cloth	2	Rachnuvus Turban	1	--	--	--	--	5
8	Quartz Tiara	Quartz	2	Blaze Tiara	1	--	--	--	--	5
8	Prismatite Tiara	Prismatite Metal	2	Blaze Tiara	1	--	--	--	--	5
9	Mercurius Crown	Mercurius Metal	2	Quartz Tiara	1	--	--	--	--	6
9	Pius Tiara	Pius Wood	2	Prismatite Tiara	1	--	--	--	--	6
10	Blessed Hat	Empyrean Cloth	1	Mage Hat	1	--	--	--	--	6
10	Vermillion Wing Piece	Amarlista	1	Eye of Avifir	1	--	--	--	--	6

*Edward cannot forge Magic Helmets.

MAGIC BOOTS

Rico

Rucha

Eugene

Michelle

Savio

Seraphina

* Males can't wear damask mules.

Eugene makes the best footwear for mages, too. The scarlet pumps operate just like the feeble cape, replenishing 1% of max MP every 5 seconds. The price you pay—taking damage equivalent to 1% of max HP every 5 seconds—is small compared to the allure of replenishing MP.

Name	Description	Value	Rarity	ATK	HIT	DEF	AGL	INT	LUC	Effects	Special Acquisition
Broken-Heeled Sandals	Sandals with broken heels caused by excessive wear.	20	1	--	--	--	--	--	--	Unbreakable	--
Cork Sandals	Sandals made of cork. Light yet durable.	80	1	--	--	2	3	--	--	--	--
Lauan Sandals	Sandals made of lauan. Offer good protection.	380	2	--	--	5	6	--	--	--	--
Balsa Sandals	Sandals made of balsa. So light it is easy to forget you're even wearing them.	650	2	--	--	8	10	--	--	--	--
Lux Sandals	Sandals made of lux. Expensive with a beautiful sheen.	1200	3	--	--	10	12	--	--	--	Complete Private Event "Stray Dog"
Silver Fur Pumps	Silk pumps adorned with silver fox fur.	2800	3	--	--	18	15	--	--	--	Complete Side Quest "Broken Heart"
Rachnuvus Pumps	Pumps made of rachnuvus webbing.	8500	5	--	--	42	10	--	--	--	--
Mage Sandals	Sandals made of rachnuvus cloth. Restore the wearer's magic power with every step.	70000	8	--	--	65	50	--	--	MP Regeneration 1%	--
Golden Fur Pumps	Silk pumps adorned with golden wolf fur.	3400	4	--	--	22	20	--	--	--	--
Lentesco Sandals	Sandals made of lentesco. Soft and comfortable.	5000	4	--	--	26	15	--	--	--	--
Placidus Sandals	Sandals made of placidus. Offer great comfort on long journeys.	6000	5	--	--	35	25	--	--	--	--
Silk Pumps	Stylish pumps made from silk. Popular among Burguss nobles.	12000	6	--	--	40	30	--	--	--	--
Malus Sandals	Sandals made of malus. Given to the mages of great accomplishment.	20000	6	--	--	45	30	--	--	--	--
Damask Mules	Mules made from damask. Stylish, with beautiful embroidery.	35000	7	--	--	50	35	--	--	--	--
Beast Fur Greaves	Greaves made from the fur of a beast. Stained crimson from the blood of the slain.	40000	8	--	--	60	45	--	--	--	--
Pius Sandals	Sandals made of pius. Increase the wearer's spirit.	75000	9	--	--	70	55	--	--	INT +20	--
Blessed Mules	Mules made from empyrean. Only permitted for aristos to wear.	92600	10	--	--	90	65	--	--	MP +10%	Must complete Private Event "Secret of Smithery" to make
Black Pumps	Pumps made from lubricus.	85000	9	--	--	80	60	--	--	--	Must complete Private Event "Secret of Smithery" to make
Scarlet Pumps	Pumps made of feeble cloth. Increase magic powers in place of energy.	46000	7	--	--	55	40	--	--	HP drain 1%, MP Regeneration 1%	--
Karathos Sandals	Sandals with the power of Karathos. Grant infinite magic power in place of speed.	115000	10	--	--	95	--	--	--	AGL-20, INT +30	Must have access to Seraphic Gate to make

Magic Boot Forging

Rarity	Creation Result	1st Ingredient	Qty.	2nd Ingredient	Qty.	3rd Ingredient	Qty.	Eugene IC Lv.	Sigmund IC Lv.	Kristofer IC Lv.
1	Broken-Heeled Sandals	Junk	1	--	--	--	--	--	1	--
1	Cork Sandals	Cork Wood	1	--	--	--	--	1	1	1
2	Lauan Sandals	Lauan Wood	1	Cork Sandals	1	--	--	2	1	1
2	Balsa Sandals	Balsa Wood	1	Lauan Sandals	1	--	--	2	2	1
3	Lux Sandals	Lux Wood	1	Balsa Sandals	1	--	--	3	3	2
3	Silver Fur Pumps	Silver Fox Fur	1	Lux Sandals	1	--	--	3	--	2
4	Golden Fur Pumps	Golden Wolf Fur	1	Silver Fur Pumps	1	--	--	3	--	2
4	Lentesco Sandals	Lentesco Wood	1	Lux Sandals	1	--	--	--	--	3
5	Placidus Sandals	Placidus Wood	1	Lentesco Sandals	1	--	--	--	--	3
5	Rachnuvus Pumps	Rachnuvus Shell	2	Placidus Sandals	1	--	--	--	--	3
6	Silk Pumps	Silk Cloth	1	Golden Fur Pumps	1	--	--	--	--	4
6	Malus Sandals	Malus Wood	1	Rachnuvus Pumps	1	--	--	--	--	4
7	Damask Mules	Damask Cloth	1	Malus Sandals	1	--	--	--	--	5
7	Scarlet Pumps	Feeble Cloth	1	Silk Pumps	1	--	--	--	--	5
8	Beast Fur Greaves	Feeble Cloth	1	Malus Sandals	1	--	--	--	--	5
8	Mage Sandals	Rachnuvus Cloth	1	Malus Sandals	1	--	--	--	--	5
9	Pius Sandals	Pius Wood	1	Mage Sandals	1	--	--	--	--	6
9	Black Pumps	Lubricus Cloth	1	Scarlet Pumps	1	--	--	--	--	6
10	Blessed Mules	Empyrean Cloth	1	Damask Mules	1	--	--	--	--	6
10	Karathos Sandals	Amarlista	1	Empyrean Cloth	2	--	--	--	--	6

*Edward cannot forge Magic Boots.

ACCESSORIES

RINGS

Everyone *

* Only Gustav can wear sovereignty ring; only Capell and Sigmund can wear Casandra ring.

Rings allow you to augment each character's individual abilities as you see fit. Kristofer fashions the best rings at IC Lv.6. These add HP and MP regeneration to any character, or drastically boost stats!

Name	Description	Value	Rarity	ATK	HIT	DEF	AGL	INT	LUC	Effects	Special Acquisition
Sandstone Ring	A scrap ring made of crumbling sandstone.	150	1	--	--	--	--	--	--	--	--
Blossom Ring	A ring made of flowers. Used by children during pretend weddings.	2	1	--	--	--	--	--	--	--	--
Bronze Ring	A ring made of bronze.	300	2	--	--	5	--	--	--	--	--
Iron Ring	A ring made of iron. Increases the wearer's accuracy.	600	2	--	10	--	--	--	--	--	--
Copper Ring	A ring made of copper. Increases the wearer's intelligence.	1500	3	--	--	--	--	10	--	--	--
Silver Ring	A ring made of silver. Increases the wearer's defense.	2800	3	--	--	10	--	--	--	--	--
Gold Ring	A ring made of gold. Increases the wearer's strength.	5000	4	10	--	--	--	--	--	--	Complete Side Quest "Son"
Mercurius Ring	A ring made of mercurius. Increases the wearer's agility.	5000	4	--	--	--	10	--	--	--	--
Lentesco Ring	A ring made of lentesco. Increases air magic power.	40000	7	--	--	--	--	5	--	Air damage +10%	--
Salamander Ring	A ring made from salamander skin. Increases fire magic power.	40000	7	--	--	--	--	5	--	Fire damage	--
Ceramic Ring	A ring made of rock from the deepest stratum below Halgita. Increases earth magic power.	40000	7	--	--	--	--	5	--	Earth damage +10%	--
Prismatite Ring	A ring made of ore from the mountains of Kolton. Increases aether magic power.	40000	7	--	--	--	--	5	--	Aether damage +10%	--
Rachnuvus Ring	A ring made of rachnuvus webbing from Casandra forests. Increases water magic power.	40000	7	--	--	--	--	5	--	Water damage +10%	--
Ring of Heart	A magic ring that continuously increases the wearer's spirit.	50000	8	--	--	--	--	--	--	MP Regeneration 1%	--
Ring of Life	A magic ring that heals the wearer's wounds.	42000	8	--	--	--	--	--	--	HP Regeneration 3%	Complete Side Quest "Looking for Jewelry"
Lunatite Ring	A ring embedded with lunatite. Gives the wearer great powers.	35000	8	--	--	--	--	--	--	MP +20%	--
Crystallite Ring	A ring made of crystallite.	35000	8	--	--	--	--	--	--	HP +20%	--
Amarlista Ring	A ring embedded with amarlista.	78000	9	--	--	--	--	5	--	Magic damage +10%	Must complete Private Event "Secret of Smithery" to make
Sovereignty Ring	A ring worn by a legendary sacred bird as a symbol of his sovereignty.	120000	9	50	--	50	--	--	--	ATK/DEF +5%	Underwater Palace Treasure Chest
Saruleus Ring	A ring embedded with a gem from the eye of Saruleus. Gives the wearer great powers.	200000	10	--	--	--	--	--	--	ATK +200, INT +20	Must have access to Seraphic Gate to make
Casandra Ring	A ring given by Svala with "Eternal Friends" inscribed on it.	--	10	--	--	--	--	--	--	HP +10%, MP +10%	Complete Side Quest "Lost Memories"

Ring Forging

Rarity	Creation Result	1st Ingredient	Qty.	2nd Ingredient	Qty.	3rd Ingredient	Qty.	Sigmund IC Lv.	Edward IC Lv.	Kristofer IC Lv.
1	Blossom Ring	Laurel	2	--	--	--	--	1	--	--
1	Sandstone Ring	Sandstone	1	--	--	--	--	1	1	1
2	Bronze Ring	Bronze Metal	1	Sandstone Ring	1	--	--	2	2	2
2	Iron Ring	Iron Metal	1	Bronze Ring	1	--	--	3	2	2
3	Copper Ring	Copper Metal	1	Bronze Ring	1	--	--	--	3	2
3	Silver Ring	Silver Metal	1	Bronze Ring	1	--	--	--	3	3
4	Gold Ring	Gold Metal	1	Silver Ring	1	--	--	--	--	3
4	Mercurius Ring	Mercurius Metal	1	Silver Ring	1	--	--	--	--	3
7	Lentesco Ring	Lentesco Wood	1	Lunatite	1	Pius Wood	1	--	--	5
7	Salamander Ring	Blaze Metal	1	Lunatite	1	Salamander Skin	1	--	--	5
7	Ceramic Ring	Ceramic	1	Lunatite	1	Prismatite Metal	1	--	--	5
7	Prismatite Ring	Prismatite Metal	1	Lunatite	1	Hearthstone	1	--	--	5
7	Rachnuvus Ring	Rachnuvus Cloth	1	Lunatite	1	Rachnuvus Shell	1	--	--	5
8	Lunatite Ring	Lunatite	1	Rachnuvus Ring	1	--	--	--	--	5
8	Crystallite Ring	Crystallite Metal	1	Rachnuvus Ring	1	--	--	--	--	5
8	Ring of Life	Malus Wood	1	Lentesco Ring	1	--	--	--	--	6
8	Ring of Heart	Pius Wood	1	Lentesco Ring	1	--	--	--	--	6
9	Amarlista Ring	Amarlista	1	Ring of Life	1	Ring of Heart	1	--	--	6
10	Saruleus Ring	Atlantis Metal	1	Dragon Eye	1	Amarlista Ring	1	--	--	6

*Eugene cannot forge Rings.

NECKLACES

Everyone

Like rings, different necklaces are effective for different types of characters. The rarest necklaces are made by Kristofer at IC Lv.6, and can block magic damage and status ailments.

Name	Description	Value	Rarity	ATK	HIT	DEF	AGL	INT	LUC	Effects	Special Acquisition
Cork Pendant	An ugly pendant that makes observers question the wearer's fashion sense.	100	1	--	--	--	--	--	--	--	--
Lei	A necklace made of flowers. Used by children during pretend weddings.	2	1	--	--	--	--	--	--	--	--
Lauan Pendant	A pendant imbued with magic to prevent falling asleep.	400	2	--	--	--	--	--	--	Anti-sleep	--
Granite Necklace	A necklace embedded with granite.	600	2	--	--	5	--	--	5	--	--
Balsa Pendant	A pendant imbued with magic to prevent getting confused.	1200	3	--	--	--	--	--	--	Anti-confusion	--
Ebony Pendant	A pendant imbued with magic to prevent being paralyzed.	1600	3	--	--	--	--	--	--	Anti-paralysis	--
Marble Necklace	A necklace embedded with marble.	3500	4	5	--	--	--	--	10	--	Complete Side Quest "The Staff of Life"
Lux Pendant	A pendant imbued with magic to prevent fainting.	3000	4	--	--	--	--	--	--	Anti-faint	--
Snake Pendant	A pendant imbued with magic to prevent being poisoned.	4000	5	--	--	--	--	--	--	Anti-poison	--
Metetite Necklace	A necklace embedded with metetite.	3800	5	--	--	--	--	5	15	--	--
Placidus Pendant	A pendant imbued with magic to prevent being silenced.	4500	6	--	--	--	--	--	--	Anti-silence	--
Malus Pendant	A pendant imbued with magic to prevent being charmed.	5500	7	--	--	--	--	--	--	Anti-charm	--
Pius Pendant	A pendant imbued with magic to prevent being cursed.	6000	7	--	--	--	--	--	--	Anti-curse	--
Blaze Necklace	A necklace imbued with magic to warm the body and prevent being frozen.	5000	6	--	--	--	--	--	--	Anti-freeze	--
Quartz Necklace	A necklace made by a famous sculptor. Imbued with magic to prevent being petrified.	6500	8	--	--	--	--	--	--	Anti-stone	--
Hearthstone Necklace	A necklace from a keeper of the netherworld. Imbued with magic to prevent being doomed.	6500	8	--	--	--	--	--	--	Anti-doom	--
Solar Necklace	A necklace imbued with the magic of light to repel any bodily contaminations.	50000	9	--	--	--	--	--	--	Anti-ailment (50%)	Must complete Private Event "Secret of Smithery" to make
Lunar Necklace	A necklace imbued with the power to nullify magic by crystallizing lunar energy.	50000	9	--	--	--	--	--	--	Anti-magic	Must complete Private Event "Secret of Smithery" to make
Karathos Necklace	A necklace with the power of Karathos.	75000	10	--	--	--	--	--	--	Anti-ailment	Must have access to Seraphic Gate to make
Saruleus Necklace	A necklace with the power of Saruleus.	80000	10	--	--	--	--	--	--	Magic damage -50%	Must have access to Seraphic Gate to make

Necklace Forging

Rarity	Creation Result	1st Ingredient	Qty.	2nd Ingredient	Qty.	3rd Ingredient	Qty.	Eugene IC Lv.	Sigmund IC Lv.	Kristofer IC Lv.
1	Lei	Laurel	2	--	--	--	--	--	1	--
1	Cork Pendant	Cork Wood	1	Insect Antenna	2	--	--	1	1	--
2	Lauan Pendant	Lauan Wood	1	Thin Wing	2	Cork Pendant	1	1	1	1
2	Granite Necklace	Granite	1	Bat Wing	2	Cork Pendant	1	2	2	1
3	Balsa Pendant	Balsa Wood	1	Bird Eye	2	Lauan Pendant	1	2	3	2
3	Ebony Pendant	Ebony Wood	1	Cactus Needle	2	Lauan Pendant	1	3	--	2
4	Marble Necklace	Marble	1	Insect Fang	2	Granite Necklace	1	3	--	2
4	Lux Pendant	Lux Wood	1	Random Beast Bone	2	Balsa Pendant	1	--	--	3
5	Snake Pendant	Silver Metal	1	Snakeskin	2	Ebony Pendant	1	--	--	3
5	Metetite Necklace	Metetite	1	Animal Fang	2	Granite Necklace	1	--	--	3
6	Placidus Pendant	Placidus Wood	1	Lizard Eye	2	Lux Pendant	1	--	--	4
6	Blaze Necklace	Blaze Metal	1	Sunstone	2	Snake Pendant	1	--	--	4
7	Malus Pendant	Malus Wood	1	Vine	2	Placidus Pendant	1	--	--	4
7	Pius Pendant	Pius Wood	1	Monster Claw	2	Blaze Necklace	1	--	--	5
8	Quartz Necklace	Quartz	1	Glutton Hide	1	Pius Pendant	1	--	--	5
8	Hearthstone Necklace	Hearthstone	1	Dragon Scale	1	Malus Pendant	1	--	--	5
9	Solar Necklace	Prismatite Metal	1	Blaze Metal	2	Hearthstone Necklace	1	--	--	6
9	Lunar Necklace	Lunatite	1	Giant Eye	2	Quartz Necklace	1	--	--	6
10	Karathos Necklace	Atlantis Metal	1	Solar Necklace	1	--	--	--	--	6
10	Saruleus Necklace	Atlantis Metal	1	Lunar Necklace	1	--	--	--	--	6

*Edward cannot forge Necklaces.

BRACELETS

Everyone *

* Only Gustav can wear oversized and dragon wristbands.

Kristofer makes the best bracelets. His best, which require IC Lv.6, grant big stat boosts to the wearer. Also note the Karathos wristband, which gives full party EXP to someone who is not in the party!

Name	Description	Value	Rarity	ATK	HIT	DEF	AGL	INT	LUC	Effects	Special Acquisition
Oversized Wristband	A wristband that seems too large for anyone to wear. Who was it possibly made for?	500	1	10	--	10	--	--	--	--	--
Satin Wristband	A wristband made from silk.	3000	5	5	5	5	--	--	--		--
Lizard Wristband	A wristband with a carving that seems to be a good omen.	1000	2	2	--	2	--	--	10	--	--
Linen Wristband	A wristband made from linen.	800	1	--	--	2	--	--	5		--
Iron Wristguard	An iron wristguard. Increases the wearer's accuracy.	2000	4	--	10	5	--	--	--	--	--
Copper Wristguard	A copper wristguard. Increases the wearer's intelligence.	2000	4	--	--	5	--	10	--	--	--
Silver Wristguard	A silver wristguard. Increases the wearer's defense.	5000	6	5	--	10	--	--	--	--	--
Quilt Wristband	A wristband made of down feather cloth.	6500	6	--	--	5	5	5	5	--	Complete Side Quest "Missing Simon"
Gold Wristguard	A gold wristguard. Increases the wearer's strength.	7500	7	10	--	5	--	--	--	--	--
Mercurius Wristguard	A crystallite wristguard. Increases the wearer's agility.	7500	7	--	--	5	10	--	--	--	Complete Side Quest "Aspiring Animal Breeder"
Feather Wristband	A wristband imbued with magic. Makes the wearer light on their feet.	25000	9	--	10	5	10	--	--		--
Wolf Wristband	A wristband imbued with magic that increases the wearer's defense.	1500	3	--	--	--	--	--	--	DEF +10%	--
Sheep Wristband	A wristband in the shape of two clasped hands. Increases the wearer's teamwork skills.	1000	2	--	--	2	--	2	10	--	--
Buffalo Wristband	A wristband with the crest of the god of war. Increases strength.	3000	3	--	--	--	--	--	--	ATK +10% Ð	--
Glutton Wristband	A wristband with the crest of the god of salvation. Increases defense.	32000	8	10	--	--	--	--	--	DEF +10%	--
Feeble Wristband	A wristband worn by a prominent sage. Increases intelligence.	40000	9	--	--	--	10	--	--	INT +5%	--
Lamé Wristband	A wristband made from damask.	75000	8	10	10	100	10	10	10	--	--
Dragon Wristband	A wristband said to grant the wearer the status of king of beasts.	60000	10	100	20	10	10	--	--	ATK/DEF +5%	Must complete Private Event "Secret of Smithery" to make
Sabris Wristband	A divine wristband passed on from Sabris. Imbued with extraordinary powers.	80000	10	5	5	5	5	5	5	HP +20%, MP +20%	Must have access to Seraphic Gate to make
Karathos Wristband	A magic wristband. Creates an emotional bond between the wearer and a distant friend.	4500	5	--	--	--	--	--	--	Main party EXP (100%)	Complete Side Quest "Letter Quest"

Bracelet Forging

Rarity	Creation Result	1st Ingredient	Qty.	2nd Ingredient	Qty.	3rd Ingredient	Qty.	Sigmund IC Lv.	Edward IC Lv.	Kristofer IC Lv.
1	Linen Wristband	Linen Cloth	3	--	--	--	--	1	1	1
2	Sheep Wristband	Sheep Hide	3	Linen Wristband	1	--	--	1	1	1
2	Lizard Wristband	Lizard Skin	3	Linen Wristband	1	--	--	2	2	2
3	Buffalo Wristband	Buffalo Hide	3	Lizard Wristband	1	--	--	3	2	2
3	Wolf Wristband	Golden Wolf Fur	3	Lizard Wristband	1	--	--	--	3	2
4	Iron Wristguard	Iron Metal	3	Iron Ring	1	--	--	--	3	3
4	Copper Wristguard	Copper Metal	3	Copper Ring	1	--	--	--	--	3
5	Karathos Wristband	Ceramic	3	Sheep Wristband	1	--	--	--	--	3
5	Satin Wristband	Silk Cloth	3	Buffalo Wristband	1	--	--	--	--	4
6	Quilt Wristband	Down Feather Cloth	3	Wolf Wristband	1	--	--	--	--	4
6	Silver Wristguard	Silver Metal	3	Silver Ring	1	--	--	--	--	5
7	Gold Wristguard	Gold Metal	3	Gold Ring	1	--	--	--	--	5
7	Mercurius Wristguard	Mercurius Metal	3	Mercurius Ring	1	--	--	--	--	5
8	Lamé Wristband	Damask Cloth	3	Quilt Wristband	1	--	--	--	--	5
8	Glutton Wristband	Glutton Hide	3	Ring of Life	1	--	--	--	--	5
9	Feeble Wristband	Feeble Cloth	3	Ring of Heart	1	--	--	--	--	5
9	Feather Wristband	Empyrean Cloth	3	Mercurius Ring	1	--	--	--	--	6
10	Dragon Wristband	Dragon Hide	3	Oversized Wristband	1	--	--	--	--	6
10	Sabris Wristband	Atlantis Metal	2	Amarlista Ring	1	--	--	--	--	6

*Eugene cannot forge Bracelets.

TALISMANS

Everyone *

* Males can't wear eternal rose; only Capell can wear the Capell, Faina, and Leif Dolls.

Master artisan of accessories, Kristofer is the best at crafting talismans as well. The useful sacrificial doll totem can be vital in dicey situations—upon death, it resurrects its wearer before becoming a (worthless) hopeless charm. Other talismans grant extra damage, stat bonuses, or resource regeneration. The best talisman that Kristofer doesn't make comes from the Seraphic Gate.

Name	Description	Value	Rarity	ATK	HIT	DEF	AGL	INT	LUC	Effects	Special Acquisition
Hopeless Charm	A strange item of which the function is unknown even to its creator.	2	1	--	--	--	--	--	--	--	--
Four-leaf Clover	A charm made from a four-leaf clover.	50	1	--	--	--	--	--	5	--	--
Harvest Coin	A coin with the goddess of fertility engraved in it. Brings wealth to the bearer.	6500	5	--	--	--	--	--	--	Gold +10%	--
Fox Tail	A charm made from the tail of a fox.	1000	3	--	--	--	--	--	--	ATK/DEF +5%	--
Wisdom Coin	A coin with the god of intelligence engraved in it. Increases learning ability.	10000	6	--	--	--	--	--	--	EXP +10%	Complete Side Quest "Minister and Fur"
Smiley Charm	A charm that brings a smile to whoever gazes upon it. A symbol of peace.	3000	3	--	--	--	--	--	--	Autoguard rate +3%	--
Rabbit's Foot	A charm made from the foot of a rabbit. Gives agility to the bearer.	200	2	--	--	--	--	--	--	AGL +20	Complete Side Quest "Child's Lost Matter"
Eagle Eye	A charm made from an eagle's eye. Imbued with the power to increase critical hits.	350	2	--	--	--	--	--	--	Critical hit rate +3%	--
Horseshoe	A charm made from a horseshoe.	5200	4	--	--	--	--	--	--	AP recovery amount x2	--
Sacrificial Doll	A doll that sacrifices its life in place of the bearer during battle.	3500	4	--	--	--	--	--	--	100% Survival (Accessory Shatter)	--
Moon Drop	A lunatite gem shaped like a water droplet. Controls the bearer's lunaglyph power.	25000	8	--	--	--	--	--	--	Tranquil Glyph	--
Crimson Moon	A lunatite gem shaped like the crimson moon. Enhances the bearer's lunaglyph power.	20000	8	--	--	--	--	--	--	Chaotic Glyph	--
Magic Amplio	A charm of a renowned mage. Enhances the bearer's magic power.	15000	6	--	--	--	--	--	--	MP +10%	--
Magic Aria	A charm of an eloquent mage. Enhances the bearer's ability to chant magic spells.	18000	7	--	--	--	--	--	--	Casting time down	--
Lunarage	A charm created by unblesseds showing anger at the moon. Repels magic.	20000	7	--	--	--	--	--	--	Magic damage -50%, MP drain 1%	Must complete Private Event "Secret of Smithery" to make
Eternal Rose	A rose corsage that never wilts. Enhances its wearer's energy and magic.	40000	9	--	--	--	--	--	--	HP Regeneration 3%, MP Regeneration 1%	Must complete Private Event "Secret of Smithery" to make
Monk's Soul	A charm imbued with magic that suppresses ambition.	100	1	--	--	--	--	--	--	0 EXP	--
King of Kings	A magic card held by a Lumper king as a symbol of its majesty.	200000	10	--	--	--	--	--	--	Magic damage +10%, Anti-ailment, AP consumption -50%	Must have access to Seraphic Gate to make
Tri-Emblem	A divine charm that grants the bearer tremendous powers.	350000	10	--	--	--	--	--	--	Anti-ailment, MP consumption -20%, Casting Time Down+	Seraphic Gate
Tri-Emplem	A divine charm that grants the bearer tremendous powers. Or does it?	--	1	--	--	--	--	--	--	--	Seraphic Gate
Capell Doll	A charm made by Faina. A strange sense of peace is felt when in possession of it.	--	10	--	--	--	--	--	--	Anti-ailment (30%)	Complete Side Quest "Promised Doll"
Faina Doll	A charm made by Faina. A doll of a little girl with a gentle smile.	--	10	--	--	--	--	--	--	Anti-doom, Anti-curse	Complete Side Quest "Promised Doll"
Leif Doll	A charm made by Faina. A doll of a little boy with a playful smile.	--	10	--	--	--	--	--	--	Anti-stone, Anti-silence	Complete Side Quest "Promised Doll"

Talisman Forging

Rarity	Creation Result	1st Ingredient	Qty.	2nd Ingredient	Qty.	3rd Ingredient	Qty.	Eugene IC Lv.	Sigmund IC Lv.	Edward IC Lv.	Kristofer IC Lv.
1	Monk's Soul	Hopeless Charm	1	--	--	--	--	--	1	1	--
2	Rabbit's Foot	Rabbit Hide	2	--	--	--	--	1	1	1	1
2	Eagle Eye	Bird Eye	2	--	--	--	--	2	1	2	2
3	Fox Tail	Silver Fox Fur	2	--	--	--	--	3	3	3	2
3	Smiley Charm	Sheep Hide	2	--	--	--	--	3	--	3	3
4	Horseshoe	Iron Metal	2	Granite	1	--	--	4	--	4	3
4	Sacrificial Doll	Miraculous Medicine	1	Novo Herb	1	Stone Statue Fragment	1	4	--	4	3
5	Harvest Coin	Gold Metal	2	Silver Metal	1	--	--	--	--	--	3
6	Wisdom Coin	Harvest Coin	1	Four-leaf Clover	1	--	--	--	--	--	4
6	Magic Amplio	Feeble Wristband	1	Giant Eye	1	--	--	--	--	--	4
7	Magic Aria	Feeble Wristband	1	Dragon Eye	1	--	--	--	--	--	4
7	Lunarage	Lunatite	2	Lunar Incense	1	Lunar Suppressant	1	--	--	--	5
8	Crimson Moon	Lunatite	2	Lunar Incense	1	Lunar Powder	1	--	--	--	5
8	Moon Drop	Amarlista	2	Lunar Suppressant	1	Lunar Suppressant X	1	--	--	--	5
9	Eternal Rose	Amarlista	2	Blossom Ring	1	Lei	1	--	--	--	6
10	King of Kings	Queen of Queens	1	Servant of Jacks	1	--	--	--	--	--	6

ITEMS

RECOVERY ITEMS

Name	Description	Value	Rarity	Effects	Special Acquisition
Red Berry Potion	Made from red berries. Slight healing of wounds.	60	1	Restores 30% of HP	--
Blue Berry Potion	Made from blue berries. Moderate healing of wounds.	150	2	Restores 50% of HP	--
Yellow Berry Potion	Made from yellow berries. Extensive healing of wounds.	500	5	Restores 70% of HP	--
Green Berry Potion	Made from green berries. Full healing of wounds.	1500	6	Restores 100% of HP	--
Red Berry Powder	Made from red berries. Slight healing of multiple party members' wounds.	650	4	Restores 30% of HP, Area effect	--
Blue Berry Powder	Made from blue berries. Moderate healing of multiple party members' wounds.	1650	6	Restores 50% of HP, Area effect	--
Yellow Berry Powder	Made from yellow berries. Extensive healing of multiple party members' wounds.	3500	7	Restores 70% of HP, Area effect	--
Green Berry Powder	Made from green berries. Full healing of multiple party members' wounds.	5000	9	Restores 100% of HP, Area effect	--
Black Berry Potion	Made from black berries. Slight healing of mental fatigue.	350	3	Restores 30% of MP	--
White Berry Potion	Made from white berries. Moderate healing of mental fatigue.	1200	6	Restores 50% of MP	--
Silver Berry Potion	Made from silver berries. Extensive healing of mental fatigue.	3500	7	Restores 70% of MP	--
Gold Berry Potion	Made from gold berries. Full healing of mental fatigue.	8500	8	Restores 100% of MP	--
Black Berry Powder	Made from black berries. Slight healing of multiple party members' mental fatigue.	1500	6	Restores 30% of MP, Area effect	--
White Berry Powder	Made from white berries. Moderate healing of multiple party members' mental fatigue.	5000	7	Restores 50% of MP, Area effect	--
Silver Berry Powder	Made from silver berries. Extensive healing of multiple party members' mental fatigue.	7200	9	Restores 70% of MP, Area effect	--
Gold Berry Powder	Made from gold berries. Full healing of multiple party members' mental fatigue.	12000	10	Restores 100% of MP, Area effect	--

Potion Alchemy

Rarity	Creation Result	1st Ingredient	Qty.	2nd Ingredient	Qty.	3rd Ingredient	Qty.	Michelle IC Lv.	Kiriya IC Lv.	Seraphina IC Lv.	Sigmund IC Lv.
1	Red Berry Potion	Red Berry	2	--	--	--	--	1	1	1	1
2	Blue Berry Potion	Blue Berry	2	--	--	--	--	2	1	2	2
5	Yellow Berry Potion	Yellow Berry	2	--	--	--	--	3	2	3	3
6	Green Berry Potion	Green Berry	2	--	--	--	--	4	3	4	--
4	Red Berry Powder	Red Berry	2	Red Berry Potion	2	--	--	3	3	3	--
6	Blue Berry Powder	Blue Berry	2	Blue Berry Potion	2	--	--	--	4	--	--
7	Yellow Berry Powder	Yellow Berry	2	Yellow Berry Potion	2	--	--	--	5	--	--
9	Green Berry Powder	Green Berry	2	Green Berry Potion	2	--	--	--	6	--	--
3	Black Berry Potion	Black Berry	2	--	--	--	--	3	2	3	3
6	White Berry Potion	White Berry	2	--	--	--	--	4	3	3	--
7	Silver Berry Potion	Silver Berry	2	--	--	--	--	5	4	4	--
8	Gold Berry Potion	Gold Berry	2	--	--	--	--	6	5	5	--
6	Black Berry Powder	Black Berry	2	Black Berry Potion	2	--	--	--	3	--	--
7	White Berry Powder	White Berry	2	White Berry Potion	2	--	--	--	4	--	--
9	Silver Berry Powder	Silver Berry	2	Silver Berry Potion	2	--	--	--	5	--	--
10	Gold Berry Powder	Gold Berry	2	Gold Berry Potion	2	--	--	--	6	--	--

DISPOSABLE ITEMS

Name	Description	Value	Rarity	Effects	Special Acquisition
Liquid Salt	A bitter liquid medicine that brings around an unconscious party member.	100	2	Cures faint	--
Coffee	A liquid medicine that awakens a sleeping member. Be sure not to get any in the eyes.	100	2	Cures sleep	--
Antidote	An herbal liquid medicine that cures any kind of poison.	100	2	Cures poison	--
Holy Water	Holy water purified by the Claridians. Neutralizes any impurities.	200	3	Cures curse	--
Para-Gone	A liquid medicine that heals paralysis. At least you'll be numb to its taste and smell.	200	3	Cures paralysis	--
Cough Drop	A magic medicine created by a minstrel to heal throat problems.	150	3	Cures silence	--
Sedative	A relaxing agent to calm down those who are confused.	150	3	Cures confusion	--
Spring Warmth	A magical medicine that casts a warm light that defrosts those who are frozen.	200	3	Cures freeze	--
Odious Eye	A medicine made from the eye of a monster. It reverses petrification.	200	3	Cures stone	--
Maiden's Scorn	A medicine that brings those who have been charmed to their senses.	150	3	Cures charm	--
Eye Drops	A medicine that cleans and refreshes the eyes to heal the unseeing.	120	2	Cures unseeing	--
Angel Earpick	A gentle earpick that cleans out the ears and heals the unhearing.	120	2	Cures unhearing	--
Aroma Oil	A soothing scented oil that removes bad smells.	120	2	Cures stink	--
Panacea	A renowned doctor's concoction, made from various ingredients. Heals any condition.	350	5	Cures all status ailments	--
Miraculous Medicine	A medicine stewed from rare herbs. Revives a fallen party member.	550	5	Revive &Ð Restores 30% of HP	--
Mysterious Medicine	A medicine made by an insane alchemist. Revives a party member to almost full health.	3000	8	Revive & Restores 60% of HP	--
Claridian Medicine	A medicine with the power of the Claridians. Revives a party member to full health.	15000	10	Revive &Ð Restores 100% of HP	--
Bottomless Pot	A divine pot with multiple cracks. Offers an endless supply of healing food.	0	10	Restores 30% of HP, Shatter (30%)	Must complete Private Event "Secret of Wrought Gold" to make

Name	Description	Value	Rarity	Effects	Special Acquisition
Kismetic Tablet	A miraculous stone tablet with multiple cracks. Gives its bearer infinite magic.	0	10	Restores 30% of MP, Shatter (30%)	Must complete Private Event "Secret of Wrought Gold" to make
Cornucopia	A magical horn with multiple cracks. Expels any bodily contaminations when blown.	0	10	Cures all status ailments, Shatter (50%)	Must complete Private Event "Secret of Wrought Gold" to make
Holy Grail	A grail with multiple cracks. Continually gushes miraculous water that revives the dead.	0	10	Revive &ÐRestores 30% of HP, Shatter (50%)	Must complete Private Event "Secret of Wrought Gold" to make
Toothbrush	A soft-bristle toothbrush that is easy on the gums. Cleans and refreshes the palate.	120	2	Cures untasting	--
Call of War	A medicine for calming the nerves of frightened rookie soldiers on the battlefield.	150	3	Cures berserk	--
Lunar Scale	A magical scale that restores any power lost due to magic.	150	3	Cures dwindle	--
Seeing Eye	A magic magnifying glass that reveals the enemy's characteristics.	30	1	Analyze	--
Horizon Crystal	A magic crystal ball that allows one to have a better view of the surrounding area.	40	1	Expand minimap	--
Sunstone	A magic stone that emits a warm light, eliminating any darkness.	50	2	Faint light	--
Lunar Suppressant	A medicine made to slightly suppress the effects of lunar power.	1000	5	Lower glyph 10%	--
Lunar Suppressant X	A medicine made to moderately suppress the effects of lunar power.	1500	7	Lower glyph 30%	--
Lunar Suppressant Z	A medicine made to greatly suppress the effects of lunar power.	3000	9	Lower glyph 50%	--
Lunar Incense	A special medicine mixed with lunar incense that slightly increases lunaglyph power.	2000	4	Raise glyph 10%	--
Lunar Powder	Powder ground from fragments of the moon. Moderately increases lunaglyph power.	3000	6	Raise glyph 30%	--
Lunar Fragment	A fragment carved from the moon. Greatly increases lunaglyph power.	3500	8	Raise glyph 50%	--
Perfume of Suspicion	A crude copy of a legendary perfume. Has a scent that evokes hatred.	0	5	Emotion down, Stench	--
Perfume of Charm	A magic perfume. Makes anyone wearing it seem attractive.	0	10	Emotion up, Perfume	--

Item Alchemy

Rarity	Creation Result	1st Ingredient	Qty.	2nd Ingredient	Qty.	3rd Ingredient	Qty.	Michelle IC Lv.	Kiriya IC Lv.	Seraphina IC Lv.	Sigmund IC Lv.
2	Coffee	Fresh Herb	1	Medical Herb	2	--	--	1	1	1	--
2	Antidote	Antidote Herb	1	Medical Herb	2	--	--	3	2	2	--
3	Holy Water	Fresh Herb	1	Medical Herb	2	--	--	3	2	3	--
3	Para-Gone	Antidote Herb	1	Medical Herb	2	--	--	3	2	3	--
3	Cough Drop	Fresh Herb	1	Medical Herb	2	--	--	2	1	1	--
3	Sedative	Fresh Herb	1	Medical Herb	2	--	--	3	2	2	--
3	Spring Warmth	Laurel	1	Medical Herb	2	--	--	4	3	3	--
3	Odious Eye	Lizard Eye	1	Medical Herb	2	--	--	4	3	4	--
3	Maiden's Scorn	Toadstool	1	Medical Herb	2	--	--	3	2	3	--
2	Eye Drops	Toadstool	1	Medical Herb	2	--	--	3	2	3	--
2	Angel Earpick	Toadstool	1	Medical Herb	2	--	--	3	2	3	--
2	Aroma Oil	Fresh Herb	1	Medical Herb	2	--	--	2	1	2	--
2	Toothbrush	Fresh Herb	1	Medical Herb	2	--	--	2	1	2	--
3	Call of War	--	--	--	--	--	--	--	--	--	--
3	Lunar Scale	Fresh Herb	1	Medical Herb	2	--	--	2	1	2	--
5	Panacea	Laurel	1	Medical Herb	2	Novo Herb	1	4	3	4	--
5	Miraculous Medicine	Novo Herb	3	Red Berry Potion	2	--	--	4	2	4	--
8	Mysterious Medicine	Miraculous Medicine	1	Novo Herb	3	Blue Berry Potion	1	--	5	6	--
10	Claridian Medicine	Mysterious Medicine	1	Novo Herb	4	Green Berry Potion	1	--	6	--	--
10	Bottomless Pot	Green Berry Potion	10	Green Berry Powder	5	Atlantis Metal	1	--	--	6	--
10	Kismetic Tablet	Gold Berry Potion	10	Gold Berry Powder	5	Atlantis Metal	1	--	--	6	--
10	Cornucopia	Panacea	10	Amarlista	2	--	--	--	--	6	--
10	Holy Grail	Miraculous Medicine	10	Claridian Medicine	3	Atlantis Metal	1	--	--	6	--
1	Seeing Eye	Bird Eye	2	--	--	--	--	1	1	--	1
1	Horizon Crystal	Seeing Eye	1	Bird Eye	2	--	--	1	1	--	2
2	Sunstone	Sandstone	1	Cork Wood	1	--	--	2	2	--	3
5	Lunar Suppressant	Silver Metal	2	Laurel	2	Vine	--	--	3	--	--
7	Lunar Suppressant X	Lunar Suppressant	1	Silver Metal	3	--	--	--	5	--	--
9	Lunar Suppressant Z	Lunar Suppressant X	1	Amarlista	1	--	--	--	6	--	--
4	Lunar Incense	Lunatite	2	Laurel	2	Toadstool	1	--	4	--	--
6	Lunar Powder	Lunar Incense	1	Lunatite	2	--	--	--	5	--	--
8	Lunar Fragment	Lunar Powder	1	Lunatite	3	--	--	--	6	--	--
5	Perfume of Suspicion	Lunar Incense	1	Aroma Oil	2	Toadstool	1	5	--	--	--
10	Perfume of Charm	Perfume of Suspicion	1	Aroma Oil	2	Laurel	1	6	--	--	--

BOOKS & SCORES

Title	Description	Value	Rarity	Effects	Special Acquisition
"Intro to Astrology"	The fortune-telling book from the famous Savio, teaching how to become a spiritual guide.	100	1	--	--
Astrology Manual	Savio's new, much-anticipated fortune-telling book. Read this to shape your life.	500	2	--	--
"Understanding Astrology"	"Unbelievable! The truth of your origins can be found within Savio's book."	1000	3	--	--
"Astrological Mysteries"	A must have! Savio's fortune- telling book will help you to become a new you.	2000	4	--	--
"Secret Arts of Astrology"	The latest issue. Savio's secrets are revealed for you to take control of your life!	3000	5	--	--
"Talk With Animals"	A work from a fresh-faced author. Rico's picture book is great for the whole family.	100	1	--	--
"My Animal Friends"	The anticipated sequel from Rico is brimming with cute drawings.	200	2	--	--
"Animal Secrets"	Highly acclaimed! Rico's latest series of work. What animals will appear?	800	3	--	--
"Heart of Animals"	Winning rave reviews! Rico's picture book series. How do animals feel?	1500	4	--	--
"Facts About Animals"	A masterpiece! This work from Rico will turn you into a master of animal psychology.	2000	5	--	--
Memoirs of a Warrior	A book of a legendary warrior who remained undefeated. Increases attack power.	25000	9	MAX ATK +4	Must complete Private Event "Secret of Writing" to make
Memoirs of a Knight	A book of a legendary knight who dedicated his life to his king. Increases defense.	25000	9	MAX DEF +4	Must complete Private Event "Secret of Writing" to make
Memoirs of a Hunter	A book of a legendary hunter who always caught his prey. Increases accuracy.	25000	9	MAX HIT +4	Must complete Private Event "Secret of Writing" to make
Memoirs of a Thief	A book of a legendary thief who could steal anything. Increases agility.	25000	9	MAX AGL +4	Must complete Private Event "Secret of Writing" to make
Memoirs of a Mage	A book of a legendary mage who mastered all magical spells. Increases intelligence.	25000	9	MAX INT +4	Must complete Private Event "Secret of Writing" to make
Memoirs of a Mercenary	A book of a legendary mercenary who survived all his battles. Increases health.	25000	8	MAX HP +20%	Must complete Private Event "Secret of Writing" to make
Memoirs of an Alchemist	A book of a legendary alchemist who sought the truth. Increases spirit.	25000	8	MAX MP +20%	Must complete Private Event "Secret of Writing" to make
"Dance of the Sword"	The book that explains how to attain Capell's battle skill, Alfheim.	0	10	Bestows Alfheim	Must complete Private Event "Secret of Writing" to make
"Memos of a Master Marksman"	The book that explains how to attain Aya's battle skill, Simorgh Zal.	0	10	Bestows Simorgh Zal	Must complete Private Event "Secret of Writing" to make
"Path of a Hero"	The book that explains how to attain Capell's battle skill, Levantine Slash.	0	10	Bestows Levantine Slash	Must complete Private Event "Secret of Writing" to make
"Live by the Sword"	The book that explains how to attain Edward's battle skill, Tempest Clash.	0	10	Bestows Tempest Clash	Must complete Private Event "Secret of Writing" to make
"Legend of a Shadow"	The book that explains how to attain Komachi's battle skill, Nightshade.	0	10	Bestows Nightshade	Must complete Private Event "Secret of Writing" to make
"Palm of the Hand"	The book that explains how to attain Touma's battle skill, Peerless Valor.	0	10	Bestows Peerless Valor	Must complete Private Event "Secret of Writing" to make
"Whispers of a Tree"	The book that explains how to attain Michelle's air magic spell, Voltsweep.	0	9	Bestows Voltsweep	Must complete Private Event "Secret of Writing" to make
"Rage of Fire"	The book that explains how to attain Eugene's fire magic spell, Pyrdance.	0	9	Bestows Pyrdance	Must complete Private Event "Secret of Writing" to make
"Molding of Earth"	The book that explains how to attain Rico's earth magic spell, Geocrush.	0	9	Bestows Geocrush	Must complete Private Event "Secret of Writing" to make
"Tide of Water"	The book that explains how to attain Michelle's water magic spell, Nekros.	0	9	Bestows Nekros	Must complete Private Event "Secret of Writing" to make
"Power of Fog"	The book that explains how to attain Rucha's water magic spell, Miasma.	0	10	Bestows Miasma	Must complete Private Event "Secret of Writing" to make
"Flow of the Land"	The book that explains how to attain Eugene's earth magic spell, Geoquake.	0	10	Bestows Geoquake	Must complete Private Event "Secret of Writing" to make
"Will of the Universe"	The book that explains how to attain Rucha's fire magic spell, Pyrgeddon.	0	10	Bestows Pyrgeddon	Must complete Private Event "Secret of Writing" to make
Training Score	A musical score that teaches Placare.	0	2	Bestows Placare	--
Prelude Score	A musical score that teaches Fortuna.	0	3	Bestows Fortuna	--
Fugue Score	A musical score that teaches Angere.	0	4	Bestows Angere	--
Fantasia Score	A musical score that teaches Alucinari.	0	5	Bestows Alucinari	--
Sonata Score	A musical score that teaches Perturbare.	0	6	Bestows Perturbare	--
Concerto Score	A musical score that teaches Valere.	0	7	Bestows Valere	--
Suite Score	A musical score that teaches Obduratus.	0	7	Bestows Obduratus	--
Overture Score	"A musical score that teaches Mare Lunaris."	0	8	Bestows Mare Lunaris	--
Capriccio Score	A musical score that teaches Irritatus.	0	8	Bestows Irritatus	--
Nocturne Score	A musical score that teaches Hypnoticus.	0	9	Bestows Hypnoticus	--
Symphony Score	A musical score that teaches Precari.	0	10	Bestows Precari	--

Book Writing

Rarity	Creation Result	1st Ingredient	Qty.	2nd Ingredient	Qty.	3rd Ingredient	Qty.	Rico IC Lv.	Savio IC Lv.	Sigmund IC Lv.
1	"Intro to Astrology"	Papyrus Paper	2	--	--	--	--	--	1	--
2	Astrology Manual	Papyrus Paper	2	Lentesco Wood	1	--	--	--	2	--
3	"Understanding Astrology"	Pulp Paper	1	Lentesco Wood	2	--	--	--	3	--
4	"Astrological Mysteries"	Parchment	1	Writer's Quill	1	--	--	--	4	--
5	"Secret Arts of Astrology"	Parchment	2	Clerk's Quill	1	--	--	--	5	--
1	"Talk With Animals"	Papyrus Paper	2	--	--	--	--	1	--	--
2	"My Animal Friends"	Papyrus Paper	2	Lentesco Wood	1	--	--	2	--	--
3	"Animal Secrets"	Pulp Paper	1	Lentesco Wood	2	--	--	3	--	--
4	"Heart of Animals"	Parchment	1	Writer's Quill	1	--	--	4	--	--
5	"Facts About Animals"	Parchment	2	Clerk's Quill	1	--	--	5	--	--
9	Memoirs of a Warrior	Halgitian Paper	3	Genius's Quill	1	--	--	6	5	--
9	Memoirs of a Knight	Halgitian Paper	3	Genius's Quill	1	--	--	6	5	--
9	Memoirs of a Hunter	Halgitian Paper	3	Genius's Quill	1	--	--	6	5	--
9	Memoirs of a Thief	Halgitian Paper	3	Genius's Quill	1	--	--	6	5	--
9	Memoirs of a Mage	Halgitian Paper	3	Genius's Quill	1	--	--	6	5	--
8	Memoirs of a Mercenary	Halgitian Paper	3	Genius's Quill	1	--	--	6	5	--
8	Memoirs of an Alchemist	Halgitian Paper	3	Genius's Quill	1	--	--	6	5	--
10	"Dance of the Sword"	Memoirs of a Knight	1	Genius's Quill	2	--	--	6	--	--
10	"Memos of a Master Marksman"	Memoirs of a Hunter	1	Genius's Quill	2	--	--	6	--	--
10	"Path of a Hero"	Memoirs of a Warrior	1	Genius's Quill	2	--	--	6	--	--
10	"Live by the Sword"	Memoirs of a Warrior	1	Genius's Quill	2	--	--	6	--	--
10	"Legend of a Shadow"	Memoirs of a Thief	1	Genius's Quill	2	--	--	6	--	--
10	"Palm of the Hand"	Memoirs of a Mercenary	1	Genius's Quill	2	--	--	6	--	--
9	"Whispers of a Tree"	Memoirs of a Mage	1	Genius's Quill	2	--	--	--	5	--
9	"Rage of Fire"	Memoirs of a Mage	1	Genius's Quill	2	--	--	--	5	--
9	"Molding of Earth"	Memoirs of a Mage	1	Genius's Quill	2	--	--	--	5	--
9	"Tide of Water"	Memoirs of a Mage	1	Genius's Quill	2	--	--	--	5	--
10	"Power of Fog"	Memoirs of an Alchemist	1	Genius's Quill	2	--	--	--	6	--
10	"Flow of the Land"	Memoirs of an Alchemist	1	Genius's Quill	2	--	--	--	6	--
10	"Will of the Universe"	Memoirs of an Alchemist	1	Genius's Quill	2	--	--	--	6	--
2	Training Score	Training Notations	1	Staff Paper	1	Musician's Quill	1	1	1	--
3	Prelude Score	Prelude Notations	1	Staff Paper	1	Musician's Quill	1	1	1	--
4	Fugue Score	Fugue Notations	1	Staff Paper	1	Musician's Quill	1	2	2	--
5	Fantasia Score	Fantasia Notations	1	Staff Paper	1	Musician's Quill	1	2	2	--
6	Sonata Score	Sonata Notations	1	Staff Paper	1	Musician's Quill	1	3	3	--
7	Concerto Score	Concerto Notations	1	Staff Paper	2	Musician's Quill	2	3	3	--
7	Suite Score	Suite Notations	1	Staff Paper	2	Musician's Quill	2	4	4	--
8	Capriccio Score	Capriccio Notations	1	Staff Paper	2	Musician's Quill	2	4	4	--
8	Overture Score	Overture Notations	1	Staff Paper	3	Musician's Quill	2	5	--	--
9	Nocturne Score	Nocturne Notations	1	Staff Paper	3	Musician's Quill	2	5	--	--
10	Symphony Score	Symphony Notations	1	Staff Paper	3	Musician's Quill	2	6	--	--

JUICES

Name	Description	Value	Rarity	Effects	Special Acquisition
Fresh Milk	A fresh and nutritious milk. Used in a variety of dishes.	100	1	Restores a little HP, Party effect	--
Fruit Milk	A milk mixed with berries. Even children enjoy drinking this tasty treat.	200	1	Restores a little MP, Party effect	--
100% Berry Juice	A juice made from one hundred percent freshly squeezed berries.	450	2	Restores 10% of HP, Sweet smell, Party effect	--
Mixed Berry Juice	A healthy juice made from a variety of berries. Watch as your tongue changes color.	650	3	Restores 10% of MP, Sweet smell, Party effect	--
Halgitian Berry Wine	A Halgitian wine made from berries fermented over a long time. Goes great with fish.	1300	4	Restores 30% of HP, Pleasant smell, Party effect	--
Fresh Herb Tea	A mixed herb drink enjoyed for its strong aroma. It doesn't taste too bad, either.	2300	5	Restores 30% of MP, Pleasant smell, Party effect	--
Royal Herb Tea	A magnificent herbal tea sweetened with royal jelly.	3800	5	Restores 50% of HP, Cures silence, Party effect	--
Honey Tea	A tea sweetened with honey. Even children can enjoy this, but be careful… it's hot!	5500	6	Restores 50% of MP, Cures freeze, Party effect	--
Burguss Fruit Liquor	A sweet liqueur with a hint of sourness from Burguss fruit. Popular with the ladies.	6200	7	Restores 70% of HP, Party effect	--
Premium Karathos	Made in Casandra. The winery closed suddenly, leaving only a few bottles remaining.	12000	8	Restores 70% of MP, Party effect	--
Thousand Year Sigh	A unique cocktail with a taste you'll never forget.	55000	9	MAX HP +10%, Party effect	--
Big Gamble	Artificial courage juice. Some drink this in times of need.	55000	9	MAX MP +10%, Party effect	--
Primo Nectar	The ultimate drink in taste, aroma, and price. Made from a special mix of spirits.	150000	10	MAX HP +10%, MAX MP +10%, Party effect	Must complete Private Event "Secret of Cooking" to make

Juice Making

Rarity	Creation Result	1st Ingredient	Qty.	2nd Ingredient	Qty.	3rd Ingredient	Qty.	Aya IC Lv.	Rucha IC Lv.	Dominica IC Lv.	Sigmund IC Lv.
1	Fruit Milk	Burguss Apple	1	Fresh Milk	1	--	--	1	1	1	1
2	100% Berry Juice	Red Berry	2	Blue Berry	1	--	--	1	1	1	1
3	Mixed Berry Juice	Blue Berry	2	Yellow Berry	1	100% Berry Juice	1	2	2	1	2
4	Halgitian Berry Wine	Halgitian Strawberry	1	Mixed Berry Juice	1	--	--	--	--	2	--
5	Fresh Herb Tea	Fresh Herb	2	Fructus Herb	1	--	--	3	3	2	--
5	Royal Herb Tea	Royal Jelly	1	Fresh Herb Tea	1	--	--	3	3	3	--
6	Honey Tea	Honey	4	Fayel Lemon	2	Royal Herb Tea	1	4	4	3	--
7	Burguss Fruit Liquor	Burguss Apple	3	White Berry	2	Halgitian Berry Wine	1	--	--	4	--
8	Premium Karathos	Casandra Banapple	2	Halgitian Berry Wine	1	Burguss Fruit Liquor	1	--	--	5	--
9	Thousand Year Sigh	Premium Karathos	1	Silver Berry	3	--	--	--	--	5	--
9	Big Gamble	Premium Karathos	1	Gold Berry	3	--	--	--	--	6	--
10	Primo Nectar	Premium Karathos	1	Thousand Year Sigh	1	Big Gamble	1	--	--	6	--

SOUPS

Name	Description	Value	Rarity	Effects	Special Acquisition
Soup Stock	A soup stock made from bones. Used in a variety of dishes, but never on its own.	150	1	Restores a little MP, Bitter taste, Party effect	--
Bee Larvae Soup	A soup made from bee larvae. Very nutritious, but has a horrible texture.	320	2	Restores some MP, Bitter taste, Party effect	--
Nutritious Snake Soup	A soup made from shed snake skin and snake meat. Full of nourishment.	600	3	Restores 10% of MP, Bitter taste, Party effect	--
Hearty Soup	A soup from Halgita. Its secret ingredient is the love put into making it.	800	4	Restores 10% of MP, Party effect	--
Stewed Lizard Scales	A strange concoction made with lizard scales. Best to gulp down with your eyes shut.	2400	5	Restores 30% of MP, Party effect	--
Dragon Soup Stock	A soup stock made from dragon bone. Finding the ingredients could be hazardous.	3000	6	Restores 30% of MP, Cures poison, Party effect	--
Deviant Fish Soup	A fish soup full of tiny bones. Tastes great, but be careful when eating it.	5000	7	Restores 50% of MP, Party effect	--
Stewed Bear Paw	A delicacy of Fayel. Those made from the right paws are highly prized.	6000	8	Restores 50% of MP, Cures curse, Party effect	--
Deluxe Crab Soup	A lavish crab soup made using crab shells. Only appreciated by nobility.	12000	9	Restores 70% of MP, Party effect	--
Witch Broth Soup	A mysterious soup made in a mysterious pot with mysterious ingredients. Eaters, beware.	24000	9	Restores 100% of MP, Perilous taste, Party effect	--
Heaven and Earth	An extravagant soup made up of ingredients from land, sea, and air. Rare even for kings.	55000	10	MAX INT +2, Party effect	Must complete Private Event "Secret of Cooking" to make

Soup Making

Rarity	Creation Result	1st Ingredient	Qty.	2nd Ingredient	Qty.	3rd Ingredient	Qty.	Rucha IC Lv.	Sigmund IC Lv.
1	Soup Stock	Random Beast Bone	2	--	--	--	--	1	1
2	Bee Larvae Soup	Beehive	1	Soup Stock	1	--	--	1	1
3	Nutritious Snake Soup	Snakeskin	2	Soup Stock	1	--	--	2	2
4	Hearty Soup	Fish Fin	2	Sliced Fish	1	Halgitian Paste	1	2	--
5	Stewed Lizard Scales	Lizard Scale	2	Soup Stock	1	Zala Rock Salt	1	3	--
6	Dragon Soup Stock	Dragon Scale	2	Hearty Soup	1	--	--	4	--
7	Deviant Fish Soup	Sliced Deviant Fish	2	Hearty Soup	1	Antidote Herb	2	4	--
8	Stewed Bear Paw	Bear Paw	2	Hearty Soup	2	--	--	5	--
9	Deluxe Crab Soup	Crab Claw	2	Crab Shell	2	Hearty Soup	1	5	--
9	Witch Broth Soup	Giant Eye	1	Toadstool	2	Stewed Bear Paw	1	6	--
10	Heaven and Earth	Dragon Meat	1	Sliced Rare Salmon	2	King Egg	1	6	--

*Aya and Dominica cannot make Soup.

POTS

Name	Description	Value	Rarity	Effects	Special Acquisition
Amateur Hot Pot	A dish made by an amateur. Made from random ingredients; you won't be wanting seconds.	80	1	Restores a little HP, Stench, Party effect	--
Oradian Chicken Hot Pot	A hot pot made with Fayel chicken. The bones are used to create the tasty broth.	250	2	Restores some HP, Restores a little MP, Party effect	--
Desert Hot Pot	A local hot pot concocted by the people of Fayel.	500	3	Restores 10% of HP, Party effect	--
Pandora's Hot Pot	Although it smells of danger, those who eat it can't help but feel great hope.	650	4	Restores 10% of HP, Cures poison, Party effect	--
Imperial Stewed Hot Pot	A wonderful-smelling dish served at feasts in Burguss Palace.	1200	5	Restores 30% of HP, Pleasant smell, Party effect	--
Cobasna Mushroom Hot Pot	A seasonal hot pot made from mushrooms picked from the Cobasna Timberlands.	1500	6	Restores 30% of HP, Party effect	--
Feast of the Immortals	The ingredients of this unique-looking and smelling dish are a mystery. Is it safe to eat?	3500	7	Restores 50% of HP, Stench, Party effect	--
Heavenly Risotto	A famous risotto that brings all who eat it to tears. Could use a little less salt.	4000	8	Restores 50% of HP, Party effect	--
Hero's Crab Gratin	A lavish crab gratin made in honor of a returning hero. The sea smell brings nostalgia.	6500	9	Restores 70% of HP, Party effect	--
Devil's Spaghetti	A dish with dragon as its main ingredient. Getting the meat is the challenge.	10000	9	Restores 100% of HP, Looks poisonous, Party effect	--
Dragon Fiesta	A dish that looks and tastes awful. Often eaten by warriors to prove their courage.	55000	10	MAX DEF +2, Party effect	Must complete Private Event "Secret of Cooking" to make

Pot Making

Rarity	Creation Result	1st Ingredient	Qty.	2nd Ingredient	Qty.	3rd Ingredient	Qty.	Dominica IC Lv.	Sigmund IC Lv.
1	Amateur Hot Pot	Mystery Meat	2	--	--	--	--	1	1
2	Oradian Chicken Hot Pot	Chicken	1	Amateur Hot Pot	1	--	--	1	1
3	Desert Hot Pot	Oradian Carrot	2	Fayel Chicken	1	Sliced Salmon	1	2	2
4	Pandora's Hot Pot	Blue Berry	2	Amateur Hot Pot	1	Zala Rock Salt	1	3	--
5	Imperial Stewed Hot Pot	Wild Rabbit Meat	2	Wild Fox Meat	1	Oradian Chicken Hot Pot	1	3	--
6	Cobasna Mushroom Hot Pot	Cobasna Lettuce	1	Pieria Mushroom	2	Toadstool	1	4	--
7	Feast of the Immortals	Random Beast Bone	3	Dragon Soup Stock	1	Pandora's Hot Pot	1	4	--
8	Heavenly Risotto	Halgitian Rice	2	White Pepper	2	Beef	2	5	--
9	Hero's Crab Gratin	Oradian Butter	3	Fresh Milk	3	Crab Meat	1	5	--
9	Devil's Spaghetti	Feast of the Immortals	1	Fayel Wheat	3	Bear Paw	1	6	--
10	Dragon Fiesta	Dragon Meat	2	Dragon Scale	2	Dragon Fang	2	6	--

*Aya and Rucha cannot make Pots.

PLATES

Name	Description	Value	Rarity	Effects	Special Acquisition
Stewed Whole Bat	A dish including a whole bat. Recommended only for the adventurous types.	65	1	Restores a little HP, Bitter taste, Party effect	--
Veggie Salad	A salad made from fresh vegetables picked from the Cobasna Timberlands.	150	2	Restores a little HP	Restores a little MP, Party effect
Kolton Omelet	A common homemade dish in Kolton.	350	4	Restores some HP	Restores some MP, Party effect
Fried Greatfowl	A dish of fried greatfowl. Frying it gets rid of the distinct smell.	800	5	Restores 10% of HP, Restores 10% of MP, Party effect	--
Deviant Fish Platter	A platter of fresh sliced fish. A popular dish among fishermen.	1800	5	Restores 30% of HP	Restores 10% of MP, Party effect
Grilled Rachnuvus	A dish of grilled rachnuvus. Commonly eaten during wartime. It smells great, but…	3500	6	Restores 10% of HP, Restores 30% of MP, Party effect	--
Fried Lizard with Veggies	Vegetables are piled up to hide the gross-looking lizard. An odd dish, but tastes great.	4500	7	Restores 30% of HP/MP, Party effect	--
Rare Salmon Hot Plate	A dish that uses an entire salmon. Salmon are very rare, making it a sought-after dish.	10000	8	Restores 50% of HP/MP, Party effect	--
Fried Demon Eye	The eye of a demon served up whole. Close your eyes and gulp it down.	18500	9	Restores 70% of HP/MP, Party effect	--
Perfected Curry	An ultimate curry made by a chef who dedicated his life to spices.	35000	9	Restores 100% of HP/MP, Party effect	--
Gourmet Barbeque	An extravagant barbecue of meat and vegetables. A real outdoors-y treat.	55000	10	MAX ATK +2, Party effect	Must complete Private Event "Secret of Cooking" to make

Plate Making

Rarity	Creation Result	1st Ingredient	Qty.	2nd Ingredient	Qty.	3rd Ingredient	Qty.	Rucha IC Lv.	Dominica IC Lv.	Sigmund IC Lv.
1	Stewed Whole Bat	Bat Wing	2	--	--	--	--	1	1	1
2	Veggie Salad	Cobasna Lettuce	1	Nolaan Potato	1	Graad Onion	1	1	1	1
4	Kolton Omelet	Lintz Tomato	1	Oradian Butter	1	Bird Egg	1	2	2	2
5	Fried Greatfowl	Chicken	2	Berry Oil	1	Fayel Lemon	1	2	2	--
5	Deviant Fish Platter	Sliced Deviant Fish	1	Sliced Fish	2	--	--	3	2	--
6	Grilled Rachnuvus	Rachnuvus Shell	2	Berry Oil	2	Sapran Green Pepper	1	3	3	--
7	Fried Lizard with Veggies	Lizard Scale	2	Reiner Garlic	2	Sapran Green Pepper	2	4	3	--
8	Rare Salmon Hot Plate	Sliced Rare Salmon	2	Sliced Salmon	2	Oradian Butter	2	4	--	--
9	Fried Demon Eye	Giant Eye	2	King Egg	2			5	--	--
9	Perfected Curry	Halgitian Rice	5	Curry Powder	4	Beef	1	5	--	--
10	Gourmet Barbeque	Prehistoric Meat	4	Sapran Green Pepper	3	Blaze Metal	3	6	--	--

*Aya cannot make Plates.

DESSERTS

Name	Description	Value	Rarity	Effects	Special Acquisition
Berry Ice Cream	The generous amount of berries used in this ice cream gives sweetness with a hint of sour.	100	1	Restores a little MP, Sweet smell, Party effect	--
Berry Tart	The finest tart made from high-quality berries. Popular among the ladies.	200	2	Restores some MP, Sweet smell, Party effect	--
Special Pudding	Often given as a gift, this is a pudding filled with love.	650	3	Restores some MP, Sweet taste, Party effect	--
Halgitian Jelly	A popular snack in Halgitian homes. Often served to guests as a treat.	1500	4	Restores 10% of MP, Sweet taste, Party effect	--
Lucky Chocolate Coin	A chocolate made to look like a lucky coin. Eating it makes one feel very lucky.	10000	5	Revive & Restores 30% of HP, Sweet taste, Party effect	--
Slime Pudding	An amazing snack that is so soft that one forgets he is even eating it.	16000	6	Revive & Restores 60% of HP, Sweet taste, Party effect	--
Rare Butter Cake	A cake made from precious eggs. Favored by nobles.	20000	7	Revive & Restores 100% of HP, Sweet taste, Party effect	--
Fruit Fiesta	An exquisite mix of famous fruits from across the land.	30000	8	Revive & Restores 30% of HP/MP, Sweet smell, Party effect	--
Emperor's Delight	A lavish dessert created by royalty. Not many people know of this treat.	40000	9	Revive & Restores 60% of HP/MP, Sweet taste, Party effect	--
Glacial Delight	Ice shaved from the glaciers of Vinphen. Its taste will blow you away.	50000	9	Revive & Restores 100% of HP/MP, Mind-numbing taste, Party effect	--
Wedding Special	Created by a first-class chef who committed his life to perfecting this flawless cake.	55000	10	MAX AGL +2, Party effect	Must complete Private Event "Secret of Cooking" to make

BREAD

Name	Description	Value	Rarity	Effects	Special Acquisition
Berry Bread	A bread made with a selection of sour berries. It seems healthy.	60	1	Cures sleep, Sour taste, Party effect	--
Cobasna Salad Sandwich	A sandwich made with vegetables from the Cobasna Timberlands.	200	2	Cures poison, Restores a little HP, Party effect	--
Toast of Dawn	A powerful herb bread that wakes you up. Great for those feeling sleepy in the morning.	350	3	Cures confusion, Restores a little MP, Party effect	--
Oradian Chicken Sandwich	A sandwich filled with Fayel chicken cooked to just the right tenderness.	400	4	Cures charm, Restores some HP, Party effect	--
Jackpot Burger	A burger made with a ridiculously wasteful set of ingredients. Eat like a king!	550	5	Cures freeze, Restores some MP, Party effect	--
Soul Roll	A bread made by a baker with all his soul. Lifts the spirit.	2300	6	Cures paralysis, Restores 30% of HP, Party effect	--
Rock Hard Stick of Bread	A rock-hard bread. There was once a rumor of a warrior killing a person with it.	3800	7	Cures stone, Restores 30% of MP, Party effect	--
Exquisite Bread Crusts	Bread crusts made from the finest ingredients. No one knows where the bread goes!	5000	8	Cures silence, Restores 50% of HP, Party effect	--
Hell's Egg Sandwich	The finest sandwich made from the finest (and rarest) of eggs.	6800	9	Cures unseeing, Restores 50% of MP, Party effect	--
Mysterious Curry Bread	Bread filled with the curry of a legendary chef. Let the spicy curry clear your system.	20000	9	Cures all status ailments, Restores 50% of HP/MP, Party effect	--
Heavenly Pancake	A heavenly pancake made using a combination of traditional techniques with great skill.	55000	10	MAX HIT +2, Party effect	Must complete Private Event "Secret of cooking" to make

Bread Making

Rarity	Creation Result	1st Ingredient	Qty.	2nd Ingredient	Qty.	3rd Ingredient	Qty.	Aya IC Lv.	Sigmund IC Lv.
1	Berry Bread	Fayel Wheat	1	Red Berry	1	--	--	1	1
2	Cobasna Salad Sandwich	Fayel Wheat	2	Veggie Salad	1	--	--	1	1
3	Toast of Dawn	Fayel Wheat	2	Berry Bread	1	Fresh Herb	1	2	2
4	Oradian Chicken Sandwich	Cobasna Salad Sandwich	1	Fayel Chicken	1	Oradian Butter	1	2	--
5	Jackpot Burger	Fayel Wheat	2	Lintz Tomato	1	Beef	1	3	--
6	Soul Roll	Fayel Wheat	1	Royal Jelly	1	Maiden's Scorn	1	3	--
7	Rock Hard Stick of Bread	Fayel Wheat	4	Prehistoric Meat	2	Oradian Butter	1	4	--
8	Exquisite Bread Crusts	Fayel Wheat	4	Berry Oil	2	Fruit Milk	2	4	--
9	Hell's Egg Sandwich	Fayel Wheat	4	King Egg	1	Veggie Salad	1	5	--
9	Mysterious Curry Bread	Fayel Wheat	4	Curry Powder	3	Oradian Carrot	2	6	--
10	Heavenly Pancake	Fayel Wheat	4	Royal Jelly	4	Berry Ice Cream	2	6	--

Rucha and Dominica cannot make Bread.

MEAT

Name	Description	Value	Rarity	Special Acquisition
Mystery Meat	Meat of random wild animals. Not fit for eating.	15	1	--
Wild Rabbit Meat	Wild rabbit meat. Slightly hard, but tastes good. Used in high-class cuisine.	20	1	--
Wild Fox Meat	Wild fox meat that isn't very tasty.	25	1	--
Chicken	Chicken used in a variety of dishes. Fayel chicken is especially world-renowned.	50	3	--
Fayel Chicken	Fayel's special breed of chicken. Used in a lot of high-class cuisine.	50	3	--
Beef	Beef, the meat of choice for all meat lovers.	80	4	--
Prehistoric Meat	A giant hunk of meat on the bone. Eating it raw would take a lot of guts.	100	4	--
Dragon Meat	The meat of a legendary creature. Strength is gained by those who eat it.	320	6	--

FISH

Name	Description	Value	Rarity	Special Acquisition
Fish Fin	Fish fin that is used in a variety of dishes.	5	1	--
Sliced Fish	Fish meat cut into easy-to-eat portions that is used in a variety of dishes.	15	2	--
Sliced Deviant Fish	Deviant fish meat that is considered a delicacy. Finding it fresh is often difficult.	30	2	--
Sliced Salmon	Fish that goes with any food. Easier to catch from the river during the winter.	50	3	--
Sliced Rare Salmon	Fish so rare that it is highly prized among fishermen.	500	6	--
Crab Claw	A giant crab claw used in a variety of dishes as well as for other purposes.	200	4	--
Crab Meat	Flavorful crab meat scooped straight out of the shell. Considered to be a delicacy.	250	5	--

VEGETABLES

Name	Description	Value	Rarity	Special Acquisition
Cobasna Lettuce	Famous lettuce cultivated in Cobasna.	10	1	--
Oradian Carrot	Carrot resistant to hot weather. Cultivated in Oradia.	12	1	--
Nolaan Potato	A potato used in a variety of dishes. A local specialty of Nolaan.	15	1	--
Graad Onion	An onion cultivated in Graad. Has a bit of a kick that leaves the cook teary-eyed.	30	2	--
Lintz Tomato	A tomato grown in the cold land of Lintz to give a delicious, sweet taste.	35	2	--
Pieria Mushroom	An edible mushroom common in the Pieria Marshlands. Slightly hallucinogenic.	40	2	--
Reiner Garlic	Famous garlic from Reiner. Adds a nice little accent to many dishes.	55	3	--
Sapran Green Pepper	A pepper cultivated in Sapran. Can even be grown in the desert. Disliked by children.	20	2	--

SPICES

Name	Description	Value	Rarity	Special Acquisition
Honey	Sweet honey stolen from honey bees.	150	1	--
Wood Syrup	A mix of sap and honey. Used in many desserts.	120	2	--
Zala Rock Salt	A high-grade salt collected from the Zalan coast. Cherished by chefs everywhere.	200	3	--
Halgitian Paste	A condiment created in Halgita by fermenting beans.	220	3	--
White Pepper	A spice picked in Kolton. Resistant to the cold.	250	3	--
Oradian Butter	A dairy product made from milk. Used in a variety of dishes and desserts.	210	3	--
Berry Oil	Fruit oil extracted from berries. Used in food as well as in medicine.	300	3	--
Royal Jelly	Valuable honey collected from beehives. Often used as a tonic.	500	5	--
Curry Powder	A mix of various spices. Recently created, it is hot, but addictive.	600	5	--

FRUITS

Name	Description	Value	Rarity	Special Acquisition
Red Berry	An unripened red berry. Too sour to eat.	30	1	--
Blue Berry	An unripened blue berry. Too hard to eat.	35	1	--
Yellow Berry	An unripened yellow berry. Too hot to eat.	50	1	--
Green Berry	An unripened green berry. Too pungent to eat.	60	2	--
Black Berry	An unripened black berry. Too bitter to eat.	80	2	--
White Berry	An unripened white berry. Too bland to eat.	120	3	--
Silver Berry	An unripened silver berry. Too salty to eat.	200	3	--
Gold Berry	An over-ripened gold berry. Too sweet to eat.	250	4	--
Burguss Apple	A famous type of apple from Burguss that grows very high in trees.	150	3	--
Fayel Lemon	A very sour lemon cultivated in Fayel. Resistant to heat.	100	3	--
Halgitian Strawberry	Grown in Halgita between spring and summer. Popular among children.	120	4	--
Kolton Melon	An expensive melon cultivated in Kolton. Not too sweet, it is a favorite among nobles.	500	5	--
Casandra Banapple	A rare fruit cultivated in Casandra. Almost like a myth around the marketplace.	300	6	--

ORE

Name	Description	Value	Rarity	Special Acquisition
Junk	Some broken object seen as worthless junk.	1	1	--
Metal Fragment	A piece of metal.	10	1	--
Stone Statue Fragment	A cracked piece of a stone statue.	30	1	--
Sandstone	A stone that is easy to process. The lowest grade of stone around.	120	2	--
Granite	The most commonly used stone due to its durability and resilience to weathering.	250	3	--
Marble	An expensive stone that breaks into sharp pieces, often used for arrow and spear heads.	500	4	--
Ceramic	Strong ceramic baked from soft clay.	750	5	--
Metetite	A heavy, moist stone. Ideal for use in the foundation of houses.	1000	6	--
Hearthstone	An incredibly light and soft stone. Good for absorbing shock.	2000	7	--
Lunatite	A stone that emits rainbow colors. Enhances lunaglyph powers.	5000	8	--
Quartz	A stone that resonates when it is struck. Aligning the waves creates a destructive force.	7000	9	--
Amarlista	A stone that dampens lunaglyph power. Although beautiful, it is said to be cursed.	10000	10	--
Bronze Metal	A metal lacking rigidness and durability. A low-grade metal, to say the least.	100	2	--
Iron Metal	The most common metal around. Many nations have gone to war to secure deposits of it.	200	2	--
Copper Metal	A soft metal that is easy to process. Durable and light, it does not rust easily.	350	3	--
Steel Metal	A harder metal than iron, but does not last quite as long.	600	3	--
Silver Metal	A rather expensive metal despite being common. Wards off evil spirits.	900	4	--
Titanium Metal	A rare metal that is prized for its hard, light, and durable properties.	1300	4	--
Gold Metal	An elastic metal that can even be processed into a thin wire.	2200	5	--
Blaze Metal	A metal that radiates heat. The hotter it gets, the harder the metal becomes.	3900	6	--
Prismatite Metal	A metal sought after by smiths everywhere. The color differs with time spent processing.	5000	7	--
Mercurius Metal	A metal usually found in liquid form. Solidified by a special process to give elasticity.	7000	8	--
Crystallite Metal	A metal said to be refined only by aristos. The more refined, the clearer it is.	15000	9	--
Atlantis Metal	A metal that is so scarce that even the basic properties of the metal are a mystery.	20000	10	Must complete Private Event "Secret of Wrought Gold" to make

Ore Alchemy

Rarity	Creation Result	1st Ingredient	Qty.	2nd Ingredient	Qty.	3rd Ingredient	Qty.	Kiriya IC Lv.	Seraphina IC Lv.	Sigmund IC Lv.
2	Sandstone	Stone Statue Fragment	2	--	--	--	--	1	1	1
3	Granite	Sandstone	2	--	--	--	--	1	1	1
4	Marble	Granite	2	--	--	--	--	2	2	--
5	Ceramic	Marble	2	--	--	--	--	3	3	--
6	Metetite	Ceramic	2	Granite	2	--	--	4	4	--
7	Hearthstone	Metetite	2	Marble	2	--	--	--	4	--
8	Lunatite	Hearthstone	2	Ceramic	2	--	--	--	5	--
9	Quartz	Lunatite	2	Hearthstone	2	--	--	--	5	--
2	Bronze Metal	Metal Fragment	2	--	--	--	--	1	1	2
2	Iron Metal	Bronze Metal	2	--	--	--	--	1	1	2
3	Copper Metal	Iron Metal	2	Sandstone	1	--	--	2	2	--
3	Steel Metal	Copper Metal	2	Granite	1	--	--	2	2	--
4	Silver Metal	Steel Metal	2	Marble	1	--	--	3	3	--
4	Titanium Metal	Silver Metal	2	Ceramic	1	--	--	4	3	--
5	Gold Metal	Titanium Metal	2	Silver Metal	1	--	--	--	4	--
6	Blaze Metal	Gold Metal	2	Sunstone	3	--	--	--	4	--
7	Prismatite Metal	Blaze Metal	2	Gold Metal	2	--	--	--	5	--
8	Mercurius Metal	Prismatite Metal	2	Blaze Metal	2	--	--	--	5	--
9	Crystallite Metal	Mercurius Metal	2	Blaze Metal	2	--	--	--	6	--
10	Atlantis Metal	Crystallite Metal	2	Amarlista	2	--	--	--	6	--

Michelle cannot make Ore Alchemy.

WOOD

Name	Description	Value	Rarity	Special Acquisition
Cork Wood	An inexpensive wood that is resistant to humidity, but wears down easily.	15	1	--
Lauan Wood	A commonly found wood. Quick growth makes it perfect for mass distribution.	150	2	--
Balsa Wood	A very soft and light wood. Extremely easy to process.	200	3	--
Ebony Wood	A wood that is as hard as steel when in cylindrical form, making application difficult.	280	3	--
Lux Wood	Regarded as being harder than the average wood. Its shine makes it a high-quality wood.	350	4	--
Lentesco Wood	An extraordinarily rubbery wood. It can be manipulated to any shape and does not burn.	400	4	--
Placidus Wood	An elastic wood ideal for use in bows. Also used to help expel evil spirits.	600	5	--
Malus Wood	A magical wood that increases in density the more it's swung around. Tastes sweet.	850	6	--
Pius Wood	A rare wood from a divine ancient tree. Its elegant aroma seems to give vitality.	1200	7	--

Wood Alchemy

Rarity	Creation Result	1st Ingredient	Qty.	2nd Ingredient	Qty.	3rd Ingredient	Qty.	Michelle IC Lv.	Kiriya IC Lv.	Seraphina IC Lv.
1	Lentesco Wood	Lauan Wood	2	--	--	--	--	1	1	1

Sigmund make Wood Alchemy.

CLOTH

Name	Description	Value	Rarity	Special Acquisition
Rabbit Hide	The hide of a small animal that gives off a pungent smell.	45	1	--
Sheep Hide	The hide of a mid-sized herbivore. Durable and used commonly across the land.	120	2	--
Lizard Skin	The skin of a reptile. Unlike most cloths, it is resistant to dry and humid conditions.	250	3	--
Buffalo Hide	The durable hide of a large herbivore.	300	4	--
Silver Fox Fur	The fur of a mid-sized mammal. Soft and warm, viewed as an expensive material.	500	4	--
Golden Wolf Fur	The fur of a wolf that can absorb impacts when kept in good condition.	150	3	--
Chameleon Skin	Magically imbued skin that blends in with its surroundings.	1000	5	--
Salamander Skin	The skin of a serpent that is resistant to fire.	2500	6	--
Glutton Hide	A magically imbued skin that absorbs impacts and is as hard as metal, but remains light.	3000	7	--
Garuda Skin	The skin of a garuda. Different layering methods change its characteristics.	800	5	--
Dragon Hide	The hide of a dragon that hardens in places according to its wearer's reflexes.	8000	8	Must complete Private Event "Secret of Wrought Gold" to make
Kenaf Cloth	A crude cloth that is thick and coarse. Rips easily like paper.	20	1	--
Ramie Cloth	A cloth in mass distribution. Made from a plant that can grow even in dry regions.	80	1	--
Barkcloth	A rough but strong cloth woven from wood fibers.	100	2	--
Cotton Cloth	A soft, absorbent cloth that gives the wearer optimum mobility.	150	2	--
Linen Cloth	A widely used cloth that breathes well. Popular in hot regions.	200	3	--
Silk Cloth	A scented cloth also known as fragrant cloth. Keeps away diseases as well as bugs.	250	4	--
Down Feather Cloth	A light and warm cloth made with feathers woven into the material.	500	5	--
Damask Cloth	A glittery cloth with bits of metals and gems sewn into it. Surprisingly smooth.	1000	6	--
Feeble Cloth	A cloth soaked in the blood of a now-extinct breed of monsters called feebles.	2000	7	--
Rachnuvus Cloth	An expensive cloth made from rachnuvae webbing. Durable and insulates well.	3500	8	--
Lubricus Cloth	A magically imbued cloth that always feels wet. Whatever touches it slips right off.	4000	9	--
Empyrean Cloth	A mysterious cloth soaked in holy water that shines like metal and reflects light.	5500	10	Must complete Private Event "Secret of Wrought Gold" to make

Cloth Alchemy

Rarity	Creation Result	1st Ingredient	Qty.	2nd Ingredient	Qty.	3rd Ingredient	Qty.	Michelle IC Lv.	Kiriya IC Lv.	Seraphina IC Lv.	Sigmund IC Lv.
3	Lizard Skin	Lizard Scale	2	--	--	--	--	2	2	2	--
5	Chameleon Skin	Lizard Scale	2	Silver Metal	1	--	--	4	2	4	--
6	Salamander Skin	Snakeskin	4	Blaze Metal	1	--	--	4	3	4	--
8	Dragon Hide	Dragon Scale	2	Salamander Skin	1	--	--	6	--	--	--
1	Kenaf Cloth	Fresh Herb	2	--	--	--	--	1	1	1	1
1	Ramie Cloth	Lauan Wood	2	--	--	--	--	1	1	1	2
2	Barkcloth	Balsa Wood	2	Lauan Wood	2	--	--	2	2	--	--
2	Cotton Cloth	Lauan Wood	4	--	--	--	--	2	2	--	--
3	Linen Cloth	Lux Wood	2	--	--	--	--	3	--	--	--
4	Silk Cloth	Rachnuvus Shell	2	--	--	--	--	3	--	--	--
6	Damask Cloth	Gold Metal	2	Silver Metal	2	Metetite	1	4	--	--	--
7	Feeble Cloth	Silver Fox Fur	4	Golden Wolf Fur	3	Bear Paw	1	4	--	--	--
8	Rachnuvus Cloth	Silk Cloth	2	Rachnuvus Shell	4	--	--	5	--	--	--
9	Lubricus Cloth	Glutton Hide	2	Metetite	3	--	--	6	--	--	--
10	Empyrean Cloth	Damask Cloth	3	Holy Water	4	--	--	6	--	--	--

HERB

Name	Description	Value	Rarity	Special Acquisition
Medical Herb	A kind of herb that is abundantly cultivated in Graad Woods.	50	1	--
Fresh Herb	A kind of herb with a shockingly potent smell.	80	2	--
Antidote Herb	A kind of herb that is used to cure a variety of poisons.	100	2	--
Novo Herb	A kind of herb that is said to have the power to revive the dead.	120	3	--
Fructus Herb	A kind of herb with a fruity scent. Added to various things to give a nice fragrance.	150	3	--
Halgitian Rice	A staple of the Halgitian diet.	200	4	--
Fayel Wheat	A cereal that is cultivated in Fayel.	200	4	--
Laurel	A kind of herb used in a variety of medicines. A symbol of honor and victory.	350	5	--
Toadstool	A mushroom that releases hallucinogenic spores.	250	4	--

PARTS

Name	Description	Value	Rarity	Special Acquisition
Insect Antenna	An insect antenna. Most people would not touch this out of choice.	2	1	--
Insect Shell	The hard shell of an insect. Light yet tough, it has many uses.	2	1	--
Thin Wing	The thin wing of an insect. Handle it gently, or it will come apart in your hands.	3	1	--
Monster Claw	A long, eerie claw.	10	1	--
Insect Fang	An insect fang. A commodity among collectors.	12	2	--
Poison Stinger	The stinger of a monster. Be careful, as it may still carry traces of poison.	15	2	--
Bat Wing	The creepy wing of a bat. Used in medicine and in cooking.	20	2	--
Beehive	A hive made by bees as their home. Sweet honey can be extracted from it.	10	2	--
Snakeskin	The shed skin of a snake. Often boiled down to be used in medicine.	15	2	--
Cactus Needle	A durable needle taken from a certain breed of cactus.	13	2	--
Vine	A flexible piece of vine that shrinks and stretches.	14	2	--
Random Beast Bone	A bone of an undetermined animal.	15	3	--
Bone Fragment	A piece of a bone that has been smashed into smithereens.	20	3	--
Animal Fang	The sharp fang of a wild animal.	10	3	--
Bird Eye	The eye of a bird that sailors use as good-luck charms.	10	3	--
Lizard Scale	The scale of a lizard. Sold in marketplaces as good-luck charms.	25	3	--
Bird Egg	A fresh egg packed full of nutrition. Used in a variety of dishes.	10	3	--
Lizard Fang	The fang of a lizard. Used in a variety of things, as it's so easy to process.	35	4	--
Lizard Eye	The eye of a lizard. Valued among nobles as a gem.	50	5	--
Rachnuvus Shell	The shell of a rachnuvus. Moderately strong and easy to process.	300	5	--
King Egg	An extremely rare chicken egg that is highly valued.	250	5	--
Crab Shell	The durable shell of a crab that is used in cooking as well as in making equipment.	200	5	--
Dragon Scale	The scale of a dragon that is fire-resistant. Valued as a material for equipment.	1000	5	--
Dragon Fang	The fang of a dragon said to be able to cut through steel. Used to make deadly weapons.	1500	6	--
Giant Eye	The eyeball of a giant demon. Even without its body, magic still resides within the eye.	1000	6	--
Bear Paw	The paw of a bear. Considered to be a delicacy in some places.	2000	7	--
Dragon Eye	The eye of a dragon that is said to have the power to see the future.	3500	7	--

PENS

Name	Description	Value	Rarity	Special Acquisition
Quill	A simple writing tool.	100	1	--
Writer's Quill	A writing tool designed so the writer does not get tired when writing long pieces.	150	2	--
Clerk's Quill	A writing tool that has long been used for creating important documents.	200	3	--
Musician's Quill	A writing tool used for composing musical masterpieces.	250	4	--
Genius's Quill	A legendary writing tool that can make any novice writer sound like a master.	300	5	Must complete Private Event "Secret of Wrought Gold" to make

Pen Alchemy

Rarity	Creation Result	1st Ingredient	Qty.	2nd Ingredient	Qty.	3rd Ingredient	Qty.	Michelle IC Lv.	Kiriya IC Lv.	Seraphina IC Lv.
2	Writer's Quill	Ebony Wood	2	Bronze Metal	1	--	--	2	2	2
3	Clerk's Quill	Writer's Quill	2	Placidus Wood	2	--	--	3	3	3
4	Musician's Quill	Malus Wood	1	Lizard Fang	1	--	--	--	4	--
5	Genius's Quill	Pius Wood	1	Dragon Fang	1	--	--	--	--	5

Sigmund cannot make Pen Alchemy.

PAPER

Name	Description	Value	Rarity	Special Acquisition
Papyrus Paper	A type of paper that has been used since long ago. Made from plants.	50	1	--
Pulp Paper	A type of paper that is commonly used. Made from timber.	80	2	--
Staff Paper	A type of paper suitable for composing music. The staff is already on the sheet.	100	3	--
Parchment	A type of paper made from animal skin. Often used for important documents.	120	4	--
Halgitian Paper	A type of strong and durable paper that was developed in Halgita.	150	5	--
Sword of Spades	A treasure possessed by the Lumpers. Carved with a spade.	0	5	--
Chalice of Hearts	A treasure possessed by the Lumpers. Carved with a heart.	0	5	--
Club of Clubs	A treasure possessed by the Lumpers. Carved with a club.	0	5	--
Coin of Diamonds	A treasure possessed by the Lumpers. Carved with a diamond.	0	5	--
Servant of Jacks	A hidden treasure possessed by the Lumper elites. Carved with a jack.	0	6	--
Queen of Queens	A hidden treasure possessed by the Lumper elites. Carved with a queen.	0	7	--

Paper Alchemy

Rarity	Creation Result	1st Ingredient	Qty.	2nd Ingredient	Qty.	3rd Ingredient	Qty.	Michelle IC Lv.	Kiriya IC Lv.	Seraphina IC Lv.
1	Papyrus Paper	Cork Wood	2	--	--	--	--	1	--	1
2	Pulp Paper	Lauan Wood	2	--	--	--	--	2	--	1
3	Staff Paper	Ebony Wood	2	--	--	--	--	3	--	2
4	Parchment	Sheep Hide	2	Buffalo Hide	2	--	--	4	--	--
5	Halgitian Paper	Kenaf Cloth	3	Lentesco Wood	2	--	--	5	--	--
7	Servant of Jacks	Sword of Spades	1	Chalice of Hearts	1	--	--	--	6	--
7	Queen of Queens	Club of Clubs	1	Coin of Diamonds	1	--	--	--	--	6

Sigmund cannot make Paper Alchemy.

QUEST/STORY ITEMS

Name	Description	Special Acquisition
Eagle Emblem Gold Coin	A gold coin given to you by a prisoner. Take it to his family in Burguss.	Side Quest: "Gold Coin"
Saruleus Flute	A divine flute endowed with the vision and spirit of Saruleus.	Story
Saruleus Amarlista	A holy stone imbued with the power of Saruleus. Dispels all impurities.	Story
Firewood	Very dry wood that will probably burn easily.	Story
Sigmund's Pendant	A broken locket worn by Sigmund. It seems there used to be a photo in it…	Story
Lunytol	Medicine to prevent turning into a vermiform. Take it to Edward quickly.	Story
Prison Key	An old key that opens the doors of Graad Prison.	Story
Cell Key	A jade key that opens the cells in Prevant Castle.	Story
Key of Prevant	A fancy key that opens the doors of Castle Prevant.	Story
Brass Bar	A brass alloy bar. It seems that something can be fitted to it.	Story
Jade Stone	A gem made of jade.	Story
Orb of Chaos	An orb with a crest that symbolizes chaos carved into it.	Story
Orb of Order	An orb with a crest that symbolizes order carved into it.	Story
Orb of Patience	An orb with a crest that symbolizes patience carved into it.	Story
Orb of Desire	An orb with a crest that symbolizes desire carved into it.	Story
Orb of Reincarnation	An orb with a crest that symbolizes reincarnation carved into it.	Story
Orb of Destruction	An orb with a crest that symbolizes destruction carved into it.	Story
Orb of Rebirth	An orb with a crest that symbolizes rebirth carved into it.	Story

Name	Description	Special Acquisition
Orb of Rebirth Fragment	A broken piece of an orb. If all the pieces are gathered, it may be possible to fix it.	Story
Mirror	A mirror that has been painstakingly polished to make it very reflective.	Story
Mirror Fragment	A shard of a mirror. If all the pieces are collected, it could make a fine mirror.	Story
Training Notations	A good piece came to mind. You'd better make a note of it…	Story
Prelude Notations	A good piece came to mind. You'd better make a note of it…	Story
Nocturne Notations	A good piece came to mind. You'd better make a note of it…	Complete Private Event "Funeral March"
Sonata Notations	A good piece came to mind. You'd better make a note of it…	--
Fantasia Notations	A good piece came to mind. You'd better make a note of it…	Story
Symphony Notations	A good piece came to mind. You'd better make a note of it…	--
Concerto Notations	A good piece came to mind. You'd better make a note of it…	Complete Private Event "Saruleus Flute"
Suite Notations	A good piece came to mind. You'd better make a note of it…	Complete Private Event "Encouraging Tone"
Capriccio Notations	A good piece came to mind. You'd better make a note of it…	Story
Fugue Notations	A good piece came to mind. You'd better make a note of it…	Story
Wooden Box	A scratched-up, locked box.	Side Quest: "Secret Lost by Tsunami"
Strange-Colored Bag	A scrunched-up bulky bag covered with dirt.	Side Quest: "Gift Lost by Tsunami"
Dentures	A full set of dentures.	Side Quest: "Dentures"
Doll	A broken doll missing its head.	Side Quest: "Junk from Tsunami Disaster"
Battered Notebook	A dirty notebook missing its latter half.	Side Quest: "Junk from Tsunami Disaster"
Piece of Wood	A rectangular piece of wood with a strange design on it.	Side Quest: "Amulet Lost by Tsunami"
Bouquet	A withered bunch of flowers tied with a ribbon.	Side Quest: "Junk from Tsunami Disaster"
Vase	A vase with a floral design on the side. It's missing its bottom.	Side Quest: "Junk from Tsunami Disaster"
Tail	A fluffy tail that seems to come from a small animal.	Side Quest: "Rat Extermination"
Rag	A big piece of cloth scrunched up in a ball.	Side Quest: "Junk from Tsunami Disaster"
Damaged Pendant	An intricately designed pendant decorated with a crimson gem.	Side Quest: "Missing Simon"
Broken Glasses	The frame is bent and the lenses are cracked.	Side Quest: "Missing Simon"
Blood of Fayel	A blood-red jewel that can be found on a Fayel monster on rare occasions.	Side Quest: "Looking for Jewelry"
Worn Bow	Aya's old practice bow.	Side Quest: "Gustav's Memories"
Bone Comb	A comb that has been well-kept.	Side Quest: "The Staff of Life"
Crested Ring	A dull silver ring.	Side Quest: "Lost Memories"
Replica of a Kylin Sword	A replica of a superior sword wielded by Halgitian aristos.	Side Quest: "Lost Katana"
Blood-Stained Seal	The seal of Veros. Stained with the blood of the sacrificed.	--
Old Ring	An old ring you found in Nolaan. Someone must have dropped it.	Side Quest: "Old Ring"
Poor Clay	Material used for pottery. Take it to the cranky old man.	Side Quest: "Pot"
Soft Clay	Material used for pottery. Take it to the cranky old man.	Side Quest: "Pot"
Golden Clay	Material used for pottery. Take it to the cranky old man.	Side Quest: "Pot"
Letter	A letter you've been asked to deliver. It's addressed to Denton in Burguss.	Side Quest: "Letter"
Potter's Wheel	A potter's wheel. Take it to the cranky old man.	Side Quest: "Delivery"
Hair Clip	A pretty hair clip. Take it to the helpful young woman at the entrance of the village.	Side Quest: "Delivery"
Iron Arm Weights	A very bulky set of iron arm weights. Someone in the village must've ordered them.	Side Quest: "Delivery"
Prescription	A prescription for back pain medicine. Take it to the item shop in Burguss.	Side Quest: "Back Pain Medicine"
Harpy Liver	The back pain medicine ingredients. Take 10 of them to the item shop in Burguss.	Side Quest: "Back Pain Medicine"
Back Pain Medicine	Special medicine for back pain. Take it to the worried old woman in Nolaan.	Side Quest: "Back Pain Medicine"
Cut of Cured Meat	Cured meat that is even loved by monsters. Take it to the twins' mother in Nolaan.	Side Quest: "Risky Delivery"
Gior Fur	An extremely rare item. Take it to the minister in Burguss Palace.	Side Quest: "Minister and Fur"
Zalacrest	A top-brand wine that has a smooth clean taste. Take it to the barkeeper in Burguss.	Side Quest: "Zalan Alcohol Brand"
Burgano Special	A famous brand of liquor with a rich and robust aroma. Loved by liquor aficionados.	Complete Side Quest "Zalan Alcohol Brand"
Toy Sword	The toy Ralph's friend lost. Take it to Ralph in Burguss.	Side Quest: "Child's Lost Matter"
Special Cocktail Recipe	A recipe for a confidence- building cocktail. Perfect for asking a girl out.	Side Quest: "Straw"
Secret Pain Reliever	Miraculous painkiller. However, it doesn't actually heal anything.	Side Quest: "Straw"
Veros's Teardrop	A stone with something mildly resembling the symbol of Veros on it. Best ask the priest.	Side Quest: "Straw"
Ring for Delivery	The mustered-up courage of a shy young man. Take this expensive ring to his love.	Side Quest: "Cupid"
Overture Notations	A good piece came to mind. You'd better make a note of it…	--
"Legend of the Creator Vol. 2"	A blessed world made by a divine god who later shunned it after mankind's feuding…	--
"Legend of the Creator Vol. 4"	The victor was given eternal life and power. The god placed him on the moon and vanished.	--
"Legend of the Creator Vol. 5"	I am Juno. Thou shalt engrave my name.	--
Torn Page of a Thick Book	This page is badly torn and cannot be read.	--
Torn Page of a Thin Book	This page is badly torn and cannot be read.	--
Torn Page of a Scratched Book	This page is badly torn and cannot be read.	--
Torn Page of a New Book	This page is badly torn and cannot be read.	--
A Voucher	Customers have the chance to purchase a special material set with this ticket.	Xbox Live
B Voucher	Customers have the chance to purchase a special material set with this ticket.	Xbox Live
C Voucher	Customers have the chance to purchase rare gear with this ticket.	Xbox Live

ENCHANTING

Capell's craft works a little differently than the others. Rather than make new gear or items, Capell uses resources to create timed bonuses for allies. Press [RB] or [LB] on the Enchantment menu to choose which ally to buff up. Items used in the enchantment are gone for good, so choose enchantments carefully. They're best when applied for short-term, difficult encounters, like boss fights—normal fighting is not usually difficult enough to warrant expending the items. Like other crafts, enchantment increases in IC level through repetitious use, unlocking more advanced recipes. Some advanced enchantments grant huge bonuses, but at great cost—once the bonus wears off, equipped weapons or body armor are permanently shattered. You can't cheat the system, either; taking off the weapon or armor before the timer runs out simply shatters the item and ends the buff prematurely. The bonuses are sizeable enough (ATK +3000, ATK ×3, or INT ×2, for example) that you might consider equipping an outdated piece of gear before enchanting. What you give up in stats swapping to a weapon or piece of armor you won't miss later, you'll more than make up from these staggering enchantments.

Enchanting

Rarity	Result	1st Ingredient	Qty.	2nd Ingredient	Qty.	3rd Ingredient	Qty.	Capell IC Lv.	Notes
3	ATK +20 (10:00)	Junk	1	Sandstone	1	--	--	1	--
5	ATK +200 (05:00)	Gold Metal	1	--	--	--	--	2	--
7	ATK +500 (05:00)	Gold Metal	2	Lizard Scale	1	--	--	3	--
8	ATK +1000 (03:00)	Gold Metal	3	Lizard Scale	2	--	--	6	--
10	ATK +3000 (Weapon Shatter) (03:00)	Gold Metal	5	Dragon Scale	1	Dragon Eye	1	6	Must have access to Seraphic Gate to make
8	ATK ×2 (HP drain 5% over time) (05:00)	Gold Ring	1	Lizard Eye	1	--	--	5	--
8	ATK ×2 (HP drain 10% with each attack) (05:00)	Gold Ring	2	Lizard Eye	2	--	--	5	--
10	ATK ×3Ð (Weapon Shatter) (03:00)	Gold Ring	3	Dragon Eye	1			6	Must complete Private Event "Secret of Enchantment" to make
5	ATK +5% (10:00)	Gold Wristguard	1	Lizard Fang	1	--	--	2	--
6	ATK +10% (05:00)	Gold Wristguard	2	Lizard Fang	2	--	--	4	--
8	ATK +30% (03:00)	Gold Wristguard	3	Dragon Fang	1	--	--	4	--
4	DEF +5% (10:00)	Bronze Metal	1	--	--	--	--	2	--
7	DEF +10% (05:00)	Silver Metal	2	--	--	--	--	3	--
8	DEF +30% (03:00)	Silver Wristguard	1	Rachnuvus Shell	1	--	--	5	--
10	DEF ×2 (Armor Shatter) (03:00)	Silver Ring	3	Crab Shell	1	--	--	6	Must have access to Seraphic Gate to make
3	HIT +5% (05:00)	Metal Fragment	2	--	--	--	--	1	--
4	HIT +10% (03:00)	Iron Metal	1	--	--	--	--	2	--
2	AGL +5% (05:00)	Metal Fragment	2	--	--	--	--	1	--
6	AGL +10% (03:00)	Mercurius Metal	1	--	--	--	--	3	--
7	INT +200 (05:00)	Granite	1	--	--	--	--	3	--
9	INT +500 (03:00)	Copper Metal	1	--	--	--	--	6	Must complete Private Event "Secret of Enchantment" to make
6	INT +5% (10:00)	Copper Metal	1	Random Beast Bone	1	--	--	3	--
8	INT +10% (05:00)	Copper Wristguard	1	--	--	--	--	4	--
9	INT +30% (03:00)	Copper Wristguard	2	--	--	--	--	5	--
10	INT +50% (MP drain 1% over time) (03:00)	Copper Wristguard	3	Random Beast Bone	1	--	--	6	--
10	INT ×2 (Weapon Shatter) (03:00)	Copper Ring	3	Giant Eye	1	--	--	6	Must have access to Seraphic Gate to make
4	LUC +5% (05:00)	Sheep Hide	1			--	--	2	--
8	LUC +10% (03:00)	Lizard Skin	1			--	--	4	--
6	ATK/DEF +5% (05:00)	Gold Metal	1	Silver Metal	1	--	--	3	--
9	ATK/DEF +10% (03:00)	Gold Ring	1	Silver Ring	1	--	--	5	--
8	ATK/HIT +10% (03:00)	Gold Wristguard	1	Iron Metal	1	--	--	5	--
5	ATK +500ÐHIT Ð50 (03:00)	Gold Ring	1	Silver Metal	2	--	--	3	--
9	ATK +1000ÐDEF Ð500 (03:00)	Gold Wristguard	1	Gold Ring	1	--	--	5	--
9	ATK ×3ÐDEF 0 (03:00)	Gold Wristguard	2	Gold Ring	1	Dragon Fang	1	5	--
8	ATK/DEF +500 (Confusion) (03:00)	Gold Wristguard	1	Silver Wristguard	1	Balsa Wood	1	4	--
7	AGL/INT +10% (05:00)	Mercurius Metal	1	Copper Metal	1	--	--	4	--
8	AGL/INT +20% (03:00)	Mercurius Ring	1	Copper Ring	1	--	--	4	--
5	Regenerate HP by 3% over time (10:00)	Blue Berry Potion	2	Yellow Berry Potion	1	--	--	3	--
6	Regenerate HP by 6% over time (05:00)	Blue Berry Powder	2	Yellow Berry Powder	1	--	--	4	--
7	Regenerate MP by 1% over time (10:00)	Black Berry Potion	2	White Berry Potion	1	--	--	4	--
8	Regenerate MP by 4% over time (03:00)	Black Berry Powder	1	--	--	--	--	5	--
4	Fire damage +30% (10:00)	Salamander Skin	1	Cork Wood	1	--	--	3	--
8	Fire damage +50% (05:00)	Blaze Metal	2	--	--	--	--	5	--
4	Water damage +30% (10:00)	Rachnuvus Shell	1	Lauan Wood	1	--	--	3	--
8	Water damage +50% (05:00)	Rachnuvus Cloth	1	--	--	--	--	5	--
4	Air damage +30% (10:00)	Lentesco Wood	2	Balsa Wood	1	--	--	3	--
8	Air damage +50% (05:00)	Pius Wood	2	--	--	--	--	5	--
4	Earth damage +30% (10:00)	Ceramic	1	Cork Wood	1	--	--	3	--
8	Earth damage +50% (05:00)	Quartz	3	--	--	--	--	5	--
4	Aether damage +30% (10:00)	Lizard Skin	1	Lauan Wood	1	--	--	3	--
8	Aether damage +50% (05:00)	Prismatite Metal	3	--	--	--	--	5	--
9	Magic damage +10% (05:00)	Amarlista	1	--	--	--	--	5	--
10	Magic damage +30% (03:00)	Amarlista	1	Lunatite	1	--	--	6	--
10	Magic damage +50%ÐDEF 0 (03:00)	Amarlista	1	Lunatite	2	--	--	6	Must complete Private Event "Secret of Enchantment" to make
3	Fire attack (10:00)	Sunstone	1	--	--	--	--	1	--
6	Fire damage -50% (10:00)	Salamander Skin	1	--	--	--	--	3	--

Enchanting

Rarity	Result	1st Ingredient	Qty.	2nd Ingredient	Qty.	3rd Ingredient	Qty.	Capell IC Lv.	Notes
8	Fire damage -100% (05:00)	Blaze Metal	1	--	--		--	4	--
10	Absorb fire (03:00)	Blaze Metal	2	Salamander Skin	2		--	6	--
3	Water attack (10:00)	Holy Water	1	--	--		--	1	--
6	Water damage -50% (10:00)	Rachnuvus Shell	1	--	--		--	3	--
8	Water damage -100% (05:00)	Rachnuvus Cloth	1	--	--		--	4	--
10	Absorb water (03:00)	Rachnuvus Cloth	2	Rachnuvus Shell	2		--	6	--
3	Air attack (10:00)	Cork Wood	1	--	--		--	1	--
6	Air damage -50% (10:00)	Lentesco Wood	2	--	--		--	3	--
8	Air damage -100% (05:00)	Malus Wood	2	--	--		--	4	--
10	Absorb air (03:00)	Pius Wood	1	Malus Wood	1		--	6	--
3	Earth attack (10:00)	Sandstone	1	--	--		--	1	--
6	Earth damage -50% (10:00)	Ceramic	1	--	--		--	3	--
8	Earth damage -100% (05:00)	Quartz	1	--	--		--	4	--
10	Absorb earth (03:00)	Quartz	2	Ceramic	2		--	6	--
3	Aether attack (10:00)	Metal Fragment	1	--	--		--	1	--
6	Aether damage -50% (10:00)	Lizard Skin	1	--	--		--	3	--
8	Aether damage -100% (05:00)	Prismatite Metal	2	--	--		--	4	--
10	Absorb Aether (03:00)	Prismatite Metal	2	Lizard Skin	2		--	6	--
8	Magic damage -50% (03:00)	Lunatite	1	--	--		--	4	--
9	Magic damage -100% (03:00)	Amarlista	1	--	--		--	5	--
10	Absorb all elements (03:00)	Amarlista	2	Lunatite	2		--	6	Must complete Private Event "Secret of Enchantment" to make
4	Anti-faint (05:00)	Lux Wood	1	--	--		--	2	--
2	Anti-sleep (05:00)	Lauan Wood	1	--	--		--	1	--
2	Anti-poison (05:00)	Snakeskin	1	--	--		--	1	--
4	Anti-curse (05:00)	Random Beast Bone	1	--	--		--	2	--
2	Anti-paralysis (05:00)	Ebony Wood	1	--	--		--	1	--
4	Anti-silence (05:00)	Placidus Wood	1	--	--		--	2	--
4	Anti-confusion (05:00)	Balsa Wood	1	--	--		--	2	--
4	Anti-freeze (05:00)	Sunstone	1	--	--		--	2	--
5	Anti-stone (05:00)	Stone Statue Fragment	1	--	--		--	2	--
4	Anti-charm (05:00)	Vine	1	--	--		--	2	--
5	Anti-doom (05:00)	Novo Herb	1	--	--		--	2	--
3	Anti-unseeing (05:00)	Bird Eye	1	--	--		--	2	--
3	Anti-unhearing (05:00)	Bat Wing	1	--	--		--	2	--
3	Anti-untasting (05:00)	Fresh Herb	1	--	--		--	2	--
6	Anti-ailment (05:00)	Giant Eye	1	--	--		--	4	--
8	Anti-magic (03:00)	Dragon Eye	1	--	--		--	6	Must have access to Seraphic Gate to make
4	Faint attack (05:00)	Lux Wood	2	Sandstone	2		--	2	--
5	Sleep attack (05:00)	Sheep Hide	2	Coffee	2	--	--	2	--
5	Poison attack (05:00)	Poison Stinger	2	Antidote	2	--	--	2	--
4	Curse attack (05:00)	Monster Claw	2	Holy Water	2	--	--	2	--
5	Paralysis attack (03:00)	Rachnuvus Shell	2	Para-Gone	2	--	--	2	--
5	Silence attack (05:00)	Placidus Wood	2	Cough Drop	2	--	--	2	--
4	Confusion attack (05:00)	Toadstool	2	Sedative	2	--	--	2	--
7	Freeze attack (03:00)	Dragon Fang	2	Spring Warmth	2	--	--	4	--
8	Stone attack (03:00)	Glutton Hide	2	Odious Eye	2	--	--	4	--
7	Charm attack (03:00)	Malus Wood	2	Maiden's Scorn	2	--	--	4	--
8	HP absorb attack (03:00)	Feeble Cloth	2	Blue Berry Potion	2	--	--	4	--
8	MP absorb attack (03:00)	Giant Eye	2	Black Berry Potion	2	--	--	4	--
9	Doom attack (03:00)	Amarlista	2	Dragon Eye	1	--	--	5	--
4	Unseeing attack (05:00)	White Pepper	2	Eye Drops	2	--	--	3	--
4	Unhearing attack (05:00)	White Pepper	1	Angel Earpick	2	--	--	3	--
8	Casting time down (05:00)	Crystallite Metal	1	Cough Drop	2	--	--	4	--
9	Casting time down+ (03:00)	Crystallite Metal	2	Cough Drop	4	--	--	5	--
3	Critical hit rate +5% (10:00)	Cactus Needle	2	--	--	--	--	2	--
4	Critical hit rate +10% (05:00)	Bird Eye	1	Cactus Needle	2	--	--	3	--
5	Autoguard rate +5% (10:00)	Insect Shell	1	--	--	--	--	2	--
6	Autoguard rate +10% (05:00)	Bronze Metal	1	--	--	--	--	3	--
9	Autoguard rate +100% Attacks prohibited (03:00)	Silver Metal	2	Rachnuvus Shell	1	--	--	5	--
5	EXP +20% (10:00)	Gold Metal	1	Silver Metal	1	--	--	3	--
6	EXP +30% (05:00)	Gold Metal	2	Silver Metal	2	--	--	3	--
8	EXP ×2ÐNo Fol (03:00)	Gold Metal	3	Silver Metal	3	--	--	4	--
4	Gold +20% (10:00)	Gold Metal	1	Steel Metal	1	--	--	3	--
5	Gold +30% (05:00)	Gold Metal	2	Steel Metal	2	--	--	3	--
7	Gold ×3ÐNo EXP (03:00)	Gold Metal	3	Steel Metal	3	--	--	4	--
7	AP recovery amount ×2 (05:00)	Insect Fang	2	Animal Fang	2	Lizard Fang	2	4	--
8	AP consumption -50% (05:00)	Insect Fang	3	Animal Fang	3	Lizard Fang	3	5	--
9	AP consumption 0 (MP drain 1% over time) (03:00)	Animal Fang	2	Lizard Fang	2	Dragon Fang	1	6	Must complete Private Event "Secret of Enchantment" to make
7	MP consumption -20% (10:00)	Dragon Scale	1	--	--	--	--	3	--
8	MP consumption -30% (05:00)	Dragon Scale	2	--	--	--	--	4	--
9	MP consumption -40% (03:00)	Dragon Hide	1	Dragon Scale	1	--	--	5	--
10	MP consumption -50% (HP drain 5% over time) (03:00)	Dragon Hide	1	Dragon Scale	1	--	--	6	--
10	MP consumption 0 (Weapon Shatter) (03:00)	Dragon Hide	1	Dragon Scale	1	--	--	6	Must have access to Seraphic Gate to make
9	Survival rate up (05:00)	Lizard Eye	1	Bird Eye	1	--	--	5	--
10	Anti-stun DEF -50% (03:00)	Dragon Eye	1	Giant Eye	1	--	--	6	--
1	Increased vision (10:00)	Bird Eye	1	--	--	--	--	1	--

SHOPS

NOLAAN

General Shop

Item	Cost
Fresh Milk	100
Red Berry Potion	60
Antidote	100
Sedative	150
Seeing Eye	30
Nolaan Potato	15
Antidote Herb	100
Four-leaf Clover	50

CASTLE PREVANT

Genma

Item	Cost
Red Berry Potion	60
Blue Berry Potion	150
Black Berry Potion	350
Coffee	100
Antidote	100
Holy Water	200
Para-Gone	200

Genma

Item	Cost
Cough Drop	150
Sedative	150
Odious Eye	200
Maiden's Scorn	150
Eye Drops	120
Angel Earpick	120
Aroma Oil	120

Genma

Item	Cost
Toothbrush	120
Lunar Scale	150
Miraculous Medicine	550
Seeing Eye	30
Horizon Crystal	40
Sunstone	50

BURGUSSTADT

General Shop

Item	Cost
Red Berry Potion	60
Blue Berry Potion	150
Black Berry Potion	350
Antidote	100
Para-Gone	200
Sedative	150
Miraculous Medicine	550
Seeing Eye	30

General Shop

Item	Cost
Sunstone	50
Gladius	500
Longsword	800
Laminated Bow	800
Acolyte Staff	350
"The Art of Making Tea"	260
Greatsword	600
Bastard Sword	1000

General Shop

Item	Cost
Novice Baton	550
Bodhran	550
Sea Axe	500
Soft Leather Jacket	750
Hard Leather Jacket	1800
Iron Scale Armor	1250
Steel Scale Armor	2650
Ramie Chiton	600

General Shop

Item	Cost
Soft Leather Cap	650
Iron Scale Helmet	1200
Granite Circlet	520
Soft Leather Boots	550
Iron Scale Greaves	950
Lauan Sandals	380
Bronze Ring	300

SAPRAN

Item Shop

Item	Cost
Fresh Milk	100
Red Berry Potion	60
Blue Berry Potion	150
Red Berry Powder	650
Black Berry Potion	350
Coffee	100
Antidote	100
Para-Gone	200
Seeing Eye	30
Horizon Crystal	40
Cork Wood	15
Lauan Wood	150

FAYEL

Item Shop

Item	Cost
Red Berry Potion	60
Blue Berry Potion	150
Red Berry Powder	650
Black Berry Potion	350
White Berry Potion	1200
Coffee	100
Antidote	100
Holy Water	200
Para-Gone	200
Cough Drop	150
Sedative	150
Spring Warmth	200
Odious Eye	200
Maiden's Scorn	150
Eye Drops	120
Angel Earpick	120
Aroma Oil	120
Toothbrush	120
Lunar Scale	150
Seeing Eye	30
Horizon Crystal	40
Chicken	50
Fayel Chicken	50
Oradian Carrot	12
Fayel Lemon	100
Fayel Wheat	200

Weapons Shop

Item	Cost
Scimitar	2000
Falchion	3200
Iron Bow	1800
Backed Bow	2600
Preaching Staff	1500
Ebony Staff	3000
"The Shadow Codex"	2400
Two-Handed Sword	2500
Claymore	4000
Marching Baton	1650
Ebony Baton	2800
Tarabuka	1250
Bayan	2500
Broad Axe	4100

Accessory Shop

Item	Cost
Bronze Ring	300
Iron Ring	600
Copper Ring	1500
Granite Necklace	600
Linen Wristband	800
Sheep Wristband	1000
Lizard Wristband	1000
Sacrificial Doll	3500

Armor Shop

Item	Cost
Hard Leather Jacket	1800
Crested Vest	2400
Silver Fur Jacket	3000
Copper Chainmail	2000
Steel Scale Armor	2650
Silver Chainmail	3400
Ramie Chiton	600
Cotton Cloak	1700
Linen Cape	2000
Hard Leather Cap	1450
Crested Mask	1600
Copper Chain Helmet	1750
Steel Scale Helmet	2000
Cotton Hat	1200
Hard Leather Boots	1100
Balsa Clogs	1800
Copper Chain Greaves	1400
Steel Scale Greaves	1750
Balsa Sandals	650
Lux Sandals	1200

PORT ZALA

General Shop

Item	Cost
Red Berry Potion	60
Blue Berry Potion	150
Red Berry Powder	650
Black Berry Potion	350
Miraculous Medicine	550

The Emporium

Item	Cost
Falchion	3200
Claymore	4000
Wolf Claws	800
Silver Fur Jacket	3000
Silver Chainmail	3400
Sacrificial Doll	3500

Trader—Faina

Item	Cost
Fresh Milk	100
Fruit Milk	200
Wild Rabbit Meat	20
Wild Fox Meat	25
Chicken	50
Fayel Chicken	50
Sliced Fish	15
Sliced Deviant Fish	30
Sliced Salmon	50
Oradian Carrot	12

Trader—Faina

Item	Cost
Nolaan Potato	15
Graad Onion	30
Sapran Green Pepper	20
Red Berry	30
Blue Berry	35
Yellow Berry	50
Green Berry	60
Fayel Lemon	100
Honey	150
Wood Syrup	120

Trader—Faina

Item	Cost
Sandstone	120
Granite	250
Marble	500
Bronze Metal	100
Iron Metal	200
Cork Wood	15
Lauan Wood	150
Rabbit Hide	45
Fayel Wheat	200

KOLTON

The Emporium	
Item	Cost
Rapier	5500
Silver Sword	10000
Longbow	6500
Bishop Staff	5000
"Fear of the Unseen"	4500
Shamshir	7500
Battle Baton	4300
Conical Drum	5000
Kris	700
Chilanum Dagger	1800
Iron Claws	2000
Panther Claws	4500
Lizard Skin Vest	4000

The Emporium	
Item	Cost
Banded Armor	4500
Gold Chainmail	6500
Linen Toga	6500
Silk Shawl	4500
Lizard Skin Cap	3500
Silver Chain Helmet	2800
Banded Headgear	4000
Linen Hat	1800
Metetite Circlet	3800
Lizard Skin Boots	5000
Banded Greaves	3500
Silver Fur Pump	2800
Golden Fur Pumps	3400

General Shop	
Item	Cost
Red Berry Potion	60
Blue Berry Potion	150
Yellow Berry Potion	500
Red Berry Powder	650
Black Berry Potion	350
White Berry Potion	1200
Coffee	100
Antidote	100
Holy Water	200
Spring Warmth	200
Miraculous Medicine	550

General Shop	
Item	Cost
Seeing Eye	30
Horizon Crystal	40
Quill	100
Writer's Quill	150
Papyrus Paper	50
Pulp Paper	80
Silver Ring	2800
Marble Necklace	3500
Silver Wristguard	5000
Sacrificial Doll	3500
Lintz Tomato	35

HALGITA

Trader—Faina	
Item	Cost
Berry Bread	60
Cobasna Salad Sandwich	200
Fayel Chicken	50
Beef	80
Prehistoric Meat	100
Sliced Fish	15
Sliced Deviant Fish	30
Cobasna Lettuce	10
Pieria Mushroom	40
Reiner Garlic	55
Halgitian Strawberry	120
Kolton Melon	500
Berry Oil	300
Metetite	1000
Hearthstone	2000
Titanium Metal	1300
Gold Metal	2200
Ebony Wood	280
Lux Wood	350
Lentesco Wood	400
Silver Fox Fur	500
Barkcloth	100
Cotton Cloth	150
Linen Cloth	200
Medical Herb	50
Fresh Herb	80
Novo Herb	120

Item Shop	
Item	Cost
Red Berry Potion	60
Blue Berry Potion	150
Yellow Berry Potion	500
Red Berry Powder	650
Black Berry Potion	350
White Berry Potion	1200
Coffee	100
Antidote	100
Holy Water	200
Para-Gone	200
Cough Drop	150
Sedative	150
Spring Warmth	200
Odious Eye	200
Maiden's Scorn	150
Eye Drops	120
Angel Earpick	120
Aroma Oil	120
Toothbrush	120
Lunar Scale	150
Panacea	350
Miraculous Medicine	550
Seeing Eye	30
Horizon Crystal	40
Musician's Quill	250
Staff Paper	100

General Shop	
Item	Cost
Fayel Chicken	50
Beef	80
Prehistoric Meat	100
Sliced Fish	15
Sliced Deviant Fish	30
Cobasna Lettuce	10
Pieria Mushroom	40
Reiner Garlic	55
Halgitian Strawberry	120
Kolton Melon	500
Halgitian Paste	220
Berry Oil	300
Medical Herb	50
Fructus Herb	150
Halgitian Rice	200
Laurel	350
Hearthstone	2000
Silver Metal	900
Titanium Metal	1300
Ebony Wood	280
Lux Wood	350

Armor Shop	
Item	Cost
Nightwhisper Garb	6000
Gold Chainmail	6500
Bronze Plate Armor	8500
Linen Toga	6500
Lizard Skin Cap	3500
Nightwhisper Hood	5500
Banded Headgear	4000
Gold Chain Helmet	5800
Silk Hat	4500
Hearthstone Boots	11000
Banded Greaves	3500
Gold Chain Greaves	5500
Lentesco Sandals	5000

Weapons Shop	
Item	Cost
Ceramic Sword	7200
Prismatite Sword	15000
Longbow	6500
Great Bow	12000
Light Staff	8500
Pilgrim Staff	12000
Estoc	9300
Katzbalger	16000
Marble Baton	8500
Silver Baton	1000
Ceramic Drum	8300
Silver Drum	9200
Kukri	7000
Baselard	10500
Tiger Claws	8000

Weapons Shop	
Item	Cost
Nightingale	3000
Kingfisher	6800
Peacock	8000
Blindeye	1800
Ogre	3500
Herosong	6200
"Endless Tale"	14500

Accessory Shop	
Item	Cost
Iron Ring	600
Copper Ring	1500
Silver Ring	2800
Gold Ring	5000
Granite Necklace	600
Quilt Wristband	6500
Rabbit's Foot	200
Eagle Eye	350

PLODHIF CAVERNS

Genma	
Item	Cost
Red Berry Potion	60
Blue Berry Potion	150
Black Berry Potion	350
Coffee	100
Antidote	100
Holy Water	200
Para-Gone	200
Cough Drop	150
Sedative	150
Spring Warmth	200
Odious Eye	200
Maiden's Scorn	150
Eye Drops	120
Angel Earpick	120
Aroma Oil	120
Toothbrush	120
Lunar Scale	150
Miraculous Medicine	550
Seeing Eye	30
Horizon Crystal	40
Sunstone	50

UNDERWATER PALACE

Genma	
Item	Cost
Red Berry Potion	60
Blue Berry Potion	150
Black Berry Potion	350
Coffee	100
Antidote	100
Holy Water	200
Para-Gone	200
Cough Drop	150
Sedative	150
Spring Warmth	200
Odious Eye	200
Maiden's Scorn	150
Eye Drops	120
Angel Earpick	120
Aroma Oil	120
Toothbrush	120
Lunar Scale	150
Miraculous Medicine	550
Seeing Eye	30
Horizon Crystal	40
Sunstone	50

SERAPHIC GATE

Genma	
Item	Cost
Red Berry Potion	60
Blue Berry Potion	150
Yellow Berry Potion	500
Green Berry Potion	1500
Red Berry Powder	650
Blue Berry Powder	1650
Black Berry Potion	350
White Berry Potion	1200
Silver Berry Potion	3500
Coffee	100
Antidote	100
Holy Water	200
Para-Gone	200
Cough Drop	150
Sedative	150
Spring Warmth	200
Odious Eye	200

Genma	
Item	Cost
Maiden's Scorn	150
Eye Drops	120
Angel Earpick	120
Aroma Oil	120
Toothbrush	120
Lunar Scale	150
Panacea	350
Miraculous Medicine	550
Seeing Eye	30
Horizon Crystal	40
Musician's Quill	250
Staff Paper	100
Lunar Suppressant	1000
Lunar Suppressant X	1500
Sacrificial Doll	3500

BESTIARY

1 *Name*: The fiend's title.

2 *Location*: In which zone the enemy is found.

3 *Stats*: Information concerning the foe's parameters and spoils upon defeat.

4 *Elemental Resistances*: The enemy's susceptibility to the elements. -50 indicates a monster absorbs an element as health, 0 indicates the element has no effect, 100 indicates standard damage, and 250 indicates extreme damage.

5 *Status Resistances*: Indicates the opponent's vulnerability to various status effects, which can be attempted through the abilities of certain allies, or through equipment or enchantments which add effects to hits. 0 indicates the foe is completely resistant, while 100 indicates the enemy is completely vulnerable. Elements are listed in the order Air—Fire—Earth—Aether—Water.

6 *Drops*: Items received upon defeat. The likelihood of a drop, period, is found under **3**. Once the game determines whether a drop will happen, a drop class is assigned based on combat. Fight efficiently and score Player Advantage multiple times for S-Class, score Player Advantage for A-Class, fight normally for B-Class, and have Enemy Advantage scored against you for C-Class. Finally, the actual drop obtained within a given class is based on percentage chance, with luck affecting the odds of rarer drops.

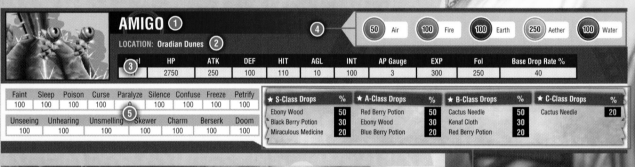

AMIGO **1**

LOCATION: Oradian Dunes **2**

4 — (50) Air · (100) Fire · (100) Earth · (250) Aether · (100) Water

3	HP	ATK	DEF	HIT	AGL	INT	AP Gauge	EXP	Fol	Base Drop Rate %
	2750	250	100	110	10	100	3	300	250	40

Faint	Sleep	Poison	Curse	Paralyze	Silence	Confuse	Freeze	Petrify
100	100	100	100	0	100	100	100	100

Unseeing	Unhearing	Unsmelling	Skewer	Charm	Berserk	Doom
100	100	100	100	100	100	100

5

★ S-Class Drops	%	★ A-Class Drops	%	★ B-Class Drops	%	★ C-Class Drops	%
Ebony Wood	50	Red Berry Potion	50	Cactus Needle	50	Cactus Needle	20
Black Berry Potion	30	Ebony Wood	30	Kenaf Cloth	30		
Miraculous Medicine	20	Blue Berry Potion	20	Red Berry Potion	20		

6

NORMAL ENEMIES

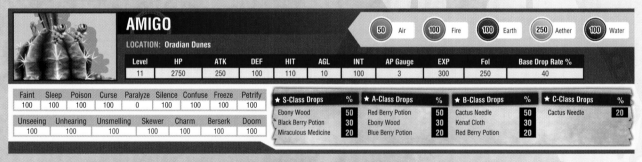

AMIGO

LOCATION: Oradian Dunes

(50) Air · (100) Fire · (100) Earth · (250) Aether · (100) Water

Level	HP	ATK	DEF	HIT	AGL	INT	AP Gauge	EXP	Fol	Base Drop Rate %
11	2750	250	100	110	10	100	3	300	250	40

Faint	Sleep	Poison	Curse	Paralyze	Silence	Confuse	Freeze	Petrify
100	100	100	100	0	100	100	100	100

Unseeing	Unhearing	Unsmelling	Skewer	Charm	Berserk	Doom
100	100	100	100	100	100	100

★ S-Class Drops	%	★ A-Class Drops	%	★ B-Class Drops	%	★ C-Class Drops	%
Ebony Wood	50	Red Berry Potion	50	Cactus Needle	50	Cactus Needle	20
Black Berry Potion	30	Ebony Wood	30	Kenaf Cloth	30		
Miraculous Medicine	20	Blue Berry Potion	20	Red Berry Potion	20		

BLOODSUCKER

LOCATION: Dragonbone Shrine

(100) Air · (100) Fire · (250) Earth · (100) Aether · (50) Water

Level	HP	ATK	DEF	HIT	AGL	INT	AP Gauge	EXP	Fol	Base Drop Rate %
3	80	28	20	25	5	10	10	20	15	40

Faint	Sleep	Poison	Curse	Paralyze	Silence	Confuse	Freeze	Petrify
100	100	100	100	30	100	100	100	100

Unseeing	Unhearing	Unsmelling	Skewer	Charm	Berserk	Doom
100	100	100	100	100	100	100

★ S-Class Drops	%	★ A-Class Drops	%	★ B-Class Drops	%	★ C-Class Drops	%
Sedative	80	Nolaan Potato	50	Bat Wing	50	Bat Wing	20
Granite	20	Granite	30	Nolaan Potato	30		
		Sedative	20	Granite	20		

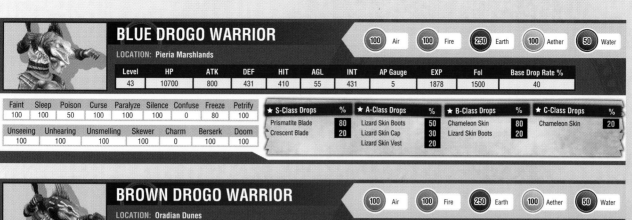

BLUE DROGO WARRIOR

LOCATION: Pieria Marshlands

100 Air	100 Fire	250 Earth	100 Aether	50 Water

Level	HP	ATK	DEF	HIT	AGL	INT	AP Gauge	EXP	Fol	Base Drop Rate %
43	10700	800	431	410	55	431	5	1878	1500	40

Faint	Sleep	Poison	Curse	Paralyze	Silence	Confuse	Freeze	Petrify
100	100	50	100	100	100	0	80	100

Unseeing	Unhearing	Unsmelling	Skewer	Charm	Berserk	Doom
100	100	100	100	0	100	100

★ S-Class Drops	%	★ A-Class Drops	%	★ B-Class Drops	%	★ C-Class Drops	%
Prismatite Blade	80	Lizard Skin Boots	50	Chameleon Skin	80	Chameleon Skin	20
Crescent Blade	20	Lizard Skin Cap	30	Lizard Skin Boots	20		
		Lizard Skin Vest	20				

BROWN DROGO WARRIOR

LOCATION: Oradian Dunes

100 Air	100 Fire	250 Earth	100 Aether	50 Water

Level	HP	ATK	DEF	HIT	AGL	INT	AP Gauge	EXP	Fol	Base Drop Rate %
38	8110	400	389	335	55	389	5	1000	820	40

Faint	Sleep	Poison	Curse	Paralyze	Silence	Confuse	Freeze	Petrify
100	100	50	100	100	100	0	80	100

Unseeing	Unhearing	Unsmelling	Skewer	Charm	Berserk	Doom
100	100	100	100	0	100	100

★ S-Class Drops	%	★ A-Class Drops	%	★ B-Class Drops	%	★ C-Class Drops	%
Lizard Skin Boots	50	Chameleon Skin	100	Lizard Skin	80	Lizard Skin	20
Lizard Skin Cap	30			Chameleon Skin	20		
Lizard Skin Vest	20						

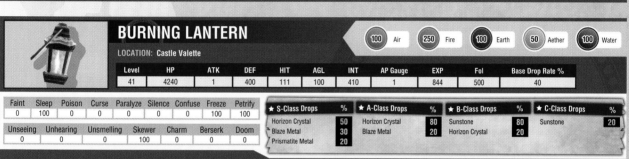

BURNING LANTERN

LOCATION: Castle Valette

100 Air	250 Fire	100 Earth	50 Aether	100 Water

Level	HP	ATK	DEF	HIT	AGL	INT	AP Gauge	EXP	Fol	Base Drop Rate %
41	4240	1	400	111	100	410	1	844	500	40

Faint	Sleep	Poison	Curse	Paralyze	Silence	Confuse	Freeze	Petrify
0	100	0	0	0	0	0	100	100

Unseeing	Unhearing	Unsmelling	Skewer	Charm	Berserk	Doom
0	0	0	100	0	0	0

★ S-Class Drops	%	★ A-Class Drops	%	★ B-Class Drops	%	★ C-Class Drops	%
Horizon Crystal	50	Horizon Crystal	80	Sunstone	80	Sunstone	20
Blaze Metal	30	Blaze Metal	20	Horizon Crystal	20		
Prismatite Metal	20						

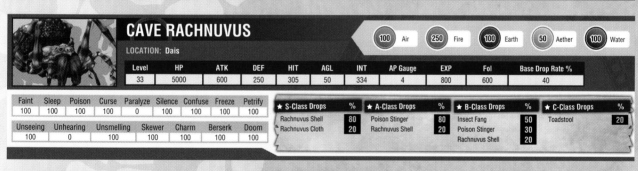

CAVE RACHNUVUS

LOCATION: Dais

100 Air	250 Fire	100 Earth	50 Aether	100 Water

Level	HP	ATK	DEF	HIT	AGL	INT	AP Gauge	EXP	Fol	Base Drop Rate %
33	5000	600	250	305	50	334	4	800	600	40

Faint	Sleep	Poison	Curse	Paralyze	Silence	Confuse	Freeze	Petrify
100	100	100	100	0	100	100	100	100

Unseeing	Unhearing	Unsmelling	Skewer	Charm	Berserk	Doom
100	0	100	100	100	100	100

★ S-Class Drops	%	★ A-Class Drops	%	★ B-Class Drops	%	★ C-Class Drops	%
Rachnuvus Shell	80	Poison Stinger	80	Insect Fang	50	Toadstool	20
Rachnuvus Cloth	20	Rachnuvus Shell	20	Poison Stinger	30		
				Rachnuvus Shell	20		

CRYSTAL GARGOYLE

LOCATION: Vesplume Tower

250 Air	100 Fire	0 Earth	100 Aether	50 Water

Level	HP	ATK	DEF	HIT	AGL	INT	AP Gauge	EXP	Fol	Base Drop Rate %
20	8000	1000	300	200	15	300	4	800	50	40

Faint	Sleep	Poison	Curse	Paralyze	Silence	Confuse	Freeze	Petrify
0	0	0	0	0	100	100	100	0

Unseeing	Unhearing	Unsmelling	Skewer	Charm	Berserk	Doom
0	0	0	100	100	100	0

★ S-Class Drops	%	★ A-Class Drops	%	★ B-Class Drops	%	★ C-Class Drops	%
Ceramic	50	Stone Statue Fragment	50	Stone Statue Fragment	50	Stone Statue Fragment	20
Steel Metal	30	Ceramic	30	Stone Statue Fragment	30		
Silver Metal	20	Steel Metal	20	Ceramic	20		

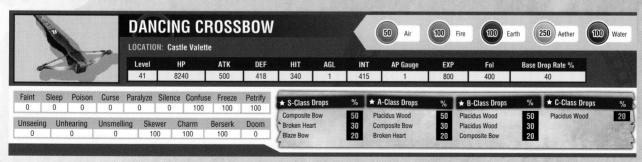

DANCING CROSSBOW

LOCATION: Castle Valette

50 Air	100 Fire	100 Earth	250 Aether	100 Water

Level	HP	ATK	DEF	HIT	AGL	INT	AP Gauge	EXP	Fol	Base Drop Rate %
41	8240	500	418	340	1	415	1	800	400	40

Faint	Sleep	Poison	Curse	Paralyze	Silence	Confuse	Freeze	Petrify
0	0	0	0	0	0	100	100	100

Unseeing	Unhearing	Unsmelling	Skewer	Charm	Berserk	Doom
0	0	0	100	100	100	0

★ S-Class Drops	%	★ A-Class Drops	%	★ B-Class Drops	%	★ C-Class Drops	%
Composite Bow	50	Placidus Wood	50	Placidus Wood	50	Placidus Wood	20
Broken Heart	30	Composite Bow	30	Placidus Wood	30		
Blaze Bow	20	Broken Heart	20	Composite Bow	20		

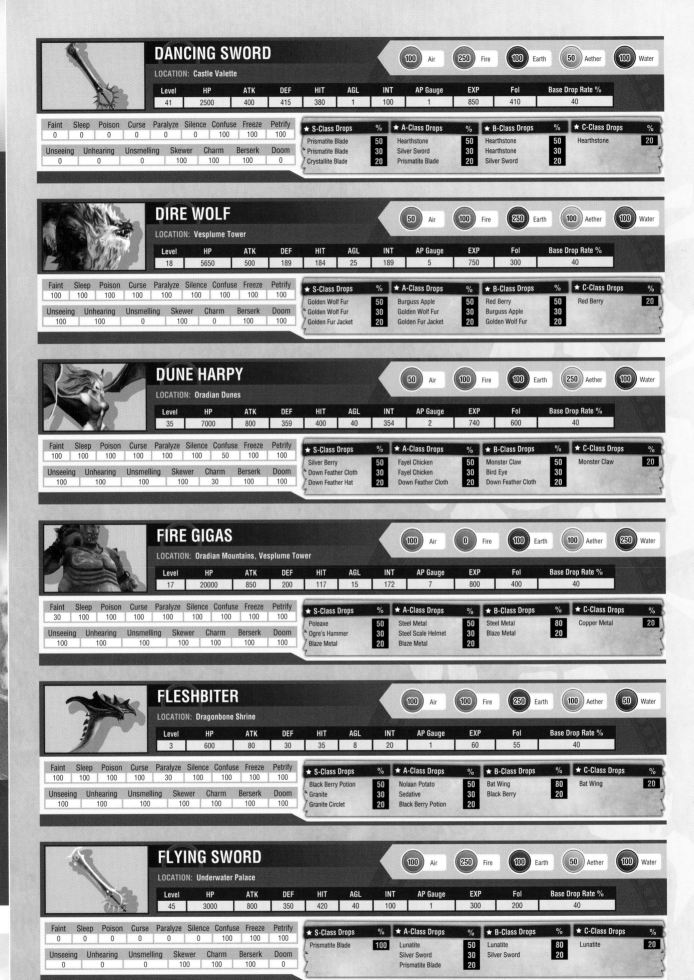

DANCING SWORD

LOCATION: Castle Valette

100 Air	250 Fire	100 Earth	50 Aether	100 Water	

Level	HP	ATK	DEF	HIT	AGL	INT	AP Gauge	EXP	Fol	Base Drop Rate %
41	2500	400	415	380	1	100	1	850	410	40

Faint	Sleep	Poison	Curse	Paralyze	Silence	Confuse	Freeze	Petrify
0	0	0	0	0	0	100	100	100

Unseeing	Unhearing	Unsmelling	Skewer	Charm	Berserk	Doom
0	0	0	100	100	100	0

★ S-Class Drops	%	★ A-Class Drops	%	★ B-Class Drops	%	★ C-Class Drops	%
Prismatite Blade	50	Hearthstone	50	Hearthstone	50	Hearthstone	20
Prismatite Blade	30	Silver Sword	30	Hearthstone	30		
Crystallite Blade	20	Prismatite Blade	20	Silver Sword	20		

DIRE WOLF

LOCATION: Vesplume Tower

50 Air	100 Fire	250 Earth	100 Aether	100 Water	

Level	HP	ATK	DEF	HIT	AGL	INT	AP Gauge	EXP	Fol	Base Drop Rate %
18	5650	500	189	184	25	189	5	750	300	40

Faint	Sleep	Poison	Curse	Paralyze	Silence	Confuse	Freeze	Petrify
100	100	100	100	100	100	100	100	100

Unseeing	Unhearing	Unsmelling	Skewer	Charm	Berserk	Doom
100	100	0	100	100	100	100

★ S-Class Drops	%	★ A-Class Drops	%	★ B-Class Drops	%	★ C-Class Drops	%
Golden Wolf Fur	50	Burguss Apple	50	Red Berry	50	Red Berry	20
Golden Wolf Fur	30	Golden Wolf Fur	30	Burguss Apple	30		
Golden Fur Jacket	20	Golden Fur Jacket	20	Golden Wolf Fur	20		

DUNE HARPY

LOCATION: Oradian Dunes

50 Air	100 Fire	100 Earth	250 Aether	100 Water	

Level	HP	ATK	DEF	HIT	AGL	INT	AP Gauge	EXP	Fol	Base Drop Rate %
35	7000	800	359	400	40	354	2	740	600	40

Faint	Sleep	Poison	Curse	Paralyze	Silence	Confuse	Freeze	Petrify
100	100	100	100	100	100	50	100	100

Unseeing	Unhearing	Unsmelling	Skewer	Charm	Berserk	Doom
100	100	100	100	30	100	100

★ S-Class Drops	%	★ A-Class Drops	%	★ B-Class Drops	%	★ C-Class Drops	%
Silver Berry	50	Fayel Chicken	50	Monster Claw	50	Monster Claw	20
Down Feather Cloth	30	Fayel Chicken	30	Bird Eye	30		
Down Feather Hat	20	Down Feather Cloth	20	Down Feather Cloth	20		

FIRE GIGAS

LOCATION: Oradian Mountains, Vesplume Tower

100 Air	0 Fire	100 Earth	100 Aether	250 Water	

Level	HP	ATK	DEF	HIT	AGL	INT	AP Gauge	EXP	Fol	Base Drop Rate %
17	20000	850	200	117	15	172	7	800	400	40

Faint	Sleep	Poison	Curse	Paralyze	Silence	Confuse	Freeze	Petrify
30	100	100	100	100	100	100	100	100

Unseeing	Unhearing	Unsmelling	Skewer	Charm	Berserk	Doom
100	100	100	100	100	100	100

★ S-Class Drops	%	★ A-Class Drops	%	★ B-Class Drops	%	★ C-Class Drops	%
Poleaxe	50	Steel Metal	50	Steel Metal	80	Copper Metal	20
Ogre's Hammer	30	Steel Scale Helmet	30	Blaze Metal	20		
Blaze Metal	20	Blaze Metal	20				

FLESHBITER

LOCATION: Dragonbone Shrine

100 Air	100 Fire	250 Earth	100 Aether	50 Water	

Level	HP	ATK	DEF	HIT	AGL	INT	AP Gauge	EXP	Fol	Base Drop Rate %
3	600	80	30	35	8	20	1	60	55	40

Faint	Sleep	Poison	Curse	Paralyze	Silence	Confuse	Freeze	Petrify
100	100	100	100	30	100	100	100	100

Unseeing	Unhearing	Unsmelling	Skewer	Charm	Berserk	Doom
100	100	100	100	100	100	100

★ S-Class Drops	%	★ A-Class Drops	%	★ B-Class Drops	%	★ C-Class Drops	%
Black Berry Potion	50	Nolaan Potato	50	Bat Wing	80	Bat Wing	20
Granite	30	Sedative	30	Black Berry	20		
Granite Circlet	20	Black Berry Potion	20				

FLYING SWORD

LOCATION: Underwater Palace

100 Air	250 Fire	100 Earth	50 Aether	100 Water	

Level	HP	ATK	DEF	HIT	AGL	INT	AP Gauge	EXP	Fol	Base Drop Rate %
45	3000	800	350	420	40	100	1	300	200	40

Faint	Sleep	Poison	Curse	Paralyze	Silence	Confuse	Freeze	Petrify
0	0	0	0	0	0	100	100	100

Unseeing	Unhearing	Unsmelling	Skewer	Charm	Berserk	Doom
0	0	0	100	100	100	0

★ S-Class Drops	%	★ A-Class Drops	%	★ B-Class Drops	%	★ C-Class Drops	%
Prismatite Blade	100	Lunatite	50	Lunatite	80	Lunatite	20
		Silver Sword	30	Silver Sword	20		
		Prismatite Blade	20				

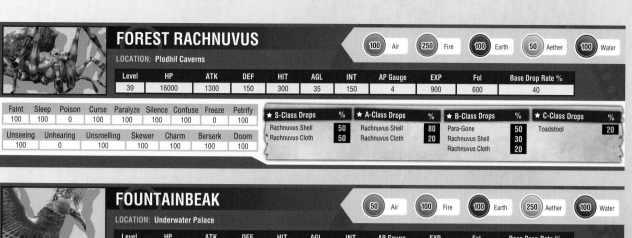

FOREST RACHNUVUS

LOCATION: Plodhif Caverns

100 Air	250 Fire	100 Earth	50 Aether	100 Water	

Level	HP	ATK	DEF	HIT	AGL	INT	AP Gauge	EXP	Fol	Base Drop Rate %
39	16000	1300	150	300	35	150	4	900	600	40

Faint	Sleep	Poison	Curse	Paralyze	Silence	Confuse	Freeze	Petrify
100	100	0	100	100	100	100	0	100

Unseeing	Unhearing	Unsmelling	Skewer	Charm	Berserk	Doom
100	0	100	100	100	100	100

★ S-Class Drops	%	★ A-Class Drops	%	★ B-Class Drops	%	★ C-Class Drops	%
Rachnuvus Shell	50	Rachnuvus Shell	80	Para-Gone	50	Toadstool	20
Rachnuvus Cloth	50	Rachnuvus Cloth	20	Rachnuvus Shell	30		
				Rachnuvus Cloth	20		

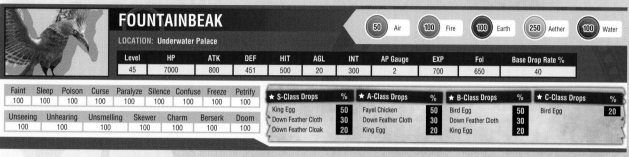

FOUNTAINBEAK

LOCATION: Underwater Palace

50 Air	100 Fire	100 Earth	250 Aether	100 Water	

Level	HP	ATK	DEF	HIT	AGL	INT	AP Gauge	EXP	Fol	Base Drop Rate %
45	7000	800	451	500	20	300	2	700	650	40

Faint	Sleep	Poison	Curse	Paralyze	Silence	Confuse	Freeze	Petrify
100	100	100	100	100	100	100	100	100

Unseeing	Unhearing	Unsmelling	Skewer	Charm	Berserk	Doom
100	100	100	100	100	100	100

★ S-Class Drops	%	★ A-Class Drops	%	★ B-Class Drops	%	★ C-Class Drops	%
King Egg	50	Fayel Chicken	50	Bird Egg	50	Bird Egg	20
Down Feather Cloth	30	Down Feather Cloth	30	Down Feather Cloth	30		
Down Feather Cloak	20	King Egg	20	King Egg	20		

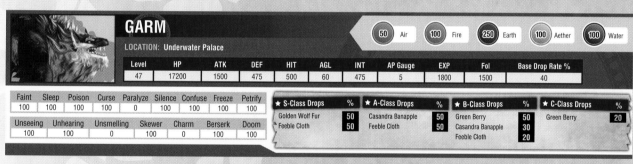

FROST GIGAS

LOCATION: Underwater Palace

100 Air	100 Fire	250 Earth	100 Aether	0 Water	

Level	HP	ATK	DEF	HIT	AGL	INT	AP Gauge	EXP	Fol	Base Drop Rate %
45	45000	1800	458	410	30	458	7	2000	1670	40

Faint	Sleep	Poison	Curse	Paralyze	Silence	Confuse	Freeze	Petrify
30	100	100	100	100	100	100	0	100

Unseeing	Unhearing	Unsmelling	Skewer	Charm	Berserk	Doom
100	100	100	100	100	100	100

★ S-Class Drops	%	★ A-Class Drops	%	★ B-Class Drops	%	★ C-Class Drops	%
Crescent Axe	50	Prismatite Metal	50	Gold Metal	50	Gold Metal	20
Ogre's Hammer	30	Prismatite Headgear	30	Prismatite Metal	30		
Crystallite Metal	20	Crystallite Metal	20	Crystallite Metal	20		

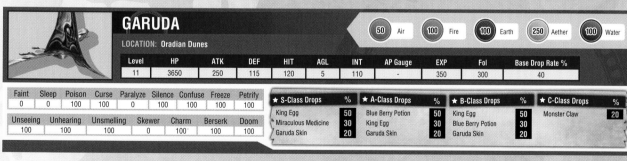

GARM

LOCATION: Underwater Palace

50 Air	100 Fire	250 Earth	100 Aether	100 Water	

Level	HP	ATK	DEF	HIT	AGL	INT	AP Gauge	EXP	Fol	Base Drop Rate %
47	17200	1500	475	500	60	475	5	1800	1500	40

Faint	Sleep	Poison	Curse	Paralyze	Silence	Confuse	Freeze	Petrify
100	100	100	100	0	100	100	100	100

Unseeing	Unhearing	Unsmelling	Skewer	Charm	Berserk	Doom
100	100	0	100	0	100	100

★ S-Class Drops	%	★ A-Class Drops	%	★ B-Class Drops	%	★ C-Class Drops	%
Golden Wolf Fur	50	Casandra Banapple	50	Green Berry	50	Green Berry	20
Feeble Cloth	50	Feeble Cloth	50	Casandra Banapple	30		
				Feeble Cloth	20		

GARUDA

LOCATION: Oradian Dunes

50 Air	100 Fire	100 Earth	250 Aether	100 Water	

Level	HP	ATK	DEF	HIT	AGL	INT	AP Gauge	EXP	Fol	Base Drop Rate %
11	3650	250	115	120	5	110	-	350	300	40

Faint	Sleep	Poison	Curse	Paralyze	Silence	Confuse	Freeze	Petrify
0	0	100	100	0	100	100	100	100

Unseeing	Unhearing	Unsmelling	Skewer	Charm	Berserk	Doom
100	100	100	0	100	100	100

★ S-Class Drops	%	★ A-Class Drops	%	★ B-Class Drops	%	★ C-Class Drops	%
King Egg	50	Blue Berry Potion	50	King Egg	50	Monster Claw	20
Miraculous Medicine	30	King Egg	30	Blue Berry Potion	30		
Garuda Skin	20	Garuda Skin	20	Garuda Skin	20		

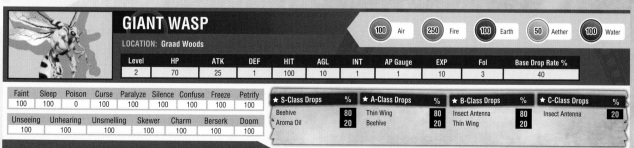

GIANT WASP

LOCATION: Graad Woods

100 Air	250 Fire	100 Earth	50 Aether	100 Water	

Level	HP	ATK	DEF	HIT	AGL	INT	AP Gauge	EXP	Fol	Base Drop Rate %
2	70	25	1	100	10	1	1	10	3	40

Faint	Sleep	Poison	Curse	Paralyze	Silence	Confuse	Freeze	Petrify
100	100	0	100	100	100	100	100	100

Unseeing	Unhearing	Unsmelling	Skewer	Charm	Berserk	Doom
100	100	100	100	100	100	100

★ S-Class Drops	%	★ A-Class Drops	%	★ B-Class Drops	%	★ C-Class Drops	%
Beehive	80	Thin Wing	80	Insect Antenna	80	Insect Antenna	20
Aroma Oil	20	Beehive	20	Thin Wing	20		

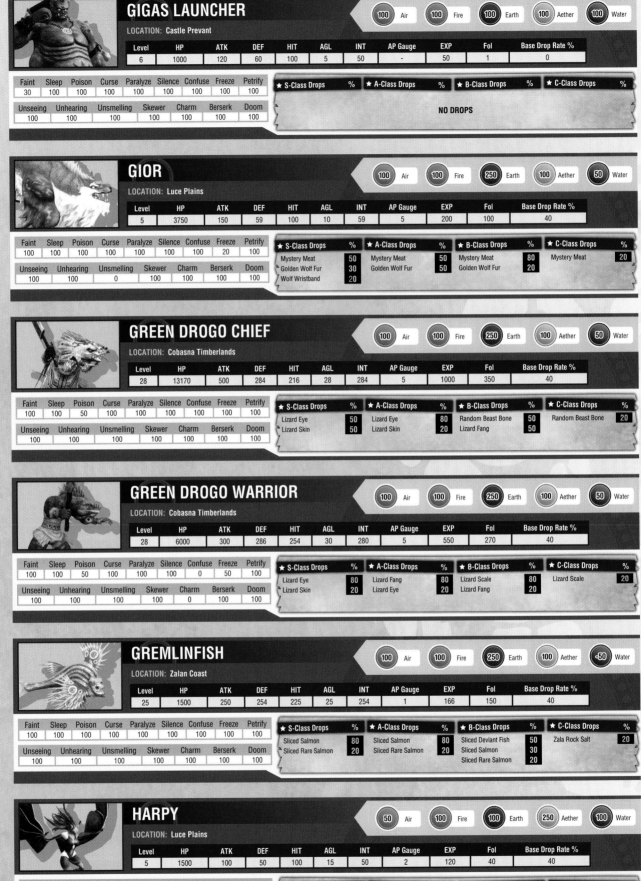

GIGAS LAUNCHER

100 Air	100 Fire	100 Earth	100 Aether	100 Water

LOCATION: Castle Prevant

Level	HP	ATK	DEF	HIT	AGL	INT	AP Gauge	EXP	Fol	Base Drop Rate %
6	1000	120	60	100	5	50	-	50	1	0

Faint	Sleep	Poison	Curse	Paralyze	Silence	Confuse	Freeze	Petrify
30	100	100	100	100	100	100	100	100

Unseeing	Unhearing	Unsmelling	Skewer	Charm	Berserk	Doom
100	100	100	100	100	100	100

★ S-Class Drops	%	★ A-Class Drops	%	★ B-Class Drops	%	★ C-Class Drops	%
		NO DROPS					

GIOR

100 Air	100 Fire	250 Earth	100 Aether	50 Water

LOCATION: Luce Plains

Level	HP	ATK	DEF	HIT	AGL	INT	AP Gauge	EXP	Fol	Base Drop Rate %
5	3750	150	59	100	10	59	5	200	100	40

Faint	Sleep	Poison	Curse	Paralyze	Silence	Confuse	Freeze	Petrify
100	100	100	100	100	100	100	20	100

Unseeing	Unhearing	Unsmelling	Skewer	Charm	Berserk	Doom
100	100	0	100	100	100	100

★ S-Class Drops	%	★ A-Class Drops	%	★ B-Class Drops	%	★ C-Class Drops	%
Mystery Meat	50	Mystery Meat	50	Mystery Meat	80	Mystery Meat	20
Golden Wolf Fur	30	Golden Wolf Fur	50	Golden Wolf Fur	20		
Wolf Wristband	20						

GREEN DROGO CHIEF

100 Air	100 Fire	250 Earth	100 Aether	50 Water

LOCATION: Cobasna Timberlands

Level	HP	ATK	DEF	HIT	AGL	INT	AP Gauge	EXP	Fol	Base Drop Rate %
28	13170	500	284	216	28	284	5	1000	350	40

Faint	Sleep	Poison	Curse	Paralyze	Silence	Confuse	Freeze	Petrify
100	100	50	100	100	100	100	100	100

Unseeing	Unhearing	Unsmelling	Skewer	Charm	Berserk	Doom
100	100	100	100	100	100	100

★ S-Class Drops	%	★ A-Class Drops	%	★ B-Class Drops	%	★ C-Class Drops	%
Lizard Eye	50	Lizard Eye	80	Random Beast Bone	50	Random Beast Bone	20
Lizard Skin	50	Lizard Skin	20	Lizard Fang	50		

GREEN DROGO WARRIOR

100 Air	100 Fire	250 Earth	100 Aether	50 Water

LOCATION: Cobasna Timberlands

Level	HP	ATK	DEF	HIT	AGL	INT	AP Gauge	EXP	Fol	Base Drop Rate %
28	6000	300	286	254	30	280	5	550	270	40

Faint	Sleep	Poison	Curse	Paralyze	Silence	Confuse	Freeze	Petrify
100	100	50	100	100	100	0	50	100

Unseeing	Unhearing	Unsmelling	Skewer	Charm	Berserk	Doom
100	100	100	100	0	100	100

★ S-Class Drops	%	★ A-Class Drops	%	★ B-Class Drops	%	★ C-Class Drops	%
Lizard Eye	80	Lizard Fang	80	Lizard Scale	80	Lizard Scale	20
Lizard Skin	20	Lizard Eye	20	Lizard Fang	20		

GREMLINFISH

100 Air	100 Fire	250 Earth	100 Aether	<50 Water

LOCATION: Zalan Coast

Level	HP	ATK	DEF	HIT	AGL	INT	AP Gauge	EXP	Fol	Base Drop Rate %
25	1500	250	254	225	25	254	1	166	150	40

Faint	Sleep	Poison	Curse	Paralyze	Silence	Confuse	Freeze	Petrify
100	100	100	100	100	100	100	100	100

Unseeing	Unhearing	Unsmelling	Skewer	Charm	Berserk	Doom
100	100	100	100	100	100	100

★ S-Class Drops	%	★ A-Class Drops	%	★ B-Class Drops	%	★ C-Class Drops	%
Sliced Salmon	80	Sliced Salmon	80	Sliced Deviant Fish	50	Zala Rock Salt	20
Sliced Rare Salmon	20	Sliced Rare Salmon	20	Sliced Salmon	30		
				Sliced Rare Salmon	20		

HARPY

50 Air	100 Fire	100 Earth	250 Aether	100 Water

LOCATION: Luce Plains

Level	HP	ATK	DEF	HIT	AGL	INT	AP Gauge	EXP	Fol	Base Drop Rate %
5	1500	100	50	100	15	50	2	120	40	40

Faint	Sleep	Poison	Curse	Paralyze	Silence	Confuse	Freeze	Petrify
100	100	100	100	100	100	50	100	100

Unseeing	Unhearing	Unsmelling	Skewer	Charm	Berserk	Doom
100	100	100	100	30	100	100

★ S-Class Drops	%	★ A-Class Drops	%	★ B-Class Drops	%	★ C-Class Drops	%
Lauan Wood	50	Lauan Wood	80	Monster Claw	50	Monster Claw	20
Lauan Sandals	30	Chicken	20	Lauan Wood	50		
Marble	20						

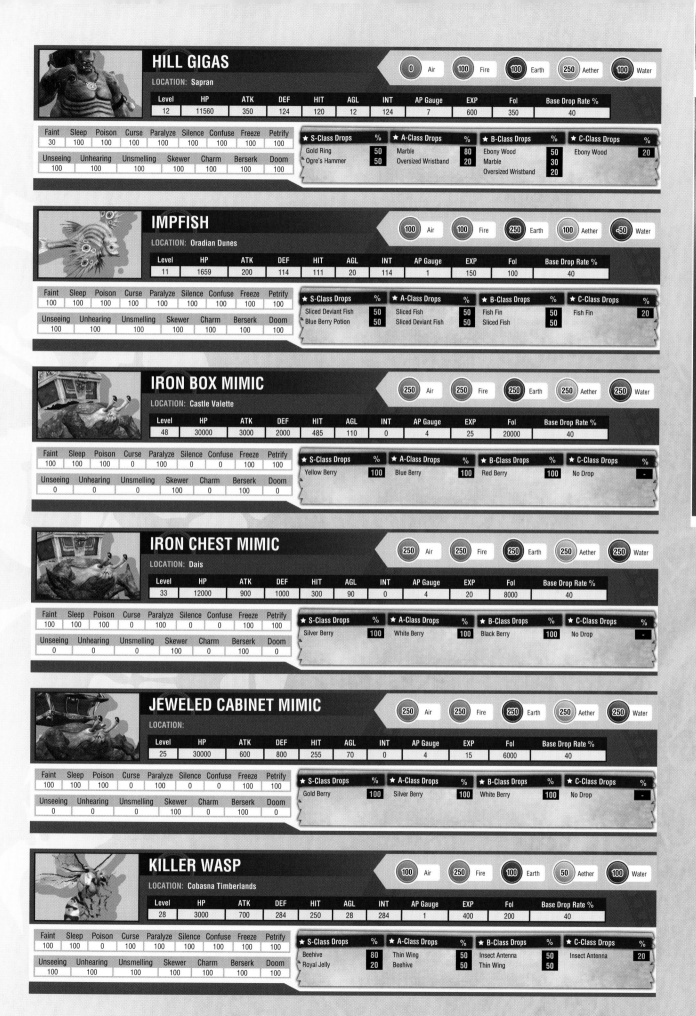

HILL GIGAS
LOCATION: Sapran

	Air		Fire		Earth		Aether		Water
0		100		100		250		100	

Level	HP	ATK	DEF	HIT	AGL	INT	AP Gauge	EXP	Fol	Base Drop Rate %
12	11560	350	124	120	12	124	7	600	350	40

Faint	Sleep	Poison	Curse	Paralyze	Silence	Confuse	Freeze	Petrify
30	100	100	100	100	100	100	100	100

Unseeing	Unhearing	Unsmelling	Skewer	Charm	Berserk	Doom
100	100	100	100	100	100	100

★ S-Class Drops	%	★ A-Class Drops	%	★ B-Class Drops	%	★ C-Class Drops	%
Gold Ring	50	Marble	80	Ebony Wood	50	Ebony Wood	20
Ogre's Hammer	50	Oversized Wristband	20	Marble	30		
				Oversized Wristband	20		

IMPFISH
LOCATION: Oradian Dunes

	Air		Fire		Earth		Aether		Water
100		100		250		100		-50	

Level	HP	ATK	DEF	HIT	AGL	INT	AP Gauge	EXP	Fol	Base Drop Rate %
11	1659	200	114	111	20	114	1	150	100	40

Faint	Sleep	Poison	Curse	Paralyze	Silence	Confuse	Freeze	Petrify
100	100	100	100	100	100	100	100	100

Unseeing	Unhearing	Unsmelling	Skewer	Charm	Berserk	Doom
100	100	100	100	100	100	100

★ S-Class Drops	%	★ A-Class Drops	%	★ B-Class Drops	%	★ C-Class Drops	%
Sliced Deviant Fish	50	Sliced Fish	50	Fish Fin	50	Fish Fin	20
Blue Berry Potion	50	Sliced Deviant Fish	50	Sliced Fish	50		

IRON BOX MIMIC
LOCATION: Castle Valette

	Air		Fire		Earth		Aether		Water
250		250		250		250		250	

Level	HP	ATK	DEF	HIT	AGL	INT	AP Gauge	EXP	Fol	Base Drop Rate %
48	30000	3000	2000	485	110	0	4	25	20000	40

Faint	Sleep	Poison	Curse	Paralyze	Silence	Confuse	Freeze	Petrify
100	100	100	0	100	0	0	100	100

Unseeing	Unhearing	Unsmelling	Skewer	Charm	Berserk	Doom
30	0	0	100	0	100	0

★ S-Class Drops	%	★ A-Class Drops	%	★ B-Class Drops	%	★ C-Class Drops	%
Yellow Berry	100	Blue Berry	100	Red Berry	100	No Drop	-

IRON CHEST MIMIC
LOCATION: Dais

	Air		Fire		Earth		Aether		Water
250		250		250		250		250	

Level	HP	ATK	DEF	HIT	AGL	INT	AP Gauge	EXP	Fol	Base Drop Rate %
33	12000	900	1000	300	90	0	4	20	8000	40

Faint	Sleep	Poison	Curse	Paralyze	Silence	Confuse	Freeze	Petrify
100	100	100	0	100	0	0	100	100

Unseeing	Unhearing	Unsmelling	Skewer	Charm	Berserk	Doom
0	0	0	100	0	100	0

★ S-Class Drops	%	★ A-Class Drops	%	★ B-Class Drops	%	★ C-Class Drops	%
Silver Berry	100	White Berry	100	Black Berry	100	No Drop	-

JEWELED CABINET MIMIC
LOCATION:

	Air		Fire		Earth		Aether		Water
250		250		250		250		250	

Level	HP	ATK	DEF	HIT	AGL	INT	AP Gauge	EXP	Fol	Base Drop Rate %
25	30000	600	800	255	70	0	4	15	6000	40

Faint	Sleep	Poison	Curse	Paralyze	Silence	Confuse	Freeze	Petrify
100	100	100	0	100	0	0	100	100

Unseeing	Unhearing	Unsmelling	Skewer	Charm	Berserk	Doom
0	0	0	100	0	100	0

★ S-Class Drops	%	★ A-Class Drops	%	★ B-Class Drops	%	★ C-Class Drops	%
Gold Berry	100	Silver Berry	100	White Berry	100	No Drop	-

KILLER WASP
LOCATION: Cobasna Timberlands

	Air		Fire		Earth		Aether		Water
100		250		100		50		100	

Level	HP	ATK	DEF	HIT	AGL	INT	AP Gauge	EXP	Fol	Base Drop Rate %
28	3000	700	284	250	28	284	1	400	200	40

Faint	Sleep	Poison	Curse	Paralyze	Silence	Confuse	Freeze	Petrify
100	100	0	100	100	100	100	100	100

Unseeing	Unhearing	Unsmelling	Skewer	Charm	Berserk	Doom
100	100	100	100	100	100	100

★ S-Class Drops	%	★ A-Class Drops	%	★ B-Class Drops	%	★ C-Class Drops	%
Beehive	80	Thin Wing	50	Insect Antenna	50	Insect Antenna	20
Royal Jelly	20	Beehive	50	Thin Wing	50		

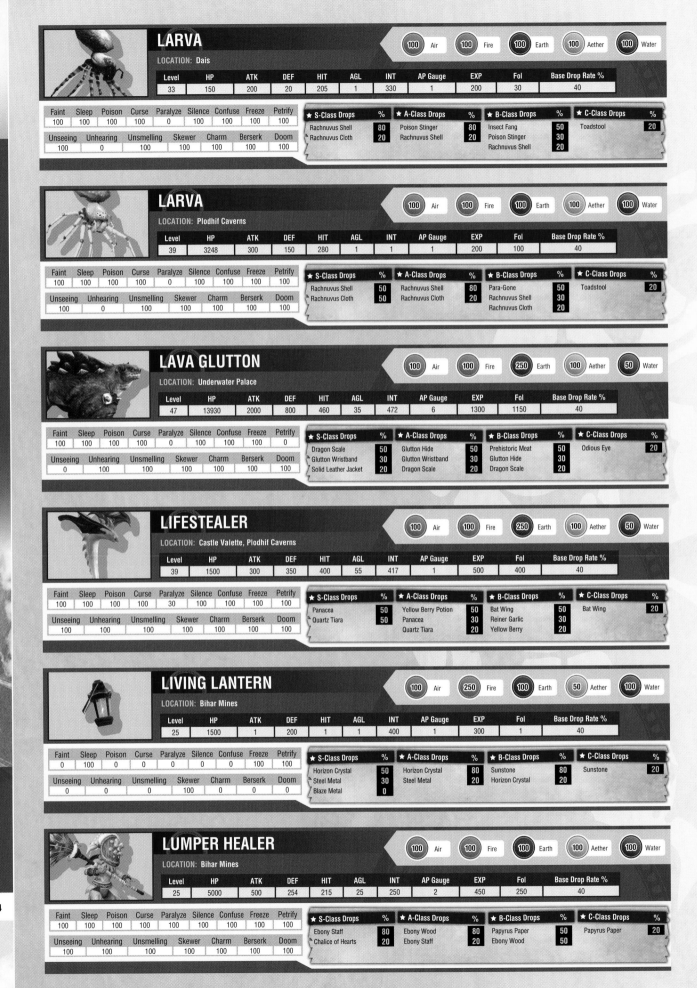

LARVA

LOCATION: Dais

	Air		Fire		Earth		Aether		Water
100		100		100		100		100	

Level	HP	ATK	DEF	HIT	AGL	INT	AP Gauge	EXP	Fol	Base Drop Rate %
33	150	200	20	205	1	330	1	200	30	40

Faint	Sleep	Poison	Curse	Paralyze	Silence	Confuse	Freeze	Petrify
100	100	100	100	0	100	100	100	100

Unseeing	Unhearing	Unsmelling	Skewer	Charm	Berserk	Doom
100	0	100	100	100	100	100

★ S-Class Drops	%	★ A-Class Drops	%	★ B-Class Drops	%	★ C-Class Drops	%
Rachnuvus Shell	80	Poison Stinger	80	Insect Fang	50	Toadstool	20
Rachnuvus Cloth	20	Rachnuvus Shell	20	Poison Stinger	30		
				Rachnuvus Shell	20		

LARVA

LOCATION: Plodhif Caverns

	Air		Fire		Earth		Aether		Water
100		100		100		100		100	

Level	HP	ATK	DEF	HIT	AGL	INT	AP Gauge	EXP	Fol	Base Drop Rate %
39	3248	300	150	280	1	1	1	200	100	40

Faint	Sleep	Poison	Curse	Paralyze	Silence	Confuse	Freeze	Petrify
100	100	100	100	0	100	100	100	100

Unseeing	Unhearing	Unsmelling	Skewer	Charm	Berserk	Doom
100	0	100	100	100	100	100

★ S-Class Drops	%	★ A-Class Drops	%	★ B-Class Drops	%	★ C-Class Drops	%
Rachnuvus Shell	50	Rachnuvus Shell	80	Para-Gone	50	Toadstool	20
Rachnuvus Cloth	50	Rachnuvus Cloth	20	Rachnuvus Shell	30		
				Rachnuvus Cloth	20		

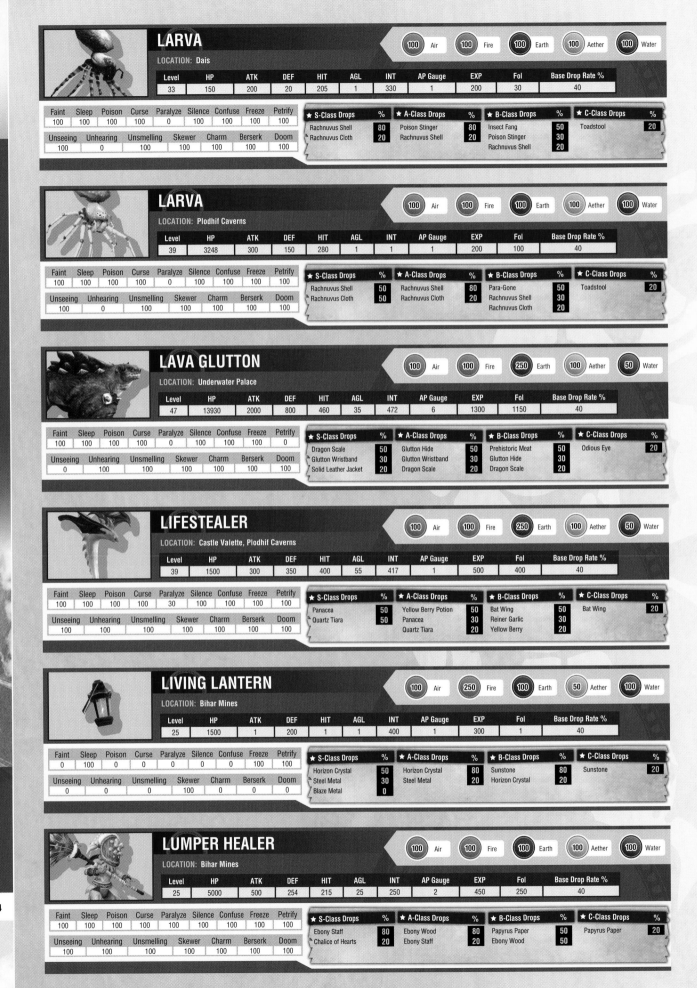

LAVA GLUTTON

LOCATION: Underwater Palace

	Air		Fire		Earth		Aether		Water
100		100		250		100		50	

Level	HP	ATK	DEF	HIT	AGL	INT	AP Gauge	EXP	Fol	Base Drop Rate %
47	13930	2000	800	460	35	472	6	1300	1150	40

Faint	Sleep	Poison	Curse	Paralyze	Silence	Confuse	Freeze	Petrify
100	100	100	100	0	100	100	100	0

Unseeing	Unhearing	Unsmelling	Skewer	Charm	Berserk	Doom
0	100	100	100	100	100	100

★ S-Class Drops	%	★ A-Class Drops	%	★ B-Class Drops	%	★ C-Class Drops	%
Dragon Scale	50	Glutton Hide	50	Prehistoric Meat	50	Odious Eye	20
Glutton Wristband	30	Glutton Wristband	30	Glutton Hide	30		
Solid Leather Jacket	20	Dragon Scale	20	Dragon Scale	20		

LIFESTEALER

LOCATION: Castle Valette, Plodhif Caverns

	Air		Fire		Earth		Aether		Water
100		100		250		100		50	

Level	HP	ATK	DEF	HIT	AGL	INT	AP Gauge	EXP	Fol	Base Drop Rate %
39	1500	300	350	400	55	417	1	500	400	40

Faint	Sleep	Poison	Curse	Paralyze	Silence	Confuse	Freeze	Petrify
100	100	100	100	30	100	100	100	100

Unseeing	Unhearing	Unsmelling	Skewer	Charm	Berserk	Doom
100	100	100	100	100	100	100

★ S-Class Drops	%	★ A-Class Drops	%	★ B-Class Drops	%	★ C-Class Drops	%
Panacea	50	Yellow Berry Potion	50	Bat Wing	50	Bat Wing	20
Quartz Tiara	50	Panacea	30	Reiner Garlic	30		
		Quartz Tiara	20	Yellow Berry	20		

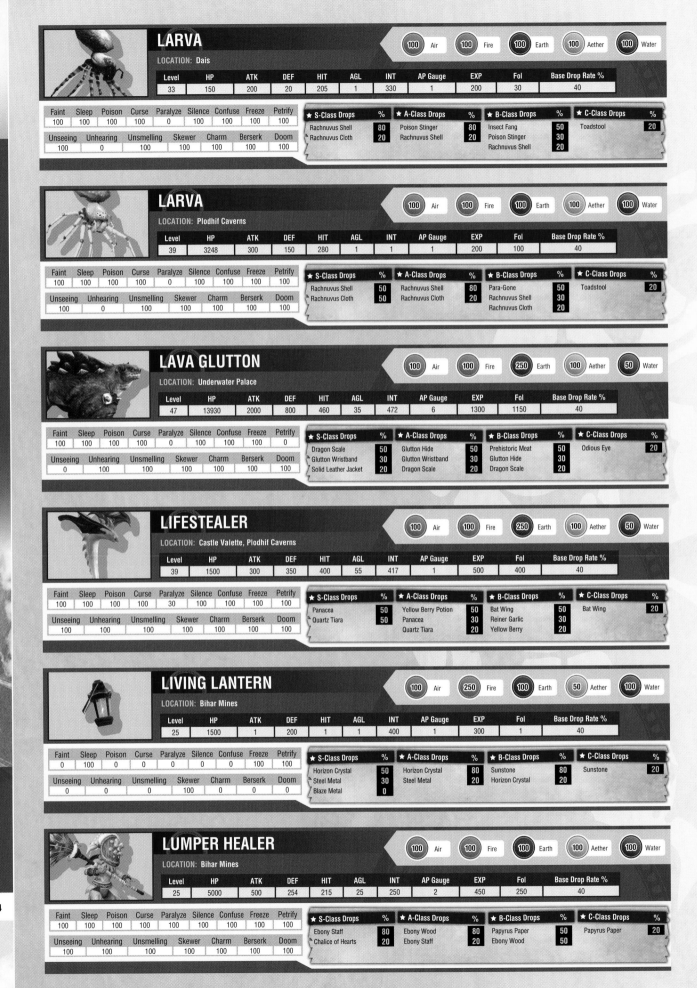

LIVING LANTERN

LOCATION: Bihar Mines

	Air		Fire		Earth		Aether		Water
100		250		100		50		100	

Level	HP	ATK	DEF	HIT	AGL	INT	AP Gauge	EXP	Fol	Base Drop Rate %
25	1500	1	200	1	1	400	1	300	1	40

Faint	Sleep	Poison	Curse	Paralyze	Silence	Confuse	Freeze	Petrify
0	100	0	0	0	0	0	100	100

Unseeing	Unhearing	Unsmelling	Skewer	Charm	Berserk	Doom
0	0	0	100	0	0	0

★ S-Class Drops	%	★ A-Class Drops	%	★ B-Class Drops	%	★ C-Class Drops	%
Horizon Crystal	50	Horizon Crystal	80	Sunstone	80	Sunstone	20
Steel Metal	30	Steel Metal	20	Horizon Crystal	20		
Blaze Metal	0						

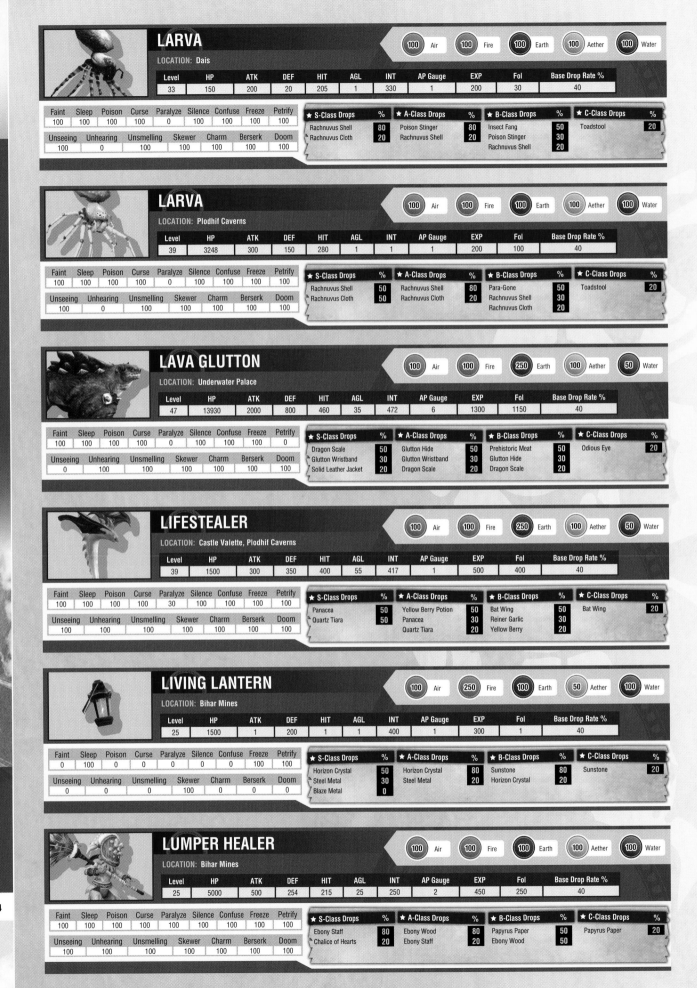

LUMPER HEALER

LOCATION: Bihar Mines

	Air		Fire		Earth		Aether		Water
100		100		100		100		100	

Level	HP	ATK	DEF	HIT	AGL	INT	AP Gauge	EXP	Fol	Base Drop Rate %
25	5000	500	254	215	25	250	2	450	250	40

Faint	Sleep	Poison	Curse	Paralyze	Silence	Confuse	Freeze	Petrify
100	100	100	100	100	100	100	100	100

Unseeing	Unhearing	Unsmelling	Skewer	Charm	Berserk	Doom
100	100	100	100	100	100	100

★ S-Class Drops	%	★ A-Class Drops	%	★ B-Class Drops	%	★ C-Class Drops	%
Ebony Staff	80	Ebony Wood	80	Papyrus Paper	50	Papyrus Paper	20
Chalice of Hearts	20	Ebony Staff	20	Ebony Wood	50		

LUMPER LEADER

LOCATION: Bihar Mines

	Air		Fire		Earth		Aether		Water
100		100		100		100		100	

Level	HP	ATK	DEF	HIT	AGL	INT	AP Gauge	EXP	Fol	Base Drop Rate %
25	12500	700	253	241	25	253	2	566	300	40

Faint	Sleep	Poison	Curse	Paralyze	Silence	Confuse	Freeze	Petrify
100	100	100	100	100	100	100	100	100

Unseeing	Unhearing	Unsmelling	Skewer	Charm	Berserk	Doom
100	100	100	100	100	100	100

★ S-Class Drops	%	★ A-Class Drops	%	★ B-Class Drops	%	★ C-Class Drops	%
Scimitar	80	Copper Metal	80	Sheep Hide	50	Sheep Hide	20
Sword of Spades	20	Scimitar	20	Copper Metal	50		

LUMPER MAGE

LOCATION: Oradian Mountains, Bihar Mines

	Air		Fire		Earth		Aether		Water
100		100		100		100		100	

Level	HP	ATK	DEF	HIT	AGL	INT	AP Gauge	EXP	Fol	Base Drop Rate %
11	1825	110	110	110	5	200	2	200	150	40

Faint	Sleep	Poison	Curse	Paralyze	Silence	Confuse	Freeze	Petrify
100	100	100	100	100	100	100	100	100

Unseeing	Unhearing	Unsmelling	Skewer	Charm	Berserk	Doom
100	100	100	100	100	100	100

★ S-Class Drops	%	★ A-Class Drops	%	★ B-Class Drops	%	★ C-Class Drops	%
Acolyte Staff	80	Ebony Wood	80	Random Beast Bone	50	Random Beast Bone	20
Club of Clubs	20	Acolyte Staff	20	Ebony Wood	50		

LUMPER MARKSMAN

LOCATION: Luce Plains, Bihar Mines

	Air		Fire		Earth		Aether		Water
100		100		100		100		100	

Level	HP	ATK	DEF	HIT	AGL	INT	AP Gauge	EXP	Fol	Base Drop Rate %
3	675	100	30	50	3	30	2	25	20	40

Faint	Sleep	Poison	Curse	Paralyze	Silence	Confuse	Freeze	Petrify
100	100	100	100	100	100	100	100	100

Unseeing	Unhearing	Unsmelling	Skewer	Charm	Berserk	Doom
100	100	100	100	100	100	100

★ S-Class Drops	%	★ A-Class Drops	%	★ B-Class Drops	%	★ C-Class Drops	%
Tracker's Bow	80	Cork Wood	80	Sandstone	50	Cork Wood	20
Coin of Diamonds	20	Tracker's Bow	20	Cork Wood	50		

LUMPER SOLDIER

LOCATION: Oradian Mountains, Bihar Mines

	Air		Fire		Earth		Aether		Water
100		100		100		100		100	

Level	HP	ATK	DEF	HIT	AGL	INT	AP Gauge	EXP	Fol	Base Drop Rate %
17	4500	350	173	174	25	166	2	300	150	40

Faint	Sleep	Poison	Curse	Paralyze	Silence	Confuse	Freeze	Petrify
100	100	100	100	100	100	100	100	100

Unseeing	Unhearing	Unsmelling	Skewer	Charm	Berserk	Doom
100	100	100	100	100	100	100

★ S-Class Drops	%	★ A-Class Drops	%	★ B-Class Drops	%	★ C-Class Drops	%
Hunting Sword	80	Copper Metal	80	Junk	50	Junk	20
Servant of Jacks	20	Hunting Sword	20	Copper Metal	50		

MANDRAGORA

LOCATION: Cobasna Timberlands

	Air		Fire		Earth		Aether		Water
0		250		50		250		50	

Level	HP	ATK	DEF	HIT	AGL	INT	AP Gauge	EXP	Fol	Base Drop Rate %
28	13170	800	286	230	28	286	4	700	290	40

Faint	Sleep	Poison	Curse	Paralyze	Silence	Confuse	Freeze	Petrify
100	100	100	0	0	100	0	100	100

Unseeing	Unhearing	Unsmelling	Skewer	Charm	Berserk	Doom
0	0	0	100	0	0	100

★ S-Class Drops	%	★ A-Class Drops	%	★ B-Class Drops	%	★ C-Class Drops	%
Barkcloth	50	Barkcloth	50	Vine	50	Vine	20
Lentesco Wood	30	Lentesco Wood	30	Antidote Herb	30		
Lentesco Sandals	20	Barkcloth	20	Lentesco Wood	20		

MANTIFISH

LOCATION: Pieria Marshlands

	Air		Fire		Earth		Aether		Water
100		100		250		100		<50	

Level	HP	ATK	DEF	HIT	AGL	INT	AP Gauge	EXP	Fol	Base Drop Rate %
43	5300	700	400	360	80	431	1	700	650	40

Faint	Sleep	Poison	Curse	Paralyze	Silence	Confuse	Freeze	Petrify
100	100	100	100	100	100	100	100	100

Unseeing	Unhearing	Unsmelling	Skewer	Charm	Berserk	Doom
100	100	100	100	100	100	100

★ S-Class Drops	%	★ A-Class Drops	%	★ B-Class Drops	%	★ C-Class Drops	%
Sliced Rare Salmon	50	Sliced Rare Salmon	80	Sliced Salmon	80	Sliced Salmon	20
Rachnuvus Ring	50	Rachnuvus Ring	20	Sliced Rare Salmon	20		

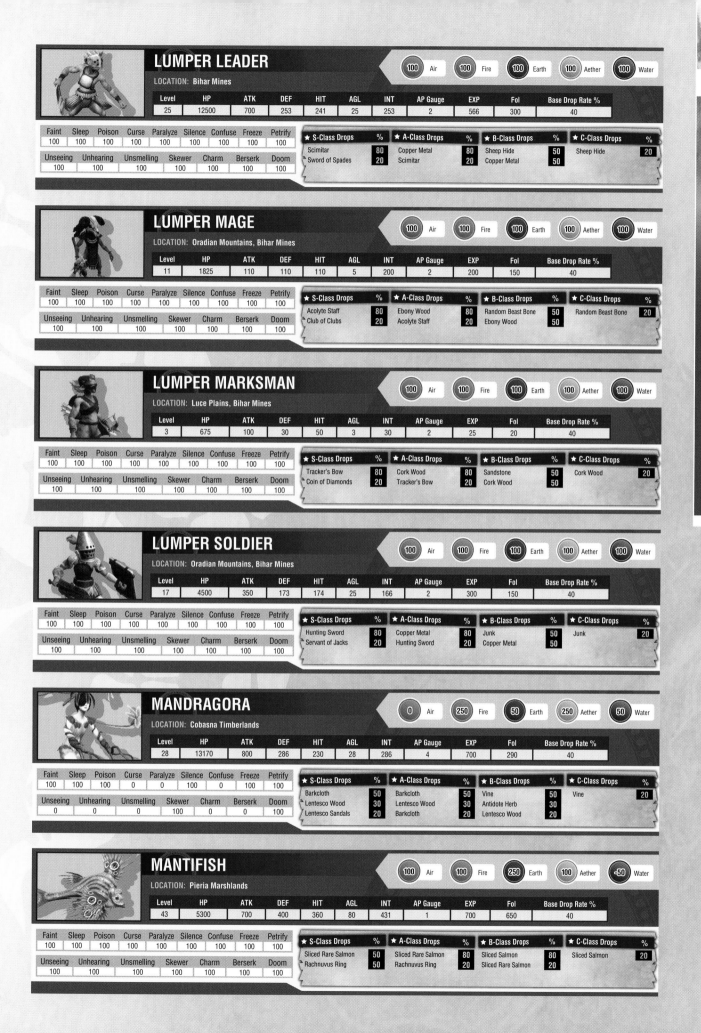

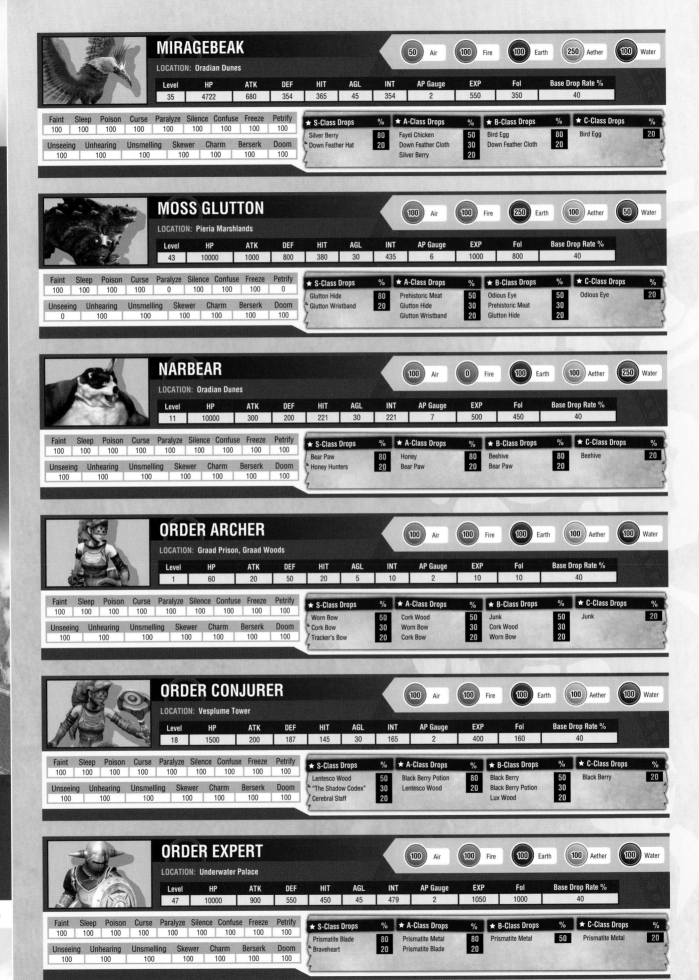

MIRAGEBEAK

LOCATION: Oradian Dunes

50 Air	100 Fire	100 Earth	250 Aether	100 Water

Level	HP	ATK	DEF	HIT	AGL	INT	AP Gauge	EXP	Fol	Base Drop Rate %
35	4722	680	354	365	45	354	2	550	350	40

Faint	Sleep	Poison	Curse	Paralyze	Silence	Confuse	Freeze	Petrify
100	100	100	100	100	100	100	100	100

Unseeing	Unhearing	Unsmelling	Skewer	Charm	Berserk	Doom
100	100	100	100	100	100	100

★ S-Class Drops	%	★ A-Class Drops	%	★ B-Class Drops	%	★ C-Class Drops	%
Silver Berry	80	Fayel Chicken	50	Bird Egg	80	Bird Egg	20
Down Feather Hat	20	Down Feather Cloth	30	Down Feather Cloth	20		
		Silver Berry	20				

MOSS GLUTTON

LOCATION: Pieria Marshlands

100 Air	100 Fire	250 Earth	100 Aether	50 Water

Level	HP	ATK	DEF	HIT	AGL	INT	AP Gauge	EXP	Fol	Base Drop Rate %
43	10000	1000	800	380	30	435	6	1000	800	40

Faint	Sleep	Poison	Curse	Paralyze	Silence	Confuse	Freeze	Petrify
100	100	100	100	0	100	100	100	0

Unseeing	Unhearing	Unsmelling	Skewer	Charm	Berserk	Doom
0	100	100	100	100	100	100

★ S-Class Drops	%	★ A-Class Drops	%	★ B-Class Drops	%	★ C-Class Drops	%
Glutton Hide	80	Prehistoric Meat	50	Odious Eye	50	Odious Eye	20
Glutton Wristband	20	Glutton Hide	30	Prehistoric Meat	30		
		Glutton Wristband	20	Glutton Hide	20		

NARBEAR

LOCATION: Oradian Dunes

100 Air	0 Fire	100 Earth	100 Aether	250 Water

Level	HP	ATK	DEF	HIT	AGL	INT	AP Gauge	EXP	Fol	Base Drop Rate %
11	10000	300	200	221	30	221	7	500	450	40

Faint	Sleep	Poison	Curse	Paralyze	Silence	Confuse	Freeze	Petrify
100	100	100	100	100	100	100	100	100

Unseeing	Unhearing	Unsmelling	Skewer	Charm	Berserk	Doom
100	100	100	100	100	100	100

★ S-Class Drops	%	★ A-Class Drops	%	★ B-Class Drops	%	★ C-Class Drops	%
Bear Paw	80	Honey	80	Beehive	80	Beehive	20
Honey Hunters	20	Bear Paw	20	Bear Paw	20		

ORDER ARCHER

LOCATION: Graad Prison, Graad Woods

100 Air	100 Fire	100 Earth	100 Aether	100 Water

Level	HP	ATK	DEF	HIT	AGL	INT	AP Gauge	EXP	Fol	Base Drop Rate %
1	60	20	50	20	5	10	2	10	10	40

Faint	Sleep	Poison	Curse	Paralyze	Silence	Confuse	Freeze	Petrify
100	100	100	100	100	100	100	100	100

Unseeing	Unhearing	Unsmelling	Skewer	Charm	Berserk	Doom
100	100	100	100	100	100	100

★ S-Class Drops	%	★ A-Class Drops	%	★ B-Class Drops	%	★ C-Class Drops	%
Worn Bow	50	Cork Wood	50	Junk	50	Junk	20
Cork Bow	30	Worn Bow	30	Cork Wood	30		
Tracker's Bow	20	Cork Bow	20	Worn Bow	20		

ORDER CONJURER

LOCATION: Vesplume Tower

100 Air	100 Fire	100 Earth	100 Aether	100 Water

Level	HP	ATK	DEF	HIT	AGL	INT	AP Gauge	EXP	Fol	Base Drop Rate %
18	1500	200	187	145	30	165	2	400	160	40

Faint	Sleep	Poison	Curse	Paralyze	Silence	Confuse	Freeze	Petrify
100	100	100	100	100	100	100	100	100

Unseeing	Unhearing	Unsmelling	Skewer	Charm	Berserk	Doom
100	100	100	100	100	100	100

★ S-Class Drops	%	★ A-Class Drops	%	★ B-Class Drops	%	★ C-Class Drops	%
Lentesco Wood	50	Black Berry Potion	80	Black Berry	50	Black Berry	20
"The Shadow Codex"	30	Lentesco Wood	20	Black Berry Potion	30		
Cerebral Staff	20			Lux Wood	20		

ORDER EXPERT

LOCATION: Underwater Palace

100 Air	100 Fire	100 Earth	100 Aether	100 Water

Level	HP	ATK	DEF	HIT	AGL	INT	AP Gauge	EXP	Fol	Base Drop Rate %
47	10000	900	550	450	45	479	2	1050	1000	40

Faint	Sleep	Poison	Curse	Paralyze	Silence	Confuse	Freeze	Petrify
100	100	100	100	100	100	100	100	100

Unseeing	Unhearing	Unsmelling	Skewer	Charm	Berserk	Doom
100	100	100	100	100	100	100

★ S-Class Drops	%	★ A-Class Drops	%	★ B-Class Drops	%	★ C-Class Drops	%
Prismatite Blade	80	Prismatite Metal	80	Prismatite Metal	50	Prismatite Metal	20
Braveheart	20	Prismatite Blade	20				

ORDER FENCER

LOCATION: Castle Valette

100 Air	100 Fire	100 Earth	100 Aether	100 Water

Level	HP	ATK	DEF	HIT	AGL	INT	AP Gauge	EXP	Fol	Base Drop Rate %
41	9000	700	500	400	55	413	2	1500	1150	40

Faint	Sleep	Poison	Curse	Paralyze	Silence	Confuse	Freeze	Petrify
100	100	100	100	100	100	100	100	100

Unseeing	Unhearing	Unsmelling	Skewer	Charm	Berserk	Doom
100	100	100	100	100	100	100

★ S-Class Drops	%	★ A-Class Drops	%	★ B-Class Drops	%	★ C-Class Drops	%
Ceramic Sword	50	Gold Metal	80	Gold Metal	50	Gold Metal	20
Prismatite Sword	30	Ceramic Sword	20				
Defender	20						

ORDER FIGHTER

LOCATION: Vesplume Tower

100 Air	100 Fire	100 Earth	100 Aether	100 Water

Level	HP	ATK	DEF	HIT	AGL	INT	AP Gauge	EXP	Fol	Base Drop Rate %
18	3630	350	180	130	18	150	2	400	180	40

Faint	Sleep	Poison	Curse	Paralyze	Silence	Confuse	Freeze	Petrify
100	100	100	100	100	100	100	100	100

Unseeing	Unhearing	Unsmelling	Skewer	Charm	Berserk	Doom
100	100	100	100	100	100	100

★ S-Class Drops	%	★ A-Class Drops	%	★ B-Class Drops	%	★ C-Class Drops	%
Copper Metal	50	Iron Metal	50	Iron Metal	80	Iron Metal	20
Falchion	30	Copper Metal	50	Copper Metal	20		
Rapier	20						

ORDER FOLLOWER

LOCATION: Luce Plains

100 Air	100 Fire	100 Earth	100 Aether	100 Water

Level	HP	ATK	DEF	HIT	AGL	INT	AP Gauge	EXP	Fol	Base Drop Rate %
7	2000	120	70	70	7	110	2	150	90	40

Faint	Sleep	Poison	Curse	Paralyze	Silence	Confuse	Freeze	Petrify
100	100	100	100	100	100	100	100	100

Unseeing	Unhearing	Unsmelling	Skewer	Charm	Berserk	Doom
100	100	100	100	100	100	100

★ S-Class Drops	%	★ A-Class Drops	%	★ B-Class Drops	%	★ C-Class Drops	%
Iron Metal	50	Iron Metal	80	Iron Metal	50	Bronze Metal	20
Gladius	30	Gladius	20				
Longsword	20						

ORDER HOUND

LOCATION: Graad Woods

50 Air	100 Fire	250 Earth	100 Aether	100 Water

Level	HP	ATK	DEF	HIT	AGL	INT	AP Gauge	EXP	Fol	Base Drop Rate %
2	600	50	50	110	10	20	5	50	30	40

Faint	Sleep	Poison	Curse	Paralyze	Silence	Confuse	Freeze	Petrify
100	100	100	100	100	100	100	100	100

Unseeing	Unhearing	Unsmelling	Skewer	Charm	Berserk	Doom
100	100	0	100	0	100	100

★ S-Class Drops	%	★ A-Class Drops	%	★ B-Class Drops	%	★ C-Class Drops	%
Burguss Apple	50	Red Berry	50	Animal Fang	50	Animal Fang	20
Golden Wolf Fur	30	Burguss Apple	30	Red Berry	30		
Golden Wolf Fur	20	Golden Wolf Fur	20	Burguss Apple	20		

ORDER JAILER

LOCATION: Graad Prison, Graad Woods, Luce Plains, Castle Prevant, Sapran

100 Air	100 Fire	100 Earth	100 Aether	100 Water

Level	HP	ATK	DEF	HIT	AGL	INT	AP Gauge	EXP	Fol	Base Drop Rate %
1	120	25	80	40	5	10	2	15	10	40

Faint	Sleep	Poison	Curse	Paralyze	Silence	Confuse	Freeze	Petrify
100	100	100	100	100	100	100	100	100

Unseeing	Unhearing	Unsmelling	Skewer	Charm	Berserk	Doom
100	100	100	100	100	100	100

★ S-Class Drops	%	★ A-Class Drops	%	★ B-Class Drops	%	★ C-Class Drops	%
Red Berry Potion	50	Hopeless Charm	50	Metal Fragment	50	Metal Fragment	20
Iron Metal	30	Red Berry Potion	30	Hopeless Charm	50		
Iron Staff	20	Iron Metal	20				

ORDER MAGE

LOCATION: Castle Valette

100 Air	100 Fire	100 Earth	100 Aether	100 Water

Level	HP	ATK	DEF	HIT	AGL	INT	AP Gauge	EXP	Fol	Base Drop Rate %
41	4000	500	380	370	41	410	2	1000	800	40

Faint	Sleep	Poison	Curse	Paralyze	Silence	Confuse	Freeze	Petrify
100	100	100	100	100	100	100	100	100

Unseeing	Unhearing	Unsmelling	Skewer	Charm	Berserk	Doom
100	100	100	100	100	100	100

★ S-Class Drops	%	★ A-Class Drops	%	★ B-Class Drops	%	★ C-Class Drops	%
Holy Staff	80	Black Berry Potion	50	White Berry	50	White Berry	20
"End of Ages"	20	White Berry Potion	30	Black Berry Potion	30		
		Holy Staff	20	White Berry Potion	20		

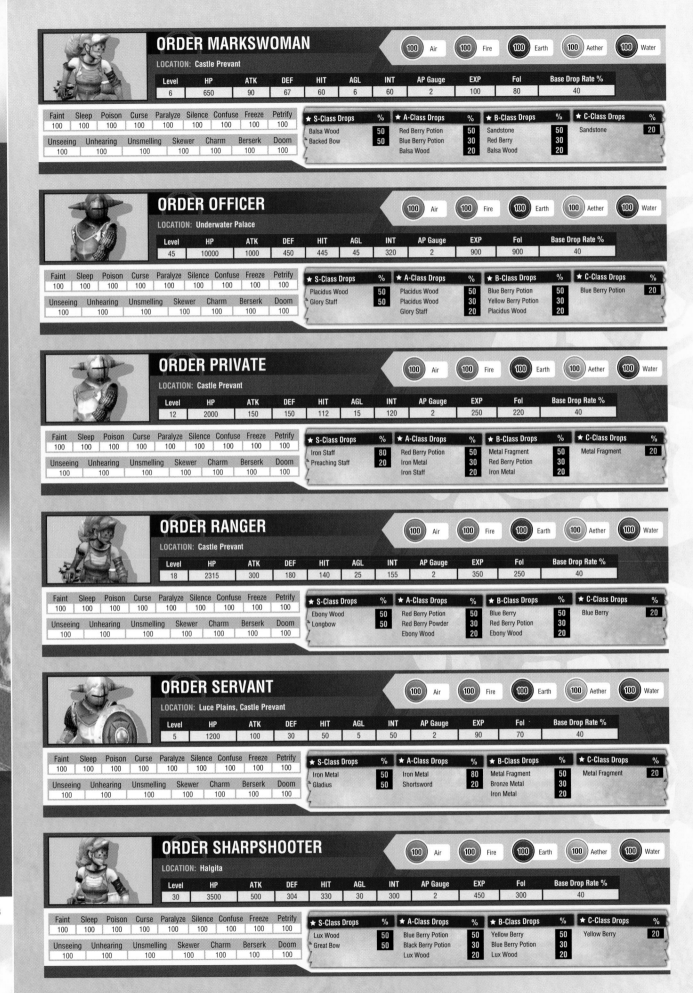

ORDER MARKSWOMAN

LOCATION: Castle Prevant

100 Air	100 Fire	100 Earth	100 Aether	100 Water

Level	HP	ATK	DEF	HIT	AGL	INT	AP Gauge	EXP	Fol	Base Drop Rate %
6	650	90	67	60	6	60	2	100	80	40

Faint	Sleep	Poison	Curse	Paralyze	Silence	Confuse	Freeze	Petrify
100	100	100	100	100	100	100	100	100

Unseeing	Unhearing	Unsmelling	Skewer	Charm	Berserk	Doom
100	100	100	100	100	100	100

★ S-Class Drops	%	★ A-Class Drops	%	★ B-Class Drops	%	★ C-Class Drops	%
Balsa Wood	50	Red Berry Potion	50	Sandstone	50	Sandstone	20
Backed Bow	50	Blue Berry Potion	30	Red Berry	30		
		Balsa Wood	20	Balsa Wood	20		

ORDER OFFICER

LOCATION: Underwater Palace

100 Air	100 Fire	100 Earth	100 Aether	100 Water

Level	HP	ATK	DEF	HIT	AGL	INT	AP Gauge	EXP	Fol	Base Drop Rate %
45	10000	1000	450	445	45	320	2	900	900	40

Faint	Sleep	Poison	Curse	Paralyze	Silence	Confuse	Freeze	Petrify
100	100	100	100	100	100	100	100	100

Unseeing	Unhearing	Unsmelling	Skewer	Charm	Berserk	Doom
100	100	100	100	100	100	100

★ S-Class Drops	%	★ A-Class Drops	%	★ B-Class Drops	%	★ C-Class Drops	%
Placidus Wood	50	Placidus Wood	50	Blue Berry Potion	50	Blue Berry Potion	20
Glory Staff	50	Placidus Wood	30	Yellow Berry Potion	30		
		Glory Staff	20	Placidus Wood	20		

ORDER PRIVATE

LOCATION: Castle Prevant

100 Air	100 Fire	100 Earth	100 Aether	100 Water

Level	HP	ATK	DEF	HIT	AGL	INT	AP Gauge	EXP	Fol	Base Drop Rate %
12	2000	150	150	112	15	120	2	250	220	40

Faint	Sleep	Poison	Curse	Paralyze	Silence	Confuse	Freeze	Petrify
100	100	100	100	100	100	100	100	100

Unseeing	Unhearing	Unsmelling	Skewer	Charm	Berserk	Doom
100	100	100	100	100	100	100

★ S-Class Drops	%	★ A-Class Drops	%	★ B-Class Drops	%	★ C-Class Drops	%
Iron Staff	80	Red Berry Potion	50	Metal Fragment	50	Metal Fragment	20
Preaching Staff	20	Iron Metal	30	Red Berry Potion	30		
		Iron Staff	20	Iron Metal	20		

ORDER RANGER

LOCATION: Castle Prevant

100 Air	100 Fire	100 Earth	100 Aether	100 Water

Level	HP	ATK	DEF	HIT	AGL	INT	AP Gauge	EXP	Fol	Base Drop Rate %
18	2315	300	180	140	25	155	2	350	250	40

Faint	Sleep	Poison	Curse	Paralyze	Silence	Confuse	Freeze	Petrify
100	100	100	100	100	100	100	100	100

Unseeing	Unhearing	Unsmelling	Skewer	Charm	Berserk	Doom
100	100	100	100	100	100	100

★ S-Class Drops	%	★ A-Class Drops	%	★ B-Class Drops	%	★ C-Class Drops	%
Ebony Wood	50	Red Berry Potion	50	Blue Berry	50	Blue Berry	20
Longbow	50	Red Berry Powder	30	Red Berry Potion	30		
		Ebony Wood	20	Ebony Wood	20		

ORDER SERVANT

LOCATION: Luce Plains, Castle Prevant

100 Air	100 Fire	100 Earth	100 Aether	100 Water

Level	HP	ATK	DEF	HIT	AGL	INT	AP Gauge	EXP	Fol	Base Drop Rate %
5	1200	100	30	50	5	50	2	90	70	40

Faint	Sleep	Poison	Curse	Paralyze	Silence	Confuse	Freeze	Petrify
100	100	100	100	100	100	100	100	100

Unseeing	Unhearing	Unsmelling	Skewer	Charm	Berserk	Doom
100	100	100	100	100	100	100

★ S-Class Drops	%	★ A-Class Drops	%	★ B-Class Drops	%	★ C-Class Drops	%
Iron Metal	50	Iron Metal	80	Metal Fragment	50	Metal Fragment	20
Gladius	50	Shortsword	20	Bronze Metal	30		
				Iron Metal	20		

ORDER SHARPSHOOTER

LOCATION: Halgita

100 Air	100 Fire	100 Earth	100 Aether	100 Water

Level	HP	ATK	DEF	HIT	AGL	INT	AP Gauge	EXP	Fol	Base Drop Rate %
30	3500	500	304	330	30	300	2	450	300	40

Faint	Sleep	Poison	Curse	Paralyze	Silence	Confuse	Freeze	Petrify
100	100	100	100	100	100	100	100	100

Unseeing	Unhearing	Unsmelling	Skewer	Charm	Berserk	Doom
100	100	100	100	100	100	100

★ S-Class Drops	%	★ A-Class Drops	%	★ B-Class Drops	%	★ C-Class Drops	%
Lux Wood	50	Blue Berry Potion	50	Yellow Berry	50	Yellow Berry	20
Great Bow	50	Black Berry Potion	30	Blue Berry Potion	30		
		Lux Wood	20	Lux Wood	20		

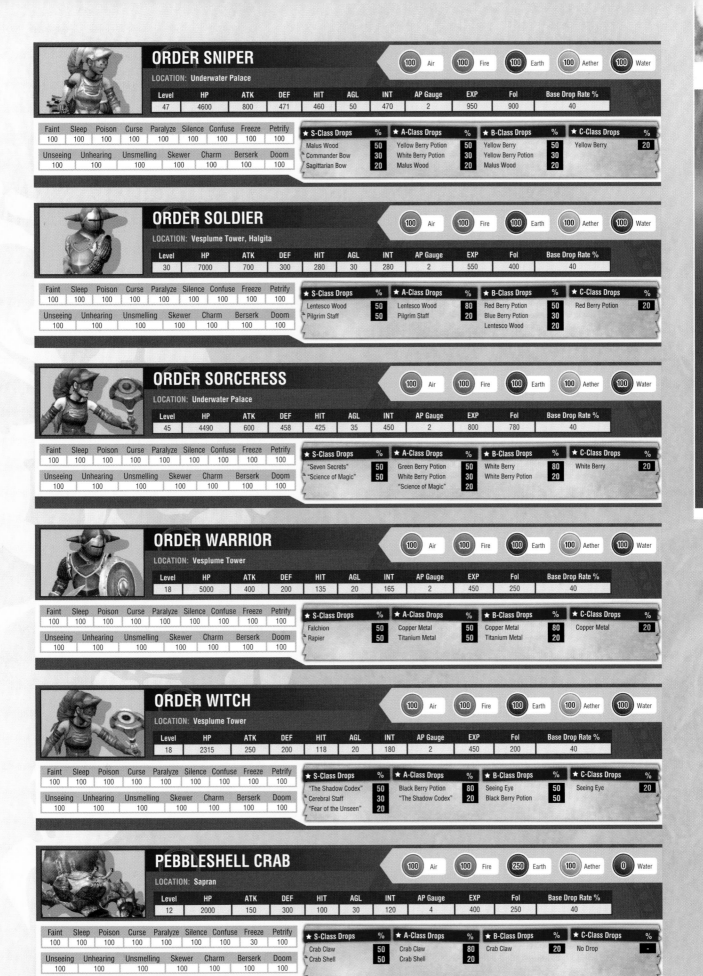

ORDER SNIPER

LOCATION: Underwater Palace

Air	Fire	Earth	Aether	Water
100	100	100	100	100

Level	HP	ATK	DEF	HIT	AGL	INT	AP Gauge	EXP	Fol	Base Drop Rate %
47	4600	800	471	460	50	470	2	950	900	40

Faint	Sleep	Poison	Curse	Paralyze	Silence	Confuse	Freeze	Petrify
100	100	100	100	100	100	100	100	100

Unseeing	Unhearing	Unsmelling	Skewer	Charm	Berserk	Doom
100	100	100	100	100	100	100

★ S-Class Drops	%	★ A-Class Drops	%	★ B-Class Drops	%	★ C-Class Drops	%
Malus Wood	50	Yellow Berry Potion	50	Yellow Berry	50	Yellow Berry	20
Commander Bow	30	White Berry Potion	30	Yellow Berry Potion	30		
Sagittarian Bow	20	Malus Wood	20	Malus Wood	20		

ORDER SOLDIER

LOCATION: Vesplume Tower, Halgita

Air	Fire	Earth	Aether	Water
100	100	100	100	100

Level	HP	ATK	DEF	HIT	AGL	INT	AP Gauge	EXP	Fol	Base Drop Rate %
30	7000	700	300	280	30	280	2	550	400	40

Faint	Sleep	Poison	Curse	Paralyze	Silence	Confuse	Freeze	Petrify
100	100	100	100	100	100	100	100	100

Unseeing	Unhearing	Unsmelling	Skewer	Charm	Berserk	Doom
100	100	100	100	100	100	100

★ S-Class Drops	%	★ A-Class Drops	%	★ B-Class Drops	%	★ C-Class Drops	%
Lentesco Wood	50	Lentesco Wood	80	Red Berry Potion	50	Red Berry Potion	20
Pilgrim Staff	50	Pilgrim Staff	20	Blue Berry Potion	30		
				Lentesco Wood	20		

ORDER SORCERESS

LOCATION: Underwater Palace

Air	Fire	Earth	Aether	Water
100	100	100	100	100

Level	HP	ATK	DEF	HIT	AGL	INT	AP Gauge	EXP	Fol	Base Drop Rate %
45	4490	600	458	425	35	450	2	800	780	40

Faint	Sleep	Poison	Curse	Paralyze	Silence	Confuse	Freeze	Petrify
100	100	100	100	100	100	100	100	100

Unseeing	Unhearing	Unsmelling	Skewer	Charm	Berserk	Doom
100	100	100	100	100	100	100

★ S-Class Drops	%	★ A-Class Drops	%	★ B-Class Drops	%	★ C-Class Drops	%
"Seven Secrets"	50	Green Berry Potion	50	White Berry	80	White Berry	20
"Science of Magic"	50	White Berry Potion	30	White Berry Potion	20		
		"Science of Magic"	20				

ORDER WARRIOR

LOCATION: Vesplume Tower

Air	Fire	Earth	Aether	Water
100	100	100	100	100

Level	HP	ATK	DEF	HIT	AGL	INT	AP Gauge	EXP	Fol	Base Drop Rate %
18	5000	400	200	135	20	165	2	450	250	40

Faint	Sleep	Poison	Curse	Paralyze	Silence	Confuse	Freeze	Petrify
100	100	100	100	100	100	100	100	100

Unseeing	Unhearing	Unsmelling	Skewer	Charm	Berserk	Doom
100	100	100	100	100	100	100

★ S-Class Drops	%	★ A-Class Drops	%	★ B-Class Drops	%	★ C-Class Drops	%
Falchion	50	Copper Metal	50	Copper Metal	80	Copper Metal	20
Rapier	50	Titanium Metal	50	Titanium Metal	20		

ORDER WITCH

LOCATION: Vesplume Tower

Air	Fire	Earth	Aether	Water
100	100	100	100	100

Level	HP	ATK	DEF	HIT	AGL	INT	AP Gauge	EXP	Fol	Base Drop Rate %
18	2315	250	200	118	20	180	2	450	200	40

Faint	Sleep	Poison	Curse	Paralyze	Silence	Confuse	Freeze	Petrify
100	100	100	100	100	100	100	100	100

Unseeing	Unhearing	Unsmelling	Skewer	Charm	Berserk	Doom
100	100	100	100	100	100	100

★ S-Class Drops	%	★ A-Class Drops	%	★ B-Class Drops	%	★ C-Class Drops	%
"The Shadow Codex"	50	Black Berry Potion	80	Seeing Eye	50	Seeing Eye	20
Cerebral Staff	30	"The Shadow Codex"	20	Black Berry Potion	50		
"Fear of the Unseen"	20						

PEBBLESHELL CRAB

LOCATION: Sapran

Air	Fire	Earth	Aether	Water
100	100	250	100	0

Level	HP	ATK	DEF	HIT	AGL	INT	AP Gauge	EXP	Fol	Base Drop Rate %
12	2000	150	300	100	30	120	4	400	250	40

Faint	Sleep	Poison	Curse	Paralyze	Silence	Confuse	Freeze	Petrify
100	100	100	100	100	100	100	30	100

Unseeing	Unhearing	Unsmelling	Skewer	Charm	Berserk	Doom
100	100	100	100	100	100	100

★ S-Class Drops	%	★ A-Class Drops	%	★ B-Class Drops	%	★ C-Class Drops	%
Crab Claw	50	Crab Claw	80	Crab Claw	20	No Drop	-
Crab Shell	50	Crab Shell	20				

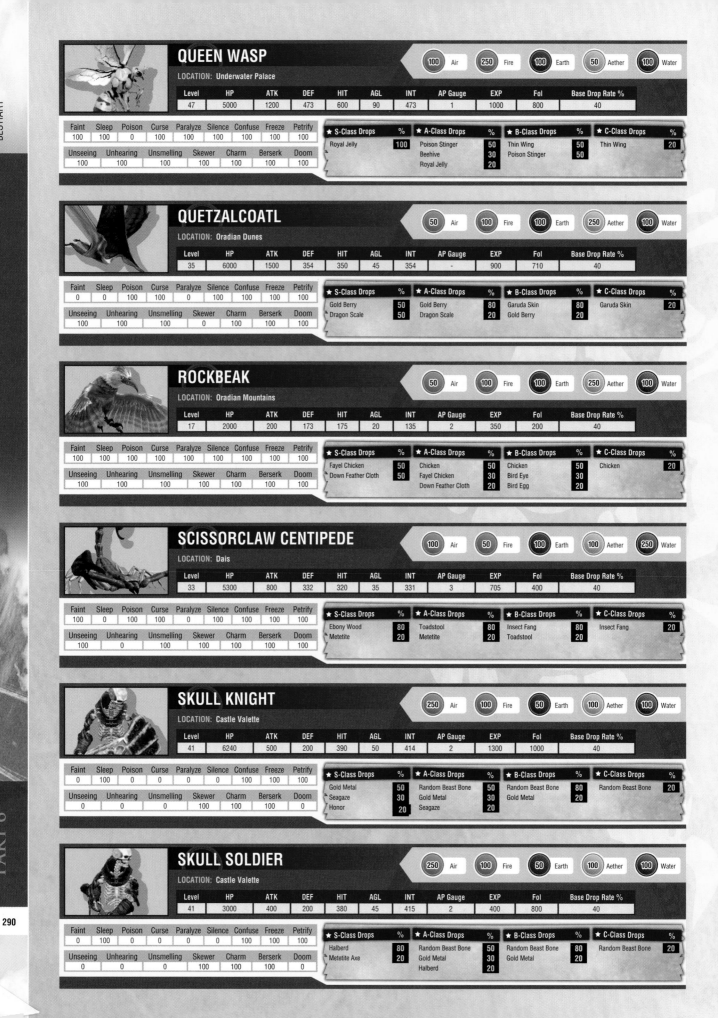

QUEEN WASP

LOCATION: Underwater Palace

| 100 Air | 250 Fire | 100 Earth | 50 Aether | 100 Water |

Level	HP	ATK	DEF	HIT	AGL	INT	AP Gauge	EXP	Fol	Base Drop Rate %
47	5000	1200	473	600	90	473	1	1000	800	40

Faint	Sleep	Poison	Curse	Paralyze	Silence	Confuse	Freeze	Petrify
100	100	0	100	100	100	100	100	100

Unseeing	Unhearing	Unsmelling	Skewer	Charm	Berserk	Doom
100	100	100	100	100	100	100

★ S-Class Drops	%	★ A-Class Drops	%	★ B-Class Drops	%	★ C-Class Drops	%
Royal Jelly	100	Poison Stinger	50	Thin Wing	50	Thin Wing	20
		Beehive	30	Poison Stinger	50		
		Royal Jelly	20				

QUETZALCOATL

LOCATION: Oradian Dunes

| 50 Air | 100 Fire | 100 Earth | 250 Aether | 100 Water |

Level	HP	ATK	DEF	HIT	AGL	INT	AP Gauge	EXP	Fol	Base Drop Rate %
35	6000	1500	354	350	45	354	-	900	710	40

Faint	Sleep	Poison	Curse	Paralyze	Silence	Confuse	Freeze	Petrify
0	0	100	100	0	100	100	100	100

Unseeing	Unhearing	Unsmelling	Skewer	Charm	Berserk	Doom
100	100	100	100	100	100	100

★ S-Class Drops	%	★ A-Class Drops	%	★ B-Class Drops	%	★ C-Class Drops	%
Gold Berry	50	Gold Berry	80	Garuda Skin	80	Garuda Skin	20
Dragon Scale	50	Dragon Scale	20	Gold Berry	20		

ROCKBEAK

LOCATION: Oradian Mountains

| 50 Air | 100 Fire | 100 Earth | 250 Aether | 100 Water |

Level	HP	ATK	DEF	HIT	AGL	INT	AP Gauge	EXP	Fol	Base Drop Rate %
17	2000	200	173	175	20	135	2	350	200	40

Faint	Sleep	Poison	Curse	Paralyze	Silence	Confuse	Freeze	Petrify
100	100	100	100	100	100	100	100	100

Unseeing	Unhearing	Unsmelling	Skewer	Charm	Berserk	Doom
100	100	100	100	100	100	100

★ S-Class Drops	%	★ A-Class Drops	%	★ B-Class Drops	%	★ C-Class Drops	%
Fayel Chicken	50	Chicken	50	Chicken	50	Chicken	20
Down Feather Cloth	50	Fayel Chicken	30	Bird Eye	30		
		Down Feather Cloth	20	Bird Egg	20		

SCISSORCLAW CENTIPEDE

LOCATION: Dais

| 100 Air | 50 Fire | 100 Earth | 100 Aether | 250 Water |

Level	HP	ATK	DEF	HIT	AGL	INT	AP Gauge	EXP	Fol	Base Drop Rate %
33	5300	800	332	320	35	331	3	705	400	40

Faint	Sleep	Poison	Curse	Paralyze	Silence	Confuse	Freeze	Petrify
100	0	100	100	0	100	100	100	100

Unseeing	Unhearing	Unsmelling	Skewer	Charm	Berserk	Doom
100	0	100	100	100	100	100

★ S-Class Drops	%	★ A-Class Drops	%	★ B-Class Drops	%	★ C-Class Drops	%
Ebony Wood	80	Toadstool	80	Insect Fang	80	Insect Fang	20
Metetite	20	Metetite	20	Toadstool	20		

SKULL KNIGHT

LOCATION: Castle Valette

| 250 Air | 100 Fire | 50 Earth | 100 Aether | 100 Water |

Level	HP	ATK	DEF	HIT	AGL	INT	AP Gauge	EXP	Fol	Base Drop Rate %
41	6240	500	200	390	50	414	2	1300	1000	40

Faint	Sleep	Poison	Curse	Paralyze	Silence	Confuse	Freeze	Petrify
0	100	0	0	0	0	100	100	100

Unseeing	Unhearing	Unsmelling	Skewer	Charm	Berserk	Doom
0	0	0	100	100	100	0

★ S-Class Drops	%	★ A-Class Drops	%	★ B-Class Drops	%	★ C-Class Drops	%
Gold Metal	50	Random Beast Bone	50	Random Beast Bone	80	Random Beast Bone	20
Seagaze	30	Gold Metal	30	Gold Metal	20		
Honor	20	Seagaze	20				

SKULL SOLDIER

LOCATION: Castle Valette

| 250 Air | 100 Fire | 50 Earth | 100 Aether | 100 Water |

Level	HP	ATK	DEF	HIT	AGL	INT	AP Gauge	EXP	Fol	Base Drop Rate %
41	3000	400	200	380	45	415	2	400	800	40

Faint	Sleep	Poison	Curse	Paralyze	Silence	Confuse	Freeze	Petrify
0	100	0	0	0	0	100	100	100

Unseeing	Unhearing	Unsmelling	Skewer	Charm	Berserk	Doom
0	0	0	100	100	100	0

★ S-Class Drops	%	★ A-Class Drops	%	★ B-Class Drops	%	★ C-Class Drops	%
Halberd	80	Random Beast Bone	50	Random Beast Bone	80	Random Beast Bone	20
Metetite Axe	20	Gold Metal	30	Gold Metal	20		
		Halberd	20				

SKULL WARRIOR

LOCATION: Underwater Palace

	Air	Fire	Earth	Aether	Water
	250	100	50	100	100

Level	HP	ATK	DEF	HIT	AGL	INT	AP Gauge	EXP	Fol	Base Drop Rate %
45	8000	850	300	450	40	280	2	600	450	40

Faint	Sleep	Poison	Curse	Paralyze	Silence	Confuse	Freeze	Petrify
0	100	0	0	0	0	100	100	100

Unseeing	Unhearing	Unsmelling	Skewer	Charm	Berserk	Doom
0	0	0	100	100	100	0

★ S-Class Drops	%	★ A-Class Drops	%	★ B-Class Drops	%	★ C-Class Drops	%
Crystallite Axe	80	Random Beast Bone	50	Random Beast Bone	80	Random Beast Bone	20
Bardiche	20	Crystallite Metal	30	Crystallite Metal	20		
		Crystallite Axe	20				

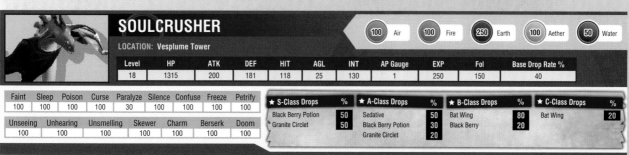

SOULCRUSHER

LOCATION: Vesplume Tower

	Air	Fire	Earth	Aether	Water
	100	100	250	100	50

Level	HP	ATK	DEF	HIT	AGL	INT	AP Gauge	EXP	Fol	Base Drop Rate %
18	1315	200	181	118	25	130	1	250	150	40

Faint	Sleep	Poison	Curse	Paralyze	Silence	Confuse	Freeze	Petrify
100	100	100	100	30	100	100	100	100

Unseeing	Unhearing	Unsmelling	Skewer	Charm	Berserk	Doom
100	100	100	100	100	100	100

★ S-Class Drops	%	★ A-Class Drops	%	★ B-Class Drops	%	★ C-Class Drops	%
Black Berry Potion	50	Sedative	50	Bat Wing	80	Bat Wing	20
Granite Circlet	50	Black Berry Potion	30	Black Berry	20		
		Granite Circlet	20				

STONE GARGOYLE

LOCATION: Castle Prevant

	Air	Fire	Earth	Aether	Water
	250	100	0	100	50

Level	HP	ATK	DEF	HIT	AGL	INT	AP Gauge	EXP	Fol	Base Drop Rate %
7	2500	350	150	100	2	10	4	200	100	40

Faint	Sleep	Poison	Curse	Paralyze	Silence	Confuse	Freeze	Petrify
0	0	0	0	0	0	100	100	0

Unseeing	Unhearing	Unsmelling	Skewer	Charm	Berserk	Doom
0	0	0	100	100	100	0

★ S-Class Drops	%	★ A-Class Drops	%	★ B-Class Drops	%	★ C-Class Drops	%
Iron Metal	50	Stone Statue Fragment	50	Stone Statue Fragment	80	Stone Statue Fragment	20
Marble	30	Iron Metal	30	Iron Metal	20		
Copper Metal	20	Marble	20				

STONESHELL CRAB

LOCATION: Zalan Coast

	Air	Fire	Earth	Aether	Water
	100	100	250	100	0

Level	HP	ATK	DEF	HIT	AGL	INT	AP Gauge	EXP	Fol	Base Drop Rate %
25	2000	300	300	235	25	25	4	200	130	40

Faint	Sleep	Poison	Curse	Paralyze	Silence	Confuse	Freeze	Petrify
100	100	100	100	100	100	100	30	100

Unseeing	Unhearing	Unsmelling	Skewer	Charm	Berserk	Doom
100	100	100	100	100	100	100

★ S-Class Drops	%	★ A-Class Drops	%	★ B-Class Drops	%	★ C-Class Drops	%
Crab Shell	50	Crab Claw	50	Crab Claw	50	Crab Claw	20
Crab Meat	50	Crab Shell	30	Crab Shell	50		
		Crab Meat	20				

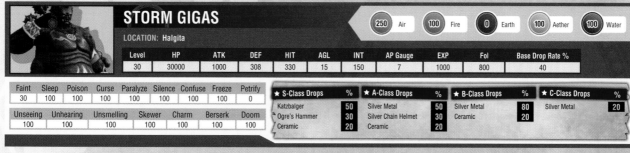

STORM GIGAS

LOCATION: Halgita

	Air	Fire	Earth	Aether	Water
	250	100	0	100	100

Level	HP	ATK	DEF	HIT	AGL	INT	AP Gauge	EXP	Fol	Base Drop Rate %
30	30000	1000	308	330	15	150	7	1000	800	40

Faint	Sleep	Poison	Curse	Paralyze	Silence	Confuse	Freeze	Petrify
30	100	100	100	100	100	100	100	0

Unseeing	Unhearing	Unsmelling	Skewer	Charm	Berserk	Doom
100	100	100	100	100	100	100

★ S-Class Drops	%	★ A-Class Drops	%	★ B-Class Drops	%	★ C-Class Drops	%
Katzbalger	50	Silver Metal	50	Silver Metal	80	Silver Metal	20
Ogre's Hammer	30	Silver Chain Helmet	30	Ceramic	20		
Ceramic	20	Ceramic	20				

SWAMP SERPENT

LOCATION: Oradian Dunes

	Air	Fire	Earth	Aether	Water
	100	100	250	100	50

Level	HP	ATK	DEF	HIT	AGL	INT	AP Gauge	EXP	Fol	Base Drop Rate %
11	3000	150	80	85	15	110	3	250	200	40

Faint	Sleep	Poison	Curse	Paralyze	Silence	Confuse	Freeze	Petrify
100	0	0	100	100	100	100	100	100

Unseeing	Unhearing	Unsmelling	Skewer	Charm	Berserk	Doom
100	100	0	100	100	100	100

★ S-Class Drops	%	★ A-Class Drops	%	★ B-Class Drops	%	★ C-Class Drops	%
Antidote	50	Bronze Metal	50	Snakeskin	80	Snakeskin	20
Snake Pendant	50	Antidote	30	Bronze Metal	20		
		Bronze Ring	20				

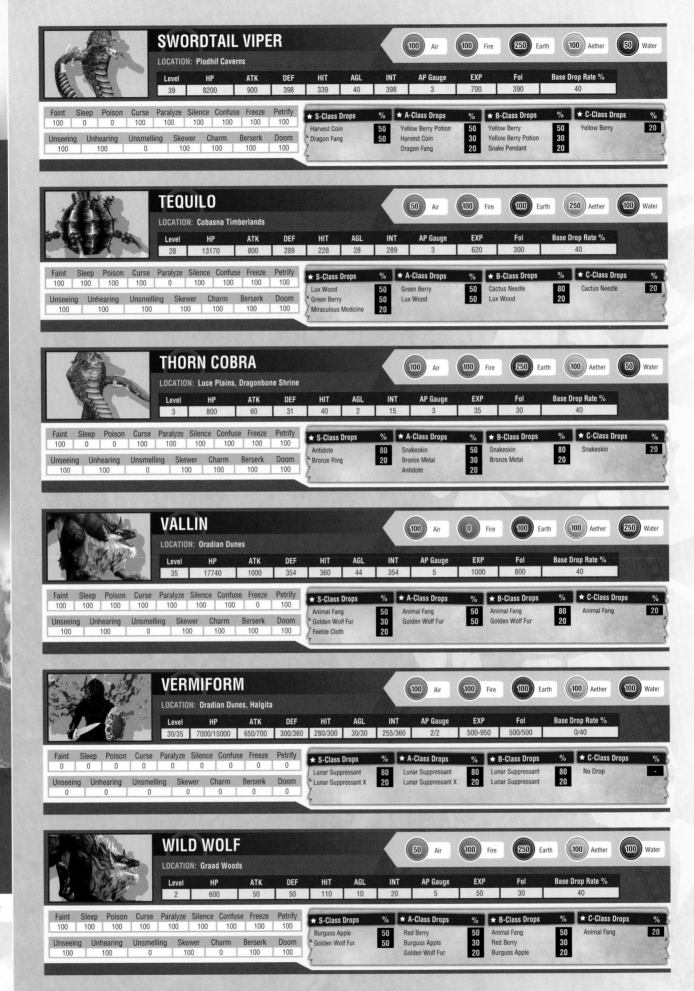

SWORDTAIL VIPER

LOCATION: Plodhif Caverns

100 Air	100 Fire	250 Earth	100 Aether	50 Water

Level	HP	ATK	DEF	HIT	AGL	INT	AP Gauge	EXP	Fol	Base Drop Rate %
39	8200	900	398	339	40	398	3	700	390	40

Faint	Sleep	Poison	Curse	Paralyze	Silence	Confuse	Freeze	Petrify
100	0	0	100	100	100	100	100	100

Unseeing	Unhearing	Unsmelling	Skewer	Charm	Berserk	Doom
100	100	0	100	100	100	100

★ S-Class Drops	%	★ A-Class Drops	%	★ B-Class Drops	%	★ C-Class Drops	%
Harvest Coin	50	Yellow Berry Potion	50	Yellow Berry	50	Yellow Berry	20
Dragon Fang	50	Harvest Coin	30	Yellow Berry Potion	30		
		Dragon Fang	20	Snake Pendant	20		

TEQUILO

LOCATION: Cobasna Timberlands

50 Air	100 Fire	100 Earth	250 Aether	100 Water

Level	HP	ATK	DEF	HIT	AGL	INT	AP Gauge	EXP	Fol	Base Drop Rate %
28	13170	800	289	228	28	289	3	620	300	40

Faint	Sleep	Poison	Curse	Paralyze	Silence	Confuse	Freeze	Petrify
100	100	100	100	0	100	100	100	100

Unseeing	Unhearing	Unsmelling	Skewer	Charm	Berserk	Doom
100	100	100	100	100	100	100

★ S-Class Drops	%	★ A-Class Drops	%	★ B-Class Drops	%	★ C-Class Drops	%
Lux Wood	50	Green Berry	50	Cactus Needle	80	Cactus Needle	20
Green Berry	50	Lux Wood	50	Lux Wood	20		
Miraculous Medicine	20						

THORN COBRA

LOCATION: Luce Plains, Dragonbone Shrine

100 Air	100 Fire	250 Earth	100 Aether	50 Water

Level	HP	ATK	DEF	HIT	AGL	INT	AP Gauge	EXP	Fol	Base Drop Rate %
3	800	60	31	40	2	15	3	35	30	40

Faint	Sleep	Poison	Curse	Paralyze	Silence	Confuse	Freeze	Petrify
100	0	0	100	100	100	100	100	100

Unseeing	Unhearing	Unsmelling	Skewer	Charm	Berserk	Doom
100	100	0	100	100	100	100

★ S-Class Drops	%	★ A-Class Drops	%	★ B-Class Drops	%	★ C-Class Drops	%
Antidote	80	Snakeskin	50	Snakeskin	80	Snakeskin	20
Bronze Ring	20	Bronze Metal	30	Bronze Metal	20		
		Antidote	20				

VALLIN

LOCATION: Oradian Dunes

100 Air	0 Fire	100 Earth	100 Aether	250 Water

Level	HP	ATK	DEF	HIT	AGL	INT	AP Gauge	EXP	Fol	Base Drop Rate %
35	17740	1000	354	360	44	354	5	1000	800	40

Faint	Sleep	Poison	Curse	Paralyze	Silence	Confuse	Freeze	Petrify
100	100	100	100	100	100	100	0	100

Unseeing	Unhearing	Unsmelling	Skewer	Charm	Berserk	Doom
100	100	0	100	100	100	100

★ S-Class Drops	%	★ A-Class Drops	%	★ B-Class Drops	%	★ C-Class Drops	%
Animal Fang	50	Animal Fang	50	Animal Fang	80	Animal Fang	20
Golden Wolf Fur	30	Golden Wolf Fur	50	Golden Wolf Fur	20		
Feeble Cloth	20						

VERMIFORM

LOCATION: Oradian Dunes, Halgita

100 Air	100 Fire	100 Earth	100 Aether	100 Water

Level	HP	ATK	DEF	HIT	AGL	INT	AP Gauge	EXP	Fol	Base Drop Rate %
30/35	7000/15000	650/700	300/360	280/300	30/30	255/360	2/2	500-950	500/500	0/40

Faint	Sleep	Poison	Curse	Paralyze	Silence	Confuse	Freeze	Petrify
0	0	0	0	0	0	0	0	0

Unseeing	Unhearing	Unsmelling	Skewer	Charm	Berserk	Doom
0	0	0	0	0	0	0

★ S-Class Drops	%	★ A-Class Drops	%	★ B-Class Drops	%	★ C-Class Drops	%
Lunar Suppressant	80	Lunar Suppressant	80	Lunar Suppressant	80	No Drop	-
Lunar Suppressant X	20	Lunar Suppressant X	20	Lunar Suppressant	20		

WILD WOLF

LOCATION: Graad Woods

50 Air	100 Fire	250 Earth	100 Aether	100 Water

Level	HP	ATK	DEF	HIT	AGL	INT	AP Gauge	EXP	Fol	Base Drop Rate %
2	600	50	50	110	10	20	5	50	30	40

Faint	Sleep	Poison	Curse	Paralyze	Silence	Confuse	Freeze	Petrify
100	100	100	100	100	100	100	100	100

Unseeing	Unhearing	Unsmelling	Skewer	Charm	Berserk	Doom
100	100	0	100	100	100	100

★ S-Class Drops	%	★ A-Class Drops	%	★ B-Class Drops	%	★ C-Class Drops	%
Burguss Apple	50	Red Berry	50	Animal Fang	50	Animal Fang	20
Golden Wolf Fur	50	Burguss Apple	30	Red Berry	30		
		Golden Wolf Fur	20	Burguss Apple	20		

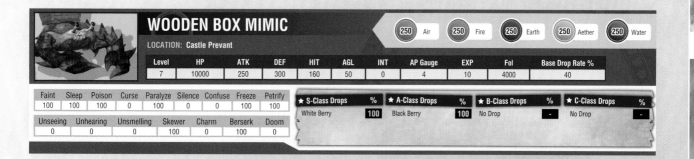

WOODEN BOX MIMIC

LOCATION: Castle Prevant

	Air		Fire		Earth		Aether		Water
250		250		250		250		250	

Level	HP	ATK	DEF	HIT	AGL	INT	AP Gauge	EXP	Fol	Base Drop Rate %
7	10000	250	300	160	50	0	4	10	4000	40

Faint	Sleep	Poison	Curse	Paralyze	Silence	Confuse	Freeze	Petrify
100	100	100	0	100	0	0	100	100

Unseeing	Unhearing	Unsmelling	Skewer	Charm	Berserk	Doom
0	0	0	100	0	100	0

★ S-Class Drops	%	★ A-Class Drops	%	★ B-Class Drops	%	★ C-Class Drops	%
White Berry	100	Black Berry	100	No Drop	-	No Drop	-

BOSSES

RAMBERT

LOCATION: Dragonbone Shrine

	Air		Fire		Earth		Aether		Water
100		100		250		100		50	

Level	HP	ATK	DEF	HIT	AGL	INT	AP Gauge	EXP	Fol	Base Drop Rate %
3	10000	90	33	100	10	15	7	500	300	0

Faint	Sleep	Poison	Curse	Paralyze	Silence	Confuse	Freeze	Petrify
50	40	80	100	0	100	100	0	0

Unseeing	Unhearing	Unsmelling	Skewer	Charm	Berserk	Doom
100	100	100	0	0	100	0

★ S-Class Drops	%	★ A-Class Drops	%	★ B-Class Drops	%	★ C-Class Drops	%
			NO DROPS				

LESTER

LOCATION: Castle Prevant

	Air		Fire		Earth		Aether		Water
50		100		100		250		100	

Level	HP	ATK	DEF	HIT	AGL	INT	AP Gauge	EXP	Fol	Base Drop Rate %
7	25000	200	150	100	50	120	-	1450	700	0

Faint	Sleep	Poison	Curse	Paralyze	Silence	Confuse	Freeze	Petrify
50	20	30	0	0	0	0	0	0

Unseeing	Unhearing	Unsmelling	Skewer	Charm	Berserk	Doom
0	0	0	0	0	0	0

★ S-Class Drops	%	★ A-Class Drops	%	★ B-Class Drops	%	★ C-Class Drops	%
			NO DROPS				

SEMBERAS

LOCATION: Sapran

	Air		Fire		Earth		Aether		Water
100		50		100		100		250	

Level	HP	ATK	DEF	HIT	AGL	INT	AP Gauge	EXP	Fol	Base Drop Rate %
12	40000	300	200	122	30	150	-	5000	1200	0

Faint	Sleep	Poison	Curse	Paralyze	Silence	Confuse	Freeze	Petrify
30	30	0	0	0	0	0	0	0

Unseeing	Unhearing	Unsmelling	Skewer	Charm	Berserk	Doom
0	0	0	0	0	0	0

★ S-Class Drops	%	★ A-Class Drops	%	★ B-Class Drops	%	★ C-Class Drops	%
			NO DROPS				

FAESPHERE (SEMBERAS)

LOCATION: Sapran

	Air		Fire		Earth		Aether		Water
100		100		100		100		100	

Level	HP	ATK	DEF	HIT	AGL	INT	AP Gauge	EXP	Fol	Base Drop Rate %
12	500	0	120	0	0	120	1	0	0	0

Faint	Sleep	Poison	Curse	Paralyze	Silence	Confuse	Freeze	Petrify
0	0	0	0	0	0	0	0	0

Unseeing	Unhearing	Unsmelling	Skewer	Charm	Berserk	Doom
0	0	0	100	0	0	0

★ S-Class Drops	%	★ A-Class Drops	%	★ B-Class Drops	%	★ C-Class Drops	%
			NO DROPS				

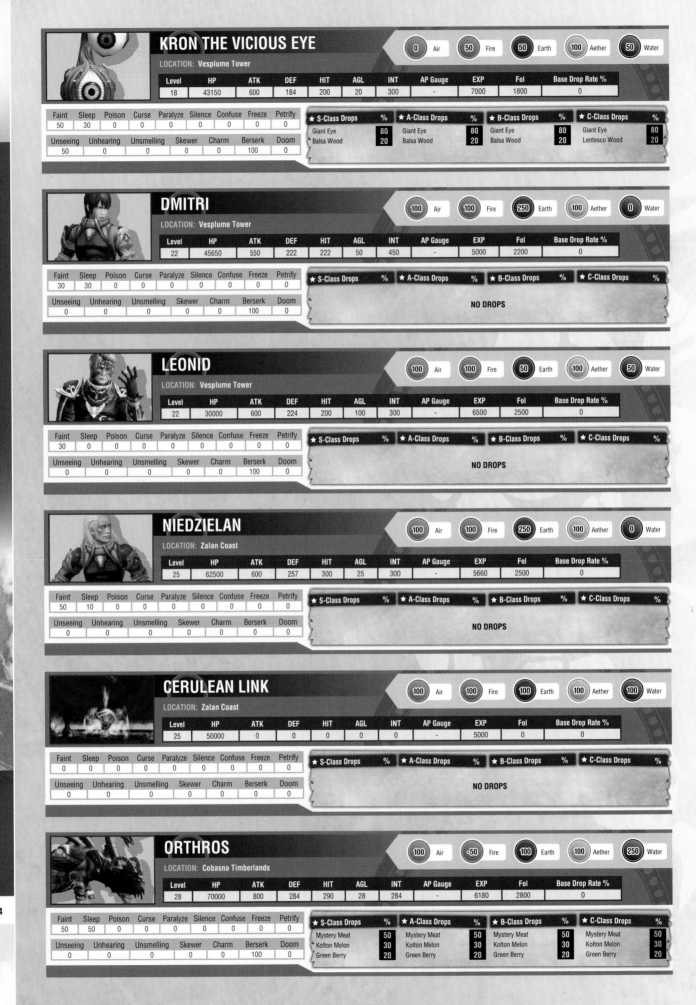

KRON THE VICIOUS EYE

LOCATION: Vesplume Tower

0 Air	50 Fire	50 Earth	100 Aether	50 Water

Level	HP	ATK	DEF	HIT	AGL	INT	AP Gauge	EXP	Fol	Base Drop Rate %
18	43150	600	184	200	20	300	-	7000	1800	0

Faint	Sleep	Poison	Curse	Paralyze	Silence	Confuse	Freeze	Petrify
50	30	0	0	0	0	0	0	0

Unseeing	Unhearing	Unsmelling	Skewer	Charm	Berserk	Doom
50	0	0	0	0	100	0

★ S-Class Drops	%	★ A-Class Drops	%	★ B-Class Drops	%	★ C-Class Drops	%
Giant Eye	80	Giant Eye	80	Giant Eye	80	Giant Eye	80
Balsa Wood	20	Balsa Wood	20	Balsa Wood	20	Lentesco Wood	20

DMITRI

LOCATION: Vesplume Tower

100 Air	100 Fire	250 Earth	100 Aether	0 Water

Level	HP	ATK	DEF	HIT	AGL	INT	AP Gauge	EXP	Fol	Base Drop Rate %
22	45650	550	222	222	50	450	-	5000	2200	0

Faint	Sleep	Poison	Curse	Paralyze	Silence	Confuse	Freeze	Petrify
30	30	0	0	0	0	0	0	0

Unseeing	Unhearing	Unsmelling	Skewer	Charm	Berserk	Doom
0	0	0	0	0	100	0

★ S-Class Drops	%	★ A-Class Drops	%	★ B-Class Drops	%	★ C-Class Drops	%
			NO DROPS				

LEONID

LOCATION: Vesplume Tower

100 Air	100 Fire	50 Earth	100 Aether	50 Water

Level	HP	ATK	DEF	HIT	AGL	INT	AP Gauge	EXP	Fol	Base Drop Rate %
22	30000	600	224	200	100	300	-	6500	2500	0

Faint	Sleep	Poison	Curse	Paralyze	Silence	Confuse	Freeze	Petrify
30	0	0	0	0	0	0	0	0

Unseeing	Unhearing	Unsmelling	Skewer	Charm	Berserk	Doom
0	0	0	0	0	100	0

★ S-Class Drops	%	★ A-Class Drops	%	★ B-Class Drops	%	★ C-Class Drops	%
			NO DROPS				

NIEDZIELAN

LOCATION: Zalan Coast

100 Air	100 Fire	250 Earth	100 Aether	0 Water

Level	HP	ATK	DEF	HIT	AGL	INT	AP Gauge	EXP	Fol	Base Drop Rate %
25	62500	600	257	300	25	300	-	5660	2500	0

Faint	Sleep	Poison	Curse	Paralyze	Silence	Confuse	Freeze	Petrify
50	10	0	0	0	0	0	0	0

Unseeing	Unhearing	Unsmelling	Skewer	Charm	Berserk	Doom
0	0	0	0	0	0	0

★ S-Class Drops	%	★ A-Class Drops	%	★ B-Class Drops	%	★ C-Class Drops	%
			NO DROPS				

CERULEAN LINK

LOCATION: Zalan Coast

100 Air	100 Fire	100 Earth	100 Aether	100 Water

Level	HP	ATK	DEF	HIT	AGL	INT	AP Gauge	EXP	Fol	Base Drop Rate %
25	50000	0	0	0	0	0	-	5000	0	0

Faint	Sleep	Poison	Curse	Paralyze	Silence	Confuse	Freeze	Petrify
0	0	0	0	0	0	0	0	0

Unseeing	Unhearing	Unsmelling	Skewer	Charm	Berserk	Doom
0	0	0	0	0	0	0

★ S-Class Drops	%	★ A-Class Drops	%	★ B-Class Drops	%	★ C-Class Drops	%
			NO DROPS				

ORTHROS

LOCATION: Cobasna Timberlands

100 Air	-50 Fire	100 Earth	100 Aether	250 Water

Level	HP	ATK	DEF	HIT	AGL	INT	AP Gauge	EXP	Fol	Base Drop Rate %
28	70000	800	284	290	28	284	-	6180	2800	0

Faint	Sleep	Poison	Curse	Paralyze	Silence	Confuse	Freeze	Petrify
50	50	0	0	0	0	0	0	0

Unseeing	Unhearing	Unsmelling	Skewer	Charm	Berserk	Doom
0	0	0	0	0	100	0

★ S-Class Drops	%	★ A-Class Drops	%	★ B-Class Drops	%	★ C-Class Drops	%
Mystery Meat	50	Mystery Meat	50	Mystery Meat	50	Mystery Meat	50
Kolton Melon	30	Kolton Melon	30	Kolton Melon	30	Kolton Melon	30
Green Berry	20	Green Berry	20	Green Berry	20	Green Berry	20

VERMIFIED EDWARD

LOCATION: Kolton

| 50 Air | 50 Fire | 100 Earth | 100 Aether | 100 Water |

Level	HP	ATK	DEF	HIT	AGL	INT	AP Gauge	EXP	Fol	Base Drop Rate %
30	20000	400	304	90	30	200	5	6530	3000	0

Faint	Sleep	Poison	Curse	Paralyze	Silence	Confuse	Freeze	Petrify
0	0	0	0	0	0	0	0	0

Unseeing	Unhearing	Unsmelling	Skewer	Charm	Berserk	Doom
0	0	0	0	0	0	0

★ S-Class Drops	%	★ A-Class Drops	%	★ B-Class Drops	%	★ C-Class Drops	%
NO DROPS							

QUEEN RACHNUVUS

LOCATION: Dais

| 100 Air | 250 Fire | 100 Earth | 50 Aether | 100 Water |

Level	HP	ATK	DEF	HIT	AGL	INT	AP Gauge	EXP	Fol	Base Drop Rate %
33	76850	900	334	350	9999	340	-	6000	3000	0

Faint	Sleep	Poison	Curse	Paralyze	Silence	Confuse	Freeze	Petrify
50	70	0	0	0	0	0	0	0

Unseeing	Unhearing	Unsmelling	Skewer	Charm	Berserk	Doom
0	0	0	0	0	0	0

★ S-Class Drops	%	★ A-Class Drops	%	★ B-Class Drops	%	★ C-Class Drops	%
Rachnuvus Shell	50	Rachnuvus Shell	50	Rachnuvus Shell	50	Rachnuvus Shell	50
Rachnuvus Cloth	50	Rachnuvus Cloth	50	Rachnuvus Cloth	50	Rachnuvus Cloth	50

HELD

LOCATION: Dais

| 50 Air | 100 Fire | 100 Earth | 250 Aether | 100 Water |

Level	HP	ATK	DEF	HIT	AGL	INT	AP Gauge	EXP	Fol	Base Drop Rate %
33	60000	600	335	333	33	330	-	0	0	0

Faint	Sleep	Poison	Curse	Paralyze	Silence	Confuse	Freeze	Petrify
30	30	0	0	0	0	0	0	0

Unseeing	Unhearing	Unsmelling	Skewer	Charm	Berserk	Doom
0	0	0	0	0	0	0

★ S-Class Drops	%	★ A-Class Drops	%	★ B-Class Drops	%	★ C-Class Drops	%
NO DROPS							

FAESPHERE (HELD)

LOCATION: Dais

| 100 Air | 100 Fire | 100 Earth | 100 Aether | 100 Water |

Level	HP	ATK	DEF	HIT	AGL	INT	AP Gauge	EXP	Fol	Base Drop Rate %
33	4000	0	300	0	0	290	1	0	0	0

Faint	Sleep	Poison	Curse	Paralyze	Silence	Confuse	Freeze	Petrify
0	0	0	0	0	0	0	0	0

Unseeing	Unhearing	Unsmelling	Skewer	Charm	Berserk	Doom
0	0	0	100	0	0	0

★ S-Class Drops	%	★ A-Class Drops	%	★ B-Class Drops	%	★ C-Class Drops	%
NO DROPS							

VERMIFIED HELD

LOCATION: Dais

| 0 Air | 100 Fire | 100 Earth | 250 Aether | 100 Water |

Level	HP	ATK	DEF	HIT	AGL	INT	AP Gauge	EXP	Fol	Base Drop Rate %
33	60000	300	230	333	33	380	-	7500	3600	0

Faint	Sleep	Poison	Curse	Paralyze	Silence	Confuse	Freeze	Petrify
0	0	0	0	0	0	0	0	0

Unseeing	Unhearing	Unsmelling	Skewer	Charm	Berserk	Doom
0	0	0	0	0	0	0

★ S-Class Drops	%	★ A-Class Drops	%	★ B-Class Drops	%	★ C-Class Drops	%
NO DROPS							

AMBER LINK

LOCATION: Dais

| 100 Air | 100 Fire | 100 Earth | 100 Aether | 100 Water |

Level	HP	ATK	DEF	HIT	AGL	INT	AP Gauge	EXP	Fol	Base Drop Rate %
33	105000	0	0	0	0	0	-	7000	0	0

Faint	Sleep	Poison	Curse	Paralyze	Silence	Confuse	Freeze	Petrify
0	0	0	0	0	0	0	0	0

Unseeing	Unhearing	Unsmelling	Skewer	Charm	Berserk	Doom
0	0	0	0	0	0	0

★ S-Class Drops	%	★ A-Class Drops	%	★ B-Class Drops	%	★ C-Class Drops	%
NO DROPS							

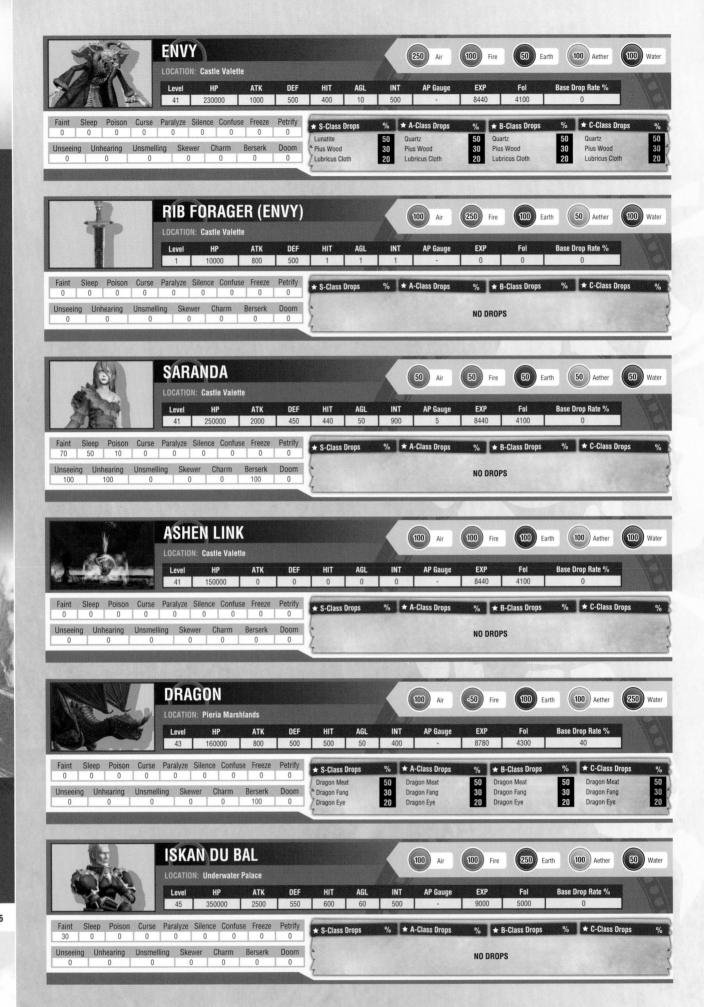

ENVY

LOCATION: Castle Valette

250 Air	100 Fire	50 Earth	100 Aether	100 Water

Level	HP	ATK	DEF	HIT	AGL	INT	AP Gauge	EXP	Fol	Base Drop Rate %
41	230000	1000	500	400	10	500	-	8440	4100	0

Faint	Sleep	Poison	Curse	Paralyze	Silence	Confuse	Freeze	Petrify
0	0	0	0	0	0	0	0	0

Unseeing	Unhearing	Unsmelling	Skewer	Charm	Berserk	Doom
0	0	0	0	0	0	0

★ S-Class Drops	%	★ A-Class Drops	%	★ B-Class Drops	%	★ C-Class Drops	%
Lunatite	50	Quartz	50	Quartz	50	Quartz	50
Pius Wood	30	Pius Wood	30	Pius Wood	30	Pius Wood	30
Lubricus Cloth	20	Lubricus Cloth	20	Lubricus Cloth	20	Lubricus Cloth	20

RIB FORAGER (ENVY)

LOCATION: Castle Valette

100 Air	250 Fire	100 Earth	50 Aether	100 Water

Level	HP	ATK	DEF	HIT	AGL	INT	AP Gauge	EXP	Fol	Base Drop Rate %
1	10000	800	500	1	1	1	-	0	0	0

Faint	Sleep	Poison	Curse	Paralyze	Silence	Confuse	Freeze	Petrify
0	0	0	0	0	0	0	0	0

Unseeing	Unhearing	Unsmelling	Skewer	Charm	Berserk	Doom
0	0	0	0	0	0	0

★ S-Class Drops	%	★ A-Class Drops	%	★ B-Class Drops	%	★ C-Class Drops	%
			NO DROPS				

SARANDA

LOCATION: Castle Valette

50 Air	50 Fire	50 Earth	50 Aether	50 Water

Level	HP	ATK	DEF	HIT	AGL	INT	AP Gauge	EXP	Fol	Base Drop Rate %
41	250000	2000	450	440	50	900	5	8440	4100	0

Faint	Sleep	Poison	Curse	Paralyze	Silence	Confuse	Freeze	Petrify
70	50	10	0	0	0	0	0	0

Unseeing	Unhearing	Unsmelling	Skewer	Charm	Berserk	Doom
100	100	0	0	0	100	0

★ S-Class Drops	%	★ A-Class Drops	%	★ B-Class Drops	%	★ C-Class Drops	%
			NO DROPS				

ASHEN LINK

LOCATION: Castle Valette

100 Air	100 Fire	100 Earth	100 Aether	100 Water

Level	HP	ATK	DEF	HIT	AGL	INT	AP Gauge	EXP	Fol	Base Drop Rate %
41	150000	0	0	0	0	0	-	8440	4100	0

Faint	Sleep	Poison	Curse	Paralyze	Silence	Confuse	Freeze	Petrify
0	0	0	0	0	0	0	0	0

Unseeing	Unhearing	Unsmelling	Skewer	Charm	Berserk	Doom
0	0	0	0	0	0	0

★ S-Class Drops	%	★ A-Class Drops	%	★ B-Class Drops	%	★ C-Class Drops	%
			NO DROPS				

DRAGON

LOCATION: Pieria Marshlands

100 Air	-50 Fire	100 Earth	100 Aether	250 Water

Level	HP	ATK	DEF	HIT	AGL	INT	AP Gauge	EXP	Fol	Base Drop Rate %
43	160000	800	500	500	50	400	-	8780	4300	40

Faint	Sleep	Poison	Curse	Paralyze	Silence	Confuse	Freeze	Petrify
0	0	0	0	0	0	0	0	0

Unseeing	Unhearing	Unsmelling	Skewer	Charm	Berserk	Doom
0	0	0	0	0	100	0

★ S-Class Drops	%	★ A-Class Drops	%	★ B-Class Drops	%	★ C-Class Drops	%
Dragon Meat	50	Dragon Meat	50	Dragon Meat	50	Dragon Meat	50
Dragon Fang	30	Dragon Fang	30	Dragon Fang	30	Dragon Fang	30
Dragon Eye	20	Dragon Eye	20	Dragon Eye	20	Dragon Eye	20

ISKAN DU BAL

LOCATION: Underwater Palace

100 Air	100 Fire	250 Earth	100 Aether	50 Water

Level	HP	ATK	DEF	HIT	AGL	INT	AP Gauge	EXP	Fol	Base Drop Rate %
45	350000	2500	550	600	60	500	-	9000	5000	0

Faint	Sleep	Poison	Curse	Paralyze	Silence	Confuse	Freeze	Petrify
30	0	0	0	0	0	0	0	0

Unseeing	Unhearing	Unsmelling	Skewer	Charm	Berserk	Doom
0	0	0	0	0	0	0

★ S-Class Drops	%	★ A-Class Drops	%	★ B-Class Drops	%	★ C-Class Drops	%
			NO DROPS				

VELD THE EVIL EYE
LOCATION: Underwater Palace

Air 0 | Fire 50 | Earth 50 | Aether 100 | Water 50

Level	HP	ATK	DEF	HIT	AGL	INT	AP Gauge	EXP	Fol	Base Drop Rate %
45	120000	1000	450	465	25	500	-	5000	4000	0

Faint	Sleep	Poison	Curse	Paralyze	Silence	Confuse	Freeze	Petrify
50	30	0	0	0	0	0	0	0

Unseeing	Unhearing	Unsmelling	Skewer	Charm	Berserk	Doom
50	0	0	0	0	100	0

★ S-Class Drops	%	★ A-Class Drops	%	★ B-Class Drops	%	★ C-Class Drops	%
Giant Eye	80	Giant Eye	80	Giant Eye	80	Giant Eye	80
Malus Wood	20	Malus Wood	20	Malus Wood	20	Malus Wood	20

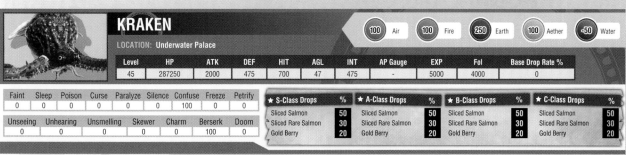

KRAKEN
LOCATION: Underwater Palace

Air 100 | Fire 100 | Earth 250 | Aether 100 | Water -50

Level	HP	ATK	DEF	HIT	AGL	INT	AP Gauge	EXP	Fol	Base Drop Rate %
45	287250	2000	475	700	47	475	-	5000	4000	0

Faint	Sleep	Poison	Curse	Paralyze	Silence	Confuse	Freeze	Petrify
0	0	0	0	0	0	100	0	0

Unseeing	Unhearing	Unsmelling	Skewer	Charm	Berserk	Doom
0	0	0	0	0	100	0

★ S-Class Drops	%	★ A-Class Drops	%	★ B-Class Drops	%	★ C-Class Drops	%
Sliced Salmon	50	Sliced Salmon	50	Sliced Salmon	50	Sliced Salmon	50
Sliced Rare Salmon	30	Sliced Rare Salmon	30	Sliced Rare Salmon	30	Sliced Rare Salmon	30
Gold Berry	20	Gold Berry	20	Gold Berry	20	Gold Berry	20

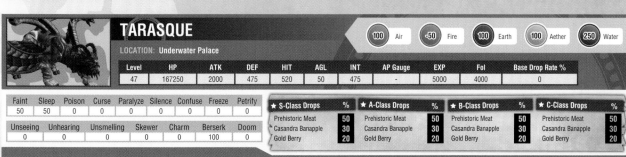

TARASQUE
LOCATION: Underwater Palace

Air 100 | Fire -50 | Earth 100 | Aether 100 | Water 250

Level	HP	ATK	DEF	HIT	AGL	INT	AP Gauge	EXP	Fol	Base Drop Rate %
47	167250	2000	475	520	50	475	-	5000	4000	0

Faint	Sleep	Poison	Curse	Paralyze	Silence	Confuse	Freeze	Petrify
50	50	0	0	0	0	0	0	0

Unseeing	Unhearing	Unsmelling	Skewer	Charm	Berserk	Doom
0	0	0	0	0	100	0

★ S-Class Drops	%	★ A-Class Drops	%	★ B-Class Drops	%	★ C-Class Drops	%
Prehistoric Meat	50	Prehistoric Meat	50	Prehistoric Meat	50	Prehistoric Meat	50
Casandra Banapple	30	Casandra Banapple	30	Casandra Banapple	30	Casandra Banapple	30
Gold Berry	20	Gold Berry	20	Gold Berry	20	Gold Berry	20

KARATHOS
LOCATION: Underwater Palace

Air 100 | Fire 100 | Earth 250 | Aether 100 | Water -50

Level	HP	ATK	DEF	HIT	AGL	INT	AP Gauge	EXP	Fol	Base Drop Rate %
47	250000	3000	500	480	10	475	-	7000	4700	0

Faint	Sleep	Poison	Curse	Paralyze	Silence	Confuse	Freeze	Petrify
0	50	0	0	0	0	0	0	0

Unseeing	Unhearing	Unsmelling	Skewer	Charm	Berserk	Doom
0	0	0	0	0	100	0

NO DROPS

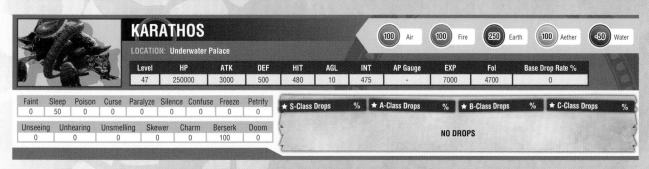

GREED
LOCATION: Underwater Palace

Air 250 | Fire 100 | Earth 50 | Aether 100 | Water 100

Level	HP	ATK	DEF	HIT	AGL	INT	AP Gauge	EXP	Fol	Base Drop Rate %
47	277777	1500	600	500	50	600	-	5000	4000	0

Faint	Sleep	Poison	Curse	Paralyze	Silence	Confuse	Freeze	Petrify
0	0	0	0	0	0	0	0	0

Unseeing	Unhearing	Unsmelling	Skewer	Charm	Berserk	Doom
0	0	0	0	0	0	0

★ S-Class Drops	%	★ A-Class Drops	%	★ B-Class Drops	%	★ C-Class Drops	%
Quartz	50	Quartz	50	Quartz	50	Quartz	50
Malus Wood	30	Malus Wood	30	Malus Wood	30	Malus Wood	30
Empyrean Cloth	20	Empyrean Cloth	20	Empyrean Cloth	20	Empyrean Cloth	20

RIB FORAGER (GREED)
LOCATION: Underwater Palace

Air 100 | Fire 250 | Earth 100 | Aether 50 | Water 100

Level	HP	ATK	DEF	HIT	AGL	INT	AP Gauge	EXP	Fol	Base Drop Rate %
1	18000	1200	600	1	1	1	-	0	0	0

Faint	Sleep	Poison	Curse	Paralyze	Silence	Confuse	Freeze	Petrify
0	0	0	0	0	0	0	0	0

Unseeing	Unhearing	Unsmelling	Skewer	Charm	Berserk	Doom
0	0	0	0	0	0	0

NO DROPS

LEONID

LOCATION: Underwater Palace

100 Air	100 Fire	50 Earth	100 Aether	50 Water	

Level	HP	ATK	DEF	HIT	AGL	INT	AP Gauge	EXP	Fol	Base Drop Rate %
47	300000	2000	600	555	70	520	-	8000	4700	0

Faint	Sleep	Poison	Curse	Paralyze	Silence	Confuse	Freeze	Petrify
30	0	0	0	0	0	0	0	0

Unseeing	Unhearing	Unsmelling	Skewer	Charm	Berserk	Doom
0	0	0	0	0	100	0

★ S-Class Drops	%	★ A-Class Drops	%	★ B-Class Drops	%	★ C-Class Drops	%
			NO DROPS				

LEONID

LOCATION: Lunar Sanctuary

100 Air	100 Fire	50 Earth	100 Aether	50 Water	

Level	HP	ATK	DEF	HIT	AGL	INT	AP Gauge	EXP	Fol	Base Drop Rate %
48	300000	2300	800	600	100	530	-	9650	6000	0

Faint	Sleep	Poison	Curse	Paralyze	Silence	Confuse	Freeze	Petrify
30	0	0	0	0	0	0	0	0

Unseeing	Unhearing	Unsmelling	Skewer	Charm	Berserk	Doom
0	0	0	0	0	100	0

★ S-Class Drops	%	★ A-Class Drops	%	★ B-Class Drops	%	★ C-Class Drops	%
			NO DROPS				

VEROS

LOCATION: Lunar Sanctuary

100 Air	100 Fire	100 Earth	100 Aether	100 Water	

Level	HP	ATK	DEF	HIT	AGL	INT	AP Gauge	EXP	Fol	Base Drop Rate %
50	100000	1500	599	1000	150	500	-	12000	10000	0

Faint	Sleep	Poison	Curse	Paralyze	Silence	Confuse	Freeze	Petrify
0	0	0	0	0	0	0	0	0

Unseeing	Unhearing	Unsmelling	Skewer	Charm	Berserk	Doom
0	0	0	0	0	0	0

★ S-Class Drops	%	★ A-Class Drops	%	★ B-Class Drops	%	★ C-Class Drops	%
			NO DROPS				

NETHERMYRMIDON (VEROS)

LOCATION: Lunar Sanctuary

100 Air	100 Fire	100 Earth	100 Aether	100 Water	

Level	HP	ATK	DEF	HIT	AGL	INT	AP Gauge	EXP	Fol	Base Drop Rate %
48	42000	1000	480	0	0	480	-	0	0	0

Faint	Sleep	Poison	Curse	Paralyze	Silence	Confuse	Freeze	Petrify
0	0	0	0	0	0	0	0	0

Unseeing	Unhearing	Unsmelling	Skewer	Charm	Berserk	Doom
0	0	0	0	0	0	0

★ S-Class Drops	%	★ A-Class Drops	%	★ B-Class Drops	%	★ C-Class Drops	%
			NO DROPS				

SUPERNHELOT (VEROS)

LOCATION: Lunar Sanctuary

100 Air	100 Fire	100 Earth	100 Aether	100 Water	

Level	HP	ATK	DEF	HIT	AGL	INT	AP Gauge	EXP	Fol	Base Drop Rate %
48	68000	1000	480	0	0	480	-	0	0	0

Faint	Sleep	Poison	Curse	Paralyze	Silence	Confuse	Freeze	Petrify
0	0	0	0	0	0	0	0	0

Unseeing	Unhearing	Unsmelling	Skewer	Charm	Berserk	Doom
0	0	0	0	0	0	0

★ S-Class Drops	%	★ A-Class Drops	%	★ B-Class Drops	%	★ C-Class Drops	%
			NO DROPS				

SERAPHIC GATE

ALRAUNE

0 Air	250 Fire	50 Earth	250 Aether	50 Water

LOCATION: Seraphic Gate

Level	HP	ATK	DEF	HIT	AGL	INT	AP Gauge	EXP	Fol	Base Drop Rate %
120	55000	3800	1080	1500	120	980	4	6000	6000	40

Faint	Sleep	Poison	Curse	Paralyze	Silence	Confuse	Freeze	Petrify
100	100	100	0	0	0	100	100	100

Unseeing	Unhearing	Unsmelling	Skewer	Charm	Berserk	Doom
0	0	0	100	0	0	100

★ S-Class Drops	%	★ A-Class Drops	%	★ B-Class Drops	%	★ C-Class Drops	%
Placidus Wood	50	Placidus Wood	50	Vine	50	Vine	20
Malus Wood	50	Malus Wood	30	Barkcloth	30		
		Pius Wood	20	Malus Wood	20		

AVALANCHE HARPY

50 Air	100 Fire	100 Earth	250 Aether	100 Water

LOCATION: Seraphic Gate

Level	HP	ATK	DEF	HIT	AGL	INT	AP Gauge	EXP	Fol	Base Drop Rate %
70	30000	2000	550	1000	40	600	2	2500	2000	40

Faint	Sleep	Poison	Curse	Paralyze	Silence	Confuse	Freeze	Petrify
100	100	100	100	100	100	50	100	100

Unseeing	Unhearing	Unsmelling	Skewer	Charm	Berserk	Doom
100	100	100	100	30	100	100

★ S-Class Drops	%	★ A-Class Drops	%	★ B-Class Drops	%	★ C-Class Drops	%
Down Feather Cloth	50	Fayel Chicken	50	Bird Eye	50	Bird Eye	20
Down Feather Hat	30	Down Feather Cloth	30	Down Feather Cloth	50		
Down Feather Cloak	20	Down Feather Cloak	20				

BLUE DROGO WARRIOR

100 Air	100 Fire	250 Earth	100 Aether	50 Water

LOCATION: Seraphic Gate

Level	HP	ATK	DEF	HIT	AGL	INT	AP Gauge	EXP	Fol	Base Drop Rate %
60	17000	1200	600	600	65	608	50	2300	1840	40

Faint	Sleep	Poison	Curse	Paralyze	Silence	Confuse	Freeze	Petrify
100	100	50	100	100	100	0	30	100

Unseeing	Unhearing	Unsmelling	Skewer	Charm	Berserk	Doom
100	100	100	100	0	100	100

★ S-Class Drops	%	★ A-Class Drops	%	★ B-Class Drops	%	★ C-Class Drops	%
Crescent Blade	80	Crescent Blade	80	Lizard Skin	50	Lizard Skin	20
Braveheart	20	Braveheart	20	Lizard Wristband	30		
				Crescent Blade	20		

BURNING LANTERN

100 Air	250 Fire	100 Earth	50 Aether	100 Water

LOCATION: Seraphic Gate

Level	HP	ATK	DEF	HIT	AGL	INT	AP Gauge	EXP	Fol	Base Drop Rate %
115	10000	500	500	1150	50	1300	1	1000	10	40

Faint	Sleep	Poison	Curse	Paralyze	Silence	Confuse	Freeze	Petrify
0	100	0	0	0	0	0	100	100

Unseeing	Unhearing	Unsmelling	Skewer	Charm	Berserk	Doom
0	0	0	100	0	0	0

★ S-Class Drops	%	★ A-Class Drops	%	★ B-Class Drops	%	★ C-Class Drops	%
Horizon Crystal	50	Horizon Crystal	80	Sunstone	80	Sunstone	20
Blaze Metal	30	Blaze Metal	20	Horizon Crystal	20		
Prismatite Metal	20						

COMBCLAW CENTIPEDE

100 Air	50 Fire	100 Earth	100 Aether	250 Water

LOCATION: Seraphic Gate

Level	HP	ATK	DEF	HIT	AGL	INT	AP Gauge	EXP	Fol	Base Drop Rate %
105	40000	2500	600	1200	50	500	3	3500	2800	0

Faint	Sleep	Poison	Curse	Paralyze	Silence	Confuse	Freeze	Petrify
100	0	100	100	0	100	100	100	100

Unseeing	Unhearing	Unsmelling	Skewer	Charm	Berserk	Doom
100	0	100	100	100	100	100

★ S-Class Drops	%	★ A-Class Drops	%	★ B-Class Drops	%	★ C-Class Drops	%
			NO DROPS				

CRYSTAL GARGOYLE

LOCATION: Seraphic Gate

Element	Value
Air	250
Fire	100
Earth	0
Aether	100
Water	50

Level	HP	ATK	DEF	HIT	AGL	INT	AP Gauge	EXP	Fol	Base Drop Rate %
130	70000	4000	1300	1600	140	1300	4	4500	3500	40

Faint	Sleep	Poison	Curse	Paralyze	Silence	Confuse	Freeze	Petrify
0	0	0	0	0	0	100	100	0

Unseeing	Unhearing	Unsmelling	Skewer	Charm	Berserk	Doom
0	0	0	100	100	100	0

★ S-Class Drops	%	★ A-Class Drops	%	★ B-Class Drops	%	★ C-Class Drops	%
Crystallite Metal	50	Crystallite Metal	50	Stone Statue Fragment	50	Stone Statue Fragment	20
Quartz	30	Quartz	30	Crystallite Metal	30		
Amarlista	20	Amarlista	20	Quartz	20		

DANCING CROSSBOW

LOCATION: Seraphic Gate

Element	Value
Air	50
Fire	100
Earth	100
Aether	250
Water	100

Level	HP	ATK	DEF	HIT	AGL	INT	AP Gauge	EXP	Fol	Base Drop Rate %
130	35000	3500	1000	1500	100	1150	1	2350	1800	40

Faint	Sleep	Poison	Curse	Paralyze	Silence	Confuse	Freeze	Petrify
0	0	0	0	0	0	100	100	100

Unseeing	Unhearing	Unsmelling	Skewer	Charm	Berserk	Doom
0	0	0	100	100	100	0

★ S-Class Drops	%	★ A-Class Drops	%	★ B-Class Drops	%	★ C-Class Drops	%
Sagittarian Bow	80	Mercurius Metal	50	Mercurius Metal	80	Mercurius Metal	20
Royal Bow	20	Sagittarian Bow	50	Sagittarian Bow	20		

DANCING SWORD

LOCATION: Seraphic Gate

Element	Value
Air	100
Fire	250
Earth	100
Aether	50
Water	100

Level	HP	ATK	DEF	HIT	AGL	INT	AP Gauge	EXP	Fol	Base Drop Rate %
115	25000	2800	800	1100	120	200	1	2900	1700	40

Faint	Sleep	Poison	Curse	Paralyze	Silence	Confuse	Freeze	Petrify
0	0	0	0	0	0	100	100	100

Unseeing	Unhearing	Unsmelling	Skewer	Charm	Berserk	Doom
0	0	0	100	100	100	0

★ S-Class Drops	%	★ A-Class Drops	%	★ B-Class Drops	%	★ C-Class Drops	%
Crescent Blade	100	Amarlista	50	Quartz	80	Quartz	20
		Prismatite Blade	30	Amarlista	20		
		Crescent Blade	20				

DUNE HARPY

LOCATION: Seraphic Gate

Element	Value
Air	50
Fire	100
Earth	100
Aether	250
Water	100

Level	HP	ATK	DEF	HIT	AGL	INT	AP Gauge	EXP	Fol	Base Drop Rate %
65	20000	1500	500	650	40	650	2	2400	1920	40

Faint	Sleep	Poison	Curse	Paralyze	Silence	Confuse	Freeze	Petrify
100	100	100	100	100	100	50	100	100

Unseeing	Unhearing	Unsmelling	Skewer	Charm	Berserk	Doom
100	100	100	100	30	100	100

★ S-Class Drops	%	★ A-Class Drops	%	★ B-Class Drops	%	★ C-Class Drops	%
Down Feather Cloth	50	Fayel Chicken	50	Bird Eye	50	Bird Eye	20
Down Feather Hat	30	Down Feather Cloth	30	Down Feather Cloth	50		
Down Feather Cloak	20	Down Feather Cloak	20				

FIRE GIGAS

LOCATION: Seraphic Gate

Element	Value
Air	100
Fire	0
Earth	100
Aether	100
Water	250

Level	HP	ATK	DEF	HIT	AGL	INT	AP Gauge	EXP	Fol	Base Drop Rate %
65	35000	2000	600	500	25	400	7	3000	2400	40

Faint	Sleep	Poison	Curse	Paralyze	Silence	Confuse	Freeze	Petrify
30	100	100	100	100	100	100	100	100

Unseeing	Unhearing	Unsmelling	Skewer	Charm	Berserk	Doom
100	100	100	100	100	100	100

★ S-Class Drops	%	★ A-Class Drops	%	★ B-Class Drops	%	★ C-Class Drops	%
Bardiche	50	Blaze Metal	50	Blaze Metal	80	Blaze Metal	20
Ogre's Hammer	30	Blaze Tiara	30	Crystallite Metal	20		
Atlantis Metal	20	Atlantis Metal	20				

FOREST RACHNUVUS

LOCATION: Seraphic Gate

Element	Value
Air	100
Fire	250
Earth	100
Aether	50
Water	100

Level	HP	ATK	DEF	HIT	AGL	INT	AP Gauge	EXP	Fol	Base Drop Rate %
135	42000	4000	1300	2100	120	1000	4	4300	3400	40

Faint	Sleep	Poison	Curse	Paralyze	Silence	Confuse	Freeze	Petrify
100	100	0	100	100	100	100	0	100

Unseeing	Unhearing	Unsmelling	Skewer	Charm	Berserk	Doom
100	0	100	100	100	100	100

★ S-Class Drops	%	★ A-Class Drops	%	★ B-Class Drops	%	★ C-Class Drops	%
Rachnuvus Shell	50	Rachnuvus Shell	80	Toadstool	50	Toadstool	20
Rachnuvus Cloth	30	Pius Wood	20	Rachnuvus Shell	30		
Pius Wood	20			Pius Wood	20		

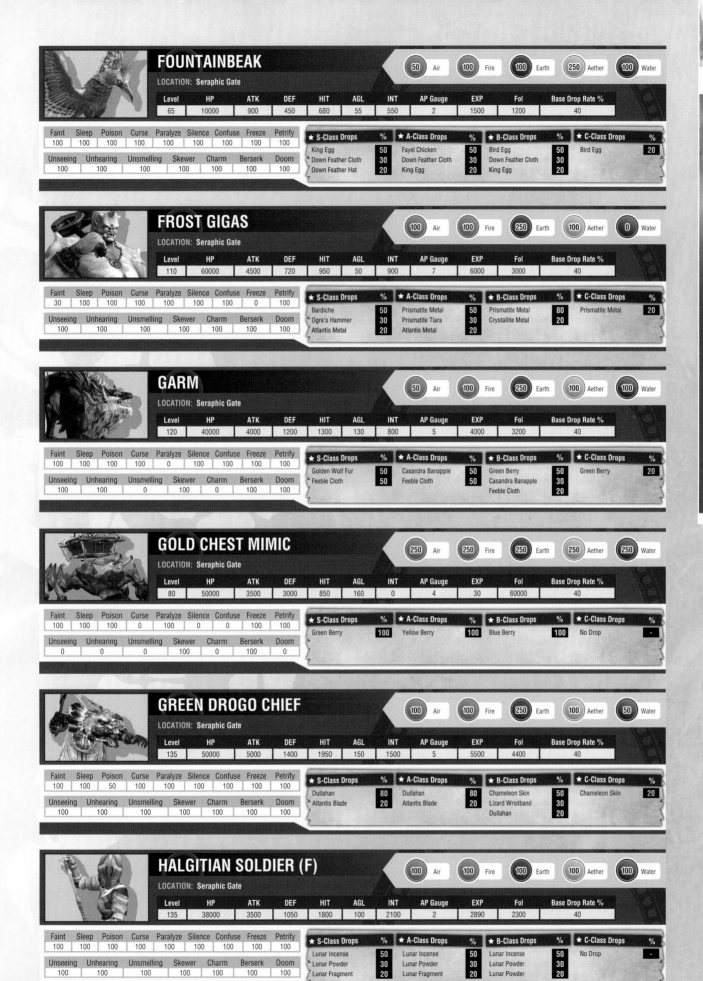

FOUNTAINBEAK

LOCATION: Seraphic Gate

	Air		Fire		Earth		Aether		Water
50		100		100		250		100	

Level	HP	ATK	DEF	HIT	AGL	INT	AP Gauge	EXP	Fol	Base Drop Rate %
65	10000	900	450	680	55	550	2	1500	1200	40

Faint	Sleep	Poison	Curse	Paralyze	Silence	Confuse	Freeze	Petrify
100	100	100	100	100	100	100	100	100

Unseeing	Unhearing	Unsmelling	Skewer	Charm	Berserk	Doom
100	100	100	100	100	100	100

★ S-Class Drops	%	★ A-Class Drops	%	★ B-Class Drops	%	★ C-Class Drops	%
King Egg	50	Fayel Chicken	50	Bird Egg	50	Bird Egg	20
Down Feather Cloth	30	Down Feather Cloth	30	Down Feather Cloth	30		
Down Feather Hat	20	King Egg	20	King Egg	20		

FROST GIGAS

LOCATION: Seraphic Gate

	Air		Fire		Earth		Aether		Water
100		100		250		100		0	

Level	HP	ATK	DEF	HIT	AGL	INT	AP Gauge	EXP	Fol	Base Drop Rate %
110	60000	4500	720	950	50	900	7	6000	3000	40

Faint	Sleep	Poison	Curse	Paralyze	Silence	Confuse	Freeze	Petrify
30	100	100	100	100	100	100	0	100

Unseeing	Unhearing	Unsmelling	Skewer	Charm	Berserk	Doom
100	100	100	100	100	100	100

★ S-Class Drops	%	★ A-Class Drops	%	★ B-Class Drops	%	★ C-Class Drops	%
Bardiche	50	Prismatite Metal	50	Prismatite Metal	80	Prismatite Metal	20
Ogre's Hammer	30	Prismatite Tiara	30	Crystallite Metal	20		
Atlantis Metal	20	Atlantis Metal	20				

GARM

LOCATION: Seraphic Gate

	Air		Fire		Earth		Aether		Water
50		100		250		100		100	

Level	HP	ATK	DEF	HIT	AGL	INT	AP Gauge	EXP	Fol	Base Drop Rate %
120	40000	4000	1200	1300	130	800	5	4000	3200	40

Faint	Sleep	Poison	Curse	Paralyze	Silence	Confuse	Freeze	Petrify
100	100	100	100	0	100	100	100	100

Unseeing	Unhearing	Unsmelling	Skewer	Charm	Berserk	Doom
100	100	0	100	0	100	100

★ S-Class Drops	%	★ A-Class Drops	%	★ B-Class Drops	%	★ C-Class Drops	%
Golden Wolf Fur	50	Casandra Banapple	50	Green Berry	50	Green Berry	20
Feeble Cloth	50	Feeble Cloth	50	Casandra Banapple	30		
				Feeble Cloth	20		

GOLD CHEST MIMIC

LOCATION: Seraphic Gate

	Air		Fire		Earth		Aether		Water
250		250		250		250		250	

Level	HP	ATK	DEF	HIT	AGL	INT	AP Gauge	EXP	Fol	Base Drop Rate %
80	50000	3500	3000	850	160	0	4	30	60000	40

Faint	Sleep	Poison	Curse	Paralyze	Silence	Confuse	Freeze	Petrify
100	100	100	0	100	0	0	100	100

Unseeing	Unhearing	Unsmelling	Skewer	Charm	Berserk	Doom
0	0	0	100	0	100	0

★ S-Class Drops	%	★ A-Class Drops	%	★ B-Class Drops	%	★ C-Class Drops	%
Green Berry	100	Yellow Berry	100	Blue Berry	100	No Drop	-

GREEN DROGO CHIEF

LOCATION: Seraphic Gate

	Air		Fire		Earth		Aether		Water
100		100		250		100		50	

Level	HP	ATK	DEF	HIT	AGL	INT	AP Gauge	EXP	Fol	Base Drop Rate %
135	50000	5000	1400	1950	150	1500	5	5500	4400	40

Faint	Sleep	Poison	Curse	Paralyze	Silence	Confuse	Freeze	Petrify
100	100	50	100	100	100	100	100	100

Unseeing	Unhearing	Unsmelling	Skewer	Charm	Berserk	Doom
100	100	100	100	100	100	100

★ S-Class Drops	%	★ A-Class Drops	%	★ B-Class Drops	%	★ C-Class Drops	%
Dullahan	80	Dullahan	80	Chameleon Skin	50	Chameleon Skin	20
Atlantis Blade	20	Atlantis Blade	20	Lizard Wristband	30		
				Dullahan	20		

HALGITIAN SOLDIER (F)

LOCATION: Seraphic Gate

	Air		Fire		Earth		Aether		Water
100		100		100		100		100	

Level	HP	ATK	DEF	HIT	AGL	INT	AP Gauge	EXP	Fol	Base Drop Rate %
135	38000	3500	1050	1800	100	2100	2	2890	2300	40

Faint	Sleep	Poison	Curse	Paralyze	Silence	Confuse	Freeze	Petrify
100	100	100	100	100	100	100	100	100

Unseeing	Unhearing	Unsmelling	Skewer	Charm	Berserk	Doom
100	100	100	100	100	100	100

★ S-Class Drops	%	★ A-Class Drops	%	★ B-Class Drops	%	★ C-Class Drops	%
Lunar Incense	50	Lunar Incense	50	Lunar Incense	50	No Drop	-
Lunar Powder	30	Lunar Powder	30	Lunar Powder	30		
Lunar Fragment	20	Lunar Fragment	20	Lunar Powder	20		

HALGITIAN SOLDIER (M)

100 Air	100 Fire	100 Earth	100 Aether	100 Water

LOCATION: Seraphic Gate

Level	HP	ATK	DEF	HIT	AGL	INT	AP Gauge	EXP	Fol	Base Drop Rate %
135	40000	4000	1200	1900	140	2000	2	3000	2400	40

Faint	Sleep	Poison	Curse	Paralyze	Silence	Confuse	Freeze	Petrify
100	100	100	100	100	100	100	100	100

Unseeing	Unhearing	Unsmelling	Skewer	Charm	Berserk	Doom
100	100	100	100	100	100	100

★ S-Class Drops	%	★ A-Class Drops	%	★ B-Class Drops	%	★ C-Class Drops	%
Lunar Suppressant	50	Lunar Suppressant	50	Lunar Suppressant	50	No Drop	-
Lunar Suppressant X	30	Lunar Suppressant X	30	Lunar Suppressant X	30		
Lunar Suppressant Z	20	Lunar Suppressant Z	20	Lunar Suppressant X	20		

HILL GIGAS

0 Air	100 Fire	100 Earth	250 Aether	100 Water

LOCATION: Seraphic Gate

Level	HP	ATK	DEF	HIT	AGL	INT	AP Gauge	EXP	Fol	Base Drop Rate %
120	70000	5000	1300	1050	100	1000	7	7000	4000	40

Faint	Sleep	Poison	Curse	Paralyze	Silence	Confuse	Freeze	Petrify
30	100	100	100	100	100	100	100	100

Unseeing	Unhearing	Unsmelling	Skewer	Charm	Berserk	Doom
100	100	100	100	100	100	100

★ S-Class Drops	%	★ A-Class Drops	%	★ B-Class Drops	%	★ C-Class Drops	%
Bardiche	50	Pius Wood	50	Pius Wood	80	Pius Wood	20
Ogre's Hammer	30	Pius Tiara	30	Crystallite Metal	20		
Atlantis Metal	20	Atlantis Metal	20				

INFERNO GLUTTON

100 Air	100 Fire	250 Earth	100 Aether	50 Water

LOCATION: Seraphic Gate

Level	HP	ATK	DEF	HIT	AGL	INT	AP Gauge	EXP	Fol	Base Drop Rate %
125	60000	5000	1500	1150	100	1050	6	5000	4800	40

Faint	Sleep	Poison	Curse	Paralyze	Silence	Confuse	Freeze	Petrify
100	100	100	100	0	100	100	100	0

Unseeing	Unhearing	Unsmelling	Skewer	Charm	Berserk	Doom
0	100	100	100	100	100	100

★ S-Class Drops	%	★ A-Class Drops	%	★ B-Class Drops	%	★ C-Class Drops	%
Dragon Meat	80	Giant Eye	80	Odious Eye	50	Odious Eye	20
Solid Leather Jacket	20	Dragon Meat	20	Giant Eye	30		
				Glutton Hide	20		

LARVA

100 Air	100 Fire	100 Earth	100 Aether	100 Water

LOCATION: Seraphic Gate

Level	HP	ATK	DEF	HIT	AGL	INT	AP Gauge	EXP	Fol	Base Drop Rate %
60	7000	1000	100	350	30	135	1	500	400	40

Faint	Sleep	Poison	Curse	Paralyze	Silence	Confuse	Freeze	Petrify
100	100	100	100	0	100	100	100	100

Unseeing	Unhearing	Unsmelling	Skewer	Charm	Berserk	Doom
100	0	100	100	100	100	100

★ S-Class Drops	%	★ A-Class Drops	%	★ B-Class Drops	%	★ C-Class Drops	%
Rachnuvus Shell	50	Rachnuvus Shell	80	Toadstool	50	Toadstool	20
Rachnuvus Cloth	30	Pius Wood	20	Rachnuvus Shell	30		
Pius Wood	20			Pius Wood	20		

LARVA

100 Air	100 Fire	100 Earth	100 Aether	100 Water

LOCATION: Seraphic Gate

Level	HP	ATK	DEF	HIT	AGL	INT	AP Gauge	EXP	Fol	Base Drop Rate %
120	20000	2800	650	1350	80	650	1	100	2	40

Faint	Sleep	Poison	Curse	Paralyze	Silence	Confuse	Freeze	Petrify
100	100	100	100	0	100	100	100	100

Unseeing	Unhearing	Unsmelling	Skewer	Charm	Berserk	Doom
100	0	100	100	100	100	100

★ S-Class Drops	%	★ A-Class Drops	%	★ B-Class Drops	%	★ C-Class Drops	%
Rachnuvus Shell	50	Rachnuvus Shell	80	Toadstool	50	Toadstool	20
Rachnuvus Cloth	30	Pius Wood	20	Rachnuvus Shell	30		
Pius Wood	20			Pius Wood	20		

LAVA GLUTTON

100 Air	100 Fire	250 Earth	100 Aether	50 Water

LOCATION: Seraphic Gate

Level	HP	ATK	DEF	HIT	AGL	INT	AP Gauge	EXP	Fol	Base Drop Rate %
95	35000	2500	600	700	85	320	6	3500	2100	40

Faint	Sleep	Poison	Curse	Paralyze	Silence	Confuse	Freeze	Petrify
100	100	100	100	0	100	100	100	0

Unseeing	Unhearing	Unsmelling	Skewer	Charm	Berserk	Doom
0	100	100	100	100	100	100

★ S-Class Drops	%	★ A-Class Drops	%	★ B-Class Drops	%	★ C-Class Drops	%
Dragon Eye	50	Dragon Eye	80	Dragon Eye	50	Giant Eye	20
Solid Leather Jacket	50	Solid Leather Jacket	20	Giant Eye	30		
				Glutton Wristband	20		

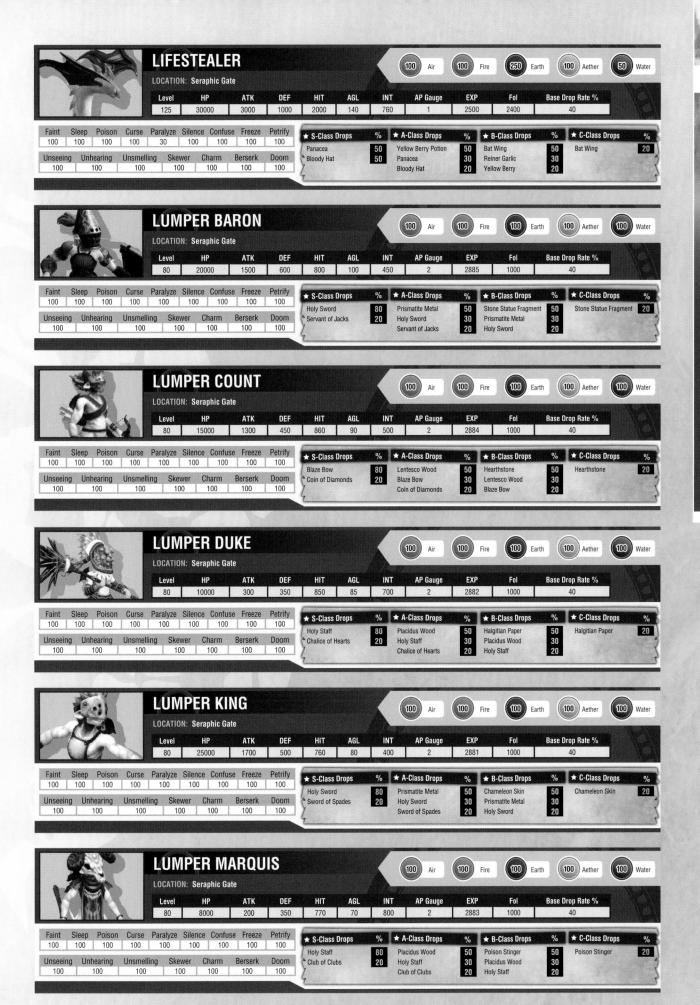

LIFESTEALER

LOCATION: Seraphic Gate

100 Air	100 Fire	250 Earth	100 Aether	50 Water

Level	HP	ATK	DEF	HIT	AGL	INT	AP Gauge	EXP	Fol	Base Drop Rate %
125	30000	3000	1000	2000	140	760	1	2500	2400	40

Faint	Sleep	Poison	Curse	Paralyze	Silence	Confuse	Freeze	Petrify
100	100	100	100	30	100	100	100	100

Unseeing	Unhearing	Unsmelling	Skewer	Charm	Berserk	Doom
100	100	100	100	100	100	100

★ S-Class Drops	%	★ A-Class Drops	%	★ B-Class Drops	%	★ C-Class Drops	%
Panacea	50	Yellow Berry Potion	50	Bat Wing	50	Bat Wing	20
Bloody Hat	50	Panacea	30	Reiner Garlic	30		
		Bloody Hat	20	Yellow Berry	20		

LUMPER BARON

LOCATION: Seraphic Gate

100 Air	100 Fire	100 Earth	100 Aether	100 Water

Level	HP	ATK	DEF	HIT	AGL	INT	AP Gauge	EXP	Fol	Base Drop Rate %
80	20000	1500	600	800	100	450	2	2885	1000	40

Faint	Sleep	Poison	Curse	Paralyze	Silence	Confuse	Freeze	Petrify
100	100	100	100	100	100	100	100	100

Unseeing	Unhearing	Unsmelling	Skewer	Charm	Berserk	Doom
100	100	100	100	100	100	100

★ S-Class Drops	%	★ A-Class Drops	%	★ B-Class Drops	%	★ C-Class Drops	%
Holy Sword	80	Prismatite Metal	50	Stone Statue Fragment	50	Stone Statue Fragment	20
Servant of Jacks	20	Holy Sword	30	Prismatite Metal	30		
		Servant of Jacks	20	Holy Sword	20		

LUMPER COUNT

LOCATION: Seraphic Gate

100 Air	100 Fire	100 Earth	100 Aether	100 Water

Level	HP	ATK	DEF	HIT	AGL	INT	AP Gauge	EXP	Fol	Base Drop Rate %
80	15000	1300	450	860	90	500	2	2884	1000	40

Faint	Sleep	Poison	Curse	Paralyze	Silence	Confuse	Freeze	Petrify
100	100	100	100	100	100	100	100	100

Unseeing	Unhearing	Unsmelling	Skewer	Charm	Berserk	Doom
100	100	100	100	100	100	100

★ S-Class Drops	%	★ A-Class Drops	%	★ B-Class Drops	%	★ C-Class Drops	%
Blaze Bow	80	Lentesco Wood	50	Hearthstone	50	Hearthstone	20
Coin of Diamonds	20	Blaze Bow	30	Lentesco Wood	30		
		Coin of Diamonds	20	Blaze Bow	20		

LUMPER DUKE

LOCATION: Seraphic Gate

100 Air	100 Fire	100 Earth	100 Aether	100 Water

Level	HP	ATK	DEF	HIT	AGL	INT	AP Gauge	EXP	Fol	Base Drop Rate %
80	10000	300	350	850	85	700	2	2882	1000	40

Faint	Sleep	Poison	Curse	Paralyze	Silence	Confuse	Freeze	Petrify
100	100	100	100	100	100	100	100	100

Unseeing	Unhearing	Unsmelling	Skewer	Charm	Berserk	Doom
100	100	100	100	100	100	100

★ S-Class Drops	%	★ A-Class Drops	%	★ B-Class Drops	%	★ C-Class Drops	%
Holy Staff	80	Placidus Wood	50	Halgitian Paper	50	Halgitian Paper	20
Chalice of Hearts	20	Holy Staff	30	Placidus Wood	30		
		Chalice of Hearts	20	Holy Staff	20		

LUMPER KING

LOCATION: Seraphic Gate

100 Air	100 Fire	100 Earth	100 Aether	100 Water

Level	HP	ATK	DEF	HIT	AGL	INT	AP Gauge	EXP	Fol	Base Drop Rate %
80	25000	1700	500	760	80	400	2	2881	1000	40

Faint	Sleep	Poison	Curse	Paralyze	Silence	Confuse	Freeze	Petrify
100	100	100	100	100	100	100	100	100

Unseeing	Unhearing	Unsmelling	Skewer	Charm	Berserk	Doom
100	100	100	100	100	100	100

★ S-Class Drops	%	★ A-Class Drops	%	★ B-Class Drops	%	★ C-Class Drops	%
Holy Sword	80	Prismatite Metal	50	Chameleon Skin	50	Chameleon Skin	20
Sword of Spades	20	Holy Sword	30	Prismatite Metal	30		
		Sword of Spades	20	Holy Sword	20		

LUMPER MARQUIS

LOCATION: Seraphic Gate

100 Air	100 Fire	100 Earth	100 Aether	100 Water

Level	HP	ATK	DEF	HIT	AGL	INT	AP Gauge	EXP	Fol	Base Drop Rate %
80	8000	200	350	770	70	800	2	2883	1000	40

Faint	Sleep	Poison	Curse	Paralyze	Silence	Confuse	Freeze	Petrify
100	100	100	100	100	100	100	100	100

Unseeing	Unhearing	Unsmelling	Skewer	Charm	Berserk	Doom
100	100	100	100	100	100	100

★ S-Class Drops	%	★ A-Class Drops	%	★ B-Class Drops	%	★ C-Class Drops	%
Holy Staff	80	Placidus Wood	50	Poison Stinger	50	Poison Stinger	20
Club of Clubs	20	Holy Staff	30	Placidus Wood	30		
		Club of Clubs	20	Holy Staff	20		

MANDRAGORA

Air	Fire	Earth	Aether	Water
0	250	50	250	50

LOCATION: Seraphic Gate

Level	HP	ATK	DEF	HIT	AGL	INT	AP Gauge	EXP	Fol	Base Drop Rate %
95	25000	2000	430	1000	150	800	4	3200	2560	40

Faint	Sleep	Poison	Curse	Paralyze	Silence	Confuse	Freeze	Petrify
100	100	100	0	0	100	100	100	100

Unseeing	Unhearing	Unsmelling	Skewer	Charm	Berserk	Doom
0	0	0	100	0	0	100

★ S-Class Drops	%	★ A-Class Drops	%	★ B-Class Drops	%	★ C-Class Drops	%
Malus Wood	50	Malus Wood	50	Laurel	80	Laurel	20
Pius Wood	50	Pius Wood	50	Pius Wood	20		

MANTIFISH

Air	Fire	Earth	Aether	Water
100	100	250	100	-50

LOCATION: Seraphic Gate

Level	HP	ATK	DEF	HIT	AGL	INT	AP Gauge	EXP	Fol	Base Drop Rate %
85	9000	1000	350	880	80	600	1	1800	1440	40

Faint	Sleep	Poison	Curse	Paralyze	Silence	Confuse	Freeze	Petrify
100	100	100	100	100	100	100	100	100

Unseeing	Unhearing	Unsmelling	Skewer	Charm	Berserk	Doom
100	100	100	100	100	100	100

★ S-Class Drops	%	★ A-Class Drops	%	★ B-Class Drops	%	★ C-Class Drops	%
Sliced Rare Salmon	50	Sliced Rare Salmon	80	Sliced Salmon	50	Sliced Salmon	20
Ring of Heart	50	Ring of Heart	20	Sliced Rare Salmon	50		

NARBEAR

Air	Fire	Earth	Aether	Water
100	0	100	100	250

LOCATION: Seraphic Gate

Level	HP	ATK	DEF	HIT	AGL	INT	AP Gauge	EXP	Fol	Base Drop Rate %
135	60000	7500	1500	1800	135	1300	7	6000	4800	40

Faint	Sleep	Poison	Curse	Paralyze	Silence	Confuse	Freeze	Petrify
100	100	100	100	100	100	100	100	100

Unseeing	Unhearing	Unsmelling	Skewer	Charm	Berserk	Doom
100	100	100	100	100	100	100

★ S-Class Drops	%	★ A-Class Drops	%	★ B-Class Drops	%	★ C-Class Drops	%
Bear Paw	80	Royal Jelly	80	Honey	80	Honey	20
Salmon Killers	20	Bear Paw	20	Bear Paw	20		

ORDER ADEPT

Air	Fire	Earth	Aether	Water
100	100	100	100	100

LOCATION: Seraphic Gate

Level	HP	ATK	DEF	HIT	AGL	INT	AP Gauge	EXP	Fol	Base Drop Rate %
110	38000	2500	450	1100	40	1500	2	3700	3690	40

Faint	Sleep	Poison	Curse	Paralyze	Silence	Confuse	Freeze	Petrify
100	100	100	100	100	100	100	100	100

Unseeing	Unhearing	Unsmelling	Skewer	Charm	Berserk	Doom
100	100	100	100	100	100	100

★ S-Class Drops	%	★ A-Class Drops	%	★ B-Class Drops	%	★ C-Class Drops	%
"End of Ages"	50	Green Berry Potion	50	Silver Berry	80	Silver Berry	20
"The Book of Judgment"	50	Silver Berry Potion	30	Silver Berry Potion	20		
		"The Book of Judgment"	20				

ORDER BOMBER

Air	Fire	Earth	Aether	Water
100	100	100	100	100

LOCATION: Seraphic Gate

Level	HP	ATK	DEF	HIT	AGL	INT	AP Gauge	EXP	Fol	Base Drop Rate %
85	20000	1500	480	860	80	800	2	2800	2240	40

Faint	Sleep	Poison	Curse	Paralyze	Silence	Confuse	Freeze	Petrify
100	100	100	100	100	100	100	100	100

Unseeing	Unhearing	Unsmelling	Skewer	Charm	Berserk	Doom
100	100	100	100	100	100	100

★ S-Class Drops	%	★ A-Class Drops	%	★ B-Class Drops	%	★ C-Class Drops	%
Pius Wood	50	Green Berry Potion	50	Green Berry	50	Green Berry	20
Commander Bow	30	White Berry Potion	30	Green Berry Potion	30		
Sagittarian Bow	20	Pius Wood	20	Pius Wood	20		

ORDER EXPERT

Air	Fire	Earth	Aether	Water
100	100	100	100	100

LOCATION: Seraphic Gate

Level	HP	ATK	DEF	HIT	AGL	INT	AP Gauge	EXP	Fol	Base Drop Rate %
110	33000	3000	1000	1050	110	1000	2	4000	3200	40

Faint	Sleep	Poison	Curse	Paralyze	Silence	Confuse	Freeze	Petrify
100	100	100	100	100	100	100	100	100

Unseeing	Unhearing	Unsmelling	Skewer	Charm	Berserk	Doom
100	100	100	100	100	100	100

★ S-Class Drops	%	★ A-Class Drops	%	★ B-Class Drops	%	★ C-Class Drops	%
Braveheart	80	Amarlista	80	Crystallite Metal	30	Crystallite Metal	20
Dullahan	20	Braveheart	20	Amarlista	20		

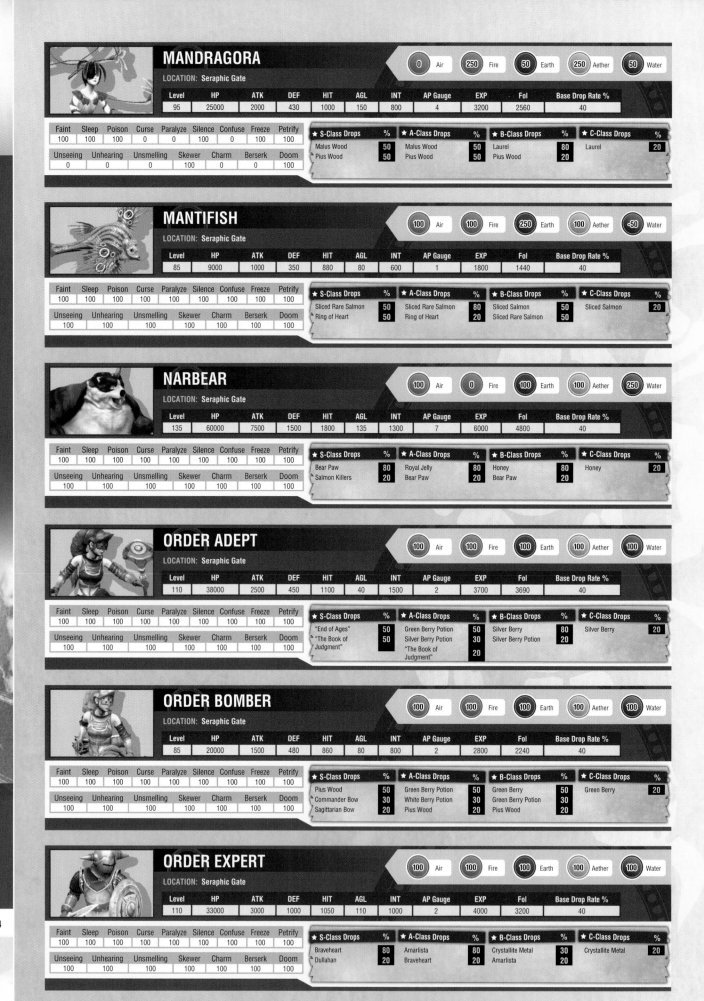

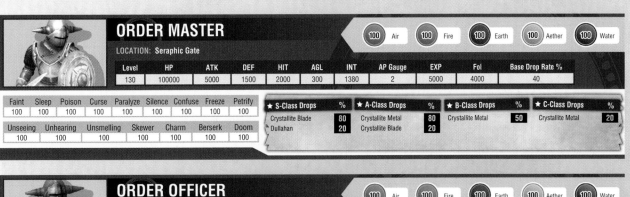

ORDER MASTER
LOCATION: Seraphic Gate

	Air	Fire	Earth	Aether	Water
	100	100	100	100	100

Level	HP	ATK	DEF	HIT	AGL	INT	AP Gauge	EXP	Fol	Base Drop Rate %
130	100000	5000	1500	2000	300	1380	2	5000	4000	40

Faint	Sleep	Poison	Curse	Paralyze	Silence	Confuse	Freeze	Petrify
100	100	100	100	100	100	100	100	100

Unseeing	Unhearing	Unsmelling	Skewer	Charm	Berserk	Doom
100	100	100	100	100	100	100

★ S-Class Drops	%	★ A-Class Drops	%	★ B-Class Drops	%	★ C-Class Drops	%
Crystallite Blade	80	Crystallite Metal	80	Crystallite Metal	50	Crystallite Metal	20
Dullahan	20	Crystallite Blade	20				

ORDER OFFICER
LOCATION: Seraphic Gate

	Air	Fire	Earth	Aether	Water
	100	100	100	100	100

Level	HP	ATK	DEF	HIT	AGL	INT	AP Gauge	EXP	Fol	Base Drop Rate %
85	22000	1500	500	800	70	620	2	2900	2320	40

Faint	Sleep	Poison	Curse	Paralyze	Silence	Confuse	Freeze	Petrify
100	100	100	100	100	100	100	100	100

Unseeing	Unhearing	Unsmelling	Skewer	Charm	Berserk	Doom
100	100	100	100	100	100	100

★ S-Class Drops	%	★ A-Class Drops	%	★ B-Class Drops	%	★ C-Class Drops	%
Malus Wood	50	Malus Wood	80	Blue Berry Potion	50	Blue Berry Potion	20
Ancient Staff	50	Ancient Staff	20	Yellow Berry Potion	30		
				Malus Wood	20		

ORDER RANGER
LOCATION: Seraphic Gate

	Air	Fire	Earth	Aether	Water
	100	100	100	100	100

Level	HP	ATK	DEF	HIT	AGL	INT	AP Gauge	EXP	Fol	Base Drop Rate %
110	30000	2500	650	1150	80	1100	2	3000	2650	40

Faint	Sleep	Poison	Curse	Paralyze	Silence	Confuse	Freeze	Petrify
100	100	100	100	100	100	100	100	100

Unseeing	Unhearing	Unsmelling	Skewer	Charm	Berserk	Doom
100	100	100	100	100	100	100

★ S-Class Drops	%	★ A-Class Drops	%	★ B-Class Drops	%	★ C-Class Drops	%
Pius Wood	50	Green Berry Potion	50	Green Berry	50	Green Berry	20
Commander Bow	30	White Berry Potion	30	Green Berry Potion	30		
Sagittarian Bow	20	Pius Wood	20	Pius Wood	20		

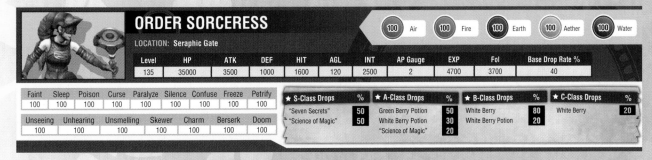

ORDER SORCERESS
LOCATION: Seraphic Gate

	Air	Fire	Earth	Aether	Water
	100	100	100	100	100

Level	HP	ATK	DEF	HIT	AGL	INT	AP Gauge	EXP	Fol	Base Drop Rate %
135	35000	3500	1000	1600	120	2500	2	4700	3700	40

Faint	Sleep	Poison	Curse	Paralyze	Silence	Confuse	Freeze	Petrify
100	100	100	100	100	100	100	100	100

Unseeing	Unhearing	Unsmelling	Skewer	Charm	Berserk	Doom
100	100	100	100	100	100	100

★ S-Class Drops	%	★ A-Class Drops	%	★ B-Class Drops	%	★ C-Class Drops	%
"Seven Secrets"	50	Green Berry Potion	50	White Berry	80	White Berry	20
"Science of Magic"	50	White Berry Potion	30	White Berry Potion	20		
		"Science of Magic"	20				

PEBBLESHELL CRAB
LOCATION: Seraphic Gate

	Air	Fire	Earth	Aether	Water
	100	100	250	100	0

Level	HP	ATK	DEF	HIT	AGL	INT	AP Gauge	EXP	Fol	Base Drop Rate %
105	35000	2300	850	1000	120	780	4	3000	2400	40

Faint	Sleep	Poison	Curse	Paralyze	Silence	Confuse	Freeze	Petrify
100	100	100	100	100	100	100	30	100

Unseeing	Unhearing	Unsmelling	Skewer	Charm	Berserk	Doom
100	100	100	100	100	100	100

★ S-Class Drops	%	★ A-Class Drops	%	★ B-Class Drops	%	★ C-Class Drops	%
Crab Shell	50	Crab Claw	50	Crab Claw	50	Crab Claw	20
Crab Meat	50	Crab Shell	30	Crab Shell	50		
		Crab Meat	20				

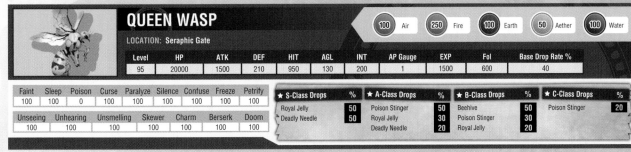

QUEEN WASP
LOCATION: Seraphic Gate

	Air	Fire	Earth	Aether	Water
	100	250	100	50	100

Level	HP	ATK	DEF	HIT	AGL	INT	AP Gauge	EXP	Fol	Base Drop Rate %
95	20000	1500	210	950	130	200	1	1500	600	40

Faint	Sleep	Poison	Curse	Paralyze	Silence	Confuse	Freeze	Petrify
100	100	0	100	100	100	100	100	100

Unseeing	Unhearing	Unsmelling	Skewer	Charm	Berserk	Doom
100	100	100	100	100	100	100

★ S-Class Drops	%	★ A-Class Drops	%	★ B-Class Drops	%	★ C-Class Drops	%
Royal Jelly	50	Poison Stinger	50	Beehive	50	Poison Stinger	20
Deadly Needle	50	Royal Jelly	30	Poison Stinger	30		
		Deadly Needle	20	Royal Jelly	20		

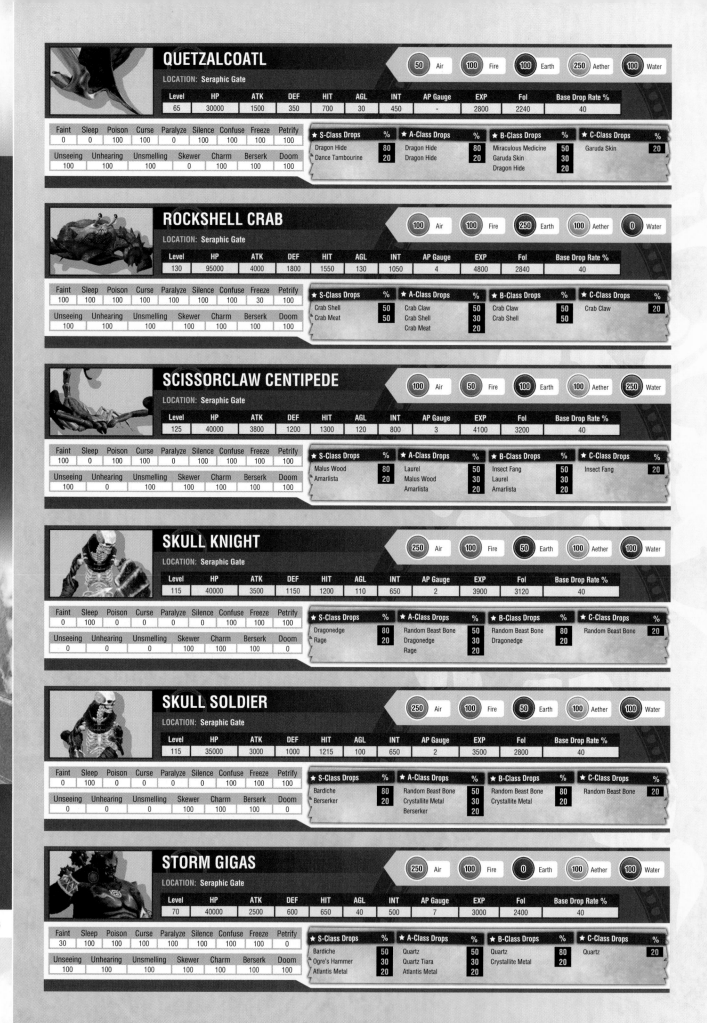

QUETZALCOATL

Air	50
Fire	100
Earth	100
Aether	250
Water	100

LOCATION: Seraphic Gate

Level	HP	ATK	DEF	HIT	AGL	INT	AP Gauge	EXP	Fol	Base Drop Rate %
65	30000	1500	350	700	30	450	-	2800	2240	40

Faint	Sleep	Poison	Curse	Paralyze	Silence	Confuse	Freeze	Petrify
0	0	100	100	0	100	100	100	100

Unseeing	Unhearing	Unsmelling	Skewer	Charm	Berserk	Doom
100	100	100	100	100	100	100

★ S-Class Drops	%	★ A-Class Drops	%	★ B-Class Drops	%	★ C-Class Drops	%
Dragon Hide	80	Dragon Hide	80	Miraculous Medicine	50	Garuda Skin	20
Dance Tambourine	20	Dragon Hide	20	Garuda Skin	30		
				Dragon Hide	20		

ROCKSHELL CRAB

Air	100
Fire	100
Earth	250
Aether	100
Water	0

LOCATION: Seraphic Gate

Level	HP	ATK	DEF	HIT	AGL	INT	AP Gauge	EXP	Fol	Base Drop Rate %
130	95000	4000	1800	1550	130	1050	4	4800	2840	40

Faint	Sleep	Poison	Curse	Paralyze	Silence	Confuse	Freeze	Petrify
100	100	100	100	100	100	100	30	100

Unseeing	Unhearing	Unsmelling	Skewer	Charm	Berserk	Doom
100	100	100	100	100	100	100

★ S-Class Drops	%	★ A-Class Drops	%	★ B-Class Drops	%	★ C-Class Drops	%
Crab Shell	50	Crab Claw	50	Crab Claw	50	Crab Claw	20
Crab Meat	50	Crab Shell	30	Crab Shell	50		
		Crab Meat	20				

SCISSORCLAW CENTIPEDE

Air	100
Fire	50
Earth	100
Aether	100
Water	250

LOCATION: Seraphic Gate

Level	HP	ATK	DEF	HIT	AGL	INT	AP Gauge	EXP	Fol	Base Drop Rate %
125	40000	3800	1200	1300	120	800	3	4100	3200	40

Faint	Sleep	Poison	Curse	Paralyze	Silence	Confuse	Freeze	Petrify
100	0	100	100	0	100	100	100	100

Unseeing	Unhearing	Unsmelling	Skewer	Charm	Berserk	Doom
100	0	100	100	100	100	100

★ S-Class Drops	%	★ A-Class Drops	%	★ B-Class Drops	%	★ C-Class Drops	%
Malus Wood	80	Laurel	50	Insect Fang	50	Insect Fang	20
Amarlista	20	Malus Wood	30	Laurel	30		
		Amarlista	20	Amarlista	20		

SKULL KNIGHT

Air	250
Fire	100
Earth	50
Aether	100
Water	100

LOCATION: Seraphic Gate

Level	HP	ATK	DEF	HIT	AGL	INT	AP Gauge	EXP	Fol	Base Drop Rate %
115	40000	3500	1150	1200	110	650	2	3900	3120	40

Faint	Sleep	Poison	Curse	Paralyze	Silence	Confuse	Freeze	Petrify
0	100	0	0	0	0	100	100	100

Unseeing	Unhearing	Unsmelling	Skewer	Charm	Berserk	Doom
0	0	0	100	100	100	0

★ S-Class Drops	%	★ A-Class Drops	%	★ B-Class Drops	%	★ C-Class Drops	%
Dragonedge	80	Random Beast Bone	50	Random Beast Bone	80	Random Beast Bone	20
Rage	20	Dragonedge	30	Dragonedge	20		
		Rage	20				

SKULL SOLDIER

Air	250
Fire	100
Earth	50
Aether	100
Water	100

LOCATION: Seraphic Gate

Level	HP	ATK	DEF	HIT	AGL	INT	AP Gauge	EXP	Fol	Base Drop Rate %
115	35000	3000	1000	1215	100	650	2	3500	2800	40

Faint	Sleep	Poison	Curse	Paralyze	Silence	Confuse	Freeze	Petrify
0	100	0	0	0	0	100	100	100

Unseeing	Unhearing	Unsmelling	Skewer	Charm	Berserk	Doom
0	0	0	100	100	100	0

★ S-Class Drops	%	★ A-Class Drops	%	★ B-Class Drops	%	★ C-Class Drops	%
Bardiche	80	Random Beast Bone	50	Random Beast Bone	80	Random Beast Bone	20
Berserker	20	Crystallite Metal	30	Crystallite Metal	20		
		Berserker	20				

STORM GIGAS

Air	250
Fire	100
Earth	0
Aether	100
Water	100

LOCATION: Seraphic Gate

Level	HP	ATK	DEF	HIT	AGL	INT	AP Gauge	EXP	Fol	Base Drop Rate %
70	40000	2500	600	650	40	500	7	3000	2400	40

Faint	Sleep	Poison	Curse	Paralyze	Silence	Confuse	Freeze	Petrify
30	100	100	100	100	100	100	100	0

Unseeing	Unhearing	Unsmelling	Skewer	Charm	Berserk	Doom
100	100	100	100	100	100	100

★ S-Class Drops	%	★ A-Class Drops	%	★ B-Class Drops	%	★ C-Class Drops	%
Bardiche	50	Quartz	50	Quartz	80	Quartz	20
Ogre's Hammer	30	Quartz Tiara	30	Crystallite Metal	20		
Atlantis Metal	20	Atlantis Metal	20				

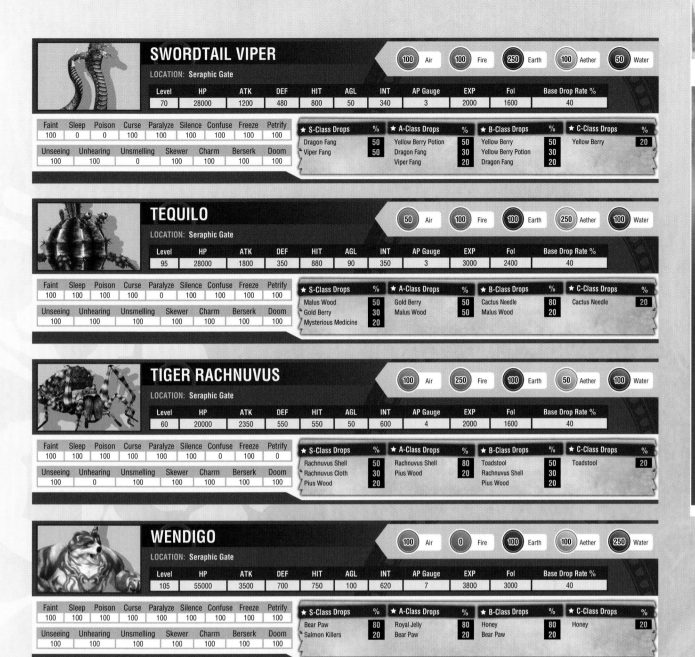

SWORDTAIL VIPER

LOCATION: Seraphic Gate

Air	Fire	Earth	Aether	Water
100	100	250	100	50

Level	HP	ATK	DEF	HIT	AGL	INT	AP Gauge	EXP	Fol	Base Drop Rate %
70	28000	1200	480	800	50	340	3	2000	1600	40

Faint	Sleep	Poison	Curse	Paralyze	Silence	Confuse	Freeze	Petrify
100	0	0	100	100	100	100	100	100

Unseeing	Unhearing	Unsmelling	Skewer	Charm	Berserk	Doom
100	100	0	100	100	100	100

★ S-Class Drops	%	★ A-Class Drops	%	★ B-Class Drops	%	★ C-Class Drops	%
Dragon Fang	50	Yellow Berry Potion	50	Yellow Berry	50	Yellow Berry	20
Viper Fang	50	Dragon Fang	30	Yellow Berry Potion	30		
		Viper Fang	20	Dragon Fang	20		

TEQUILO

LOCATION: Seraphic Gate

Air	Fire	Earth	Aether	Water
50	100	100	250	100

Level	HP	ATK	DEF	HIT	AGL	INT	AP Gauge	EXP	Fol	Base Drop Rate %
95	28000	1800	350	880	90	350	3	3000	2400	40

Faint	Sleep	Poison	Curse	Paralyze	Silence	Confuse	Freeze	Petrify
100	100	100	100	0	100	100	100	100

Unseeing	Unhearing	Unsmelling	Skewer	Charm	Berserk	Doom
100	100	100	100	100	100	100

★ S-Class Drops	%	★ A-Class Drops	%	★ B-Class Drops	%	★ C-Class Drops	%
Malus Wood	50	Gold Berry	50	Cactus Needle	80	Cactus Needle	20
Gold Berry	30	Malus Wood	50	Malus Wood	20		
Mysterious Medicine	20						

TIGER RACHNUVUS

LOCATION: Seraphic Gate

Air	Fire	Earth	Aether	Water
100	250	100	50	100

Level	HP	ATK	DEF	HIT	AGL	INT	AP Gauge	EXP	Fol	Base Drop Rate %
60	20000	2350	550	550	50	600	4	2000	1600	40

Faint	Sleep	Poison	Curse	Paralyze	Silence	Confuse	Freeze	Petrify
100	100	100	100	100	100	0	100	0

Unseeing	Unhearing	Unsmelling	Skewer	Charm	Berserk	Doom
100	0	100	100	100	100	100

★ S-Class Drops	%	★ A-Class Drops	%	★ B-Class Drops	%	★ C-Class Drops	%
Rachnuvus Shell	50	Rachnuvus Shell	80	Toadstool	50	Toadstool	20
Rachnuvus Cloth	30	Pius Wood	20	Rachnuvus Shell	30		
Pius Wood	20			Pius Wood	20		

WENDIGO

LOCATION: Seraphic Gate

Air	Fire	Earth	Aether	Water
100	0	100	100	250

Level	HP	ATK	DEF	HIT	AGL	INT	AP Gauge	EXP	Fol	Base Drop Rate %
105	55000	3500	700	750	100	620	7	3800	3000	40

Faint	Sleep	Poison	Curse	Paralyze	Silence	Confuse	Freeze	Petrify
100	100	100	100	100	100	100	100	100

Unseeing	Unhearing	Unsmelling	Skewer	Charm	Berserk	Doom
100	100	100	100	100	100	100

★ S-Class Drops	%	★ A-Class Drops	%	★ B-Class Drops	%	★ C-Class Drops	%
Bear Paw	80	Royal Jelly	80	Honey	80	Honey	20
Salmon Killers	20	Bear Paw	20	Bear Paw	20		

SERAPHIC GATE BOSSES

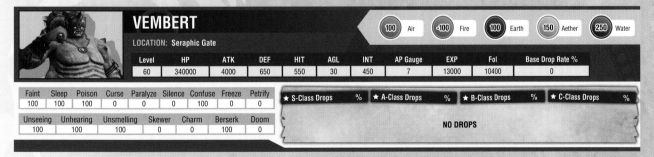

VEMBERT

LOCATION: Seraphic Gate

Air	Fire	Earth	Aether	Water
100	-100	100	150	250

Level	HP	ATK	DEF	HIT	AGL	INT	AP Gauge	EXP	Fol	Base Drop Rate %
60	340000	4000	650	550	30	450	7	13000	10400	0

Faint	Sleep	Poison	Curse	Paralyze	Silence	Confuse	Freeze	Petrify
100	100	100	0	0	0	100	0	0

Unseeing	Unhearing	Unsmelling	Skewer	Charm	Berserk	Doom
100	100	100	0	0	100	0

★ S-Class Drops	%	★ A-Class Drops	%	★ B-Class Drops	%	★ C-Class Drops	%
			NO DROPS				

SHADOW SIGMUND

LOCATION: Seraphic Gate

	Air		Fire		Earth		Aether		Water
100		100		100		100		100	

Level	HP	ATK	DEF	HIT	AGL	INT	AP Gauge	EXP	Fol	Base Drop Rate %
70	130000	2000	900	720	150	750	5	15000	49610	0

Faint	Sleep	Poison	Curse	Paralyze	Silence	Confuse	Freeze	Petrify
50	0	0	0	0	0	0	0	0

Unseeing	Unhearing	Unsmelling	Skewer	Charm	Berserk	Doom
0	0	0	0	0	100	0

★ S-Class Drops	%	★ A-Class Drops	%	★ B-Class Drops	%	★ C-Class Drops	%

NO DROPS

WYVERN

LOCATION: Seraphic Gate

	Air		Fire		Earth		Aether		Water
100		-50		100		100		250	

Level	HP	ATK	DEF	HIT	AGL	INT	AP Gauge	EXP	Fol	Base Drop Rate %
70	500000	3000	1000	1000	60	700	-	25000	20000	0

Faint	Sleep	Poison	Curse	Paralyze	Silence	Confuse	Freeze	Petrify
0	0	0	0	0	0	0	0	0

Unseeing	Unhearing	Unsmelling	Skewer	Charm	Berserk	Doom
0	0	0	0	0	100	0

★ S-Class Drops	%	★ A-Class Drops	%	★ B-Class Drops	%	★ C-Class Drops	%

NO DROPS

LEVIATHAN

LOCATION: Seraphic Gate

	Air		Fire		Earth		Aether		Water
100		100		250		100		-50	

Level	HP	ATK	DEF	HIT	AGL	INT	AP Gauge	EXP	Fol	Base Drop Rate %
85	425000	2000	550	900	88	600	-	28000	23000	0

Faint	Sleep	Poison	Curse	Paralyze	Silence	Confuse	Freeze	Petrify
0	0	0	0	0	0	100	0	0

Unseeing	Unhearing	Unsmelling	Skewer	Charm	Berserk	Doom
0	0	0	0	0	100	0

★ S-Class Drops	%	★ A-Class Drops	%	★ B-Class Drops	%	★ C-Class Drops	%

NO DROPS

PELUDA

LOCATION: Seraphic Gate

	Air		Fire		Earth		Aether		Water
100		-50		100		100		250	

Level	HP	ATK	DEF	HIT	AGL	INT	AP Gauge	EXP	Fol	Base Drop Rate %
95	350000	3500	510	1000	100	900	-	30000	24000	0

Faint	Sleep	Poison	Curse	Paralyze	Silence	Confuse	Freeze	Petrify
50	50	0	0	0	0	0	0	0

Unseeing	Unhearing	Unsmelling	Skewer	Charm	Berserk	Doom
0	0	0	0	0	100	0

★ S-Class Drops	%	★ A-Class Drops	%	★ B-Class Drops	%	★ C-Class Drops	%

NO DROPS

GABRIEL CELESTE

LOCATION: Seraphic Gate

	Air		Fire		Earth		Aether		Water
100		100		100		100		100	

Level	HP	ATK	DEF	HIT	AGL	INT	AP Gauge	EXP	Fol	Base Drop Rate %
110	1000000	5000	1200	2000	100	3000	-	40000	32000	0

Faint	Sleep	Poison	Curse	Paralyze	Silence	Confuse	Freeze	Petrify
0	0	0	0	0	0	0	0	0

Unseeing	Unhearing	Unsmelling	Skewer	Charm	Berserk	Doom
0	0	0	0	0	0	0

★ S-Class Drops	%	★ A-Class Drops	%	★ B-Class Drops	%	★ C-Class Drops	%

NO DROPS

FAESPHERE (GABRIEL CELESTE)

LOCATION: Seraphic Gate

	Air		Fire		Earth		Aether		Water
100		100		100		100		100	

Level	HP	ATK	DEF	HIT	AGL	INT	AP Gauge	EXP	Fol	Base Drop Rate %
110	10000	0	500	1	1	1100	1	0	0	0

Faint	Sleep	Poison	Curse	Paralyze	Silence	Confuse	Freeze	Petrify
0	0	0	0	0	0	0	0	0

Unseeing	Unhearing	Unsmelling	Skewer	Charm	Berserk	Doom
0	0	0	100	0	0	0

★ S-Class Drops	%	★ A-Class Drops	%	★ B-Class Drops	%	★ C-Class Drops	%

NO DROPS

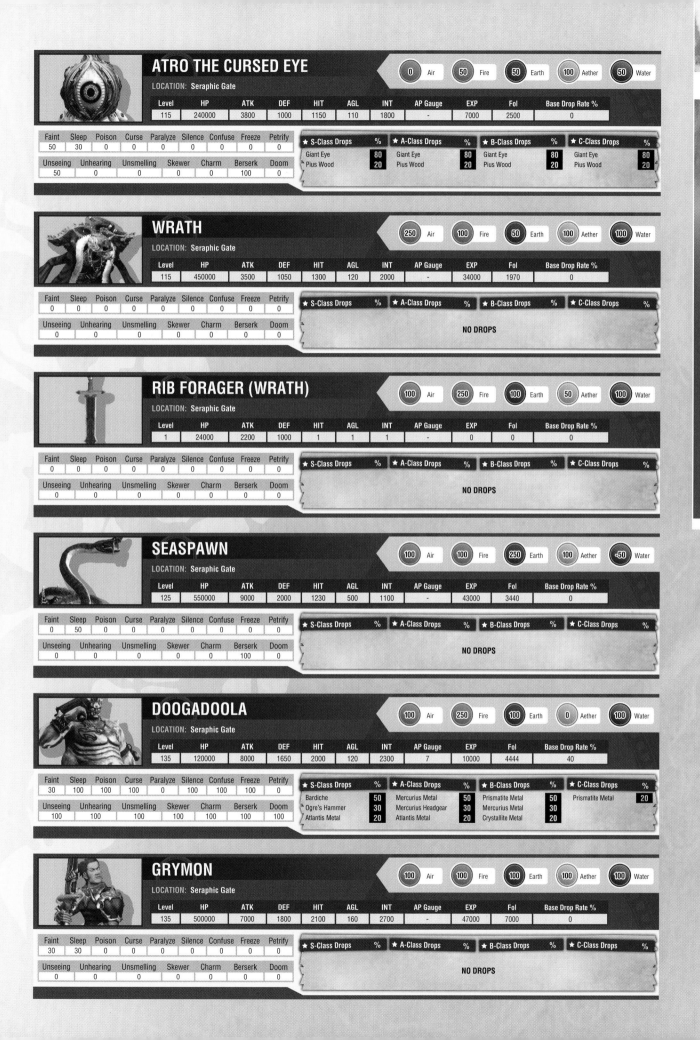

ATRO THE CURSED EYE

LOCATION: Seraphic Gate

0 Air	50 Fire	50 Earth
100 Aether	50 Water	

Level	HP	ATK	DEF	HIT	AGL	INT	AP Gauge	EXP	Fol	Base Drop Rate %
115	240000	3800	1000	1150	110	1800	-	7000	2500	0

Faint	Sleep	Poison	Curse	Paralyze	Silence	Confuse	Freeze	Petrify
50	30	0	0	0	0	0	0	0

Unseeing	Unhearing	Unsmelling	Skewer	Charm	Berserk	Doom
50	0	0	0	0	100	0

★ S-Class Drops	%	★ A-Class Drops	%	★ B-Class Drops	%	★ C-Class Drops	%
Giant Eye	80	Giant Eye	80	Giant Eye	80	Giant Eye	80
Pius Wood	20	Pius Wood	20	Pius Wood	20	Pius Wood	20

WRATH

LOCATION: Seraphic Gate

250 Air	100 Fire	50 Earth
100 Aether	100 Water	

Level	HP	ATK	DEF	HIT	AGL	INT	AP Gauge	EXP	Fol	Base Drop Rate %
115	450000	3500	1050	1300	120	2000	-	34000	1970	0

Faint	Sleep	Poison	Curse	Paralyze	Silence	Confuse	Freeze	Petrify
0	0	0	0	0	0	0	0	0

Unseeing	Unhearing	Unsmelling	Skewer	Charm	Berserk	Doom
0	0	0	0	0	0	0

★ S-Class Drops	%	★ A-Class Drops	%	★ B-Class Drops	%	★ C-Class Drops	%
			NO DROPS				

RIB FORAGER (WRATH)

LOCATION: Seraphic Gate

100 Air	250 Fire	100 Earth
50 Aether	100 Water	

Level	HP	ATK	DEF	HIT	AGL	INT	AP Gauge	EXP	Fol	Base Drop Rate %
1	24000	2200	1000	1	1	1		0	0	0

Faint	Sleep	Poison	Curse	Paralyze	Silence	Confuse	Freeze	Petrify
0	0	0	0	0	0	0	0	0

Unseeing	Unhearing	Unsmelling	Skewer	Charm	Berserk	Doom
0	0	0	0	0	0	0

★ S-Class Drops	%	★ A-Class Drops	%	★ B-Class Drops	%	★ C-Class Drops	%
			NO DROPS				

SEASPAWN

LOCATION: Seraphic Gate

100 Air	100 Fire	250 Earth
100 Aether	-50 Water	

Level	HP	ATK	DEF	HIT	AGL	INT	AP Gauge	EXP	Fol	Base Drop Rate %
125	550000	9000	2000	1230	500	1100	-	43000	3440	0

Faint	Sleep	Poison	Curse	Paralyze	Silence	Confuse	Freeze	Petrify
0	50	0	0	0	0	0	0	0

Unseeing	Unhearing	Unsmelling	Skewer	Charm	Berserk	Doom
0	0	0	0	0	100	0

★ S-Class Drops	%	★ A-Class Drops	%	★ B-Class Drops	%	★ C-Class Drops	%
			NO DROPS				

DOOGADOOLA

LOCATION: Seraphic Gate

100 Air	250 Fire	100 Earth
0 Aether	100 Water	

Level	HP	ATK	DEF	HIT	AGL	INT	AP Gauge	EXP	Fol	Base Drop Rate %
135	120000	8000	1650	2000	120	2300	7	10000	4444	40

Faint	Sleep	Poison	Curse	Paralyze	Silence	Confuse	Freeze	Petrify
30	100	100	100	0	100	100	100	0

Unseeing	Unhearing	Unsmelling	Skewer	Charm	Berserk	Doom
100	100	100	100	100	100	100

★ S-Class Drops	%	★ A-Class Drops	%	★ B-Class Drops	%	★ C-Class Drops	%
Bardiche	50	Mercurius Metal	50	Prismatite Metal	50	Prismatite Metal	20
Ogre's Hammer	30	Mercurius Headgear	30	Mercurius Metal	30		
Atlantis Metal	20	Atlantis Metal	20	Crystallite Metal	20		

GRYMON

LOCATION: Seraphic Gate

100 Air	100 Fire	100 Earth
100 Aether	100 Water	

Level	HP	ATK	DEF	HIT	AGL	INT	AP Gauge	EXP	Fol	Base Drop Rate %
135	500000	7000	1800	2100	160	2700	-	47000	7000	0

Faint	Sleep	Poison	Curse	Paralyze	Silence	Confuse	Freeze	Petrify
30	30	0	0	0	0	0	0	0

Unseeing	Unhearing	Unsmelling	Skewer	Charm	Berserk	Doom
0	0	0	0	0	0	0

★ S-Class Drops	%	★ A-Class Drops	%	★ B-Class Drops	%	★ C-Class Drops	%
			NO DROPS				

FAESPHERE (GRYMON)

LOCATION: Seraphic Gate

100 Air	100 Fire	100 Earth
100 Aether	100 Water	

Level	HP	ATK	DEF	HIT	AGL	INT	AP Gauge	EXP	Fol	Base Drop Rate %
135	20000	1	500	1	1	2000	1	0	0	

Faint	Sleep	Poison	Curse	Paralyze	Silence	Confuse	Freeze	Petrify
0	0	0	0	0	0	0	0	0

Unseeing	Unhearing	Unsmelling	Skewer	Charm	Berserk	Doom
0	0	0	100	0	0	0

★ S-Class Drops	%	★ A-Class Drops	%	★ B-Class Drops	%	★ C-Class Drops	%
NO DROPS							

LEONID

LOCATION: Seraphic Gate

100 Air	100 Fire	50 Earth
100 Aether	50 Water	

Level	HP	ATK	DEF	HIT	AGL	INT	AP Gauge	EXP	Fol	Base Drop Rate %
150	1800000	8000	2000	2000	180	3500	-	50000	15000	0

Faint	Sleep	Poison	Curse	Paralyze	Silence	Confuse	Freeze	Petrify
30	0	0	0	0	0	0	0	0

Unseeing	Unhearing	Unsmelling	Skewer	Charm	Berserk	Doom
0	0	0	0	100	0	0

★ S-Class Drops	%	★ A-Class Drops	%	★ B-Class Drops	%	★ C-Class Drops	%
NO DROPS							

FAESPHERE (LEONID)

LOCATION: Seraphic Gate

100 Air	100 Fire	100 Earth
100 Aether	100 Water	

Level	HP	ATK	DEF	HIT	AGL	INT	AP Gauge	EXP	Fol	Base Drop Rate %
110	20000	1800	500	1000	20	1300	1	1700	680	0

Faint	Sleep	Poison	Curse	Paralyze	Silence	Confuse	Freeze	Petrify
0	0	0	0	0	0	0	0	0

Unseeing	Unhearing	Unsmelling	Skewer	Charm	Berserk	Doom
0	0	0	100	0	0	0

★ S-Class Drops	%	★ A-Class Drops	%	★ B-Class Drops	%	★ C-Class Drops	%
NO DROPS							

ETHEREAL QUEEN

LOCATION: Seraphic Gate

100 Air	100 Fire	100 Earth
100 Aether	100 Water	

Level	HP	ATK	DEF	HIT	AGL	INT	AP Gauge	EXP	Fol	Base Drop Rate %
200	2500000	8500	2500	2400	150	4500	-	70000	20000	0

Faint	Sleep	Poison	Curse	Paralyze	Silence	Confuse	Freeze	Petrify
0	0	0	0	0	0	0	0	0

Unseeing	Unhearing	Unsmelling	Skewer	Charm	Berserk	Doom
0	0	0	0	0	0	0

★ S-Class Drops	%	★ A-Class Drops	%	★ B-Class Drops	%	★ C-Class Drops	%
NO DROPS							

FAESPHERE (ETHEREAL QUEEN)

LOCATION: Seraphic Gate

100 Air	100 Fire	100 Earth
100 Aether	100 Water	

Level	HP	ATK	DEF	HIT	AGL	INT	AP Gauge	EXP	Fol	Base Drop Rate %
200	2500000	8500	2500	2400	150	4500	-	70000	20000	0

Faint	Sleep	Poison	Curse	Paralyze	Silence	Confuse	Freeze	Petrify
0	0	0	0	0	0	0	0	0

Unseeing	Unhearing	Unsmelling	Skewer	Charm	Berserk	Doom
0	0	0	100	0	0	0

★ S-Class Drops	%	★ A-Class Drops	%	★ B-Class Drops	%	★ C-Class Drops	%
NO DROPS							

APPENDICES
MULTI-PARTY GRADING

At four points throughout the story, the party engages in massive battles involving multiple parties. You'll only directly control Capell's party, but you'll determine the setup of the other parties. This setup determines the letter grade, or rank, received at the end of the multi-party event, which then dictates what sort of rewards the group obtains. To achieve better ranks—nabbing more EXP, Fol, and better items—there are a few guidelines to follow. First, fill every party slot possible, and while you *can* bring along fewer characters than allowed, it only hurts your rank. Second, favor higher-level characters over lower-level ones. Third, equip everyone with the rarest gear possible. This guide's Items chapter notes the "rarity" ranking of every item in the game. This is a hidden stat, but it has a direct bearing on multi-party event ranking. The rarer equipment for everyone, the better. Finally, different personal skills impact the grade either positively or negatively if certain characters are brought along. For example, Castle Valette is essentially a mausoleum. Komachi likes dark places, while Eugene and Kristofer fear them. Having Komachi for Castle Valette helps rank, while having Kristofer or Eugene along hurts it. The rewards for great ranks are nice (especially for Fol and EXP, the latter of which applies to everyone equally, even if they're not in the party), but don't fret too much if you get a low rank and miss out—none of the rewards are exclusive to multi-party battles.

Sapran

Helpful Personal Skills: True Leader (Sigmund), Enduring (Balbagan), Thoughtful? (Edward)

Harmful Personal Skills: Coward (Michelle)

Rank	EXP Earned	Fol	Items
A	3000	1800	Metal fragment, red berry potion, iron metal, crab claw, ebony wood, and two randomly from: marble, black berry potion, bronze ring
B	2800	1600	Metal fragment, red berry potion, iron metal, crab claw, ebony wood, and one randomly from: marble, black berry potion, bronze ring
C	2500	1400	Metal fragment, red berry potion, iron metal, crab claw, ebony wood
D	2000	1200	Metal fragment, red berry potion, iron metal
E	1500	1000	Metal fragment, red berry potion

Vesplume Tower

Helpful Personal Skills: True Leader (Sigmund), Enduring (Balbagan), Lucky (Aya, Balbagan)

No Harmful Skills

Rank	EXP	Fol	Items
A	5000	12000	Golden wolf fur, steel metal, black berry potion, yellow berry potion, and two randomly from: memoirs of a warrior, rapier, giant eye
B	4600	11500	Golden wolf fur, steel metal, black berry potion, yellow berry potion, and one randomly from: memoirs of a warrior, rapier, giant eye
C	4200	11000	Golden wolf fur, steel metal, lux wood, black berry potion, yellow berry potion
D	4000	10000	Golden wolf fur, steel metal, lux wood
E	3800	9000	Golden wolf fur, steel metal

Castle Valette

Helpful Personal Skills: Linguist (Savio, Eugene), Shady Lady (Komachi)

Harmful Personal Skills: Nyctophobic (Eugene, Kristofer)

Rank	EXP Earned	Fol	Items
A	18000	100000	Random beast bone, feeble cloth, giant eye, holy water, mysterious medicine, and two randomly from: memoirs of a mage, "Apocalypse of Darkness," dominance staff
B	15000	90000	Random beast bone, feeble cloth, giant eye, holy water, mysterious medicine, and one randomly from: memoirs of a mage, "Apocalypse of Darkness," dominance staff
C	13000	85000	Random beast bone, feeble cloth, giant eye, holy water, mysterious medicine
D	10000	78000	Random beast bone, feeble cloth, giant eye
E	9200	75000	Random beast bone, feeble cloth

Underwater Palace

Helpful Personal Skills: Coach (Eugene), Disciplinary (Edward, Dominica), Cunning Linguist (Savio, Eugene)

Harmful Personal Skills: Coward (Michelle), Big Coward (Rucha)

Rank	EXP	Fol	Items
A	20000	120000	Green berry powder, crystallite metal, pius wood, giant eye, lunatite, and two randomly from: empyrean cloth, dragon hide, memoirs of an alchemist
B	18000	100000	Green berry powder, crystallite metal, pius wood, giant eye, lunatite, and one randomly from: empyrean cloth, dragon hide, memoirs of an alchemist
C	17000	90000	Green berry powder, crystallite metal, pius wood, giant eye, lunatite
D	16000	85000	Green berry powder, crystallite metal, pius wood
E	15000	78000	Green berry powder, crystallite metal

SITUATION BONUSES

Throughout the game, fulfilling certain parameters grants bonus EXP or items to the party. The game doesn't tell you when a Situation Bonus is available…but this walkthrough does! A few Situation Bonuses also double as achievements. Beware scanning the Situation Bonus or achievement lists before you're very familiar with *Infinite Undiscovery*, as some spoilers are present within the descriptions.

Location	Requirement	Reward
Graad Prison	Destroyed all barricades.	Full HP and MP recovery!
Graad Woods	Shot down all Burguss apples.	Obtained a bottle of blue berry potion!
Luce Plains	Reached Nolaan without being hit.	Bonus 500 EXP!
Dragonbone Shrine	Found the secret room.	Bonus 1000 EXP!
Luce Plains	Opened the castle gate within 3 minutes.	Bonus 3000 EXP!
Castle Prevant	Freed all Burguss soldiers.	Bonus 3500 EXP!
Castle Prevant	Defeated Lester within 2 minutes.	Obtained a yellow berry potion and a white berry potion!
Sapran	Liberated Sapran within 3 minutes.	Bonus 5000 EXP!
Sapran	Defeated Semberas within 2 minutes.	Obtained some granite and some steel metal!
Oradian Dunes	Delivered all the unblesseds safely.	Bonus 7500 EXP!
Oradian Dunes	Rescued Leif without him getting hit.	Obtained some all-purpose medicine and miraculous medicine!
Oradian Dunes	Rescued Gustav without him getting hit.	Bonus 8500 EXP!
Oradian Mountains	Defeated more than 5 enemies using rocks.	Bonus 10000 EXP!
Vesplume Tower	Defeated Kron within 1 minute.	Obtained some blue berry powder and a giant eye!
Vesplume Tower	Defeated Dmitri within 2 minutes.	Obtained some lentesco wood and some down feather cloth!
Zalan Coast	Smashed the chain without being swept away.	Bonus 20000 EXP!
Kolton	Defeated the mysterious foe within 1 minute.	Obtained some blue berry powder!
Kolton	Stopped Edward within 3 minutes.	Bonus 20000 EXP!
Halgita	Reached Svala within 3 minutes.	Obtained some malus wood!
Dais	Used stalactite to finish Rachnuvae Queen.	Obtained some rachnuvae cloth!
Dais	Defeated Held within 2 minutes.	Obtained the memoirs of a mage!
Oradian Dunes	Reached Sapran within 3 minutes.	Bonus 30000 EXP!
Castle Valette	Solved Chamber of Elements w/ no mistakes.	Full HP and MP recovery!
Castle Valette	Defeated Saranda within 2 minutes.	Obtained some lunatite and some mercurius metal!
Pieria Marshlands	Defeated the dragon within 2 minutes.	Obtained a dragon eye and a dragon fang!
Underwater Palace	Didn't finish off Iskan via Capell.	Bonus 35000 EXP!
Underwater Palace	Didn't finish off Leonid via Capell.	Bonus 40000 EXP!
Lunar Sanctuary	Defeated Leonid within 2 minutes.	Obtained some amarlista!

ACHIEVEMENTS

As with any Xbox 360 title, *Infinite Undiscovery* is packed with achievements you can unlock to boost your Gamerscore. A few are storyline-focused, but the majority of them are combat-or-crafting-related accomplishments. Avoid scanning this list too thoroughly before you're very familiar with the game, as a few achievement descriptions constitute spoilers. The titles of these achievements are bolded; don't read them before you beat the game!

Achievement	Description	Gamerscore	Acquisition
Surprise!	Launched your first surprise attack.	5	Simple enough—score Player Advantage once.
Blitzkrieg	Launched 10 surprise attacks.	10	Score Player Advantage 10 times. This achievement almost certainly can be obtained naturally through normal gameplay.
Infinitely Unobservant	Allowed the enemy to surprise you 10 times.	10	Let foes score Enemy Advantage 10 times. By the time you finish the game this may have happened on its own, but if not it's easy to achieve on purpose.
Groundbreaking	Executed a 30-hit ground combo.	20	Score a 30+ hit combo on a standing opponent. This likely unlocks through normal gameplay eventually, especially as better skills and spells become available. Otherwise, to coax this along, use a Connect skill that hits many times and doesn't knock down or launch, like leveled-up Astro or Raven Venom, and fill in the gaps between casts with Dancing Rhapsody. After two or three repetitions, voila, achievement unlocked!
Aerial Acrobat	Executed a 20-hit aerial combo.	20	Score 20+ hits on a launched foe. Also likely achieved through normal gameplay. Otherwise, simply launch the enemy with Crescendo Spike or Cutting Gavotte, then juggle with Dancing Rhapsody to Cutting Gavotte while using Connect skills like Sparrowrain. Wash, rinse, repeat. Light flying enemies, like lifestealers, are the easiest to keep aloft.
Down to Earth	Executed a 20-hit down combo.	20	The other combo achievements are almost guaranteed to unlock through incidental gameplay—it would be harder *not* to get them. This achievement is much more difficult, however. Only for a very brief window can you combo foes while they're floored, and foes cannot be "Overkilled" while grounded (whereas you can pound on standing or juggled foes for as long as you can keep it up). With a party built around multi-hit attacks, use a skill like Diminuendo Dive that knocks down while timing a Connect skill that hits many times, like Edward's Swordsquall, to strike just after the foe is floored. Toss in a multi-hit skill of Capell's, like Marching Boots, and hope a third ally joins in the fun at the right moment. Most enemies cannot withstand such an assault, so repeated attempts might have to wait for the stouter enemies in the Seraphic Gate (or an Infinity mode playthrough).
Stalwart	Learned every battle skill.	30	Most skills are acquired simply by leveling up. A few choice skills are obtained only from skill books, however. You'll need Rico at IC Lv.6 to craft these. The Private Event "Secret of Writing" must also be completed.
Sagacious	Learned every spell.	30	Like skills, spells are mostly acquired through leveling up. Savio crafts some exclusive spell books at IC Lv.6, after the Private Event "Secret of Writing" is completed.
Artistic	Learned every tune.	30	Apart from a few learned through the story, most scores must be made from notations found in treasure chests or earned through Side Quests and Private Events. Getting Rico to IC Lv.6 is also required.
Compulsive	Obtained every item.	50	Obviously, this achievement takes some time. It requires getting everyone to IC Lv.6 and completely clearing out the Seraphic Gate—probably many times for raw materials. Don't miss the instrumental sword in Castle Valette, necessary for some late sword recipes.
Mister Chef	Obtained level 4 cooking skills.	5	Compared to later IC skill levels, Lv.4 is relatively painless. Rucha, Aya, and Dominica can get cooking this high.
Claridian Chef	Obtained level 6 cooking skills.	10	Continue skilling up IC level with Rucha, Aya, or Dominica to unlock this achievement.
Creme de la Crème	Cooked a Heaven and Earth dish.	30	After getting Rucha to IC Lv.6 and completing the Private Event "Secret of Cooking," save the game and have her combine 1 dragon meat, 2 sliced rare salmon, and 1 king egg. If she fails, reload and try again.
Aspiring Chemist	Obtained level 4 alchemy skills.	5	Michelle, Kiriya, and Seraphina are capable of achieving IC Lv.4.
Claridian Mind	Obtained level 6 alchemy skills.	10	Grind Michelle, Kiriya, or Seraphina up to alchemy IC Lv.6 for this achievement.
Mad Scientist	Alchemized a holy grail.	30	Get Seraphina to IC Lv.6, complete the Private Event "Secret of Wrought Gold," then have her combine 10 miraculous medicines, 3 Claridian medicines, and 1 atlantis metal for this achievement. As with Creme de la Crème, save before attempting the synth, as you won't want to lose rare ingredients on a failed attempt.
Goldsmith	Obtained level 4 forging skills.	5	Eugene, Edward, and Kristofer can achieve forging IC Lv.4, thus unlocking this achievement.
Claridian Hammer	Obtained level 6 forging skills.	10	Eugene, Edward, and Kristofer can attain forging IC Lv.6.
Hephaestus's Hammer	Forged an azureal blade.	30	Edward crafts the game's best weapon, but not before he has IC Lv.6. You must also have Seraphic Gate access, which only occurs after beating the main game on at least Normal difficulty. Save before combining 2 amarlistas, 1 gram, and 1 emblazoned sword.
Bestselling Author	Obtained level 4 writing skills.	5	Rico and Savio are the scribes in this outfit. Get either of them to IC Lv.4 for 5 Gamerscore.
Claridian Scribe	Obtained level 6 writing skills.	10	Push Rico or Savio to writing IC Lv.6 for this achievement.
Summa Cum Laude	Wrote "Will of the Universe."	30	After completing the Private Event "Secret of Writing" and getting Savio to IC Lv.6, have him combine 1 memoirs of an alchemist and 2 genius's quills to receive this tome, and 30 Gamerscore.
High Enchanter	Obtained level 4 enchanting skills.	5	Capell is the only enchanter, and he gets started on his tradeskill later than everyone else does on theirs. Get him enchanting IC Lv.4 for this achievement.
Claridian Hand	Obtained level 6 enchanting skills.	10	Push Capell all the way to enchanting IC Lv.6 for this achievement.

Achievement	Description	Gamerscore	Acquisition
Social Butterfly	Connected with every character.	10	The last additions to the party are Touma and Komachi, relatively late in the normal game. Once they're available, simply Connect with both and you're done. Make sure you Connect with Sigmund during disc 1; if you miss the chance, you'll have to wait until the Seraphic Gate for another opportunity.
Filthy Rich	Obtained 99,999,999 Fol.	20	Like the Compulsive achievement, this one takes a lot of diligence and many trips through the Seraphic Gate. Sell any extra craft results—that you won't need for other IC recipes, of course!
Hero of the Millennium	Defeated 1000 enemies.	20	This achievement is a matter of time. If you don't avoid combat excessively and play through the Seraphic Gate after a normal playthrough, it comes naturally.
Bad Influence	Allowed nine characters to vermify.	30	Once the lunar rain begins effecting characters toward the end of the game, they'll become incredibly threatening monsters if overexposed. Your party members can be very hard to deal with in this state, but you must let it happen nine times for the achievement. Get Percipere up immediately to defeat their vermified forms, and don't let them transform while you're busy dealing with other monsters too…this scenario virtually guarantees a visit to the Game Over screen (sacrificial dolls notwithstanding)!
Time for Glasses?	Played for over 40 hours.	30	Depending on your level of exploration and Side Quest completion with a Normal difficulty playthrough, *Infinite Undiscovery* takes between 20-40 hours to complete. Add in a Seraphic Gate playthrough or two after the main game is done, and this achievement unlocks.
Barrel of Lulz	Detonated every explosive barrel in Graad Prison.	15	Graad Prison is the first area in the game. Use Aya's Ravaging Raptor Connect skill to destroy all barrels from a distance, out of harm's way. Don't miss any barrels you didn't use blowing Vembert over the railing.
On the Run	Reached Nolaan without taking any damage.	30	After Aya falls ill, Capell must carry her across Luce Plains while a crazed wyvern spews flame after him. Getting nailed by the flames (or the Lumper foes in the area) negates the achievement. You might simply run and get lucky with not getting hit, but you can also use stone pillars as cover between fireball volleys. Making it to Nolaan unscathed also scores a Situation Bonus.
Rock, Stock, and Barrel	Defeated ten enemies using a catapult at Castle Prevant.	30	The catapults can be aimed at the gate…or they can be aimed at the ogres standing atop the battlements on either side. Nail 10 of them for the achievement, but note that going for this probably means you won't score the Situation Bonus for breaching the gate within 3 minutes. If you're a completionist who wants both, save just before the battle, take your time getting this achievement, then re-load the save and play the battle again with speed in mind.
Capell to the Rescue	Rescued all the Burguss soldiers in Castle Prevant.	30	Keys must be found, but also crafted, inside Castle Prevant in order to spring everyone on your side free from containment. This also scores a Situation Bonus.
Guardian	Reached a safe haven without letting any unblesseds perish.	30	Be extremely diligent in your protection of the unblesseds, never straying from the slowly-moving group, to get this achievement (and a Situation Bonus). Try to keep AP high so you can launch any enemy that comes near—a foe thrown into the air isn't attacking anyone. The sand fish provide the biggest threat here, as you might not notice if one swims under the desert and pops up into the group behind you. Continually scan the helpless Sapran citizens for surprise attacks.
For the Children	Rescued Leif before he got injured.	30	You must rescue Leif from the garuda in the Oradian dunes before he is injured. Act quickly, Connect with Aya, and use Ravaging Raptor to bring the beast down.
Reckless Driver	Defeated ten enemies using a mine cart in the Bihar Mines.	30	Bihar Mines is a completely optional area crawling with Lumpers. By striking a mine cart with a weapon, you'll send it quickly along its rail path. Lumpers along the way will be defeated. Take 10 of them for a ride for this achievement.
The Tide of Battle	Destroyed the Cerulean Chain without being hit by the tsunami once.	20	During the battle with Niedzielan along the Zalan Coast, hide behind the rock barriers whenever a tsunami approaches to avoid damage. Avoiding tsunamis throughout the fight also scores a Situation Bonus.
Imperial Guard	Reached Empress Svala within 3 minutes.	20	Rush up the stairs to the throne room during the battle in Halgita without pausing to fight any soldiers or gigas along the way to nab this achievement. This also scores a Situation Bonus.
Marathon Man	Reached Sapran within 3 minutes.	20	Like the previous achievement, once it's apparent that Sapran is in danger, simply hightail it there without pausing for combat. This also scores a Situation Bonus.
Azure Avenger	Destroyed the Azure Chain.	10	Unlocks naturally through story.
Orange Officer	Destroyed the Orange Chain.	10	Unlocks naturally through story.
Crimson Crusader	Destroyed the Crimson Chain.	10	Unlocks naturally through story.
Cerulean Savior	Destroyed the Cerulean Chain.	10	Unlocks naturally through story.
Amber Ace	Destroyed the Amber Chain.	10	Unlocks naturally through story.
Ashen Assailant	Destroyed the Ashen Chain.	10	Unlocks naturally through story.
Vengeance at Last	Defeated the Dreadknight.	30	Unlocks naturally through story.
Deicide	Defeated Veros.	45	Unlocks naturally through story.
Big Daddy's Back	Sigmund joined your party in the Seraphic Gate.	49	Defeat Sigmund in the Seraphic Gate. See the Seraphic Gate section for more info. In short: brush up on your Deflect Drive skills!
Cherubic Gatekeeper	Defeated Ethereal Queen in Hard mode.	30	Hard mode is unlocked by defeating Normal difficulty. Enemies have their stats multiplied by 1.2 in Hard mode; this puts the queen at 3 million HP instead of 2.5! Hard mode is not significantly more difficult than Normal, however; if you cleared the Seraphic Gate on Normal, this achievement is just a matter of time.
Seraphic Gatekeeper	Defeated Ethereal Queen in Infinity mode.	1	This is a taller order by far than defeating the queen on Hard difficulty. In Infinity mode, enemies have their stats multiplied by 1.8. Instead of 2.5 million HP, she'll have 4 million. She'll also be even more capable of eviscerating your entire party at will. The maximum level for characters in this game is 255, and it's not really unreasonable to need it considering Infinity mode's difficulty. Boost your IC levels as well, so azureal blade and other excellent weapons, especially those with HP/MP regeneration, are in hand. This will almost certainly be your last achievement, and just about the hardest-earned single achievement point on Xbox Live!

PERSONAL SKILLS

Personal skills, accessible through the skills menu, show interesting insights into Capell's thoughts on his allies. Capell's thoughts change over time based on level gains, story events, Private Events, and crafting levels. Often these "skills" are just extra flavor for the story, but a few have meaning for gameplay—such as those that explain which party members a character prefers to group with, which animals he or she dislikes fighting, or how he or she reacts in adverse situations. *Tread carefully* here if you haven't completed *Infinite Undiscovery*, as this section is absolutely *riddled* with spoilers…in fact, don't look through these at all until you're done!

CAPELL

Title Type	Title	Capell says…
Title 1	Soother	A traveling musician with little renown and no glory.
Title 1	Transporter	Carrying Aya is making my arms really tired…
Title 1	Babysitter	Now I'm looking after two kids? Does their mother have any shame?
Title 1	Chain Gang	Traveling around and cutting chains.
Title 1	Hero of Light	Looks like I get to be Sigmund!
Title 1	False Hero	I might not be a real hero, but what's so bad about that?
Title 1	Unblessed	Sure we've got the support of each nation, but what good is that?
Title 1	Prince	Wow, so I'm a prince…But that doesn't change who I am. I'm just Capell.
Title 2	Unwieldy	Looks like I'm pretty decent with a sword!
Title 2	Cutless	Chopping apart small woodland creatures is a simple task.
Title 2	Scabbard	Still improving. I'm about as good as most of the Order peons now.
Title 2	Swordsman	Almost nobody can beat me now.
Title 2	Elite Swordsman	A master of the sword. It's time to open up a school.
Title 2	Swordmaster	The greatest swordsman on the face of the planet.
Title 2	Oversword	I feel almost…over-leveled…Naw, it's just my imagination……Right?
IC	Apprentice	Level 1 IC enchanting. I'm just a beginner.
IC	Journeyman	Level 2 IC enchanting. I'm getting used to things.
IC	Enchanter	Level 3 IC enchanting. A master of simple enchantments.
IC	High Enchanter	Level 4 IC enchanting. A master of most enchantments.
IC	Master Enchanter	Level 5 IC enchanting. Best enchanter around.
IC	Claridian Hand	Level 6 IC enchanting. I leave a little bit of me in everything I enchant.
Trait 1	Versatile	I'm pretty good at everything, and very good at nothing.
Trait 2	Dullard	I'm lazy and proud of it! Why do anything today that I can put off until tomorrow?
Trait 2	Go-getter	I can do anything when I put my mind to it!
Trait 3	Strongman	My arms and legs might look weak, but I'm pretty tough!
Trait 4	Lady's Man	I'm not picky when it comes to women. I love them all!
Trait 4	Older Lady's Man	Older women are so much more…mature.
Trait 4	Brash Lady's Man	Overemotional and angsty girls are nice, too…
Trait 4	Aya's Man	Aya's my girl!
Palate	Fruit Lover	I love fruit! I could eat an apple for breakfast, lunch, and dinner!
Palate	Fruit Hater	I ate too much fruit…and now it makes me…sick…ugh…

AYA

Title Type	Title	Capell says…
Title 1	Acrobat	Did she come out of the ceiling!?
Title 1	Patient	She doesn't look so good. I wonder if she's sick, or if it's just the lighting?
Title 1	Friend	Thanks for not hating me!
Title 1	Princess	A princess!? Royalty is way out of my league!
Title 1	Confidant	You can tell me anything, even the bad stuff.
Title 1	Partner	Maybe she'll understand…
Title 1	Vengeful	If someone takes something from you, then you've just got to take as well.
Title 1	Beloved	Wait, do I have to say it? Aya, I…I…I lo…
Title 2	Lousy Shot	She sure misses a lot with that bow.
Title 2	Poor Shot	She spends more on arrows than she gets from killing monsters.
Title 2	Hunter	She's getting pretty good. I think she makes a decent hunter.
Title 2	High Hunter	She doesn't miss much anymore.
Title 2	Bowmaster	She can hit any enemy's weak point without even aiming!
Title 2	Bowmistress	Did she just hit that apple from a mile away? Wow!
Title 2	Royal Failure	What about dance lessons or history class? She IS a princess after all!
IC	Kitchen Scrub	Level 2 IC cooking. She sure likes to cook. Good with bread and desserts.
IC	Cook	Level 3 IC cooking. Her cooking's pretty good! Good with bread and desserts.
IC	Chef	Level 4 IC cooking. She must know every recipe! Good with bread and desserts.
IC	Master Chef	Level 5 IC cooking. She's a world-class chef now. Good with bread and desserts.
IC	Claridian Chef	Level 6 IC cooking. The Claridians line up for food! Good with bread and desserts.
Trait 1	Lucky	Looks like she gets a strength boost when she surprises enemies now!
Trait 2	Commoner	She's actually pretty normal.
Trait 3	Bear Fan	She really seems to like bears.
Trait 3	Bear Lover	All she ever thinks about is bears!
Trait 3	Bear Otaku	Does she…I-I-love bears!?
Trait 4	Reptile Hater	Look how scared she gets of reptiles! She can't even get close to them!
Trait 5	Bug Hater	She's really scared of bugs! It's like she can't even look at them!

EUGENE

Title Type	Title	Capell says…
Title 1	Some Guy	There's something about the tone of his voice…and how he moves his hands…
Title 1	The Man	He looks like the one who keeps everybody organized.
Title 1	Conniving	It looks like he's planning something…
Title 1	Sigmund's Aide	Did he just call Sigmund Siggy?
Title 1	Supportive	I'm gonna need his help if I want to get a hang of this Sigmund act.
Title 1	Halgitian Priest	I didn't know he was important in Halgita.
Title 1	Crucial	I'm going to need his thinking skills to complete my goals.
Title 1	Big Brother	He's always there when you need him, but never too close for comfort.
Title 2	Guide	His ideas aren't too bad.
Title 2	Trainer	He says some really inspirational stuff sometimes.
Title 2	Coach	His skills and knowledge help out the whole Liberation Force.
Title 2	Adviser	Look at him fight, cast spells, and even dance a step now and then. THAT'S talent.
Title 2	Consultant	Magic is at the core of his strategy.
Title 2	Counsellor	He knows what everybody is going to do before they know themselves!
Title 2	Guru	It's like he can control the battlefield with his eyes!
IC	Bronzesmith	Level 2 IC forging. He can keep the fire going. Good with cloth and skins.
IC	Silversmith	Level 3 IC forging. He's getting a little better now. Good with cloth and skins.
IC	Goldsmith	Level 4 IC forging. He's finally a decent smith. Good with cloth and skins.
IC	Mastersmith	Level 5 IC forging. The greatest smith of our age! Good with cloth and skins.
IC	Claridian Hammer	Level 6 IC forging. Awe-inspiring anvil prowess! Good with cloth and skins.
CS	Linguist	Where did he learn to read all those ancient signs and symbols?
CS	Cunning Linguist	He knows every tongue, old and new. He's a true weaver of language.
Trait 1	Avid Bather	I've never seen anybody else take a bath three times a day before.
Trait 2	Fisherman	He always looks happy when he talks about fishing. I bet he's in a club.
Palate	Alcohol Hater	It seems he can't handle alcohol. Ha-ha! Look at that! He got sick just by smelling some.
Trait 3	Nyctophobic	He can't concentrate in the dark. It seems to lower his strength.
Trait 3	Scaredy Cat	He's doing a little better in the dark, but his strength still suffers.

MICHELLE

Title Type	Title	Capell says…
Title 1	Confused	Oh, man! I hope she mistakes me for Sigmund again! That felt really good!
Title 1	Sexy	She…she really needs to do something about always… hugging, but…do I really mind?
Title 1	Fashionable	She's having a hard time out in the desert with her make-up.
Title 1	Gentle	She's a lot stronger than I first thought.
Title 1	Multifaceted	She can be a little cold.
Title 1	Passionate	Sometimes it looks like she tries too hard, but she's a really good person.
Title 1	Resolved	I think I can depend on her for the foundation of our cause.
Title 1	Embracing	All of my fears and doubts pale to the pleasure of being wrapped in her embrace.
Title 2	Initiate	Her hugs make my pain go away.
Title 2	Stitcher	Now she can do some basic healing.
Title 2	Healer	She can handle most of the healing now. Very dependable!
Title 2	Pro Healer	She can heal my wounds and lift my spirits!
Title 2	High Healer	No gashes too deep! No bones too broken! She can fix it all.
Title 2	Miracle Healer	Who's afraid of dying with a healer this skilled around!?
Title 2	Love Doctor	There's something about the feel of her hand on my forehead when she takes my temperature…
IC	Herbalist	Level 2 IC alchemy. She has a lot to learn. Good with herbs and medicine.
IC	Pharmacist	Level 3 IC alchemy. A beginner alchemist. Good with herbs and medicine.
IC	Chemist	Level 4 IC alchemy. Knows a lot about alchemy. Good with herbs and medicine.
IC	Alchemist	Level 5 IC alchemy. She really knows her stuff! Good with herbs and medicine.
IC	Claridian Mind	Level 6 IC alchemy. She knows all there is to know! Good with herbs and medicine.
CS	Beauty	She's such a hottie. She makes men shiver in their loincloths.
Trait 1	Coward	She's not really into confrontation.
Trait 2	Tea Taster	She really enjoys serving tea as well as drinking it. She's awfully picky about taste, though.
Trait 3	Cuddly	She seems to like fighting beside Sigmund and me.
Trait 4	Flyer Despiser	She must have been traumatized in her youth. She can't get close to flying creatures.
Trait 4	Flyer Hater	She's not only scared of airborne foes, she despises them!

KIRIYA

Title Type	Title	Capell says…
Title 1	Scary	This guy is weird, plain and simple.
Title 1	Hermit	He's really smart! How'd he learn all that stuff?
Title 1	Sharp Tongue	Does everybody get an attitude like that by reading books?
Title 1	Freak	I guess he's not that weird after all. …He's a freak!
Title 1	Rationalist	So he CAN say something that isn't insulting!
Title 1	Too Much	He needs to get a little bit more control over his words and his actions.
Title 1	Ally	He and I are after the same thing.
Title 1	Starseer Cadet	I've got a feeling he's going to follow in Savio's footsteps.
Title 2	Scholar	Well he says he's a scholar, so I guess he is.
Title 2	Academic	He's studying a little bit, but he's also spending a lot of time with the weights.
Title 2	Researcher	Now all he does is field research and combat training.
Title 2	Field Researcher	He's really strong now. But what about the books?
Title 2	Undecided	Didn't he say he was a scholar?
Title 2	Scything Scholar	His skills with the scythe are unparalleled! I hope he knows what he's doing.
Title 2	Fickle Sickle	It's about time to stop calling yourself a scholar.
IC	Chemist	Level 4 IC alchemy. Knows a lot about alchemy.
IC	Alchemist	Level 5 IC alchemy. He really knows his stuff!
IC	Claridian Mind	Level 6 IC alchemy. He knows all there is to know!
CS	Scavenger	He's good at locating items where we already found something.
Trait 1	Medicinal Master	With him around, we can use medicine a lot more effectively.
Trait 2	Elitist	He only likes to talk to other smart people. He doesn't get along well with normal people.
Trait 3	Picky	He hates a lot of stuff.
Trait 3	Fussy	He hates EVERYTHING.
Palate	Vegetable Lover	So he likes vegetables…Maybe if I mix some in with his meal, his mood will improve.

SIGMUND

Title Type	Title	Capell says…
Title 1	Look-alike	Wow, we DO look alike!
Title 1	Well-known	They even know about him out in a small village like Nolaan!
Title 1	Wounded Hero	Hey, shouldn't he be more careful?
Title 1	Hero of Light	He's looking a lot better now after the lunar rite.
Title 1	Chaincutter	How did he know I would be able to cut the chain?
Title 1	True Leader	He's a great leader. I know why everybody follows him so loyally.
Title 1	Legacy	He'll always be remembered.
Title 1	Father	Now I know… He must have known about us all along… That's why he was so kind…
Title 2	Hero?	I wonder if all the stories about him are true.
Title 2	Hero	He really IS a hero!
Title 2	Superhero	He's no ordinary hero…
Title 2	Great Hero	So when he meets people, does he want them to shake his hand or kneel before him?
Title 2	Shining Hero	His courage and valor burn so brightly it makes my eyes hurt!
Title 2	Liberator	He's the most famous man alive! Babies come out of the oven knowing his name!
Title 2	Living Legend	He's a man of peerless strength. Even his foes worship the ground he walks on.
CS	Observant	He's really good at figuring out the enemy's weak points.
Trait 1	Authority Figure	His presence alone gives us strength!
Trait 2	Feral Wolf	When he's in danger, he gets even stronger than usual!
Trait 3	Calm & Cool	He's always relaxed and has a handle on the situation.
Palate 1	Soup Lover	He really likes soup, and it's really effective when used on him.
Palate 2	Tomato Hater	Who would have thought his only weak point would be a vegetable? Oh the irony!

EDWARD

Title Type	Title	Capell says…
Title 1	Bad Attitude	He's got such an attitude…
Title 1	Sigmund's Fan	All he ever does is talk about Sigmund!
Title 1	Spoiled Brat	I don't mind too much, but he should really be more tactful, especially when giving orders.
Title 1	Patient	Now he's sick. Oh no!
Title 1	Vermiform	Don't give up, Ed! We'll fix you!
Title 1	Comrade	He's accepted everything there is to accept about me.
Title 1	Pawn	Yes, his piece fits perfectly in my plans.
Title 1	Best Friend	We always know what the other is thinking. It's like we have telepathy!
Title 2	Tadpole	Keep on trying, little man!
Title 2	Page Boy	His skill with the sword is grand—at least when it comes to polishing the blade! Ha!
Title 2	Squire	He's pretty helpful and can follow most instructions.
Title 2	Heroguard	Now he's ready to stand by the hero and fight!
Title 2	Lieutenant	Even the hero depends on him now.
Title 2	Guardian	Now he's stronger than the hero! He's a master of defense!
Title 2	Lionheart	Maybe he should be the main character now…
IC	Bronzesmith	Level 2 IC forging. He can keep the fire going. Good with metals.
IC	Silversmith	Level 3 IC forging. He's getting a little better now. Good with metals.
IC	Goldsmith	Level 4 IC forging. He's finally a decent smith. Good with metals.
IC	Mastersmith	Level 5 IC forging. The greatest smith of our age! Good with metals.
IC	Claridian Hammer	Level 6 IC forging. Awe-inspiring anvil prowess! Good with metals.
Trait 1	Disciplinary	He's a pretty good leader. Knows how to take control of a group.
Trait 2	Thoughtful?	Though he's harsh with his words, he cares. His strength rises when an ally falls.
Trait 3	Serious	He's just too serious! Even serious about being serious!
Trait 3	Adamant	He's so serious about fighting that he sometimes gets a little experience point bonus.
Trait 4	Sigmundite	He worships Sigmund like a god!
Palate	Pepper Hater	He hates peppers. He won't even touch them.
Palate	Pepper Despiser	Don't even think about putting peppers in his food! The sight of them alone makes him retch!

KOMACHI

Title Type	Title	Capell says…
Title 1	Guild Girl	She seems to be a member of the Nightwhisper Guild.
Title 1	Touma's Servant	She's a nightwhisper assigned to protecting Touma's family.
Title 1	Wise Whisper	She's pretty smart. I wonder if she studied with Touma.
Title 1	Loving Servant	She's so obvious about it, but he just doesn't get it. I almost feel bad for her.
Title 1	Swift Servant	With her, my enemies won't be safe anywhere, not even in the shadows.
Title 1	Touma Forever	An aristo will never respond to your feelings. Never!
Title 1	Sacrificial Lamb	Well if I can't use her for anything else, I'll just make sure she's useful in battle.
Title 1	Ideal Servant	She's so loyal to him, even though he offers nothing. I hope her heart reaches him.
Title 2	Rookie	She still needs a lot more training.
Title 2	Mightwhisper	Well she can hold her breath underwater for ten minutes now. She's improving.
Title 2	Nightwhisper	She's fast. Really fast.
Title 2	Nightwhisper Ace	Physically, she's in amazing shape.
Title 2	Sonic Nightwhisper	Now she's outracing cheetahs!
Title 2	High Nightwhisper	Soon she'll be able to control the shadows! And hold fancy light shows!
Title 2	Incognito	You know a nightwhisper's good when you'd never guess she was one. It's hard to tell she's in disguise!!!
CS 1	Trapmaster	She should be able to handle locked treasure chests or traps.
CS 1	High Trapmaster	Locked treasure chests or traps are no problem. She can even detect their location!
CS 2	Rummager	She's good at locating items where we already found something.
CS 2	High Rummager	She's really good at locating items where we already found something.
Trait 1	Loyal Servant	She's more effective in battle when she's fighting beside her beloved Touma.
Trait 2	Shady Lady	Though she's more relaxed in dark places, it says nothing about her personality.
Trait 3	Edgy	She likes being off to the side, but she's not the least bit antisocial!
Trait 4	Undead Hater	Her legs go all wobbly when undead monsters are nearby.
Trait 4	Undead Despiser	She's no good against the undead! I better finish any off quickly for her!

RICO

Title Type	Title	Capell says…
Title 1	Twerp 1	Where did this…kid come from? Seriously…
Title 1	Overactive	He's pretty brave…for a little kid.
Title 1	Admirable	Wow, even after what happened to his father, he's pretty tough.
Title 1	Bratty	He's sure got an attitude. It's probably all the adults he has to deal with.
Title 1	Childish	Look at him! He's so cute! Just a little kid!
Title 1	Big Boy	He's pretty mature for his age. I guess I can't make fun of him…too much.
Title 1	Useless	I can't get anything out of this kid.
Title 1	Future Hero	Someday he might even be a bigger hero than Sigmund was.
Title 2	Rabbit Tamer	Small and weak animals are the only ones who listen to what he has to say.
Title 2	Lion Tamer	He can give animals simple instructions now.
Title 2	Beastmaster	Looks like most animals are listening to him.
Title 2	Beastmaster 2	Now he can even get animals to help him in battle!
Title 2	Beastmaster 3	I didn't even know those were animals! He's the boss of everybody!
Title 2	Claridian Tamer	Even the Claridians kneel before him!
Title 2	Bathmaster	He's mastered the ancient art of having a grizzly bear wash his back in the bathtub. Astounding!
IC	Scribbler	Level 1 IC writing. Look at him pretend he knows how to use a pen and paper.
IC	Amateur	Level 2 IC writing. His prose and poetry reek of amateurism.
IC	Writer	Level 3 IC writing. He could make a little money with his writing now.
IC	Bestseller	Level 4 IC writing. The offers keep on pouring in! Who's his agent?
IC	Wordsmith	Level 5 IC writing. It's almost time he started lecturing at an academy.
IC	Claridian Scribe	Level 6 IC writing. Each of his words is worth a thousand pictures.
CS	Beastspeaker	Look at that! He can talk to friendly animals!
Trait 1	Hyper	What did he eat? He doesn't stop moving!
Trait 1	Hyperactive	He doesn't stop moving! But sometimes he finds stuff.
Trait 2	Twin	He's in a much better mood whenever Rucha is with him.
Trait 3	Bug Fan	He gets all excited when he sees a bug.
Trait 3	Bug Lover	Bugs make him wild! He won't listen to a thing I say after one shows up.
Palate	Vegetable Hater	He stays far, far away from vegetables.
Palate	Fish Lover	He hates his vegetables, but at least he likes fish.

RUCHA

Title Type	Title	Capell says…
Title 1	Twerp 2	Where did this…kid come from? Give me a break…
Title 1	Overachiever	I know she's worried about her dad, but she should be more careful.
Title 1	Commendable	Even after everything that's happened, she's still so positive.
Title 1	Little Lady	How does she know about THAT?
Title 1	Just a Kid	It's good to see her act her age once in a while.
Title 1	Young Adult	She's no ordinary kid or grown-up. She's a young adult!
Title 1	Useless	I can't get anything out of this kid.
Title 1	Future Heroine	She's going to be beautiful when she grows up.
Title 2	Trainee	She's a summoner in training studying up on magic.
Title 2	Jr. Summoner	She's getting better at magic. Good luck with the summoning!
Title 2	Summoner	She's great with magic now! Good luck with the summoning!
Title 2	Jr. Mage	Her magic's perfect! Good luck with the summoning!
Title 2	High Mage	No other mage can compete with her anymore. Good luck with the summoning!
Title 2	Magemaster	Her sorcery will go down in history. Good luck with the summoning!
Title 2	Overmagicker	Weren't you going to be a summoner? What happened with that?
IC	Mama's Girl	Level 1 IC cooking. A fan of salt and pepper. Good with soup and platters.
IC	Kitchen Scrub	Level 2 IC cooking. She sure likes to cook. Good with soup and platters.
IC	Cook	Level 3 IC cooking. Her cooking's pretty good! Good with soup and platters.
IC	Chef	Level 4 IC cooking. She must know every recipe! Good with soup and platters.
IC	Master Chef	Level 5 IC cooking. She's a world-class chef now. Good with soup and platters.
IC	Claridian Chef	Level 6 IC cooking. The Claridians line up for food! Good with soup and platters.
CS	Scavenger	She's good at locating items where we already found something.
Trait 1	Big Coward	She gets really confused when the enemy launches a surprise attack.
Trait 1	Coward	She gets confused when the enemy launches a surprise attack.
Trait 2	Twin	She's in a much better mood whenever Rico is with him.
Trait 3	Mime	Look at that! Did she just imitate one of Rico's spells!?
Palate	Hot Hater	Hot food seems to make her tongue numb.

KRISTOFER

Title Type	Title	Capell says...
Title 1	Lech	He's only got one thing on his mind…and it's dirty.
Title 1	Womanizer	It's amazing how he can act completely different around men and women.
Title 1	Lustful	So does he go for ANYTHING that's pretty?
Title 1	Desperado	So does he go for ANYONE that's pretty? (gulp)
Title 1	Irrelevant	This guy is useless.
Title 1	Impassioned	Well he's sure passionate about what he does.
Title 1	Darling	He calls her darling? Does he have no shame?
Title 1	Committed	Although his words might make you think otherwise, he's pretty serious about Seraphina.
Title 2	Nogunner	Why's he carry that thing around? He couldn't shoot the broad side of a barn with training wheels on.
Title 2	Lowgunner	Well his accuracy is up to 30%. I guess he's somewhat useful.
Title 2	Midgunner	Up to 80%. He's pretty dependable now.
Title 2	Topgunner	He never misses! What improvement!
Title 2	Quickgunner	He's great at rapid fire now. Groups of enemies are kept at bay with ease!
Title 2	Machinegunner	So incredibly…fast. I don't know which is more impressive, his shooting speed or reloading time!
Title 2	Supergunner	I bet I could blindfold him, and he'd still shoot an apple off Gustav's head from a mile away.
IC	Goldsmith	Level 4 IC forging. He's finally a decent smith. Good with metals.
IC	Mastersmith	Level 5 IC forging. The greatest smith of our age! Good with metals.
IC	Claridian Hammer	Level 6 IC forging. Awe-inspiring anvil prowess! Good with metals.
Trait 1	Operator	He's really good at operating machines, especially vehicles.
Trait 2	Flippant	He's thoughtless to the bone!
Trait 2	Devoted	Even though he talks to all the ladies, I think there's one that's extra special.
Trait 3	Playboy	He's a natural lady's man. All he can do is think about picking up women.
Trait 3	Mega Playboy	He's beyond help. He doesn't even listen to me anymore. Maybe if I was a woman…
Palate	Spicy Lover	He likes his food like his women: hot!
Trait 4	Nyctophobic	He can't concentrate in the dark. It seems to lower his strength.
Trait 4	Scaredy Cat	He's doing a little better in the dark, but his strength still suffers.

BALBAGAN

Title Type	Title	Capell says...
Title 1	Brawny	He's got muscles. I'll give him that much.
Title 1	Burly	It's kind of funny how typecast he is as the strong guy.
Title 1	Sturdy	I think his brain is made out of muscle, too! Motor cortex to the max!
Title 1	Strapping	His muscles are so sweaty they're…they're…blinding!
Title 1	Reliable	I guess you're worth more than the weight of your muscle in gold ingot.
Title 1	Unreliable	Sorry for letting you down…
Title 1	Returner	He might be worth something. He never tires in battle.
Title 1	Jolly Giant	If there's anybody who's honest about themselves, it's him.
Title 2	Musclehead	He's as strong as ten men!
Title 2	Mr. Muscles	He's almost too strong to fight properly!
Title 2	Sir Muscles	He's finally figured out how to use his strength effectively!
Title 2	Lord Muscles	Watch him swing the most titanic of weapons with ease!
Title 2	King Muscles	He can become one with his weapon and cleave mountains asunder!
Title 2	Musclestorm	All he has to do is hit his foes with his pinky finger, and they go flying!
Title 2	Loose Cannon	His footsteps stir the seas and his breath topples towers. Eight out of ten bars deny him entrance.
Trait 1	Brutish	He's just so strong! He can smash anything!
Trait 2	Lucky	It looks like he becomes stronger after a successful surprise attack…
Trait 3	Enduring	So the longer a battle drags on, the stronger he gets…
Trait 4	Child at Heart	He's just a big—very big—kid at heart!
Palate 1	Meat-eater	He loves his meat dripping and undercooked.
Palate 2	Drinker	The cause and the solution to all life's headaches.
Palate 2	Heavy Drinker	He sure drinks a lot. I hope his memories aren't suffering for it…
Palate 2	Lush	He's looking pretty rough around the edges in the morning.

TOUMA

Title Type	Title	Capell says...
Title 1	Aristocrat	He looks like he was brought up well—in harsh contrast to a certain princess I know…
Title 1	Sigmund's Friend	What!? He's an old friend of Sigmund's? My cover's blown!
Title 1	Well-educated	He knows a lot for having grown up pampered. He must be really experienced.
Title 1	Innocent	Th-that's not what I was expecting… Don't tell me he's…
Title 1	Emblematic	I know he's not bad, but his kind…
Title 1	Blockhead	People like him don't understand…
Title 1	Despised	It's not his fault, but…but…
Title 1	Altruistic	He would sacrifice himself in an instant to save another. A true nobleman.
Title 2	Naive	He's taking his first few steps in bushido.
Title 2	Youth	He takes good care of himself and does everything in moderation.
Title 2	Warrior	His policy seems to be that preparation is important and results can come later.
Title 2	Noble	No complaints from me about his strength. I just hope he realizes for himself how much he's grown.
Title 2	Samurai	He's a true warrior. No one can deny that.
Title 2	Samurai Lord	One of seven legendary samurai…
Title 2	Super Shogun	Why does he call himself that?
CS	Dashing	He's a fine and strapping lad. Any woman would want a chance to talk with him.
Trait 1	Survivor	It looks like his true powers come out when he's in difficult situations.
Trait 2	Wise Leader	He's more effective in battle when he's fighting beside his servant Komachi.
Trait 3	Dedicated	It's out of more than duty that he protects the empress.
Trait 4	Mask Fan	Masks help him block out distractions and focus on battle.
Trait 4	Mask Lover	Now he likes to collect masks.
Trait 4	Mask Otaku	He's a master of masks now! He knows every type and even how to make them!
Palate	Vegetable Lover	He gets excited when he eats his vegetables!

SAVIO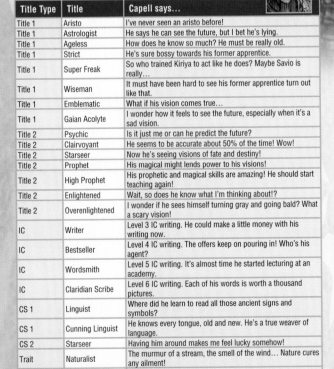

Title Type	Title	Capell says...
Title 1	Aristo	I've never seen an aristo before!
Title 1	Astrologist	He says he can see the future, but I bet he's lying.
Title 1	Ageless	How does he know so much? He must be really old.
Title 1	Strict	He's sure bossy towards his former apprentice.
Title 1	Super Freak	So who trained Kiriya to act like he does? Maybe Savio is really…
Title 1	Wiseman	It must have been hard to see his former apprentice turn out like that.
Title 1	Emblematic	What if his vision comes true…
Title 1	Gaian Acolyte	I wonder how it feels to see the future, especially when it's a sad vision.
Title 2	Psychic	Is it just me or can he predict the future?
Title 2	Clairvoyant	He seems to be accurate about 50% of the time! Wow!
Title 2	Starseer	Now he's seeing visions of fate and destiny!
Title 2	Prophet	His magical might lends power to his visions!
Title 2	High Prophet	His prophetic and magical skills are amazing! He should start teaching again!
Title 2	Enlightened	Wait, so does he know what I'm thinking about!?
Title 2	Overenlightened	I wonder if he sees himself turning gray and going bald? What a scary vision!
IC	Writer	Level 3 IC writing. He could make a little money with his writing now.
IC	Bestseller	Level 4 IC writing. The offers keep on pouring in! Who's his agent?
IC	Wordsmith	Level 5 IC writing. It's almost time he started lecturing at an academy.
IC	Claridian Scribe	Level 6 IC writing. Each of his words is worth a thousand pictures.
CS 1	Linguist	Where did he learn to read all those ancient signs and symbols?
CS 1	Cunning Linguist	He knows every tongue, old and new. He's a true weaver of language.
CS 2	Starseer	Having him around makes me feel lucky somehow!
Trait	Naturalist	The murmur of a stream, the smell of the wind… Nature cures any ailment!
Palate 1	Sweets Lover	He loves his sweets!
Palate 2	Vegetable Hater	He loves nature but hates vegetables? How odd.

VIC

Title Type	Title	Capell says...
Title 1	Snoop	He must have some good sources.
Title 1	Savvy Boy	He's real tight with his money.
Title 1	Boy?	W-wait a minute…He…he is a he, right?
Title 1	Fraternal Boy	Even though he grew up alone with his brother, he talks about him a little bit too much.
Title 1	Lil' Capell	So now he wants to be like me!?
Title 1	Lil' Capellette	Does he like dressing up as a girl?
Title 1	Disposable	Was he really helpful at all?
Title 1	Lil' Buddy	I wonder if he's got feelings for somebody. I'll back him up!
Title 2	Snoop?	He knows a lot, but is it all on the level?
Title 2	Pickpocket	He's pretty good with his hands.
Title 2	Spy	He's good with intel and also pretty reliable in battle.
Title 2	Master Spy	He seems to be well-known in the shadier parts of society.
Title 2	Assassin	I bet he never loses in hide-and-seek.
Title 2	High Assassin	If he started a business, I bet he'd have clients knocking the door down to get to him.
Title 2	Night Maven	Hey! Where'd he go!? So stealthy!
CS 1	Trapmaster	He should be able to handle locked treasure chests or traps.
CS 1	High Trapmaster	Locked treasure chests or traps are no problem. He can even detect their location!
CS 2	Bargaineer	Sometimes he can get us a 10% off deal at shops!
CS 2	High Bargaineer	Sometimes he can get us a 20% off deal at shops!
Trait 1	Enduring	So the longer a battle drags on, the stronger he gets…
Trait 2	Fraternal	Having him around makes me feel lucky somehow!
Trait 3	Shrewd	He thinks twice about using consumable items.
Trait 3	Stingy	He sometimes thinks twice about using consumable items.
Trait 4	Selachophobic	So aquatic monsters lower his strength?
Trait 4	Selachophobic 2	He's still bad with aquatic monsters.

GUSTAV

Title Type	Title	Capell says...
Title 1	Great Big Bear	He's bigger than I expected.
Title 1	Angry Bear	I don't think he likes me very much.
Title 1	Aya's Bear	So can he tell when Aya's been hurt? In a special bear kind of way?
Title 1	Bearmobile	I think those kids spend a little too much time playing with the bear.
Title 1	Handy Bear	He's so quick! This is great!
Title 1	Boisterous Bear	Sometimes I feel like he might be my greatest rival.
Title 1	Wild Animal	All he's good for is protecting Aya.
Title 1	Aya's Friend	He better take good care of Aya!
Title 2	Bear	Grrr.
Title 2	Big Bear	Grrrrrr.
Title 2	Tough Bear	Grar!
Title 2	Brazen Bear	Grrr. Grar!
Title 2	Boss Bear	Grar! Grooo!
Title 2	King Bear	Grooo! Grooo!
Title 2	Bear of Bears	Graaar! Grooo!
CS	Tracker	Sometimes he can find materials when there are no enemies around.
CS	High Tracker	He can find materials when there are no enemies around.
Trait 1	Grinenbearit	When he's in danger, he gets even stronger than usual!
Trait 2	Bear-handed	Of course he's powerful! He's a bear!
Trait 3	Aya's Man	He likes to fight alongside Aya! Grooo!
Trait 4	Capellivore	He just doesn't seem as useful when I'm nearby…
Trait 4	Nonchalant	I think he just tried to bite me when I got close to Aya!
Palate	Fish Lover	Look at him eat those fish! They have a good effect on him!

DOMINICA

Title Type	Title	Capell says...
Title 1	Big Sis	She's pretty cool, but seems a bit too bossy.
Title 1	Dependable	She fights for what she believes in no matter what.
Title 1	Sharp Tongue	She says some pretty mean stuff without blinking an eye.
Title 1	Aya's Guardian	She really cares about Aya.
Title 1	Lethal Weapon	She's valuable in battle.
Title 1	Unrequited	She should know better than to think one of them could understand our feelings…
Title 1	Emir's Avenger	She has her right to vengeance, but I don't have to help.
Title 1	Future In-law?	You never know.
Title 2	Weakling	She's too weak to be of any use.
Title 2	Hireling	I wouldn't think of hiring her unless the cost was really low.
Title 2	Freelance	She looks like she's earned the respect of other mercenaries.
Title 2	Sellsword	She's been through a lot of battles now. A very reliable ally.
Title 2	Mercenary	She's an authentic and respected mercenary.
Title 2	Warlord	Her presence alone sends tremors through the enemy ranks!
Title 2	Overpriced	She's good…TOO good! I can't afford her anymore! Anybody got a coupon?
IC	Cook	Level 3 IC cooking. Her cooking's pretty good! Good with booze and bowls.
IC	Chef	Level 4 IC cooking. She must know every recipe! Good with booze and bowls.
IC	Master Chef	Level 5 IC cooking. She's a world-class chef now. Good with booze and bowls.
IC	Claridian Chef	Level 6 IC cooking. The Claridians line up for food! Good with booze and bowls.
Trait 1	Disciplinary	She's great at commanding a group.
Trait 2	Harsh Mistress	She can be a little rough sometimes, but it's only because she cares.
Trait 2	Maidenlike	Although she doesn't show it very much, she has a gentle side, too.
Trait 3	Collector	Although she doesn't wear it much, she's got a penchant for jewelry.
Palate 1	Drinker	She likes alcohol.
Palate 1	Big Drinker	She loves alcohol!
Palate 2	Sweets Hater	She can't stand sweets. Maybe she got too much sugar from all the drinks?

SERAPHINA

Title Type	Title	Capell says...
Title 1	Porcelain Doll	She's so pretty, she's like a doll.
Title 1	Humorous	She's got her own very special brand of humor.
Title 1	Exquisite Beauty	She's so pretty, she looks like a doll even when she's not standing still.
Title 1	Problematic	I don't want anything to do with her kind.
Title 1	Spirited	So just because she hides her feelings doesn't mean she doesn't really have them…
Title 1	Kris Lover?	So maybe she does have feelings for Kris?
Title 1	Elegant Beauty	She's pretty, even when she's joking around with Kris.
Title 1	Eternal Beauty	I bet she'll be pretty like this forever!
Title 2	Street Performer	She's got a couple tricks up her sleeves.
Title 2	Witch	She's got a few spells mastered now.
Title 2	Magician	Now she can cast all kinds of magic!
Title 2	Enchantress	Her potential for destroying things is increasing.
Title 2	Sorceress	There can't be very many other magic users with her skill and power.
Title 2	High Sorceress	In terms of raw destructive power, she's number one.
Title 2	Kolt Revolver	She's too dangerous! She's got to be kept under close watch by the government!
IC	Chemist	Level 4 IC alchemy. Knows a lot about alchemy. Good at making magic gear.
IC	Alchemist	Level 5 IC alchemy. She really knows her stuff! Good at making magic gear.
IC	Claridian Mind	Level 6 IC alchemy. She knows all there is to know! Good at making magic gear.
Trait 1	Tranquil	She's really resistant to status ailments. It must be her strong mentality.
Trait 2	Stoic	It's impossible to read her face!
Trait 2	Shy Girl	So she's pretty shy after all!
Trait 3	Composed	She's got a calm and dignified aura.
Trait 3	Stubborn	She's actually pretty stubborn. Once she's made up her mind, there's no changing it!
Palate 1	Soup Lover	She really likes soup. Look at her slurp!
Palate 2	Chicken Hater	She doesn't like eating chicken, or even fighting them!

PERSONAL SKILLS

OFFICIAL STRATEGY GUIDE

Written by Rick Barba and Joe Epstein

DK/BradyGames, a division of Penguin Group (USA) Inc.
800 East 96th Street, 3rd Floor
Indianapolis, IN 46240

ISBN: 978-0-7440-1036-7

Printing Code: The rightmost double-digit number is the year of the book's printing; the rightmost single-digit number is the number of the book's printing. For example, 08-1 shows that the first printing of the book occurred in 2008.

11 10 09 08   4 3 2 1

Printed in the USA.

BRADYGAMES STAFF

Publisher
David Waybright

Editor-In-Chief
H. Leigh Davis

Licensing Manager
Mike Degler

Marketing Manager
Debby Neubauer

CREDITS

Editor Title
Chris Hausermann

Screenshot Editor
Michael Owen

Book Designer
Keith Lowe

Production Designer
Tracy Wehmeyer
Wil Cruz

ACKNOWLEDGEMENTS

Rick Barba would like to thank:

My co-author Joe Epstein and editor Chris Hausermann for good-natured companionship and calm, sure direction during what turned into a marathon project. Special thanks to the folks at Square Enix in Los Angeles for their gracious hospitality, open access, and invaluable input.

Joe Epstein would like to say:

Even if it's just two dudes' names on the cover, many more people contributed to the production of this book, and even more people, ideas, objects, and animals contributed to keeping those two dudes (somewhat) sane. I'd like to extend a huge thanks, a hug, a high-five, 20% gratuity, concert tickets, a back massage, and whatever else* to:

Rick Barba for sharing his Maker's Mark, and helping me push the boulder up the hill; Leigh Davis and David Waybright for the comfy digs in L.A.; Chris Durrance and Mark Provost for keeping me entertained remotely via Facebook and email; Liz Ellis for timely-as-usual translation assistance; Katie Goodyear for always being a great friend, even when the going gets tough(er than usual); Chris Hausermann, Keith Lowe and everyone at BradyGames for consistently turning six or seven hundred pages of manuscript into something that resembles a book; Daniel Maniago for waxing philosophical about life and fighters over dinner, giving me something to think about that wasn't Astro; Michael Owen for the saving throw when I nuked my dev 360; Everyone at Square Enix QA and Localization for their incredible hospitality and assistance; Mia Vo for the delicious breakfast frisbees and being the sweetest, sexiest partner a professional dork could want; finally, Astro for being amazing, the Courtyard Mariott on Mariposa for having a whirlpool hot tub, the Penny Arcade guys for putting on a damn good show, and Karma for being the best dog ever.

*some of these offers may be rhetorical.